We the People

We the People

A Concise Introduction to American Politics

NINTH EDITION

Thomas E. Patterson

Bradlee Professor of Government and the Press
John F. Kennedy School of Government
Harvard University

McGraw Hill
Connect Learn Succeed™

The McGraw·Hill Companies

Published by McGraw-Hill, an imprint of The McGraw-Hill Companies, Inc., 1221 Avenue of the Americas, New York, NY 10020.

This book is printed on acid-free paper.

2 3 4 5 6 7 8 9 0 DOC/DOC 1 0 9 8 7 6 5 4 3 2 1

ISBN: 978-0-07-337906-7
MHID: 0-07-337906-9

Vice President, Editorial: *Michael Ryan*
Director, Editorial: *Beth Mejia*
Sponsoring Editor: *Mark Georgiev*
Marketing Manager: *Patrick Brown*
Director of Development: *Nancy Crochiere*
Developmental Editor: *Laura Wilk*
Production Editor: *Regina Ernst*
Manuscript Editor: *Amy Marks*
Design Manager: *Jeanne Schreiber*
Cover Designer: *Jeanne Schreiber*
Senior Photo Editor: *Nora Agbayni*
Photo Research: *Toni Michaels/PhotoFind*
Buyer II: *Louis Swaim*
Composition: *10/12 Palatino by Aptara®, Inc.*
Printing: *45# New Era Matte Plus, R.R. Donnelley*

Cover Photo: George Debold/SuperStock

Credits: The credits section for this book begins on page 694 and is considered an extension of the copyright page

Library of Congress Cataloging-in-Publication Data

Patterson, Thomas E.
We the people / Thomas Patterson. —9th ed.
p. cm.
Includes bibliographical references and index.
ISBN-13: 978-0-07-337906-7 (alk. paper)
ISBN-10: 0-07-337906-9 (alk. paper)
1. United States—Politics and government. I. Title.
JK276.P38 2011
320.473—dc22 2010042595

The Internet addresses listed in the text were accurate at the time of publication. The inclusion of a Web site does not indicate an endorsement by the authors or McGraw-Hill, and McGraw-Hill does not guarantee the accuracy of the information presented at these sites.

www.mhhe.com

To
Alex and Leigh

About the Author

Thomas E. Patterson is Bradlee Professor of Government and the Press in the John F. Kennedy School of Government at Harvard University. He was previously Distinguished Professor of Political Science in the Maxwell School of Citizenship at Syracuse University. Raised in a small Minnesota town near the Iowa and South Dakota borders, he attended South Dakota State University as an undergraduate and served in the military in Vietnam before enrolling at the University of Minnesota, where he received his Ph.D. in 1971.

He is the author of numerous books and articles, which focus mainly on elections and the media. His book *The Vanishing Voter* (2002) describes and explains the long-term decline in Americans' electoral participation. An earlier book, *Out of Order* (1994), received national attention when President Clinton said every politician and journalist should be required to read it. In 2002, *Out of Order* received the American Political Science Association's Graber Award for the best book of the past decade in political communication. Another of Patterson's books, *The Mass Media Election* (1980), received a *Choice* award as Outstanding Academic Book, 1980–1981. Patterson's first book, *The Unseeing Eye* (1976), was selected by the American Association for Public Opinion Research as one of the fifty most influential books of the past half century in the field of public opinion.

His research has been funded by major grants from the National Science Foundation, the Markle Foundation, the Smith-Richardson Foundation, the Ford Foundation, the Knight Foundation, The Carnegie Corporation, and the Pew Charitable Trusts.

CONTENTS

Chapter Twelve

Chapter Thirteen

Preface

Learning to Think Politically

Political thinking enables citizens to act responsibly, whether in casting a vote, forming an opinion about a public policy, or contributing to a political cause. It enables us, as citizens, to gather and weigh evidence, to apply foundational principles to current events, and to consider historical context when evaluating contemporary issues. In short, it allows us to have informed judgment. This text aims to help you learn how to think about politics. By introducing you to the tools that political scientists use, you will work through the process of forming a knowledgeable view about a political issue.

Tools for Political Thinking: What Political Science Can Contribute

Fortunately, political science provides many tools to help you think effectively and accurately around political issues. This text will not tell you *what* to think politically. There is no correct way of thinking when it comes to the "what" of politics. People differ in their political values and interests, and thus also in their political views.

Instead, this text will help you learn *how* to think politically by providing you with analytical tools that can sharpen your understanding of American politics. The tools are derived from **political science**—the systematic study of government and politics—and help you think critically about:

- Reliable information about how the U.S. political system operates;
- Systematic generalizations about major tendencies in American politics;
- Terms and concepts that precisely describe key aspects of politics.

These tools enable you, as a citizen, to dig more deeply into political developments than would otherwise be possible.

PEDAGOGICAL ELEMENTS FOR POLITICAL THINKING

We the People has developed a series of activities and exercises to help increase your command of political thinking tools.

★ **POLITICAL THINKING** Demonstrates step by step how to apply a political thinking tool—a concept or principle—to better understand and evaluate a political event.

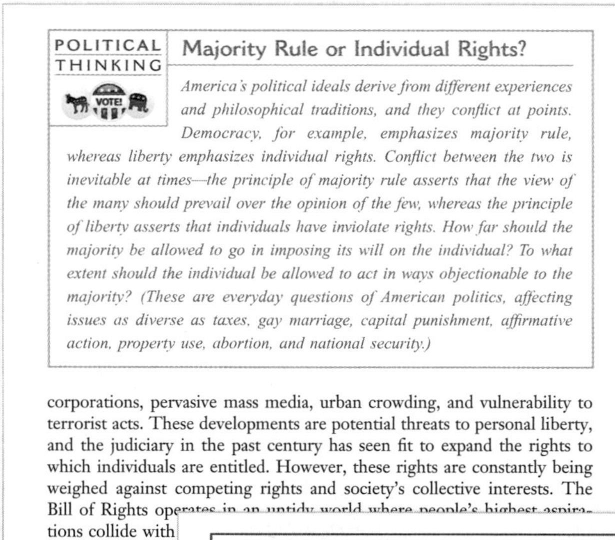

POLITICAL THINKING

Majority Rule or Individual Rights?

America's political ideals derive from different experiences and philosophical traditions, and they conflict at points. Democracy, for example, emphasizes majority rule, whereas liberty emphasizes individual rights. Conflict between the two is inevitable at times—the principle of majority rule asserts that the view of the many should prevail over the opinion of the few, whereas the principle of liberty asserts that individuals have inviolate rights. How far should the majority be allowed to go in imposing its will on the individual? To what extent should the individual be allowed to act in ways objectionable to the majority? (These are everyday questions of American politics, affecting issues as diverse as taxes, gay marriage, capital punishment, affirmative action, property use, abortion, and national security.)

corporations, pervasive mass media, urban crowding, and vulnerability to terrorist acts. These developments are potential threats to personal liberty, and the judiciary in the past century has seen fit to expand the rights to which individuals are entitled. However, these rights are constantly being weighed against competing rights and society's collective interests. The Bill of Rights op
tions collide with

See page 107.

★ **HOW THE US DIFFERS: Political Thinking through Comparisons** Encourages you to think outside our borders and reflect more broadly on how our national political priorities compare to those of other democracies.

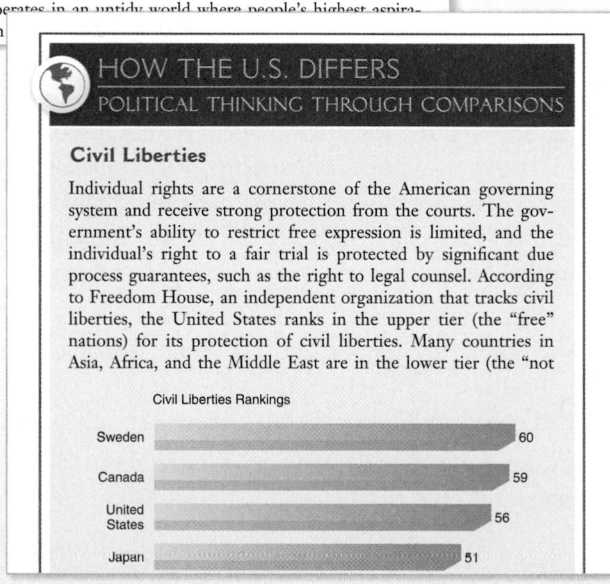

Civil Liberties

Individual rights are a cornerstone of the American governing system and receive strong protection from the courts. The government's ability to restrict free expression is limited, and the individual's right to a fair trial is protected by significant due process guarantees, such as the right to legal counsel. According to Freedom House, an independent organization that tracks civil liberties, the United States ranks in the upper tier (the "free" nations) for its protection of civil liberties. Many countries in Asia, Africa, and the Middle East are in the lower tier (the "not

See page 113.

★ **HOW THE 50 STATES DIFFER: Political Thinking through Comparisons** Uses color-coded maps to illustrate issues relevant to each chapter, enabling you to build analytical skills that help you understand how and why our 50 "united" states differ.

HOW THE 50 STATES DIFFER
POLITICAL THINKING THROUGH COMPARISONS

Incarceration Rates

Although the states are required under the Constitution to uphold defendants' rights, their criminal justice systems differ markedly in other respects. Sentencing laws are an example. States differ in their sentencing practices—most obviously in the application of the death penalty. Some states prohibit it, and others apply it liberally. Texas, Florida, and Virginia are far and away the leaders in its application. Roughly a third of all executions in the past quarter-century have taken place in Texas alone. States also differ substantially in the proportion of their residents who are in prison. Louisiana has the highest incarceration rate, with 865 inmates for every 100,000 residents. Mississippi, Texas, Oklahoma, and Alabama are the other states in the top five. Maine has the lowest

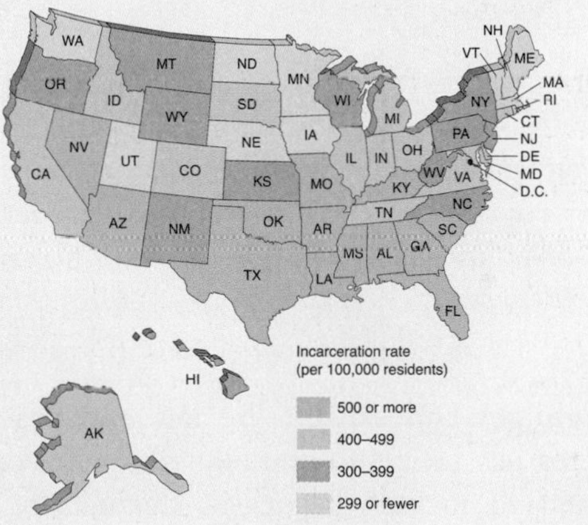

Continued

See page 135.

This revision of the text is the most thorough ever. More than 80 instructors provided chapter reviews, which helped identify areas where the text could be strengthened from the perspective of the student reader. The reviews—more than one review per chapter and several reviews in the case of some chapters—also guided the substantive revisions.

The text has been thoroughly updated to include significant recent developments, including the 2010 midterm elections, the Obama presidency, and the economic recession, as well as major recent policy and political developments such as health care reform, financial regulation, the conflict in Afghanistan, and the rise of the Tea Party. Every chapter includes significant updates and revisions. A few of them of them have been thoroughly reworked. The most heavily revised chapters include the following:

Chapter-by-Chapter Updates

Chapter 1, Political Thinking: Becoming a Responsible Citizen

Rewritten to reflect the text's emphasis on political thinking, this chapter introduces the concept of political thinking and explains why it is the basis for responsible citizenship. The second part of the chapter introduces students to major concepts, such as power and democracy, and describes leading theories of political power.

Chapter 4, Civil Liberties: Protecting Individual Rights

Rewritten to highlight and explain the law and practice of individual rights, this chapter has been substantially reorganized. The chapter has also been updated to include key cases during the two most recent Supreme Court terms, such as the Second Amendment case, *McDonald v. Chicago (2010)*.

Chapter 5, Equal Rights: Struggling toward Fairness

Completely rewritten, this chapter now starts with the origins, key provisions, and impact of major civil rights policies, such as the 1964 Civil Rights Act. The chapter then turns to a section entitled "The Continuing Struggle for Equality," which examines key groups in a contemporary context—their present circumstances, problems, and political efforts.

Chapter 6, Public Opinion and Political Socialization: Shaping the People's Voice

This chapter has been reorganized. It begins with the impact of political socialization on public opinion, before going into how Americans "think about" politics, and then into a section on polling and the public opinion measurement. The chapter concludes with a new section that assesses the influence of public opinion on policy.

Chapter 11, Congress: Balancing National Goals and Local Interests

The new version more fully addresses the heightened level of partisanship in Congress. A section on the threat that primary elections pose to moderate incumbents has been added. The outcome of the 2010 midterm elections is included.

Chapter 13, The Federal Bureaucracy: Administering the Government

This chapter includes updated scholarship and examples, including the Minerals Management Service's lax oversight of offshore drilling, which contributed to the Gulf oil spill and exemplifies agency capture. The chapter includes a major addition: a full section on the budgetary process that includes the role played by federal agencies. Discussions of the Senior Executive Service (SES) and Administrative Law Judges are new to this edition.

Chapter 15, Economic and Environmental Policy: Contributing to Prosperity

The section on environmental policy has been expanded, with particular attention to global warming and energy policy. The current economic recession is addressed in the context of fiscal and monetary policy. Updates include the financial regulation legislation enacted by Congress in 2010.

Chapter 16, Welfare and Education Policy: Providing for Personal Security and Need

The health care reform law passed by Congress in 2010 is discussed from a policy and political perspective. Pending problems of out-year expenditures on social security, Medicare and Medicaid receive increased attention in the new edition.

Chapter 17, Foreign Policy: Protecting the American Way

The chapter's revisions include, among other things, the troop surge in Afghanistan and the evolving economic relationship between the United States and China. Transnational terrorism and counterinsurgency have been added to the section on defense preparedness.

YOUR SUGGESTIONS ARE INVITED

We the People has been in use in college classrooms for nearly twenty years. During that time, the text (including its full-length edition, *The American Democracy*) has been adopted at roughly a thousand colleges and universities. I am extremely grateful to all who have used it. I am particularly indebted to the many instructors and students who have sent me corrections or recommendations. Professor Paul David in the University of Nevada system, for example, pointed out a mistaken entry on Nevada state politics. Joe Sheeler, a student at the University of Maryland, caught an error in a date in one of the chapters. You can contact me at the John F. Kennedy School, Harvard University, Cambridge, MA 02138, or by email: thomas_patterson@harvard.edu.

Thomas E. Patterson

Supplements Package

This text is accompanied by supplementary materials. Please contact your local McGraw-Hill representative or McGraw-Hill Customer Service (800-338-3987) for details concerning policies, prices, and availability, as some restrictions may apply.

For Students and Instructors

Online Learning Center

www.mhhe.com/pattersonwtp9e
The book's website includes separate instructor and student areas. The instructor area contains the instructor's manual, test bank, and PowerPoints, while the student area hosts a wealth of study materials such as chapter outlines, chapter objectives, multiple choice and essay quizzes, flashcards, and weblinks. All chapter-by-chapter material has been updated for the new edition.

For Instructors

Instructor's Manual/Test Bank/PowerPoints

Available online, the instructor's manual includes the following for each chapter: learning objectives, focus points and main points, a chapter summary, a list of major concepts, and suggestions for complementary lecture topics. The test bank consists of approximately fifty multiple-choice questions and five suggested essay topics per chapter, with page references given alongside the answers.

PowerPoints and CPS questions are also available to instructors via the book's website.

Create

Craft your teaching resources to match the way you teach! With McGraw-Hill Create, www.mcgrawhillcreate.com, you can easily rearrange chapters, combine material from other content sources, and quickly upload content you have written like your course syllabus or teaching notes. Find the content you need in Create by searching through thousands of leading McGraw-Hill textbooks. Arrange your book to fit your teaching style. Create even allows you to personalize your book's appearance by selecting the cover and adding your name, school, and course information. Order a Create book and you'll receive a complimentary print review copy in 3–5 business days or a complimentary electronic review copy (eComp) via email in about one hour. Go to www.mcgrawhillcreate.com today and register. Experience how McGraw-Hill Create empowers you to teach your students your way.

CourseSmart e-Textbook

This text is available as an eTextbook at www.CourseSmart.com. At CourseSmart your students can take advantage of significant savings off the cost of a print textbook, reduce their impact on the environment, and gain access to powerful web tools for learning. CourseSmart eTextbooks can be viewed online or downloaded to a computer. The eTextbooks allow students to do full text searches, add highlighting and notes, and share notes with classmates. CourseSmart has the largest selection of eTextbooks available anywhere. Visit www.coursesmart.com to learn more and to try a sample chapter.

For Students

Study Material

Through the book's Online Learning Center, students have free access to the following materials: chapter outlines, chapter objectives, multiple choice and essay quizzes, flashcards, and weblinks. In addition, the site offers a Presidential Timeline, a Spanish-English Glossary, and guidelines for avoiding plagiarism.

Acknowledgments

For this new, ninth edition of *We the People*, I received an enormous amount of sound advice. Reviewers are the lifeblood of a text, and I was fortunate to have the assistance of a skilled group of scholars. I am deeply grateful to each of them for their help:

Alan Abramowitz, *Community College of Baltimore County*
Martin Adamian, *California State University, Los Angeles*
Larry Adams, *Hartnell College*
John Anene, *Central Florida Community College*
Mohammad "Mo" Bahramzadeh, *Arizona Western College*
J. Robert Baker, *Wittenberg University*
Lee Ballestero, *Moorpark College*
Kedron Bardwell, *Simpson College*
Jordan Barkalow, *Bridgewater State University*
Helen Boutrous, *Mount St. Mary's College*
Robert Bromber, *University of Maryland-University College*
Jane Bryant, *John A. Logan College*
Steven Campbell, *University of South Carolina, Lancaster*
Sue Chiki, *Hocking College*
Gene Chintala, *Tiffin University*
Milton Clarke, *Los Medanos College*
James W. Closs, *Gordon College*
Scott Crosby, *Valencia Community College*
Lane Crothers, *Illinois State University*
Timothy Dale, *University of Wisconsin, Green Bay*
Laura De La Cruz, *El Paso Community College*
Marsa Detscher, *Edison State College*
John L. Diehl, *Bucks County Community College*
David Dillman, *Abilene Christian University*
Pat Dunham, *Duquesne University*
Marie Eisenstein, *Indiana University Northwest*
Kevin Eoff, *Palo Verde College*
Traci Fahimi, *Irvine Valley College*
Jasmine Farrier, *University of Louisville*

Paul Frank, *Sacramento City College*
Lawrence Fuell, *Shoreline Community College*
Terence M. Garrett, *The University of Texas at Brownsville*
Sarah Allen Gershon, *Georgia State University*
David Goetsch, *Northwest Florida State College*
Kate Greene, *University of Southern Mississippi*
Andrew Grossman, *Albion College*
Dan Guerrant, *Middle Georgia College*
Margaret Gunnell, *Butte College*
Willie Hamilton, *Mt. San Jacinto College*
Scott Hartman, *University of Akron-Wayne College*
Brian Harward, *Allegheny College*
Meredith Heiser, *Foothill College*
Lisa Herrington, *San Jose City College*
Eric Herzik, *University of Nevada, Reno*
Timothy G. Hill, *Doane College*
David Hobbs, *Los Medanos College*
Tom Hogen-Esch, *California State University, Northridge*
Michael Hoover, *Seminole State College of Florida*
Tseggai Isaac, *Missouri University of Science & Technology*
Jean-Gabriel Jolivet, *Southwestern College*
Doris J. Jones, *Tarrant County College*
Wayne A. Jones, *Virginia State University*
Larry Jordan, *Vernon College*
Eric Juenke, *University of Colorado, Boulder*
Jeff Justice, *Tarleton State University*
Akis Kalaitzidis, *University of Central Missouri*
Perry Knop, *John A. Logan College*
Paul Labedz, *Valencia Community College*
June Lang, *Suffolk County Community College*
Matt Lees, *Southeastern Illinois College*
Julie Lester, *Macon State College*
Angela K. Lewis, *University of Alabama at Birmingham*
Jason Lindsey, *St. Cloud State University*
Jason MacDonald, *West Virginia University*
W. R. Mack, *University of Southern Indiana*
W. Dale Mason, *University of New Mexico, Gallup*
Jim Matson, *Beaufort County Community College*
Cherry McCabe, *Shasta College*
Stephen McDougal, *University of Wisconsin, La Crosse*

Mark Milewicz, *Gordon College*
Cheri Miller, *Cuyahoga Community College*
Christopher Mobley, *Chattanooga State Community College*
Todd Myers, *Grossmont College*
Thomas Nisley, *Southern Polytechnic State University*
Anthony Nownes, *University of Tennessee*
Gabriel Ondetti, *Missouri State University*
Patricia Ann Owens, *Wabash Valley College*
Henry Patterson, *Lorain County Community College*
Richard M. Pearlstein, *Southeastern Oklahoma State University*
Andrew Pieper, *Kennesaw State University*
John R. Pottenger, *University of Alabama in Huntsville*
Chapman Rackaway, *Fort Hays State University*
Daniel J. Reagan, *Ball State University*
Michelle Rodriguez, *San Diego Mesa College*
Paul Rozycki, *Mott Community College*
Michael Sanchez, *San Antonio College*
Allen K. Settle, *California Polytechnic State University*
Greg Shaw, *Illinois Wesleyan University*
Lorraine Smith, *Northern Essex Community College*
Mark Caleb Smith, *Cedarville University*
Michael Sonnleitner, *Portland Community College*
Chris Soper, *Pepperdine University*
James Stone, *Mt. San Antonio College*
Margaret Stout, *West Virginia University*
William H. Taylor, *Terra State Community College*
James Terry, *Harrisburg Area Community College*
Bob Thompson, *Arcadia University*
Karl Trautman, *Central Maine Community College*
Adewole Umoja, *Los Angeles Southwest College*
Ewa Unoke, *Kansas City Kansas Community College*
Denise Vaughan, *Bellevue College*
Troy Vidal, *Columbus State University*
M. Theron Waddell, *Jr.*, *Galveston College*
Steve Walker, *Northwest College*
Donna Wasserman, *Washtenaw Community College*
Gwyneth I. Williams, *Webster University*
Robert Willoughby, *University of Arkansas, Ft. Smith*
Tony Wohlers, *Cameron University*
Maryann Zihala, *Ozarks Technical Community College*

I also want to thank those at McGraw-Hill who contributed to the ninth edition. Mark Georgiev, my editor, began the discussion that led to the focus on "political thinking." It is the most substantial adjustment in the life of the text, and the one destined to have the most impact on students. I am deeply grateful for Mark's guidance.

At Harvard, I had the diligent and cheerful support of Camille Stevens, Annalese Duprey, and Heather McKinnon. I owe each of them a deep thanks.

Thomas Patterson

CHAPTER 1

POLITICAL THINKING: BECOMING A RESPONSIBLE CITIZEN

"The worth of the state, in the long run, is the worth of the individuals composing it."

JOHN STUART MILL[1]

As U.S. troops moved into position along the Iraq border, pollsters were busy asking Americans what they thought about the prospect of war with Iraq. A narrow majority expressed support for an attack on Iraq without United Nations approval if President George W. Bush deemed it necessary. But Americans' level of support for war varied with their knowledge of the enemy.

Contrary to fact, about half of the American public believed that Iraq was aligned with al Qaeda, the terrorist group that had attacked the United States on September 11, 2001. Some of these Americans mistakenly thought that Iraq helped plan the attacks; others erroneously believed that Iraq was equipping al Qaeda.[2] Some Americans even claimed that Iraqi pilots were flying the passenger jets that slammed into the World Trade Center towers and the Pentagon on that tragic September day.[3]

Compared with Americans who knew that Iraqi leader Saddam Hussein and al Qaeda were avowed enemies, those who falsely believed they were allies were more than twice as likely to support an American attack on Iraq.[4] Some of these individuals undoubtedly had other reasons for backing the invasion. Hussein was a tyrant who had brutalized his own people and thwarted United Nations resolutions calling for inspection of his weapons systems. But their belief that Iraq was in league with al Qaeda terrorists was pure fiction and hardly a reasonable basis for supporting an invasion.

The journalist Walter Lippmann worried that most citizens are unprepared to play the role democracy assigns them. They live in the real world but think in an imagined one. "While men are willing to admit that there are two sides to a question," Lippmann noted, "they do not believe that there are two sides to what they regard as fact."[5] In a self-governing society, citizens are expected to act on behalf of themselves and others. But how can they govern themselves if they are out of touch with reality?

Lippmann's worry has been confirmed by dozens of scholarly studies. "The research," Mark Bauerlein writes, "piles gloomy fact upon gloomy fact."[6] Political scientists Bruce Ackerman and James Fishkin put it bluntly: "If six decades of modern public opinion research establish anything, it is that the general public's political ignorance is appalling by any standard."[7]

In March 2003, by order of President George W. Bush, U.S. forces attacked Iraq. Support for the invasion was highest among Americans who mistakenly believed that Iraq was an ally of the al Qaeda terrorist network. Seen here is a view of U.S. troops through a bullet hole in a window.

The sparse nature of the public's information is apparent in a 2010 Pew Research Center survey that asked Americans about the health care reform bill that Congress was considering. The legislation had been headline news for months and had been stalled for much of that period by the Senate requirement of sixty votes to break a filibuster and bring the bill to the Senate floor for a vote. When asked how many votes were needed to break a Senate filibuster—whether it was 51, 60, 67, or 75—only 26 percent of the respondents gave the correct response. When asked whether the Senate majority leader was Harry Reid, Al Franken, Mitch McConnell, or Hillary Clinton, only 39 percent made the correct pick, Harry Reid. A larger number, 44 percent, said they did not know who held the post. Ten percent guessed it was Hillary Clinton, who was actually the secretary of state. Young adults were particularly likely to be uninformed about the Senate. Among 18- to 29-year-olds, a mere 14 percent knew that it takes sixty votes to break a Senate filibuster, and a bare 16 percent recognized Harry Reid as the Senate majority leader.

Uninformed citizens are not without opinions. Some of them speak out more often and more loudly than people who are informed. But their view of the world is wildly at odds with the reality of it. They are like the ancient mariners who, thinking the world was flat, stayed close to shore, believing they would sail off the edge if they ventured farther out to sea.

Learning to Think Politically

This text aims to help students, as citizens, learn how to think about politics. Political thinking is not the mere act of voicing an opinion. **Political thinking** involves the careful gathering and sifting of information in the process of forming a knowledgeable view about a political issue. Political thinking enables citizens to act responsibly, whether in casting a vote, forming an opinion about a public policy, or contributing to a political cause.

Political thinking is not defined by its endpoint. Equally thoughtful individuals can reach opposite conclusions about the same issue. Political thinking is defined instead by the process through which conclusions are reached. Political thinking involves the application of relevant information to the problem at hand. Information disciplines the thought process, forcing the individual to grapple with the reality of the situation. Opinions not reached in this way are likely to be incomplete at best, perhaps even wildly off base. "Ignorance of the [facts]," Bauerlein notes, "is a fair gauge of deeper deficiencies."[8]

Responsible citizenship was what English philosopher John Stewart Mill had in mind when he said that democracy is the best form of

Civic Literacy Quiz

Each year, the Intercollegiate Studies Institute (ISI) administers a civic literacy quiz to a sample of Americans, including college seniors. The average score is about 50 percent, with college seniors doing only somewhat better than average. The following are a few of the questions that were asked in a recent ISI quiz:

1. Which of the following are the inalienable rights referred to in the Declaration of Independence?
   a. life, liberty, and property
   b. honor, liberty, and peace
   c. liberty, health, and community
   d. life, respect, and equal protection
   e. life, liberty, and the pursuit of happiness
2. What are the three branches of government?
   a. executive, legislative, and judicial
   b. executive, legislative, and military
   c. bureaucratic, military, and industry
   d. federal, state, and local
3. Which of the following is a tool of the Federal Reserve?
   a. raising or lowering income taxes
   b. increasing or decreasing unemployment benefits
   c. buying or selling government securities
   d. increasing or decreasing government spending
4. The United States Electoral College
   a. trains those aspiring to higher political office.
   b. was established to supervise the first televised presidential debates.
   c. is part of Congress.
   d. is a constitutionally mandated assembly that elects the president.
   e. was ruled undemocratic by the Supreme Court.
5. The Bill of Rights explicitly prohibits
   a. prayer in public schools.
   b. discrimination based on race, sex, or religion.
   c. private gun ownership.
   d. establishing an official religion for the United States.
   e. the president from vetoing a line item in a spending bill.
6. Name one right or freedom guaranteed by the first amendment.
   a. the right to bear arms
   b. the right to due process
   c. freedom of religion
   d. the right to counsel
7. Which of the following fiscal policy combinations would a government most likely follow to stimulate economic activity when the economy is in a severe recession?
   a. increasing both taxes and spending
   b. increasing taxes and decreasing spending
   c. decreasing taxes and increasing spending
   d. decreasing both taxes and spending
8. Name two countries that were our enemies during World War II.
   a. Canada and Mexico
   b. Germany and Japan
   c. England and Spain
   d. China and Russia
9. What part of the government has the power to declare war?
   a. Congress
   b. the president
   c. the Supreme Court
   d. the Joint Chiefs of Staff
10. A progressive tax
   a. encourages more investment from those with higher incomes.
   b. is illustrated by a 6 percent sales tax.
   c. requires those with higher incomes to pay a higher ratio of taxes to income.
   d. requires every income class to pay the same ratio of taxes to income.
   e. earmarks revenues for poverty reduction.

Answers: 1. e 2. a 3. c 4. d 5. d 6. c 7. c 8. b 9. a 10. c

Source: From Intercollegiate Studies Institute, Inc. Reprinted with permission.

government. Any form of government, Mill asserted, should be judged on its ability to promote the individual "as a progressive being."[9] It was on this basis that Mill rejected authoritarianism and embraced democracy. Authoritarian governments suppress individuality, forcing people to think and act in prescribed ways or risk punishment. Democracy liberates the individual. People are given the freedom to act as they please, as long as their actions are not harmful to others.

Barriers to Political Thinking

Although democracy provides the *opportunity* for personal development, the individual bears the responsibility for using that opportunity. In this sense, democracy is double-edged. By liberating individuals, democracy frees them to make choices. They can develop and hone the habit of political thinking. Or they can devise cockeyed visions of reality. There is nothing to stop them from thinking the world is flat rather than round.

The major barrier to political thinking is the unwillingness of citizens to make the effort. Political thinking requires close attention to politics, a responsibility that many people refuse to accept. They are, as James David Barber said, "dangerously unready when the time comes for choice."[10]

Others pay close attention, but they do so in unproductive ways. A paradox of modern communication is that, although political information is more widely available than ever before, it is also less trustworthy than ever before. Two decades ago, the "knowledge gap" was defined largely by the amount of attention that people paid to the news. Citizens who followed the news closely were much better informed on average than those who did not.[11] The pattern still holds but with a qualification: some of today's leading news sources are purveyors of unreliable information.

Half of adult Americans now get most of their news from cable television, talk shows, or Internet blogs.[12] Most of these outlets—whether on the left or right—have dropped all but the pretense of accuracy. They rarely tell flat-out lies, but they routinely slant information to fit their purpose while burying contradictory facts. Once in a while, they expose a truth that mainstream news outlets have missed or were too timid to tackle. For the most part, however, they are in the business of concocting versions of reality that will lure an audience and promote a cause. "The talk show culture," media analyst Ellen Hume notes, "is a blur of rumor, fact, propaganda, and infotainment."[13]

Political leaders also "spin" their messages. Although this has always been true, the scale of the effort today is unlike anything that has gone before.[14] The White House press office, for example, was once run by a single individual. It is now a communication machine that reaches deep into the federal agencies and involves scores of operatives, each of whom

The Daily Show's Jon Stewart is one of the few talk show hosts to acknowledge his program's shortcomings. "It's style over substance," Stewart says.

is intent on putting a presidential slant on the day's news.[15] In the period before the Iraq war, the Bush administration, through its hold on the intelligence agencies, tightly controlled the messages coming from the U.S. government. Iraq and al Qaeda were lumped together as targets of the war on terror, leading some Americans—most of them Republicans—to conclude that Iraq and al Qaeda were indistinguishable. During the recent economic downturn, the Obama administration put a favorable slant on the impact of its economic stimulus program, leading some Americans—most of them Democrats—to conclude that the administration had saved and created more jobs than it actually had.

Research suggests that faulty perceptions are becoming more prevalent, and that changes in communication are primarily to blame.[16] During the buildup to the Iraq invasion, for example, individuals who got their news from cable television shows were the most misinformed about the relationship between Iraq and al Qaeda. On average, their level of misinformation exceeded even that of citizens who paid only sporadic attention to news. Daily newspaper readers had a firmer grasp on the Iraq situation, but their numbers are shrinking.[17]

The audience appeal of the "new news," to use journalist Marvin Kalb's term, is understandable.[18] People are keen to receive messages that confirm what they already believe. It is not surprising that liberal bloggers and talk show hosts have an audience made up of mostly liberals, whereas conservative bloggers and talk show hosts have a largely conservative audience. Such exposure, however, tends to intensify rather than expand people's thinking. "When people find themselves in groups of like-minded types," legal scholar Cass Sunstein writes, "they are especially likely to move to extremes."[19]

Citizens cannot know whether their ideas are sound until they have heard alternative views and weighed them against their own. The test of an opinion is not whether it sounds good by itself but whether it makes sense when held up against opposing views. "He who knows only his one side of the case knows little of that," Mill wrote. "His reasons may be good, and no one may have been able to refute them. But if he is equally unable to refute the reasons of the opposite side, if he does not so much as know what they are, he has no ground for preferring either opinion."[20]

What Political Science Can Contribute to Political Thinking

This text will not try to tell you *what* to think politically. There is no correct way of thinking when it comes to the "what" of politics. People differ in their political values and interests and, thus, also in their political opinions.

Instead, this text will help you learn *how* to think politically by providing you with analytical tools that can sharpen your understanding of American politics. The tools are derived from **political science**—the systematic study of government and politics. Political science has developed largely through the work of scholars, but political practitioners and writers have also contributed. One of America's foremost political scientists was the chief architect of the U.S. Constitution and later a president. Even today, James Madison's essays on constitutional design (two of which can be found in this book's appendixes) are masterpieces of political science.

As a discipline, political science is descriptive and analytical—that is, it attempts to depict and explain politics. This effort takes place through various frameworks, including rational choice theory, institutional analysis, historical reasoning, behavioral studies, legal reasoning, and cultural analysis. Political science offers a set of analytical tools that can increase one's ability to think politically:

- Reliable information about how the U.S. political system operates
- Systematic generalizations about major tendencies in American politics
- Terms and concepts that precisely describe key aspects of politics

These tools enable the citizen to delve more deeply into political developments than would otherwise be possible.

Take, for instance, President Barak Obama's inability in 2010 to persuade Congress to enact a wholesale overhaul of the nation's health care system. The United States remains the only fully industrialized Western democracy that does not provide health insurance for all its citizens. Although Obama was able to persuade Congress to enact significant changes in the U.S. health care system, he failed to obtain the comprehensive reform he had sought. News coverage attributed the shortcoming to several factors, most notably the intense opposition of insurance companies and the Senate filibuster rule that enabled the Republican minority to impede the Democratic majority.

Although these factors were undeniably important, an equally large obstacle was America's belief in individualism. This belief has roots in the country's origins as a wilderness society. Land was plentiful, and there was no aristocracy to stifle the ambitions of ordinary people. From this experience grew the idea that people ought to make it on their own. It was a very different outlook than the one that prevailed in Europe, where one's place in life was determined by whether one was born into the tiny aristocracy, the small middle class, or the huge peasant mass. The European experience created a belief that one's place in society was largely beyond personal control, which, when democracy emerged centuries later, spawned the belief that government has a responsibility for the economic well-being of the less fortunate.

The enduring impact of these different legacies can be seen in the fact that the United States spends much less per capita on social welfare programs than do European democracies (see Figure 1-1). It is not that Americans are so well off that they have no need for health insurance or other economic support from government. Compared with Britain, France, Germany, Italy, the Netherlands, Spain, Sweden, Switzerland, and other Western European countries, the United States has in both relative and absolute terms the largest number of hungry, sick, homeless, and poor people. Nevertheless, the United States ranks below nearly all these countries in government spending on social welfare. Americans do not necessarily have less sympathy than Europeans for the less advantaged, but they have resisted an extensive role for government out of a belief that

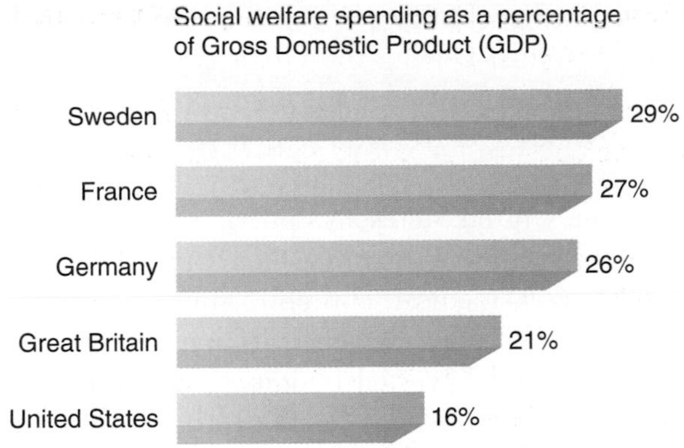

figure 1-1 SOCIAL WELFARE SPENDING IN THE UNITED STATES AND SELECTED EUROPEAN DEMOCRACIES

The United States spends less on social welfare than do European Democracies. *Source:* Organization for Economic Cooperation and Development, 2010.

able-bodied individuals should take responsibility for their economic security and out of a conviction that government assistance erodes self-reliance.

The distinctiveness of this cultural belief can be seen in opinion surveys. In a 2009 Pew Research Center survey, only 24 percent of Americans expressed "complete agreement" when asked whether government has a responsibility "to take care of people who can't take care of themselves."[21] The Germans were closest to the Americans in their response to this question, but nearly twice as many of them, 45 percent, said they agreed completely with the idea that the state is obligated to take care of the poor. Roughly 50 percent of the French and Italians held this opinion. In Britain 59 percent did so.[22]

POLITICAL THINKING

Is Government Responsible for the Disadvantaged?

In the 2009 Pew Research Center survey cited in the text, Americans were asked whether government has a responsibility "to take care of people who can't take care of themselves." Only 24 percent of the respondents said they "completely agree" with the statement. The other options offered to respondents were "mostly agree," "mostly disagree," and "completely disagree." Which response best describes your opinion? What factors have contributed to your outlook (for example, family situation, community attitudes, religious beliefs, political party identification, work experience)?

America's individualistic culture is not an absolute barrier to government assistance programs. During the Great Depression, and at the urging of President Franklin D. Roosevelt, Congress enacted social security for retirees, even though critics attacked it as European socialism and un-American. Social security is now widely popular and embraced by both political parties. The United States also provides, for example, health care for seniors; temporary unemployment benefits for the jobless; and a degree of food, housing, medical, and child support for the poor.

Nevertheless, America's individualistic culture has meant that proposals to expand social welfare will be greeted by intense opposition from some and deep skepticism from others. As the legislative battle over Obama's health care proposal unfolded, opinion polls showed a steady decline in its public support.[23] A 2010 Gallup poll taken a few days after Congress had enacted health care reform found that 65 percent of Americans believed the legislation "will expand the government's role in the healthcare system too much."[24]

Obama is not the first American president to discover the limits of public support for universal government-funded health insurance. Franklin Roosevelt and Lyndon Johnson backed away from proposing comprehensive government-based health insurance because of a conviction that it could not be achieved. Harry Truman in the late 1940s and Bill Clinton in the early 1990s made all-out efforts to achieve it, but failed. Over the decades, Americans have expressed varying levels of dissatisfaction with the country's health care system, but there has been one constant during this period. Never has a majority expressed a willingness to entrust health insurance fully to government—an arrangement that Europeans take for granted.[25]

By contrast, Americans place a greater emphasis than Europeans on personal advancement through education. If individuals are to be entrusted with their own welfare, as Americans believe, they must be given a reasonable chance to succeed on their own. The United States has led the way in education, first by pioneering the idea of universal public schooling, and then by creating the world's most elaborate system of higher education, which now includes more than three thousand two-year and four-year institutions. In some European countries, access to college is readily available only to those from higher-income families. Although some young Americans do not have a realistic prospect of attending college, the nation's college system is relatively open. Nearly 40 percent of young Americans enroll in college, double the rate of Western Europe. About a fourth of America's adult citizens now have a college degree, the world's highest rate. Even West Virginia—the American state with the lowest proportion of college graduates—has a higher percentage of residents with a bachelor's degree than does the typical European country (see "How the 50 States Differ").

HOW THE 50 STATES DIFFER

POLITICAL THINKING THROUGH COMPARISONS

A College Education

Reflecting their cultural beliefs of individualism and equality, Americans have developed the world's largest college system. Every state has at least eight colleges within its boundaries. No European democracy has as many colleges as either California or New York—each of which has more than 300 institutions of higher education. The extensive U.S. college system has enabled large numbers of Americans to earn a college degree. Among adults aged twenty-five years or older, roughly one in four is a college graduate. Even the states that rank low on this indicator have a higher percentage of college graduates than do most European countries.

Q: *Why do the northeastern and western coastal states have a higher percentage of adults with college degrees?*

A: *The northeastern and western coastal states are more affluent and urbanized than most states. Accordingly, young people in these states can better afford the costs of college and are more likely to pursue careers that require a college degree.*

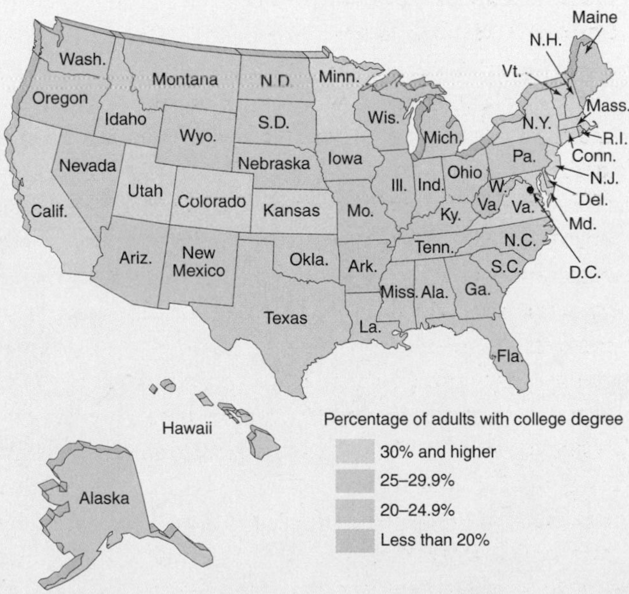

Source: U.S. Census Bureau, 2010. Based on percentage of adults twenty-five years of age or older with a college degree.

America's distinctive cultural beliefs are only one of the elements that affect the nation's politics, as subsequent chapters show. The rest of this chapter introduces concepts and distinctions that are basic to an informed understanding of politics.

Politics and Power in America

Political scientist Harold Lasswell described politics as a conflict over "who gets what, when, and how."[26] Politics would be a simple matter if everyone thought alike and could have everything they pleased. But people do not think alike, and society's resources are limited. Conflict is the inevitable result. **Politics** is the means by which society settles its conflicts and allocates the resulting benefits and costs.

Those who prevail in political conflicts are said to have **power,** a term that refers to the ability of persons, groups, or institutions to influence political developments.[27] Power is basic to politics. Actors who have enough power can provide or refuse health benefits, block or impose gun control, raise or cut taxes, permit or prohibit abortions, protect or take away private property, impose or relax trade barriers, and make war or declare peace. With so much at stake, it is not surprising that Americans, like people elsewhere, seek political power.

Iranians took to the streets to protest their authoritarian regime's rigging of the country's 2009 election. Authorities responded with mass beating and arrests. Some of those arrested were tortured and convicted in staged trials.

table 1-1 AMERICA'S GOVERNING SYSTEMS AND RELATED SOURCES OF POWER

The American polity system is, at once, a democratic system, a constitutional system, and a free market system, each of which fosters particular sources of power.

System	Description and Implications
Democratic	A system of majority rule through elections; empowers majorities (majoritarianism), groups (pluralism), and officials (authority).
Constitutional	A system based on rule of law, including legal protections for individuals; empowers individuals by enabling them to claim their rights in court (judicial action).
Free market	An economic system that centers on the transactions between private parties; empowers business firms (corporate power) and the wealthy (elitism).

French philosopher Michel Foucault called politics "war by other means,"[28] a phrase that literally describes politics in some countries. *Authoritarian governments* openly repress their political opponents as a means of staying in power. The most extreme form of authoritarian government, *totalitarianism*, admits to no limits on its power: the state controls the media, directs the economy, dictates what can and cannot be taught in schools, defines family relations, and decides which religions—if any—can be practiced openly. Authoritarian governments are characterized by one-party rule, although some of them allow a semblance of party competition. Iran's ruling party, for example, conducted a sham election in 2009, stuffing the ballot boxes to assure its victory and then brutally attacking those who took to the streets in protest.

The United States has "rules" designed to keep politics within peaceful bounds. These rules—democracy, constitutionalism, and a free market—determine which side will prevail when conflict occurs, as well as what is off limits to the winning side (see Table 1-1).

A Democratic System

The word *democracy* comes from the Greek words *demos*, meaning "the people," and *kratis*, meaning "to rule." In simple terms, **democracy** is a form of government in which the people govern, either directly or through elected representatives. A democracy is thus different from an *oligarchy* (in which control rests with a small group, such as top-ranking military officers or a few wealthy families) and from an *autocracy* (in which control rests with a single individual, such as a king or dictator).

In practice, democracy has come to mean majority rule through the free and open election of representatives. More direct forms of democracy exist, such as town meetings in which citizens vote directly on issues affecting them, but the impracticality of such an arrangement in a large society has made majority rule through elections the operative form of democratic government, including that of the United States (see Chapter 2).

When American lawmakers respond to the wishes of the majority, the result is **majoritarianism**—the situation in which the majority effectively determines what government does.[29] When Congress enacted the American Recovery and Reinvestment Act (ARRA) in 2009, for example, it was responding to majority demand. The near collapse of the nation's financial sector had sent the economy into a downward spiral. Unemployment was rising, as were home foreclosures, which contributed to the worst economic recession in decades. Americans wanted government to act, and Congress responded with the ARRA, a $787 billion spending bill designed to stimulate the economy.

Majoritarianism has limits, however. The public as a whole takes an interest in only a few of the hundreds of policy decisions that officials make each year (see Chapter 6). Even if they wanted, policymakers would have difficulty determining the majority's desires on most issues. Accordingly, most policies are formulated in response to the groups that have an immediate interest in the issue. Farmers, for example, have more influence over agricultural price-supports than do other groups, even though farm subsidies have far-reaching effects, including the price that shoppers

POLITICAL THINKING

VOTE!

Just Like Kansas City?

In 1940, Senator Kenneth Wherry exclaimed soberly, "With God's help, we will lift Shanghai up and up, every up, until it is just like Kansas City." Like many Americans before and since, Wherry assumed that the American system of government could be transplanted anywhere in the world. The United States has recently helped to create governments in Afghanistan and Iraq that are based on democratic principles, such as free and open elections. Is democracy likely to flourish in these countries? Can democracy be implanted in countries that have a tradition of authoritarian rule or where the population is deeply divided along religious, ethnic, or tribal lines?

pay for food. Some political scientists, like Yale's Robert Dahl, argue that democracies more often operate as pluralistic (multi-interest) systems than as majoritarian systems.[30] **Pluralism** holds that, on most issues, the preference of the special interest largely determines what government does (see Chapter 9).

A democratic system also bestows another form of power. Although officials are empowered by the majority, they also exercise power in their own right as a result of the positions they hold. When President Obama decided in 2009 to increase troop levels in Afghanistan, he did so despite polls that showed most Americans would have preferred a reduction in U.S. forces there.[31] In making the decision, Obama was exercising his constitutional authority as commander-in-chief of the armed forces. Such grants are a special kind of power. **Authority** is the recognized right of officials to exercise power. Members of Congress, judges, and bureaucrats, as well as the president, routinely make authoritative decisions, only some of which are a response to power asserted by the majority or special interests.

A Constitutional System

In a democracy, the votes of the majority prevail over those of the minority. If this principle was unlimited, the majority could treat the minority with impunity, depriving it even of its liberty or property. As fanciful as this prospect might seem, it preoccupied the writers of the U.S. Constitution. The history of democracies was filled with examples of majority tyranny, and the nation's early experience was no exception. In 1786, debtors had gained control of Rhode Island's legislature and made paper money a legal means of paying debts, even though contracts called for payment in gold. Creditors were then hunted down and held captive in public places so that debtors could come and pay them in full with worthless paper money. A Boston newspaper wrote that Rhode Island ought to be renamed Rogue Island.

To guard against oppressive majorities, the writers of the Constitution devised an elaborate system of checks and balances, dividing authority among the legislative, executive, and judicial branches so that each branch could check the power of the others (see Chapter 2). The Bill of Rights was added to the Constitution a few years later as a further check on the majority. Congress would be prohibited, for example, from enacting laws that abridge freedom of speech, press, or religion. These limits reflect the principle of **constitutionalism**—the idea that there are lawful restrictions on government's power. Officials are obliged to act within the limits of the law, which include protections of individual rights.

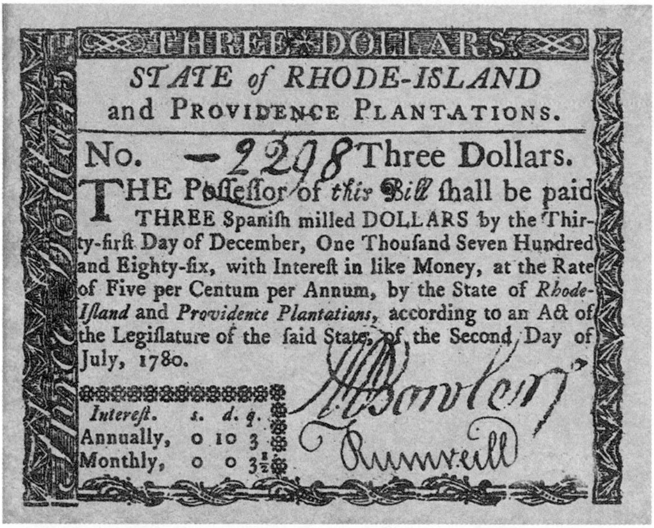

Rhode Island was nicknamed "Rogue Island" for its disregard of property rights. Shown here is the Rhode Island three-dollar bank note, which came to be worth no more than the paper on which it was printed and yet was used to pay off gold debts.

Compared with European constitutions, the U.S. Constitution places a greater number of restraints on majority power, a reflection of the country's origins. Even before Americans gained self-determination through victory in the Revolutionary War, their wilderness society provided a level of personal liberty unimaginable in aristocratic Europe. Ordinary people had no reason to accept inferior status when greater freedom was as close as the next area of unsettled land. As the political scientist Louis Hartz observed, the United States was "born free."[32]

The Bill of Rights in combination with an independent judiciary and a firm attachment to private property have made **judicial action**—the use of the courts as a means of asserting rights and interests—a channel through which ordinary citizens exercise power. Americans have an expansive view of their rights and turn more readily to the courts to make their claims than do people elsewhere (see Chapters 4 and 5).[33] A handwritten note by a penniless convict, for example, triggered the U.S. Supreme Court's landmark *Gideon v. Wainwright* ruling. Clarence Gideon had been made to stand trial in Florida without the aid of a lawyer for breaking into a pool hall. When he appealed his conviction, the Supreme Court concluded that his Sixth Amendment right to counsel had been violated. The ruling established a new policy: if the accused is too poor to hire a lawyer, the government must provide one.

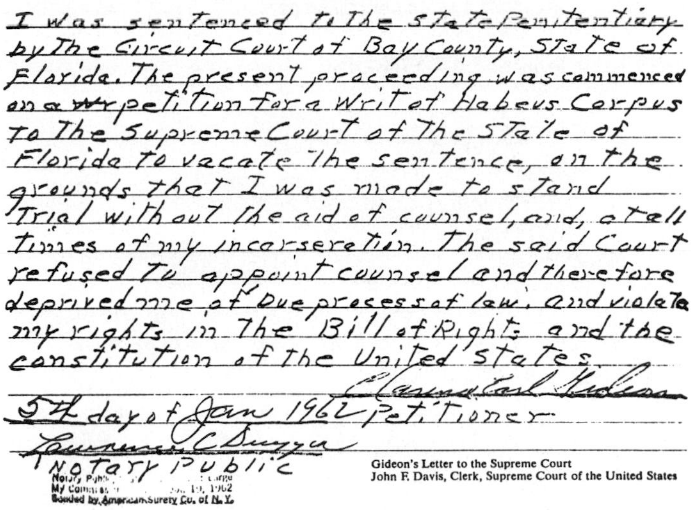

I was sentenced to The state Penitentiary by The Circuit Court of Bay County, State of Florida. The present proceeding was commenced on a petition for a Writ of Habeus Corpus to The Supreme Court of The State of Florida to vacate The sentence, on the grounds that I was made to stand Trial without the aid of counsel, and, at all times of my incarseration. The said Court refused to appoint counsel and therefore deprived me of Due process of law, and violate my rights in The Bill of Right and the constitution of the United states.

Clarence Earl Gideon

5th day of Jan 1962 Petitioner

Notary Public

Gideon's Letter to the Supreme Court
John F. Davis, Clerk, Supreme Court of the United States

The handwritten letter that Clarence Gideon (insert) sent to the Supreme Court in 1962. The letter led eventually to the *Gideon* decision, in which the Court held that states must provide poor defendants with legal counsel (see Chapter 4). Seen by many people at the time as judicial activism, the ruling is now fully accepted.

The significance of legal action in the United States can be seen from the size of its legal profession.[34] On a per-capita basis, there are roughly twice as many lawyers in the United States as in Britain, Italy, and Germany, and five times as many as in France (see Figure 1-2). The United States, as political scientist James Q. Wilson has noted, is "not more litigious because we have more lawyers; we have more lawyers because we are so litigious."[35]

A Free Market System

Politics is not confined to the halls of government. Many of society's costs and benefits are allocated through the private sector, although economic systems differ in the degree of government intervention. Under *communism*, which characterized the former Soviet Union and is practiced most fully today in North Korea, the government owns most or all major industries and also takes responsibility for overall management of the economy, including production quotas, supply points, and pricing. Under *socialism*, as it is practiced today in Sweden and other countries, government does not attempt to manage the overall economy, but owns a number of major industries and guarantees every individual a minimal standard of living. In contrast, a **free market system** operates mainly on private transactions. Firms are largely free to make their own production, distribution, and pricing decisions, and individuals depend largely on themselves for economic security.

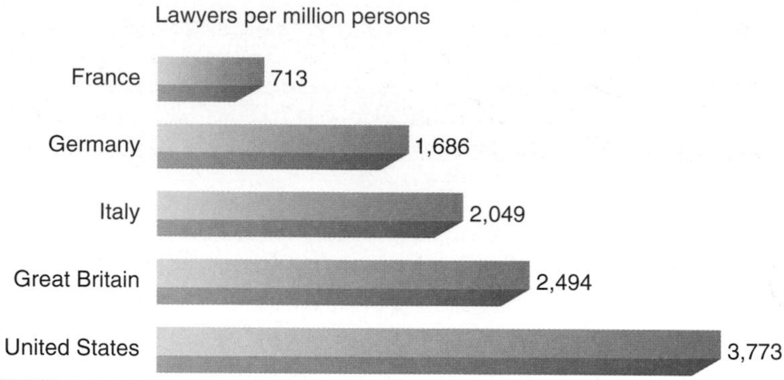

figure 1-2 NUMBER OF LAWYERS

Reflecting its emphasis on individual rights and interests, the United States has more lawyers than do other Western democracies. *Source:* American Bar Association and Council of European Lawyers data, as of 2007.

The U.S. economy is chiefly a free market system, although government intervenes through regulatory, taxing, and spending policies. The nation's economy is similar in this respect to that of most European democracies, but is nonetheless distinctive in the extent to which private transactions determine the allocation of economic costs and benefits. The tax rate is lower in America than in European countries because the U.S. government makes less effort through taxation to redistribute income from the rich to the poor in the form of economic assistance, such as government-provided health care (see "How the U.S. Differs").

Enormous concentrations of wealth and power exist in the U.S. private sector, primarily in the hands of large corporations, like Google, Ford, and Bank of America. **Corporate power** operates in part through the influence that firms have with policymakers. Roughly two-thirds of all lobbyists in the nation's capital represent business firms, which also contribute heavily to political candidates. Corporate power can also be seen in the workplace, where U.S. firms have greater control over wages and working conditions than do firms in other Western democracies. The annual income of a minimum-wage worker, for instance, is roughly $15,000 in the United States, compared with roughly $18,000 in France and $22,000 in Great Britain.[36]

Wealth is also the foundation of **elitism**, which refers to the power exercised by well-positioned and highly influential individuals. Sociologist C. Wright Mills concluded that corporate elites, operating behind the scenes, have more control over economic policy than do "the politicians

HOW THE U.S. DIFFERS
POLITICAL THINKING THROUGH COMPARISONS

Tax Rates

The United States was labeled "the country of individualism par excellence" by William Watts and Lloyd Free in their book *State of the Nation.* They were referring to the emphasis that Americans place on economic self-reliance and free markets.

In European democracies, such views also prevail but are moderated by a greater acceptance of tax and social policies that redistribute wealth. The differences between American and European culture reflect their differing political traditions. Colonial America was an open country ruled by a foreign power, and its revolution was fought largely over the issue of personal liberty. In the European revolutions, economic and social equality was also at issue, because wealth was held by hereditary aristocracies. Europeans' concern with equality was gradually translated into a willingness to use government as a means of economic redistribution. An example is government-paid medical care for all citizens, which is provided throughout nearly the whole of Europe and Canada,

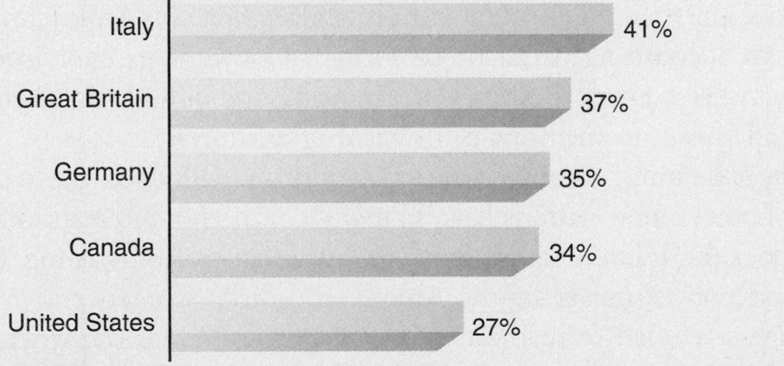

Continued

but not in the United States. More than 40 million Americans are without health insurance.

Such differences affect tax rates, as the figure on page 19 indicates. As measured by the total amount of individual taxes relative to a country's gross domestic product (GDP), the tax rate in the United States is lower than in Canada and Europe, reflecting the degree to which the various countries seek through taxes to provide economic security to the less-well-off.

Q: *Government spending includes programs other than economic assistance for the less-well-off. In which policy area do you think the United States spends significantly more than do European democracies?*

A: *Military spending by the United States far exceeds that of European nations. The United States spends more than 6 percent of its annual GDP on defense, compared with less than 3 percent for the average European country.*

Source: Organization for Economic Cooperation and Development, 2010.

in the visible government."[37] Some scholars share Mills' view, although differing in their assessments of just how much power elites have and whether elites exercise it for purely selfish reasons.[38] Some of them have concluded that elites, in part to protect their privileged positions and in part from a sense of public duty, pursue policies that serve society's broader interests as well as their own.[39]

Who Governs?

This text's perspective is that a full explanation of American politics requires an accounting of all these forms of power—as exercised by the majority, interest groups, elites, corporations, individuals through judicial action, and those in positions of governing authority.

In fact, a defining characteristic of American politics is the widespread sharing of power. Few nations have as many competing interests and institutions as does the United States. Power in America is also dynamic. For most of the first two centuries of the American nation, women and minorities were nearly excluded from the exercise of power. When the writers of the Constitution began the document with the words, "We the People," they did not have everyone equally in mind. Women and minorities are now part of the play of politics, and their influence is sure to increase in coming years.

The Text's Organization

American politics operates within a constitutional system that defines how power is to be obtained and exercised. This system is the focus of the next few chapters, which examine how, in theory and practice, the Constitution defines the institutions of governments and the rights of individuals. The discussion then shifts to the political role of citizens and of the intermediaries that enable citizens to act together and connect them to government. These subjects are explored in chapters on public opinion, political participation, political parties, interest groups, and the news media. The functioning of governing officials is then addressed in chapters on the nation's elective institutions—the Congress and the presidency—and its appointive institutions—the federal bureaucracy and the federal courts. These chapters describe how these institutions are structured but aim chiefly to explain how their actions are affected by internal and external factors, as well as by the constitutional system in which they operate.

Throughout the text, but particularly in the concluding chapters, attention is given to **public policies,** which are the decisions of government to pursue particular courses of action. No aspect of a nation's politics is more revealing of how it is governed than are its policies—everything from how it chooses to educate its children to how it chooses to use its military power.

Underlying the text's discussion is the recognition of how difficult it is to govern effectively and how important it is to try. It cannot be said too often that the issue of governing is the most difficult issue facing a democratic society. It also cannot be said too often that governing is a quest rather than a resolved issue. Political scientist E. E. Schattschneider said it clearly: "In the course of centuries, there has come a great deal of agreement about what democracy is, but nobody has a monopoly on it and the last word has not been spoken."[40]

Summary Self-Test www.mhhe.com/pattersonwtp9e

Political thinking is the careful gathering and sifting of information in the process of forming knowledgeable views of political developments. Political thinking is a key to responsible citizenship, but many citizens avoid it by virtue of paying scant attention to politics. The tools of political science can contribute to effective political thinking.

Politics is the process by which it is determined whose values will prevail in society. The basis of politics is conflict over scarce resources and competing values. Those who have power win out in this conflict and are able to control governing authority and policy choices. In the United States, no one faction controls all power and policy. Majorities govern on some issues, while other issues are dominated by groups, elites, corporations, individuals through judicial action, or officials who hold public office.

Politics in the United States plays out through rules of the game that include democracy, constitutionalism, and free markets. Democracy is rule by the people, which in practice refers to a representative system of government in which the people rule through their elected officials. Constitutionalism refers to rules that limit the rightful power of government over citizens. A free market system assigns private parties the dominant role in determining how economic costs and benefits are allocated.

Key Terms

authority (*p. 15*)
constitutionalism (*p. 15*)
corporate power (*p. 18*)
democracy (*p. 13*)
elitism (*p. 18*)
free market system (*p. 17*)
judicial action (*p. 16*)
majoritarianism (*p. 14*)
pluralism (*p. 15*)
political science (*p. 7*)
political thinking (*p. 3*)
politics (*p. 12*)
power (*p. 12*)
public policies (*p. 21*)

Suggested Readings

Bellamy, Richard. *Political Constitutionalism.* Cambridge, England: Cambridge University Press, 2007. A wide-ranging assessment of constitutionalism that goes beyond a narrowly legalistic perspective.

Domhoff, G. William. *Who Rules America? Challenges to Corporate and Class Dominance*, 6th ed. New York: McGraw-Hill, 2009. A critical assessment of American government by a contemporary proponent of elite theory.

Foley, Michael. *American Credo: The Place of Ideas in American Politics.* New York: Oxford University Press, 2007. An analysis of the political influence of Americans' core beliefs.

Friedman, Milton. *Capitalism and Freedom.* Chicago: University of Chicago Press, 2002. A treatise (originally published in 1962) on free markets by one of the twentieth century's leading economists.

Galston, William A. *The Practice of Liberal Pluralism.* New York: Cambridge University Press, 2004. A careful look at how pluralism works in practice.

Mill, John Stuart. *On Liberty.* White Plains, N.Y.: Longman Publishers, 2006. A classic theory (originally published in 1859) of personal liberty and democracy.

Page, Benjamin I., and Lawrence R. Jacobs. *Class War?: What Americans Really Think about Economic Inequality.* Chicago: University of Chicago Press, 2009. A careful assessment of Americans' economic attitudes, including how they think about individualism.

Stout, Jeffrey. *Democracy and Tradition.* Princeton, N.J.: Princeton University Press, 2004. An analysis of the moral claims associated with democracy.

Welch, Bryant. *State of Confusion: Political Manipulation and the Assault on the American Mind.* New York: Thomas Dunne Books, 2008. A look at the psychology and tactics of contemporary efforts to manipulate public opinion.

List of Websites

www.conginst.org A site that provides up-to-date survey data on the American public.

www.loc.gov The Library of Congress website; provides access to more than 70 million historical and contemporary U.S. documents.

www.realclearpolitics.com A site filled with information about current issues and developments in American politics.

www.stateline.org A University of Richmond/Pew Charitable Trusts site dedicated to providing citizens with information on major policy issues.

Politics in Theory and Practice

Thinking: How does the division of power in the U.S. political system contribute to limited government? How do the provisions for representative government (the various methods of choosing national officials) contribute to limited government?

Participating: The classroom provides an everyday opportunity to develop a skill that is basic to effective citizenship—the ability to speak clearly and persuasively. To the Greek philosopher Aristotle, rhetoric was the defining skill of citizenship. Aristotle did not define rhetoric as it is often used today, as a derisive term for speech that is long on wind and short on reason. Rather, he saw rhetoric as a tool in the search for truth, a form of persuasion that flourishes when people exchange ideas. The college classroom is a place to develop rhetorical skills. Speak up in the classroom when you have a point to make and can support it. Rhetorical skills are honed only through practice, and few settings offer more opportunities for practice than the classroom.

Extra Credit

For up-to-the-minute *New York Times* articles, interactive simulations, graphics, study tools, and more links and quizzes, visit the text's Online Learning Center at **www.mhhe.com/pattersonwtp9e**.

NATIONAL JOURNAL

Children of the Great Recession

The April sun shines brightly over the career development center at California State University. Yet, despite the perfect weather, the center's conference room is crammed with students taking notes intently. Judy Narcisse, a counselor at the center, is running a workshop on résumé writing.

Gesturing toward a PowerPoint presentation on a large screen, Narcisse marches her charges through the basics. Her tone is casual, and her humor deadpan, but her advice is hard-headed. "If you're going to leave your cellphone number, don't have rap music on your voice mail," she explains. "You can't say, 'Hey, this is Naomi! Give me a holla!' "

As Narcisse speaks, heads bob and pens scribble. Her students at this heavily Hispanic and Asian, working-class university of about 20,000 located east of downtown Los Angeles are attentive to a fault. "What if I don't have enough experience to fill a piece of paper?" one young woman asks. Print your résumé with wider margins or a larger font size, Narcisse replies. She is full of such practical suggestions: Find internships, she recommends, attend career fairs, volunteer, proofread your résumé. At times, Narcisse sounds like a coach delivering a halftime pep talk. "We're in a tough economic market," she says bluntly. "You're going to have to hustle."

The message is not lost on these children of the Great Recession, or on the massive Millennial Generation they embody. The Millennials, best defined as people born between 1981 and 2002, are now the largest generation in the United States, with nearly 92 million members according to the latest Census Bureau figures. They are the most diverse generation in American history (more than two-fifths are nonwhite, according to the census), and they are en route to possibly becoming the best-educated: About half of Millennial men and 60 percent of Millennial women older than 18 have at least some college education. They are frequently described as a civic generation, more oriented toward public service and volunteerism and more instinctively optimistic than any cohort of young people since the fabled GI Generation that fought World War II and built postwar America.

And now their great expectations are colliding with diminished circumstances. Millions in the generation are navigating the transition to adulthood through the howling gale of the worst economic downturn since the Depression. Federal statistics tell a bracing story. The unemployment rate among 20-to-24-year-olds stood at nearly 16 percent in March, more than double the level of three years earlier, before the recession began. For those 25 to 29, unemployment stood at 11.5 percent, also more than double the level of three years ago. For teenagers, 20-something African-Americans and Hispanics, and young people without a college degree, the unemployment rates spike as high as 28 percent—debilitating levels of the kind that Americans haven't seen in decades.

Even in this dire climate, some Millennials are finding new ways to weather the storm, displaying the instinct for pragmatic problem-solving that generational theorists consider one of their defining characteristics. They are flocking into service-oriented alternatives such as Teach for America or partnering with peers to launch innovative entrepreneurial ventures.

But for many others, the working world has become an inscrutable maze of part-time jobs, temporary gigs, and full-time positions that abruptly dissolve into layoffs and start the entire disorienting cycle again. Such widespread uncertainty could impose lasting costs, measured not only in diminished opportunity and earnings for the Millennials themselves, but lost productivity and multiplying social challenges for American society at large. "If the jobless recovery . . . drags on for three or four years, then I think we will face some large problems that we haven't faced since the Great Depression," says Robert Reich, who served as Labor secretary in the Clinton administration. "Young people are just not going to form the habits and attachments to work that their older siblings or parents have had, and that could conceivably create a whole variety of social problems."

Many Millennials are blazing innovative paths through the Great Recession. Alexander Develov, a senior finishing this spring at business-oriented Babson College in Wellesley, Mass., for instance, has already started a business that provides online video marketing services. "The recession is fantastic for somebody trying to start a business," he says. "You can't raise as much money, but you can get the best people."

Other Millennials are choosing to ride out the labor market's squalls by pursuing more education. Community college applications have soared 17 percent in the past two years—although the increase is driven in part by older people seeking new skills after layoffs. Demand at community colleges is so high that Bunker Hill Community College in Boston has been forced to add classes on a graveyard shift that begins at 11 p.m. Many young people with four-year degrees are seeking further education as well, although this reliance on graduate school as a harbor could prove a mixed blessing: While some experts say that acquiring more skills almost always pays off, others worry that students will simply accumulate more debt without obtaining the experience they need to begin moving up the workplace escalator. "Graduate school never solved a labor market problem," says Phil Gardner of Michigan State.

But arguably this generation's most distinctive response to hard times is not entrepreneurship or extended education but rather a pursuit of public service, in all of its variations—a trend that was evident even before the recession struck. Edna Medford, who has spent more than two decades teaching history at Howard, sees the impulse toward service as a defining characteristic of this generation. "In the last couple of years, there is a return to that whole idea of being willing to commit to the larger group," she says. "It's truly refreshing."

In many respects, the economic challenges facing young people are simply a more acute version of the threats confronting all Americans in this sharp downturn. And, as a result, many of the questions about how to create more opportunity for young Americans inevitably become tangled in the larger debates between the political parties about how to promote more prosperity for society overall—that is, whether the economy is more likely to respond to an agenda focused mostly on tax cuts and deregulation or one centered on government investment in areas such as education and alternative energy.

Yet in some ways the problems confronting the Millennial Generation are unique. Although unemployment has increased among all age groups, younger workers are falling out of the workforce much more rapidly than older workers—and more rapidly than they did in previous recessions. In fact, federal statistics show that the share of young people either working or actively looking for work was declining through the first part of the past decade, even before the recession hit. Such data suggest a growing problem in connecting young people to the world of work—in effect, a breakdown in the process of getting them to step onto the escalator. "They are just simply delaying their careers and their labor force connections," laments Reich. "It's a social problem if young people, fresh out of school . . . can't get into the labor force and have to sit around for a year or two or more."

What's Your Opinion?

Do you identify with the Millennial Generation and its concerns as described in the article? How secure do you feel about a career after your education?

CHAPTER 2

Constitutional Democracy: Promoting Liberty and Self-Government

"Why has government been instituted at all? Because the passions of man will not conform to the dictates of reason and justice, without constraint."

ALEXANDER HAMILTON[1]

At noon on January 21, 2009, Barack Obama raised his right hand and took the oath of office as president of the United States. In the inaugural address that followed, Obama spoke of renewing the American dream. He called upon his fellow citizens to join in "common purpose," to uphold the principles of a "free" and "equal" people, and to respect "the rule of law and the rights of man, a charter expanded by the blood of generations."

Americans, he said, must "carry forward that precious gift, the God-given promise that all are equal, all are free, and all deserve a chance to pursue their full measure of happiness." Obama concluded his address by telling today's Americans to pursue "the great gift of freedom and [deliver] it safely to future generations."

The ideas that guided Obama's speech would have been familiar to any generation of Americans. The same ideas have been invoked when Americans have gone to war, declared peace, celebrated national holidays, launched major policy initiatives, and asserted new rights.[2] The ideas expressed in Obama's speech were the same ones that shaped the speeches of George Washington and Abraham Lincoln, Susan B. Anthony and Franklin D. Roosevelt, Martin Luther King, and Ronald Reagan.

The ideas were there at the nation's beginning, when Thomas Jefferson put them into words in the Declaration of Independence. They had been nurtured by the colonial experience in the New World, which offered the settlers a degree of liberty, equality, and self-government unimaginable in Europe. When the Revolutionary War settled the issue of American independence in the colonists' favor, they faced the question of how to turn their ideals into a system of government. The Constitution of the United States became the instrument for that effort. The framers of the Constitution sought to create a **limited government**—one that is subject to strict legal limits on the uses of power, so that it would not threaten the people's liberty. They also sought to establish a system of **self-government**—one in which the people would be the ultimate source of governing authority and would have a voice in their governing.

The challenge facing the framers was that, although limited government and self-government can be reinforcing, they can also conflict. Self-government requires that the majority through its elected representatives have the power to rule. However, limited government requires that majority rule stop at the point where it infringes on the legitimate rights and interests of the minority. This consideration led the framers to forge a Constitution that provides for majority rule but has built-in restrictions on the power of the majority and its elected representatives.

This chapter describes how the principles of self-government and limited government are embodied in the Constitution and explains the tension between them. The chapter also indicates how these principles have

In his inaugural address, Barack Obama invoked America's founding ideals, as America's leaders have done throughout the nation's history.

been modified in practice in the course of American history. The main points presented in this chapter are these:

- *America during the colonial period developed traditions of limited government and self-government.* These traditions were rooted in governing practices, political theory, and cultural values.
- *The Constitution provides for limited government mainly by defining lawful powers and by dividing those powers among competing institutions.* The Constitution, with its Bill of Rights, also prohibits government from infringing on individual rights. Judicial review is an additional safeguard.
- *The Constitution in its original form provided for self-government mainly through indirect systems of election of representatives.* The framers' theory of self-government was based on the notion that political power must be separated from immediate popular influences if sound policies are to result.
- *The idea of popular government—in which the majority's desires have a more direct and immediate impact on governing officials—has gained strength since the nation's beginning.* Originally, the House of Representatives was the only institution subject to direct vote of the people. This mechanism has been extended to other institutions and, through primary elections, even to the nomination of candidates for public office.

Before the Constitution: The Colonial and Revolutionary Experiences

Early Americans' admiration for limited government stemmed from their British heritage. Unlike other European governments of the time, Britain did not have an absolute monarchy. Parliament was an independent body with lawmaking power and local representation. Many of the colonial charters conferred upon Americans "the rights of Englishmen," which included, for example, the right to trial by jury.

The colonies also had experience in self-government. Each colony had an elected representative assembly, which was subject to British oversight but nevertheless had important legislative powers. Moreover, most colonists were Protestants, and many of them belonged to sects that had self-governing congregations.

The American Revolution was partly a rebellion against Britain's failure to uphold the colonies' established traditions. After the French and Indian War (1754–1763), during which colonists fought alongside British soldiers to drive the French out of the western territories, the British government for the first time imposed heavy taxes on the colonies. The war with France, which was also waged in Europe, had created a budget crisis in Britain. Taxing the colonies was a way to reduce the debt, so Parliament levied a stamp tax on colonial newspapers and business documents. The colonists were not represented in Parliament, and they objected. "No taxation without representation" was their rallying cry.

Although Parliament backed down and repealed the Stamp Act, it then passed the Townshend Act, which imposed taxes on all glass, paper, tea, and lead sold in the colonies. The colonists again objected, and Parliament again backed down, except for the tax on tea, which Britain retained to show that it was still in charge of colonial affairs. The tea tax sparked an act of defiance that became known as the Boston Tea Party. In December 1773, under the cover of darkness, a small band of patriots disguised as Native Americans boarded an English ship in Boston Harbor and dumped its cargo of tea overboard.

In 1774, the colonists met in Philadelphia at the First Continental Congress to formulate their demands on Britain. They asked for their own councils for the imposition of taxes, an end to the British military occupation, and a guarantee of trial by local juries. (British authorities had resorted to shipping "troublemakers" to London for trial.) King George III rejected their demands, and British troops and colonial minutemen clashed at Lexington and Concord on April 19, 1775. Eight colonists died on the Lexington green in what became known as "the shot heard 'round the world." The American Revolution had begun.

The Declaration of Independence

Although grievances against Britain were the immediate cause of the American Revolution, ideas about the proper form of government also fueled the rebellion.[3] Building on the writings of Thomas Hobbes,[4] John Locke claimed that government is founded on a **social contract**. Locke asserted that people living in a state of nature enjoy certain **inalienable rights** (or **natural rights**), including those of life, liberty, and property, which are threatened by individuals who steal, kill, and otherwise act without regard for others. To protect against such individuals, people agree among themselves to form a government (the social contract). They submit to the government's authority in return for the protection it can provide, but, in doing so, they retain their natural rights, which the government is obliged to respect. If it fails to do so, Locke contended, people can rightfully rebel against it.[5]

Locke's idea of natural rights had strong appeal in America because the settlers enjoyed a degree of freedom unthinkable in Europe. There was in America no heredity nobility that controlled nearly all the land and laid claim to special rights and privileges. The New World's great distance from Europe and its vast stretches of open territory gave ordinary people a level of personal liberty and property ownership unimaginable in the Old World.

Thomas Jefferson declared that Locke "was one of the three greatest men that ever lived, without exception," and Jefferson paraphrased Locke's ideas in passages of the Declaration of Independence, including those asserting that "all men are created equal," that they are entitled to "life, liberty, and the pursuit of happiness," that governments derive "their just powers from the consent of the governed," and that "it is the right of the people to alter or abolish" a tyrannical government. The Declaration was a call to revolution rather than a framework for a new form of government, but the ideas it contained—liberty, equality, individual rights, self-government, lawful powers—became the basis, eleven years later, for the Constitution of the United States. (The Declaration of Independence and the Constitution are reprinted in their entirety in this book's appendixes.)

The Articles of Confederation

A **constitution** is the fundamental law that defines how a government will legitimately operate—the method for choosing its leaders, the institutions through which these leaders will work, the procedures they must follow in making policy, and the powers they can lawfully exercise. The U.S. Constitution is exactly such a law; it is the highest law of the land. Its provisions define how power is to be acquired and how it can be used.

The first government of the United States, however, was based not on the Constitution but on the Articles of Confederation. The Articles, which were adopted during the Revolutionary War, created a very weak national government that was subordinate to the states. Under the Articles, each state retained its full "sovereignty, freedom, and independence." The colonies had always been governed separately, and their people considered themselves Virginians, New Yorkers, Pennsylvanians, and so on as much as they thought of themselves as Americans. Moreover, they were wary of a powerful central government. The American Revolution was sparked by grievances against the arbitrary policies of King George III, and Americans were in no mood to replace him with a strong national authority of their own making.

Drafting the Declaration of Independence, a painting by J. L. Ferris. Benjamin Franklin, John Adams (seated, center), and Thomas Jefferson (standing) drafted the historic document. Jefferson was the principal author; he inserted the inspirational words about liberty, equality, and self-government. Jealous of the attention that Jefferson received, Adams declared that there wasn't anything in Jefferson's words that others hadn't already said. Later, they became bitter political rivals, with Jefferson defeating Adams in the presidential election of 1800. Still later, they reconciled and corresponded frequently. They died on the same day, July 4, 1826, the fiftieth anniversary of the writing of the Declaration of Independence.

Under the Articles of Confederation, the national government had no judiciary and no independent executive. All authority was vested in the Congress, but it was largely a creature of the states. Each of the thirteen states had one vote in Congress, and each state appointed its congressional representatives and paid their salary. Legislation could be enacted only if nine of the thirteen agreed to it. The rule for constitutional amendments was even more imposing. The Articles of Confederation could be amended only if each state agreed.

The Articles prohibited Congress from levying taxes, so it had to ask the states for money. It was slow to arrive, if it arrived at all. During one period, Congress requested $12 million from the states but received only $3 million. By 1786, the national government was so desperate for funds that it sold the navy's ships and reduced the army to fewer than a thousand soldiers—this at a time when Britain had an army in Canada and Spain had one in Florida. Congress was also prohibited from interfering with the states' trade policies, so it was powerless to forge a national economy. States, free to do what they wanted, tried to cripple their competitors. Connecticut, for example, placed a higher tariff on goods manufactured in neighboring Massachusetts than it did on the same goods shipped from England.

The American states had stayed together out of necessity during the Revolutionary War. They would have lost to the British if each state had tried to fend for itself. Once the war ended, however, the states felt free to go their separate ways. Several states sent representatives to Europe to negotiate their own trade agreements. New Hampshire, with its eighteen-mile coastline, established a separate navy. In a melancholy letter to Thomas Jefferson, George Washington wondered whether the United States deserved to be called "a nation."

A Nation Dissolving

In late 1785 at his Mount Vernon home, Washington met with leaders of Virginia and Maryland to secure an agreement between the two states on commercial use of the Potomac River. During the meeting, they decided on the desirability of a commerce policy binding on all the states, which would require an amendment to the Articles of Confederation. With this goal in mind, Virginia and Maryland invited the other eleven states to join them in a convention to be held in Annapolis in the spring.

A revolt in western Massachusetts added urgency to the situation. A ragtag army of two thousand farmers armed with pitchforks marched on county courthouses to prevent foreclosures on their land. Many of the farmers were veterans of the Revolutionary War; their leader, Daniel Shays, had been a captain in the American army. They had been given assurances during the Revolution that their land, which sat unploughed because they were away at war, would not be confiscated for unpaid debts and taxes. They were also promised the back pay owed to them for their military service. (Congress had run out of money during the Revolution.) Instead, they received no back pay, and heavy new taxes were levied on their farms. Many farmers faced not only losing their property but being sent to prison for unpaid debts.

Shays's Rebellion frightened wealthy interests, who called on the governor of Massachusetts to put down the revolt. He in turn asked Congress for help, but it had no army to send. The governor finally raised enough money to hire a militia that put down the uprising, but Shays's Rebellion made it clear that Congress and the army were abysmally weak and that civil unrest was spreading.

When the Annapolis Convention met in the spring, only five states sent delegates, which meant no action could be taken on changing the Articles. However, James Madison and Alexander Hamilton convinced the delegates to adopt a resolution calling for a convention "to render the Constitution of the Federal government adequate to the exigencies of Union." Congress concurred and scheduled a constitutional convention of all the states in Philadelphia while placing a restriction on it: the delegates were to meet for "the sole and express purpose of revising the Articles of Confederation."

POLITICAL THINKING

How Powerful Should Government Be?

The American political tradition includes a suspicion of government power, expressed in the adage "That government is best which governs least." Government sometimes tries to do too much. But can government also do too little? What is the lesson of the government under the Articles of Confederation? Is the issue of government's power a question, not of how much or how little power, but whether its power is equal to its responsibilities?

Negotiating toward a Constitution

The delegates to the Philadelphia constitutional convention ignored the instructions of Congress, instead drafting a plan for an entirely new form of government. Prominent delegates (among them George Washington, Benjamin Franklin, and James Madison) were determined from the outset to establish an American nation built on a stronger central government.

The Great Compromise: A Two-Chamber Congress

Debate at the constitutional convention of 1787 began over a plan put forward by the Virginia delegation, which was dominated by strong nationalists. The **Virginia Plan** (also called the **large-state plan**) included separate judicial and executive branches as well as a two-chamber Congress that would have supreme authority in all areas "in which the separate states are incompetent," particularly defense and interstate trade. Members of the lower chamber would be chosen by the voters, while members of the upper chamber would be selected by members of the lower chamber from lists of nominees provided by their respective state legislatures. In both chambers, the heavily populated states would have a greater number of representatives than would the lightly populated ones. Small states such as Delaware and Rhode Island would be allowed only one representative in the lower chamber, while large states such as Massachusetts and Virginia would have more than a dozen.

The Virginia Plan was sharply attacked by delegates from the smaller states. They rallied around a counterproposal made by New Jersey's William Paterson. The **New Jersey Plan** (also called the **small-state plan**) called for a stronger national government than that provided for by the Articles of Confederation. It would have the power to tax and to regulate commerce among the states. In most other respects, however, the Articles would remain in effect. Congress would have a single chamber in which each state, large or small, would have a single vote.

The debate over the two plans dragged on for weeks before the delegates reached what is now known as the **Great Compromise**. It provided for a bicameral (two-chamber) Congress. One chamber, the House of Representatives, would be apportioned on the basis of population. States with larger populations would have more House members than states with smaller populations, although each state would have at least one representative. The other chamber, the Senate, would be apportioned on the basis of an equal number of senators (two) for each state. This compromise was critical. The small states would not have agreed to join a union in which their vote was always weaker than that of large states, a fact reflected in Article V of the Constitution: "No state, without its consent, shall be deprived of its equal suffrage in the Senate."

The Three-Fifths Compromise: Issues of Slavery and Trade

Differences between the interests of northern states and southern states forced a second major compromise, this time over the issues of slavery and trade.

The South's delegates were concerned that northern representatives in Congress would tax or even bar the importation of slaves. A decade earlier, at the insistence of southern states, a statement critical of slavery had been deleted from Jefferson's initial draft of the Declaration of Independence, and southern delegates to the Philadelphia convention were determined to block any attempts to end slavery through a new constitution.

The southern delegates were also concerned that the North, which included more states and had a larger population, would use its numerical majority in the House and Senate to enact tax policies injurious to the South. Most of the nation's manufacturing was based in the North, and if Congress sought to protect it by placing a heavy tax (tariff) on manufactured products imported from Europe, the higher cost of these imports would be borne by the South, which was more dependent on them. If Congress also imposed a heavy tariff on the export of agricultural goods, which would make them more expensive and therefore less attractive to foreign buyers, the South would again bear most of the tax burden because it provided most of the agricultural goods shipped abroad, such as cotton and tobacco.

After extended debate, a compromise was reached. Congress would have the authority to tax imports but would be prohibited from taxing exports. Congress also would be prohibited until 1808 from passing laws to end the slave trade. However, the most controversial trade-off was the so-called **Three-Fifths Compromise**. For purposes of apportionment of taxes and seats in the U.S. House of Representatives, each slave was to count as less than a full person. Northern delegates had argued against the counting of slaves because they did not have legal rights. Southern delegates wanted to count them as full persons for purposes of apportioning House seats (which would have the effect of increasing the number of southern representatives) and to count them as nonpersons for purposes of apportioning taxes (which would have the effect of decreasing the amount of federal taxes levied on the southern states). The delegates finally settled on a compromise that included both taxation and apportionment but counted each slave as three-fifths of a person. Although the southern states did not get all that they wanted, they got the better end of the bargain. If slaves had not been counted at all, the southern states would have had only slightly more than 35 percent of the House seats. With the compromise, they held nearly 45 percent of the seats, giving them considerable influence over national policy.

These compromises have led critics to claim that the framers of the Constitution had no objections to slavery. In fact, most of the delegates were deeply troubled by it, recognizing the stark inconsistency between the practice of slavery and the nation's professed commitment to liberty and equality. "It is inconsistent with the principles of the Revolution," Maryland's Luther Martin stated. George Mason, a Virginian and a slaveholder, said: "[Slaveholders] bring the judgment of heaven on a country."[6] Benjamin Franklin and Alexander Hamilton were among the delegates who were involved in antislavery organizations.

Yet the southern states' dependence on slavery was a reality that had to be confronted if there was to be a union of the states. The northern states had few slaves, whereas the southern economies were based on slavery (see Figure 2-1). John Rutledge of South Carolina asked during the convention debate whether the North regarded southerners as "fools."

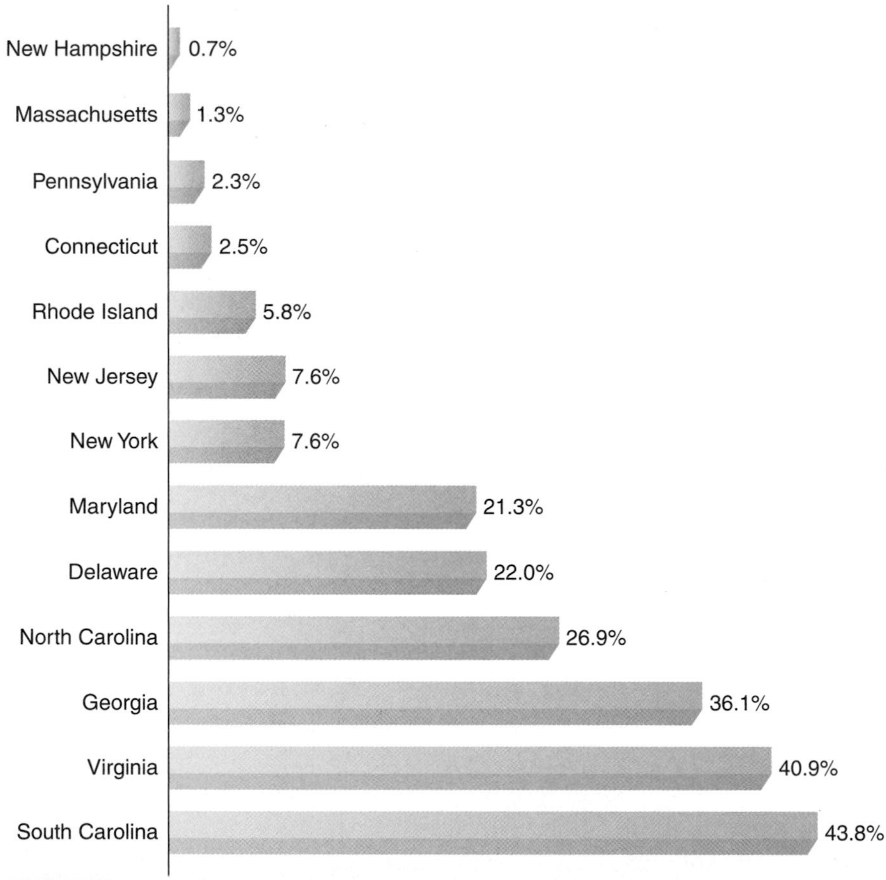

figure 2-1 AFRICAN AMERICANS AS A PERCENTAGE OF STATE POPULATION, 1790

At the time of the writing of the Constitution, African Americans (most of whom were slaves) were concentrated in the southern states. *Source:* U.S. Census Bureau.

Southern delegates insisted that their states would form a separate union rather than join one that banned slavery.

A Strategy for Ratification

The compromises over slavery and the structure of the Congress took up most of the four months that the convention was in session. Some of the other issues were the subject of remarkably little debate. Decisions on the structure of the federal judiciary and bureaucracy, for example, were largely delegated to Congress.

The last issue that had to be decided was a process for ratifying the proposed constitution. The delegates realized that all their work would amount to nothing if the states could not be persuaded to adopt the new constitution. They also recognized that ratification would be difficult; many state leaders would oppose giving strong powers to the national government. Moreover, Congress had not authorized a complete restructuring of the federal government. In fact, in authorizing the Philadelphia convention, Congress had stated that any proposed change in the Articles of Confederation would have to be "agreed to in Congress" and then "confirmed by [all] the states."

This 1790s colored engraving by William Birch depicts a Philadelphia street scene. Philadelphia's role in the birth of the American nation is rivaled only by Boston's contribution.

In a bold move, the delegates ignored Congress's instructions and established their own ratification process. The document was to be submitted to the states, where it would become law if approved by at least nine states in special ratifying conventions of popularly elected delegates. It was a masterful strategy. There was little hope that all thirteen state legislatures would approve the Constitution, but nine states through conventions might be persuaded to ratify it. Indeed, North Carolina and Rhode Island were steadfastly opposed to the new union and did not ratify the Constitution until the other eleven states had ratified it and begun the process of establishing the new government.

The Ratification Debate

The debate over ratification was historic. The **Anti-Federalists** (as opponents of the Constitution were labeled) raised arguments that still echo in American politics. They claimed that the national government would be too powerful and would threaten self-government in the separate states and the liberty of the people. Many Americans had an innate distrust of centralized power and worried that the people's liberty could be eclipsed as easily by a distant American government as it had been by the British king.

The fact that the Constitution contained no bill of rights heightened this concern. Did its absence indicate that the central government would be free to define for itself what the people's rights would be? Patrick Henry expressed outrage at the omission, saying: "The necessity of a Bill of Rights appears to be greater in this government than ever it was in any government before." The proposed constitution, Henry noted, would require the states to surrender to Congress the powers of taxation, spending, and the military "without a Bill of Rights, without check, limitation, or control." The consequences in his mind were dire: "our republic will be lost, and tyranny must and will arise."

Looking ahead, the Anti-Federalists saw a central government controlled by political elites. The Anti-Federalists admired state governments for having legislatures in which the members were not greatly different in wealth from the voters who elected them. New York's Melancton Smith, a powerful public speaker, argued that such representatives are "more competent" than "those of a superior class" whose concerns were far removed from the realities of most people's lives. The election districts in the new Congress would be so large that ordinary people would not have much contact with their representatives, or they with the people they represented. "I am convinced," Smith said, that members of Congress will become "the natural aristocracy of the country. . . . The government will fall into the hands of the few and the great. This will be a government of repression."

The presidency was another source of contention. The office of chief executive did not exist under the Articles of Confederation, and some worried that it would degenerate into an American monarchy. The fact that the president would be chosen by electors appointed by the states (the Electoral College) lessened but did not eliminate this concern.

Even the motives of the men who wrote the Constitution came under attack. They were men of wealth and education who had acted in response to debtors' riots. Would the Constitution become a tool by which the wealthy ruled over those with little or no money? And who would bear the burden of additional taxation? For Americans struggling with local and state tax payments, the thought of also paying national taxes was not appealing.

The Anti-Federalists acknowledged the need for more economic cooperation between the states and for a stronger common defense, but they opposed the creation of a strong national government as the mechanism, arguing that a revision of the Articles of Confederation could accomplish these goals without the risk of establishing an overly powerful central government. (The Anti-Federalist argument is discussed further in Chapter 3.)

The **Federalists** (as the Constitution's supporters called themselves) responded with a persuasive case of their own. Their strongest arguments were set forth by James Madison and Alexander Hamilton, who along with John Jay wrote a series of essays (*The Federalist Papers*) that were published in a New York City newspaper under the pen name Publius. Madison and Hamilton argued that the government of the Constitution would correct the defects of the Articles; it would have the power necessary to forge a secure and prosperous union. At the same time, because of restrictions on its powers, the new government would endanger neither the states nor personal liberty. In *Federalist* Nos. 47, 48, 49, 50, and 51, for example, Madison explained how the separation of national institutions was designed both to empower and to restrict the federal government. (The Federalist argument is discussed further in Chapter 3.)

Whether the ratification debate changed many minds is unclear. Historical evidence suggests, however, that a majority of ordinary Americans opposed the Constitution's ratification. But their voice in the state ratifying conventions was smaller than that of wealthier interests, which in the main supported the change. The pro-ratification forces were also bolstered by the assumption that George Washington, the country's most trusted and popular leader, would become the first president. In the view of historians, this assumption, and the fact that Washington had presided over the Philadelphia convention, tipped the balance in favor of ratification.

Delaware was the first state to ratify the Constitution, and Connecticut, Georgia, and New Jersey soon followed, an indication that the Great Compromise had satisfied some of the small states. In the early summer of 1788, New Hampshire became the ninth state to ratify. The Constitution was law. But neither Virginia nor New York had ratified it, and a stable union without these two large states was almost unthinkable. As large in area as many European countries, they conceivably could have survived as independent nations. In fact, they nearly did choose a separate course. In both states, the Constitution passed only after Federalists said they would support changing it to include a bill of rights.

The Framers' Goals

The Englishman James Bryce ranked America's Constitution as its greatest contribution to the practice of government. The Constitution offered the world a new model of government in which a written document defining the government's lawful powers would represent a higher authority than the dictates of any political leader or institution.

The Constitution embodied the framers' vision of a proper government for the American people (see Table 2-1). One of the framers' goals was the creation of a national government strong enough to meet the nation's needs, particularly in the areas of defense and commerce. Another goal was to preserve the states as governing entities. Accordingly, the framers established a system of government (federalism) in which power is divided

table 2-1 Major Goals of the Framers of the Constitution

1. To establish a government strong enough to meet the nation's needs—an objective sought through substantial grants of power to the federal government in areas such as defense and commerce (see Chapter 3)
2. To establish a government that would not threaten the existence of the separate states—an objective sought through federalism (see Chapter 3) and through a Congress connected to the states through elections
3. To establish a government that would not threaten liberty—an objective sought through an elaborate system of checks and balances
4. To establish a government based on popular consent—an objective sought through provisions for the direct and indirect election of public officials

between the national government and the states. Federalism is discussed at length in Chapter 3, which also explains how the Constitution laid the foundation for a strong national government.

The framers' other goals were to establish a national government that was restricted in its lawful uses of power (limited government) and that gave the people a voice in their governance (self-government). These two goals and the story of how they were written into the Constitution are the focus of the rest of this chapter.

Protecting Liberty: Limited Government

The framers of the Constitution sought a national government that could act decisively but not one that would act irresponsibly. History had taught them to mistrust unrestricted majority rule. In times of stress or danger, popular majorities had often acted recklessly, trampling on the liberty of others. In fact, **liberty**—the principle that individuals should be free to act and think as they choose, provided they do not infringe unreasonably on the freedom and well-being of others—was the governing ideal that the framers sought most to uphold. Americans enjoyed an unparalleled level of personal freedom as a result of their open society, and the framers were determined that it not be sacrificed to either European-style monarchy or mob-driven democracy.

The threat to liberty was inherent in government because of its coercive power. Government's unique characteristic is that it alone can legally arrest, imprison, or even kill people who violate its directives. Force is not the only basis by which government maintains order, but without it, lawless individuals would prey on innocent people. The dilemma is that government itself can use force to intimidate or brutalize its opponents. "It is a melancholy reflection," James Madison wrote to Thomas Jefferson shortly after the Constitution's ratification, "that liberty should be equally exposed to danger whether the government has too much or too little power."[7]

Grants and Denials of Power

The framers chose to limit the national government in part by confining its scope to constitutional **grants of power** (see Table 2-2). Congress's lawmaking powers are specifically listed in Article I, Section 8 of the Constitution. Seventeen in number, these listed powers include, for example,

table 2-2 CONSTITUTIONAL PROVISIONS FOR LIMITED GOVERNMENT

The U.S. Constitution creates an elaborate governing structure designed to protect against the abusive exercise of power—in short, to create a limited government.

Mechanism	Purpose
Grants of power	Powers granted to the national government; accordingly, powers not granted it are denied it unless they are necessary and proper to the carrying out of the granted powers.
Separated institutions	The division of the national government's power among three power-sharing branches, each of which is to act as a check on the powers of the other two.
Federalism	The division of political authority between the national government and the states, enabling the people to appeal to one authority if their rights and interests are not respected by the other authority.
Denials of power	Powers expressly denied to the national and state governments by the Constitution.
Bill of Rights	The first ten amendments to the Constitution, which specify rights of citizens that the national government must respect.
Judicial review	The power of the courts to declare governmental action null and void when it is found to violate the Constitution.
Elections	The power of the voters to remove officials from office.

the powers to tax, to establish an army and navy, to declare war, to regulate commerce among the states, to create a national currency, and to borrow money. Powers *not* granted to the government by the Constitution are in theory denied to it. In a period when other governments had unrestricted powers, this limitation was remarkable.

The framers also used **denials of power** as a means to limit government, prohibiting certain practices that European rulers had routinely used to oppress political opponents. The French king, for example, could imprison a subject indefinitely without charge. The U.S. Constitution prohibits such action: citizens have the right to be brought before a court under a writ of habeas corpus for a judgment as to the legality of their confinement. The Constitution also forbids Congress and the states from passing ex post facto laws under which citizens can be prosecuted for acts that were legal at the time they were committed.

Although not strictly a further denial of power, the framers made the Constitution difficult to amend, thereby making it hard for those in office to increase their power by changing the rules. An amendment could be proposed only by a two-thirds majority in both chambers of Congress or by a national constitutional convention called by two-thirds of the state legislatures. Such a proposal would then become law only if ratified by three-fourths of state legislatures or state conventions. (Over the course of the nation's history, all amendments have been proposed by Congress and only one amendment—the Twenty-First, which repealed the prohibition on alcohol—was ratified by state conventions. The others were ratified by state legislatures.)

Using Power to Offset Power

Although the framers believed that grants and denials of power could act as controls on government, they had no illusion that written words alone would suffice. As a consequence, they sought to limit government by dividing its powers among separate branches.[8]

Decades earlier, the French theorist Montesquieu had argued that the power of government could be controlled by dividing it among separate branches rather than investing it entirely in a single individual or institution. His concept of a **separation of powers** was widely admired in America, and when the states drafted new constitutions after the start of the Revolutionary War, they built their governments around the ideal. Pennsylvania was an exception, and its experience only seemed to prove the necessity of separated powers. Unrestrained by an independent judiciary or executive, Pennsylvania's all-powerful legislature ignored basic rights and freedoms: Quakers were disenfranchised for their religious beliefs, conscientious objectors to the Revolutionary War were prosecuted, and the right of trial by jury was eliminated.

In *Federalist* No. 10, Madison asked why governments often act according to the interests of overbearing majorities rather than according to principles of justice. He attributed the problem to "the mischiefs of faction." People, he argued, are divided into opposing religious, geographical, ethnic, economic, and other factions. These divisions are natural and desirable in that free people have a right to their personal opinions and interests. Yet if a faction gains full power, it will seek to use government to advance itself at the expense of all others. (*Federalist* No. 10 is widely regarded as the finest political essay ever written by an American. It is reprinted in this book's appendixes.)

Out of this concern came the framers' special contribution to the doctrine of the separation of powers. They did not believe that it would be enough, as Montesquieu had proposed, to divide the government's authority strictly along institutional lines, granting all legislative power to the legislature, all judicial power to the courts, and all executive power to the presidency. This total separation would make it too easy for a single faction to exploit a particular type of political power. A faction that controlled the legislature, for example, could enact laws ruinous to other interests. A safer system would be one in which each branch had the capacity to check the power of the others. This system would require separate but overlapping powers. Because no one faction could easily gain control over all institutions, factions would have to work together, a process that would result in compromise and moderation.[9]

Separated Institutions Sharing Power: Checks and Balances

The framers' concept of divided powers has been described by political scientist Richard Neustadt as the principle of **separated institutions sharing power**.[10] The separate branches are interlocked in such a way that an elaborate system of **checks and balances** is created (see Figure 2-2). No institution can act decisively without the support or acquiescence of the other institutions. Legislative, executive, and judicial powers in the American system are divided in such a way that they overlap: each of the three branches of government checks the others' powers and balances those powers with powers of its own.

As natural as this system now might seem to Americans, most democracies are of the parliamentary type, with executive and legislative power combined in a single institution rather than vested in separate ones. In a parliamentary system, the majority in the legislature selects the prime minister, who then serves as both the legislative leader and the chief executive (see "How the U.S. Differs" on pages 46–47).

Shared Legislative Powers Under the Constitution, Congress has legislative authority, but that power is partly shared with the other branches and thus is checked by them. The president can veto acts of Congress, recommend legislation, and call special sessions of Congress. The president also has the power to execute—and thereby interpret—the laws Congress makes.

The Supreme Court has the power to interpret acts of Congress that are disputed in legal cases. The Court also has the power of judicial

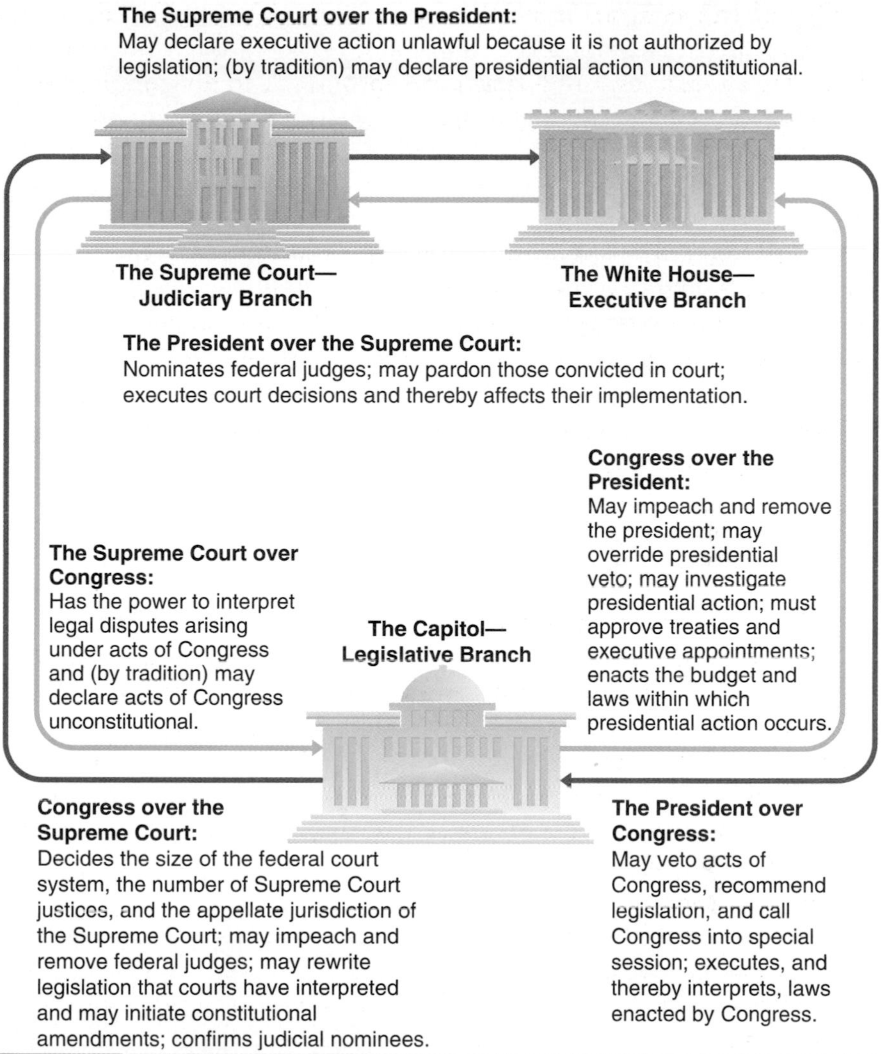

figure 2.2 THE SYSTEM OF CHECKS AND BALANCES

This elaborate system of divided spheres of authority was provided by the U.S. Constitution as a means of controlling the power of government. The separation of powers among the branches of the national government, federalism, and the different methods of selecting national officers are all part of this system.

review: it can declare laws of Congress void when it finds that they are not in accord with the Constitution.

Within Congress, there is a further check on legislative power: for legislation to be passed, a majority in each chamber of Congress is required. Thus, the Senate and the House of Representatives can block each other from acting.

HOW THE U.S. DIFFERS
POLITICAL THINKING THROUGH COMPARISONS

Checks and Balances

All democracies place constitutional limits on the power of government. The concept of rule by law, for example, is characteristic of democratic governments but not of authoritarian regimes. Democracies differ, however, in the extent to which political power is restrained through constitutional mechanisms. The United States is an extreme case in that its government rests on an elaborate system of constitutional checks and balances. The system employs a separation of powers among the executive, legislative, and judicial branches. It also includes judicial review, the power of the courts to invalidate actions of the legislative or executive branch. These constitutional restrictions on power are not part of the governing structure of all democracies.

Most democracies have parliamentary systems, which invest both executive and legislative leadership in the office of prime minister. Britain is an example of this type of system. Parliament under the leadership of the prime minister is the supreme authority in Britain. Its laws are not subject to override by Britain's high court, which has no power to review the constitutionality of parliamentary acts.

In parliamentary systems, moreover, either there is only one legislative chamber or, if there are two, power resides primarily in one chamber. The British House of Lords, for example, has only a limited ability to check the actions of the British House of Commons, which the prime minister heads. In the United States, the two legislative chambers—the House and the Senate—are coequal bodies. Because legislation can be enacted only with the approval of both houses, each serves as a check on the other.

Q: *The framers of the Constitution saw checks and balances as a means of fostering political moderation. Look at the nations in the chart on page 47 and notice the number of checks and balances in their governing systems. Is there a relationship between the number of checks and balances they have and their tendency toward political moderation?*

	Separation of Legislative and Executive Branches?	Two Coequal Legislative Chambers?	Judicial Review?
Great Britain			
Canada			✓
Germany			✓
Japan			✓
France	✓		
Mexico	✓	✓	✓
United States	✓	✓	✓

✓ Yes   (blank) No

A: *There is no clear relationship. Great Britain, for example, is often cited as an example of political moderation although it lacks an elaborate system of checks and balances. By contrast, Mexico, which has such a system, is often held up as an example of political extremes. This fragmentary evidence does not mean that checks and balances are ineffective in controlling power, but the evidence does suggest that other factors, such as a country's political culture, must also be taken into account in any full explanation of political moderation.*

Shared Executive Powers Executive power is vested in the president but is constrained by legislative and judicial checks. The president's power to make treaties and appoint high-ranking officials, for example, is subject to Senate approval. Congress also has the power to impeach and remove the president from office. In practical terms, Congress's greatest checks on executive action are its lawmaking and appropriations powers. The executive branch cannot act without laws that authorize its activities or without the money that pays for these activities.

The judiciary's major check on the presidency is its power to declare an action unlawful because it is not authorized by the laws that the executive claims to be implementing.

Shared Judicial Powers Judicial power rests with the Supreme Court and with lower federal courts, which are subject to checks by the other branches of the federal government. Congress is empowered to establish the size of the federal court system, to restrict the Supreme Court's appellate jurisdiction in some circumstances, and to impeach and remove federal judges from office. More important, Congress can rewrite legislation that the courts have misinterpreted and can initiate amendments when it disagrees with court rulings on constitutional issues.

The president has the power to appoint federal judges with the consent of the Senate and to pardon persons convicted in the courts. The president also is responsible for executing court decisions, a function that provides opportunities to influence the way rulings are carried out.

The Bill of Rights

Although the delegates to the Philadelphia convention discussed the possibility of placing a list of individual rights (such as freedom of speech and the right to a fair trial) in the Constitution, they ultimately decided that such a list was unnecessary because of the doctrine of expressed powers: government could not lawfully engage in actions, such as the suppression of speech, that were not authorized by the Constitution. Moreover, the delegates argued that a bill of rights was undesirable because government might feel free to disregard any right that was inadvertently left off the list or that might emerge in the future.

These arguments did not persuade leading Americans who believed that no possible safeguard of liberty should be omitted. Of particular concern was the fact that the Constitution, unlike the Articles of Confederation, granted the federal government direct authority over individual citizens and yet did not contain a list of their rights. "A bill of rights," Jefferson argued, "is what the people are entitled to against every government on earth, general or particular, and what no just government should refuse or rest on inference." Jefferson had included a bill of rights in the constitution he wrote for Virginia at the outbreak of the Revolutionary War, and all but four states had followed Virginia's example.

Ultimately, the demand for a bill of rights led to its addition to the Constitution. Madison himself introduced a series of amendments during the First Congress, ten of which were soon ratified by the states. These amendments, traditionally called the **Bill of Rights**, include rights such as freedom of speech and religion and due process protections (such as the right to a jury trial) for persons accused of crimes. (These rights, termed *civil liberties*, are discussed in Chapter 4.)

The Bill of Rights is a precise expression of the concept of limited government. In consenting to be governed, the people agree to accept the authority of government in certain areas but not in others; the people's constitutional rights cannot lawfully be denied by government officials.

Judicial Review

The writers of the Constitution both empowered and limited government. But who was to decide whether officials were operating within the limits of their constitutionally authorized powers? The framers did not specifically entrust this power to a particular branch of government, although they did grant the Supreme Court the authority to decide on "all cases arising under this Constitution." Moreover, at the ratifying conventions of at least eight of the thirteen states, it was claimed that the judiciary would have the power to nullify actions that violated the Constitution.[11]

Nevertheless, because the Constitution did not explicitly grant the judiciary this authority, the principle had to be established in practice. The opportunity arose with an incident that occurred after the election of 1800, in which John Adams lost his bid for a second presidential term after a bitter campaign against Jefferson. Between November 1800, when Jefferson was elected, and March 1801, when he was inaugurated, the Federalist-controlled Congress created fifty-nine additional lower-court judgeships, enabling Adams to appoint loyal Federalists to the positions before he left office. However, Adams's term expired before his secretary of state could deliver the judicial commissions to all the appointees. Without this authorization, an appointee could not take office. Knowing this, Jefferson told his secretary of state, James Madison, not to deliver the commissions. William Marbury was one of those who did not receive his commission, and he asked the Supreme Court to issue a writ of mandamus (a court order directing an official to perform a specific act) that would force Madison to deliver it.

Marbury v. Madison (1803) became the foundation for judicial review by the federal courts. Chief Justice John Marshall wrote the *Marbury* opinion, which declared that Marbury had a legal right to his commission. The opinion also said, however, that the Supreme Court could not issue him a writ of mandamus because it lacked the constitutional authority to do so. Congress had passed legislation in 1789 that gave the Court this power, but Marshall noted that the Constitution prohibits Congress from expanding the Supreme Court's authority except through a constitutional amendment. That being the case, Marshall argued, the legislation that

James Madison has been called "the father of the Constitution." Madison himself rejected that label, but he was the framer who saw most clearly how the new government should be structured. Through his *Federalist* essays, Madison was also instrumental in securing ratification of the Constitution. Madison would go on to serve as the nation's fourth president.

provided the authorization was constitutionally invalid.[12] In striking down this act of Congress on constitutional grounds, the Court asserted its power of **judicial review**—that is, the power of the judiciary to decide whether a government official or institution has acted within the limits of the Constitution and, if not, to declare its action null and void.

Marshall's decision was ingenious because it asserted the power of judicial review without creating the possibility of its rejection by either the executive or the legislative branch. In declaring that Marbury had a right to his commission, the Court in effect said that President Jefferson had failed in his constitutional duty to execute the laws faithfully. However, because it did not order Jefferson to deliver the commission, he was deprived of the opportunity to disregard the Court's ruling. At the same time, the Court reprimanded Congress for passing legislation that exceeded its constitutional authority. But Congress also had no way to retaliate. It could not force the Court to accept the power to issue writs of mandamus if the Court itself refused to do so.

Providing for Self-Government

"We the People" is the opening phrase of the Constitution. It expresses the idea that in the United States the people will have the power to govern themselves. In a sense, there is no contradiction between this idea and the Constitution's provisions for limited government, because individual *liberty* is an essential element of *self-government*. If people cannot express themselves freely, they cannot be truly self-governing. In another sense, however, the contradiction is clear: restrictions on the power of the majority are a denial of its right to govern society as it sees fit.

The framers believed that the people deserved and required a voice in their government, but they worried that the people would become inflamed by a passionate issue or fiery demagogue and act rashly. To the framers, the great risk of popular government was **tyranny of the majority:** the people acting as an irrational mob that tramples on the rights of the minority. The history of unfettered democracies was not encouraging, leading James Madison to say in *Federalist* No. 10 that they "have ever been spectacles of turbulence and contention; have ever been found incompatible with personal security or the rights of property; and have in general been as short in their lives as they have been violent in their deaths."

Democracy versus Republic

No form of self-government could eliminate completely the threat to liberty of majority tyranny, but the framers believed that the danger would be greatly diminished by creating a republican government as opposed to a democratic government.[13] Today, the terms *democracy*, *republic*, and *representative government* are often used interchangeably to refer to a system of government in which political power rests with the people through their ability to choose representatives in free and fair elections. To the writers of the Constitution, however, a democracy and a republic were different forms of government.

By the term **democracy**, the framers meant a government in which the power of the majority is unlimited, whether exercised directly (as in the case of town meetings open to all citizens) or through a representative body. The majority's will is absolute. Should it decide to act tyrannically—to run roughshod over the minority—there is nothing in the law to stop it. By the term **republic**, the framers meant a government that consists of carefully designed institutions that are responsive to the majority but not captive to it. It is representative democracy in a true sense, but the people's representatives decide policy through institutions that are structured in ways that foster deliberation, slow the decision process, and operate within constraints that protect individual rights. A republic is designed, not to prevent the people from having a say in their governing, but to filter popular sentiment in ways that reduce the likelihood of hasty, ill-conceived, and reckless policies. To the framers, the Constitution's separation of powers and other limits on power were features of the republican form of government, as opposed to the democratic form, which places no limits on the majority.[14]

The framers believed that a republic, to work well in practice, requires virtuous representatives—lawmakers who have an enlightened sense of the public interest. Their outlook mirrored that of the English theorist Edmund Burke. In his *Letter to the Sheriffs of Bristol* in 1777, Burke argued that representatives should act as the public's **trustees;** representatives are obliged to serve the interest of those who elect them, but the nature of this interest is for the representatives, not the voters, to decide. Burke was concerned with the ease with which a majority can behave like a mob, and he argued that representatives should not surrender their judgment to irrational majorities.

Limited Popular Rule

The Constitution provided that all power would be exercised through representative institutions. There was no provision for any form of direct popular participation in the making of policy decisions. In view of the fact that the United States was much too large to be governed directly by the people in popular assemblies, a representative system was a necessity. However, the framers went beyond this point, creating a system of representation that placed most federal officials a step removed from the people they represented (see Table 2-3).

The House of Representatives was the only institution that would be based on direct popular election—its members would be elected to serve for two years by a vote of the people. Frequent and direct election of House members was intended to make government responsive to the concerns of popular majorities.

table 2-3 METHODS OF CHOOSING NATIONAL LEADERS

Fearing the concentration of political power, the framers devised alternative methods of selection and terms of service for national officials.

Office	Method of Selection	Term of Service
President	Electoral College	4 years
U.S. senator	State legislature	6 years (one-third of senators' terms expire every 2 years)
U.S. representative	Popular election	2 years
Federal judge	Nominated by president, approved by Senate	Indefinite (subject to "good behavior")

U.S. senators would be appointed by the legislatures of the states they represented. Because state legislators were popularly elected, the people would be choosing their senators indirectly. Every two years, a third of the senators would be appointed to six-year terms. The Senate was expected to check and balance the House. The Senate, by virtue of the less frequent and indirect election of its members, was expected to be less responsive to popular pressure.

Presidential selection was an issue of considerable debate at the Philadelphia convention. Direct election of the president was twice proposed and twice rejected because it would link executive power directly to popular majorities. The framers finally chose to have the president selected by the votes of electors (the so-called **Electoral College**). Each state would have the same number of **electoral votes** as it had members in Congress and could select its electors by a method of its choosing. The president would serve four years and be eligible for reelection.

The framers decided that federal judges and justices would be appointed rather than elected. They would be nominated by the president and confirmed through approval by the Senate. Once confirmed, they would "hold their offices during good behavior." In effect, they would be allowed to hold office for life unless they committed a crime. The judiciary was an unelected institution that would uphold the rule of law and serve as a check on the elected branches of government.[15]

These differing methods of selecting national officeholders would not prevent a determined majority from achieving unchecked power, but control could not be attained quickly. Unlike the House of Representatives, institutions such as the Senate, presidency, and judiciary would not yield to an impassioned majority in a single election. The delay would reduce the chance that government would degenerate into mob rule driven by momentary passions.

Altering the Constitution: More Power to the People

The framers' conception of self-government was at odds with what the average American in 1787 would have expected.[16] Self-government was an ideal that had led tens of thousands of ordinary farmers, merchants, and tradesmen to risk their lives in the American Revolution. The ensuing state constitutions had put the ideal into practice. Every state but South Carolina held annual legislative elections, and several states also chose their governors through direct annual election.

Not long after ratification of the Constitution, Americans began to challenge the Constitution's restrictions on majority rule (see Table 2-4).

table 2-4 MEASURES TAKEN TO MAKE GOVERNMENT MORE RESPONSIVE TO POPULAR MAJORITIES

The U.S. Constitution created barriers designed to limit direct popular influence on government. Subsequent changes were designed to lower these barriers and increase the power of voting majorities.

Earlier Situation	Subsequent Development
Separation of powers, as a means of dividing authority and blunting passionate majorities	Political parties, as a means of uniting authorities and linking them with popular majorities
Indirect election of all national officials except House members, as a means of buffering officials from popular influence	Direct election of U.S. senators and popular voting for president (linked to electoral votes), as a means of increasing popular control of officials
Nomination of candidates for public office through political party organizations	Primary elections, as a direct means of selecting party nominees

Jeffersonian Democracy: A Revolution of the Spirit Thomas Jefferson was among the prominent Americans who questioned the Constitution's limited provisions for self-government. In a letter to Madison, he objected to its system of representation, voicing the Anti-Federalist's fear that federal officials would lose touch with the people and discount their interests. His concern intensified when John Adams became president after Washington's retirement. Under Adams, the national government increasingly favored the nation's wealthy interests. Adams publicly indicated that the Constitution was designed for a governing elite and hinted that he might use force to suppress dissent.[17] Jefferson asked whether Adams, with the aid of a strong army, intended to deprive ordinary people of their rights. Jefferson challenged Adams in the next presidential election and, upon defeating him, hailed his victory as the "Revolution of 1800."

Although Jefferson was a champion of the common people, he had no clear vision of how a popular government might work in practice. He saw Congress, not the presidency, as the institution better suited to representing majority opinion.[18] He also had no illusions about the ability of a largely uneducated population to play a substantial governing role and feared the consequences of inciting the masses to rise against the rich. Jeffersonian democracy was mostly a revolution of the spirit. Jefferson

The constitution in its original form restricted the use of the vote as the means of selecting federal officials, but subsequent reforms extended its use. Here voters stand in a long line waiting to cast their ballot at a polling place in Madison, Mississippi.

taught Americans to look on national government institutions as belonging to all, not just to the privileged few.[19]

Jacksonian Democracy: Linking the People and the Presidency Not until the election of Andrew Jackson in 1828 did the nation have a powerful president who was willing and able to involve the public more fully in government. Jackson carried out the constitutional revolution that Jeffersonian democracy had foreshadowed.

Jackson recognized that the president was the only official who could legitimately claim to represent the people as a whole. Unlike the president, members of Congress were elected from separate states and districts rather than from the entire country. Yet the president's claim to popular leadership was weakened by the fact that the president was chosen by electors rather than by the voters. To connect the presidency more closely to the people, Jackson urged the states to award their electoral votes to the candidate who wins the state's popular vote. Soon thereafter, nearly all states adopted this method. This arrangement, still in effect, places the selection of the president in the voters' hands in most elections. The candidate who gets the most popular votes nationally is also likely to finish first in enough states to win a majority of the electoral votes. Since

Jackson's time, only three candidates—Rutherford B. Hayes in 1876, Benjamin Harrison in 1888, and George W. Bush in 2000—have won the presidency after losing the popular vote. (The Electoral College is discussed further in Chapter 12.)

The Progressives: Senate and Primary Elections The Progressive Era of the early 1900s brought another wave of democratic reforms. The Progressives rejected the Burkean idea of representatives as trustees, instead embracing the idea of representatives as **delegates**—officeholders who are obligated to carry out the expressed opinions of the people they represent.

The Progressives sought to place power more directly in the hands of the people.[20] They succeeded in changing the way some state and local governments operate. Progressive reforms at state and local levels include the initiative and the referendum, which enable citizens to vote directly on legislative issues (see "How the 50 States Differ"). Another Progressive reform is the recall election, which enables citizens through petition to force an officeholder to submit to reelection before the regular expiration of his or her term. (In 2003, a recall election enabled actor Arnold Schwarzenegger to become California's governor.)

The Progressives also instigated two changes in federal elections. One was the **primary election**, which gives rank-and-file voters the power to select party nominees. In the early 1900s, nearly all states adopted the primary election as a means of choosing nominees for at least some federal and state offices. Prior to this change, nominees were selected by party leaders. The second change was the direct election of U.S. senators, who before the ratification of the Seventeenth Amendment in 1913 were chosen by state legislatures and were widely perceived as agents of big business (the Senate was nicknamed the "Millionaires' Club"). Senators who stood to lose their seats in a direct popular vote had blocked earlier attempts to change the Constitution. However, as a result of several developments, including revelations that a number of senators owed their seats to corporate bribes, the Senate was finally persuaded to support the amendment.

The Progressive Era even spawned attacks on the framers. A prominent criticism was laid out in historian Charles S. Beard's *An Economic Interpretation of the Constitution*.[21] Arguing that the Constitution grew out of wealthy Americans' fears of the debtor rebellions, Beard claimed that the Constitution's elaborate systems of power and representation were devices for keeping power in the hands of the rich. As evidence, Beard cited the Constitution's protections of property and referred to Madison's notes on the Philadelphia convention, which showed that property concerns were high on the framers' agenda. Beard further noted that not one of the

HOW THE 50 STATES DIFFER

POLITICAL THINKING THROUGH COMPARISONS

Direct Democracy: The Initiative and Popular Referendum

In some states, by gathering enough signatures on a petition, citizens can directly enact or defeat legislation through their votes in an election. This action can occur through either an initiative (in which citizens place a legislative proposal of their own choosing on the ballot) or a popular referendum (in which citizens place an act of the state legislature on the ballot, which the voters can then accept or reject). A popular referendum is different from a legislative referendum, in which the state legislature itself places a proposal on the ballot for the voters to accept or reject. All states have a form of the legislative referendum, but only some states, as indicated in the map below, have the initiative and the popular referendum.

Q: *Why are the northeastern and southern states less likely than states in other regions to have the initiative and popular referendum?*

A: *The initiative and popular referendum were introduced in the early 1900s by the Progressives, who sought to weaken the power of political bosses and give voters a larger voice in their governance. In the Northeast, party machines had enough strength in state legislatures to block their enactment. In the South, these devices were blocked by the white establishment, which feared that blacks and poor whites would make use of them.*

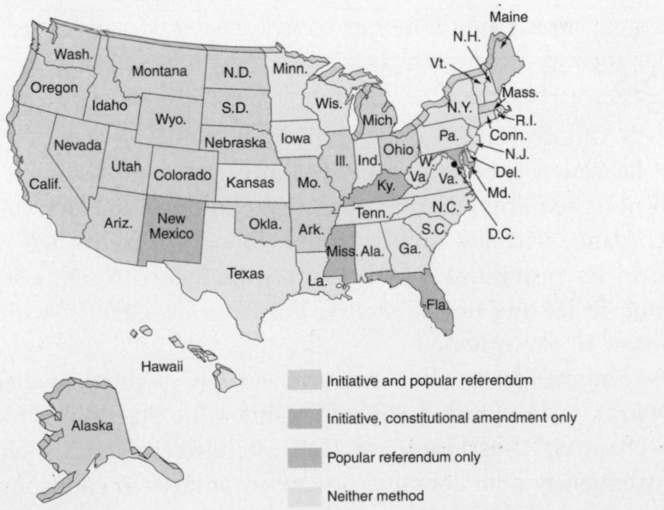

Source: From Initiative and Referendum Institute, University of Southern California. Reprinted with permission.

delegates was a workingman or farmer. Most of the framers had large landholdings, controlled substantial interests, or were major credit holders.

Beard's thesis was challenged by other historians, and he later acknowledged that he had not taken the framers' full array of motives into account. Their conception of separation of powers, for example, was a governing principle that had earlier been incorporated into state constitutions. Nevertheless, Beard held onto his claim that the Constitution was designed to protect the interests of the wealthy rather than to promote self-government.

Beard's claim has some validity, but to say that the framers were foes of democracy is inaccurate. Although they did not have great trust in popular rule, they were determined to balance the need to create a system of self-government with the need to create a system of limited government. Convinced that unchecked majority rule was likely to devolve into tyranny, the framers devised institutions that were responsive to majority opinion but not slaves to it.

POLITICAL THINKING

Trustees or Delegates?

Theorists and practitioners have long argued over the proper role of elected representatives. What is your view? Should they behave as trustees, who act in what they think is society's best interest, even if their judgment conflicts with that of their constituents? Or should they perform as delegates, who act in accordance with the expressed desires of those they represent?

CONSTITUTIONAL DEMOCRACY TODAY

The type of government created in the United States in 1787 could accurately be called a **constitutional democratic republic**. It is **constitutional** in its requirement that power gained through elections be exercised in accordance with law and with due respect for individual rights; **democratic** in its provisions for majority influence through elections; and a **republic** in its mix of deliberative institutions, each of which moderates the power of the others.[22]

By some standards, the American system of today is a model of *self-government*.[23] The United States schedules the election of its larger legislative chamber (the House of Representatives) and its chief executive more frequently than does any other democracy. In addition, it is the only major democracy to rely extensively on primary elections rather than party organizations for the selection of party nominees. The principle of direct popular election to office, which the writers of the Constitution regarded as a method to be used sparingly, has been extended further in the United States than anywhere else.

By other standards, however, the U.S. system is less democratic than some. Popular majorities must work against the barriers to power devised by the framers—divided branches, staggered terms of office, and separate constituencies. In fact, the link between an electoral majority and a governing majority is less direct in the American system than in nearly all other democratic systems. In the European parliamentary democracies, for example, legislative and executive power are not divided, are not subject to close check by the judiciary, and are acquired through the winning of a legislative majority in a single national election. The framers' vision was a different one, dominated by a concern with liberty and therefore with controls on political power. It was a response to the experiences they brought with them to Philadelphia in the summer of 1787.

SUMMARY Self-Test www.mhhe.com/pattersonwtp9e

The Constitution of the United States is a reflection of the colonial and revolutionary experiences of the early Americans. Freedom from abusive government was a reason for the colonies' revolt against British rule, but the English tradition also provided ideas about government, power, and freedom that were expressed in the Constitution and, earlier, in the Declaration of Independence.

The Constitution was designed in part to provide for a limited government in which political power would be confined to proper uses. The framers wanted to ensure that the government they were creating would not itself be a threat to freedom. To this end, they confined the national government to expressly granted powers and also denied it certain specific powers. Other prohibitions on government were later added to the Constitution in the form of stated guarantees of individual liberties in the Bill of Rights. The most significant constitutional provision for limited government, however, was a separation of powers among the three branches. The powers given to each branch enable it to act as a check on the exercise of power by the other two, an arrangement that during the nation's history has in fact served as a barrier to abuses of power.

The Constitution, however, made no mention of how the powers and limits of government were to be judged in practice. In its historic ruling in *Marbury v. Madison,* the Supreme Court assumed the authority to review the constitutionality of legislative and executive actions and to declare them unconstitutional and thus invalid.

The framers of the Constitution, respecting the idea of self-government but distrusting popular majorities, devised a system of government that they felt would temper popular opinion and slow its momentum so that the public's "true interest" (which includes a regard for the rights and interests of the minority) would guide public policy. Different methods were advanced for selecting the president, the members of the House and the Senate, and federal judges as a means of insulating political power against momentary majorities.

Since the adoption of the Constitution, the public gradually has assumed more direct control of its representatives, particularly through measures that affect the way officeholders are chosen. Presidential popular voting (linked to the Electoral College), direct election of senators, and primary elections are among the devices aimed at strengthening the majority's influence. These developments are rooted in the idea, deeply held by ordinary Americans, that the people must have substantial direct influence over their representatives if government is to serve their interests.

Key Terms

Anti-Federalists (*p. 38*)
Bill of Rights (*p. 48*)
checks and balances (*p. 44*)
constitution (*p. 30*)
constitutional democratic republic (*p. 58*)
delegates (*p. 56*)
democracy (according to the framers) (*p. 51*)
denials of power (*p. 42*)
Electoral College (*p. 53*)
electoral votes (*p. 53*)
Federalists (*p. 39*)
grants of power (*p. 41*)
Great Compromise (*p. 34*)
inalienable (natural) rights (*p. 29*)
judicial review (*p. 50*)
liberty (*p. 41*)
limited government (*p. 27*)
New Jersey (small-state) Plan (*p. 34*)
primary election (*p. 56*)
republic (*p. 51*)
self-government (*p. 27*)
separated institutions sharing power (*p. 44*)
separation of powers (*p. 43*)
social contract (*p. 29*)
Three-Fifths Compromise (*p. 35*)
trustees (*p. 32*)
tyranny of the majority (*p. 51*)
Virginia (large-state) Plan (*p. 34*)

Suggested Readings

Beard, Charles S. *An Economic Interpretation of the Constitution.* New York: Macmillan, 1941. Argues that the framers had selfish economic interests uppermost in their minds when they wrote the Constitution.

Bradburn, Douglas. *The Citizenship Revolution: Politics and the Creation of the American Union, 1774–1804.* Charlottesville: University of Virginia Press, 2009. A careful assessment of how Americans came to think of themselves as belonging to a union of states.

Ellis, Joseph J. *Founding Brothers: The Revolutionary Generation.* New York: Vintage, 2002. A riveting account of the lives of America's leading founders.

Federalist Papers. Many editions, including a one-volume paperback version edited by Isaac Kramnick (New York: Penguin, 1987). A series of essays written by Alexander Hamilton, James Madison, and John Jay under the pseudonym Publius; the essays, published in a New York newspaper in 1787–1788, explain the Constitution and support its ratification.

McGerr, Michael. *A Fierce Discontent: The Rise and Fall of the Progressive Movement in America, 1870–1920.* New York: Free Press, 2005. Assessment of the Progressive movement's contribution to American democracy.

Ostrom, Vincent. *The Political Theory of a Compound Republic: Designing the American Experiment.* Lanham, MD.: Lexington Books, 2007. An analysis of the logic of the Constitution as its writers envisioned it.

Pottinger, John R. *Reaping the Whirlwind: Liberal Democracy and the Religious Axis.* Washington, D.C.: Georgetown University Press, 2007. A thoughtful examination of the historical and contemporary relationship between religious expression and liberal democracy.

Sheehan, Colleen A. *James Madison and the Spirit of Republican Self-Government.* New York: Cambridge University Press, 2009. An account of Madison's analysis of the conditions under which self-government would thrive in America.

Tocqueville, Alexis de. *Democracy in America*, vols. 1 and 2, ed. J. P. Mayer. New York: Doubleday/Anchor, 1969. A classic analysis (originally published 1835–1840) of American democracy by an insightful French observer.

Wilentz, Sean. *The Rise of American Democracy: Jefferson to Lincoln.* New York: Norton, 2005. An account of how democratic ideas triumphed over aristocratic ones.

List of Websites

www.nara.gov The National Archives site; includes an in-depth look at the history of the Declaration of Independence.

http://odur.let.rug.nl/~usa/P/aj7/about/bio/jackxx.htm A site that focuses on Andrew Jackson and his role in shaping U.S. politics.

http://avalon.law.yale.edu/subject_menus/constpap.htm Includes documents on the Constitution, the American Revolution, and the constitutional convention.

http://avalon.law.yale.edu/subject_menus/jeffpap.htm A site that includes the papers of Thomas Jefferson, as well as his autobiography.

Politics in Theory and Practice

Thinking: Explain the types of power that result from each of America's major system of governing: democracy, constitutionalism, and free markets?

Participating: Knowledge and judgment are components of effective and responsible participation. From what sources do you get most of your political information? Are they reliable sources in the sense of placing a premium on accuracy? How frequently do you encounter opposing arguments or opinions? How carefully do you listen to them? When forming political opinions, do you tend to reflect upon your choices or do you tend to make snap judgments?

Extra Credit

For up-to-the-minute *New York Times* articles, interactive simulations, graphics, study tools, and more links and quizzes, visit the text's Online Learning Center at **www.mhhe.com/pattersonwtp9e**.

NATIONAL JOURNAL

Judicial Factions and the Constitution

The news from the recent oral argument in the Supreme Court's biggest pending case was that the five conservative justices seem poised to make the Second Amendment right to bear arms applicable to state and local gun controls, as well as federal. In the process, they will strike down the unusually strict handgun bans in Chicago and Oak Park, Ill.

But debate about the gun case, *McDonald v. City of Chicago*, has ranged far beyond guns. It has spawned an alliance of convenience among distinguished scholars in the progressive and conservative-libertarian camps.

Both have filed amicus briefs that take the gun-rights side while mainly seeking to expand other rights as well.

The detailed constitutional arguments show with unusual clarity why efforts to expand rights—whether favored by conservatives or liberals, or both—typically boil down to a bare-majority judicial faction using highly debatable theories to override democratic governance.

Many of the briefs in the gun case urge the Court to revive the 14th Amendment's open-ended but long-moribund "privileges or immunities" clause and use it as a new fount of judicial power to strike down enactments imposed by majority rule. But the privileges-or-immunities alliance breaks down when its members are pressed on which laws should be struck down and which rights should be expanded or created.

Conservative libertarians who want the courts to reject economic regulations stress the considerable evidence that the authors of the privileges or immunities clause wanted to protect property and contract rights as well as gun rights.

Progressive scholars, on the other hand, see the same principles evolving over 142 years to mandate judicial protection of welfare rights—called "the new property" by some—as well as privacy, abortion, gay rights, assisted suicide, and other liberal favorites about which nobody was thinking when the 14th Amendment was adopted in 1868.

Both groups are armed with powerful historical evidence that the 1873 precedent that gutted the privileges or immunities clause, the Slaughterhouse Cases, misread the intent of the amendment's framers. The precedent also paved the way for subsequent decisions that helped Southern whites subjugate freed slaves by, among other things, disarming them and leaving them defenseless against the Ku Klux Klan.

But the justices who spoke during the oral argument on McDonald—including those pushing to expand gun rights—were hostile to the privileges-or-immunities justification. Justice Antonin Scalia deprecated the clause as "the darling of the professoriate."

Why so dismissive? Were the justices showing respect for a deeply rooted, 137-year-old precedent, as several argued? Well, sure. They always show respect for precedent—except when they don't. Were they showing judicial restraint, by passing up a chance to grab more power? Doubtful. None of the nine justices has shown much modesty in finding support for his or her own policy preferences in the Constitution.

Were they worried about what their ideological adversaries (and future adversaries) might do with an open-ended license to conjure up new "privileges or immunities" by refracting selected fragments of historical evidence through their own philosophies?

That's my guess. The justices know that whatever clarity the text of this and other constitutional clauses may have once had has receded over many decades, as the clarity of a road sign recedes in the rearview mirror. They also know that the future content of a revived privileges or immunities clause would likely hinge on nothing more objective than the ideological leanings and policy preferences of future justices and the presidents who pick them.

You want the Court to comb through 19th-century history and find a mandate for unfettered capitalism? Vote Republican. You want it to impose welfare rights, with a heavy dose of judicial empathy? Vote Democratic. And hope for well-timed vacancies and long-lived justices who share your policy preferences.

Meanwhile, the notion of constitutional rights as immutable principles protecting our liberties from majoritarian tyranny morphs into rule by whichever faction happens to have a one-vote majority on the Supreme Court.

Shifting majorities have long advanced their own views incrementally by reading ambiguous historical evidence as supporting causes ranging from gun rights to gay rights, both of which have been put over the top by Justice Anthony Kennedy's conservative leanings on the former and liberal leanings on the latter.

But none of the nine—except perhaps Justice Clarence Thomas, who was silent as usual during the argument in the gun case—seems prepared to risk giving a privileges-or-immunities blank check to whichever faction may control the Court in the future.

Some history: The 14th Amendment was adopted in 1868, after many months of congressional hearings, primarily to give freed slaves the rights of full citizens and give Congress the power to override oppressive state and local laws, especially in the South.

Here's the critical language for purposes of the current debate: "No state shall make or enforce any law which shall abridge the privileges or immunities of citizens of the United States; nor shall any state deprive any person of life, liberty, or property, without due process of law; . . ."

Historical evidence strongly suggests that the first clause was intended to make applicable against the states and their localities all provisions of the first 10 amendments (the Bill of Rights)—which had previously limited only the federal government—and perhaps also an unspecified number of other, unenumerated rights.

But the Supreme Court virtually nullified this broad language in the 1873 Slaughterhouse Cases by narrowing it to a few "privileges" and "immunities" rooted in federal citizenship, such as the right to be protected while at sea.

Subsequent decisions using similar logic helped facilitate the subjugation of blacks in the South for most of the next century. These rulings also help explain why most of the Bill of Rights, including the First Amendment, was not applied to state or local governments until the 1920s and thereafter.

By then, the Supreme Court had found another way to apply provisions of the Bill of Rights—almost all of them, eventually—against the states, along with other judicially recognized (or, critics say, judicially invented) rights including family privacy, contraception, and abortion. The Court construed the 14th Amendment's due process clause as "selectively incorporating" against the states those rights that the justices deemed fundamental to American liberty.

This "substantive due process" doctrine has been assailed by many conservative critics—especially since Roe v. Wade—and some liberals as a judicial power grab inconsistent with the language of the due process clause, which by its terms guarantees only procedural fairness.

But advocates of expansive judicial power to create new rights—liberals and conservative libertarians alike—have responded with strong evidence that the long-buried privileges or immunities clause was originally understood to give courts even broader powers than the due process clause.

Despite this evidence, Scalia, the great originalist, suggested that ancient and deeply rooted precedents trump original meaning. "Even I have acquiesced" in the legitimacy of substantive due process, he said, even though "I think it's wrong."

A deeper question, in my view, is this: Why should the words of a few congressional leaders more than 140 years ago—as seen through the diverse, distorting lenses of current Supreme Court majorities—trump the views of elected majorities today? As Justice Stephen Breyer asked, why should equivocal evidence of what was intended in 1868 wipe out a handgun ban thought by Chicago's elected leaders to have saved hundreds of 21st-century lives?

These fundamental questions about the 14th Amendment have come to the fore because of a big 5-4 decision in 2008. The Court held for the first time that the Second Amendment protects a right to "keep and bear arms" not only for service in now-defunct state militias—as had long been widely assumed—but also for self-defense against intruders and other, so-far-unspecified, individual uses.

The 2008 decision struck down the District of Columbia's broad handgun ban, while noting that other gun controls imposed by the federal government and its enclaves would be upheld if deemed reasonable by the courts. It left open the question before the Court now: Did the 14th Amendment make the same (or similar) gun rights applicable against state and local regulation?

I could see no clear winner in the 2008 decision's learned but clashing interpretations of the Second Amendment. "It seems almost perverse," I wrote then, "to be assessing what gun controls to allow based not on examining how best to save lives but on seeking to read the minds of the men who ratified the Bill of Rights well over 200 years ago."

It's almost as hard to read the minds of those who wrote the 14th Amendment 142 years ago. They do seem to have intended to protect the rights of freed slaves and others to have guns to defend themselves against KKK terror. But the rest, or most of it, is in the eye of the beholder.

What's Your Opinion?

How do you think the "privileges and immunities" clause in the 14th Amendment should be read? Should it protect only a few narrowly defined rights, or is it more expansive?

To what extent do you think the intentions of framers of the Constitution, including its amendments, should be taken into account by the federal courts? Should the Supreme Court really try to determine—and weigh—what lawmakers intended in 1789 or 1868?

CHAPTER 3

FEDERALISM: FORGING A NATION

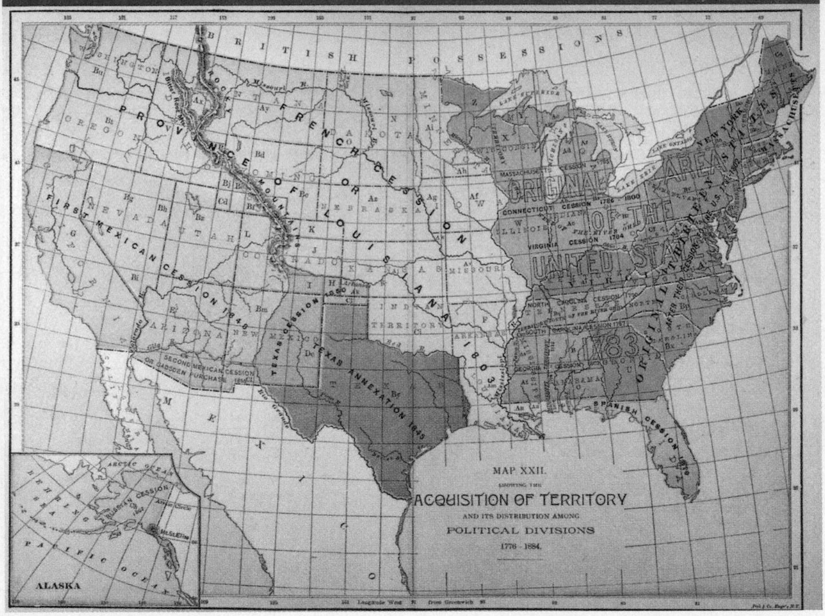

> “The question of the relation of the states to the federal government is the cardinal question of our Constitutional system. It cannot be settled by the opinion of one generation, because it is a question of growth, and each successive stage of our political and economic development gives it a new aspect, makes it a new question.”
>
> WOODROW WILSON[1]

A few weeks into his presidency and to the dismay of some supporters, Barack Obama endorsed the reauthorization of the No Child Left Behind Act (NCLB). The teachers' unions were hoping that the program would be scrapped, or at least altered greatly. Obama acknowledged the need for some adjustments but said NCLB's goal—higher standards and greater accountability for the public schools—is the right one.

NCLB was first enacted in 2003, at the urging of President George W. Bush. NCLB requires the states to test their public school students annually as a condition of receiving federal aid. Supporters of NCLB claim that strict federal testing standards are necessary if schools are to improve and be held accountable for performance. Opponents claim NCLB undermines the schools' mission by forcing faculty "to teach to the test" and by burdening administrators with test-related paperwork.

NCLB is arguably the largest federal intrusion on how local schools operate. Education has traditionally been under the control of state and local governments. Even today, they provide more than 90 percent of education funding, while also determining most of the educational standards, from teachers' qualifications to the length of the school year. NCLB is a sharp break from the state-centered tradition of education. A bipartisan commission of the National Conference of State Legislatures had scathing words for NCLB, saying it was based on "questionable constitutional underpinnings," was "overly rigid" and "thinly funded," and "coerced" states by requiring participation as a condition of receiving federal education funds.[2] Utah was among the states that refused to comply with NCLB provisions that were not adequately funded.

The controversy surrounding NCLB is one of thousands of disagreements over the course of American history that have hinged on whether national or state authority should prevail. Americans possess what amounts to dual citizenship: they are citizens both of the United States and of the state where they reside. The American political system is a *federal system*, in which constitutional authority is divided between a national government and state governments. Each government is assumed to derive its powers directly from the people and therefore to have sovereignty (final authority) over the policy responsibilities assigned to it. The federal system consists of nation *and* states, indivisible yet separate.[3]

POLITICAL THINKING

National Testing, Good Idea or Bad?

The No Child Left Behind Act (NCLB) requires states to administer nationally standardized tests to their public school students as a condition for receiving federal education funds. Do you think these tests improve public education, or do you think they weaken it by reducing teachers' flexibility? Do you think the national government through NCLB is meddling in a policy area that properly belongs to states and localities?

The relationship between the nation and the states was the most pressing issue when the Constitution was written and has been a divisive issue ever since. In one case, the Civil War, it nearly caused the dissolution of the United States. And throughout the nation's history, federalism has been a source of contention between the Republican and Democratic parties, though they have shifted sides when it served their political goals. This chapter examines federalism—its creation through the Constitution, its evolution during the nation's history, and its current status. The main points presented in the chapter are these:

- *The power of government must be equal to its responsibilities.* The Constitution was needed because the nation's preceding system (under the Articles of Confederation) was too weak to accomplish its expected goals, particularly those of a strong defense and an integrated economy.
- *Federalism—the Constitution's division of governing authority between two levels, nation and states—was the result of political bargaining.* Federalism was not a theoretical principle, but rather a compromise made necessary in 1787 by the prior existence of the states.
- *Federalism is not a fixed principle for allocating power between the national and state governments, but rather a principle that has changed over time in response to political needs and partisan ideology.* Federalism has passed through several distinct stages in the course of the nation's history.
- *Contemporary federalism tilts toward national authority, reflecting the increased interdependence of American society.*

Federalism: National and State Sovereignty

At the time of the writing of the Constitution, some of America's top leaders were dead set against the creation of a stronger national government. When rumors began to circulate that the Philadelphia convention was devising just such a government, Virginia's Patrick Henry said that he "smelt a rat." His fears were confirmed when he obtained a copy of the draft constitution. "Who authorized them," he asked, "to speak the language of 'We, the People,' instead of 'We, the States'?"

The question of "people versus states" was precipitated by the failure of the Articles of Confederation. It had created a union of the states, and they alone had authority over the people (see Chapter 2). The national government could not tax or conscript citizens, nor could it regulate their economic activities. Its directives applied only to the states, and they often ignored them. Georgia and North Carolina, for example, contributed no money at all to the national treasury between 1781 and 1786, and the federal government had no way to force them to pay. The only feasible

Patrick Henry was a leading figure in the American Revolution ("Give me liberty or give me death!"). He later opposed ratification of the Constitution on grounds that the national government should be a union of states and not also of people.

solution to this problem was to give the federal government direct authority over the people. If individuals are ordered to pay taxes, most of them will do so rather than accept the alternative—imprisonment or confiscation of their property.

At the same time, the writers of the Constitution wanted to preserve the states. The states had their own constitutions and a governing history extending back to the colonial era. And although their residents thought of themselves as Americans, many of them identified more strongly with their states. When Virginia's George Mason said that he would never agree to a constitution that abolished the states, he was speaking for nearly all the delegates.

These two realities—the need to preserve the states and the need for a national government with direct authority over the people—led the framers to invent an entirely new system of government. Before this point in history, **sovereignty** (supreme and final governing authority) had been regarded as indivisible. By definition, a government cannot be sovereign if it can be overruled by another government. Nevertheless, the framers divided sovereignty between the national government and the states, a system now know as **federalism**. Each level—the national government and the state governments—directly governs the residents within its assigned territory. Each level has authority that is not subject to the other's approval. And each level is constitutionally protected. The national government cannot abolish a state, and the states cannot abolish the national government.

In 1787, other nations in the world were governed by a **unitary system**, in which sovereignty is vested solely in the national government. Local or regional governments in a unitary system do not have sovereignty. They have authority only to the degree that it is granted by the national government, which can also withdraw any such grant. (This situation applies to America's local governments. They are not sovereign, but instead derive their authority from their respective state governments, which can, though it occurs rarely, even choose to abolish a local unit of government.)

Federalism is also different from a **confederacy**, which was the type of government that existed under the Articles of Confederation. In a confederacy, the states alone are sovereign. They decide the authority, even the continuing existence, of the central government. Confederacies have been rare in human history, but the government of the Articles was not the first. The ancient Greek city-states and medieval Europe's Hanseatic League were of this type.

The federal system established in 1787 divides the responsibilities of government between the nation and the states (see Figure 3-1). The system gives states the power to address local issues in ways of their choosing; they have primary responsibility, for example, for public education and police protection. The national government, on the other hand, is

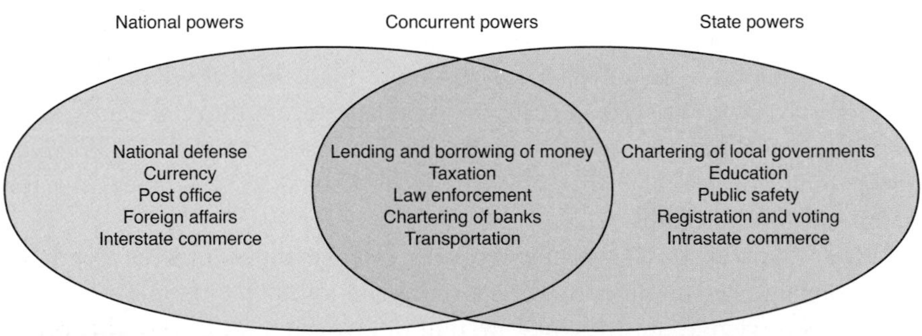

figure 3-1 FEDERALISM AS A GOVERNING SYSTEM: EXAMPLES OF NATIONAL, STATE, AND CONCURRENT POWERS

The American federal system divides sovereignty between a national government and the state governments. Each is constitutionally protected in its existence and authority, although their powers overlap somewhat even in areas granted to one level (for example, the federal government has a role in education policy).

responsible for matters of national scope, such as military defense and the currency. The national and state governments also have some concurrent powers (that is, powers exercised over the same policy areas). Each of them has, for example, the power to raise taxes and borrow money.

The Argument for Federalism

The strongest argument for federalism in 1787 was that it would correct the defects in the Articles. Two of the defects were particularly troublesome: the national government had neither the power to tax nor the power to regulate commerce among the states. Without money from taxes, the national government lacked the financial means to maintain an army strong enough to prevent encroachment by European powers or to maintain a navy strong enough to protect America's merchant ships from harassment and attack by foreign navies and pirates. And without the ability to regulate commerce, the national government could neither promote the general economy nor prevent trade wars between the states. New York and New Jersey were among the states that imposed taxes on goods shipped into their state from other states.

Although it is sometimes claimed that "the government which governs least is the government that governs best," the Articles proved otherwise. The problems with the too-weak national government were severe: public disorder, economic chaos, and an inadequate defense. Although the problems were widely recognized, many Americans in 1787 feared that a strong central government would eventually swallow up the states. An outspoken Anti-Federalist (as opponents of the Constitution were called) proclaimed: "[The states] will eventually be absorbed by our grand continental vortex, or dwindle into petty corporations, and have power over little else than yoking hogs or determining the width of cart wheels."[4]

The challenge of providing a response fell to James Madison and Alexander Hamilton. During the ratification debate, they argued in a series of essays (the so-called *Federalist Papers*) that a federal system would protect liberty and moderate the power of government.

Protecting Liberty Although theorists such as John Locke and Montesquieu had not proposed a division of power between national and local authorities as a means of protecting liberty, the framers argued that federalism was a part of the system of checks and balances.[5] Alexander Hamilton wrote in *Federalist* No. 28 that the American people could shift their loyalties back and forth between the national and state governments in order to keep each under control. "If [the people's] rights are invaded by either," Hamilton wrote, "they can make use of the other as the instrument of

HOW THE U.S. DIFFERS
POLITICAL THINKING THROUGH COMPARISONS

Federal versus Unitary Governments

Federalism involves the division of sovereignty between a national government and subnational (state) governments. It was invented in the United States in 1787 to maintain the preexisting American states while establishing an effective central government. Since then, other countries have established a *federal* government, but most countries continue to have a *unitary* government, in which all sovereignty is vested in the national government.

Even within these alternative political systems, differences exist. In Germany's federal system, for example, the states have limited lawmaking powers but exercise broad authority in determining how national laws will be implemented. By comparison, the U.S. federal system grants substantial lawmaking powers to the states except in specified areas such as national defense and currency. Unitary systems also differ. In Britain, the national government has delegated substantial authority to regions; Scotland, for example, has its own parliament, which exercises lawmaking powers. In France's unitary government, on the other hand, political authority is highly centralized.

In nearly all federal systems, the national legislature has two chambers—one apportioned by population (as in the case of the U.S. House of Representatives) and one apportioned by geographical area (as in the case of the U.S. Senate). The U.S. Senate is a pure federal institution in the sense that each state has the same number of senators. In some federal systems, such as Germany's, the states are not equally represented even in the legislative chamber that is apportioned on the basis of geography rather than population:

Q: *Federal systems typically have a two-chamber legislature. Unitary systems, on the other hand, typically have a single legislative chamber. Why?*

A: *In a unitary system, there is no constitutional need for a second legislative chamber based on geographical subdivisions (states), as is the case with a federal system.*

Country	Form of Government
Canada	Federal
France	Unitary
Germany	Federal
Great Britain	Modified unitary
Italy	Modified unitary
Japan	Unitary
Mexico	Modified federal
Sweden	Unitary
United States	Federal

redress." In *Federalist* No. 46, Madison argued that the national government would not be a threat to liberty because people had a stronger allegiance to their state, which would serve as a barrier to federal encroachment. And if a state should somehow fail to respect people's rights and interests, they could appeal to the national government. "The people ought not surely to be precluded," Madison wrote, "from giving most of their confidence where they may discover it to be the most due."

Moderating the Power of Government To the Anti-Federalists, the sacrifice of the states' power to the nation was as unwise as it was unnecessary. They claimed that a distant national government could never serve the people's interests as well as the states could. Liberty *and* self-government, the Anti-Federalists argued, were enhanced by state-centered government. In support of their contention, they turned to Montesquieu, who had concluded that a small republic is more likely than a large one to serve people's interests. When government encompasses a large area, he argued, its leaders lose touch with the people and disregard their welfare.

In *Federalist* No. 10, James Madison took issue with this claim. He argued that whether a government serves the common good is a function not of its size but of the range of interests that share political power. The problem with a small republic, Madison claimed, is that it can have a dominant faction—whether it be landholders, financiers, an impoverished majority, or some other group—that is strong enough to control government and use it for selfish purposes. A large republic is less likely to have an all-powerful faction. If financiers are strong in one area of a large republic, they are likely to be weaker elsewhere. The same will be true of farmers, merchants, laborers, and other groups. A large republic, Madison concluded, would blunt attempts by a single group to control it, which would force groups to cooperate. In making this claim, Madison was arguing not for central authority but for limited government, which he believed would result if power was shared widely. "Extend the sphere," said Madison, "and you take in a greater variety of parties and interests; you make it less probable that a majority of the whole will have a common motive to invade the rights of other citizens."

The Powers of the Nation and the States

The U.S. Constitution addresses the lawful authority of the national government, which is provided through *enumerated and implied powers.* Authority that is not granted to the national government is left—or "reserved"—to the states. Thus, the states have *reserved powers.*

Enumerated Powers and the Supremacy Clause Article I of the Constitution grants to Congress seventeen **enumerated (expressed) powers.** The framers expected these powers to establish a government strong enough to forge a union that was secure in its defense and stable in its economy. Congress's powers, for example, to regulate commerce among the states, to create a national currency, and to borrow money would provide a foundation for a sound national economy. Its power to tax, combined with its authority to establish an army and navy and to declare war, would enable it to provide for the common defense.

In addition, the Constitution prohibits the states from actions that would encroach on national powers. Article I, Section 10, prohibits the states from making treaties with other nations, raising armies, waging war, printing money, or entering into commercial agreements with other states without the approval of Congress.

The writers of the Constitution recognized that the lawful exercise of national authority would at times conflict with the laws of the states. In such instances, national law was intended to prevail. Article VI of the Constitution grants this dominance in the so-called **supremacy clause**, which provides that "the laws of the United States . . . shall be the supreme law of the land."

Implied Powers: The Necessary and Proper Clause The writers of the Constitution recognized that government, if it was to be effective, had to be capable of adjusting to change. A weaknesses of the Articles was that the national government was prohibited from exercising powers not expressly granted it, which limited its ability to meet the country's changing needs after the end of the Revolutionary War. To avoid this problem with the new government, the framers included in Article I of the Constitution the **"necessary and proper" clause** or, as it later came to be known, the **elastic clause.** It gives Congress the power "to make all laws which shall be necessary and proper for carrying into execution the foregoing [enumerated] powers." This clause gives the national government **implied powers**: powers that are not listed in the Constitution but are related to the exercise of powers that are listed.

Reserved Powers: The States' Authority The supremacy and "necessary and proper" clauses were worrisome to the Anti-Federalists. The two clauses stoked their fear of an overly powerful national government because they provided a constitutional basis for expanding the government's authority. Such concerns led them to demand a constitutional amendment that would protect states' rights and interests. Ratified in 1791 as the Tenth Amendment to the Constitution, it reads: "The powers not delegated to the United States by the Constitution, nor prohibited by it to the States, are reserved to the States." The states' powers under the U.S. Constitution are thus called **reserved powers.**

Federalism in Historical Perspective

Since ratification of the Constitution over two centuries ago, no aspect of it has provoked more frequent or bitter conflict than federalism. By establishing two levels of sovereign authority, the Constitution created two centers of power and ambition, each of which was sure to claim disputed areas as belonging to it. Ambiguities in the Constitution have also contributed to conflict between the nation and the states. The document does not delineate, for example, the dividing line between *inter*state commerce (which the national government is empowered to regulate) and *intra*state commerce (which is reserved for regulation by the states).

Not surprisingly, federalism has been a contentious and dynamic system, its development determined less by constitutional language than by the strength of partisan interests and by the country's changing needs. Federalism can be viewed as having progressed through three historical eras, each of which has involved a different relationship between the nation and the states. At the same time, each era has ended with a national government that was stronger than at the start of the era. Over the long term, the United States has undergone a process of **nationalization**—an increase in national authority. The shift is due primarily to economic growth and political action.

An Indestructible Union (1789–1865)

The issue during the first era—which lasted from the time the Constitution went into effect (1789) until the end of the Civil War (1865)—was the Union's survival. Given America's state-centered history before the Constitution, it was inevitable that the states would dispute national policies that threatened their interests.

The Nationalist View: McCulloch v. Maryland An early dispute over federalism arose when President George Washington's secretary of the treasury, Alexander Hamilton, proposed that Congress establish a national bank. Hamilton and his supporters claimed that because the federal government had constitutional authority to regulate currency, it had the "implied power" to establish a national bank. Thomas Jefferson, Washington's secretary of state, opposed the bank on the grounds that its activities would enrich the wealthy at the expense of ordinary people. Jefferson claimed the bank was unlawful because the Constitution did not expressly authorize it. Jefferson said: "I consider the foundation of the Constitution as laid on this ground that 'all powers not delegated to the United States by the Constitution, nor prohibited by it to the states, are preserved to the states or to the people.' . . . To take a single step beyond the boundaries thus drawn . . . is to take possession of a boundless field of power, no longer susceptible of any definition."

Of the framers, Alexander Hamilton had the clearest vision of what was needed to create a strong national government. As secretary of the treasury under President Washington, Hamilton succeeded in getting Congress to establish a national bank and to consolidate state debts at the federal level. Thereafter, creditors at home and abroad put their trust in the federal government rather than the state governments.

Jefferson's argument failed to sway Congress. In 1791, it established the First Bank of the United States, granting it a twenty-year charter. Although Congress did not renew the bank's charter when it expired in 1811, Congress decided in 1816 to establish the Second Bank of the United States. State and local banks did not want competition from a national bank and sought help from their state legislatures. Several states, including Maryland, levied taxes on the national bank's operations within their borders, hoping to drive it out of existence by making it unprofitable. James McCulloch, who was in charge of the Maryland branch of the national bank, refused to pay the Maryland tax and the resulting dispute was heard by the Supreme Court.

The chief justice of the Supreme Court, John Marshall, was a fervent nationalist, and in *McCulloch v. Maryland* (1819) the Court ruled decisively in favor of national authority. It was reasonable to infer, Marshall concluded, that a government with powers to tax, borrow money, and regulate commerce could establish a bank in order to exercise those powers effectively. Marshall's argument was a clear statement of *implied powers*—the idea that through the "necessary and proper" clause the national government's powers extend beyond a narrow reading of its enumerated powers.

Marshall's ruling also addressed the meaning of the Constitution's supremacy clause. The state of Maryland had argued that, even if the national government had the authority to establish a bank, a state had the authority to tax it. The Supreme Court rejected Maryland's position, concluding that valid national law overrides conflicting state law. Because the national government had the power to create the bank, it also could protect the bank from state actions, such as taxation, that might destroy it.[6]

The *McCulloch* decision served as precedent for later rulings in support of national power. In *Gibbons v. Ogden* (1824), for example, the Marshall-led Court rejected a New York law granting one of its residents a monopoly on a ferry that operated between New York and New Jersey, concluding that New York had encroached on Congress's power to regulate commerce among the states. The Court asserted that Congress's commerce power was not limited to trade between the states, but to all aspects of that trade, including the transportation of goods. Accordingly, congressional action on interstate commerce overrides any and all conflicting state law. "The power over commerce," the Court said, "is vested in Congress as absolutely as it would be in a single government."[7]

Marshall's opinions asserted that legitimate uses of national power took precedence over state authority and that the "necessary and proper" clause and the commerce clause were broad grants of national power. As a nationalist, Marshall provided the U.S. government with the legal justification for expanding its power in ways that fostered the development of the United States as a nation rather than as a collection of states. This constitutional vision was of utmost significance. As Justice Oliver Wendell Holmes Jr. noted a century later, the Union would not have survived if each state had been allowed to decide for itself which national laws it would obey.[8]

The States'-Rights View: The Dred Scott *Decision* Although John Marshall's rulings strengthened national authority, the issue of slavery posed a growing threat to the Union's survival. Westward expansion and immigration into the northern states were tilting power in Congress toward the free states, which increasingly signaled their determination to outlaw slavery at some future time. Fearing the possibility, southern leaders did what others have done throughout American history: they developed a constitutional interpretation fitted to their political purpose. John C. Calhoun declared that the United States was founded upon a "compact" between the states. The national government, he said, was "a government of states . . . not a government of individuals."[9] This line of reasoning led Calhoun to his famed "doctrine of nullification," which declared that a state has the constitutional right to nullify a national law.

A first dispute over federalism was whether the Constitution allowed the creation of a Bank of the United States (shown here in an early-nineteenth-century painting). The Constitution had a clause authorizing the printing of currency but not the establishment of a bank itself.

In 1832, South Carolina invoked this doctrine, declaring "null and void" a tariff law that favored northern interests. President Andrew Jackson called South Carolina's action "incompatible with the existence of the Union," a position that was strengthened when Congress authorized Jackson to use military force if necessary against South Carolina. The state backed down when Congress amended the tariff act to soften its impact on the South. The clash foreshadowed the Civil War, a confrontation of far greater consequence. Although war would not break out for another three decades, the dispute over states' rights was intensifying.

The Supreme Court's infamous *Dred Scott* decision (1857), written by Chief Justice Roger Taney, an ardent states'-rights advocate, inflamed the dispute. Dred Scott, a slave who had lived in the North for four years, applied for his freedom when his master died, citing a federal law—the Missouri Compromise of 1820—that made slavery illegal in a free state or territory. The Supreme Court ruled against Scott, claiming that persons of African descent were barred from citizenship and thereby could not sue for their freedom in federal courts. The Court also invalidated the Missouri Compromise. The Court ruled that slaves were property, not people. Accordingly, since the Constitution forbid Congress to deny owners their property rights, Congress did not have the power to outlaw slavery in any part of the United States.[10]

The Taney Court's decision provoked outrage in the North and contributed to a sectional split in the nation's majority party, the Democrats. In 1860, the Democratic Party's northern and southern wings nominated separate candidates for the presidency, which split the Democratic vote, enabling the Republican candidate, Abraham Lincoln, to win the presidency with only 40 percent of the popular vote. Lincoln had campaigned on a platform that called, not for an immediate end to slavery, but for its gradual abolition through payments to slaveholders. Nevertheless, southern states saw Lincoln's election as a grave threat to their way of life. By the time Lincoln assumed office, seven southern states, led by South Carolina, had left the Union. Four more states were to follow. In justifying his decision to wage war on the secessionists, Lincoln said, "The Union is older than the states." In 1865, the superior strength of the Union army settled by force the question of whether national authority is binding on the states.

Dual Federalism and Laissez-Faire Capitalism (1865–1937)

Although the North's victory in the Civil War preserved the Union, new challenges to federalism were surfacing. Constitutional doctrine held that

The American Civil War was the bloodiest conflict the world had yet known. Ten percent of fighting-age males died in the four-year war, and uncounted others were wounded. The death toll—618,000 (360,000 from the North, 258,000 from the South)—exceeded that of the American war dead in World War I, World War II, the Korean War, and the Vietnam War combined. This death toll was in a nation with a population only one-tenth the size it is today. Shown here, in one of the earliest war photos ever taken, are the bodies of soldiers killed at the battle of Antietam.

certain policy areas, such as interstate commerce and defense, belonged exclusively to the national government, whereas other policy areas, such as public health and intrastate commerce, belonged exclusively to the states. This doctrine, known as **dual federalism**, was based on the idea that a precise separation of national and state authority was both possible and desirable. "The power which one possesses," said the Supreme Court, "the other does not."[11]

American society, however, was in the midst of changes that raised questions about the suitability of dual federalism as a governing concept. The Industrial Revolution had given rise to large business firms, which were using their economic power to dominate markets and exploit workers. Government was the logical counterforce to this economic power. Which level of government—state or national—would regulate business?

There was also the issue of the former slaves. The white South had lost the war but was hardly of a mind to share power with the newly freed slaves. Would the federal government be allowed to intervene in state affairs to ensure the fair treatment of African Americans?

Dual federalism became a barrier to an effective response to these issues. From the 1860s through the 1930s, the Supreme Court held firm to the idea that there was a sharp line between national and state authority and, in both areas, a high wall of separation between government and the economy. The era of dual federalism was characterized by state supremacy in racial policy and business supremacy in commerce policy.

The Fourteenth Amendment and State Discretion Ratified after the Civil War, the Fourteenth Amendment was intended to protect the newly freed slaves from discriminatory action by state governments. A state was prohibited from depriving "any person of life, liberty, or property without due process of law," from denying "any person within its jurisdiction the equal protection of the laws," and from abridging "the privileges or immunities of citizens of the United States."

Supreme Court rulings in subsequent decades, however, undermined the Fourteenth Amendment's promise of liberty and equality for all. In 1873, for example, the Court held that the Fourteenth Amendment did not substantially limit the power of the states to determine the rights to which their residents were entitled.[12] Then, in *Plessy v. Ferguson* (1896), the Court issued its infamous "separate but equal" ruling. A black man, Homer Adolph Plessy, had been convicted of violating a Louisiana law that required white and black citizens to ride in separate railroad cars. The Supreme Court upheld his conviction, concluding that state governments could force blacks to use separate facilities as long as the facilities were "equal" in quality to those reserved for use by whites. "If one race be inferior to the other socially," the Court concluded, "the Constitution of the United States cannot put them on the same plane." The lone dissenting justice in the case, John Marshall Harlan, had harsh words for his colleagues: "Our Constitution is color-blind and neither knows nor tolerates classes among citizens. . . . The thin disguise of 'equal' accommodations . . . will not mislead anyone nor atone for the wrong this day done."[13]

With its *Plessy* decision, the Supreme Court sanctioned government-based racial segregation in the South. Black children were forced into separate public schools that seldom had libraries and usually had few teachers. Public hospitals for blacks had few doctors and nurses and almost no medical supplies and equipment. The *Plessy* ruling had become a justification for the separate and *unequal* treatment of black Americans.[14]

POLITICAL THINKING

Protector of Rights, Nation or States?

During the debate over ratification of the Constitution, Americans argued over whether liberty and equality would be better protected by the states or by the nation. The Anti-Federalists argued that a small republic was closer to the people and therefore would do more to uphold individual rights. James Madison, arguing on behalf of the Federalists, countered by saying that a large republic was preferable because its wide diversity of interests would force groups to compromise and therefore contribute to political moderation and tolerance. Historically, which level of government do you think has been more protective of liberty and equality? (The history of racial discrimination should be part of your assessment.) In terms of contemporary politics, which level of government—federal or state—is more protective of liberty and equality?

Judicial Protection of Business After the Civil War, the Supreme Court also gave nearly free rein to business. A majority of the Court's justices were proponents of laissez-faire capitalism (which holds that business should be "allowed to act" without interference), and they interpreted the Constitution in ways that restricted government's attempts to regulate business activity. In 1886, for example, the Court decided that corporations were "persons" within the meaning of the Fourteenth Amendment, and thereby were protected from substantial regulation by the states.[15] In other words, a constitutional amendment that had been enacted to protect newly freed slaves from being treated as second-class persons was ignored for that purpose but used instead to protect fictitious persons—business corporations.

The Court also weakened the national government's regulatory power by narrowly interpreting its commerce power. The Constitution's **commerce clause** says that Congress shall have the power "to regulate commerce" among the states. However, the clause does not spell out the economic activities included in the grant of power. When the federal government invoked the Sherman Antitrust Act (1890) in an attempt to break up a monopoly on the manufacture of sugar, the Supreme Court blocked the action, claiming that interstate commerce covered only the "transportation" of goods, not their "manufacture."[16] Manufacturing was deemed part of intrastate commerce and thus, according to the dual federalism doctrine,

During the era of racial segregation in the South, this sign at the entrance to the Memphis public zoo meant that it was Tuesday —the only day black people were allowed to go to the zoo. On the other six days of the week, the sign excluded black people from entering. The Memphis zoo was typical of life in the South during the so-called Jim Crow era that followed the Civil War. Such policies were upheld by federal courts despite prohibitions against discrimination set forth in the U.S. Constitution.

subject to state regulation only. However, because the Court had previously decided that the states' regulatory powers were limited by the Fourteenth Amendment, the states were not allowed to regulate manufacturing activity in a significant way.

Although some business regulation was subsequently allowed, the Supreme Court remained an obstacle to efforts to curb abusive business practices. An example is the case of *Hammer v. Dagenhart* (1918), which arose from a 1916 federal act that prohibited the interstate shipment of goods produced by child labor. The act had public support in that factory owners were exploiting children, working them for long hours at low pay. Nevertheless, the Court invalidated the law, ruling that the Tenth Amendment gave the states, and not the federal government, the power to regulate factory practices.[17] However, in an earlier case, *Lochner v. New York*

(1905), the Court had prevented states from regulating labor practices, concluding that such action violated owners' property rights.[18]

In effect, the Court had negated the principle of self-government. Neither the people's representatives in Congress nor their representatives in the state legislatures were allowed to regulate business activity. America's corporations, with the Supreme Court as their protector, were in control.[19]

National Authority Prevails The Democratic Party with its working-class base attacked the Court's position, and its candidates increasingly called for greater regulation of business and more rights for labor. Progressive Republicans like Theodore Roosevelt also fought against uncontrolled business power, but the Republican Party as a whole was ideologically committed to unregulated markets and to a small role for the federal government. Accordingly, when the Great Depression began in 1929, Republican president Herbert Hoover refused to use federal authority to put people back to work. Adhering to his party's free-market philosophy, Hoover argued that the economy would soon rebound on its own and that government intervention would only delay the recovery.

In the 1932 election, voters elected as president the Democratic candidate, Franklin D. Roosevelt, who recognized that the economy had become a national one. More than 10 million workers (compared to one million in 1860) were employed by industry, whose products were marketed throughout the nation. Urban workers typically were dependent on landlords for their housing, on farmers and grocers for their food, and on corporations for their jobs. Farmers were more independent, but they too were increasingly a part of a larger economic network. Farmers' income depended on market prices and shipping and equipment costs.[20] Economic interdependence meant that, when the depression hit in 1929, its effects could not be contained. At the depths of the Great Depression, one-fourth of the nation's workforce was unemployed and another fourth could find only part-time work.

The states by tradition had responsibility for helping the unemployed, but they were nearly penniless because of declining tax revenues and the huge demand for welfare assistance. Franklin Roosevelt's New Deal programs were designed to ease the hardship. The 1933 National Industry Recovery Act (NIRA), for example, established a federal jobs program and enabled major industries to coordinate their production decisions. Economic conservatives strenuously opposed such programs, accusing Roosevelt of leading the country into socialism. They found an ally in the Supreme Court. In *Schecter Poultry Corp. v. United States* (1935), just as it had done in previous New Deal cases, the Supreme Court in a 5-4 ruling declared the NIRA to be unconstitutional.[21]

Frustrated by the Court's rulings, Roosevelt in 1937 sought to exploit the fact that the Constitution gives Congress the power to determine the number of Supreme Court justices. Although the number had stayed at nine justices for seven decades, there was no constitutional barrier to enlarging the number, which, in fact, had been altered several times in the nation's early years. Roosevelt asked Congress to pass legislation that would allow a president to nominate a new justice whenever a seated member passed the age of seventy and a half. Since some of the justices had already reached that age, the legislation would enable Roosevelt to appoint enough new justices to swing the Court to his side. Congress hesitated to do so, but the attempt ended with the "switch in time that saved nine." For reasons that have never been fully clear, Justice Owen Roberts switched sides on New Deal cases, giving the president a 5-4 majority on the Court.

Within months, the Court upheld the 1935 National Labor Relations Act, which gave employees the right to organize and bargain collectively.[22] In passing the legislation, Congress claimed that disputes between labor and management disrupted the nation's economy and therefore could be regulated through the commerce clause. In upholding the act, the Supreme Court endorsed Congress's reasoning.[23] In a subsequent ruling, the Court declared that Congress's commerce power is "as broad as the needs of the nation."[24] Congress would be allowed to regulate *all* aspects of commerce. During this same period, the Court also loosened its restrictions on Congress's power to tax and spend.[25]

The Supreme Court had finally acknowledged the obvious: that an industrial economy is not confined by state boundaries and must be subject to national regulation. It was a principle that business also increasingly accepted. The nation's banking industry, for example, was saved from almost complete collapse in the 1930s by the creation of a federal regulatory agency, the Federal Deposit Insurance Corporation (FDIC). By insuring depositors' savings against loss, the FDIC stopped the panic withdrawals that had already ruined thousands of the nation's banks.

Subsequent Supreme Court decisions altered the constitutional doctrine of federalism in other policy areas, including civil rights. In *Brown v. Board of Education* (1954), for example, the Supreme Court held that states could not force black children to attend public schools separate from those for white children (see Chapter 5).[26] National citizenship—the notion that Americans should be equal in their rights and opportunities regardless of the state in which they reside—became a more encompassing idea than it had previously been.

Contemporary Federalism (since 1937)

Since the 1930s, the relation of the nation to the states has changed so fundamentally that dual federalism is no longer even a roughly accurate description of the American situation. An understanding of today's federalism requires the recognition of two countervailing developments. The larger one is a long-term *expansion* of national authority that began in the 1930s and continues to this day. The national government now operates in many policy areas that were once almost exclusively within the control of states and localities. The national government does not dominate in these policy areas, but it does play a significant role.

Many of the national initiatives trace to the 1960s as part of President Lyndon Johnson's Great Society program. A Democrat in the mold of Franklin Roosevelt, Johnson believed that federal power should be used to assist the economically disadvantaged. Traditional divisions of responsibility between the nation and the states were of less concern to Johnson than the policy goals that could be met though federal action. However, unlike Roosevelt's New Deal, which dealt mostly with the economy, Johnson's Great Society dealt mostly with social welfare issues, which have an indirect constitutional basis. The Constitution does not grant Congress the power to regulate "social welfare." However, Congress may tax and spend for that purpose, which was the basis of the Great Society. Johnson's presidency was marked by dozens of new federal assistance grants to states for programs in health care, public housing, nutrition, public assistance, urban development, education, and other social welfare issues traditionally reserved to state and localities. Johnson's initiatives were both creative and coercive: creative in the large number of new federal programs and coercive in the restrictions placed on states and localities as a condition of their receipt of federal funds.

A smaller and more recent development is the attempt to "pass down" authority from the national level to the state and local levels in selected areas. Known as *devolution*, this development peaked in the 1990s. Although it has since receded, devolution remains a component of contemporary federalism, as is discussed later in the chapter.

Interdependency and Intergovernmental Relations

Interdependency is a reason why national authority has increased dramatically. Modern systems of transportation, commerce, and communication transcend local and state boundaries. These systems are national—and even

Shown here is a pelican saturated with oil from the oil spill that occurred in the Gulf of Mexico in 2010. The federal, state, and local governments worked together in the relief effort. Cooperative federalism is a term used to describe these joint efforts, although they are also a source of tension. Some local and state officials criticized the federal government's response to the oil spill, saying it acted too slowly.

international—in scope, which means that problems affecting Americans living in one part of the country are likely to affect Americans living elsewhere. This situation has required Washington to assume a larger policy role. National problems typically require national solutions.

Interdependency has also encouraged national, state, and local policymakers to work together to solve policy problems. This collaborative effort has been described as **cooperative federalism**.[27] The difference between the older dual federalism and cooperative federalism has been likened to the difference between a layer cake, whose levels are separate, and a marble cake, whose levels flow together.[28]

Cooperative federalism is based on shared policy responsibilities rather than sharply divided ones. An example is the Medicaid program, which was created in 1965 as part of President Johnson's Great Society initiative and provides health care for the poor. The Medicaid program is jointly funded by the national and state governments, operates within eligibility standards set by the national government, and gives states some latitude in determining recipients' benefits. The Medicaid program is not an isolated example.

Literally hundreds of policy programs today are run jointly by the national and state governments. In many cases, local governments are also involved. These programs have the following characteristics:

- Jointly funded by the national and state governments (and sometimes by local governments)
- Jointly administered, with the states and localities providing most of the direct service to recipients and a national agency providing general administration
- Jointly determined, with both the state and national governments (and sometimes the local governments) having a say in eligibility and benefit levels and with federal regulations, such as those prohibiting discrimination, imposing a degree of uniformity on state and local efforts

Cooperative federalism should not be interpreted to mean that the states are powerless and dependent.[29] States have retained most of their traditional authority in areas such as education, health, public safety, and roadways. Nevertheless, the federal government's involvement in policy areas traditionally reserved for the states has increased its policy influence and diminished state-to-state policy differences. Before the enactment of the federal Medicaid program in 1965, for example, poor people in many states were not entitled to government-paid health care. Afterward, most poor people were eligible for health benefits regardless of where they resided.

Government Revenues and Intergovernmental Relations

The interdependency of American society—the fact that developments in one area affect what happens elsewhere—is one of three major reasons the federal government's policy role has expanded greatly since the early twentieth century. A second reason is that Americans want government services. Whenever an area of the country is hit by a natural disaster, for example, its residents seek relief from Washington. Moreover, whenever a federal program, such as student loans or farm supports, has been established, its recipients will fight to keep it. As a consequence, federal programs rarely end while new ones get added each year. A third reason is the federal government's superior taxing capacity. States and localities are in a competitive situation with regard to taxation. A state with high corporate and personal income taxes will lose firms and people to states with lower taxes. Firms and people are less likely to move to another country in search of lower taxes. The result is that the federal government raises

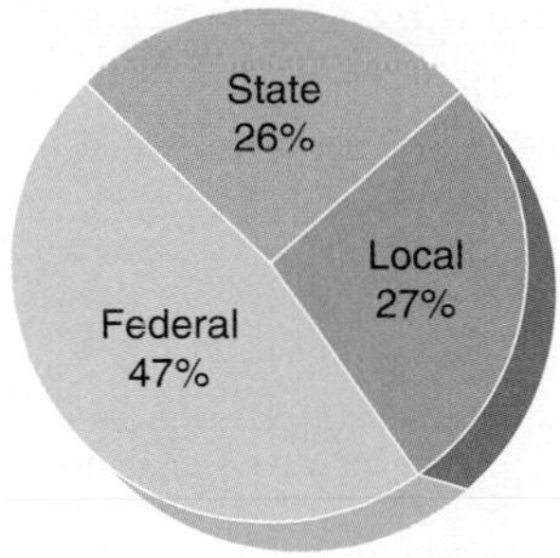

figure 3-2 FEDERAL, STATE, AND LOCAL SHARES OF GOVERNMENT TAX REVENUE

The federal government raises almost as much tax revenues as do all state and local governments combined. *Source:* U.S. Department of Commerce, 2010.

roughly as much in tax revenue as do all fifty states and the thousands of local governments combined (see Figure 3-2).

Fiscal Federalism The federal government's revenue-raising advantage has made money a basis for relations between the national government and the states and localities. **Fiscal federalism** refers to the expenditure of federal funds on programs run in part through state and local governments.[30] The federal government provides some or all of the money through **grants-in-aid** (cash payments) to states and localities, which then administer the programs. The pattern of federal assistance to states and localities is shown in Figure 3-3. Federal grants-in-aid have increased dramatically since the mid-1950s. Roughly one in every five dollars spent by local and state governments in recent decades has been raised not by them, but by the federal government in Washington (see "How the 50 States Differ").

Cash grants to states and localities have increased Washington's policy influence. State and local governments can reject a grant-in-aid, but if they accept it they must spend it in the way specified by Congress. Also, because most grants require states to contribute matching funds, the federal programs in effect determine how states will allocate some of their own tax dollars. Further, federal grants have pressured state and local officials to adopt national goals, such as the elimination of racial and other forms of discrimination. A building constructed with the help of federal funds, for example, must be accessible to persons with disabilities. Nevertheless, federal grants-in-aid also serve the policy interests of state and local officials. Although these officials often complain that federal grants contain too many restrictions and infringe

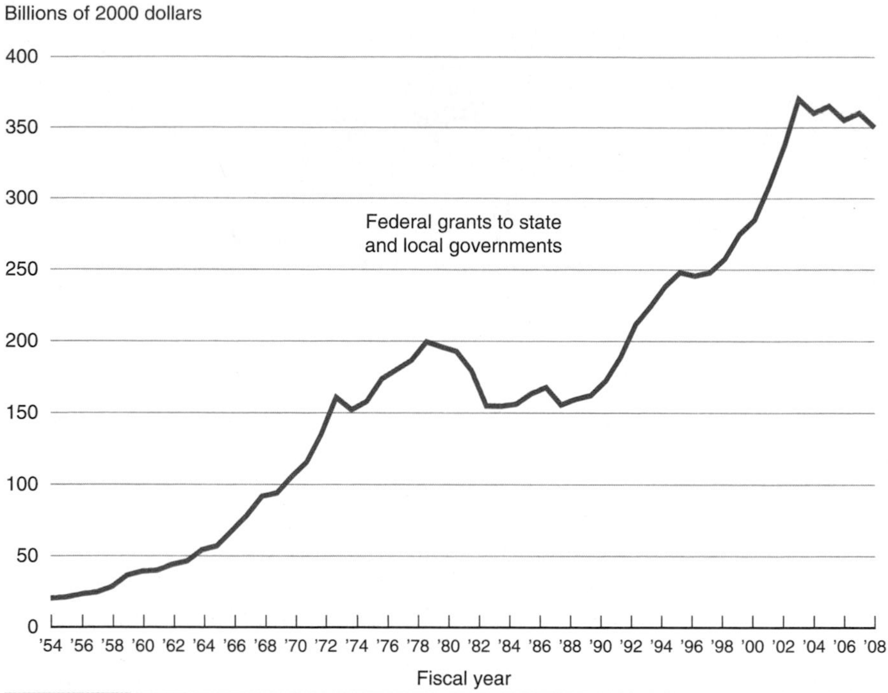

figure 3-3 FEDERAL GRANTS TO STATE AND LOCAL GOVERNMENTS

Federal aid to states and localities has increased dramatically since the 1950s. *Source:* Office of Management and Budget, 2010. Figure is based on constant (2000) dollars in order to control for the effects of inflation.

too much on their authority, most of them are eager to have the money because it permits them to offer services they could not otherwise afford. During the congressional debate in 2009 over a bill that would stimulate the nation's ailing economy, the majority of state governors, Republican and Democratic alike, urged passage of the bill. It contained more than $100 billion to help states cover their widening budget and program deficits. Said one observer: "For governors, it's free money—they get the benefits and they don't have to pay the costs of raising the revenues."[31]

Categorical and Block Grants State and local governments receive two major types of assistance—categorical grants and block grants—which differ in the extent to which Washington defines the conditions of their use. **Categorical grants**, the more restrictive type, can be used only for a designated activity. An example is funds directed for use in school lunch programs. These funds cannot be diverted to other school purposes, such

HOW THE 50 STATES DIFFER
POLITICAL THINKING THROUGH COMPARISONS

Federal Grants-in-aid to the States

Federal assistance accounts for a significant share of state revenue, but the variation is considerable. New Mexico (with a third of its total revenue coming from federal grants-in-aid) is at one extreme. Nevada (a seventh of its revenue) is at the other.

Q: *Why do states in the South, where anti-Washington sentiment is relatively high, get more of their revenue from the federal government than do most other states?*

A: *Many federal grant programs are designed to assist low-income people, and poverty is more widespread in the South. Moreover, southern states traditionally have provided fewer government services, and federal grants accordingly constitute a larger proportion of their budgets.*

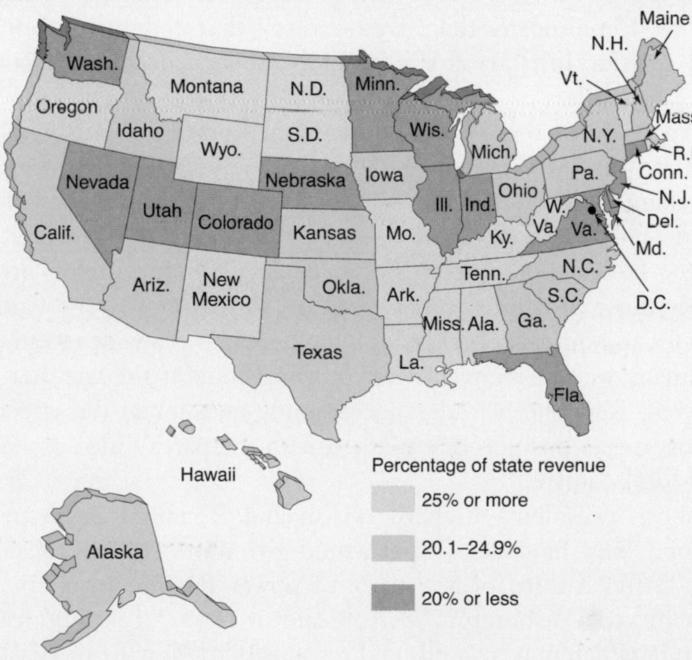

Source: U.S. Census Bureau, 2008.

as the purchase of textbooks or the hiring of teachers. **Block grants** are less restrictive. The federal government specifies the general area in which the funds must be used, but state and local officials select the specific projects. A block grant targeted for the health area, for example, might give state and local officials the authority to decide whether to use the money for hospital construction, medical equipment, the training of nurses, or some other health care activity.

State and local officials prefer federal money that comes with fewer strings attached and thus favor block grants. In contrast, members of Congress have at times preferred categorical grants, because this type of assistance gives them greater control over how state and local officials spend federal funds. Recently, however, officials at all levels have looked to block grants as the key to a more workable form of federalism. This development is a part of a process known as devolution.

Devolution

Devolution embodies the idea that American federalism can be strengthened by a partial shift in power from the federal government to the state and local governments.[32] Devolution rests on a belief—held more strongly by Republicans than Democrats—that federal authority has extended too far into areas traditionally governed through state and local governments.

The expansion of the federal government's domestic policy role from the 1930s onward was largely initiated by Democratic lawmakers, with strong backing from the public. The New Deal and Great Society programs had broad public support at the outset. After the 1960s, however, public support for federal domestic spending declined. Some of the programs, particularly those providing welfare benefits to the poor, were widely seen as too costly, too bureaucratic, and too lax—there was a widespread perception that many welfare recipients were getting benefits they neither needed nor deserved. Republican leaders increasingly questioned the effectiveness of the programs, a position that meshed with the party's ideology of lower taxes and local control.

Republican presidents Richard Nixon and Ronald Reagan proposed versions of a "new federalism" that would give more control to states and localities. "After a third of a century of power flowing from the people and the states to Washington," Nixon said in 1969, "it is time for a new federalism in which power, funds and responsibility flow from Washington and the states back to the people." Nixon's approach centered on the policy of *revenue sharing*, whereby the federal government would simply give money to the states for them to use as they saw fit. Unlike block or categorical grants, revenue sharing placed almost no restrictions on how the money would be spent. Congress, which was controlled by a Democratic majority, provided some funding for revenue sharing, though less than Nixon proposed. State and local governments used most of the money to fund their normal operations, which is not what Congress had in mind, and the program was eventually terminated.

In issuing an executive order to implement his idea of a new federalism, Reagan said: "Federalism is rooted in the knowledge that our political liberties are best assured by limiting the size and scope of national government." Reagan promoted the use of block grants as opposed to categorical grants and placed strict limits on federal agencies' activities. They were prohibited from submitting to Congress any legislative proposal that would "regulate the states in ways that would interfere" with their "traditional governmental functions." Reagan also ordered that any new federal regulation affecting the states was to be kept "to the minimum level."

The Republican Revolution When the Republican Party scored a decisive victory in the 1994 congressional elections, Speaker of the House Newt Gingrich declared that "1960s-style federalism is dead." Republican lawmakers proposed to cut some federal programs, but, even more, they sought to increase state and local control. Congressional Republicans passed legislation to reduce *unfunded mandates*—federal programs that require action by states or localities but provide no or insufficient funds to pay for it. For example, states and localities are required by federal law to make their buildings accessible to the physically handicapped, but Washington pays only part of the cost of these accommodations. In the Unfunded Mandates Reform Act of 1995, Congress eliminated some of these mandates, although under threat of a veto by Democratic president Bill Clinton, kept those relating to civil rights. The GOP-controlled Congress also took action to lump additional categorical grants into block grants, thereby giving states more control over how federal money would be spent.

The most significant change occurred in 1996, when Congress enacted the sweeping Welfare Reform Act. Opinion polls at the time indicated that a majority of Americans felt that government was spending too much on welfare and that too many welfare recipients were exploiting the system. The Welfare Reform Act tightened spending and eligibility. The legislation's key element, the Temporary Assistance for Needy Families (TANF) block grant, ended the decades-old federal program that granted cash assistance to every poor family with children. TANF restricts a family's eligibility for federal assistance to five years, and after two years, a family head normally has to go to work for the benefits to continue. Moreover, TANF gives states wide latitude in setting benefit levels, eligibility criteria, and other regulations affecting aid to poor families. TANF also places states in charge of developing training and education programs that will move people off of welfare and into jobs. (TANF and other aspects of the 1996 welfare reform legislation are discussed further in later chapters.)

The 1996 Welfare Reform Act was informed partly by state efforts to find new approaches to welfare. Wisconsin's program, which had job training and placement at its core, was instrumental in shaping provisions of the 1996 federal law. This type of influence was not new. Proponents of federalism have long held that states are "laboratories" for trying new policy approaches, which, if successful, can be adapted for use by other states or the federal government.

The Supreme Court's Contribution to Devolution After the 1930s, the Supreme Court held that the line between "traditional" and "nontraditional" state functions was legally vague and that states should rely on the political process rather than the courts for protection against what they regarded as unwarranted federal encroachment. Reasoning that members of Congress are elected from states and districts within states, the Court said that the states should look to these elected officials for protection from national actions that "unduly burden the states."[33]

The Court's position began to change as a result of the appointment of more conservative justices to the Court by Reagan and his Republican successor, George H. W. Bush. In the view of these justices, Congress had overstepped its constitutional authority in some areas.[34] In *United States v. Lopez* (1995), the Court cited the Tenth Amendment in striking down a federal law that prohibited the possession of guns within one thousand feet of a school. Congress had invoked the commerce power in passing the bill, but the Republican-dominated Supreme Court ruled that the ban had "nothing to do with commerce, or any sort of economic activity."[35] Two years later, in *Printz v. United States* (1997), the Court struck down a provision of the federal Handgun Violence Prevention Act (the so-called Brady bill) that required local law enforcement officers to conduct background checks on prospective handgun buyers. The Court said the provision violated the Tenth Amendment because it required state employees—in this case, police officers—to "enforce a federal regulatory program."[36] Congress can require federal employees to take such action, but it cannot order state employees to do so. They work for the state, not the federal government.

The Court has also used the Eleventh Amendment to limit Congress's authority over state governments. The Eleventh Amendment—sometimes called the "sovereign immunity amendment"—protects a state from being sued in federal court by a private citizen, unless the state agrees to the suit. The amendment has limits; it does not protect a state from suit in federal court when the state is alleged to have violated a right guaranteed by the U.S. Constitution, such as the right of the accused to have legal counsel. But the Supreme Court recently has used the Eleventh Amendment to restrict the scope of a few federal laws. In *Kimel v. Board of Regents* (2000), for example, the Supreme Court held that age discrimination, unlike racial and sexual discrimination, is not among the rights guaranteed under the Constitution and that Florida was not bound by federal law in deciding the age policies that apply to state employees.[37] Shortly thereafter, in *Board of Trustees of the University of Alabama v. Garrett* (2001), the Court made a similar ruling in regard to a federal law banning discrimination against the disabled.[38] (It should be noted that these rulings apply only to state *employees*. Other residents of a state are subject to federal laws banning discrimination on the basis of age or disability.)

Nationalization, the More Powerful Force Along with the 1996 Welfare Reform Act and other legislation, these Supreme Court rulings contributed to a shift in policy and power to the states. These actions did not, however, constitute a wholesale change in American federalism. Federal grants-in-aid continued to flow from Washington to the states, shaping and funding many of their activities. As for the Supreme Court, it has continued to uphold the principle established in the 1930s that Congress's taxing, spending, and commerce powers are broad and substantial.

Moreover, the devolution movement slowed dramatically after passage of the 1996 Welfare Reform Act. One of Republican president George W. Bush's first domestic policy initiatives, for instance, was the No Child Left Behind Act, which thrust federal authority more deeply than ever into local and state education policy. Bush argued that the United States needed a *national* education standard if it was to meet the challenge of the global economy. The terrorist attacks of September 11, 2001, led to further expansions of federal authority, including the creation in 2002 of the Department of Homeland Security, a cabinet-level federal agency with policing and emergency responsibilities traditionally belonging to states and localities.

The economic crisis triggered by the near-collapse of the financial markets in 2008 contributed to a further increase in national power. As the crisis worsened, President Bush provided federal funds to bail out the troubled banks and other financial institutions. When President Barack Obama took office in 2009, he and the Democratic-controlled Congress bailed out the U.S. automobile industry and then enacted a nearly $800 billion economic stimulus bill. A significant portion of the stimulus money went to states and localities; their budgets were in the red because the economic downturn had produced a drop in their tax revenues.

The Republican governors of Alaska, Mississippi, Louisiana, and South Carolina—over the objections of some Republicans in their states—said they would refuse to take federal stimulus funds. Other Republican governors urged passage of the stimulus bill and some, like Florida's Charlie Crist, actively lobbied for it. In the end, all states accepted federal money, although they did so in varying degrees, which is their option under federalism. The key point, however, is that the states faced a stark choice: if they did not take the federal money, they would have to cut programs, lay off state and local employees, and forego the new jobs that would be created by the federally funded stimulus projects, such as new roadways and schools. The realities of the economic downturn were far stronger than partisan ideology or federalism theory in determining how states responded to the stimulus legislation.

The economic crisis also shifted power from the business sector to Washington. Risky ventures and financial greed had combined to place the nation's major financial institutions on the verge of collapse. The national government kept them afloat through hundreds of billions of dollars in loans and stock purchases but, in doing so, maintained oversight of their activities.

As these examples would indicate, the features of modern life—an economy that is complex and integrated, a public that is insistent on its rights and accustomed to government services, a global environment that is filled with challenges and opportunities—have placed ever greater demands on the national government. The American states will never again enjoy the prominence, power, and autonomy they once did. American federalism is necessarily a far different governing system today than it was prior to the 1930s.[39] The change can be seen even in the structure of the federal government. Five cabinet departments—Health and Human Services, Housing and Urban Development, Transportation, Education, and Homeland Security—were created after the 1930s to administer federal programs in policy areas traditionally reserved to the states. Although the states remain powerful governing bodies, they operate within a system of expanded federal authority. Nationalization has been inevitably and irrevocably the long-term trend in American federalism.

In the 1990s, some policy responsibilities were shifted from the federal government to the states, a process called *devolution*. This trend stalled after 2000 for several reasons, including the terrorist attacks of September 11, 2001, which required a national response. Part of that response was a larger role for the federal government in the area of public safety. Shown here is a scene familiar to air travelers. The screening of airline passengers is the responsibility of federal officers rather than state or local police.

The Public's Influence: Setting the Boundaries of Federal-State Power

Public opinion has had a decisive influence on the ebb and flow of federal power during the past century. As Americans' attitudes toward the federal government and the states changed, the balance of power between these two levels of government also shifted. Every major change in federalism has been driven by a major shift in public support toward one level of government or the other.

During the Great Depression, when it was clear that the states would be unable to help, Americans turned to Washington for relief. For people without jobs, the fine points of the Constitution were of little consequence. They needed assistance, and would take it from whichever level of government could provide it. President Roosevelt's New Deal programs, which offered both jobs and income security, were a radical departure from the past, but quickly gained public favor. A 1936 Gallup poll indicated, for example, that 61 percent of Americans supported Roosevelt's social security program, whereas only 27 percent opposed it. This support reflected a new public attitude: the federal government, not the states, was expected to take the lead in protecting Americans from economic hardship.[40]

The second great wave of federal social programs—Lyndon Johnson's Great Society—was also driven by public demands. Income and education levels had risen dramatically after the Second World War, and Americans wanted more and better services from government.[41] When the states were slow to respond, Americans pressured federal officials to act. The Medicare and Medicaid programs, which provide health care for the elderly and the poor, respectively, are examples of the Johnson administration's response. A 1965 Gallup poll indicated that two-thirds of Americans approved of federal involvement in the provision of medical care, despite the fact that health was traditionally the states' responsibility.

Public opinion was also behind the rollback of federal authority in the 1990s. In a 1994 Times Mirror survey, 66 percent of respondents expressed the view that most officials in Washington did not care what people like them were thinking. An even larger proportion felt that the federal government had become too large and intrusive. Americans' dissatisfaction with federal programs and spending provided the springboard for the Republican takeover of Congress in the 1994 midterm election, which led to policies aimed at devolving power to the states, including the widely popular 1996 Welfare Reform Act.[42]

In similar fashion, Americans backed the economic stimulus bill that Barack Obama and the Democratic Congress enacted in early 2009. According to a Gallup poll, 70 percent of Americans believed that the stimulus bill was "critically important" or "important" to the nation's economic recovery. The public had reservations about the scale of the spending but this worry was secondary at the time. A year later, as the federal deficit continued to mount, polls indicated that a majority of Americans believed the government in Washington was spending too freely. Campaigning on the theme of a smaller federal government, Republican candidates ran strongly in the 2010 midterm election.

The public's role in determining the boundaries between federal and state power would come as no surprise to the framers of the Constitution. For them, federalism was a pragmatic issue, one to be decided by the nation's needs rather than by inflexible rules. Alexander Hamilton suggested that Americans would shift their loyalties between the nation and the states according to whichever level seemed more likely to serve their immediate purpose. James Madison said much the same thing in predicting that Americans would look to whichever level of government was more responsive to their interests. Indeed, each succeeding generation of Americans has seen fit to devise a balance of federal and state power suited to its needs.

SUMMARY Self-Test www.mhhe.com/pattersonwtp9e

A foremost characteristic of the American political system is its division of authority between a national government and state governments. The first U.S. government, established by the Articles of Confederation, was essentially a union of the states.

In establishing the basis for a stronger national government, the U.S. Constitution also made provision for safeguarding state interests. The result was the creation of a federal system in which sovereignty was vested in both national and state governments. The Constitution enumerates the general powers of the national government and grants it implied powers through the "necessary and proper" clause. Other powers are reserved to the states by the Tenth Amendment.

From 1789 to 1865, the nation's survival was at issue. The states found it convenient at times to argue that their sovereignty took precedence over national authority. In the end, it took the Civil War to cement the idea that the United States was a union of people, not of states. From 1865 to 1937, federalism reflected the doctrine that certain policy areas were the exclusive responsibility of the national government, whereas responsibility in other policy areas belonged exclusively to the states. This constitutional position validated the laissez-faire doctrine that big business was largely beyond governmental control. It also allowed the states to discriminate against African Americans in their public policies. Federalism in a form recognizable today began to emerge in the 1930s.

In the areas of commerce, taxation, spending, civil rights, and civil liberties, among others, the federal government now plays an important role, one that is the inevitable consequence of the increasing complexity of American society and the interdependence of its people. National, state, and local officials now work closely together to solve the nation's problems, a situation known as cooperative federalism. Grants-in-aid from Washington to the states and localities have been the chief instrument of national influence. States and localities have received billions in federal assistance; in accepting federal money, they also have accepted both federal restrictions on its use and the national policy priorities that underlie the granting of the money.

Throughout the nation's history, the public through its demands on government has influenced the boundaries between federal and state power. The devolutionary trend of the 1990s, for example, was sparked by Americans' sense that a rollback in federal power was desirable, whereas the subsequent expansion of federal power has been a response to Americans' concerns about terrorism and economic recovery.

Key Terms

block grants (*p. 92*)
categorical grants (*p. 90*)
commerce clause (*p. 82*)
confederacy (*p. 70*)
cooperative federalism (*p. 87*)
devolution (*p. 92*)
dual federalism (*p. 80*)
enumerated (expressed) powers (*p. 74*)
federalism (*p. 69*)
fiscal federalism (*p. 89*)
grants-in-aid (*p. 89*)
implied powers (*p. 75*)
nationalization (*p. 76*)
"necessary and proper" (elastic) clause (*p. 75*)
reserved powers (*p. 75*)
sovereignty (*p. 69*)
supremacy clause (*p. 74*)
unitary system (*p. 70*)

Suggested Readings

Blackmon, Douglas A. *Slavery by Another Name: The Re-Enslavement of Black Americans from the Civil War to World War II.* New York: Anchor Books, 2009. An examination of the Jim Crow era, including how federalism worked against the rights and interests of African Americans.

Chopra, Pran. *Supreme Court versus the Constitution: A Challenge to Federalism.* Thousand Oaks, CA.: Sage Publications, 2006. A look at the Supreme Court's view of federalism.

Cornell, Saul. *The Other Founders: Anti-Federalism and the Dissenting Tradition in America.* Chapel Hill: University of North Carolina Press, 1999. An analysis of Anti-Federalist thought, its origins, and its legacy.

Edling, Max M. *A Revolution in Favor of Government.* New York: Oxford University Press, 2003. Argues that the framers intended the Constitution to create a strong government.

Elkins, Stanley, and Eric McKitrick. *The Age of Federalism: The Early American Republic, 1788–1800.* New York: Oxford University Press, 1993. An award-winning book on the earliest period of American federalism.

Garry, Patrick M. *An Entrenched Legacy: How the New Deal Constitutional Revolution Continues to Shape the Role of the Supreme Court.* State College: Pennsylvania State University Press, 2008. An analysis showing the durability of the constitutional changes in federalism established in the 1930s.

LaCroix, Alison L. *The Ideological Origins of American Federalism.* Cambridge, MA.: Harvard University Press, 2010. An examination of the normative ideas, as opposed to the pragmatic ones, that contributed to federalism's adoption.

Nugent, John D. *Safeguarding Federalism: How States Protect Their Interests in National Policymaking.* Norman: University of Oklahoma Press, 2009. An assessment of how states promote their interest in the context of federal initiatives.

Ross, William G. *A Muted Fury: Populists, Progressives, and Labor Unions Confront the Courts, 1890–1937*. Princeton, N.J.: Princeton University Press, 1993. A valuable study of the political conflict surrounding the judiciary's laissez-faire doctrine in the period 1890–1937.

LIST OF WEBSITES

http://lcweb2.loc.gov/ammem/amlaw/lawhome.html A site containing congressional documents and debates from 1774 to 1873.

www.csg.org The site of the Council of State Governments; includes current news from each of the states and basic information about their governments.

http://avalon.law.yale.edu/subject_menus/fed.asp A documentary record of the *Federalist Papers*, the Annapolis convention, the Articles of Confederation, the Madison debates, and the U.S. Constitution.

POLITICS IN THEORY AND PRACTICE

Thinking: How have interdependency and the federal government's superior taxing power contributed to a larger policy role for the national government? Do you think these factors will increase or decrease in importance in the future? What will this trend mean for the future of American federalism? (You might find it helpful to think about these questions in the context of a specific policy area, such as the terrorist threat facing the country.)

Participating: The U.S. federal system of government offers an array of channels for political participation. Vital governing decisions are made at the national, state, and local levels, all of which provide opportunities for citizens to make a difference and also to build skills, such as public speaking and working with others, that will prove valuable in other areas of life. You have a participatory arena close at hand: the college campus. Most colleges and universities support a variety of activities in which students can engage. Student government is one such opportunity; another is the student newspaper. Most colleges and universities offer a wide range of groups and sponsored programs, from debate clubs to fraternal organizations. If you are not now active in campus groups, consider joining one. If you join—or if you already belong to such a group—take full advantage of the participatory opportunities it provides.

EXTRA CREDIT

For up-to-the-minute *New York Times* articles, interactive simulations, graphics, study tools, and more links and quizzes, visit the text's Online Learning Center at **www.mhhe.com/pattersonwtp/9e**.

NATIONAL JOURNAL

Dependent States Usher in a New Federalism

Education Secretary Arne Duncan had some harsh words for Wisconsin's education laws during a November visit to Madison. He complained that the state's policies, particularly its cap on charter schools and its refusal to use test data in evaluating teachers, were antiquated, unacceptable, and even "ridiculous."

Rather than take offense, his hosts acted quickly to appease him.

The very next day, Wisconsin's Assembly and Senate passed a package of four bills designed to bring the state in line with Duncan's vision. In so doing, Wisconsin became the 10th state in 2009 to alter its education laws to please the Education secretary.

The reason is money. Last year's economic stimulus law provided Duncan with $4.35 billion to give to states that pursue innovations in education. The so-called Race to the Top fund is competitive: All the states want a share of the money, and the Education secretary can give out the aid largely as he sees fit, without having to rely on any set formula.

But there is not enough money to go around, which is why the states are doing everything they can to satisfy Duncan. No other Education secretary has ever had that much cash at his disposal. "There's no question those of us in Wisconsin want to have as strong an application as we can to get at the $4.35 billion," said John Lehman, who chairs the state Senate Education Committee. "It is true that there is a big carrot that got people thinking."

The Obama administration has been using a lot of carrots to elicit support for its policy goals, from forcing states to accept new Medicaid recipients to cracking down on distracted drivers. With states facing their worst financial outlook in decades, they are becoming increasingly reliant on money from Washington. "It wouldn't surprise me if federal funding ends up being 40 percent of state budgets" during the current fiscal year, said Marcia Howard, executive director of Federal Funds Information for States, which on behalf of state legislators and governors tracks federal grant money. Federal dollars—dominated by Medicaid funds—made up just over 25 percent of state spending as recently as 2008 before jumping to 30 percent for the fiscal year that ended in most states last June.

With so much money being transferred from Washington to state capitals, the administration is practicing what might be called golden-rule federalism: Whoever has the gold makes the rules. "The fact that states are so broke offers unprecedented opportunities for the federal government to intrude into areas that were strictly the purview of states," said Sujit CanagaRetna, a senior fiscal analyst with the Council of State Governments.

President Obama thus presents a paradox when it comes to federalism. Barely five years out of the Illinois Legislature, he has expressed more genuine interest in collaborating with the lower levels of government than perhaps any other president since Jimmy Carter. Several Cabinet secretaries have been working together to craft joint programs to find a more coherent approach to matching federal efforts with local programs. Obama's Office of Management and Budget and the newly created White House Office of Urban Affairs are pushing all federal departments and agencies to do likewise.

But at the same time, Obama is clearly presiding over a greater centralization of power and policy-making in Washington. It was inevitable that states would have to cede ground that they had been able to hold for themselves in recent years, given a president determined to set his own mark in a swath of domestic policy areas, such as education and health care. But the states' growing dependence on Washington for aid has greatly accelerated the shift.

And their ability to set their own courses as independent actors is diminishing. "This is an administration that doesn't take the states and locals as it finds them—it has an agenda," says Paul Posner, a federalism expert at George Mason University. "The agenda they have is not framed in terms of helping state and local governments with their problems, but in pushing their own goals."

It has always been the case that when states and local governments cut spending, they try to spare federal programs. After all, if the federal government is paying 50 percent of a program's cost, they would have to cut $2 in spending just to save $1 for their own treasury. Not surprisingly, state budgets have long been subject to federal whims, both through the creation of programs that impose new mandates and the simple expansion of the federal government.

If state spending tended to increase during federal expansions under Democratic administrations, Republican presidents took a different tack. Under the Nixon and Reagan models, block grants meant offering states less money but more flexibility. Their proposals had the dual purpose of reining in spending and giving states more authority.

It's the opposite of Obama's approach, which is more in line with Lyndon Johnson's during the Great Society—finding innovative ways to use grants to get states and localities to pursue federal policy goals. "In the absence of reauthorization of some of the grant programs, the Obama administration is using regulations to impose their agenda," said Marcia Howard of Federal Funds Information for States, a joint project of the NCSL and the governors association. "You could call it a heavy federal hand, but it's more inducements, using more carrots than sticks to get states to do what they'd like them to do."

In response, many state officials complain that federal priorities are starting to crowd out their own. This may sound a little ungrateful. The influx of federal dollars may be edging out other parts of state budgets on a percentage basis, but it's not as if their absence would allow states to spend more in areas such as corrections or parks. As things now stand, states would simply have less to spend.

Some states have heatedly invoked the 10th Amendment in stressing supposed limits on federal policy-making. Legislative chambers in Texas and North Dakota approved resolutions last year proclaiming state sovereignty and demanding an immediate end to federal mandates not enumerated in the U.S. Constitution.

But it looks increasingly as if the Republican governors who opposed the stimulus—and appeared at the time merely to be seeking to score partisan points—had a valid argument. South Carolina's Mark Sanford, Mississippi's Haley Barbour, and others noted that it would be a mistake to accept federal money that obligates them to continue the spending when the federal pipeline runs dry a year or two later. As that time draws nearer on such programs as unemployment insurance and energy-efficiency block grants, more of their colleagues are worried about what they'll do when the funding drops off.

Obama's instincts are not those of a centralizer, however. Nearly every state and local government lobbying group readily concedes that outreach and access are much improved on his watch. They say that his administration attempts to take a collaborative approach whenever it can, with a special interest in reshaping the interaction between the federal government and metropolitan regions.

Obama went so far in May as to issue a memorandum directing federal agencies not to pre-empt state and local laws when they didn't have to (although he certainly didn't diminish their authority to do so). His administration has deferred to lower levels of government in areas where it was conducive to constituency politics. In October, the Justice Department announced that it would (in most cases) not prosecute suppliers of medical marijuana who were in compliance with state laws. Four months earlier, EPA signed off on a waiver long sought by California and 13 other states to regulate greenhouse-gas emissions from vehicles.

Like every administration—and more quickly than most—Obama's White House may have recognized that it needs state and local governments to carry out much of its program. But despite its care in consulting with them and in seeking ways to foster regional economic growth, this administration mostly treats state and local governments in just that way—as a means for carrying out its own agenda.

The Obama administration approach may be most evident when it comes to education. The administration is spending record amounts on education, and it clearly expects states to get with its program when it comes to ideas such as lifting caps on the number of charter schools and using standardized test data in evaluating teachers. "States were complaining under Bush because they had all these education mandates with no funding," said David Wyss, chief economist for Standard & Poor's. "At least with Obama they're getting the funding to match the mandates, but the mandates are increasing."

In certain ways, education-reform activists are glad that Duncan is showing states a firm hand. Recent experience, they note, suggests that the federal government can require states to do certain things—but it can't make states do them well. Bush's 2002 No Child Left Behind law required states to use standardized tests to ensure that a rising share of their student populations were proficient in language arts and math. But the law left it up to the states to determine what "proficiency" meant, and it's clear that many of them have gamed the system to guarantee that more of their students can pass.

The question remains whether education—a classic example of a state and local responsibility that the federal government has been involved in for only 50 years—is best run by an agenda driven out of Washington. "It's absolutely the case that the administration is taking enormous liberties with its ability to use emergency funds, especially the stimulus, to push states into policy adoption," said Frederick Hess, director of education policy studies at the American Enterprise Institute.

"If one believes that there's sufficient expertise and farsightedness in Washington, that the key is to cudgel these recalcitrant states into behaving, then I'm sure this is encouraging," Hess said. "It so happens that I actually like what they're pushing states to do, but my concern is that this model of federal leadership is problematic. The question of federalism depends on whether one actually believes there is value in the checks and balances, and the states as the laboratories of democracy."

What's Your Opinion?

Do you agree with the Texas and North Dakota legislatures that Washington's extension of grant money contingent on cooperation with its agenda violates the Constitutional separation of state and federal powers? Why or why not? When do you think it is appropriate for Washington to help shape the state agenda, and when do you think the federal government should stay out? What are the critical differences?

CHAPTER 4

CIVIL LIBERTIES: PROTECTING INDIVIDUAL RIGHTS

"A bill of rights is what the people are entitled to against every government on earth, general or particular, and what no just government should refuse, or rest on inference."

THOMAS JEFFERSON[1]

Robert and Sarisse Creighton and their three children were asleep when FBI agents and local police broke into their home in the middle of the night. Brandishing guns, the officers searched the house for a relative of the Creightons who was suspected of bank robbery. When asked to show a search warrant, the officers said, "You watch too much TV." The suspect was not there, and the agents and officers left as abruptly as they had entered. The Creightons sued the FBI agent in charge, Russell Anderson, for violating their Fourth Amendment right against unlawful search.

The Creightons won a temporary victory when the U.S. Circuit Court of Appeals for the Eighth Circuit—noting that individuals are constitutionally protected against warrantless searches unless officers have good reason ("probable cause") for a search and unless they have good reason ("exigent circumstances") for conducting that search without a warrant—concluded that Anderson had been derelict in his duty. In the judgment of the appellate court, Anderson should have sought a warrant from a judge, who would have decided whether a search of the Creightons' home was justified.

The Supreme Court of the United States overturned the lower court's ruling. The Court's majority opinion stated: "We have recognized that it is inevitable that law enforcement officials will in some cases reasonably but mistakenly conclude that probable cause is present, and we have indicated that in such cases those officials . . . should not be held personally liable." Justice John Paul Stevens and two other justices dissented. Stevens accused the Court's majority of showing "remarkably little fidelity" to the Fourth Amendment.[2] Civil liberties groups claimed that the Court's decision gave police an open invitation to invade people's homes on the slightest pretext. For their part, law enforcement officials praised the decision, saying that a ruling in the Creightons' favor would have made them hesitant to pursue a suspect for fear of being sued if the search failed to find anything.

As this case illustrates, issues of individual rights are complex and political. The Fourth Amendment protects Americans not from *all* searches but from *unreasonable* searches. The public would be unsafe if law officials could never pursue a suspect into a home. Yet the public would also be unsafe if police could invade homes any time they wanted. The challenge for a civil society is to establish a level of police authority that meets the demands of public safety without infringing unduly on personal freedom. The balance point, however, is always subject to dispute. Did Agent Anderson have sufficient cause for a warrantless search of the Creightons' home? Or was his evidence so weak that his forcible entry constituted an unreasonable search? Not even the justices of the Supreme Court could agree on these questions. Six justices sided with Anderson, and three backed the Creightons' position.

This chapter examines issues of **civil liberties**—specific individual rights, such as freedom of speech, that are constitutionally protected against infringement by government. Although the term *civil liberties* is sometimes used synonymously with the term *civil rights*, they can be distinguished. Civil liberties refer to specific *individual* rights, such as protection against self-incrimination, whereas civil rights have to do with whether members of differing groups—racial, sexual, religious, and the like—are treated equally by government and, in some cases, by private parties. Issues of civil rights are addressed in the next chapter.

Civil liberties issues have become increasingly complex. The framers of the Constitution could not possibly have foreseen the United States of the early twenty-first century, with its huge national government, enormous

POLITICAL THINKING

Majority Rule or Individual Rights?

America's political ideals derive from different experiences and philosophical traditions, and they conflict at points. Democracy, for example, emphasizes majority rule, whereas liberty emphasizes individual rights. Conflict between the two is inevitable at times—the principle of majority rule asserts that the view of the many should prevail over the opinion of the few, whereas the principle of liberty asserts that individuals have inviolate rights. How far should the majority be allowed to go in imposing its will on the individual? To what extent should the individual be allowed to act in ways objectionable to the majority? (These are everyday questions of American politics, affecting issues as diverse as taxes, gay marriage, capital punishment, affirmative action, property use, abortion, and national security.)

corporations, pervasive mass media, urban crowding, and vulnerability to terrorist acts. These developments are potential threats to personal liberty, and the judiciary in the past century has seen fit to expand the rights to which individuals are entitled. However, these rights are constantly being weighed against competing rights and society's collective interests. The Bill of Rights operates in an untidy world where people's highest aspirations collide with their worst passions, and it is at this juncture that issues of civil liberties arise. Should a murder suspect be entitled to recant a confession? Should the press be allowed to print military secrets whose publication might jeopardize national security? Should extremist groups be allowed to publicize their messages of prejudice and hate? Such questions are among the subjects of this chapter, which focuses on these points:

- *Freedom of expression is the most basic of democratic rights, but like all rights, it is not unlimited.*
- *"Due process of law" refers to legal protections (primarily procedural safeguards) designed to ensure that individual rights are respected by government.*
- *Over the course of the nation's history, Americans' civil liberties have been broadened in law and more fully protected by the courts.* Of special significance has been the Supreme Court's use of the Fourteenth Amendment to protect individual rights from action by state and local governments.
- *Individual rights are constantly being weighed against the demands of majorities and the collective needs of society.* All political institutions are involved

in this process, as is public opinion, but the judiciary plays a central role and is the institution that is typically most protective of civil liberties.

The Constitution: The Bill of Rights and the Fourteenth Amendment

The Constitution's failure to enumerate individual freedoms led to demands for the **Bill of Rights** (see Chapter 2). Enacted in 1791, these first ten amendments to the Constitution specify certain rights of life, liberty, and property that the federal government is obliged to protect (see Table 4-1). Among these rights are freedom of speech, press, assembly, and religion (First Amendment); the right to bear arms (Second Amendment); protection against unreasonable search and seizure (Fourth Amendment); protection against self-incrimination and double jeopardy (Fifth Amendment); right to a jury trial, to an attorney, and to confront witnesses (Sixth Amendment); and protection against cruel and unusual punishment (Eight Amendment).

The Supreme Court has assumed responsibility for defining what the Bill of Rights guarantees will mean in practice. In some areas, the Court has devised specific tests to determine whether authorities have acted properly. A test applied in the area of free speech, for example, is whether general rules (such as restrictions on the time and place of a political rally) are reasonable and are applied fairly. Government officials would fail to meet this standard if they allowed rallies only on a particular day of the week or if they were more accommodating to groups they like than to those they dislike.

Originally, the guarantees in the Bill of Rights applied only to the actions of the national government. When this limitation on the Bill of Rights was challenged in *Barron v. Baltimore* (1833), the Supreme Court upheld it, saying that the first ten "amendments contain no expression indicating an intention to apply them to the state governments."[3] As a result, the Bill of Rights originally had little meaning in the daily lives of ordinary Americans because state governments have authority over most of the activities, such as law enforcement, in which individual rights are at issue.

Selective Incorporation of Free Expression Rights

Today, most of the rights contained in the Bill of Rights *are* protected from action by the state governments. This development occurred slowly and in stages.

table 4-1 THE BILL OF RIGHTS: A SELECTED LIST OF CONSTITUTIONAL PROTECTIONS

The Bill of Rights refers to the first ten amendments to the Constitution, which include protections of individual rights.

First Amendment

Speech: You are free to say almost anything except that which is obscene, slanders another person, or has a high probability of inciting others to take imminent lawless action.

Assembly: You are free to assemble, although government may regulate the time and place for reasons of public convenience and safety, provided such regulations are applied evenhandedly to all groups.

Religion: You are protected from having the religious beliefs of others imposed on you, and you are free to believe what you like.

Fourth Amendment

Search and seizure: You are protected from unreasonable searches and seizures, although you forfeit that right if you knowingly waive it.

Arrest: You are protected from arrest unless authorities have probable cause to believe that you have committed a crime.

Fifth Amendment

Self-incrimination: You are protected against self-incrimination, which means that you have the right to remain silent and to be protected against coercion by law enforcement officials.

Double jeopardy: You cannot be tried twice for the same crime if the first trial results in a verdict of innocence.

Due process: You cannot be deprived of life, liberty, or property without proper legal proceedings.

Sixth Amendment

Counsel: You have a right to be represented by an attorney and can demand to speak first with an attorney before responding to questions from law enforcement officials.

Prompt and reasonable proceedings: You have a right to be arraigned promptly, to be informed of the charges, to confront witnesses, and to have a speedy and open trial by an impartial jury.

Eighth Amendment

Bail: You are protected against excessive bail or fines.

Cruel and unusual punishment: You are protected from cruel and unusual punishment, although this provision does not protect you from the death penalty or from a long prison term for a minor offense.

Thomas Jefferson was critical of the framers of the Constitution for their failure to include a listing of individual rights. At the urging of Jefferson and other leading Americans, the first Congress passed a set of amendments (the Bill of Rights) aimed at protecting these rights. Earlier, Jefferson had drafted a bill of rights for the state of Virginia's constitution.

Immediately after the Civil War, several southern states enacted laws denying newly freed slaves the rights held by whites, such as the right to own property and to travel freely. Congress responded by proposing a constitutional amendment designed to protect the rights of former slaves. The former Confederate states with the exception of Tennessee refused to ratify it. Congress then passed the Reconstruction Act, which placed the southern states under military rule until they ratified the amendment and adopted state constitutions that conformed with the U.S. Constitution. In 1868, the Fourteenth Amendment was ratified. It includes a **due process clause** that says "no state shall . . . deprive any person of life, liberty, or property, without due process of law." In the ensuing decades, with the tacit consent of the Supreme Court (see Chapter 3), the southern states ignored the clause.

Then, in 1925, the Supreme Court invoked the Fourteenth Amendment's due process clause in a free speech case. In *Gitlow v. New York* (1925), the Supreme Court upheld a New York law that made it illegal to advocate the violent overthrow of the U.S. government. In doing so, however, the Court held that states do *not* have complete authority over what their residents can say and write. The Court said: "For present purposes we may and do assume that freedom of speech and of the press—which are protected by the First Amendment from abridgement by Congress—are among the fundamental personal rights and "liberties" protected by the due process clause of the Fourteenth Amendment from impairment by the states."[4]

By interpreting the Fourteenth Amendment's due process clause to protect a First Amendment right, the Court positioned itself to broaden the protection to include all First Amendment rights. Within a dozen years, the Court heard a set of free-expression cases that allowed it to do just that. The Court invalidated state laws restricting expression in the areas of speech (*Fiske v. Kansas*), press (*Near v. Minnesota*), religion (*Hamilton v. Regents, University of California*), and assembly and petition (*DeJonge v. Oregon*).[5] The *Near* decision is the best known of these rulings. Jay Near was the publisher of a Minneapolis weekly newspaper that regularly made defamatory statements about blacks, Jews, Catholics, and labor union leaders. His paper was closed down on the basis of a Minnesota law banning "malicious, scandalous, or defamatory" publications. Near appealed the shutdown on the grounds that it infringed on freedom of the press, and the Supreme Court ruled in his favor, saying that the Minnesota law was "the essence of censorship."[6]

In these cases, the Supreme Court engaged in what came to be known as **selective incorporation**—the process by which certain of the rights contained in the Bill of Rights become applicable through the Fourteenth Amendment to actions by the state governments. In *Gitlow*, for example, the Court selectively incorporated the First Amendment guarantee of free expression into the Fourteenth Amendment, enabling citizens who believe their free expression rights were violated by a state to sue it in federal court. (The incorporation process is called *selective* because the Supreme Court has chosen to protect some Bill of Rights guarantees from state action but not others. Even today, for example, the Seventh Amendment right to a jury trial in civil cases is not binding on the states).

Selective Incorporation of Fair Trial Rights

As the Supreme Court was moving to protect free-expression rights from state action in the 1920s and 1930s, it held back on doing the same for the rights of the accused. The Court claimed that free-expression rights were more deserving of federal protection because they are "the indispensable condition of nearly every other form of freedom."[7] The Court did make an exception, however, in capital punishment cases, holding that states had to provide legal counsel to defendants who were too poor to hire one. The ruling came in *Powell v. Alabama* (1932), a case involving eight African American men who were sentenced to death without benefit of counsel on trumped-up rape charges.[8]

The Supreme Court's position on the rights of the accused in state courts changed abruptly in the 1960s. Advances in public education and communication had made Americans more aware of their rights, and the civil rights movement dramatized the fact that the poor and minorities had fewer rights in practice than did other Americans. In response, the

Supreme Court in the 1960s began to protect the rights of the accused from action by the states.

The selective incorporation process began with *Mapp v. Ohio* (1961). Police forcibly entered the home of Dollree Mapp, a black woman, saying they had a tip she was harboring a fugitive. After discovering that the fugitive was not there, they handcuffed her and began rummaging through her closets. In the basement, they found a chest that contained obscene photographs. Mapp was arrested and convicted of violating an Ohio law that prohibited the possession of such material. The Supreme Court overturned her conviction, ruling that police had acted unconstitutionally, citing the Fourth Amendment, which reads in part: "The right of the people to be secure in their persons, houses, papers, and effects, against unreasonable searches and seizures, shall not be violated. . . ." The Court concluded that evidence acquired through an unconstitutional search cannot be used to obtain a conviction in state courts.[9]

During the 1960s, the Court also ruled that defendants in state criminal proceedings must be provided a lawyer in felony cases if they cannot afford to hire one,[10] cannot be compelled to testify against themselves,[11] have the right to remain silent and to have legal counsel at the time of arrest,[12] have the right to confront witnesses who testify against them,[13] must be granted a speedy trial,[14] have the right to a jury trial in criminal proceedings,[15] and cannot be subjected to double jeopardy.[16]

Through these decisions, and the earlier ones involving free expression, the Supreme Court has broadly protected Bill of Rights guarantees from action by the states. The following sections examine more closely the law and practice of Americans' civil liberties.

Freedom of Expression

Freedom of expression is widely regarded as the most basic of individual rights. As Justice Harlan Fisk Stone argued in 1938, a government that can silence those who speak out against it has the power to control elections and to abridge other rights.[17]

The First Amendment provides for **freedom of expression**—the right of individual Americans to hold and communicate thoughts of their choosing. For many reasons, such as a desire to conform to social pressure or a fear of harassment, Americans do not always choose to express themselves freely. Moreover, freedom of expression, like other rights, is not absolute in practice. It does not entitle individuals to say whatever they want to whomever they want. Free expression can be denied, for example, if it endangers national security, wrongly damages the reputation of others,

HOW THE U.S. DIFFERS

POLITICAL THINKING THROUGH COMPARISONS

Civil Liberties

Individual rights are a cornerstone of the American governing system and receive strong protection from the courts. The government's ability to restrict free expression is limited, and the individual's right to a fair trial is protected by significant due process guarantees, such as the right to legal counsel. According to Freedom House, an independent organization that tracks civil liberties, the United States ranks in the upper tier (the "free" nations) for its protection of civil liberties. Many countries in Asia, Africa, and the Middle East are in the lower tier (the "not

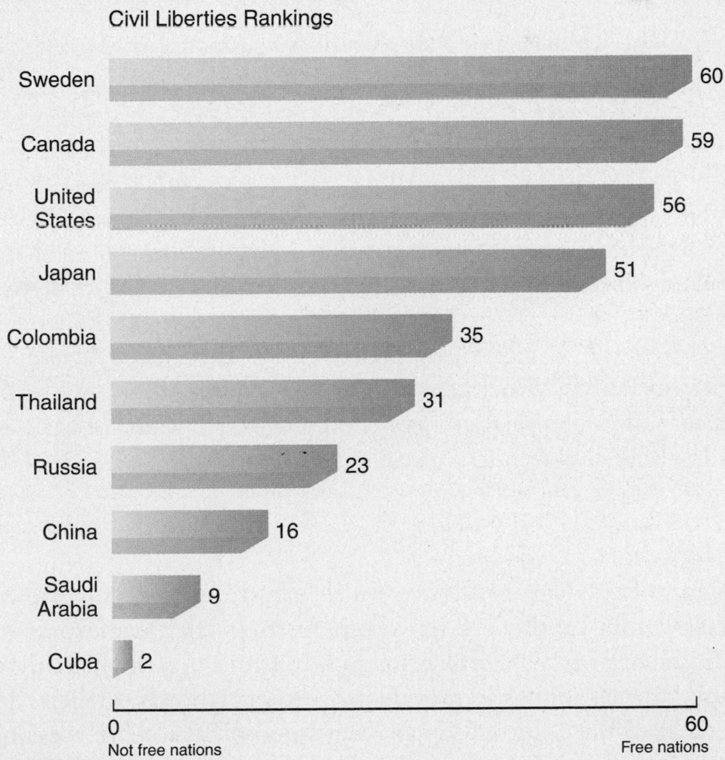

Continued

free") as a result, for example, of their use of force against political opponents. The middle-tier nations (the "partly free") provide some protection of civil liberties but engage in political repression and inadequately protect the rights of the accused. In determining its civil liberties rankings, Freedom House evaluates countries for their policies in four areas: freedom of expression, associational and organizational rights, rule of law, and personal autonomy and individual rights. The highest possible score across these dimensions is "60." The United States received a score of "56," placing it slightly below a few countries, including Canada. The United States lost points for its record on labor rights and treatment of minorities. The chart on page 113 shows how the United States compares with selected other countries on the Freedom House index.

Q: *What do the "not free" countries on the chart have in common?*

A: *The "not free" countries in the chart are characterized by one-party rule.*

Source: From Freedom House (2010). Reprinted with permission.

or deprives others of their basic rights. Nevertheless, the First Amendment provides for freedom of expression by prohibiting laws that would unreasonably abridge the freedoms of conscience, speech, press, assembly, and petition.

Free expression is vigorously protected by the courts. Today, under most circumstances, Americans can freely express their political views without fear of governmental interference or retribution. In earlier times, Americans were less free to express their opinions.

The Early Period: The Uncertain Status of the Right of Free Expression

The first attempt by the U.S. government to restrict free expression was the Sedition Act of 1798, which made it a crime to print harshly critical newspaper stories about the president or other national officials. Thomas Jefferson called the Sedition Act an "alarming infraction" of the Constitution and, upon replacing John Adams as president in 1801, pardoned those who had been convicted under it. Nevertheless, the Sedition Act was not tested in a Supreme Court case, which left open the question of whether Congress had the power to regulate free expression and, if so, how far its power extended. The Supreme Court also did not rule on the question during the Civil War era, when the government substantially restricted free expression. In this instance, Congress passed legislation barring the Court from hearing appeals of free expression cases, and the Court accepted the limitation.[18]

In 1919, the Court finally ruled on a free-expression case. The defendant had been convicted under the 1917 Espionage Act, which prohibited forms of dissent, including the distribution of antiwar leaflets that could harm the nation's effort in World War I. In *Schenck v. United States* (1919), the Court unanimously upheld the constitutionality of the Espionage Act. In the opinion written by Justice Oliver Wendell Holmes, the Court said that Congress could restrict speech that was "of such a nature as to create a clear and present danger" to the nation's security. In a famous passage, Holmes argued that not even the First Amendment would permit a person to falsely yell "Fire!" in a crowded theater and create a panic that could kill or injure innocent people.[19]

Although the *Schenck* decision upheld a law that limited free expression, it also established a constitutional standard—the **clear-and-present-danger test**—for determining when government could legally do so. According to the test, the government has to clearly demonstrate that spoken or written expression presents a clear and present danger before it can prohibit the expression.

The Modern Period: Protecting Free Expression

Until the twentieth century, the tension between national security interests and free expression was not a pressing issue in the United States. The country's great size and ocean barriers provided protection from potential enemies, minimizing concerns about internal subversion. World War I, however, intruded on America's isolation, and World War II brought it to an abrupt end. Since then, Americans' rights of free expression have been defined largely in the context of national security concerns.

Free Speech In the period after World War II, many Americans believed that the Soviet Union was bent on destroying the United States, and the Supreme Court allowed government to limit subversive expression. In 1951, for example, the Court upheld the convictions of eleven members of the U.S. Communist Party who had been prosecuted under a federal law that made it illegal to advocate the forceful overthrow of the U.S. government.[20]

By the late 1950s, however, fear of internal communist subversion was subsiding, and the Supreme Court changed its stance.[21] Ever since, it has held that national security must be endangered before government can lawfully prohibit citizens from speaking out. During this period, which includes the Vietnam and Iraq wars, not a single individual has been convicted solely for criticizing the government's war policies. (Some dissenters have been found guilty on other grounds, such as inciting a riot or assaulting a police officer.)

As was noted previously, the Supreme Court in the 1920s moved to protect speech from actions by the states. It has continued to do so. A defining free speech case is *Brandenburg v. Ohio* (1969). In a speech delivered at a Ku Klux Klan rally, Clarence Brandenburg said that "revenge" might have to be taken if the national government "continues to suppress the white Caucasian race." He was convicted under an Ohio law, but the Supreme Court reversed the conviction, saying a state cannot prohibit speech that advocates the unlawful use of force unless it meets a two-part test: it must be "directed at inciting or producing imminent lawless action" and it must be "likely to produce such action."[22] This test—the likelihood of **imminent lawless action**—is a refinement of the clear-and-present-danger test and a more restrictive one. It is rare for words alone to launch a riot, rampage, or other substantial form of lawless action.

The imminent lawless action test effectively gives Americans the freedom to voice nearly any political opinion they desire. This freedom extends to hate speech. In a unanimous 1992 opinion, the Court struck down a St. Paul, Minnesota, ordinance making it a crime to engage in speech likely to arouse "anger or alarm" on the basis of "race, color, creed, religion or gender." The Court said that the First Amendment prohibits government from "silencing speech on the basis of its content."[23] This protection of hate *speech* does not, however, extend to hate *crimes*, such as assault, motivated by racial or other prejudice. A Wisconsin law that provided for increased sentences for hate crimes was challenged as a violation of the First Amendment. In a unanimous 1993 opinion, the Court said that the law was aimed, not at free speech, but at "conduct unprotected by the First Amendment."[24]

The Supreme Court's protection of **symbolic speech** has been less substantial than its protection of verbal speech. For example, the Court in 1968 upheld the conviction of a Vietnam War protester who had burned his draft registration card. The Court concluded that the federal law prohibiting the destruction of draft cards was intended to protect the military's manpower needs and not to prevent people from criticizing government policy.[25] Nevertheless, the Supreme Court has generally

Protest is a constitutionally protected activity. No recent group has used it more effectively than the Tea Party movement. Taking its name from the famed Boston Tea Party of the Revolutionary War era, the Tea Party launched its protest activities in a major way on April 15, 2009—the deadline for filing federal income taxes. The Tea Party's protests are aimed at reducing government spending and taxation.

protected symbolic speech. In 1989, for example, the Court ruled that the symbolic burning of the American flag is a lawful form of expression. The ruling came in the case of Gregory Lee Johnson, who had set fire to a flag outside the hall in Dallas where the 1984 Republican National Convention was being held. The Supreme Court rejected the state of Texas's argument that flag burning is, in every instance, an imminent danger to public safety. "If there is a bedrock principle underlying the First Amendment," the Court ruled in the *Johnson* case, "it is that the Government may not prohibit the expression of an idea simply because society finds the idea itself offensive or disagreeable."[26]

Free Assembly In a key case involving freedom of assembly, the U.S. Supreme Court in 1977 upheld a lower-court ruling against local ordinances of Skokie, Illinois, that had been invoked to prevent a parade there by the American Nazi Party.[27] Skokie had a large Jewish population, including survivors of Nazi Germany's concentration camps. The Supreme Court held that the right of free expression takes precedence over the mere *possibility* that the exercise of that right might have undesirable consequences. Before government can lawfully prevent a speech or rally, it must demonstrate that the event will likely cause harm and also must demonstrate that it lacks an alternative way (such as assigning police officers to control the crowd) to prevent the harm from happening.

The Supreme Court has recognized that freedoms of speech and assembly may conflict with the routines of daily life. Accordingly, individuals do not have the right to hold a public rally at a busy intersection during rush hour, nor do they have the right to immediate access to a public auditorium or the right to turn up the volume on loudspeakers to the point where they can be heard miles away. The Court allows public officials to regulate the time, place, and conditions of public assembly, provided the regulations are reasonable and are applied fairly to all groups, including those that espouse unpopular views.[28]

In general, the Supreme Court has held that any government effort to regulate the *content* of a message is suspect. In the flag-burning case, for example, Texas was regulating the content of the message—contempt for the flag and the principles it represents. Texas could not have been regulating the act itself, for the Texas government's own method of disposing of worn-out flags is to burn them. But a content-neutral regulation (no public rally can be held at a busy intersection during rush hour without a permit) is acceptable as long as it is reasonable and is not used to discriminate against certain groups or ideas.

Press Freedom and Prior Restraint Freedom of the press also receives strong judicial protection. In *New York Times Co. v. United States* (1971), the Court ruled that the *Times*'s publication of the "Pentagon Papers" (secret government documents revealing that officials had deceived the public about aspects of the Vietnam War) could not be blocked by the government, which claimed that publication would harm the war effort. The documents had been obtained illegally by antiwar activists, who then gave them to the *Times*. The Court ruled that "any system of prior restraints" on the press is unconstitutional unless the government can clearly justify the restriction.[29]

The unacceptability of **prior restraint**—government prohibition of speech or publication before it occurs—is basic to the current doctrine of free expression. The Supreme Court has said that any attempt by government to prevent expression carries "a 'heavy presumption' against its constitutionality."[30] News organizations are legally responsible after the fact for what they report or say (for example, they can be sued by an individual whose reputation is wrongly damaged by their words), but government ordinarily cannot prevent a news organization from reporting whatever it wants to report. One of the few exceptions is wartime reporting; in some circumstances, the government can censor news reports that contain information that might compromise a military operation or endanger the lives of American troops.

Libel and Slander The constitutional right of free expression is not a legal license to avoid responsibility for the consequences of what is said or written. If false information harmful to a person's reputation is published (**libel**) or spoken (**slander**), the injured party can sue for damages. If it were easy for public officials to claim defamation and win large amounts of money, individuals and news organizations would be reluctant to criticize those in power. As it happens, slander and libel laws in the United States are based on the assumption that society has an interest in encouraging citizens and news organizations to express themselves freely. Accordingly, public officials can be criticized nearly at will without fear that the writer or speaker will have to pay them damages for slander or libel. (The courts are less protective of the writer or speaker when allegations are made about a private citizen. What is said about private individuals is considered to be less basic to the democratic process than what is said about public officials.)

The Supreme Court has held that true statements disseminated by the media have "full constitutional protection."[31] In other words, factually accurate statements, no matter how damaging they might be to a public official's career or reputation, are a protected form of expression. Even false or conjectural statements enjoy considerable legal protection. In *New York Times Co. v. Sullivan* (1964), the Supreme Court overruled an Alabama state court that had found the *New York Times* guilty of libel for publishing an advertisement that claimed Alabama officials had mistreated student civil rights activists. Although only some of the allegations were true, the Supreme Court backed the *Times*, saying that libel of a public official requires proof of actual malice, which was defined as a knowing or reckless disregard for the truth.[32] It is very difficult to prove that a publication recklessly or deliberately disregarded the truth. In fact, no federal official has won a libel judgment against a news organization in the four decades since the *Sullivan* ruling.

Obscenity Obscenity is a form of expression that is not protected by the First Amendment and thus can legally be prohibited. However, the

Supreme Court has found it difficult to develop a legal test for distinguishing obscene material from sexually oriented material that adults have a right to see or possess. No test had the support of a majority on the Court until *Miller v. California* (1973). In this ruling, the Court held that for material to be judged obscene, it had to meet a three-part test: first, the material must depict sexual conduct in a "patently offensive" way; second, the material must be precisely described in law as obscene; and third, the material "taken as a whole" must appeal to "prurient interest" and have "no redeeming social value." In determining whether material is patently offensive, the standard should be "contemporary community standards," based on the locale. The Court said that what might offend residents of "Mississippi might be found tolerable in Las Vegas."[33] The Court subsequently ruled that material cannot be judged obscene simply because the "average" local resident might object to it. "Community standards" were to be judged in the context of a "reasonable person"—someone with a broad enough outlook to evaluate the material on its overall merit rather than its most objectionable feature. The Court later also modified its content standard, saying that the material must be of a "particularly offensive type."[34]

These efforts illustrate the Court's difficulty in developing a tight legal standard that can be applied consistently so that the outcome of an obscenity trial does not rest on the personal opinions of a judge or jury members. Even the justices of the Supreme Court, when examining allegedly obscene material in the case before them, have disagreed on whether it appealed to prurient interest and was without redeeming social value.

The Supreme Court has distinguished between obscene materials in public places and those in the home. A unanimous ruling in 1969 held that what adults read and watch in the privacy of their homes cannot be made a crime.[35] The Court created an exception to this rule in 1990 by upholding an Ohio law making it a crime to possess pornographic photographs of children.[36] The Court reasoned that the purchase of such material encourages producers to use children in the making of pornographic materials, which is a crime. In a 2008 decision, the Court extended the ban by upholding a 2003 federal statute that makes it a crime to offer or solicit child pornography, even if the material is based on computer-generated or digitally altered images that merely appear to be those of children. Writing for the majority in the Court's 7-2 decision, Justice Antonin Scalia said: "Offers to provide or requests to obtain child pornography are categorically excluded from the First Amendment."[37]

Children have also been a consideration in court cases involving material transmitted on cable television or over the Internet. On several occasions, Congress has passed legislation (for example, the 1998 Child Online

Protection Act) that would restrict the transmission of sexually explicit material that children can access. The Supreme Court has held that the restrictions, though well intentioned, have been so broad that they would ban material adults have a constitutional right to view if they so choose.[38] The Court has directed officials to find less restrictive ways to keep such material from being seen by children. An example is the federal requirement that cable operators, if a subscriber requests it, must scramble the signal of channels that convey sexually explicit material.

Freedom of Religion

Free religious expression is the precursor of free political expression, at least within the English tradition of limited government. England's Glorious, or Bloodless, Revolution of 1689 centered on the issue of religion and resulted in the Act of Toleration, which gave members of Protestant sects the right to worship freely and publicly. The First Amendment reflects this tradition; it protects religious freedom, as well as freedom of speech, press, assembly, and petition.

In regard to religion, the First Amendment reads: "Congress shall make no law respecting an establishment of religion, or prohibiting the free exercise thereof." It will be noted that this statement contains two clauses, one referring to the "establishment of religion" (the establishment clause) and one referring to the "free exercise" of religion (the free-exercise clause). Each clause has been the subject of Supreme Court rulings.

The Establishment Clause

The **establishment clause** has been interpreted by the courts to mean that government may not favor one religion over another or support religion over no religion. (This position contrasts with that of a country such as England, where Anglicanism is the official, or "established," state religion, though no religion is prohibited.)

To this end, the Court in recent decades has prohibited religious teachings and observances in public schools. A leading case was *Engel v. Vitale* (1962), which held that the establishment clause prohibits the reciting of prayers in public schools.[39] A year later, the Court struck down Bible readings in public schools.[40] Efforts to bring religion into the schools in less direct ways have also been invalidated. For example, an Alabama law attempted to circumvent the prayer ruling by permitting public schools to set aside one minute each day for silent prayer or meditation. In 1985, the Court declared the law unconstitutional, ruling that "government

The First Amendment's protection of free expression includes religious freedom, which has led the courts to hold that government cannot in most instances promote or interfere with religious practices.

must pursue a course of complete neutrality toward religion."[41] The Court in 2000 reaffirmed the ban by extending it to include organized student-led prayer at public school football games.[42]

The Supreme Court has also banned religious displays on public property when the purpose of such a display is overtly religious and lacks a historical context. Because of the prominence of religion in American life, many public buildings display religious symbols. For instance, a statue of Moses holding the Ten Commandments stands in the rotunda of the Library of Congress building, which opened in 1897. Legal challenges to such displays have rarely succeeded. In *Van Orden v. Perry* (2005), for example, the Supreme Court rejected a suit asking for the dismantling of a display of the Ten Commandments on a monument at the Texas State Capitol. The Court noted that the display had been installed nearly a half-century earlier, had been paid for by a nonreligious group, and had not previously been the subject of dispute.[43] On the other hand, in *McCreary County v. American Civil Liberties Union* (2005), the Supreme Court struck down displays of the Ten Commandments on the walls of two Kentucky courthouses. The displays were recent and had initially hung by themselves on the courtroom walls. Only after county officials were sued did they mount a few historical displays alongside the religious ones. The Supreme Court concluded that the officials had religious purposes in mind when they erected the displays and had to remove them.[44]

Although the Court can be said to have applied the *wall of separation doctrine* (a strict separation of church and state) in these rulings, it has also relied upon what is called the *accommodation doctrine*. This doctrine allows government to aid religious activity if no preference is shown toward a particular religion and if the assistance is of a secular nature. For example, the Court has allowed states to provide busing for children who attend religious schools. In deciding whether government assistance for such activities is lawful, the Court at times has applied a test articulated in *Lemon v. Kurtzman* (1971), a case involving state funding of the salaries of religious school instructors who teach secular subjects, such as math and English. In its ruling, the Court articulated a three-point test that has come to be known as the **Lemon test**. Government action must meet all three conditions for it to be acceptable:

> First, the statute must have a secular legislative purpose; second, its principal or primary effect must be one that neither advances nor inhibits religion . . . ; finally, the statute must not foster "an excessive government entanglement with religion."[45]

In the *Lemon* case, the Court held that state funding of religious school teachers failed the test. The Court concluded that such payments involve "excessive government entanglement with religion" because an instructor, even though teaching a subject such as math or science, might use the classroom as an opportunity to promote religious teachings. In contrast, the Court in another case allowed states to pay for math, science, and other secular textbooks used in church-affiliated schools, concluding that the textbooks had little if any religious content in them.[46]

In a key 2002 decision, however, the Supreme Court upheld an Ohio law that allows students in Cleveland's failing public schools to receive a tax-supported voucher to attend a private or parochial school. The Court's majority argued in *Zelman v. Simmons-Harris* that the program did not violate the establishment clause because students had a choice between secular and religious education. Four members of the Court dissented with the majority's reasoning. Justice John Paul Stevens said the ruling went beyond accommodation and had in effect removed a "brick from the wall that was once designed to separate religion from government."[47]

The Free-Exercise Clause

The First and Fourteenth Amendments also prohibit government interference with the free exercise of religion. The **free-exercise clause** has been interpreted to mean that Americans are free to hold any religious belief of their choosing. Americans are not always free, however, to act on their belief. The Supreme Court has allowed government interference when the exercise of religious belief conflicts with otherwise valid law. Examples include the prohibition on the practice of polygamy by those of the Mormon faith and court-ordered medical care for children with life-threatening illnesses whose parents have denied them treatment on religious grounds. A more recent example is *Employment Division v. Smith* (1990), in which the Supreme Court upheld Oregon's refusal to grant unemployment benefits to a person fired for using peyote, even though its use was a ritual of the person's religion.[48]

In some instances, the free exercise of religion clashes with the prohibition on the establishment of religion, and the Supreme Court is forced to choose between them. In 1987, for example, the Court overturned a Louisiana law that required creationism (the Bible's account of how God created the world in seven days) to be taught along with the theory of evolution in public school science courses. The Court concluded that creationism is a religious doctrine, not a scientific theory, and that its inclusion in public school curricula violates the establishment clause by promoting a religious belief.[49] In 2005, a federal judge blocked a Pennsylvania public school district from requiring intelligent design (the belief that God has guided evolution) to be taught in science classes. The judge ruled that intelligent design is a disguised version of creationism, that it has no basis in science, and that the teaching of it would violate the establishment clause.[50] Certain religious groups claim that such decisions violate the free-exercise clause because some children are required to study a version of creation—evolution—that contradicts their religious belief about the origin of life.

The Right to Bear Arms

The Second Amendment to the Constitution says: "A well regulated Militia, being necessary to the security of a free State, the right of the people to keep and bear Arms, shall not be infringed." The amendment is widely understood to prevent the federal government from abolishing state militias (such as National Guard units), but there has been disagreement over whether the amendment also gives individuals the right to possess weapons outside their use in military service.

Remarkably, more than two centuries passed before the Supreme Court squarely addressed the issue of how the Second Amendment is to be interpreted. The decision came in *District of Columbia v. Heller* (2008). In its ruling, the Court said that "the Second Amendment protects an individual right to possess a firearm unconnected with service in a militia, and to use that arm for traditionally lawful purposes, such as self-defense within the home." The ruling struck down a District of Columbia law that had banned the possession of handguns but not rifles or shotguns within the district's boundaries. Writing for the 5-4 majority, Justice Antonin Scalia said that the justices were "aware of the problem of handgun violence in this country." But Scalia concluded: "The enshrinement of constitutional rights necessarily takes certain policy choices off the table. These include the absolute prohibition of handguns held and used for self-defense in the home."[51] In a sharply worded dissent, Justice John Paul Stevens said the majority had devised a ruling that fit its partisan agenda rather than what the framers intended. Stevens declared: "When each word in the text is given full effect, the Amendment is most naturally read to secure to the people a right to use and possess arms in conjunction with service in a well-regulated militia. So far as it appears, no more than that was contemplated by its drafters or is encompassed within its terms."

Although the *Heller* decision was a victory for advocates of gun rights, the District of Columbia is federal territory and there was a question whether the Supreme Court, through selective incorporation, would extend the ruling to include state and local gun laws. In *McDonald v. Chicago* (2010), the Court did so. As in the *Heller* decision, the Court's majority was careful to say that some gun restrictions are permitted, such as limits on gun ownership by those convicted of a felony. Nevertheless the Court did not provide clear or comprehensive guidelines on which restrictions are constitutionally permissible and which are not, leaving the issue to be decided through future court cases.

The Right of Privacy

Until the 1960s, Americans' constitutional rights were confined largely to those listed in the Bill of Rights. This situation prevailed despite the Ninth Amendment, which reads, "The enumeration in the Constitution, of certain rights, shall not be construed to deny or disparage others retained by the people." In 1965, however, the Supreme Court added to the list of individual rights, declaring that Americans have "a right of privacy." This judgment arose from the case of *Griswold v. Connecticut*, which challenged a state law prohibiting the use of condoms and other birth control devices, even by married couples. The Supreme Court struck down the statute, concluding that a state had no business interfering with a married couple's decision regarding contraception. The Court did not invoke the Ninth Amendment but reasoned instead that the freedoms in the Bill of Rights imply an underlying **right of privacy**. The Court held that individuals have a "zone of [personal] privacy" that government cannot lawfully invade.[52]

Although the right of privacy has not been applied broadly by the Supreme Court, it has been invoked in two major areas—a woman's right to choose an abortion and consensual relations among same-sex adults.

Abortion

The right of privacy was the basis for the Supreme Court's ruling in *Roe v. Wade* (1973), which gave women full freedom to choose abortion during the first three months of pregnancy. In overturning a Texas law banning abortion except to save the life of the mother, the Court said that the right of privacy is "broad enough to encompass a woman's decision whether or not to terminate her pregnancy."[53]

The *Roe* decision was met with praise by some Americans and condemnation by others, provoking a still-continuing debate. Americans are sharply divided over the abortion issue and have been throughout the nearly four decades since *Roe*. The dispute has included violent confrontations at abortion clinics. In 1994, Congress passed a law that makes it illegal to block the entrance to abortion clinics or otherwise prevent people from entering. (The Supreme Court upheld the law, concluding that it regulated actions as opposed to words and thus did not violate free speech rights.[54])

After the *Roe* ruling, antiabortion activists sought a constitutional amendment that would ban abortion, but failed in that effort, prompting them to pursue alternatives. They persuaded the Missouri legislature to pass a law that prohibited abortions from being performed in the state's publicly funded medical facilities, a policy that the Supreme Court upheld in *Webster v. Reproductive Health Services* (1989).[55] The *Webster* decision was followed by a Pennsylvania abortion case, *Planned Parenthood v. Casey* (1992), which antiabortion advocates had hoped would reverse the *Roe* precedent. Instead, by a 5-4 margin, the Supreme Court upheld a constitutional right to abortion, concluding that "the essential holding of *Roe v. Wade* should be retained and once again reaffirmed."[56] At the same time, the Court upheld the part of the Pennsylvania law that requires a minor to have parental or judicial consent before obtaining an abortion. Any such restriction, the Court said, is constitutional as long as it does not impose an "undue burden" on the woman. A decade later, the Court struck down a New Hampshire parental-consent law because it had no exception in the case of a medical emergency. The omission, the Court ruled, could place an "undue burden" on a pregnant minor who faced a life-threatening emergency.[57]

In *Gonzales v. Carhart* (2007), the Supreme Court for the first time upheld a ban on the use of a particular type of abortion. At issue was the federal Partial-Birth Abortion Ban Act, passed by Congress in 2003. The law provides for a fine and prison term for physicians who perform an abortion during the birth process even if the mother's life or health is endangered. In an earlier case, *Stenberg v. Carhart* (2000), the Supreme Court had invalidated a nearly identical Nebraska law.[58] However, the Nebraska case was decided by a narrow 5-4 margin, with Justice Sandra Day O'Connor providing the swing vote. By the time the 2007 case reached the Supreme Court, O'Connor had retired, and her replacement, the more conservative Samuel Alito, voted the other way, resulting in a 5-4 vote upholding the congressional ban. Writing for the majority, Justice Anthony Kennedy said that the federal act did not place an "undue burden" on women. In her dissenting opinion, Justice Ruth Bader Ginsburg, the lone woman on the Court, called the decision "alarming," arguing that it ignored established legal precedent and put women's lives and health at risk.[59]

Consensual Sexual Relations among Same-Sex Adults

Although the Supreme Court's 1965 *Griswold* ruling on contraceptive use was widely said to have taken "government out of people's bedrooms," a clear exception remained. All states prohibited sexual relations between consenting adults of the same sex. A number of states eliminated this prohibition over the next two decades, and others stopped enforcing it. Nevertheless, in a 1986 Georgia case, *Bowers v. Hardwick*, the Supreme Court held that the right of privacy did not extend to consensual sexual relations among adults of the same sex.[60]

In 2003, the Court reversed itself and in the process struck down the sodomy laws of the thirteen states that still had them. In *Lawrence v.*

Gay rights proponents won a civil liberties lawsuit when the Supreme Court in 2003 overturned a state ban on sexual relations among consenting adults of the same sex.

Texas, the Court in a 6-3 vote concluded that Texas's sodomy law violated "the right of privacy" implied by the grant of liberty in the Fourteenth Amendment's due process clause. The Court said: "The petitioners are entitled to respect for their private lives. The State cannot demean their existence or control their destiny by making their private sexual conduct a crime."[61] The decision was hailed by gay and lesbian rights groups but condemned by some religious groups, who said it opened the door to same-sex marriage (see Chapter 5).

Rights of Persons Accused of Crime

Due process refers to legal protections that have been established to preserve the rights of individuals. The most significant of these protections is **procedural due process**; the term refers primarily to procedures that authorities must follow before a person can lawfully be punished for an offense. No system of justice is foolproof. Even in the most careful systems, innocent people have been wrongly accused, convicted, and punished with imprisonment or death. But the scrupulous application of procedural safeguards, such as a defendant's right to legal counsel, greatly increases the likelihood of a fair trial. "The history of liberty has largely been the history of the observance of procedural guarantees," said Justice Felix Frankfurter in *McNabb v. United States* (1943).[62]

The U.S. Constitution offers procedural safeguards designed to protect a person from wrongful arrest, conviction, and punishment. According to Article I, Section 9, a person taken into police custody is entitled to seek a writ of habeas corpus, which requires law enforcement officials to bring the suspect into court and to specify the legal reason for the detention. The Fifth and Fourteenth Amendments provide generally that no person can be deprived of life, liberty, or property without due process of law. Specific procedural protections for the accused are listed in the Fourth, Fifth, Sixth, and Eighth Amendments.[63]

Suspicion Phase: Unreasonable Search and Seizure

In 1766, Parliamentary leader William Pitt forcefully expressed a principle of English common law: "The poorest man may, in his cottage, bid defiance to all the forces of the Crown. It may be frail; its roof may shake; the wind may blow through it; the rain may enter; but the King of England may not enter; all his force dares not cross the threshold."[64] In the period immediately preceding the American Revolution, few things provoked more anger among the colonists than Britain's disregard for the sanctity of the home. British soldiers regularly forced their way into colonists' houses, looking for documents or other evidence of anti-British activity.

The Fourth Amendment was included in the Bill of Rights to prohibit such actions by the U.S. government. The Fourth Amendment reads: "The right of the people to be secure in their persons, houses, papers, and effects, against unreasonable searches and seizures, shall not be violated, and no Warrants shall issue, but upon probable cause, supported by Oath of Affirmation, and particularly describing the place to be searched, and the persons or things to be seized."

The Fourth Amendment does not provide blanket protection against search and seizure. A person caught in the act of a crime can be arrested (seized) on the spot and can be searched for weapons and incriminating evidence. The Fourth Amendment does, however, provide protection against speculative or arbitrary police action. If someone is suspected of a crime, the police ordinarily have to obtain a search warrant from a judge before they can act. If the judge finds the evidence unconvincing, the warrant is denied.

Recent decisions have lowered the standard police must meet to lawfully search a person. Previously, the Court had held that police must have a substantial basis ("probable cause") for believing that an individual had committed a crime before they could stop, apprehend, and search the person. In *Whren v. United States* (1996), however, the Court upheld the conviction of an individual who had been found with drugs sitting in plain view in the front seat of his car. The police had no evidence (no "probable cause") indicating that drugs were in the car, but they had a hunch that the driver was a drug dealer and used a minor traffic infraction as a pretext to stop his car. The Supreme Court accepted the defense's arguments that the police had no concrete evidence to back their suspicion, that the traffic infraction was not the real reason he was stopped, and that police usually do not stop a person for the infraction in question (turning a corner without signaling). However, the Court concluded that the officers' motive was irrelevant as long as an officer in some situations might reasonably stop a car for the infraction in question.[65] The ruling gave police more latitude in stopping suspected individuals. It also reaffirmed an earlier decision upholding the admissibility of evidence found in plain sight (*the plain view doctrine*) even when the evidence relates to an infraction other than the one for which the individual was stopped.[66]

The Supreme Court also allows warrantless searches in some circumstances. It has held, for example, that police roadblocks to check drivers for signs of intoxication are legal as long as the action is systematic and not arbitrary (for example, stopping only young drivers would be

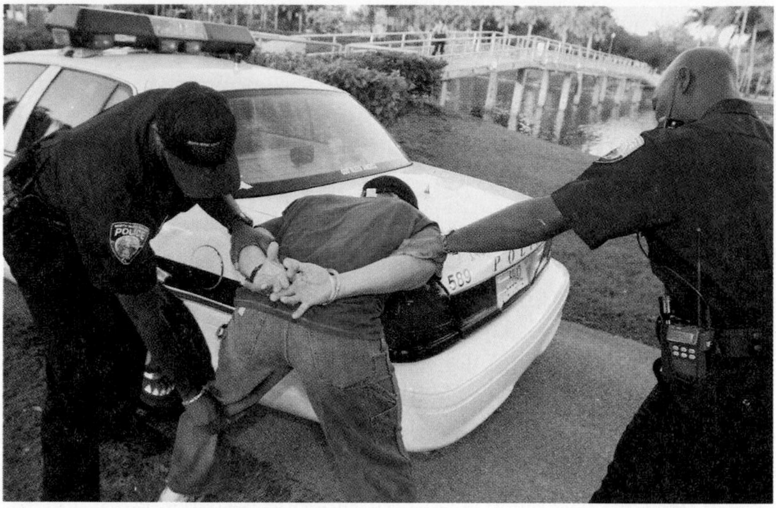

Most of the controversies surrounding procedural due process involve the conduct of police officers. They operate under constitutional restraints in terms of apprehending, searching, and questioning suspects. If they ignore these restraints, evidence they obtain is not admissable in court in some instances.

unconstitutional, whereas stopping all drivers is acceptable). The Court justified this decision by saying that roadblocks serve an important highway safety objective.[67] However, the Court does not allow police roadblocks to check for drugs. In *Indianapolis v. Edmund* (2001), the Court held that narcotics roadblocks serve a general law enforcement purpose rather than one specific to highway safety and therefore violate the Fourth Amendment's requirement that police have suspicion of wrongdoing before they can search an individual's auto.[68] The Court has also held that police cannot use thermal-imaging devices to scan homes to detect the presence of heat sources that might reveal the production of illegal drugs. Ordinarily, police cannot physically enter a home without a search warrant, and the Court reasoned that the same procedure should apply to searches based on modern technology.[69]

The Fourth Amendment protects individuals in their persons as well as in their homes and vehicles. In *Ferguson v. Charleston* (2001), for example, the Court held that patients in public hospitals cannot be forced to take a test for illegal drugs if the purpose is to report to police those patients who test positive. Such action, said the Court, constitutes an illegal search of the person.[70] Authorities have more leeway when it comes to students in public schools. For example, in *Board of Education of Independent School District No. 92 of Pottawatomie County v. Earls* (2002), the Court held that random drug testing of high school students involved in extracurricular activities does not violate the ban on unreasonable searches.[71] In general, the Court has usually deferred to school administrators on grounds that they are responsible for student safety, which can be endangered if drugs, weapons, and other dangerous items make their way into schools.

Arrest Phase: Protection against Self-Incrimination

The Fifth Amendment says, in part, that an individual cannot "be compelled in any criminal case to be a witness against himself." This provision is designed to protect individuals from the age-old practice of coerced confession. Trickery and torture can lead people to confess to acts they never committed.

At the time of arrest, police cannot legally begin their interrogation until the suspect has been warned that his or her words can be used as evidence. This warning requirement emerged from *Miranda v. Arizona* (1966), which centered on Ernesto Miranda's confession to kidnapping and rape during police questioning. The Supreme Court overturned his conviction on the grounds that police had not informed him of his right to remain silent and to have legal assistance. The Court reasoned that suspects have a right to know their rights. The Court's ruling led to the formulation of the "Miranda warning" that police are now required to read to suspects: "You have the right to remain silent. . . . Anything you say can and will be used against you in a court of law. . . . You have the right to an attorney." (Miranda was subsequently retried and convicted on the basis of evidence other than his confession.)

The Miranda warning has been effective in protecting the rights of the accused. The benefit has accrued mainly to the poor and uneducated, who are less likely than the well-to-do or the highly educated to be aware of their rights. In a 2000 case, *Dickerson v. United States*, the Supreme Court reaffirmed the *Miranda* decision, saying that it was an established "constitutional rule" that Congress could not abolish by ordinary legislation.[72] The Court further strengthened the Miranda precedent in *Missouri v. Siebert* (2004). This ruling came in response to a police strategy of questioning suspects before informing them of their Miranda rights and then questioning them a second time in a more formal way, often with the use of a tape or video recorder. In such instances, suspects who admitted wrongdoing in the first round of questioning often did so also in the second round. The Court concluded that the police strategy was intended "to undermine the Miranda warnings" and was a violation of suspects' rights.[73] In 2010, however, the Supreme Court weakened the Miranda warning to some extent. In one ruling, the Court held that suspects who invoke their rights can be questioned at a later time if they have been released from custody and are read their rights again before the questioning begins.[74] In another case, the Court ruled that police, after reading suspects their Miranda rights, can question them if they fail to ask for an attorney or fail to express their intent to remain silent.[75] Previously, the Court had held that suspects must "knowingly and intelligently waive" their rights before they can be questioned.

Trial Phase: The Right to a Fair Trial

The right to a fair trial is basic to any reasonable notion of justice. If the trial process is arbitrary or biased against the defendant, justice is denied. It is sometimes said the American justice system is based on the principle that it is better to let one hundred guilty parties go free than to convict one innocent person. The system does not actually work that way. Once a person has been arrested and charged with a crime, prosecutors are determined to get a conviction. Defendants in such instances have fair-trial guarantees that are designed to protect them from wrongful conviction.

Legal Counsel and Impartial Jury Under the Fifth Amendment, suspects charged with a *federal* crime cannot be tried unless indicted by a grand jury. The grand jury hears the prosecution's evidence and decides whether it is strong enough to allow the government to try the suspect. This protection has not been incorporated into the Fourteenth Amendment. As a result, states are not required to use grand juries, although roughly half of them do so. In the rest of the states, the prosecutor usually decides whether to proceed with a trial.

The Sixth Amendment provides a right to legal counsel before and during trial. But what if a person cannot afford a lawyer? For most of the nation's history, poor people had no choice but to act as their own attorneys. In *Johnson v. Zerbst* (1938), the Supreme Court held that criminal defendants in federal cases must be provided a lawyer at government expense if they cannot afford legal counsel.[76] The Court extended this requirement to include state felony cases with its ruling in *Gideon v. Wainwright* (1963). This case centered on Clarence Gideon, who had been convicted in a Florida court of breaking into a pool hall. He had asked for a lawyer, but the trial judge denied the request, forcing Gideon to act as his own attorney. He appealed his conviction, and the Supreme Court overturned it on grounds that he did not have adequate legal counsel.[77]

Criminal defendants also have the right to a speedy trial and to confront witnesses against them. At the federal level and sometimes at the state level, they have a right to jury trial, which is to be heard by an "impartial jury." The Court has ruled that a jury's impartiality can be compromised if the prosecution stacks a jury by race or ethnicity.[78] There was a period in the South when blacks accused of crimes against whites were always tried by all-white juries, which invariably returned a guilty verdict. The jury's makeup can be an issue for other reasons as well. In *Witherspoon v. Illinois* (1968), for example, the Supreme Court invalidated Illinois's policy of allowing the prosecution an unlimited number of challenges in capital cases. The prosecution used the challenges to remove from the jury anyone who expressed even the slightest qualms about sentencing the defendant to death if found guilty. To allow that practice, the Court ruled, is to virtually guarantee "a verdict of death." "Whatever else might be said of capital punishment," the Court said, "it is at least clear that its imposition by a hanging jury cannot be squared with the Constitution."[79]

The Exclusionary Rule An issue in some trials is the admissibility of evidence obtained in violation of the defendant's rights. The **exclusionary rule** bars the use of such evidence in some circumstances. The rule was formulated on a limited basis in a 1914 Supreme Court decision and was devised to deter police from violating people's rights. If police know that illegally obtained evidence will be inadmissible in court, they presumably will be less inclined to obtain it. As the Court wrote in *Weeks v. United States* (1914): "The tendency of those who execute the criminal laws of the country to obtain convictions by means of unlawful searches and enforced confessions . . . should find no sanction in the judgment of the courts."[80]

In the 1960s, the liberal-dominated Supreme Court expanded the exclusionary rule to the point where almost any illegally obtained evidence was inadmissible in federal or state court. Opponents accused the Court of "coddling criminals," and the appointment of more conservative justices to the Court led to a weakening of the exclusionary rule in the 1980s. In *United States v. Leon* (1984), the Court ruled that evidence discovered under a faulty warrant was admissible because the police had acted in "good faith."[81] This position was reaffirmed in *Herring v. United States* (2008), a case in which police, acting on an arrest warrant issued by another jurisdiction, found firearms and drugs in the individual's truck, only to later discover that the warrant was invalid because it had expired.[82] The *good faith exception* holds that otherwise excludable evidence can be admitted in trial if police believed they were following proper procedures.

A second principle by which tainted evidence can be admitted is the *inevitable discovery exception*. It was developed in the case of *Nix v. Williams* (1984). An eyewitness account had led police to believe that Williams had kidnapped a young girl. Police obtained a warrant and arrested him at a distant location. While being transported by police, despite verbal assurances to his lawyer that he would not be questioned en route, Williams was interrogated and told police where the girl's body could be found. When Williams appealed his conviction, the Court acknowledged that his rights had been violated but concluded that police had other evidence that would have enabled them to find the girl's body. "Exclusion of physical evidence that would have inevitably been discovered adds nothing to either the integrity or fairness of a criminal trial," the Court said.[83]

As some observers see it, the Court has sought to weaken the exclusionary rule without going so far as to allow police to do whatever they please. Other observers believe the Court has narrowed the exclusionary rule nearly to the point where it applies only to the most outrageous forms of police misconduct. The Court's majority has said that defendants can seek other remedies when the police violate their constitutional rights, such as suing the police for monetary damages. In a 2006 dissent, Justice Stephen Breyer criticized this reasoning, saying that the Court's majority could not "cite a single reported case" in which someone whose rights had been violated by police officers had been awarded an amount of money worth the time and effort required to get it.[84]

Sentencing Phase: Cruel and Unusual Punishment

Most issues of criminal justice involve *procedural* due process. However, adherence to proper procedures does not necessarily produce reasonable outcomes. The Eighth Amendment was designed to address this issue. It prohibits "cruel and unusual punishment" of those convicted of crime. The Supreme Court has applied several tests in determining whether punishment is cruel and unusual, including whether it is "disproportionate to the offence," violates "fundamental standards of good conscience and fairness," and is "unnecessarily cruel."

However, the Supreme Court has typically let Congress and the state legislatures determine the appropriate penalties for crime. Thus, the Supreme Court in 1991 upheld a conviction under a Michigan law that mandated life imprisonment without parole for a nonviolent first offense involving 1.5 pounds of cocaine.[85] More recently, the Court upheld a conviction under California's "three strikes and you're out" law that sent a twice previously convicted felon to prison for life without parole for shoplifting videotapes worth $100.[86]

On the other hand, the Supreme Court has recently employed the Eighth Amendment to narrow the use of the death penalty. In *Atkins v. Virginia*

HOW THE 50 STATES DIFFER

POLITICAL THINKING THROUGH COMPARISONS

Incarceration Rates

Although the states are required under the Constitution to uphold defendants' rights, their criminal justice systems differ markedly in other respects. Sentencing laws are an example. States differ in their sentencing practices—most obviously in the application of the death penalty. Some states prohibit it, and others apply it liberally. Texas, Florida, and Virginia are far and away the leaders in its application. Roughly a third of all executions in the past quarter-century have taken place in Texas alone. States also differ substantially in the proportion of their residents who are in prison. Louisiana has the highest incarceration rate, with 865 inmates for every 100,000 residents. Mississippi, Texas, Oklahoma, and Alabama are the other states in the top five. Maine has the lowest

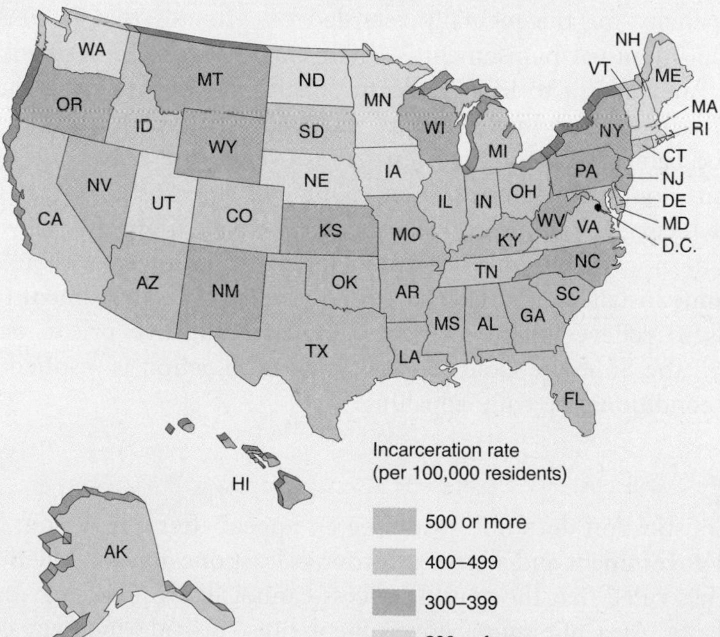

Continued

incarceration rate—159 inmates per 100,000 residents. On a per-capita basis, Louisiana imprisons more than five times as many of its residents as does Maine. Minnesota, North Dakota, Rhode Island, and Utah are the other states that rank in the lowest five in terms of number of inmates.

Q: *What do many of the states with low incarceration rates have in common?*

A: *Most of these states are relatively affluent and rank high on indicators of educational attainment, which are correlated with lower crime rates. Most of these states also have relatively small minority-group populations. Studies have found that minority-group defendants are more likely than white defendants to be convicted and, when convicted, to receive a lengthier sentence.*

Source: U.S. Department of Justice, 2010.

(2002) and again in *Panetti v. Quarterman* (2007), the Court outlawed the death penalty for the mentally retarded on grounds that it constitutes "cruel and unusual punishment."[87] The Court also recently invoked the Eighth Amendment to ban the death penalty in cases involving juveniles and for crimes other than murder.[88] In 2010, the Supreme Court broadened the ban on extreme punishment of juveniles to include life without parole in nonhomicide cases. The ruling grew out of a Florida case in which a teenager, who had previously been convicted of robbery, was sentenced to life without parole for participating in a home invasion.[89]

In some instances, courts have applied the Eighth Amendment to force officials to relieve inmate overcrowding and improve prison facilities, although the Supreme Court has said that such action is justified only if prison conditions are truly appalling.[90]

Appeal: One Chance, Usually

The Constitution does not guarantee an appeal after conviction, but the federal government and all states permit at least one appeal. The Supreme Court has ruled that the appeal process cannot discriminate against poor defendants. At a minimum, government must provide indigent convicts with the legal resources to file a first appeal.

Prisoners who believe their constitutional rights have been violated by state officials can appeal their conviction to a federal court. A 1960s

Supreme Court case gave prisoners the right to have their appeal heard in federal court unless they had "deliberately bypassed" the opportunity to first make their appeal in state courts.[91] This precedent was overturned in 1992 when the Court held that inmates can lose the right to a federal hearing even if a lawyer's mistake is the reason they failed to first present their appeal properly in state courts.[92] In *Bowles v. Russell* (2007), the Court in a 5-4 decision went so far as to deny an appeal in a case in which the deadline for filing the appeal was missed because a federal judge had given the inmate's lawyer the wrong date.[93]

The greatest restriction on appeals is a federal law that bars in most instances a second federal appeal by a state prison inmate.[94] Upheld by the Supreme Court in *Felker v. Turpin* (1996), this law is designed to prevent frivolous and multiple federal court appeals. State prisoners had used appeals to contest even small issues, and some inmates—particularly those on death row—had filed appeal after appeal. An effect was the clogging of the federal courts and a delay in hearing other cases. The Supreme Court has ruled that, except in unusual cases,[95] it is fair to ask inmates to first pursue their options in state courts and then to confine themselves to a single federal appeal.

Crime, Punishment, and Police Practices

Although the exclusionary rule and the appeals process have been weakened, there has not been a return to the lower procedural standards that prevailed prior to the 1960s. Most of the key precedents established in that decade remain in effect, including the most important one of all: the principle that procedural protections guaranteed to the accused by the Bill of Rights must be observed by the states as well as by the federal government.

Supreme Court rulings have affected police practices. The Miranda warning, for example, is respected by most police departments. Nevertheless, numerous studies, some of which have been conducted by state governments, have found that constitutional rights are applied arbitrarily, or even ignored completely, by some law enforcement officials. *Racial profiling* (the assumption that certain groups are more likely to commit particular crimes) is a common police practice and results in the unequal treatment of minorities.[96] One study found, for example, that 80 percent of the motorists stopped and searched by Maryland State Police on Interstate 95 were minorities and only 20 percent were white, despite the fact that white motorists constituted 75 percent of all drivers and were just as likely as minority motorists to violate the traffic laws. African Americans refer mockingly to a traffic infraction they call DWB—"driving while black."

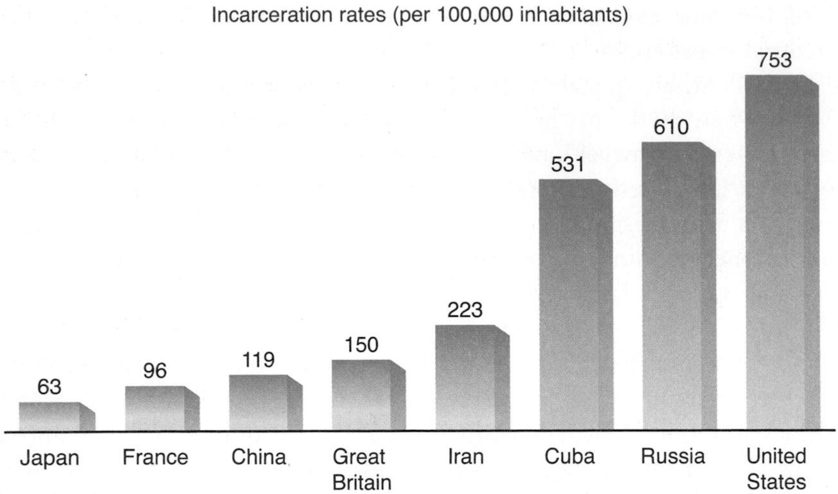

figure 4-1 INCARCERATION RATES, BY COUNTRY

The United States is the world leader in terms of the number of people it places behind bars. More than half of the people in U.S. prisons were convicted of nonviolent offenses, such as drug use or property theft. *Source:* From National Council on Crime and Delinquency (2010). Reprinted with permission.

Sentencing policies are also an issue. Being "tough on crime" is popular with some voters, and most state legislatures during the past two decades have enacted stiffer penalties for crime while also limiting the ability of judges to reduce sentences, even for nonviolent crime when the perpetrator has no prior criminal record. As a result, the number of federal and state prisoners has more than doubled since 1990. Many U.S. prisons are overflowing with inmates. In 2009, a federal court ordered California to release nearly 40,000 inmates within two years because of prison overcrowding. In fact, on a per-capita basis, the United States has the largest prison population in the world (Figure 4-1). Russia is the only country that is even close to the United States in terms of the percentage of its citizens who are behind bars.

As the human and financial costs of keeping so many people in prison have risen, debate over America's criminal justice system has intensified. The incarceration of nonviolent drug offenders is one such issue. U.S. drug policy is at odds with that of other Western countries, which rely more heavily on treatment programs than on prisons in dealing with drug offenders. Critics also cite studies showing that minorities and the poor receive harsher sentences than do middle-class white persons convicted of comparable crimes. An example is the disparity in sentences for those convicted of powder-cocaine and crack-cocaine offenses. African Americans make up roughly three-fourths of crack-cocaine defendants whereas whites make up about three-fourths of powder-cocaine defendants. Federal law calls for nearly twice as much prison time for a crack-cocaine conviction as for a powder-cocaine conviction involving comparable amounts of cocaine.[97] In 2007, the Supreme Court gave judges the authority to reduce crack-cocaine sentences below the federal guidelines to bring them closer into line with powder-cocaine sentences.[98]

Rights and the War on Terrorism

In time of war, the courts have upheld government policies that would not be permitted in peacetime. After the Japanese attack on Pearl Harbor in 1941, for example, President Franklin D. Roosevelt ordered the forced relocation of tens of thousands of Japanese Americans living on the West Coast to detention camps in Arizona, Utah, and other inland locations. Congress endorsed the policy, and the Supreme Court upheld it in *Korematsu v. United States* (1944).[99] Another Supreme Court ruling during World War II denied a U.S. citizen arrested as a Nazi collaborator a court trial after the government decided to try him before a military tribunal.[100] After the terrorist attacks of September 11, 2001, the Bush administration invoked precedents such as these in declaring that customary legal protections would not be afforded to individuals it deemed to have engaged in terrorist activity.

POLITICAL THINKING

Sacrificing Liberty to War?

Soon after the terrorist attacks on New York and Washington of September 11, 2001, Congress enacted the USA Patriot Act, which gives the federal government the power to examine medical, financial, and education records on the basis of a minimum standard of suspicion; to detain individuals for short periods without tangible evidence of wrongdoing; to deport noncitizens who have even minimal association with suspected terrorist groups; and to secretly search homes and offices in some instances. Such actions are not unprecedented during periods of national insecurity. During the early years of the cold war with the Soviet Union, for example, Congress passed the Smith Act, which made it illegal for Americans to advocate the overthrow of the U.S. government, even though the First Amendment says that "Congress shall make no law . . . abridging freedom of speech, or of the press. . . ." How far during times of heightened worry about national security are you willing to let government depart from the usual protections of individual rights?

Detention of Enemy Combatants

The Bush administration soon announced its policy for handling captured "enemy combatants"—individuals judged to be engaged in, or in support of, hostile military actions against U.S. military forces. Some of these prisoners were sent to a detention facility created at the U.S. Naval Base at Guantanamo Bay on the tip of Cuba. Others were imprisoned in Afghanistan, Iraq, and elsewhere. Requests by lawyers and international agencies like the Red Cross to see the detainees were denied or strictly limited. Some prisoners were subject to abusive treatment, although the practice was denied by U.S. officials until photographic and other evidence surfaced.

In 2004, the Supreme Court issued its first ruling on these practices, holding that the Guantanamo Bay detainees had the right to challenge their detention in court. The Court reasoned that the naval base, though in Cuba, is on land leased to the United States and therefore under the jurisdiction of U.S. courts.[101] In a second 2004 case (*Hamdi v. Rumsfeld*), the Court ruled that one of the Guantanamo Bay detainees, who was a U.S. citizen by virtue of having been born in the United States though he was raised in Saudi Arabia, had the right to be heard in U.S. courts.

Shown here is the detention center at the U.S. naval base at Guantanamo Bay where enemy detainees from the Afghanistan and Iran conflicts were held pending trial by miltary commission. In *Hamdan v. Rumsfeld* (2006), the Supreme Court ruled that the commissions, which had been established by the Bush administration, violated U.S. and international law.

The Court said: "As critical as the government's interest may be in detaining those who actually pose an immediate threat to the national security of the United States during ongoing international conflict, history and common sense teach us that an unchecked system of detention carries the potential to become a means of oppression and abuse of others who do not present that sort of threat."[102]

Two years later, the Supreme Court issued its sharpest rebuke of the Bush administration's detention policies. In a ruling nearly unprecedented in its challenge to a president's wartime authority, the Court held that the detainees were protected both by the U.S. Uniform Code of Military Justice and by the Geneva Conventions. At issue was the Bush administration's use of secret military tribunals to try detainees. In *Hamdan v. Rumsfeld* (2006), the Court ruled that the tribunals were unlawful because they did not provide even minimal protections of detainees' rights.[103] Then, in a 2008 ruling, the Court struck down a provision of an act of Congress that had been passed two years earlier at the Bush administration's insistence. The provision had denied federal courts the authority to hear appeals from prisoners who sought to challenge their detentions. Writing for the majority in a 5-4 decision, Justice Anthony Kennedy said: "The laws and Constitution are designed to survive, and remain in force, in extraordinary times."[104]

Surveillance of Suspected Terrorists

After the September 11 terrorist attacks and in response to the Bush administration's request for expanded surveillance powers, Congress passed the USA Patriot Act, which lowered the standard for judicial approval of wiretapping when terrorist activity was at issue. The law also allowed information from intelligence surveillance to be shared with criminal investigators when evidence was found of criminal activity unrelated to terrorism. Previously, such information could be shared only when obtained by the stricter standards that apply to criminal investigations. The new law also gave government increased authority to examine medical, financial, and student records and allowed the government in some situations to secretly search homes and offices (so-called "sneak and peek" searches).

The Bush administration promised to act with restraint in its exercise of the new powers, and congressional oversight committees were generally satisfied with its actions until the *New York Times* revealed in late 2005 that President Bush without judicial approval had secretly authorized the National Security Agency (NSA) to wiretap international phone calls and e-mail messages originating in the United States. Such wiretaps are expressly prohibited by the Foreign Intelligence Surveillance Act (FISA) of 1978. Bush rejected allegations that he had broken the law, saying that he had acted legally under his wartime powers as commander-in-chief and under authority implicitly granted him by the Patriot Act. When Barack Obama became president, some observers expected him to disclose the NSA's warrantless wiretap activities. Instead, the Obama administration declared that release of the information "would cause exceptionally grave harm to national security."

The Courts and a Free Society

The United States was founded on the idea that individuals have an innate right to liberty—to speak their minds, to worship freely, to be secure in their homes and persons, to be assured of a fair trial. Americans embrace these freedoms in the abstract. In particular situations, however, many Americans think otherwise. A 2010 CNN survey found, for example, that more than two in five Americans think that individuals arrested by police on suspicion of terrorism should not be read their Miranda rights.

The judiciary is not isolated from the public mood. Judges inevitably must balance society's need for security and public order against the rights of the individual. Nevertheless, relative to elected officials, police officers, or the general public, judges are typically more protective of individual rights. How far the courts will go in protecting a person's rights depends on the facts of the case, the existing status of the law, prevailing social needs, and the personal views of the judges (see Chapter 14). Nevertheless, most judges and justices regard the protection of individual rights as a constitutional imperative, which is the way the framers saw it. The Bill of Rights was created to transform the abstract idea that individuals have inalienable rights to life, liberty, and happiness into a set of specified constitutional rights, thereby bringing them under the protection of courts of law.[105]

Summary

Self-Test www.mhhe.com/pattersonwtp9e

The Bill of Rights was added to the Constitution shortly after its ratification. These amendments guarantee certain political, procedural, and property rights against infringement by the national government.

The guarantees embodied in the Bill of Rights originally applied only to the national government. Under the principle of selective incorporation of these guarantees into the Fourteenth Amendment, the courts extended them to state governments, though the process was slow and uneven. In the 1920s and 1930s,

First Amendment guarantees of freedom of expression were given protection from infringement by the states. The states continued to have wide discretion in criminal proceedings until the early 1960s, when most of the fair-trial rights in the Bill of Rights were given federal protection.

Freedom of expression is the most basic of democratic rights. People are not free unless they can freely express their views. Nevertheless, free expression may conflict with the nation's security needs during times of war and insurrection. The courts at times have allowed government to limit expression substantially for purposes of national security. In recent decades, however, the courts have protected a wide range of free expression in the areas of speech, press, and religion. They have also established a right of privacy, which in some areas, such as abortion, remains a source of controversy and judicial action.

Due process of law refers to legal protections that have been established to preserve individual rights. The most significant form of these protections consists of procedures designed to ensure that an individual's rights are upheld (for example, the right of an accused person to have an attorney present during police interrogation). A major controversy in this area is the breadth of the exclusionary rule, which bars the use in trials of illegally obtained evidence.

The war on terrorism that began after the attacks on September 11, 2001, has raised new issues of civil liberties, including the detention of enemy combatants, the use of harsh interrogation techniques, and warrantless surveillance. The Supreme Court has not ruled on all such issues but has generally held that the president's war-making power does not include the authority to disregard provisions of statutory law, treaties (the Geneva Conventions), and the Constitution.

Civil liberties are not absolute but must be judged in the context of other considerations (such as national security or public safety) and against one another when different rights conflict. The judicial branch of government, particularly the Supreme Court, has taken on much of the responsibility for protecting and interpreting individual rights. The Court's positions have changed with time and conditions, but the Court is usually more protective of civil liberties than are elected officials or popular majorities.

Key Terms

Bill of Rights (*p. 108*)
civil liberties (*p. 106*)
clear-and-present-danger test (*p. 115*)
due process clause (of the Fourteenth Amendment) (*p. 110*)
establishment clause (*p. 121*)
exclusionary rule (*p. 133*)
free-exercise clause (*p. 123*)
freedom of expression (*p. 112*)
imminent lawless action test (*p. 116*)
Lemon test (*p. 123*)
libel (*p. 119*)
prior restraint (*p. 118*)
procedural due process (*p. 128*)
right of privacy (*p. 125*)
selective incorporation (*p. 111*)
slander (*p. 119*)
symbolic speech (*p. 116*)

Suggested Readings

Abraham, Henry J. *Freedom and the Court.* New York: Oxford University Press, 2003. A comprehensive analysis of the Supreme Court's work on civil rights and civil liberties.

Ackerman, Bruce. *Before the Next Attack: Preserving Civil Liberties in an Age of Terrorism.* New Haven, CT.: Yale University Press, 2007. A thoughtful analysis of how Western democracies should treat civil liberties in the era of global terrorism.

Gup, Ted. *Nation of Secrets: The Threat to Democracy and the American Way of Life.* New York: Doubleday, 2007. An award-winning book that documents government's effort to hide from public view an ever-increasing amount of information on its activities.

Hull, N. E. H., and Peter Charles Hoffer. *Roe v. Wade: The Abortion Rights Controversy in American History.* Lawrence: University Press of Kansas, 2001. A thorough assessment of both sides of the abortion conflict, beginning with the *Roe v. Wade* decision.

Krimsky, Sheldon, and Tania Simoncelli. *Genetic Justice: DNA Data Banks, Criminal Investigations, and Civil Liberties.* New York: Columbia University Press, 2010. A cross-national look at DNA evidence in the context of civil liberties.

Perry, Michael J. *Religion in Politics: Constitutional and Moral Perspectives.* New York: Oxford University Press, 1997. A legal and philosophical analysis of the role of religion in politics.

Schwarz, John E. *Freedom Reclaimed: Rediscovering the American Vision.* Baltimore, MD.: Johns Hopkins University Press, 2005. An impassioned argument for an expansive view of liberty, both from and through government action.

Stone, Geoffrey. *War and Liberty: An American Dilemma: 1790 to the Present.* New York: Norton, 2007. A historical assessment of the tension between civil liberties and national security.

List of Websites

www.fepproject.org The site of the Free Expression Policy Project; includes information and opinions on a wide range of free-expression policy issues.

www.aclu.org The American Civil Liberties Union site; provides information on current civil liberties and civil rights issues, including information on recent and pending Supreme Court cases.

www.findlaw.com/casecode/supreme.html An excellent source of information on Supreme Court and lower-court rulings.

www.ncjrs.org The site of the National Criminal Justice Reference Service, a federally funded organization that compiles information on a wide range of criminal-justice issues.

Politics in Theory and Practice

Thinking: What is the process of selective incorporation, and why is it important to the rights you have today?

Participating: Although their right of free expression is protected by law, Americans often choose not to exercise this right for fear of social pressure or official-reprisal. Yet constitutional rights tend to wither when people fail to exercise them. The failure of citizens to speak their mind, Alexis de Tocqueville said, reduces them "to being nothing more than a herd of timid and industrious animals of which government is the shepherd." Think of an issue that you care about but that is unpopular on your campus or in your community. Consider writing a letter expressing your opinion to the editor of your college or local newspaper. (Practical advice: Keep the letter short and to the point; write a lead sentence that will get readers' attention; provide a convincing and courteous argument for your position; be sure to sign the letter and provide a return address so the editor can contact you if there are questions.)

Extra Credit

For up-to-the-minute *New York Times* articles, interactive simulations, graphics, study tools, and more links and quizzes, visit the text's Online Learning Center at **www.mhhe.com/pattersonwtp9e**.

NATIONAL JOURNAL

Courts Could Void Arizona's New Law

President Obama had it about right, in my view, when he called Arizona's new immigration law, which requires police to check the ID of people they suspect are in the state illegally, "misguided" and a threat to "basic notions of fairness" and to "trust between police and our communities."

Similar misgivings—filtered through a legal doctrine called "field pre-emption"—seem more likely than not to persuade the courts to strike the law down.

But please, let's can the hysteria. The problems with this law—and with copycat proposals in at least 10 other states—are a far cry from the images of Nazi Germany, apartheid, and the Jim Crow South conjured up by leftists who would denounce any effort to discourage illegal immigration.

To correct some misconceptions:

- The solid majority support for the law among Arizonans—and the 51 percent support among other Americans who told Gallup pollsters that they had heard of the Arizona law—is not driven by racism. It's driven by frustration with the federal government's failure to protect Arizona and other border states from seeing their neighborhoods, schools, hospitals, and prisons flooded by illegal immigrants. Worse, "It's terrifying to live next door to homes filled with human traffickers, drug smugglers, AK-47s, pit bulls, and desperate laborers stuffed 30 to a room, shoes removed to hinder escape," as Eve Conant reported in Newsweek.
- Although it's true, and most unfortunate, that absent robust administrative safeguards the Arizona law could lead to racial profiling by police, it certainly does not require racial profiling. Indeed, a package of revisions signed on April 30 by Arizona Gov. Jan Brewer seeks to prohibit racial profiling. The revisions did this by deleting the word "solely" from the original, April 23, law's provision barring investigation of "complaints that are based solely on race, color, or national origin."
- Nor does the new law, as revised, empower police officers to stop anyone they choose and demand to see their papers. Rather, it authorizes such demands only after "any lawful stop, detention, or arrest made by a law enforcement official," and only if "reasonable suspicion exists"—apart from ethnicity—that the person "is an alien and is unlawfully present in the United States." Some of the law's language could tempt police to demand papers from people suspected of petty violations of civil ordinances such as having an overgrown lawn, but it's unclear how that will play out in practice.
- Neither is it fair to say—as did a New York Times editorial—that Arizona's "defining the act of [an alien's] standing on its soil without papers as a criminal act is repellant." In fact, since 1952, the law of the United States has defined the act of an alien's standing on its soil without papers as a criminal act.

So is there a problem with Arizona stepping in to enforce its own identical copy of a federal law that the feds barely attempt to enforce?

Actually, there is a problem. It's more subtle than suggested by the dependably hyperbolic Times editorial page. But it may well persuade the courts to find the new Arizona law unconstitutional.

The Supreme Court has long held that by adopting a comprehensive regulatory regime for immigration matters, Congress has manifested an intent to "pre-empt the field" and thus to sweep away state laws addressing the same issues.

To be sure, federal immigration laws do not specify that states may not do what Arizona has done. Nor do they conflict directly with the Arizona law. So the pre-emption challenges now being prepared by civil-rights groups and others are not sure to succeed.

But they aren't sure to lose, either. The Supreme Court has held that federal law regulates immigration so comprehensively as to pre-empt any state law—even one purporting to help enforce federal law—that "stands as an obstacle to the accomplishment and execution of the full purposes and objectives of Congress." So said the justices, in Hines v. Davidowitz, in 1941.

The strongest argument for federal pre-emption of the Arizona law is that Congress has carefully balanced the need to pursue the most-dangerous criminals among the estimated 12 million to 20 million illegal immigrants in the U.S. against the risk of harm from overly aggressive or arbitrary pursuit of hard-working people who immigrated—legally or illegally—years ago.

The justices may well hold that "Congress would prefer to have U.S. agents making the decisions about what individuals are realistic suspects," says a leading Supreme Court litigator who declined to speak for attribution, "and not having potential vigilante groups (even if they are wearing a badge) running around sweeping up individuals, many of whom are here legally."

Another consideration is the pre-eminence of the federal government in matters touching on foreign affairs. Mexican President Felipe Calderon, among others, has sharply condemned Arizona's action.

Although a 1976 decision, *De Canas v. Bica,* recognized an exception to the pre-emption doctrine for state laws regulating conduct of only "peripheral concern" to the federal immigration laws, the issues raised by the new Arizona law seem more than peripheral.

All of this may sound rather technical and abstract, and you may wonder: Is that really the way that judges and justices think? Don't they worry about how the Arizona law will affect the lives of real people?

Of course they do. But that begs the question of which real people have the best claim on what Obama used to call judicial "empathy." The hard-working Mexicans and Central Americans whose crime (a misdemeanor, under both federal and Arizona law) was sneaking across the border long ago to seek a piece of the American dream? The legal immigrants and children of immigrants who fear being hassled by racial-profiling police? The other Arizonans who feel that they are being overrun by illegal immigrants and fear that the murderous Mexican drug lords' reign of terror is starting to spread across the border?

Principled judges and justices are less comfortable making such open-ended value judgments—or, to be precise, making them overtly—than they are following precedents that weigh such apparent abstractions as whether an admittedly failed federal regulatory regime should pre-empt a chaotic collection of inconsistent state laws that might, or might not, deepen the dysfunction.

The bottom line is that it's a pretty good bet that the four more-liberal justices, including any successor to retiring Justice John Paul Stevens, would vote to strike down the Arizona law. And even if all of the four more-conservative justices went the other way—no sure bet—swing-voting Justice Anthony Kennedy might well vote with the liberals.

A Supreme Court decision striking down the Arizona law would be most likely if there were evidence by the time the case reached the justices of police abuses so serious and widespread that the only effective remedy would be wholesale invalidation.

And therein lies a paradox: If civil-rights groups and other plaintiffs succeed in persuading lower federal courts to block the law from taking effect—and thus from spawning any police abuses—they may well hurt their own chances of prevailing in the Supreme Court.

So they might be wise to wait for evidence of real police abuses rather than rushing to sue over potential abuses—which seem somewhat less likely after the April 30 revisions than before. But the race to raise funds by piling lawsuits atop hyperbolic rhetoric is on.

The Obama administration faces a similar quandary, and others, in deciding whether to file its own court challenge.

Homeland Security Secretary Janet Napolitano testified that the Arizona law will "detract from and siphon [federal] resources that we need to concentrate on those . . . who have committed the most serious crimes." But she could avoid that outcome—while taking some political heat—simply by instructing federal agents not to cooperate with Arizona police in enforcing the new law.

Meanwhile, an extraordinarily broad coalition of immigrant, civil-liberties, business, and other groups—including virtually all of those attacking the new Arizona law—has urged the Supreme Court to review and strike down another Arizona immigration law, which was adopted in 2007 to punish employers of illegal immigrants.

The justices asked Solicitor General Elena Kagan more than six months ago to take a position on the plaintiffs' petition. She has not yet responded.

Might the delay have something to do with the fact that it was Napolitano, then governor of Arizona, who signed the 2007 law? Or the fact that Kagan, a leading contender to fill Stevens's seat, will be savaged by many conservatives if she attacks either Arizona law and by many liberals if she defends either of them?

Inquiring minds in Congress will want to know.

What's Your Opinion?

How do the author's opinions expressed in this article compare to your own? Do you think Arizona's law represents an infringement of civil liberties? Solicitor General Elena Kagan did in fact fill Justice Stevens' seat this year. Explain the politics of the situation as the columnist lays them out. Why might conservatives have savaged Kagan for taking a strong position on Arizona's law, and why do liberals oppose the law so much in the first place?

CHAPTER 5

Equal Rights: Struggling toward Fairness

"I have a dream that one day this nation will rise up and live out the true meaning of its creed: "We hold these truths to be self-evident: that all men are created equal."

Martin Luther King Jr.[1]

The producers of ABC television's *Primetime Live* put hidden cameras on two young men, equally well dressed and groomed, and then sent them on different routes to do the same things—search for an apartment, shop for a car, look at albums in a record store. The cameras recorded people's reactions to the two men. One was more often greeted with smiles and quick service, while the other was more often greeted with suspicious looks and was sometimes made to wait. Why the difference? The explanation was straightforward: the young man who was routinely well received was white; the young man who was sometimes treated poorly was black.

The Urban Institute conducted a more substantial experiment. It included pairs of specially trained white and black male college students who were comparable in all respects—education, work experience, speech patterns, physical builds—except for their race. The students responded individually to nearly five hundred classified job advertisements in Chicago and Washington, D.C. The black applicants got fewer interviews and received fewer job offers than did the white applicants. An Urban Institute spokesperson said, "The level of reverse discrimination [favoring blacks over whites] that we found was limited, was certainly far lower than many might have been led to fear, and was swamped by the extent of discrimination against black job applicants."[2]

These two experiments suggest why some Americans are still struggling to achieve equal rights. In theory Americans have equal rights, but in reality they are not now equal nor have they ever been. African Americans, women, Hispanic Americans, the disabled, Jews, Native Americans, Catholics, Asian Americans, gays and lesbians, and members of other minority groups have been victims of discrimination in fact and in law. The nation's creed—"all men are created equal"—has encouraged minorities to demand equal treatment. But inequality is built into almost every aspect of U.S. society. For example, compared with whites, African Americans with correctable health problems are significantly less likely to receive coronary artery bypass surgery, to receive a kidney transplant, or to undergo surgery for early-stage lung cancer.[3]

This chapter focuses on **equal rights**, or **civil rights**—terms that refer to the right of every person to equal protection under the laws and equal access to society's opportunities and public facilities. As Chapter 4 explained, civil liberties refer to specific *individual* rights, such as freedom of speech, that are protected from infringement by government. Equal rights, or civil rights, are a question of whether individual members of differing *groups*, such as racial, gender, and ethnic groups, are treated equally by government and, in some instances, by private parties.

Although the law refers to the rights of individuals first and to those of groups in a secondary and derivative way, this chapter concentrates on groups because the history of civil rights has been largely one of group claims to equality. The catchphrase of nearly every group's claim to a more equal standing in American society has been "equality under the law." When secure in their legal rights, people are positioned to pursue equality in other arenas, such as the economic sector. This chapter examines the major laws relating to equality, and the conditions that led to their adoption. The chapter concludes with a brief look at some of the continuing challenges facing America's historically disadvantaged groups. The chapter emphasizes these points:

- *Americans have attained substantial equality under the law.* They have, in legal terms, equal protection under the laws, equal access to accommodations and housing, and an equal right to vote. Discrimination by law against persons because of race, sex, religion, or ethnicity has been virtually eliminated.
- *Legal equality for all Americans has not resulted in de facto equality.* African Americans, women, Hispanic Americans, and other traditionally disadvantaged groups have a disproportionately small share of America's opportunities and benefits. Existing inequalities, discrimination, and political pressures still are major barriers to their full equality.
- *Disadvantaged groups have had to struggle for equal rights.* African Americans, women, Native Americans, Hispanic Americans, Asian Americans, and others have had to fight for their rights in order to come closer to equality with white males.

Equality through Law

Equality has always been the least developed of America's founding concepts. Not even Thomas Jefferson, who had a deep admiration for the "common man," believed that a precise meaning could be given to the claim of the Declaration of Independence that "all men are created equal."[4] Nevertheless, the promise contained in that phrase has placed history on the side of those seeking greater equality. Every civil rights movement, from suffrage for males without property in the 1830s to gay rights today, has derived moral strength from the nation's pledge of equality for all.

Nevertheless, America's history reveals that disadvantaged groups have rarely achieved a greater measure of equality without a struggle.[5] The policies that protect these groups today are the result of intense and sustained political action that forced entrenched interests to relinquish or share their privileged status.

The Fourteenth Amendment: Equal Protection

The Fourteenth Amendment, which was ratified in 1868 after the Civil War, declares in part that no state shall "deny to any person within its

Two police dogs attack a black civil rights activist (*center left*) during the 1963 Birmingham demonstrations. Such images of hatred and violence shook many white Americans out of their complacency about the plight of African Americans.

jurisdiction the equal protection of the laws." The **equal-protection clause** is a basis for equal treatment under the law, but nearly a century lapsed before the courts applied the clause in a substantial way. After federal troops withdrew from the South in 1877, the region's white majority took control, enacting laws that prohibited blacks from using the same public facilities as whites.[6] In *Plessy v. Ferguson* (1896), the Supreme Court endorsed these laws, ruling that "separate" public facilities for the two races did not violate the Constitution as long as the facilities were "equal."[7] The *Plessy* decision became a justification for the separate and *unequal* treatment of African Americans (see Chapter 3). Black children were forced, for example, to attend separate schools that rarely had libraries or enough teachers.

These practices were challenged through legal action, but not until the late 1930s did the Supreme Court begin to respond. In a first ruling, the Court held that blacks must be allowed to use public facilities reserved for whites in cases where they did not have separate facilities. When Oklahoma, which had no law school for blacks, was ordered to admit Ada Sipuel as a law student in 1949, it created a separate law school for her—she sat alone in a roped-off corridor of the state capitol building. The white students, meanwhile, continued to meet at the University of Oklahoma's law school in Norman, twenty miles away. The Supreme

Court then ordered the law school to admit her to regular classes. The law school did so but roped off her seat from the rest of the class and stenciled the word *colored* on it. She was also forced to eat alone in a roped-off area of the law school's cafeteria. In her memoir, Sipuel wrote that, although the law school itself was less than welcoming, some law students helped out, including those who gave her notes from classes she had missed while studying alone at the capitol building.[8]

Segregation in the Schools Substantial judicial intervention on behalf of African Americans finally occurred in 1954 with *Brown v. Board of Education of Topeka.* The case began when Linda Carol Brown, a black child in Topeka, Kansas, was denied admission to an all-white elementary school that she passed every day on her way to her all-black school, which was twelve blocks farther away. In a unanimous decision, the Court invoked the Fourteenth Amendment's equal protection clause, declaring that racial segregation of public schools "generates [among black children] a feeling of inferiority as to their status in the community that may affect their hearts and minds in a way unlikely ever to be undone. . . . Separate educational facilities are inherently unequal."[9]

A 1954 Gallup poll indicated that a sizable majority of southern whites opposed the *Brown* decision, and billboards were erected along southern roadways that called for the impeachment of Chief Justice Earl Warren. In the so-called "Southern Manifesto," southern congressmen urged their state governments to "resist forced integration by any lawful means." Rioting broke out in 1957 when Arkansas's governor called out the state's National Guard to prevent black students from entering Little Rock's high school. They achieved entry only after President Dwight D. Eisenhower used his power as commander in chief to place the Arkansas National Guard under federal control.

Although the *Brown* decision banned forced segregation in the public schools, it did not require states to take active steps to integrate their schools. Most children attended neighborhood schools, and because most residential neighborhoods were racially segregated, so too were the schools. Even as late as fifteen years after *Brown*, 95 percent of black children were attending schools that were mostly or entirely black.

In 1971, the Supreme Court endorsed the busing of children as a remedy for segregated schools. The Court held in *Swann v. Charlotte-Mecklenburg County Board of Education* (1971) that the busing of children out of their neighborhoods for the purpose of achieving racially integrated schools was constitutionally permissible in cases where previous acts of racial discrimination contributed to school segregation. "The basis of our decision," the Court said, "[is] the prohibition of the Fourteenth Amendment that no state shall deny to any person within its jurisdiction the equal protection of the laws."[10] Few Court decisions have provoked the outcry that followed *Swann*. A 1972 University of Michigan survey indicated that more than 80 percent of white Americans disapproved of forced busing. Angry demonstrations lasting weeks took place in Charlotte. When busing was ordered in Detroit and Boston, the protests turned violent as white demonstrators burned buses and beat black residents. Unlike *Brown*, which affected mainly the South, *Swann* also applied to northern communities where blacks and whites lived separately because of discriminatory real estate practices.

Racial busing had mixed results. Studies found that busing improved school children's racial attitudes and improved minority children's performance on standardized tests without diminishing the performance of white classmates.[11] On the other hand, the policy forced many children to spend long hours each day riding buses to and from school. Busing also contributed to white flight to the suburbs, which were protected by a 1974 Supreme Court decision that prohibited busing across school districts except where district boundaries had been deliberately drawn to keep the races apart.[12] As white students fled from urban schools, it became harder to achieve racial balance through busing and harder to convince taxpayers to fund these schools adequately.

In the 1990s, the Supreme Court ordered cutbacks in busing, saying that it was meant to be a temporary solution[13] and that communities were free to use alternatives, such as increased spending on schools in poor neighborhoods.[14] Then, in 2007, the Supreme Court essentially declared an end to forced busing. At issue were voluntary (as opposed to court-ordered) busing programs in Seattle and Louisville that took race, neighborhood, and student preference into account in assigning students to particular schools. The large majority of students were placed in their schools of choice, but some were forced to go elsewhere, which led to lawsuits on their behalf. In a 5-4 decision, the Supreme Court ruled they had been denied equal protection under the Fourteenth Amendment. Writing for the majority, Chief Justice John Roberts said, "Before *Brown*, schoolchildren were told where they could and could not go to school based on the color of their skin. The school districts in [Seattle and Louisville] have not carried the heavy burden of demonstrating that we should allow this once again—even for very different reasons." In the dissenting opinion, Justice Stephen Breyer said, "It is a cruel distortion of history to compare Topeka, Kansas in the 1950s to Louisville and Seattle in the modern day."[15]

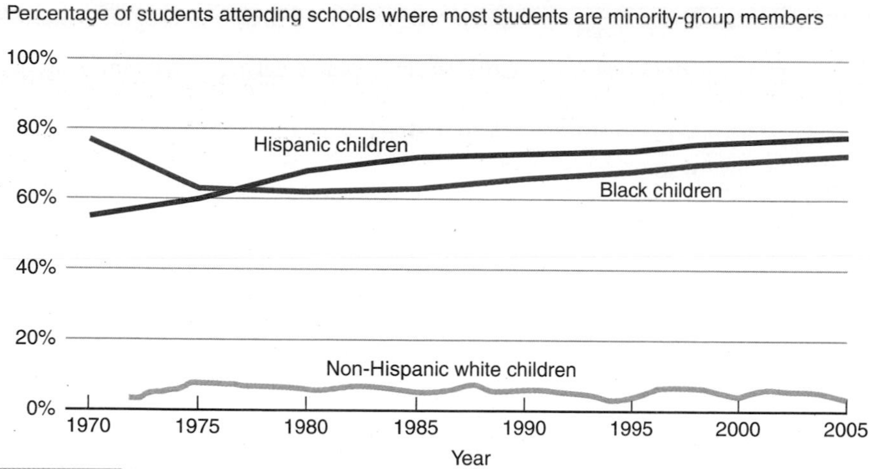

figure 5-1 SEGREGATION RATES IN PUBLIC SCHOOLS

In the past two decades, racial and ethnic segregation in America's public schools has increased. More than two-thirds of black and Hispanic children today attend a school in which most of the students are members of a minority group. An increase in the number of non-Hispanic white students attending private schools and a decrease in racial busing are factors in the trend. *Source:* U.S. Department of Education, 2010.

Segregation in America's public schools is increasing. As a result of the end of racial busing and white flight to private and suburban schools, America's schools are becoming less racially diverse (see Figure 5-1). Today, only 30 percent of Hispanic and black children attend a school that is predominately white, compared with 40 percent at the height of the busing era.

Judicial Tests of Equal Protection The Fourteenth Amendment's equal-protection clause does not require government to treat all groups or classes of people equally in all circumstances. The judiciary allows inequalities that are "reasonably" related to a legitimate government interest. In applying this **reasonable-basis test**, the courts require government only to show that a particular law is reasonable. For example, twenty-one-year-olds can legally drink alcohol but twenty-year-olds cannot. The courts have held that the goal of reducing fatalities from alcohol-related accidents involving young drivers is a valid reason for imposing an age limit on the purchase and consumption of alcohol.

The reasonable-basis test does not apply to racial or ethnic classifications (see Table 5-1). Any law that treats people differently because of race or ethnicity is subject to the **strict-scrutiny test**, which presumes that the table 5-1 LEVELS OF COURT REVIEW FOR LAWS THAT TREAT AMERICANS DIFFERENTLY

In reviewing the constitutionality of laws that treat people differently, the judiciary applies different tests, depending on the nature of the classification—for example, whether the law in question classifies people on the basis of race or income.

Test	Application	Standard Used
Strict scrutiny	Race, ethnicity	Suspect category—assumed unconstitutional in the absence of an overwhelming justification
Intermediate scrutiny	Gender	Almost suspect category—assumed unconstitutional unless the law serves a clearly compelling and justified purpose
Reasonable basis	Other categories (such as age and income)	Not suspect category—assumed constitutional unless no sound rationale for the law can be provided

law is unconstitutional unless government can provide a compelling basis for it. The strict-scrutiny test has virtually eliminated race and ethnicity as permissible classifications when the effect is to place a hardship on a racial or ethnic minority. The Supreme Court's position is that race and national origin are **suspect classifications**—in other words, laws that classify people differently on the basis of their race or ethnicity are presumed to have discrimination as their purpose.

Although the notion of suspect classifications was implicit in earlier cases, including *Brown*, the Court did not use those words until *Loving v. Virginia* (1967). The state of Virginia had a law that prohibited white residents from marrying a person of a different race. When Richard Loving, a white man, and Mildred Jeter, a woman of African American and Native American descent, went to Washington, D.C., to get married and then returned home to Virginia, police invaded their home and arrested them. The state of Virginia claimed that its ban on interracial marriage did not violate the equal protection clause because the penalty for the offense—a prison sentence of one to five years—was the same for both the white and the non-white spouse. The Supreme Court ruled otherwise, saying the Virginia law was "subversive of the principle of equality at the heart of the Fourteenth Amendment." The Court concluded that the law was based solely on "invidious racial discrimination" and that any such "classification" was unconstitutional.[16]

When women began to assert their rights more forcefully in the 1970s, the Supreme Court indicated that it might expand the scope of strict scrutiny to include gender. In *Craig v. Boren* (1976), however, the Court ruled that gender classifications are permissible if they serve "important governmental objectives" and are "substantially related" to the achievement of those objectives.[17] The Court thus placed gender classifications in an intermediate (or almost suspect) category; such classifications are to be scrutinized more closely than some others (for example, income or age) but are allowable if government can adequately justify the policy. In *Rostker v. Goldberg* (1980), the Court upheld such a classification, ruling that the male-only draft registration law served the important objective of excluding women from *involuntary* combat duty.[18]

Since then, however, the Supreme Court has struck down nearly all the gender-based laws it has reviewed. A leading case is *United States v. Virginia* (1996), in which the Court invalidated the male-only admissions policy of Virginia Military Institute (VMI), a 157-year-old state-supported college. The state had created an alternative program for women at another college, but the Court said it was no substitute for VMI's unique education. In its ruling, the Court said that Virginia had failed to provide an "exceedingly persuasive" argument for its policy. This standard would appear to be a stricter one than the "important governmental objectives" standard applied earlier. However, the Court did not explicitly say it was toughening the standard for gender classifications. (The VMI decision had the effect of also ending the all-male admissions policy of the Citadel, a state-supported military college in South Carolina.)[19]

The Civil Rights Act of 1964

The Fourteenth Amendment prohibits discrimination by government but not by private parties. As a result, for a long period in American history, private employers could freely discriminate in their hiring practices, and owners of restaurants, hotels, theaters, and other public accommodations could legally bar black people from entering. That changed with passage of the 1964 Civil Rights Act. Based on Congress's power to regulate commerce, the legislation entitles all persons to equal access to public accommodations. The legislation also bars discrimination on the basis of race, color, religion, sex, or national origin in the hiring, promotion, and wages of employees of medium-size and large firms. A few forms of job discrimination are still lawful under the Civil Rights Act. For example, an owner-operator of a small business can discriminate in hiring his or her coworkers, and a church-related school can take the religion of a prospective teacher into account.

The Black Civil Rights Movement The impetus behind the 1964 Civil Rights Act was the black civil rights movement. Without it, the legislation would undoubtedly have come later, and possibly have been less sweeping.

During World War II, African American soldiers fought against Nazi racism only to return to an America where racial discrimination was legal, widespread, and oppressive.[20] The contradiction was stark and led to growing demands for change, which intensified after an incident in Montgomery, Alabama, on December 1, 1955. Upon leaving work that day, Rosa Parks boarded a bus for home, taking her seat as required by law in the section reserved for blacks. When all the seats for white passengers were occupied, the bus driver ordered Parks to give her seat to a white passenger. She refused, whereupon she was arrested and fined. The incident provoked outrage in Montgomery's black community, which organized a boycott of the city's bus system. A young pastor at a local Baptist church, Dr. Martin Luther King Jr., led the boycott, which spread quickly to other cities. African Americans also conducted sit-ins at lunch counters that served only whites. The black civil rights movement was now fully under way and would persist for more than a decade. A peak moment occurred in 1963 with the March on Washington for Jobs and Freedom, which attracted 250,000 marchers, one of the largest gatherings in the Capital's history. In his speech to the crowd, King said: "I have a dream that my four little children will one day live in a nation where they will not be judged by the color of their skin but by the content of their character."[21]

Martin Luther King Jr. is the only American of the twentieth century to be honored with a national holiday. The civil rights leader was the pivotal figure in the movement to gain legal and political rights for black Americans. The high point was a triumphal gathering of a quarter million supporters on the Washington Mall. The recipient of the Nobel Peace Prize in 1964 (the youngest person ever to receive that honor), King was assassinated in Memphis in 1968 as he was preparing to lead a march on behalf of the city's sanitation workers.

The momentum of the March on Washington carried over into Congress, where major civil rights legislation was languishing in House committee. Although opponents employed every possible legislative maneuver in an effort to block it, it finally cleared the House the following February. Senate maneuvering and debate—including a fifty-five-day filibuster—took another four months. Finally, in early July, President Lyndon Johnson signed into law the Civil Rights Act of 1964.

Resistance to the Civil Rights Act was widespread. Many restaurants, hotels, and other establishments refused to serve black customers. An Atlanta restaurant owner, Lester Maddox, responded to the legislation by standing outside his restaurant brandishing a handgun, threatening to shoot any African American who entered. Maddox was elected governor of Georgia three years later, but lawsuits against Maddox and other defiant proprietors slowly ended resistance to the new law, with the effect that overt forms of discrimination in the area of public accommodations gradually ceased. Even today, some restaurants and hotels may provide better service to white customers, but outright refusal to serve African Americans or other minority-group members is rare. Any such refusal violates federal law and can be proven in many instances. Discrimination in job decisions is harder to prove, and the Civil Rights Act has been less effective in stopping it, as is discussed in a later section.

The Movement for Women's Rights The black civil rights movement inspired other disadvantaged groups to become more demanding of their rights. Women were the most vocal and successful of these groups.

The United States carried over from English common law a political disregard for women, forbidding them to vote, hold public office, or serve on juries.[22] Upon marriage, a woman essentially lost her identity as an individual and could not own and dispose of property without her husband's consent. Even a wife's body was not fully hers. A wife's adultery was declared by the Supreme Court in 1904 to be a violation of the husband's property rights.[23]

The first large and well-organized attempt to promote women's rights came in 1848 in Seneca Falls, New York. Lucretia Mott and Elizabeth Cady Stanton had been barred from the main floor of an antislavery convention and decided to organize a women's rights convention. Thereafter, the struggle for women's rights became closely aligned with the abolitionist movement. However, when Congress wrote the Fifteenth Amendment after the Civil War, women were not included in its provisions despite promises to the contrary. The Fifteenth Amendment declared only that the right to vote could not be abridged on account of race or color. Not until passage of the Nineteenth Amendment in 1920 did women acquire the right to vote.

The Nineteenth Amendment's ratification encouraged women's leaders in 1923 to propose a constitutional amendment granting equal rights to women. Congress rejected the proposal but fifty years later approved the Equal Rights Amendment (ERA) and submitted it to the states for ratification. The ERA failed by three states to receive the required three-fourths majority.[24] Women did succeed in other efforts, however. Among the congressional measures were the Equal Pay Act of 1963, which prohibits sex discrimination in salary and wages by some categories of employers; Title IX of the Education Amendment of 1972, which prohibits sex discrimination in education; and the Equal Credit Act of 1974, which prohibits sex discrimination in the granting of financial credit. Women are also protected by Title VII of the Civil Rights Act of 1964, which bans gender discrimination in employment, a topic that is discussed in a later section.

Hispanic Americans and the Farm Workers' Strikes Although the Civil Rights Act of 1964 was largely a response to the black civil rights movement, Hispanics also had their political movement. Its centerpiece was the farm workers' strikes of the late 1960s and the 1970s, which sought labor rights for migrant workers. Migrants were working long hours for low pay, were living in shacks without electricity or plumbing, and were unwelcome in many local schools as well as in some local hospitals. Farm owners at first refused to bargain with the workers, but a well-organized national boycott of California grapes and lettuce forced the state to pass a law giving migrant workers the right to bargain collectively. The strikes were led in California by Cesar Chavez, who himself grew up in a Mexican American migrant family. Chavez's tactics were copied with less success in other states, including Texas.[25]

The Hispanic civil rights movement lacked the scope of the black civil rights movement but brought about some policy changes, including a congressional act that requires states to provide bilingual ballots in local areas with large numbers of non-English-speaking minorities.

Native Americans and Their Long-Delayed Rights The civil rights movement of the 1960s at first did not include Native Americans. It was not the first time they had been left behind. Native Americans were not granted official citizenship until passage of an act of Congress in 1924. By then, their population had fallen to less than one million, down from the estimated 10 million alive at the time the white settlers arrived. In the whole of human history, no people had suffered such a great popula-

During the 1960s civil rights era, Native Americans voiced long-standing grievances, often in dramatic ways. The abandoned federal prison on Alcatraz Island in San Francisco Bay was the site of the first major protest. For nineteen months beginning in late 1969, Native Americans from tribes across the country occupied the prison. From there, the protest spread to other locations, including Washington, D.C., and Wounded Knee, South Dakota.

tion loss in such a short period. Diseases brought by white settlers took the heaviest toll, but wars and massacres also contributed. As part of a policy of westward expansion, settlers and U.S. troops alike mercilessly drove the eastern Indians from their ancestral lands to the Great Plains and then seized most of these lands as well.

In 1972, Native American leaders organized the "Trail of Broken Treaties," a caravan that journeyed from California to Washington, D.C., to protest federal policy. Upon arriving in Washington, they occupied the Bureau of Indian Affairs, renaming it the Native American Embassy. The occupation ended when the government agreed to establish a committee to investigate their grievances. The next year, armed Native Americans took control of the village of Wounded Knee on a Sioux reservation in South Dakota; over the next two months they exchanged sporadic gunfire with U.S. marshals that left two Native Americans dead and one marshal paralyzed. Eight decades earlier at Wounded Knee, U.S. cavalry had shot to death three hundred disarmed Sioux men, women, and children.

In 1974, Congress passed legislation that granted Native Americans living on reservations greater control over federal programs that affect them. Six years earlier, Congress had enacted the Indian Bill of Rights, which gives Native Americans on reservations constitutional guarantees similar to those held by other Americans.

Asian Americans and Immigration Chinese and Japanese laborers were brought to the western states during the late 1800s to work in mines and to build railroads. When the need for this labor declined, Congress in 1892 suspended Asian immigration on grounds that Asians were inferior. Over the next four decades, informal arrangements kept all but a few Asians from entering the country. In 1923, President Calvin Coolidge asked Congress for a permanent ban on Chinese immigration, saying that people "who do not want to be partakers in the American spirit ought not to settle in America." Seven years later, Congress completely blocked the entry of Japanese. Japan had protested a California law that prohibited persons of Japanese descent from buying property in the state. Rather than trying to finesse what was called "the California problem," Congress bluntly told Japan that its people were not wanted in the United States.[26]

Not until 1965 did Congress, as part of its broader civil rights agenda, lift restrictions on Asian immigration. Tight limits on Hispanic immigration were also lifted at this time, and since then, more than 70 percent of immigrants have come from Latin America and Asia.

Asian Americans were not politically active to any great extent during the 1960s. Their rights were expanded primarily by court rulings and legislation, including the 1964 Civil Rights Act, made in response to pressure from other minority groups. However, in *Lau v. Nichols* (1974), a case initiated by a Chinese American family, the Supreme Court ruled unanimously that placing public school children for whom English is a second language in regular classrooms without special assistance violates the Civil Rights Act because it denies them the opportunity to obtain a proper education.[27] The Court did not mandate bilingual instruction, but the *Lau* decision prompted many schools to offer it. Since then, however, some states have restricted its use. For example, California's Proposition 227, enacted in 1998, requires most children for whom English is a second language to take courses taught in English after a single year in school.

POLITICAL THINKING

Should Private Discrimination Be Allowed?

The Fifth and Fourteenth Amendments prohibit discrimination by government, but not by private organizations. The courts have ruled that social clubs and other private organizations are often within their rights in discriminating against individuals because of color, gender, creed, national origin, and other characteristics. How far would you go in limiting discrimination by private organizations?

The Voting Rights Act of 1965

Free elections are the bedrock of American democracy, but the right to vote has only recently become a reality for many Americans, particularly African Americans. Although the 1870 Fifteenth Amendment granted blacks the right to vote, southern whites invented an array of devices, from whites-only primaries to rigged literacy tests, to keep blacks from registering and voting. In the mid-1940s, for example, there were only 2,500 registered black voters in the entire state of Mississippi, even though its black population numbered half a million.[28]

Racial barriers to voting began to crumble in the mid-1940s when the Supreme Court declared that whites-only primary elections were unconstitutional.[29] Two decades later, the Twenty-fourth Amendment outlawed the poll tax, which was a fee that an individual had to pay in order to register to vote. However, the major step toward electoral participation by African Americans was passage of the Voting Rights Act of 1965, which forbids discrimination in voting and registration. The legislation empowers federal agents to register voters and, as interpreted by the courts, prohibits the use of literacy tests as a registration requirement. The Voting Rights Act had an immediate impact on black participation. In the ensuing presidential election, black turnout in the South increased by 20 percentage points and has continued to rise, affecting state and local elections in addition to federal elections (see "How the 50 States Differ").

Congress has renewed the Voting Rights Act several times, most recently in 2006. The act includes a provision that requires states and localities to clear with federal officials any electoral change that has the effect, intended or not, of reducing the voting power of a minority group. This requirement, for example, has prevented states from creating election districts that deliberately dilute the minority vote. A recent example is *League of United*

HOW THE 50 STATES DIFFER
POLITICAL THINKING THROUGH COMPARISON

Black and Latino Representation in State Legislatures

For a long period in U.S. history, there were almost no minorities among the ranks of state legislators. Minorities are still under-represented relative to their numbers in the population. Although one in every three Americans is a minority-group member, only one in eight state legislators comes from a minority group. Of these legislators, about two-thirds are African American.

Q: *What accounts for differences between the states in the percentage of minority-group members in their legislatures?*

A: *States with large populations of minorities tend to have a larger percentage of legislators from minority groups. Alabama and Mississippi have large black populations and have the highest proportion of African American legislators. New Mexico, with its large Hispanic population, has the highest proportion of Latino lawmakers.*

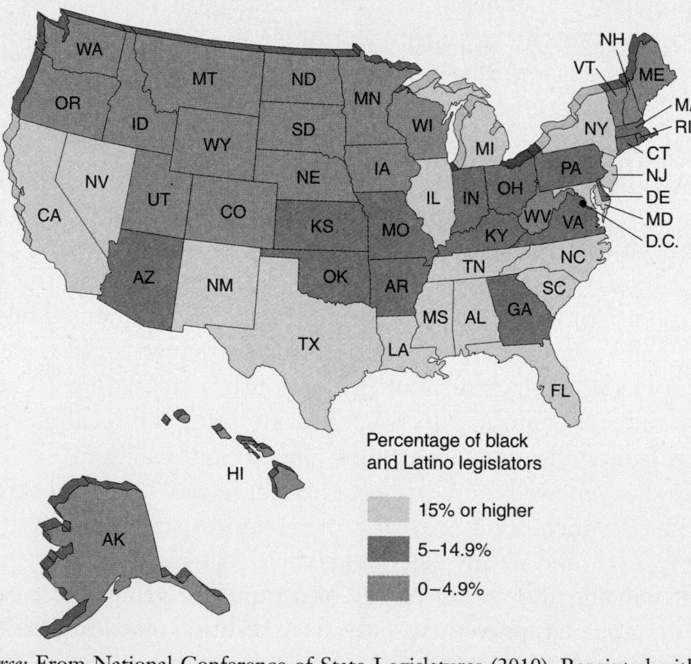

Source: From National Conference of State Legislatures (2010). Reprinted with permission.

Latin American Voters v. Perry (2006), a case involving Texas's 23rd congressional district, the boundaries of which were drawn in a way designed to make Hispanics a minority of the voters within the district. In ordering the state of Texas to redraw the district, the Supreme Court said, "The troubling blend of politics and race—and the resulting vote dilution of a group that was beginning to [overcome] prior electoral discrimination—cannot be sustained."[30] However, the court also does not allow election districts to be created for the sole purpose of giving control to a minority group. In some areas, a district will naturally have a minority group as the voting majority, which is acceptable. States are not permitted, however, to draw district lines in a way deliberately intended to create a district that has a minority group as its majority. Any such districting, the Court has ruled, violates the equal-protection rights of white voters.[31]

The Civil Rights Act of 1968

In 1968, Congress passed civil rights legislation designed to prohibit discrimination in housing. A building owner cannot refuse to sell or rent housing because of a person's race, religion, ethnicity, or sex. An exception is allowed for owners of small multifamily dwellings who reside on the premises.

Despite legal prohibitions on discrimination, housing in America remains highly segregated. Only a third of African Americans live in a neighborhood that is mostly white. One reason is that the annual income of most black families is substantially below that of most white families. Another reason is banking practices. At one time, banks contributed to housing segregation by *redlining*—refusing to grant mortgage loans in certain neighborhoods. This practice drove down the price of homes in these neighborhoods, which led to an influx of African Americans and an exodus of whites. The 1968 Civil Rights Act prohibits redlining, but many of the segregated neighborhoods it helped to create still exist. Moreover, minority status continues to be a factor in the lending practices of some banks. A report of the U.S. Conference of Mayors indicated that, among applicants with average or slightly higher incomes relative to their community, whites were roughly twice as likely to be granted a mortgage as were Hispanics or African Americans.[32]

Affirmative Action

Changes in the law seldom have large or immediate effects on how people behave. For example, although the 1964 Civil Rights Act prohibited discrimination in employment on the basis of race, color, religion, sex, or national origin, disadvantaged group members did not suddenly obtain jobs for which they were qualified. Many employers continued to prefer white male employees. Other employers adhered to established employment procedures that kept women and minorities at a disadvantage. Membership in many union locals, for example, was handed down from father to son. Moreover, the Civil Rights Act did not require employers to prove that their employment practices were not discriminatory. Instead, the burden of proof was on the woman or minority-group member who was denied a job. It was costly and usually difficult for an individual to prove in court that gender or race was the reason for not being hired or promoted. Moreover, a victory in court applied only to the individual in question; it did not help other women and minorities faced with job discrimination.

Affirmative action programs were devised as a remedy for such problems. **Affirmative action** refers to deliberate efforts to provide full and equal opportunities in employment, education, and other areas for members of traditionally disadvantaged groups. Affirmative action applies only to organizations—such as universities, agencies, and construction firms—that receive federal funding or contracts. These organizations are required to establish programs designed to ensure that all applicants are treated fairly. They also bear a burden of proof. If an organization grants a disproportionate share of opportunities to white males, it must show that the pattern is the result of necessity (such as the nature of the job or the locally available labor pool) and not the result of systematic discrimination.

Although most equality-oriented policies have been established through congressional or judicial action, affirmative action is an exception. It was established by executive action. The term "affirmative action" first appeared in an executive order issued in 1961 by President John F. Kennedy, who directed federal contractors to "take affirmative action to ensure that applicants are employed . . . without regard to their race, creed, color, or national origin." In 1967, President Lyndon Johnson extended affirmative action to include women and summarized the policy's goal: "We seek . . . not just equality as a right and a theory, but equality as a fact and a result." *Equality of result* was a new concept. Other major civil rights policies had sought to eliminate **de jure discrimination**, which is discrimination based on law, as in the case of the state laws requiring black and white children to attend separate schools during the pre-*Brown* period. Affirmative action policy sought to alleviate **de facto discrimination**—the fact that disadvantaged groups have fewer opportunities and benefits because of prejudice and social and economic conditions, such as less access to higher education.

Few issues have sparked more controversy than has affirmative action, and even today the public has a mixed response to it. Most Americans support programs designed to ensure that historically disadvantaged groups receive equal treatment, but oppose programs that would give them preferential treatment. Preference programs are deeply divisive. Whereas nearly 60 percent of African Americans and more than 50 percent of Hispanics support them, only slightly more than 20 percent of whites do so.[33]

Policies that pit individuals against each other typically end up in the Supreme Court, and affirmative action is no exception. In *University of California Regents v. Bakke* (1978), the Court issued its first affirmative action ruling. A white male, Alan Bakke, had been rejected by a medical school that admitted minority applicants with significantly lower test scores. The Court ruled that the medical school, because it had reserved a fixed number ("a quota") of admissions for minority applicants, had violated Bakke's right to equal protection. However, the Court did not strike down affirmative-action admissions per se, saying instead that race could be among the factors take into account by schools in their effort to create a diverse student body.[34] In a later case, the Court endorsed quotas in a different context, upholding a federal policy that "set aside" a certain percentage of federally funded construction projects for minority-owned firms.[35]

The scope of affirmative action was narrowed in the 1980s. Recent appointees to the Supreme Court had taken it in a conservative direction, and they provided the votes to limit the policy. In 1986, for example, the Court held that preferential treatment for minorities can be justified only in organizations that had perpetrated "longstanding or egregious discrimination."[36] Nearly a decade later, in *Adarand v. Pena* (1995), the Supreme Court halted the general use of quotas in the granting of federal contracts. Calling such programs "a highly suspect tool," the Court said that "past discrimination in a particular industry cannot justify the use of an unyielding racial quota" that gives an automatic advantage to minority owners of construction firms who were not themselves the direct victims of that discrimination.[37]

The *Adarand* decision fueled hopes among affirmative action opponents that the Supreme Court might end the policy entirely. In 2003, however, the Court narrowly upheld its use. At issue were two University of Michigan admission policies: its point system for undergraduate admission, which granted 20 points (out of a total of 150 possible points) to minority applicants, and its law school admission process, in which race (along with other factors such as work experience and extracurricular activities) was taken into account in admission decisions. By a 6-3 vote in *Gratz v. Bollinger*, the Supreme Court invalidated Michigan's undergraduate admissions policy because its point system assigned a specific weight to race.[38] However, by a 5-4 vote in *Grutter v. Bollinger*, the Court upheld the law school's program, concluding it was being applied sensibly and

The University of Michigan was the focus of national attention in 2003 as a result of its affirmative action admissions programs. Shown here are demonstrators from both sides of the issue. In its 2003 ruling, the Supreme Court upheld the use of race as a factor in admissions but rejected the use of a "point system" as the method of applying it.

fostered Michigan's "compelling interest in obtaining the educational benefits that flow from a diverse student body."[39]

Although affirmative action remains in effect, the Supreme Court's narrow 5-4 majority in the Michigan law school case suggests that it is not a settled issue, as a 2009 ruling would indicate. In *Ricci v. DeStefano*, a sharply divided Supreme Court held that, once an organization has established an equal opportunity program, it cannot reverse course if minorities are adversely affected. At issue was a promotion test that the city of New Haven administered to firefighters. None of the city's black firefighters scored high enough to be considered for promotion and, after an exhaustive assessment of the exam's contents, the city concluded it had been biased and rescinded the results. The white firefighters who passed the exam then sued, and the

Supreme Court ruled in their favor, concluding that New Haven had violated the 1964 Civil Rights Act's prohibition on discrimination by employers. Writing for the majority, Justice Anthony Kennedy said "once [a] process has been established and employers have made clear their selection criteria, they may not then invalidate the test results, thus upsetting an employee's legitimate expectation not to be judged on the basis of race." In her dissent, Justice Ruth Bader Ginsberg, after noting the history of racial discrimination in the New Haven fire department, wrote that the Court's majority was endorsing the legitimacy of a "fire department in which members of racial and ethnic minorities are rarely seen in command positions."[40]

Attempts to equalize opportunity in other ways have also been disputed. An example is the Texas Ten Percent Plan. In recognition of the variation in the quality and diversity of its schools, the state of Texas guarantees placement in a University of Texas institution to any Texas high school student graduating in the top 10 percent of his or her class. This policy was initially uncontroversial, but opposition grew as a result of a belief that students at weaker high schools have an unfair advantage and because of growing enrollment pressure at the most popular campus, the University of Texas at Austin. In 2009, the Texas legislature renewed the program for five years and capped the number of 10-percent admissions at the Austin campus. The fact is, almost every conceivable method of allocating society's benefits—whether through the public sector or the private sector, and however fair or uncontroversial it might at first appear—inevitably leaves some Americans feeling as if they were treated unfairly. At that point, such policies become political and legal issues.[41]

The Continuing Struggle for Equality

Although progress has been made toward a more equal America, civil rights problems involve deeply rooted conditions, habits, and prejudices. As a consequence, America's traditionally disadvantaged groups are still substantially unequal in their daily lives. The following discussion describes some, though hardly all, of the problems these groups confront.

African Americans

Martin Luther King Jr.'s dream of an equal society for black Americans remains elusive.[42] Poverty is a persistent problem in the black community, affecting everyone from the very old to the very young. The median net worth of households headed by retired black people is less than $20,000, compared with roughly $200,000 for retired white people. Among adults of employment age, the jobless rate of African Americans is twice that of white Americans. As for black children, roughly 40 percent live below the government-defined poverty line, compared with about 10 percent of white children. Nearly a third of black children, compared with a twentieth of white children, live in extremely poor families—those with incomes that are 50 percent or more below the poverty line. Such families live on less than $10,000 a year. The mortality rate of black infants is two-and-a-half times higher than that of white babies.[43]

Even the legal rights of African Americans do not, in practice, match the promise of the civil rights movement. Studies have found that African Americans accused of crime are more likely than white Americans to be convicted, and they are more likely to receive stiffer sentences for comparable offenses. The U.S. Department of Justice found, for example, that among persons convicted of drug felonies in state courts, half of black defendants received prison sentences, compared with a third of white defendants.[44] Crime rates are also substantially higher in the black community, a finding attributable in part to higher unemployment and lower education rates. An effect is that Africans Americans make up more than 40 percent of all prison inmates, even though they account for only one-eighth of the U.S. population. Based on current incarceration rates, more than one in four black males will spend time in prison, which is higher than the number projected to finish college. By comparison, Hispanic males have about a one in six chance of going to prison, and non-Hispanic white males have a one in twenty-three chance.[45]

A distinguishing characteristic of the black community, and a source of controversy within it, is the status of the family. Compared with other children, many fewer black children grow up in a household with both parents (see Figure 5-2). More than half of black children grow up in a single-parent family, and 8 percent grow up in a home where neither parent is present. The African American entertainer Bill Cosby was widely criticized within the black community when he suggested that many of its problems trace to the unwillingness of many black fathers to meet their family responsibilities. When Barack Obama made the same point during the 2008 presidential campaign, he was attacked by black leader Jesse Jackson, who said that the problem of absentee fathers is largely the result of job and criminal-justice discrimination. Nearly everyone within the black community agrees, however, that black children are harmed by the disintegration of the black family—the proportion of black children living with a single parent or no parent has nearly doubled since the 1960s. Those who grow up in a single-parent household are substantially more likely to have inadequate nutrition, not finish high school, not attend college, end up in prison, and be unemployed.

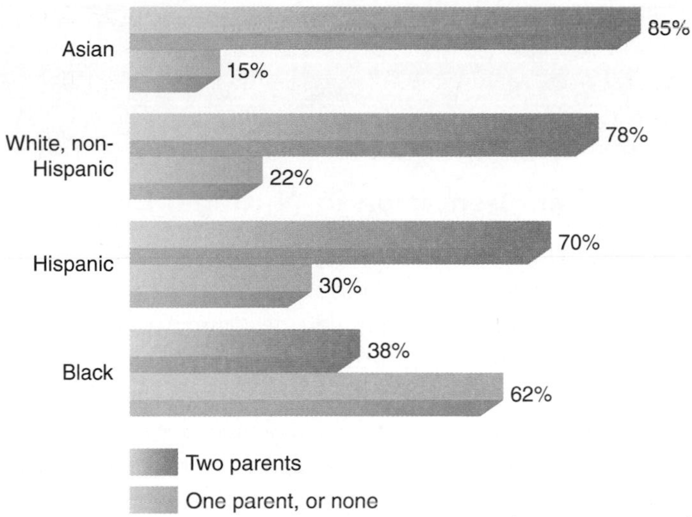

figure 5-2 FAMILY STRUCTURE, BY RACE AND ETHNICITY

Most American children live in two-parent households. The major exception is black children, who are more likely to be raised in a single-parent family. *Source:* U.S. Census Bureau, 2010.

One area in which African Americans have made substantial progress since the 1960s is elective office. Although the percentage of black elected officials is still far below the proportion of African Americans in the population, it has risen sharply in recent decades.[46] There are now roughly five hundred black mayors and more than forty black members of Congress. The most stunning advance, of course, was the election of Barack Obama in 2008 as the first African American president.

Women

Women, too, have made substantial gains in the area of appointive and elective offices. In 1981, President Ronald Reagan appointed the first woman to serve on the Supreme Court, Sandra Day O'Connor. When the Democratic Party in 1984 chose Geraldine Ferraro as its vice presidential nominee, she became the first woman to run on the national ticket of a major political party. Sarah Palin became the second when she ran as the 2008 Republican vice presidential nominee. Hillary Clinton nearly won the 2008 Democratic presidential nomination, which would have been the first time that a woman headed a major party's national ticket. Nevertheless, women are still a long way from attaining political parity.[47] Women occupy roughly one in six congressional seats and one in five statewide and city council offices (see "How the U.S. Differs").

HOW THE U.S. DIFFERS
POLITICAL THINKING THROUGH COMPARISON

Women's Representation in National Legislatures

For a long period in world history, women were largely barred from holding positions of political power. The situation has changed dramatically in recent decades, and women now hold more seats in national legislatures than at any time in history. Yet in only a few countries have they even approached parity with men. The Scandinavian countries (of which Sweden is an example) rank highest in terms of the percentage of female lawmakers. Other northern European countries have lower levels, but their levels are higher than that of the United States, as the figure below indicates.

Q: *Why does the United States have fewer women in its national legislature than do European democracies?*

A: *Public opinion in the United States does not differ greatly from that in Europe on the issue of women in public office. An explanation for why Europe has more women legislators is its reliance on proportional representation. In this system, the parties get seats in proportion to the votes they receive in the election, and the parties decide which party*

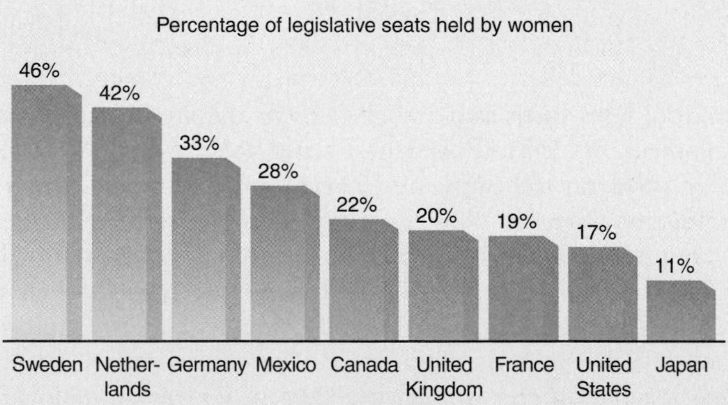

Source: From Inter-Parliamentary Union, Women in National Parliaments (2010). Reprinted with permission. www.ipu.org.

members will occupy the seats. The parties tend to balance their selections, including a balance of men and women, in order to attract as many votes as possible. In the United States, candidates compete directly for the vote, and the candidate who gets the most votes in a district wins the seat. There is no systematic method for assuring the election of a designated proportion of women candidates. (Chapter 8 provides a fuller explanation of the difference between proportional representation and single-member districts as methods of election.)

In recent decades, increasing numbers of women have entered the job market. They are six times more likely today than a half century ago to work outside the home and have made inroads in male-dominated occupations. Women now comprise, for example, nearly half of graduating lawyers and physicians. The change in women's work status is also reflected in general education statistics. A few decades ago, more men than women were enrolled in college. Today, the reverse is true. A recent U.S. Education Department report showed that women are ahead of men in more than just college enrollment; they are also more likely to complete their degree, to do it in a shorter period, and to get better grades.[48]

Nevertheless, women have not achieved job equality. Women increasingly hold managerial positions, but, as they rise through the ranks, they can encounter the so-called *glass ceiling*, which refers to the invisible but nonetheless real barrier that some women face when firms choose their top executives. Of the five hundred largest U.S. corporations, less than 5 percent are headed by women. Women also earn less than men: the average pay for full-time female employees is about 80 percent of that for full-time male employees. One reason is that many of the jobs traditionally held by women, such as office assistant, pay less than many of the jobs traditionally held by men, such as truck driver. Attempts by women's groups to change this tendency have been largely unsuccessful. Only a few firms and municipalities have established *comparable worth policies* whereby women and men get equal pay for jobs that require a similar level of training or education.[49]

Sexual harassment can also mar the work experience of women. Lewd comments and unwelcome advances are a workplace reality for many American women. The courts with increasing firmness have held that companies and government agencies are liable if they fail to create a work environment in which this kind of behavior is discouraged and punished.[50] A recent Supreme Court decision also made it easier for employees to sue an organization that retaliates against them for filing a sexual harassment complaint. The case involved a woman who, after filing such a complaint, was removed from her position as a forklift operator and assigned a less desirable job in the company.[51]

Women gained a major victory in the workplace in 1993 when Congress passed the Family and Medical Leave Act. It provides for up to twelve weeks of unpaid leave for employees to care for a new baby or a seriously ill family member. Upon return from leave, the employee ordinarily must be given the original or an equivalent job position with equivalent pay and benefits. These provisions apply to men as well as women, but women were the instigating force behind the legislation and are the primary beneficiaries in that they usually bear the larger share of responsibility for newborn or sick family members.

Most single-parent families are headed by women, and about one in four of these families lives below the poverty line, which is five times the level of two-parent families (see Figure 5-3). The situation has been described as "the feminization of poverty." Especially vulnerable are single-parent families headed by women who work in a nonprofessional field. Women without a college education or special skills often cannot find jobs that pay significantly more than the child-care expenses they incur if they work outside the home. Adding to their burden is the fact that some of them receive no or only token child-support payments from the father.

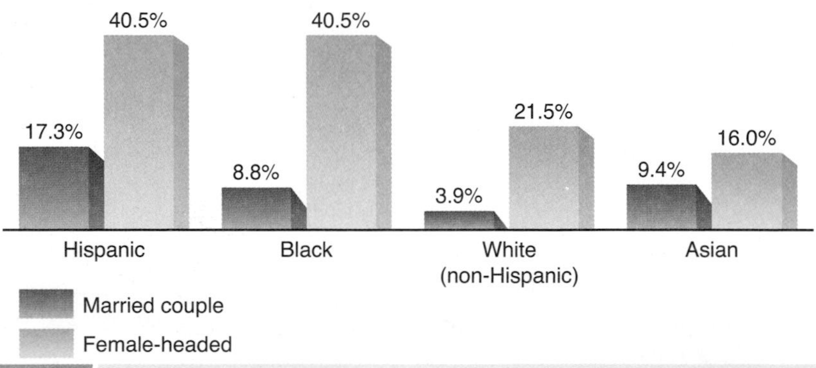

figure 5-3 PERCENTAGE OF FAMILIES LIVING IN POVERTY, BY FAMILY COMPOSITION AND RACE/ETHNICITY

Poverty is far more prevalent among female-headed households and African American and Hispanic households. *Source:* U.S. Census Bureau, 2008.

Native Americans

Full-blooded Native Americans, including Alaska Natives, currently number more than 2 million, about half of whom live on or close to reservations set aside for them by the federal government. State governments have no direct authority over federal reservations, and the federal government's authority is defined by the terms of its treaty with the particular tribe. U.S. policy toward the reservations has varied over time, but the current policy is aimed at fostering self-government and economic self-sufficiency.[52] Preservation of Native American culture is another policy goal.[53] For example, children in schools run by the Bureau of Indian Affairs can now be taught in their native language. At an earlier time, English was required. Nevertheless, tribal languages have declined sharply in use. Of the larger tribes, the Navajo and Pueblo are the only ones in which a majority of the people still speak their native language at home. Ninety percent or more of the Cherokee, Chippewa, Creek, Iroquois, and Lumbee speak only English.

Native Americans have filed suit to reclaim lost ancestral or treaty lands and have won a few settlements. In 2006, for example, land that had once belonged to the Seneca tribe in New York was returned to it after property owners agreed to vacate their property in return for cash settlements from New York State. However, such settlements are infrequent, cover relatively small areas, and offer no promise of substantial future grants of land.

In recent years, some tribes have erected gaming casinos on reservation land. The world's largest casino, Foxwoods, is operated by the Mashantuket Pequots in Connecticut. Casinos have brought economic opportunities to the Native Americans living on or near the reservations where they are located. The employment level of these Native Americans has increased by a fourth and their income has increased substantially.[54] However, the casinos have also brought controversy—traditionalists argue that the casinos are creating a gaming culture that, whatever its economic benefits, is eroding tribal traditions. Political scientist W. Dale Mason notes that the gaming issue has also created conflict between tribal governments and the state governments. The tribes claim the legal right to conduct their own affairs while the states claim the power to regulate gambling within their borders. Revenue is also an issue. Tribal gaming is largely beyond the states' taxing power. Congress has taken measures to give states a degree of control over tribal gaming, but tensions remain. "What remains to be seen," Mason writes, "is whether the historic tribal-state conflict can be alleviated and replaced by a new era of trust and cooperation."[55]

Although casino gambling has raised Native Americans' average income level, it is still far below the national average. Native Americans are a disadvantaged group by other indicators as well. For example, they are less than half as likely as other Americans to have completed college, and their infant mortality rate far exceeds the national average.[56]

Hispanic Americans

Hispanic Americans—that is, people of Spanish-speaking background—are one of the nation's oldest ethnic groups. Hispanics helped colonize California, Texas, Florida, New Mexico, and Arizona before those areas were annexed by the United States. Most Hispanics, however, are immigrants or the children or grandchildren of immigrants.

Hispanics are the fastest-growing minority in the United States and recently surpassed African Americans as the nation's largest racial or ethnic minority group. Nearly 50 million Hispanics live in the United States, more than twice the number of two decades ago. They have emigrated to the United States primarily from Mexico and the Caribbean islands, mainly Cuba and Puerto Rico. About half of all Hispanics in the United States were born in Mexico or claim a Mexican ancestry. Hispanics are concentrated in their states of entry. Florida, New York, and New Jersey have large numbers of Caribbean Hispanics, whereas California, Texas, Arizona, and New Mexico have many Mexican immigrants. Hispanics, mostly of Mexican descent, constitute more than half of the population of Los Angeles.

POLITICAL THINKING

VOTE!

A Common Language?

In the 1960s, U.S. immigration laws were changed to allow record numbers of Hispanics to enter the country. The Hispanic community has expanded and flourished, particularly in the American Southwest. A point of contention is whether Hispanics should be required to use English as the first language in school and in the conduct of government-related business. English-first advocates say that a common language is critical to the nation's unity and have pressed for federal legislation that would mandate English as the official language of the United States. Other advocates say that such a mandate is at odds with the inclusive spirit of the nation's history as a diverse society. What's your opinion on the issue?

A significant number of Hispanics—10 million or more by some estimates—are in the United States illegally. Most of them crossed into the United States from Mexico in search of jobs. U.S. authorities have had only limited success in stopping the influx, and illegal immigration has become a leading political issue. It is also a divisive issue, so much so that those within Congress who favor a softer line in dealing with illegal aliens have been unable to reach agreement with those who favor a harder line on a comprehensive approach to the problem.

Illegal immigration exploded into the headlines in 2010 when the state of Arizona enacted legislation that called for police to check for evidence of legal status whenever in the course of duty they stopped a person for another reason. If the person was an illegal alien, he or she would be detained, charged with a state crime, and turned over to federal authorities for deportation. In response, Hispanics organized protest rallies in communities throughout Arizona and elsewhere, claiming that the law was a thinly disguised assault on the Latino community. Most Americans, however, supported the Arizona law. A Pew Research Center poll found that Americans, by a margin of two to one, believed local police should be required to ascertain the citizenship of individuals they encounter in the course of duty.

On the other hand, Americans have divided opinions on the question of the long-term answer to illegal immigration. Polls indicate that most Americans favor a path to citizenship for illegal aliens who have been in the country for a relatively long period if they meet certain conditions, including holding a job, paying back taxes, and having no criminal record. However, most Americans also believe that border security should be tightened greatly, that new illegal entrants should be deported immediately, and that employers who hire undocumented aliens should face stiff penalties.

Hispanics' average annual income is substantially below the national average, but the consequences are buffered somewhat by the fact that the family is the foundation of the Hispanic culture. As compared with black Americans, Hispanics are nearly twice as likely to live in a two-parent family, often a two-income family. As a result, fewer Hispanic families live below the poverty line. Health researchers have concluded that family structure also helps to account for the fact that Hispanics are healthier and have a longer life expectancy than would be expected based on their education and income levels.

More than four thousand Hispanic Americans hold public office. Hispanics have been elected to statewide office in several states, including New Mexico and Arizona, and roughly two-dozen Hispanic Americans currently serve in the House of Representatives. In 2009, Sonia Sotomayor was appointed to serve on the U.S. Supreme Court, becoming the first Hispanic to do so. The political influence of Hispanic Americans is increasing and will continue to do so. At present, about half of all Hispanics are not registered to vote, and only about a third actually vote, limiting the group's political power. Nevertheless, the sheer size of the Hispanic population in states such as Texas and California will make the group a potent political force in the years to come.

Asian Americans

Asian Americans now number about 12 million, or roughly 4 percent of the total U.S. population. Most Asian Americans live on the West Coast, particularly in California. China, Japan, Korea, India, Vietnam, and the Philippines are the ancestral homes of most Asian Americans.

Asian Americans are an upwardly mobile group.[57] Most Asian cultures emphasize family-based self-reliance, which, in the American context, includes an emphasis on academic achievement. For example, Asians make up a disproportionate share of the students at California's leading public universities, which base admission primarily on high school grades and standardized test scores. Asian Americans have the highest percentage of two-parent families of any racial group, which, in combination with educational attainment, has led to their emergence in the past two decades as the group with the highest median family income. The median Asian American family's income exceeds $60,000, which is about $10,000 more than that of the median non-Hispanic white family and almost double that of the median black or Hispanic family.

Nevertheless, Asian Americans are still underrepresented in certain areas of the workplace. According to U.S. government figures, Asian Americans account for about 5 percent of professionals and technicians, which is slightly more than their percentage of the population. Yet they have not attained a proportionate share of top business positions; they hold less than 2 percent of managerial jobs.

Asian Americans are also underrepresented politically, even by comparison with Hispanics and blacks.[58] Fewer than ten Asian Americans currently serve in the Congress. Not until 1996 was an Asian American elected governor of a state other than Hawaii, and not until 2000 did an Asian American hold a presidential cabinet position. A prominent Asian-American politician today is Bobby Jindal, who became a leading figure in Republican politics upon winning Louisiana's 2007 race for governor.

Gays and Lesbians

The Civil Rights Act of 1964 classified women and minorities as legally protected groups, which has made it easier for them to pursue their claims in federal court. Other disadvantaged groups do not have the same high level of legal protection, but they have increasingly resorted to judicial action, none more so than gays and lesbians.[59]

They gained a significant legal victory when the Supreme Court in *Romer v. Evans* (1996) struck down a Colorado constitutional amendment that nullified all existing and any new legal protections for homosexuals. In a 6-3 ruling, the Court said that the Colorado law violated the Fourteenth Amendment's equal-protection clause by subjecting individuals to employment and other forms of discrimination simply because of their sexual orientation. The Court concluded that the law had no reasonable purpose and was motivated entirely by hostility toward homosexuals.[60] In *Lawrence v. Texas* (2003), the Court handed gays and lesbians another victory by invalidating state laws that prohibited sexual relations between consenting adults of the same sex (see Chapter 4).[61]

Gays and lesbians have also suffered setbacks. In 2000, for example, the Supreme Court held that the Boy Scouts, as a private organization that has a right to free association, can ban gays because the Scout creed forbids homosexuality.[62] A more controversial issue has been whether gays and lesbians should be allowed to serve in the armed services. Beginning in the 1990s, gays and lesbians were permitted to serve under the military's "don't ask, don't tell" (or, "don't harass, don't pursue") policy. As long as they did not by word or action reveal their sexual preference, they could enlist and stay in the military. In turn, service members were prohibited from trying to entrap suspected gays and lesbians. In 2010, a federal judge ruled that the policy violated gays and lesbians' constitutional rights and ordered the military to stop action to remove from service those gays and lesbians whose sexual orientation had become known. Some observers believe the Supreme Court will review the lower court's decision, unless Congress acts first to change the policy.

Gay and lesbian couples have had some success in acquiring the rights and privileges afforded opposite-sex couples. Some states, cities, and firms have extended employee benefits, such as health insurance, to their employees' same-sex partners. Other benefits, such as inheritance and hospital visitation rights, are reserved by state law for married couples and their families. In 2000, Vermont became the first state to legalize the civil union of same-sex couples, thereby granting them the same rights under Vermont law as opposite-sex couples have. Four years later, upon order of the state's high court, Massachusetts gave same-sex couples the right to marry, becoming the first state to do so. A handful of states now permit same-sex marriage, and a few additional ones have granted legal recognition to same-sex marriages performed in other states. On the other hand, more than two dozen states, by either statute or constitutional provision, have recently enacted laws that limit marriage to opposite-sex couples.

Same-sex marriages and civil unions are not recognized under federal law, with the result that these couples do not have the same federal benefits as opposite-sex married couples—such as the opportunity to file a joint tax return or receive social security benefits upon the death of a spouse. In 1996, Congress passed the Defense of Marriage Act (DOMA), which defines marriage as "a legal union of one man and one woman as husband and wife." The law authorizes states to deny marital rights to a same-sex couple that has been granted these rights by another state. Under the U.S. Constitution's "full faith and credit clause," states are required to recognize the laws and contracts of other states, although Congress can create exceptions, as it did with DOMA. An attempt in 2006 by congressional conservatives to initiate a constitutional amendment to ban same-sex marriage, even in states that have it, fell far short of receiving the required two-thirds vote in the House and the Senate.

Nevertheless, the American public has become more accepting of gay and lesbian relationships. A slight majority of Americans now say they support civil unions. Support for same-sex marriage is substantially weaker but has been increasing, led by younger adults. A 2009 CNN poll found that more than half of young adults, but only a fourth of senior citizens, would support the legalization of same-sex marriage (see Figure 5-4).

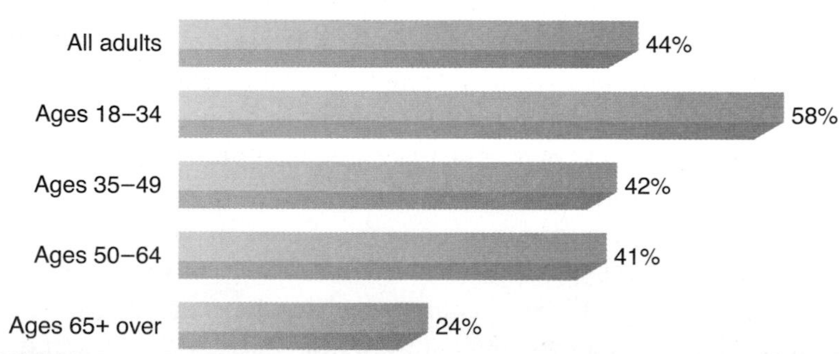

figure 5-4 OPINIONS ON SAME-SEX MARRIAGE, BY AGE

Americans are more likely to say they oppose same-sex marriage than to say they favor it, though opinions vary considerably by age groups; a majority of young adults say they support it. *Source:* CNN Poll, 2009.

Other Disadvantaged Groups

The Age Discrimination Act of 1975 and the Age Discrimination in Employment Act of 1967 prohibit discrimination against older workers in hiring for jobs in which age is not a critical factor in job performance. More recently, mandatory retirement ages for most jobs have been eliminated by law. However, age discrimination is not among the forms of discrimination prohibited by the U.S. Constitution, and the courts have given government and employers leeway in establishing age-based policies.[63] Forced retirement for reasons of age is permissible if justified by the nature of a particular job or the performance of a particular employee. Commercial airline pilots, for example, are required by law to retire at sixty-five years of age and must pass a rigorous physical examination to continue flying after they reach the age of sixty.

Discrimination against the disabled is also not among the forms of discrimination prohibited by the Constitution, but the disabled are protected through statutes. In 1990, for example, Congress passed the Americans with Disabilities Act, which grants employment and other protections to the disabled. Government entities are required, for instance, to take reasonable steps, such as installing access ramps, to make public buildings and services available to the disabled.[64] Earlier, through the Education for All Handicapped Children Act of 1975, Congress required that schools provide all children, however severe their disability, with a free and appropriate education. Before the legislation, four million children with disabilities were getting either no education or an inappropriate one (as in the case of a blind child who is not taught Braille).

Other groups could be described in this section. The United States has, for example, a long history of religious discrimination, targeted at various times and places against Catholics, Jews, Mormons, Muslims, various Protestant sects, and others. Numerous ethnic groups, including the Irish, the Italians, and the Poles, have likewise faced severe discrimination. Space precludes the discussion of the various forms of discrimination in America, but the point of any such discussion would be the same: equality has been America's most elusive ideal.

Discrimination: Superficial Differences, Deep Divisions

In 1944, Swedish sociologist Gunnar Myrdal gained fame for his book *An American Dilemma*, whose title referred to deep-rooted racism in a country that idealized equality.[65] Americans have never fully faced the contradiction,

table 5-2 TELLING THE AMERICAN STORY TO CHILDREN

Americans' values and myths are reflected in their preferences in teaching children about the nation's history.

In teaching the American story to children, how important is the following theme?	Essential/ Very Important	Somewhat Important	Somewhat Unimportant/ Very Unimportant/ Leave It Out of the Story
With hard work and perseverance, anyone can succeed in America.	83%	14%	4%
Our founders limited the power of government so government would not intrude too much into the lives of its citizens.	74	19	8
America is the world's greatest melting pot in which people from different countries are united into one nation.	73	21	5
America's contribution is one of expanding freedom for more and more people.	71	22	6
Our nation betrayed its founding principles by cruel mistreatment of blacks and American Indians.	59	24	17
Our founders were part of a male-dominated culture that gave important roles to men while keeping women in the background.	38	28	35

Source: Used by permission of the Survey of American Political Culture, James Davison Hunter and Carol Bowman, directors, Institute for Advanced Studies in Culture, University of Virginia.

as a University of Virginia survey illustrates. It found that American adults are far more likely to want children to be taught about the nation's achievements than its shortcomings, including its treatment of minorities and women (see Table 5-2). Selective memory can be found among all peoples, but the tendency to recast history is perhaps exaggerated in the American case because Americans' beliefs are so idealistic. How could a nation that claims to be the model of human equality have barred the Chinese, enslaved the blacks, massacred the Indians, and subordinated women?

Equality is a difficult idea in practice because it requires people to shed preconceived notions about how other people think, behave, and feel. People have difficulty looking beyond superficial differences—whether those differences relate to skin color, national origin, religious preference, gender, age, disability, or lifestyle.[66] Myrdal called discrimination "America's curse." He could have broadened the generalization. Discrimination is civilization's curse, as is clear from the thousands of ethnic, national, and religious conflicts that have marred human history. But America carries a special responsibility because of its high ideals. In the words of Abraham Lincoln, the United States is a nation "dedicated to the proposition that all men are created equal."

SUMMARY Self-Test www.mhhe.com/pattersonwtp9e

During the past half-century, the United States has undergone a revolution in the legal status of its traditionally disadvantaged groups, including African Americans, women, Native Americans, Hispanic Americans, and Asian Americans. Such groups are now provided equal protection under the law in areas such as education, employment, and voting. Discrimination by race, sex, and ethnicity has not been eliminated from American life, but it is no longer substantially backed by the force of law. This advance was achieved against strong resistance from established interests, which only begrudgingly and slowly responded to demands for equality in law.

Traditionally disadvantaged Americans have achieved fuller equality primarily as a result of their struggle for greater rights. The Supreme Court has been an instrument of change for disadvantaged groups. Its ruling in *Brown v. Board of Education* (1954), in which racial segregation in public schools was declared a violation of the Fourteenth Amendment's equal-protection clause, was a major breakthrough in equal rights. Through its affirmative action and other rulings, such as those providing equal access to the vote, the Court has also mandated the active promotion of social, political, and economic equality. However, because civil rights policy involves large issues concerned with social values and the distribution of society's opportunities and benefits, questions of civil rights are inherently contentious. For this reason, legislatures and executives have been deeply involved in such issues. The history of civil rights includes landmark legislation, such as the 1964 Civil Rights Act and 1965 Voting Rights Act.

In more recent decades, civil rights issues have receded from the prominence they enjoyed during the 1960s. The scope of affirmative action programs has narrowed, and the use of forced busing to achieve racial integration in America's public schools has been nearly eliminated. At the same time, new issues have emerged, including the question of whether same-sex couples will have the same rights as opposite-sex couples.

The legal gains of disadvantaged groups over the past half-century have not been matched by material gains. Although progress in areas such as education, income, and health care have been made, it has been slow. Tradition, prejudice, and the sheer difficulty of social, economic, and political progress stand as formidable obstacles to achieving a more equal America.

Key Terms

affirmative action (*p. 166*)
civil rights (*p. 150*)
de facto discrimination (*p. 166*)
de jure discrimination (*p. 166*)
equal-protection clause (*p. 152*)
equal rights (*p. 150*)
reasonable-basis test (*p. 155*)
strict-scrutiny test (*p. 155*)
suspect classifications (*p. 156*)

Suggested Readings

Anderson, Terry H. *The Pursuit of Fairness: A History of Affirmative Action.* New York: Oxford University Press, 2005. A comprehensive look at the affirmative action issue.

Blackmon, Douglas A. *Slavery by Another Name: The Re-Enslavement of Black Americans from the Civil War to World War II.* New York: Doubleday, 2008. A historical analysis of the Jim Crow era.

Feagin, Joe R. *The White Racial Frame: Centuries of Racial Framing and Counter-Framing.* New York: Routledge, 2009. A comprehensive look at past and present racial stereotypes that contribute to discrimination.

Fong, Timothy P. *Contemporary Asian American Experience: Beyond the Model Minority.* Upper Saddle River, N.J.: Prentice-Hall, 2009. A comprehensive look at today's Asian Americans, including their political empowerment.

Ganz, Marshall. *Why David Sometimes Wins: Leadership, Organization, and Strategy in the California Farm Worker Movement.* New York: Oxford University Press, 2009. An account of how Cesar Chavez succeeded in organizing California's agricultural workers, most of whom were Mexican Americans.

Garcia, F. Chris, and Gabriel Sanchez. *Hispanics and the U.S. Political System: Moving into the Mainstream.* Upper Saddle River, N.J.: Prentice-Hall, 2007. A broad examination of Hispanics' growing influence on American politics.

Lawless, Jennifer L., and Richard L. Fox. *It Takes a Candidate: Why Women Don't Run for Office.* New York: Cambridge University Press, 2005. An assessment of why fewer women than men seek public office.

Reeves, Keith. *Voting Hopes or Fears? White Voters, Black Candidates, and Racial Politics in America*. New York: Oxford University Press, 1997. A critical assessment of race and politics in American society.

Rimmerman, Craig A., and Clyde Wilcox. *The Politics of Same-Sex Marriage*. Chicago: University of Chicago Press, 2007. A careful assessment of the political forces surrounding the same-sex marriage issue.

Wilkins, David E. *American Indian Politics and the American Political System*. Lanham, MD.: Rowman & Littlefield, 2006. A comprehensive look at tribal governance and its connection to the American political process.

List of Websites

www.airpi.org The website of the American Indian Policy Center, which was established by Native Americans in 1992; includes a political and legal history of Native Americans and examines current issues affecting them.

www.naacp.org The website of the National Association for the Advancement of Colored People (NAACP); includes historical and current information on the struggle of African Americans for equal rights.

www.nclr.org The website of the National Council of La Raza, an organization dedicated to improving the lives of Hispanics; contains information on public policy, immigration, citizenship, and other subjects.

www.cawp.rutgers.edu The website of the Center for the American Woman and Politics at Rutgers University's Eagleton Institute of Politics.

Politics in Theory and Practice

Thinking: What role have political movements played in securing the legal rights of disadvantaged groups? How has the resulting legislation contributed to a furtherance of these groups' rights?

Participating: Think of a disadvantaged group that you would like to assist. It could be one of the federal government's designated groups (such as Native Americans), one of the other groups mentioned in the chapter (such as the disabled), or some other group (such as the homeless). Contact a college, community, national, or international organization that seeks to help this group and volunteer your assistance. (The Internet provides the names of thousands of organizations, such as Habitat for Humanity, that are involved in helping the disadvantaged.)

Extra Credit

For up-to-the-minute *New York Times* articles, interactive simulations, graphics, study tools, and more links and quizzes, visit the text's Online Learning Center at **www.mhhe.com/pattersonwtp9e**.

NATIONAL JOURNAL

New Meaning to the Pledge, "With Liberty and Justice for All"

Suppose you were a furry or feathery creature, confined to a cramped crate or a tiny cage, with your sole purpose in life to produce eggs for some human's plate—or to end up on that plate yourself. Don't you think your keepers should at least provide you with enough room to turn around freely, lie down, stand up, and stretch your limbs?

Well, you don't get to vote on this question. American members of species homo sapiens are voting on this matter, however, and they seem to favor awarding you these minimal rights, available to any convicted murderer on death row. In 2008, a California ballot initiative to write the "turn around freely, lie down" language into law for farm animals passed with 63.5 percent of the vote, despite intense opposition from agricultural interests arguing that complying with this costly standard would drive producers out of the state.

And such rights for the millions of animals on so-called factory farms are but one prong of an ambitious agenda. Other goals include a federal agency to safeguard and advance the interests of animals; legal standing for animals, with humans as their representatives, to file lawsuits to prevent violations of animal-protection laws; a federal law to end to the use of chimpanzees in "invasive research" at U.S. facilities; and humanlike rights for chimpanzees, gorillas, and other highly intelligent creatures that Charles Darwin, for one, believed possess rich emotional lives. Science, through the work of primatologist Jane Goodall and other pioneers, is confirming that view.

Take notice, for it is often the case with social causes that the marginal becomes the mainstream. That was the course of things in the movements demanding civil rights for women, for African-Americans, and, most recently, for gays and lesbians. Animal-rights activists are studying the history of those causes, and they are applying the lessons to their legal and political strategies. Look for intensified political, economic, and cultural warfare as advocates for animals seek nothing less than to include nonhuman creatures in America's promise of liberty and justice for all.

Although it is possible to talk about the cause in terms of "protection" or "welfare," the prism of "rights" is an apt one, as this is the concept that energizes the movement and ties its various facets into a coherent philosophical whole. The impetus has migrated from heartfelt sentiment for animals' well-being to a more elemental and sweeping concern for their plight as a matter of justice. The basic challenge is that the law still regards animals as "property," Joyce Tischler, a founder of the Animal Legal Defense Fund, said in an interview.

What theorists want to construct is a world that is less humancentric than the world, at least our Western world, traditionally has been. These advocates seek a world-view that is more regardful of animals as beings occupying an important position on the planet.

It's clear that the cause drives its opponents bonkers. "They want to take meat, milk, and eggs away from the diet of Americans and, indeed, people of the world," said Jack Fisher, executive vice president of the Ohio Farm Bureau.

"Most families now are two or three generations removed from rural life," Bud

Pidgeon, president and CEO of the U.S. Sportsmen's Alliance, lamented. His group, which supports hunters and trappers, often finds itself in battle against the major animal rights' advocates like the Humane Society. "They don't have a connection with wildlife or where their food products come from," he said.

Each camp has its strengths and weaknesses. Opponents of animal rights have a firmer base in Washington, including on Capitol Hill, where they hold a commanding influence on the Agriculture committees. The Humane Society, meanwhile, is pushing legislation requiring that any food purchased for federal government programs come from animals raised with enough room to "stand up, lie down," and all the rest. This is not small stuff: Washington spends more than $1 billion a year on food for the armed services, federal prisons, and other programs, according to the Humane Society. Once enacted, of course, that mandate could be the fulcrum for legislation to apply this standard to all food purchased in the U.S.

Outside of Washington, the public-relations campaign to paint the Humane Society as an extremist organization may be making some headway. Animal-rights activists in such culturally conservative states as Idaho and Texas now worry that Humane Society backing of any initiatives could come with too much political baggage.

For the most part, though, the landscape beyond the Beltway is hospitable to the animal-rights camp. Advocacy groups can take their message over the heads of politicians directly to pet-owning citizens, and they can do so in creative, imaginative ways that capture the spirit of their cause without sounding shrill and smarmily self-righteous. For the California ballot initiative, Proposition 2, proponents produced a brilliant piece of image-making—an animated video with a pig, surrounded by fellow creatures in their tiny cages, belting out, "There's a proposition, to save us from this hell," to the tune of Stevie Wonder's song "Superstition." As intended, the video went viral on the Internet, according to the Humane Society's Shapiro. It's difficult to watch it without a smile.

But animal rights is not only about federal laws, state ballot initiatives, and city council ordinances. At the cutting edge, and perhaps most fundamentally, the cause is about extracting support and sustenance from the common law, the set of principles that serve as the bedrock for the freedoms now taken for granted in Western societies.

Consider this plausible future: A day when the high court of some U.S. state grants a nonhuman animal—say, a chimpanzee confined to a zoo or a biomedical facility—a fundamental right to liberty, according to the ancient principle of common law that no one should be confined against his or her will without just cause.

Making that day a reality is now the consuming work of a prominent animal-rights lawyer, Steven M. Wise, director of the Nonhuman Rights Project in Coral Springs, Fla. Wise, who was born in Baltimore in 1950, taught the first class in animal law at Harvard Law School in 2000. Regarding "animal rights" as too vague a term, he prefers to speak in terms of the rights of particular species, so that the rights of horses might not be the same as the rights of chimps.

At the Nonhuman Rights Project, one goal is to identify a "plaintiff," probably a chimpanzee, on whose behalf Wise's group could file a lawsuit based on the common law writ of habeas corpus. As Wise noted, the habeas corpus writ was famously used to free slaves in the British Empire, a parallel that he views as apt to his own "abolitionist" cause.

A second objective of the Nonhuman Rights Project is to identify the most congenial venue for the lawsuit, which Wise said could be filed as soon as 2011 or 2012. For example, it might make sense to target a state Supreme Court dominated by female judges, on the theory that women are more likely to believe that nonhuman animals have legal rights. (Women make up nearly three quarters of grassroots animal rights activists.) Or it might be better to go to a state whose Supreme Court has overturned an anti-gay marriage statute, on the theory that such a panel has a demonstrated commitment to a right that traditionalists have opposed.

Should a state Supreme Court grant a writ of habeas corpus and the state's legislature permit the writ to stand, the freed animal might be viewed much like the law regards a 3-year-old child, as "an incompetent rights-bearer," Wise said, and hence put into the hands of a qualified guardian. "Yes, I do expect to live to see this happen," he said.

Consider how far the movement has come over the past 30 years. The ranks of law schools offering courses in animal law have grown from a handful more than a decade ago to more than 100 today. The number of states that treat animal abuse as a felony has increased from eight in the 1980s to 46 today. A bill requiring a public register to identify animal abusers, a parallel to Megan's Law for sex offenders, cleared the Tennessee Senate, and similar measures have been introduced in California, Louisiana, and New York. Chicago provides for court-appointed special advocates for animals in cases of animal-protection violations.

Animals are finding friends in high places, even in inhospitable Washington: In his days as a legal scholar, Cass Sunstein, now head of the Office of Information and Regulatory Affairs in the Obama White House, supported the idea that animals should have the right to bring lawsuits to prevent violations of the law.

And surely Shapiro had reason to smile when a recent report of a commission established by the Pew Charitable Trusts—hardly a citadel of extremist thinking—cited U.S. industrial agricultural practices for "inhumane treatment" and called for industry-wide adoption of the "five freedoms" for farm animals: freedom from hunger and thirst; freedom from discomfort; freedom from pain, injury, or disease; freedom to express normal behavior; and freedom from fear and distress.

As Ohio farmers reconsider their animal-confinement practices, it may make sense to "give some social-conscience relief to customers," Fisher conceded. "They want changes. So many people consider themselves a mother or father to a pet," and "we have to understand that."

The animal-rights movement gives the lie to the trope that we are living in a post-modern world in which meaning is fragmented and values are relative. These advocates burn with an old-fashioned Enlightenment fervor—an unhealthy zeal, critics believe—in this quest to extend liberty to nonhuman beings. The ridicule that sometimes greets their cause is unlikely to deter it, because in this respect, too, there is a comforting precedent.

At the close of the 18th century, one savant scoffed at the idea of equal rights for women by penning a satirical treatise in favor of the "rights of brutes." It was, an animal-rights advocate later observed, "a notable instance of how the mockery of one generation may become the reality of the next." The generational tides just may be flowing in favor of the animal rightists.

What's Your Opinion?

What civil rights, if any, do you think nonhuman animals should have? What rights, if any, should be reserved for humans? Do you think the best tactic for the animal rights movement is to borrow the language and strategies of previous civil-rights struggles in this country? Why or why not?

CHAPTER 6

PUBLIC OPINION AND POLITICAL SOCIALIZATION: SHAPING THE PEOPLE'S VOICE

> "Towering over Presidents and [Congress] . . . public opinion stands out, in the United States, as the great source of power, the master of servants who tremble before it."
>
> JAMES BRYCE[1]

As President Barack Obama weighed the recommendation of his military advisors to increase the number of troops in Afghanistan, Americans were divided on the best course of action. Polls indicated that they were nearly evenly split in their opinion as to whether the Afghan war was worth fighting. Those loyal to the president's party were the least supportive of a troop buildup. By a 58 percent to 31 percent margin, Democrats were against expanding the U.S. military mission in Afghanistan.[2]

In a nationally televised address on December 1, 2009, President Obama announced his decision on Afghanistan, saying he would send an additional 30,000 troops to what he called the "epicenter of the violent extremism practiced by al Qaeda." The surge would raise the number of American forces in Afghanistan to nearly 100,000. Obama promised a quick deployment of the troops, so that they would be in position to mount combat operations the following spring. At the same time, Obama announced that America's commitment to Afghanistan was not open ended. "After 18 months," he said, "our troops will begin to come home." During the eighteen-month period, U.S. forces would train and equip Afghan police and military units, so that the Afghans themselves could take responsibility for the war effort.

Polls taken soon after Obama's speech indicated that most Americans had liked what they heard. By a margin of 58 percent to 37 percent, they expressed approval of his decision to send more troops to Afghanistan. Support for his policy was strongest among Republicans—71 percent of them expressed approval. But Democrats, too, were swayed by his announcement. Roughly as many of them, 47 percent to 46 percent, were in support of the troop increase as opposed to it. Democrats strongly approved of the eighteen-month deadline for the withdrawal of U.S. troops; 82 percent said they favored the deadline.[3]

Obama's Afghanistan buildup is a telling example of the influence of public opinion on government: public opinion rarely forces officials to take a particular course of action. If President Obama had decided that the deployment of more troops to Afghanistan was unwise, public opinion would have likely supported that policy. In this sense, public opinion is seldom an exact guide to policy. As long as the policy seems reasonable, political leaders ordinarily have leeway in choosing a course of action.

This chapter discusses public opinion and its influence on U.S. politics. In this text, **public opinion** is viewed as the politically relevant opinions held by ordinary citizens that they express openly.[4] Their expression could be verbal, as when a citizen voices an opinion to a neighbor or responds to a question asked over the phone in an opinion poll. But the expression need not be verbal. It can also take the form, for example, of participation in a protest demonstration or casting a vote in an election. The key point is that people's private thoughts become public opinion when they are revealed to others.

A major theme of the chapter is that public opinion is a powerful yet inexact force.[5] The policies of the U.S. government cannot be understood apart from public opinion; at the same time, public opinion is not a precise determinant of public policies. The main points made in this chapter are these:

- *Public opinion consists of those views held by ordinary citizens that are openly expressed.* Public officials have various means of gauging public opinion but increasingly use public opinion polls for this purpose.

- *The process by which individuals acquire their political opinions is called political socialization.* This process begins during childhood, when, through family and school, people acquire many of their basic political values and beliefs. Socialization continues into adulthood, during which time the news media, peers, and political leaders are among the major influences.
- *Americans' political opinions are shaped by several frames of reference, including partisanship, ideology, and group attachments.*
- *Public opinion has an important influence on government but ordinarily does not determine exactly what officials will do.*

Political Socialization: The Origins of Americans' Opinions

People's opinions form in response to events, issues, and problems that catch their attention or are enduring enough to retain their interest. But opinions also reflect people's interests and values. Developments invariably provoke different responses, depending on people's prior beliefs. A particularly striking example is the differing opinions of Republicans and Democrats toward U.S. military intervention in Kosovo in 1999 and in Iraq in 2003. Democrats were more supportive of the first war, whereas Republicans were more supportive of the second war. Although differences in the nature and purpose of these wars might partially explain this split, partisanship clearly does. The first of these conflicts was initiated by a Democratic president, Bill Clinton. The second was begun by a Republican president, George W. Bush.

Partisanship is a learned response. People are not born as Democrats or as Republicans, but instead they acquire these attachments. This learning is called **political socialization**. Just as a language, a religion, or an athletic skill is acquired through a learning process, so too are people's political orientations.

Some political opinions are widely shared and deeply ingrained. They are part of what social scientists call **political culture**, a term that refers to the characteristic and deep-seated beliefs of a particular people about government and politics.[6] Americans are unusual, for example, in their commitment to liberty, equality, and self-government—the ideals that defined their nation's founding and were expressed so forcefully in the Declaration of Independence. The Frenchman Alexis de Tocqueville was among the first to see how thoroughly these beliefs had permeated American society. "Habits of the heart" was how he described them.[7]

Other political opinions are fleeting or conflicting. A few years ago, no issue mattered more to Americans than the war in Iraq. Those who supported the war and those who opposed it had intense views on the conflict. Today, it is difficult to get Americans to pay attention to what is happening in Iraq. Issues come and go and, as they do, so do the opinions they provoke.

In every case, however, opinions are a result of the political socialization process. Opinions do not develop out of thin air. They stem from what people have learned, over the long run or in the immediate context. When Congress in 2010 addressed the issue of regulating financial institutions, most Americans had an opinion about it. These views owed in part to what Congress was proposing to do, but they also owed to people's thoughts about the crash of the financial markets in 2008 and to people's attitudes toward government and business, which were largely formed before the crash.

Broadly speaking, the process of political socialization has two distinguishing characteristics. First, although socialization continues throughout life, most people's political outlooks are influenced by childhood learning. Basic ideas about which political party is better, for example, are often formed uncritically in childhood, in much the same way that belief in the superiority of a particular religion—typically, the religion of one's parents—is acquired. A second characteristic of political socialization is that its effect is cumulative. Political orientations usually grow firmer with age. Early learning affects later learning because people's beliefs affect how new information is interpreted. Prior attitudes serve as a psychological screen through which new information is filtered, as in the case of the contrasting responses of Republicans and Democrats to the wars in Kosovo and Iraq.

The political socialization process takes place through a number of **agents of socialization**. They can be divided between primary and secondary agents. Primary agents interact closely and regularly with the individual, usually early in life, as in the case of the family. Secondary agents have a less intimate connection with the individual and are usually more important later in life, as in the case of work associates. It is helpful to consider briefly how various primary and secondary agents affect political learning.

Primary Socializing Agents: Family, School, and Church

The family is a powerful primary agent because it has a near-monopoly on the attention of the young child, who places great trust in what a parent says. By the time children reach adulthood, many of the beliefs and

Agents of socialization, which include coworkers, influence people's opinions.

values that will stay with them throughout life are firmly in place. Indeed, as sociologist Herbert Hyman concluded from his research: "Foremost among agencies of socialization into politics is the family."[8] Many adults are Republicans or Democrats today almost solely because their parents backed that party. They can give all sorts of reasons for preferring their party to the other, but the reasons came later in life. The family also contributes to basic orientations that, while not directly political, have political significance. American children, for example, often have a voice in family decisions, contributing to a sense of social equality.[9]

The school, like the family, affects children's basic political beliefs. Teachers at the elementary level praise the country's political institutions and extol the exploits of national heroes such as George Washington, Abraham Lincoln, and Martin Luther King.[10] Although teachers in the middle and high school grades present a more nuanced version of American history, they tend to emphasize the nation's great moments—for example, its decisive role in the two world wars. U.S. schools are more instrumental in building support for the nation and its cultural beliefs than are the schools in most other democracies. The Pledge of Allegiance, which is recited daily in many U.S. schools, has no equivalent in Europe. Schools there do not open the day by asking students to take a pledge of national loyalty.

Religious organizations are a powerful socializing agent for some children. Although many American children do not experience religion or do so only fleetingly, others attend church regularly. Scholars have not studied the influence of religion on childhood political socialization as closely as they have studied the influence of families or schools.[11] Nevertheless, religion can have a formative influence on children's attitudes, including beliefs about society's obligations to the poor and the unborn.

Secondary Socializing Agents: Peers, Media, and Leaders

With age, additional socializing agents come into play. An individual's peers—friends, neighbors, coworkers, and the like—become sources of opinion. Research indicates that many individuals are unwilling to deviate too far politically from what their peers think. In *The Spiral of Silence*, Elisabeth Noelle-Neumann shows that individuals tend to withhold opinions that are at odds with those of the people around them. If nearly everyone in a group favors legalizing same-sex marriage, for example, a person who believes otherwise is likely to remain silent. As a result, the group's dominant opinion will appear to be more widely held than it actually is, which can persuade those with lightly held opinions to adopt the group opinion as their own.[12]

The mass media are also a powerful socializing agent. Politics for the average citizen is a second-hand affair, observed mainly through the media rather than directly. In the words of journalist Walter Lippmann, "the pictures in our heads of the world outside" owe substantially to how that world is portrayed for us by the media.[13] For example, heavy exposure to crime on television, whether through news or entertainment, can lead people to believe that society itself is more dangerous than it actually is.[14] The example illustrates the media's *agenda-setting effect*—the tendency of people to assign importance to topics that are emphasized by the media. (This effect and others are discussed more fully in Chapter 10.)

Individuals in positions of authority are also sources of opinion.[15] In the American case, no authority figure has more influence on public opinion than does the president. After the terrorist attacks of September 11, 2001, for example, many Americans were confused about who the enemy was and how America should respond. Their opinions became firmer a few days later when President George W. Bush in a nationally televised speech identified al Qaeda members as the perpetrators and declared that America would attack Afghanistan if it continued to provide

HOW THE U.S. DIFFERS
POLITICAL THINKING THROUGH COMPARISONS

National Pride

One indicator of Americans' political socialization is the pride they express in their nationality. Americans rank high on this indicator, as shown by the following chart, which is based on polls conducted by the World Values Survey. The percentages are the proportion of respondents in each country who said they were "very proud" or "proud" of their nationality.

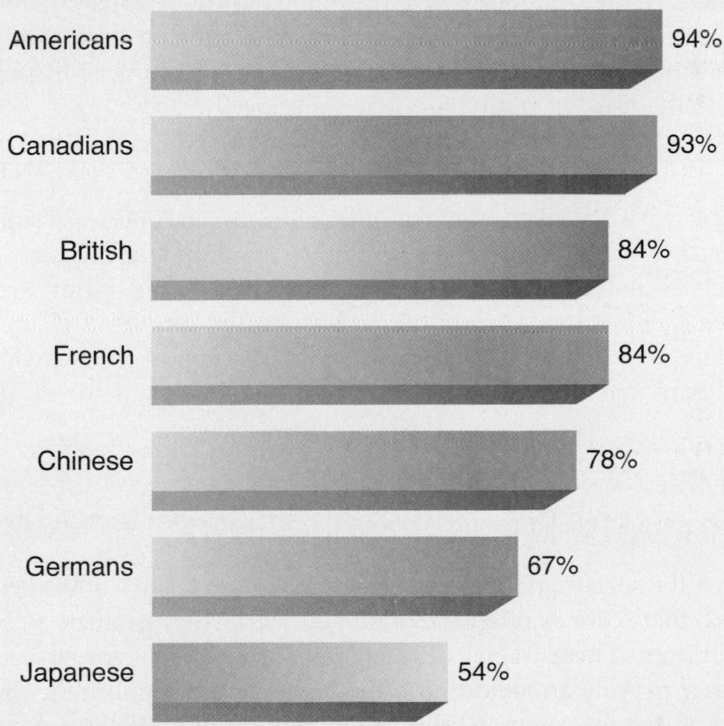

Americans are justifiably proud of their nation. It is the oldest continuous democracy in the world, an economic powerhouse, and a diverse yet harmonious society. What Americans may not rec-

Continued

ognize, because it is so much a part of everyday life in America, is the degree to which they are bombarded with messages and symbols of their nation's greatness. Political socialization in the United States is not the rigid program of indoctrination that some societies impose on their people. Nevertheless, Americans receive a thorough political education. Their country's values are impressed on them by every medium of communication: newspapers, daily conversations, television, movies, books, magazines, and so on.

The words and symbols that regularly tell Americans of their country's greatness are important to its unity. In the absence of a common ancestral heritage to bind them, Americans need other methods to instill and reinforce the idea that they are one people. America's political ideals have this effect, as do everyday reminders such as the flying of the flag on homes and private buildings, a practice that is almost uniquely American. (Elsewhere, flags are typically displayed only on public buildings.)

them sanctuary. Polls indicated that nine of every ten Americans supported Bush's stance on Afghanistan. On the other hand, political leaders' ability to influence public opinion depends on their standing. After President Bush led America into a costly war in Iraq on the erroneous claim that it had weapons of mass destruction, his political support weakened, as did his ability to persuade Americans that the war in Iraq was worth fighting.

Frames of Reference: How Americans Think Politically

Through the socialization process, citizens acquire frames of reference (or schemas) that serve as reference points by which they evaluate issues and developments. These frames of reference are important for two reasons. First, they provide an indication of how people think politically. Second, they are a basis for common cause. The opinions of millions of Americans would mean almost nothing if everyone's opinions were different from those of all others. If enough people share the same frame of reference, however, they have strength in numbers and have a chance of exerting political influence.

The subject of how Americans think politically fills entire books. Outlined here are three of the major frames of reference through which

Americans evaluate political developments: partisanship, ideological leanings, and group attachments.

Party Identification

Partisanship is the major frame of political reference for many Americans. **Party identification** refers to a person's ingrained sense of loyalty to a political party. Party identification is not formal membership in a party but rather an emotional attachment to it—the feeling that "I am a Democrat" or "I am a Republican." Scholars and pollsters measure party identification with a question of the following type: "Generally speaking, do you think of yourself as a Republican, a Democrat, an Independent, or what?" About two-thirds of adults call themselves either Democrats or Republicans. Of the one-third who prefer the label "Independent," most say they lean toward one party or the other and usually vote for that party's candidates. In short, most self-described independents have a partisan tendency.

Early studies of party identification concluded that it was highly stable and seldom changed over the course of adult life.[16] Subsequent studies have shown that party loyalty is more fluid than originally believed; it can be influenced by the issues and candidates of the moment.[17] Nevertheless, many adults remain lifelong Republicans or Democrats even as political conditions or their personal lives change in ways that might logically lead them to identify with the other party. Historically, major shifts in the party attachments of large numbers of Americans have occurred only in the context of a momentous upheaval. Even then, the shift has usually been concentrated among younger adults because their partisanship tends to be less firmly rooted. During the Great Depression, for example, Franklin Roosevelt's New Deal prompted many younger Republicans, but relatively few older ones, to transfer their loyalty to the Democratic Party.

Once acquired, partisanship affects what people "see." *Selective perception* is the process whereby people selectively choose from incoming information those aspects that support what they already believe. Studies of presidential debates have found, for example, that Republicans and Democrats are watching the same candidates but "seeing" different ones. When their party's candidate is speaking, they tend to see sincerity and strength. When the other party's candidate is speaking, they tend to see evasiveness and weakness.[18]

In the everyday world of politics, no source of opinion divides Americans more clearly than does their partisanship. Figure 6-1 provides examples, but these show only a few of the differences. On nearly every major political issue, Republicans and Democrats hold views that differ at least

Shown here is a scene from one of the 2008 presidential debates between John McCain and Barack Obama. When watching political debates, Republicans and Democrats engage in selective perception. Their partisan and candidate loyalties affect what they "see," which is why most of them conclude that their preferred candidate won the debate.

somewhat. In many cases, such as spending programs for the poor, the differences are substantial. In a 2009 Pew Research Center poll, for example, 77 percent of Democrats, as compared with 46 percent of Republicans, said that government should provide more assistance to the poor. Even developments that have little to do with policy can provoke a partisan response. When the news broke that President Obama had been awarded the 2009 Nobel Peace Prize, Republicans were twice as likely as Democrats to say he did not deserve it. Three-fourths of Republicans said "politics" rather than merit was behind the award.[19]

For most people, partisanship is not blind faith in their party. Although some Republicans and Democrats reflexively embrace their candidates and policies, party loyalties have roots in party policies. The Democratic Party, for example, has been the driving force behind social welfare and workers' rights policies, whereas the Republican Party has spearheaded pro-business and tax reduction policies. The fact that most union workers are Democrats and most people in business are Republicans is hardly a coincidence.[20] Partisanship is examined in additional detail at various points later in this book, particularly in Chapters 7, 8, 11, and 12.

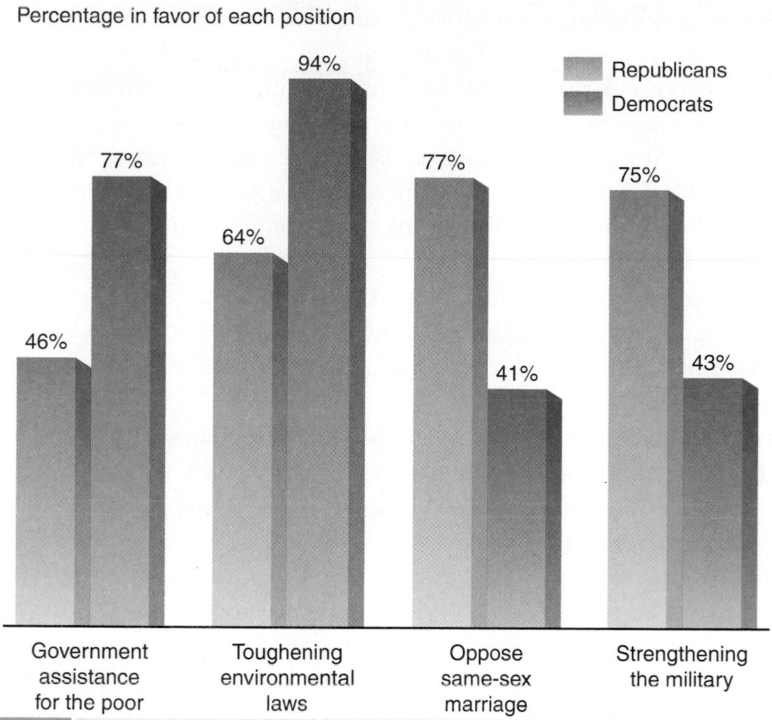

figure 6-1 PARTISANSHIP AND ISSUE OPINIONS

Republicans and Democrats differ significantly in their policy opinions and priorities. *Source:* Pew Research Center for the People and the Press (2010). Reprinted with permission.

Political Ideology

Karl Marx's collaborator, Friedrich Engels, said that he saw no real chance of communism taking root in the United States. Writing in 1893, Engels said America's workers lacked sufficient class consciousness, being concerned instead about getting ahead on their own.[21] In broader historical terms, Americans did not embrace any of the large twentieth-century ideologies—communism, fascism, or socialism—that captured the imagination of many Europeans. Historian Daniel Boorstin argued that Americans are pragmatists at heart, driven less by allegiance to ideology than by a desire to find workable solutions to problems.[22]

Of course, political ideology does not have to take an extreme form, as it did in the case of Soviet communism or German fascism. People can be said to have a political **ideology** if they hold to a coherent set of political beliefs. In assessing ideology, researchers look for a *consistent* pattern of opinions across a broad range of issues. Some Americans meet this test, but most do not. Farmers are an example. Farmers are more likely than most Americans to oppose government benefit programs for the economically vulnerable, but they strongly support farm subsidies. Their opposition to government assistance disappears when they are the recipients. On the basis of such evidence, researchers have concluded that no more than a fourth of Americans have opinions consistent enough to be judged as having a true political ideology.[23]

By a looser definition, however, Americans can be said to have ideological leanings. Most Americans have a clear opinion about how fully government should involve itself in economic and social policy. Some Americans believe, for instance, that government should play a substantial role in the distribution of economic benefits, working to ensure that the less advantaged get a fair share of society's wealth. Such individuals can be labeled **economic liberals**. Other Americans believe that the government should leave the distribution of economic benefits largely to the workings of the free market. Such individuals can be described as **economic conservatives**. Differing views on the proper role of government also exist on social and cultural issues, such as school prayer, same-sex marriage, abortion, and criminal justice. **Cultural (social) liberals** would leave lifestyle choices to the individual. In contrast, **cultural (social) conservatives** are those who would use government to promote traditional values, such as enacting laws that restrict marriage to opposite-sex couples.

Although it is sometimes said that liberals believe in big government while conservatives believe in small government, this claim is misplaced, as the foregoing discussion would indicate. Conservatives prefer a smaller role for government on economic issues but want to use government power to uphold cultural traditions. The reverse is true of liberals. Each group wants government to be active or inactive, depending on which approach furthers its policy goals.

There is no logical reason, of course, why an economic conservative also has to be a cultural conservative. Although most economic conservatives are cultural conservatives, some are not. In the Rocky Mountain states, in particular, many economic conservatives are cultural liberals. They believe government should refrain from undue intervention in the economic marketplace *and* in people's private lives. The term **libertarian** is typically used to characterize someone with these beliefs. Similarly, some economic liberals are cultural conservatives. They want to employ government power to achieve economic redistribution *and* to uphold traditional values. The term **populist** is typically used to describe a person with these beliefs.

POLITICAL THINKING

What Is Your Ideology?

The Gallup poll measures Americans' ideology by posing two sets of alternatives: 1) Some people think the government should make greater use of its taxing and spending power to help the less-well-off while other people think government should do less in this realm, leaving economic benefits to be distributed largely through the marketplace. 2) Some people think the government should make greater use of its power to promote traditional values in our society while other people think government should do less in this realm, leaving decisions about lifestyle to each individual. According to Gallup, a conservative *thinks government should do less in the economic realm but do more to promote traditional values; a* liberal *thinks government should do more to help the less-well-off but do less in promoting traditional values; a* libertarian *would like government to do less in both areas; and a* populist *would like government to do more in both realms. Do you ever use one of these labels to describe yourself? Is it the same one that would be assigned to you by the Gallup method? If not, how would you explain the difference?*

Thus, although only a minority of citizens can be classified as true ideologues, ideological tendencies are a useful way of looking at how Americans think about government. These tendencies are also useful in describing changes in public attitudes. When the U.S. economy went into a tailspin in 2008, the number of Americans who said in polls they wanted government to assist the economically disadvantaged increased. Such shifts occur periodically. During the Great Depression of the 1930s, there was a sharp increase in the number of Americans who wanted government to do more to help the poor. On the other hand, when Ronald Reagan was in office during the 1980s, Americans' views on government's economic role shifted the other way.

Group Orientations

Many Americans see politics through the lens of a group affinity. Their identity or self-interest is tied to the group, and they respond accordingly when a policy issue arises that affects it. Issues surrounding social security, for example, usually evoke a stronger response from senior citizens than from younger adults. Later chapters examine group tendencies more fully, but it is useful here to describe briefly a few groupings—religion, economic class, region, race and ethnicity, gender, and age.

Religion Religious beliefs have long been a source of solidarity among group members and a source of conflict with outsiders. As Catholics and Jews came to America in large numbers in the nineteenth and early twentieth centuries, they encountered intense hostility from some Protestants. Today, Catholics, Protestants, and Jews hold similar opinions on many policy issues. Nevertheless, important religious differences remain, although the alignment shifts as the issue shifts.[24] Fundamentalist Protestants and Roman Catholics are more likely to oppose legalized abortion than are so-called mainline Protestants and Jews, a split that partly reflects differing religious beliefs about whether human life begins at conception or later in the development of the fetus. Religious beliefs also affect opinions on poverty programs. Support for such programs is higher among Catholics and Jews than among Protestants. An obligation to help the poor is a central theme of Catholic and Jewish teachings, whereas self-reliance is a central theme in the teachings of some Protestant denominations.

The most powerful religious force in today's politics is the so-called religious right, which consists mostly of individuals who see themselves as born-again Christians and who view the Bible as infallible truth. Their opinions on issues such as gay rights, abortion, and school prayer differ

Religion is a powerful socializing force in American life. Churches, synagogues, mosques, and temples are places where Americans acquire values and beliefs that can affect their opinions about politics.

significantly from those of the population as a whole. A *Time*/CNN survey found that born-again Christians are a third more likely than other Americans to agree that "the Supreme Court and the Congress have gone too far in keeping religious and moral values like prayer out of our laws, schools, and many areas of our lives."[25]

Economic Class Economic class has less influence on political opinion in the United States than in Europe, but income and education levels do affect Americans' opinions on some issues. Welfare assistance programs and business regulation, for example, have more support among lower-income Americans, whereas higher-income Americans are more supportive of tax cuts.

An obstacle to class-based politics in the United States is that people with similar incomes but differing occupations do not share the same outlook. Support for collective bargaining, for example, is higher among factory workers than among small farmers, white collar workers, and workers in the skilled crafts, even though the average income of each of these groups is similar. The interplay of class and opinion is examined more closely in Chapter 9, which discusses interest groups.

Region For a period in U.S. history, region was the defining dimension in American politics. The North and South were divided over the issues of race and states' rights. Racial progress has diminished the regional divide, as has the relocation to the South of millions of Americans from the Northeast and Midwest. The newcomers are generally less conservative than natives to the region. Nevertheless, regional differences continue to exist on some issues, including social welfare and civil rights. The differences are large enough that when analysts talk about "red states" (Republican bastions) and "blue states" (Democratic bastions), they are generally referring to regions. The red states are clustered in the South, Great Plains, and Rocky Mountains. The blue states are found mostly in the Northeast, the northern Midwest, and the West Coast.

Race and Ethnicity As was discussed in Chapters 4 and 5, race and ethnicity affect opinions on civil rights and civil liberties issues. Blacks and Hispanics, for example, are generally more supportive of affirmative action and less trusting of police and the judicial system than are non-Hispanic whites. Blacks and Hispanics also tend to differ from non-Hispanic whites on economic assistance programs, although this difference mostly reflects differences in their income and education levels.

Gender Men and women tend to think alike on many issues, including abortion rights, but tend to disagree on others.[26] Polls have found, for

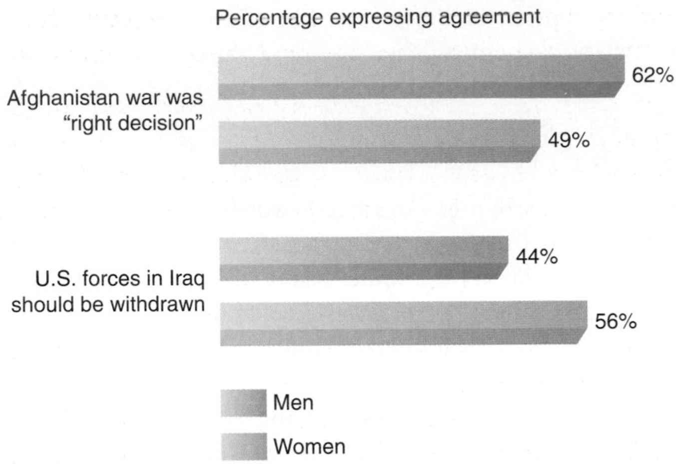

figure 6-2 GENDER AND MILITARY CONFLICTS

Compared with men, women are somewhat less inclined to support military force as a means of resolving international conflicts. This difference has been evident in polls Gallup support for the Afghanistan and Iraq wars, as these examples illustrate. *Source:* (In order of questions): Gallup poll, August 2007; ABC News/*Washington Post* poll, November 2005.

example, a consistent difference of about 10 percentage points between women and men on support for affirmative action. The difference is even larger on some social welfare issues, such as poverty and education assistance. Women tend to have more liberal opinions on these issues, reflecting in part their greater economic vulnerability and their greater role in child care. A recent *Washington Post*/ABC News poll found, for example, that women were 20 percent more likely than men to favor increased spending for public education. Women and men also differ on national security policy, with men more likely than women to support the use of military force (see Figure 6-2). Support for the Iraq and Afghanistan wars, for example, was consistently higher among men than women.

Generations and Age As a generation comes of age, it encounters a different political environment than its predecessors, with the result that its political views will differ somewhat from those of earlier generations. Those Americans who came of age during World War II, for example, acquired a sense of civic duty unmatched by the preceding generation or by any generation since. On the other hand, those who came of age during the Vietnam War era were more mistrustful of government than the generation before them or the one that followed. Americans of different ages also respond differently to age-related policies. In her book *Young v. Old*, political scientist Susan MacManus notes, for example, that senior citizens tend to oppose increases in public school funding while younger adults, particularly those with children, tend to support school spending.[27]

Crosscutting Cleavages Although group loyalties have an impact on people's opinions, this influence is diminished when identification with one group is offset by identification with other groups. In a pluralistic society such as the United States, groups tend to be "crosscutting"—that is, each group includes individuals who also belong to other groups, where they can encounter different people and opinions. Crosscutting cleavages encourage individuals to appreciate and understand political differences, which fosters political moderation. By comparison, in societies such as Northern Ireland, where group loyalties are reinforcing rather than crosscutting, opinions are intensified by personal interactions. Catholics and Protestants in Northern Ireland live largely apart from each other, differing not only in their religious beliefs but also in their income levels, residential neighborhoods, ethnic backgrounds, and loyalties to the government. The result has been widespread mistrust between Northern Ireland's Catholics and Protestants and a willingness on the part of some on each side to resort to violence.

THE MEASUREMENT OF PUBLIC OPINION

In a democracy, the central issue of public opinion is its impact on the governing process. Does government heed public opinion? Before addressing this question, it is helpful to discuss how political leaders find out about public opinion. Woodrow Wilson once said that he had spent much of his adult life in government and yet had never seen a "government." What Wilson was saying, in effect, was that government is a system of relationships. A government is not tangible in the way that a building is. So it is with public opinion. No one has ever seen a "public opinion," and thus it cannot be measured directly. It must be assessed indirectly.

Election returns are a traditional method for assessing public opinion (see "How the 50 States Differ"). Politicians routinely draw conclusions about what citizens are thinking by whether they voted and how they voted. Letters to the editor in newspapers and the size of crowds at mass demonstrations are among the other means of judging public opinion. All these indicators are useful guides for policymakers. Each of them, however, is a limited guide to what is on people's minds. Election returns indicate how many votes each candidate received but do not indicate why voters acted as they did. As for letter writers and demonstrators, their opinions tend to be atypical of the population as a whole. Fewer than 5 percent of

HOW THE 50 STATES DIFFER

POLITICAL THINKING THROUGH COMPARISONS

Party Loyalties in the States

The strength of the major parties varies substantially among the states. One indicator of party dominance is the degree to which the party identification of state residents favors one party or the other. In opinion polls, party identification is measured by a question of the following type: "Generally speaking, do you think of yourself as a Republican, a Democrat, an Independent, or what?" In 2009, the Gallup Organization used the results of its daily tracking polls to estimate the state-by-state distribution of Republican and Democratic identifiers. Nationwide, more Americans identify with the Democratic Party than the Republican Party, but the variation across states is considerable, For the map below, the fifty states (plus the District of Columbia) have been divided into three equal groups, ranging from the most Democratic to

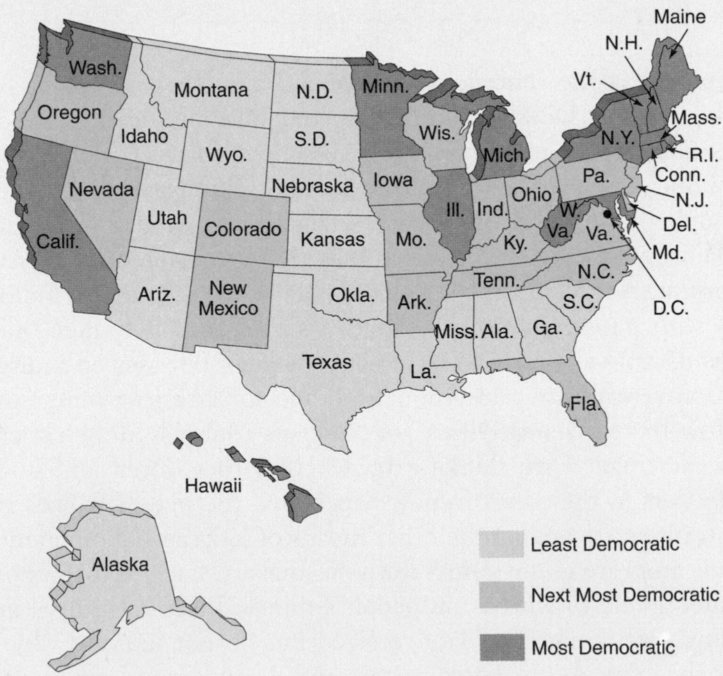

the least Democratic based on the difference between the percentage of respondents who said they were Democrats and the percentage who said they were Republicans. By this indicator, Republican strength is concentrated in the South, the Plains, and the Rockies, whereas Democratic strength is concentrated in the Northeast and the upper Midwest. According to the Gallup indicator, Massachusetts, Hawaii, Maryland, Vermont, and Rhode Island (in that order) are the most heavily Democratic states, whereas Utah, Wyoming, Idaho, Alaska, and Alabama (in that order) are the most heavily Republican states.

Q: *Why is the concentration of Republicans particularly high in some states of the South, the Great Plains, and the Rocky Mountains?*

A: *The South swung Republican after the Democratic Party took the lead on civil rights in the 1960s. The Great Plains and Rocky Mountain areas have traditionally been Republican, a reflection in part of the rugged individualism that defined their early settlement and contributed to a preference for small government.*

Source: Adapted from Gallup Organization data.

Americans each year participate in a mass demonstration or write a letter to the editor. Studies have found that their opinions are more intense and often more extreme than those of other citizens.[28]

Public Opinion Polls

Today, opinion polls or surveys are the primary method for estimating public sentiment.[29] In a **public opinion poll**, a relatively few individuals—the **sample**—are interviewed in order to estimate the opinions of a whole **population**, such as the residents of a city or country.

How is it possible to measure the thinking of a large population on the basis of a relatively small sample of that population? How can interviews with, say, one thousand Americans provide a reliable estimate of what millions of them are thinking? The answer is found in the laws of probability. Consider the hypothetical example of a huge jar filled with a million marbles, half of them red and half of them blue. If a blindfolded person reaches into the jar, the probability of selecting a marble of a given color is fifty-fifty. And if one thousand marbles are chosen in this random way, it is likely that about half of them will be red and about half will be blue. Opinion sampling works in the same way. If respondents are chosen at random from a population, their opinions will approximate those of the population as a whole.

Random selection is the key to scientific polling, which is theoretically based on *probability sampling*—a sample in which each individual in the population has a known probability of being chosen at random for inclusion. The key is random selection. Individuals do not step forward to be interviewed; they are selected at random to be part of the sample. A scientific poll is thereby different from an Internet survey that invites visitors to a site to participate. Any such survey is biased because it includes only individuals who use the Internet, who happen for one reason or another to visit the particular site, and who decide to complete the survey. A scientific poll is also different from the "people-in-the-street" interviews that news reporters sometimes conduct. Although a reporter may say that the opinions of those interviewed represent the views of the local population, this claim is clearly faulty. Interviews conducted on a downtown street at the noon hour, for example, will include a disproportionate number of business employees on their lunch breaks. Stay-at-home mothers, teachers, and factory workers are among the many groups that would be underrepresented in such a sample.

The science of polling is such that the size of the sample, as opposed to the size of the population, is the key to accurate estimates. Although it might be assumed that a much larger sample would be required to poll accurately the people of the United States as opposed to, say, the residents of Georgia, the sample requirements are nearly the same. Consider again the example of a huge jar filled with marbles, half of them red and half of them blue. If one thousand marbles were randomly selected, about half would be red and about half would be blue, regardless of whether the jar held one million, 10 million, or 100 million marbles. On the other hand, the size of the sample—the number of marbles selected—would matter. If only ten marbles were drawn, it might happen that five would be of each color but, then again, it would not be unusual for six or seven of them to be of the same color. In fact, the odds are about 1 in 20 that eight or more would be of the same color. However, if one thousand marbles were drawn, it would be highly improbable for six hundred of the marbles, much less seven or eight hundred of them, to be of the same color. The odds of drawing even six hundred of the same color are about 1 in 100,000.

The accuracy of a poll is expressed in terms of **sampling error**—the degree to which the sample estimates might differ from what the population actually thinks. The larger the sample, the smaller the sampling error, which is usually expressed as a plus-or-minus percentage. For example, a properly drawn sample of one thousand individuals has a sampling error of roughly plus or minus 3 percent. Thus, if 55 percent of a sample of one thousand respondents say they intend to vote for the Republican presidential candidate, there is a high probability that between 52 percent and 58 percent (55 percent plus or minus 3 percent) of all voters actually plan to vote Republican. It should be noted that if the poll had found the candidates separated by 1 percentage point, it would be mathematically incorrect to claim that one of them is "leading." The 1-point difference is smaller than the poll's 3-point sampling error.

The impressive record of the Gallup poll in predicting the outcome of presidential elections indicates that the theoretical accuracy of polls can be matched in practice. The Gallup Organization has polled voters in every presidential election since 1936 (nineteen elections in all) and has erred badly only once: it stopped polling several weeks before the 1948 election and missed a late voter shift that carried Harry Truman to victory.

President Harry Truman holds up the early edition *Chicago Tribune* with the headline "Dewey Defeats Truman." The *Tribune* was responding to analysts' predictions that Dewey would win the 1948 election. A Gallup poll a few weeks before the election had shown Dewey with a seemingly insurmountable lead. The Gallup Organization decided that it did not need to conduct another poll closer to the election, a mistake it has not since repeated.

Problems with Polls

Although pollsters assume that their samples are drawn from a particular population, such as all citizens of adult age, pollsters rarely have a list of all individuals in the population from which to sample. An expedient alternative is a sample based on telephone numbers. Pollsters use computers to randomly pick telephone numbers (including now also cell-phone numbers), which are dialed by interviewers to reach households. Within each of these households, a respondent is then randomly selected. Because the computer is as likely to pick one telephone number as any other, a sample selected in this way is assumed to be representative of the whole population. Nevertheless, some Americans do not have phones, and many of those who are called will not be home or refuse to participate. Such factors reduce the accuracy of telephone polling. Indeed, pollsters are concerned about the future of telephone polling. The refusal rate has increased sharply in recent decades.

The accuracy of polling is also diminished when respondents are asked about unfamiliar issues. Although respondents may answer the question anyway in order not to appear uninformed, their responses cannot be regarded as valid. Scholars label such responses "non-opinions." Less often, respondents will have an opinion but choose not to reveal it. On sensitive topics, interviewees will sometimes give what they regard as the socially correct response. For example, although turnout in presidential elections rarely exceeds 60 percent, 75 percent or more of respondents in postelection polls will claim to have voted. Some of them are not being truthful, but they are unwilling to tell the interviewer that they neglected to vote. Respondents are also not always truthful when it comes to expressing opinions that relate to race, gender, or ethnicity. Until recent years, in high-profile election campaigns pitting a white candidate against a black candidate, the polls regularly overestimated the black candidate's support. The best known example is the 1982 California governor's race, in which Tom Bradley, the Los Angeles mayor and a black man, led comfortably in the polls but lost narrowly on election day. Exit polls showed that fewer whites voted for Bradley than claimed they would in pre-election polls. "The Bradley Effect" became the term for the tendency of black candidates to receive fewer votes than the polls predicted. Recently, however, the polls of opposite-race contests have had roughly the same accuracy as same-race contests. In 2008, Barack Obama ran slightly ahead of the polls during the primaries but slightly behind them in the November election.

Question order and wording can also affect poll results. If respondents are asked their candidate preference at the outset of a survey, the results can differ from those obtained when they are asked at the end of the survey, after they have responded to other questions about the campaign. These questions can trigger thoughts that affect the choice of respondents who have a weak candidate preference at the start of the interview. In addition, how a question is framed, whether it is accompanied by relevant facts, and how the alternatives are worded can affect people's responses. Consider the issue of the death penalty. Do Americans favor or oppose its use? As it turns out, the answer depends to some extent on how the issue is worded. Respondents in some Gallup polls have been asked the question: "Are you in favor of the death penalty for a person convicted of murder?" Respondents in other Gallup polls have been asked a different version: "If you could choose between the following two approaches, which do you think is the better penalty for murder—the death penalty or life imprisonment, with absolutely no possibility of parole?" The two versions produce different results. When asked the first question, Americans by roughly two-to-one say they favor the death penalty. When asked the second question, Americans are evenly divided on whether the death sentence is the proper penalty.[30]

Despite these and other issues of polling, the poll or survey is the most relied-upon method of measuring public opinion. More than one hundred organizations are in the business of conducting public opinion polls. Some, like the Gallup Organization, conduct polls that are released to the news media by syndication. Most large news organizations also have their own in-house polls; one of the most prominent of these is the CBS News/*New York Times* poll. Other polling firms specialize in conducting surveys for candidates and officeholders.

The Influence of Public Opinion on Policy

As yet unaddressed in the discussion is a central question about public opinion: what is its impact on the policies of government? The question does not have a firm or simple answer, either in theory or in practice.

Writers have long disagreed about the impact that public opinion *should* have on government. Some have contended that almost any opinion that citizens hold, except the most fleeting or malignant, deserves to be taken into account by officials, who otherwise would promote policies that are out of line with the public's thinking. This tradition was expressed pointedly by George Gallup, a pioneer in the field of polling: "The task of the leader is to decide how best to achieve the goals set by the people."

Other writers have argued that public opinion is too whimsical and uninformed to be a basis for sound government. "Effective government," journalist Walter Lippmann wrote, "cannot be conducted by legislators and officials who, when a question is presented, ask themselves first and last not what is the truth and which is the right and necessary course, but 'What does the Gallup Poll say?'"

There is also disagreement over the impact public opinion actually has on government. Policies are complex, as are the factors that go into them. It is not a simple matter to pinpoint the influence of public opinion on particular public policies, and analysts do not entirely agree on what the evidence indicates. Nevertheless, most studies have concluded that public opinion exerts a strong influence on policymakers, though it varies across situations and issues.

Limits on the Public's Influence

Even if officials were intent on governing by public opinion, they would face obstacles, including inconsistencies in citizens' policy preferences. In polls, for example, Americans say they want a balanced federal budget. Yet only a minority say they would support the cuts in costly programs like social security and defense that would be necessary to bring the budget into closer balance. Nor are most citizens willing to balance the budget through a large tax increase. In the entire history of polling, there has never been a national survey in which a majority of respondents said their taxes should be raised significantly. In a 2006 Gallup poll, for example, 48 percent of respondents claimed that taxes were too high, and only 2 percent said taxes were too low.[31]

Many citizens also lack an understanding of issues, even vitally important ones. In the buildup to the U.S. invasion of Iraq in 2003, for example, polls revealed that more than half of adult Americans wrongly believed that Iraq had close ties to the al Qaeda terrorist network. Moreover, despite widespread opposition to the American invasion in most other countries, one in four Americans believed that world opinion supported the invasion. Americans who held these mistaken views were more likely than other Americans to support sending U.S. troops into Iraq.[32]

Only a minority of citizens can truly be said to be politically well informed. Even a college education is no guarantee that a citizen will have more than a passing familiarity with public affairs. The Intercollegiate Studies Institute surveyed 14,000 college students in 2007, giving them a multiple-choice exam to test their "civic literacy." The average college student received a grade of F, answering barely half of the questions correctly. Even historical facts of great moment eluded many students. Only 46 percent of college seniors, for example, could identify the phrase "We hold these truths to be self-evident, that all men are created equal" as being part of the Declaration of Independence.[33] An earlier survey of Ivy League students found that one-third could not identify the British prime minister, half could not name both U.S. senators from their state, and three-fourths could not identify Abraham Lincoln as the author of the phrase "a government of the people, by the people, and for the people."[34]

POLITICAL THINKING

Are Citizens Fit for Democracy?

Nearly a century ago, two of America's leading thinkers—the journalist Walter Lippmann and the philosopher John Dewey—engaged in a spirited debate on whether citizens could play the role that democracy assigns to them. Lippmann and Dewey were in agreement that citizens' ability to think sensibly about politics was undermined by the numbing distraction of the entertainment media, the inattentiveness of many citizens to public affairs, and the propaganda efforts of political elites and special interests. But Lippmann and Dewey diverged sharply on the public's potential. Lippmann doubted that the public could live up to democracy's demands. Dewey contended that advances in public education and communication would enable citizens to realize their public potential. Which argument comes closer to your own thinking?

Of course, citizens do not have to be fully informed to have a reasonable opinion about some issues.[35] Knowing only that the economy is performing poorly, a citizen could reasonably believe that government should take action to fix it. The fact that the citizen is unaware of the government's economic policy options would not render his or her opinion irrelevant. As one research team noted: "It is true that individual Americans have a weak grasp on the essentials of economics and economic policy, and it is also true that Americans, in the aggregate, are highly sensitive to real economic performance."[36]

On the other hand, there are issues where information is nearly a prerequisite to a sound opinion. The health care reform legislation that Congress debated in 2009–2010, for example, had cost and coverage provisions that affected people in different ways. Yet many Americans had no awareness of these provisions or were misinformed about them.

A Gallup poll found, for instance, that nearly a third of the public mistakenly believed that the legislation included government committees (the so-called "death panels") that would decide which elderly patients would receive life-saving treatment and which would not. Those who held this erroneous belief were more likely than other citizens to oppose the legislation. Many of these individuals might have opposed it anyway for other reasons, but mistaken beliefs are not the basis for sound judgment.

Public Opinion and the Boundaries of Action

Such considerations led political scientist V. O. Key to conclude that the role of public opinion is to place boundaries on the actions of political leaders.[37] The public is seldom attentive enough or informed enough to dictate exactly what officials will do. However, politicians must operate within the limits of what the public deems reasonable and acceptable.

Certain policy actions are outside the boundaries of public acceptability. Opinions on some issues are so settled that officials have little chance of success if they try to work against them. During his first presidential term, Ronald Reagan proposed a major overhaul of the social security system, but he quickly backed down in the face of widespread public opposition from senior citizens. During his second term, George W. Bush attempted to privatize aspects of social security, only to back down in the face of determined resistance. The founder of social security, Franklin D. Roosevelt, understood that public opinion would preserve the program. "No damn politician," he reportedly said, "can ever scrap my social security program." Roosevelt recognized that, by having social security benefits funded by payroll taxes, workers would feel they had rightfully earned their retirement benefits and would fight to keep them.

Issues vary in the degree to which they engage the public and the extent to which they provoke strong feelings. The greater the level of public involvement, the more likely officials will respond to public sentiment. In a study spanning four decades, Benjamin Page and Robert Shapiro found that changes in public opinion were usually followed by a corresponding change in public policy. As the public shifted its view, policy tended to shift in the same direction, particularly on issues that engaged large numbers of citizens.[38] Political scientist John Kingdon reached a similar conclusion, saying that when public opinion is intense and unmistakable as to a preferred course of action, politicians nearly always follow it.[39]

President Barack Obama had leeway in terms of what the American public would accept on the issue of the U.S. troop presence in Afghanistan. Political leaders are constrained by public opinion but seldom are forced by it to take a specific course of action.

Nevertheless, even on issues that engage the public, leaders usually have a degree of discretion. As political scientists Jeff Manza and Fay Lomax Cook noted from their study of public opinion: "[W]ithin the broad parameters established by public opinion, politicians and policy entrepreneurs often have substantial room to maneuver. . . ."[40] When the economy goes into a tailspin, for example, Americans expect officials to take decisive action. However, Republican leaders typically like to respond with measures such as tax cuts and interest-rate adjustments, whereas Democratic leaders tend to rely on measures such as increased unemployment benefits and spending-level adjustments. Each approach can boost the economy, but they differ in their impact. The Republican approach helps mainly business interests and upper-income citizens whereas the Democratic approach helps mainly labor interests and lower-income citizens.

Officials also acquire latitude when the public is divided in its opinions. When significant numbers of citizens are aligned on each side of an issue, officials cannot easily satisfy both sides. However, this situation often is not politically difficult because the split falls largely along party lines. The 2009–2010 health care reform issue was of this type, enabling most members of Congress to take positions aligned with the views of most of their party's voters. A February 2010 Gallup poll, for example, found that Republican identifiers by more than three-to-one opposed comprehensive health care reform whereas Democratic identifiers by more than three-to-one favored it.

On issues that fail to attract widespread public attention, leaders have considerable room to maneuver. On most policy issues, "the public"—if one means by that the whole citizenry—has no discernible opinion. The typical issue does not attract the attention of anywhere near a majority of citizens, much less provoke most of them to form an opinion about the proper course of action. Agricultural conservation programs, for example, are of keen interest to some farmers, hunters, and environmentalists but of little or no concern to most people. This pattern is so pervasive that opinion analysts have described America as a nation of *many* publics.[41] On less salient issues, political leaders typically respond to the opinions of the "public" that feels most strongly about the issue in question.

Leaders and Public Opinion

The fact that public opinion and public policy coincide at points does not necessarily mean that officials are choosing policies on the basis of what citizens would prefer. Officials often go to great lengths to win public support for their policies.[42]

If leaders succeed in persuading the public to accept their point of view, policy and opinion will coincide but they will do so because leaders have been able to influence public opinion. A case in point is the period leading up to the U.S. invasion of Iraq in 2003. Although Americans had been hearing about Iraqi leader Saddam Hussein for years and had concluded that he was a tyrant and a threat, they were unsure whether an attack on Iraq made sense. Polls indicate that some Americans preferred to give United Nations inspectors ample time to investigate Iraq's weapons program before an invasion decision was made. Other Americans expressed support for an invasion only if the United States had the backing of its European allies. Still others thought that, if a war was launched, it should be conducted entirely through the air. However, over the course of a roughly six-month period, the Bush administration pressed the case for war, which gradually increased public support for it.[43] When the war began, polls showed that President Bush's decision to use ground and air forces against Iraq had the backing of 70 percent of Americans.

Such instances have led some analysts to claim that major policies more fully reflect the preferences of leaders than those of citizens.[44] The linguist Noam Chomsky, for example, claims that public opinion is largely the product of elite manipulation or, as he calls it, "manufactured consent."[45] Nevertheless, systematic studies have found that policy usually changes in the direction of public opinion, rather than the reverse. On high-profile issues, in particular, public opinion tends to affect policy to a greater degree than policymakers' agendas affect public opinion. On the basis of their study of more than 350 policy-opinion relationships, Page and Shapiro concluded, "When Americans' policy preferences shift, it is likely that congruent changes in policy will follow."[46] In their more recent but similarly extensive study of the opinion-policy linkage, Robert Erikson, Michael MacKuen, and James Stimson found the same pattern, concluding that "public opinion influences policy."[47]

SUMMARY

Self-Test www.mhhe.com/pattersonwtp9e

The process by which individuals acquire their political opinions is called political socialization. During childhood, the family, schools, and church are important sources of basic political attitudes, such as beliefs about the parties and the nature of the U.S. political and economic systems. Many of the basic orientations that Americans acquire during childhood remain with them in adulthood, but socialization is a continuing process. Adults' opinions are affected mostly by peers, the news media, and political leaders. Events themselves also have a significant short-term influence on opinions.

The frames of reference that guide Americans' opinions include political ideology, although most citizens do not have a strong and consistent ideological attachment. In addition, individuals develop opinions as a result of group orientations—notably, religion, economic class, region, race and ethnicity, gender, and age. Partisanship is a major source of political opinions; Republicans and Democrats differ in their voting behavior and views on many policy issues.

Public opinion can be defined as those opinions held by ordinary citizens that they openly express. Public officials have many ways of assessing public opinion, such as the outcomes of elections, but they have increasingly come to rely on public opinion polls. There are many possible sources of error in polls, and surveys sometimes present a misleading portrayal of the public's views. However, a properly conducted poll can be an accurate indication of what the public is thinking.

Public opinion has a significant influence on government but seldom determines exactly what government will do in a particular instance. Public opinion serves to constrain the policy choices of officials but also is subject to their efforts to mold and channel what the public is thinking. Evidence indicates that officials are particularly attentive to public opinion on highly visible and controversial issues of public policy.

Key Terms

agents of socialization (*p. 192*)
cultural (social) conservatives (*p. 200*)
cultural (social) liberals (*p. 200*)
economic conservatives (*p. 200*)
economic liberals (p. *200*)
ideology (*p. 199*)
libertarians (*p. 200*)
party identification (*p. 197*)
political culture (*p. 191*)
political socialization (*p. 191*)
population (*p. 207*)
populists (*p. 200*)
public opinion (*p. 190*)
public opinion poll (*p. 207*)
sample (*p. 207*)
sampling error (*p. 209*)

Suggested Readings

Alvarez, R. Michael, and John Brehm. *Hard Choices, Easy Answers: Values, Information, and American Public Opinion.* Princeton: Princeton University Press, 2002. An analysis arguing that what citizens know about politics is assessed in the context of their values and beliefs.

Asher, Herbert. *Polling and the Public*, 8th ed. Washington, D.C.: CQ Press, 2010. A guide to public opinion poll methods and analysis.

Canes-Wrone, Brandice. *Who Leads Whom? Presidents, Policy, and the Public.* Chicago: University of Chicago Press, 2005. A look at recent presidents and their policies in the context of public opinion.

Erikson, Robert S., Michael B. MacKuen, and James A. Stimson. *The Macro Polity.* New York: Cambridge University Press, 2008. A careful and thorough analysis of the influence of public opinion on policy.

Foley, Michael. *American Credo: The Place of Ideas in American Politics.* New York: Oxford University Press, 2007. A careful look at Americans' core beliefs.

Green, Donald, Bradley Palmquist, and Eric Schickler. *Partisan Hearts and Minds.* New Haven, CT.: Yale University Press, 2002. An analysis concluding that partisanship powerfully affects how citizens respond to candidates and issues.

Jacobs, Lawrence, and Robert Shapiro. *Politicians Don't Pander.* Chicago: University of Chicago Press, 2000. An analysis concluding that politicians are not driven by polls.

Stimson, James. *Tides of Consent: How Public Opinion Shapes American Politics.* New York: Cambridge University Press, 2004. An analysis of trends in public opinion and their political impact.

Whitaker, Lois Duke, ed. *Voting the Gender Gap.* Urbana: University of Illinois Press, 2008. An edited volume that explores the voting divide between men and women.

Zaller, John R. *The Nature and Origins of Mass Opinion.* New York: Cambridge University Press, 1992. A superb analysis of the nature of public opinion.

List of Websites

www.gallup.com The website of the Gallup Organization, America's oldest and best-known polling organization.

www.people-press.org The website of the Pew Research Center for the People and the Press; includes an abundance of recent polling results, including cross-national comparisons.

www.realclearpolitics.com A site that has numerous up-to-date polls from a variety of organizations and on a variety of topics.

www.publicagenda.org The nonpartisan Public Agenda's site; provides opinions, analyses, and educational materials on current policy issues.

Politics in Theory and Practice

Thinking: What factors limit the influence of public opinion on the policy choices of public officials?

Participating: Studies have regularly found that Americans, in relative and in absolute terms, are substantially uninformed about the issues affecting their state, nation, and the world. As a result, Americans' opinions about policy issues and problems are not as informed as they could and should be. Citizenship entails responsibilities, one of which is to stay informed about problems and developments that affect the community, the state, and the nation. As an informed citizen, you will be better able to make judgments about policy issues, to choose wisely when voting during elections, and to recognize situations that call for greater personal involvement. Fortunately, you have access to one of the most substantial news systems in the world. News about public affairs is virtually at your fingertips—through your computer, on television, and in the newspaper. Spending only a small amount of time each day following the news will help you to be a more effective and involved citizen.

Extra Credit

For up-to-the-minute *New York Times* articles, interactive simulations, graphics, study tools, and more links and quizzes, visit the text's Online Learning Center at **www.mhhe.com/pattersonwtp9e**.

NATIONAL JOURNAL

Anger Management

Toward the end of 2009, about three weeks before he quit his uphill bid for a sixth term in the U.S. Senate, Democrat Christopher Dodd of Connecticut reflected on the vagaries of anger among the citizens of his state, who are worried about jobs and housing prices, the collapse of Wall Street, and America's wars in faraway lands. It was a ripe subject, for, as Dodd readily acknowledged, "people are angry, and angry at me." He provoked their wrath when Countrywide Financial gave him a VIP discount for a home mortgage—and even more when he neglected to mind the financial store as Senate Banking chairman and turned his energies to a futile quest for the 2008 Democratic presidential nomination.

National Journal shared with Dodd a sampling of the scathing things that his Connecticut constituents were saying about him. From a hair stylist: "He's worthless. I'm trying to be very, very nice." From a small-business owner: "I hope the bastard gets wiped right off the map. Whoever he's running against, I'm voting for that person."

The senator, in response, suggested that the anger was less personal than it seemed. "You and I have never seen anything like this," he said of the awful economy, in particular. "Their reflection about how they feel about people in public life," he said of his state's citizens, "is more of a reflection of how they feel about life."

That was a philosophical answer and not a bad one, even if it served to get him off the hook a bit. Anger is one of the trickiest of all political and social sentiments. Although it is easy enough to take a thermometer reading of public anger—and everyone can agree that the mercury stands at a high level right now—it is devilishly hard to predict the path that the anger will take.

This much is certain: Woe to anyone in the public arena who fails to take the anger seriously. Just look at the indelible example of Democrat Martha Coakley, beaten in the January 19 special election to fill the late Edward Kennedy's Senate seat in Massachusetts. Coakley, the commonwealth's attorney general, ran a lackadaisical campaign, allowing the insurgent Republican candidate, Scott Brown, to become the vessel for popular anger and pull off a historic upset in one of the nation's bluest states.

And one other lesson: In this incendiary environment, almost anyone can become a convenient target of blame and be singed by a sudden burst of flames. Federal Reserve Board Chairman Ben Bernanke's appointment to a new term, which at first looked like a lock, ran into trouble from senators desperate to protect their own political hides who are faulting him for reckless policies leading to 2008's financial meltdown.

Today's mad-as-hell "tea partiers" may be a full-throttle example of this personal anger. They are a prime case in point, circa 2010, of a venerable tendency for anger to find outward expression in the political culture. Although it would be nice to think that hope and optimism typically inspire political movements, in reality, movements such as these are likelier to start with raw anger, like oxygen to fire.

Furious citizens started the tea party movement as a spontaneous protest against Washington's taxpayer-financed bailouts of Wall Street banks and industrial giants such as General Motors. Although a conservative, anti-government hue tints the movement, it was not, at least in the beginning, self-consciously partisan. Tea partiers were steamed at George W. Bush's Treasury for its rescue of the banks; they are steamed at the Obama administration for what they say is Washington's effort to take over the health care system.

A primal anger, especially when it motivates a crowd acting in unison, is often associated with idiocy—so it is not surprising that the media often portray tea partiers as a gaggle of bumbling and blustery know-nothings, captive to rancid prejudices about President Obama and all other targets of their free-floating animus. This portrait, though, misses a certain canny intelligence in the tea party movement.

Chris Ford, a leader of the tea party movement in Connecticut, is without doubt an angry guy. His rage is focused on the big-spending, high-taxing, self-aggrandizing political establishment in Washington. But he is certainly not a yahoo. The folks who show up at the Connecticut tea party rallies, Ford said, are like him, "independent-contractor" types who either develop survival skills or go out of business. The group includes "carpenters, electricians, masons, restaurant owners, [and] printing company owners," he said.

Ford expresses his anger slyly, in humor and mockery. At the end of 2008, he and his tea party comrade-in-arms, Art McNally, a retired computer consultant, created the "Dump Dodd" campaign, exemplified in a button with a picture of "Joe the Voter" unloading a white-haired, money-bag-clutching Dodd from the back of a dump truck. "We're portraying Dodd as more of an incompetent buffoon," Ford explained. "He's not evil."

Ford and McNally are Republican-leaning political conservatives, but the Dump Dodd movement struck a chord with some grumpy Connecticut Democrats as well. Dodd's hasty January exit gratified the duo, naturally, but it has only boosted their appetite for more scalps. "We got Dodd to turn and run," McNally said in a phone interview the week after Dodd's retirement announcement. "We're not stopping. November 2010, we want to get rid of all incumbents. In Connecticut, it happens, they are all Democrats."

Another vulnerable Senate Democrat, Majority Leader Harry Reid of Nevada, is also high on the hit list of tea party activists. In their favor is an especially sour climate in Nevada, where unemployment exceeds the national average and nearly two-thirds of all mortgaged residential properties are under water—that is, worth less than their outstanding loan balance. Tea party activists contributed significantly to Brown's improbable victory in the Massachusetts special election as well. Sen. Barbara Boxer of California, a Democrat elected in 1992, could also prove vulnerable to the tea partiers' efforts to oust incumbents.

The latest question confronting the tea party movement is whether it can make the kind of transition that often trips up campaigns born of reflexive grassroots anger—the shift from a purely "anti" focus to a positive one, with efficient organizational machinery. The tea party folks most ardently hope for seismic change, "a revolution" that takes down the ruling political elite, as Ford said. But no such revolution appears in sight, for all the anger on the streets.

A more likely prospect is for the tea partiers to take over the Republican Party—or a least to become a weighty presence in it, much as disaffected conservative Christian evangelicals, long on the political margins, did in the 1970s and 1980s when they became a crucial bloc in Ronald Reagan's coalition. Should the tea partiers' plans not work out, they can always form a new political party, but that is a difficult route in a system stacked to favor the two established parties.

Liberal anger, too, is a live current, especially evident in attacks on Wall Street, a staple of the liberal blogosphere in sources such as The Huffington Post, whose namesake founder, Arianna Huffington, is spearheading a campaign for Americans to move their savings from large financial institutions to small, Main Street, community banks because "too-big-to-fail banks are profiting from bailout dollars and government guarantees, and growing bigger," as she wrote on her website.

Even though The Huffington Post reliably comes from the left, those words could just have easily been written by a tea party activist. For that matter, Obama's Treasury secretary, Timothy Geithner, who orchestrated the bailout of AIG, the insurance giant, while he was president of the Federal Reserve Bank of New York, is as much an object of scorn among the populist Left as among the populist Right.

And yet it is almost inconceivable that the anti-Wall Street, anti-Washington anger shared by the Left and Right in America will fuse into a joint campaign—liberals and conservatives are too invested in their ritual flogging of each other for that to happen. The future of anger-driven political movements in the United States remains captive to their imaginative limitations and their knee-jerk impulses—to the relief, no doubt, of the cowering targets at which they take common aim.

Sometimes it turns out this way. A movement begins in earnest, but not-especially-well-focused, anger and is taken over by a potentate—a particular kind of leader, unusually gifted in dealing with the masses, in seeming to channel their passions. That leader may or may not be a true representative of the flock, whose members tend to oscillate between an ingrained suspicion of any person in high authority and a yearning for the leadership that such a person might supply. Sarah Palin is the best example—she turned off some tea party activists by seeking a reported $100,000 speaking fee.

The Ross Perot movement was the most recent to display this dynamic. Perot, a little guy with jug ears and a squeaky voice, managed to take hold of a slice of an irate citizenry turned off by both parties and by Washington's profligacy. His strong performance in the 1992 presidential election set the bar for the anger candidate. He garnered nearly 20 million votes, about half as many as the losing Republican, George H.W. Bush, received, and 19 percent of the electorate.

In 2008, Obama, too, attracted a cultlike following on the campaign trail, with supporters motivated, yes, by his idealistic appeal for change but also by an intense anger at President George W. Bush personally and at Republicans generally over the Iraq invasion and other perceived evil deeds. But Obama has not really governed as a potentate; his flock is almost nowhere to be seen; his White House is as much invested in the nitty-gritty of negotiations on Capitol Hill as in bringing out the president for one of his trademark big speeches. Once a vessel for anger, Obama now risks becoming one of its prime targets, with a job-approval rating dipping below 50 percent.

Anger can be irrational, a reaction to slights that are more imagined than real. Today's public anger, though, is nothing like that. Americans have been a dealt a body blow, and their anger is righteous.

What's Your Opinion?

What do you think motivates political anger in America? Are Americans angry about particular politicians, about a political philosophy, a set of policies, or about something harder to track? Do you think political anger is a good or a bad thing?

CHAPTER 7

Political Participation: Activating the Popular Will

"We are concerned in public affairs, but immersed in our private ones."

WALTER LIPPMANN[1]

The stakes in the 2010 midterm elections could not have been much higher. Partisan wrangling between Republicans and Democrats in Congress had characterized nearly every legislative issue, and public confidence in Congress had reached an all-time low. Polls showed that the House and Senate races were close enough that either party could wind up in control of Congress. Yet barely more than 40 percent of eligible voters bothered to vote in the November congressional election. Of the roughly 200 million Americans of voting age, fewer than half that number cast a ballot, even though both parties waged intensive get-out-the-vote campaigns.

Voting is a form of **political participation**—involvement in activities intended to influence public policy and leadership. Political participation involves other activities in addition to voting, such as joining political groups, writing to elected officials, demonstrating for political causes, and giving money to political candidates. Such activities contribute to a properly functioning democratic society. The concept of self-government is based on the idea that citizens have a right and a duty to participate in public affairs. Democracies differ, however, in their levels of political participation. The United States is an unusual case. Compared with other Western democracies, it has relatively low levels of voter participation. Yet it has relatively high levels of citizen participation in political and civic organizations. This chapter describes and explains this participation paradox. The chapter's main points are the following:

- *Voter turnout in U.S. elections is low in comparison with that of other Western democracies.* The reasons include U.S. election laws, particularly those pertaining to registration requirements and the scheduling of elections.
- *Most citizens do not participate actively in politics in ways other than voting.* Only a minority of Americans can be classified as political activists. Nevertheless, Americans are more likely than citizens of other democracies to contribute time and money to political and community organizations.
- *Most Americans make a distinction between their personal lives and public life.* This outlook reduces their incentive to participate and contributes to a pattern of participation dominated by citizens of higher income and education.

Voter Participation

At the nation's founding, **suffrage**—the right to vote—was limited to property-owning males. Thomas Paine ridiculed this restriction in *Common Sense*. Observing that a man whose only item of property was a jackass would lose his right to vote if the jackass died, Paine asked, "Now tell me, which was the voter, the man or the jackass?" Fifty years elapsed before the property restriction was lifted in all the states.

Women did not secure the vote until 1920, with the ratification of the Nineteenth Amendment. Decades earlier, Susan B. Anthony had tried to vote in her hometown of Rochester, New York, asserting that it was her right as a U.S. citizen. She was arrested for "illegal voting" and told that her proper place was in the home. By 1920, men had run out of excuses for denying the vote to women. As Senator Wendell Phillips observed, "One of two things is true: either woman is like man—and if she is, then a ballot based on brains belongs to her as well

After a hard-fought, decades-long campaign, American women finally won the right to vote in 1920.

as to him. Or she is different, and then man does not know how to vote for her as she herself does."[2]

African Americans had to wait nearly fifty years longer than women to secure their right to vote. Blacks seemed to have gained that right after the Civil War with passage of the Fifteenth Amendment, but they were disenfranchised in the South by intimidation and electoral trickery, including whites-only primaries, rigged literacy tests, and poll taxes. Not until the 1960s were the last legal barriers to equal suffrage for African Americans swept away through congressional and court action (see Chapter 5).

In 1971, the Twenty-sixth Amendment extended voting rights to include citizens eighteen years of age or older. Previously, nearly all states had restricted voting to those twenty-one years of age or older.

Factors in Voter Turnout: The United States in Comparative Perspective

Today nearly any American adult—rich or poor, man or woman, black or white—who is determined to vote can legally and actually do so. Nearly all Americans embrace the symbolism of the vote, saying that they have a duty to vote in elections. Nevertheless, many Americans shirk their duty. Millions choose not to vote regularly, a tendency that sets Americans

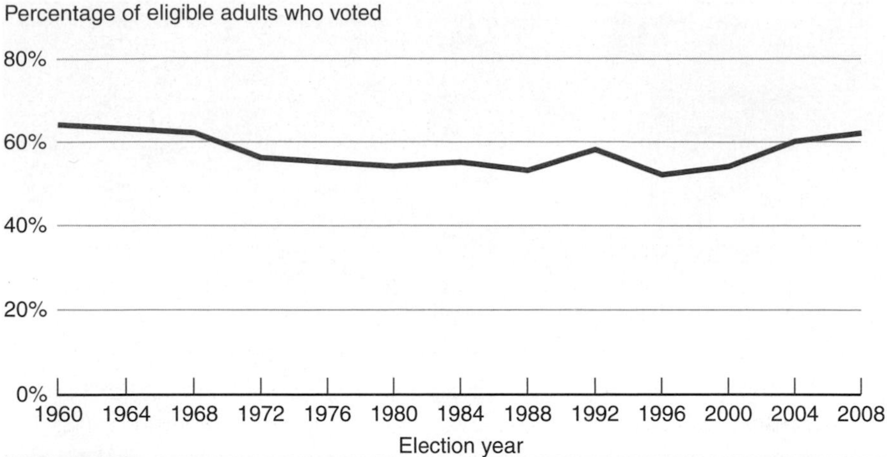

figure 7-1 VOTER TURNOUT IN PRESENTIAL ELECTIONS, 1960–2008

After 1960, as indicated by the proportion of eligible voters who voted, turnout declined steadily. In the past two decades, turnout has fluctuated, depending on the issues at stake in the particular election. *Source:* U.S. Census Bureau.

apart from citizens of most other Western democracies. Since the 1960s, **voter turnout**—the proportion of adult citizens who actually vote in a given election—has averaged about 55 percent in presidential elections (see Figure 7-1). Turnout is even lower in the midterm congressional elections that take place between presidential elections. Midterm election turnout has not reached 50 percent since 1920 and has hovered around 40 percent in recent decades. Turnout in local elections is even lower. In many places, less than 20 percent of eligible voters participate.

There is, however, an upward trend in presidential election voting. Turnout rebounded sharply in the presidential elections of 2004 and 2008 when compared to those of 1996 and 2000. In fact, turnout in 2008 was the highest since the 1960s. Turnout was also up in the 2008 presidential primaries, driven mainly by participation in the close Democratic race between Barack Obama and Hillary Clinton. Although only a third of eligible adults participated in the 2008 primaries, the voting rate was the highest since the 1970s. African Americans and young adults were among the groups with the sharpest increases in turnout.[3]

Voter participation is lower in the United States than in other democracies (see "How the U.S. Differs"). In recent decades, turnout in national elections has averaged more than 90 percent in Belgium and more than 80 percent in France, Germany, and Denmark.[4] America's lower turnout is largely the result of registration requirements and the frequency of elections.

HOW THE U.S. DIFFERS

POLITICAL THINKING THROUGH COMPARISONS

Voter Turnout

The United States ranks near the bottom among the world's democracies in the percentage of eligible citizens who participate in national elections. One reason for the low voter turnout is that individual Americans are responsible for registering to vote, whereas in most other democracies voters are registered automatically by government officials. In addition, unlike some other democracies, the United States does not encourage voting by holding elections on the weekend or by imposing penalties, such as fines, on those who do not participate.

Another factor affecting voter turnout rate in the United States is the absence of a major labor or socialist party, which would serve to bring lower-income citizens to the polls. America's individualist

Country	Approximate Voter Turnout	Automatic Registration?	Social Democrat, Socialist, or Labor Party?	Election Day a Holiday or Weekend Day?
Belgium	90%	Yes	Yes	Yes
Germany	85	Yes	Yes	Yes
Denmark	85	Yes	Yes	No
Italy	80	Yes	Yes	Yes
Austria	80	Yes	Yes	Yes
France	80	No	Yes	Yes
Great Britain	60	Yes	Yes	No
Canada	60	Yes	Yes	No
Japan	60	Yes	Yes	Yes
United States	55	No	No	No

Source: Developed from multiple sources. Turnout percentages are a rough average of national elections during the past two decades.

Continued

culture and its electoral system (see Chapter 8) have inhibited the establishment of a major labor or socialist party. In democracies where such parties exist, the turnout difference between upper- and lower-income groups is relatively small. In the United States, the gap in the turnout levels of lower- and upper-income persons is substantial.

Q: *How might American election campaigns differ if voter turnout was as high in the United States as in most European democracies?*

A: *If turnout in U.S. elections was in the 80- to 90-percent range, voters with less income and education would comprise a much larger share of the electorate, and candidates would have to pay more attention to their policy concerns. As it stands, most candidates aim their appeals at middle-income voters. Such voters constitute a substantially larger share of the electorate in the United States than in Europe.*

Registration Requirements Before Americans are allowed to vote, they must be registered—that is, their names must appear on an official list of eligible voters. **Registration** began around 1900 as a way of preventing voters from casting more than one ballot on election day. Multiple balloting had become a tactic of big-city party machines—"vote early and often" was their mantra. Although registration reduced illegal voting, it also placed a burden on honest citizens. Because they had to register beforehand, citizens who forgot or otherwise failed to do so were unable to vote. Turnout in U.S. elections declined steadily after registration began.

Although other democracies also require registration, they place the responsibility on government. When someone moves to a new address, for example, the postal service will notify registration officials of the change. The United States—in keeping with its individualistic culture—is one of the few democracies in which registration is the individual's responsibility. Moreover, registration requirements have traditionally been set by the state governments, and some states make it relatively difficult for citizens to qualify. Registration periods and locations usually are not highly publicized.[5] Eligibility can also be a problem. In most states, a citizen must reside at an address for a minimum period, usually thirty days, before becoming eligible to register. Scholars estimate that turnout would be roughly 10 percentage points higher in the United States if it had European-style registration.[6]

States with a tradition of convenient registration laws have higher turnout than other states. A few states, including Idaho, Maine, and Minnesota, allow people to register at their polling places on election day. Their turnout rates are more than 10 percentage points above the national average. States with the most restrictive registration laws—for example, those that require residents to register at least two or three weeks before election day—have turnout rates well below the national average. Several of these states are in the South, which, even today, has the lowest turnout rate of any region (see "How the 50 States Differ").

In 1993, in an effort to increase registration levels nationwide, Congress enacted a voting registration law known as "motor voter." It requires states to allow people to register when applying for a driver's license or public assistance. Registration is not automatic in these situations; the citizen must voluntarily fill out the registration form. Moreover, the motor voter law does not help citizens who do not drive or do not otherwise have contact with a proper state agency. The law has resulted in some new voters but fewer than its proponents envisioned.

A newer device, voter identification cards, serves to depress voter turnout. Legislatures in a few states have enacted laws requiring citizens to have a government-issued photo ID in order to register and vote. Proponents of these laws—most of whom are Republicans—say government-issued photo identification is needed to prevent voter fraud. Opponents of these laws—most of whom are Democrats—say the voter ID requirement is a thinly disguised effort to keep lower-income people, many of whom don't have a driver's license or passport, from voting. In every instance, the voter identification card requirement has been enacted by a Republican-controlled state legislature.

Georgia's legislature passed such a law, which required citizens without a government-issued photo ID, such as a driver's license or passport, to obtain a voter identification card, which would cost them twenty dollars and expire after five years. To obtain the card, they had to produce a certified copy of their birth certificate and other documents and could obtain it only by going to a Department of Motor Vehicles office. Georgia Democrats challenged the law, citing scholarly studies that have found that fraudulent voting due to false identity claims is rare.[7] A federal judge invalidated Georgia's twenty-dollar fee requirement, which the Georgia legislature then eliminated while retaining the photo ID requirement. In 2008, the U.S. Supreme Court

HOW THE 50 STATES DIFFER
POLITICAL THINKING THROUGH COMPARISONS

Voter Turnout in Presidential Elections

The United States has a lower rate of voter turnout than most Western democracies. Within the United States, however, the state-to-state variation is substantial. In a few states, including Minnesota and New Hampshire, nearly seven in ten adults vote in presidential elections. In contrast, there are a few states, including Hawaii and Texas, where barely more than four in ten adults vote in presidential elections.

Q: *Why do states in the South and Southwest have relatively low turnout rates?*

A: *Southern states have more poverty and a tradition of more restrictive registration laws (dating to the Jim Crow era of racial segregation). Both factors are associated with lower voting rates. A large immigrant population is also associated with lower turnout, which helps to account for the lower voting rate in southwestern states.*

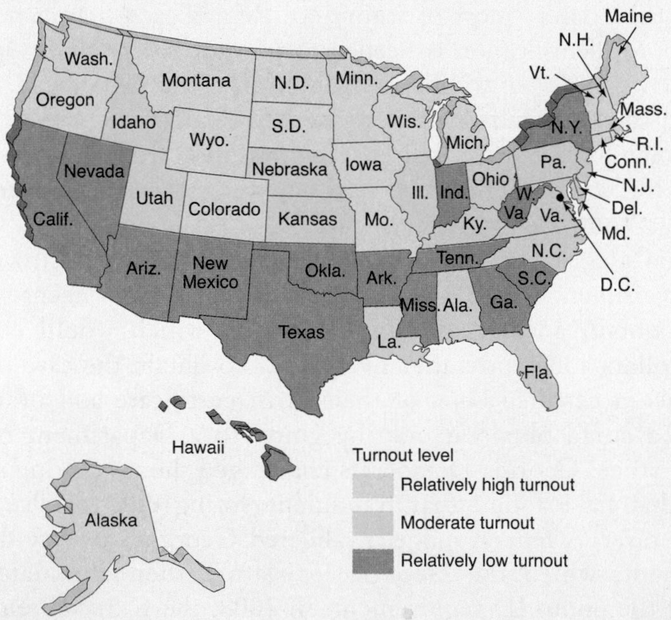

Source: Compiled by author from various sources; based on recent midterm and presidential elections.

ruled on a case involving Indiana's voter identification card law, which is similar to Georgia's. Writing for the Court's 6-3 majority, Justice John Paul Stevens said states have a "valid interest" in improving election procedures and deterring fraud. The Court acknowledged that Indiana Republicans had a partisan motivation in enacting the law but argued that the law "should not be disregarded simply because partisan interests may have provided one motivation for the votes of individual legislators." In a dissenting opinion that focused on Indiana's poorer residents, Justice David Souter said the law "threatens to impose nontrivial burdens on [their] voting rights."[8]

Frequency of Elections Just as America's registration system places a burden on voters, so, too, does its election schedule. The United States holds elections more often than other nations. No other democracy has elections for the lower chamber of its national legislature (the equivalent of the U.S. House of Representatives) as often as every two years, and no democracy schedules elections for chief executive more frequently than every four years.[9] In addition, most state and local elections in the United States are scheduled separately from federal elections. Over three-fourths of the states elect their governors in nonpresidential election years, and most U.S. cities hold elections of municipal officials in odd-numbered years. Finally, the United States uses primary elections to select the party nominees. In other democracies, party leaders pick them.

Americans are asked to vote two to three times as often as Europeans, which increases the likelihood that they will not participate every time.[10] Moreover, elections in the United States have traditionally been scheduled on Tuesday, forcing most adults to find time before or after work to get to the polls. Many European nations hold their elections on Sunday or declare election day a national holiday, making it easier for working people to vote.

Why Some Americans Vote and Others Do Not

Even though turnout is lower in the United States than in other major Western democracies, some Americans vote regularly while others seldom or never vote. Among the explanations for these individual differences are education and income, age, and civic attitudes.

Education and Income College-educated and upper-income Americans have above-average voting rates. They have the financial resources and communication skills that encourage participation and make it personally

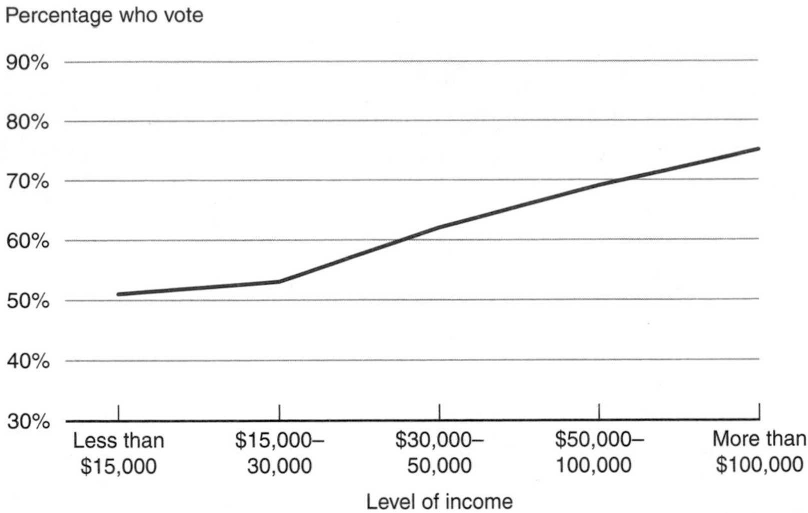

figure 7-2 VOTER TURNOUT AND LEVEL OF INCOME, 2008

Americans of lower income are much less likely to vote than those of higher income. The gap in these voting rates is greater in the United States than in other western democracies. *Source:* U.S. Census Bureau, 2010.

rewarding. Nevertheless, the United States is unusual in the degree to which education and income are related to voter participation. Europeans with less education and income vote at only slightly lower rates than those with more education and income. By comparison, Americans with a college degree or high income are 50 percent more likely to vote in a presidential election than are those who did not finish high school or have a low income (see Figure 7-2).

Why the great difference between the United States and Europe? For one thing, Europeans with less income and education are encouraged to participate by the presence of class-based organizations and appeals—strong socialist or labor parties, politically oriented trade unions, and class-based political ideologies. The United States has never had a major socialist or labor party. Although the Democratic Party represents the working class and the poor to a degree, it is chiefly responsive to middle-class voters, who hold the balance of power in U.S. elections.[11] In addition, Americans with less income and education are the people most adversely affected by the country's registration system. Many of them do not own cars or homes and are thus less likely to be registered in advance of an election. They are also less familiar with registration locations and requirements.[12]

POLITICAL THINKING

Does America's Two-Party System Depress Turnout?

Most European democracies have three or more significant political parties that are shaped around class and social divisions, and sometimes along religious and ethnic divisions as well. Labor and socialist parties abound in Europe, as do middle-class, environmental, and right-wing parties. Accordingly, Europeans voters have a broad range of choices, which some analysts cite as a reason why voter turnout in Europe is higher than in the United States, where voters basically have only two choices, the Republican and Democratic parties. What significance do you attach to the difference in the European and American party systems? Would you be more inclined to vote if you had more choices? What type of alternative party—religious, environmental, labor, or whatever—might be particularly attractive to you?

Age Young adults are substantially less likely than middle-aged and older citizens to vote. Even senior citizens, despite the infirmities of old age, have a far higher turnout rate than do voters under the age of thirty. The difference is greater in local and state elections than in presidential elections. Only a small percentage of young adults vote regularly in local elections.

In the 2004 presidential election, and again in the 2008 election, turnout among younger voters increased substantially from that of previous recent presidential elections. Underlying this increase was the Iraq war, which mobilized college-educated young adults especially. Most of them opposed the way the Bush administration was conducting the war, and they participated in unusually high numbers. Nevertheless, the voting rate of young adults was still below that of older adults, who are more likely to live in the same residence from one election to the next and thus do not need to reregister in order to vote. Older voters are also more likely to own their homes and to have children, which heightens their sense of having a stake in election outcomes.

Civic Attitudes **Apathy**—a lack of interest in politics—typifies some citizens. They rarely if ever vote. Just as some people would not attend the Super Bowl even if it was free and being played across the street, some Americans would not bother to vote even if a ballot were delivered to their

Susan B. Anthony is nearly synonymous with women's right to vote. Her first crusade was with the temperance movement, which sought to ban the sale of alcohol because of the hardship alcoholism imposed on women and children. She next joined the antislavery movement. After the Civil War, Anthony teamed up with fellow activist Elizabeth Cady Stanton to demand equal pay and voting rights for women. She was twice arrested for trying to vote in her hometown of Rochester, New York. She died a decade before women gained the right to vote in the United States, but her contribution to the cause of women's suffrage was unmatched.

door. Still other Americans refrain from voting because of **alienation**—a feeling of powerlessness rooted in the belief that government pays no attention to their interests. Many of these citizens regard voting as a waste of time, convinced that government won't respond to their concerns even if they do vote.

In contrast, some Americans have a keen sense of **civic duty**—a belief that they ought to participate in public affairs. Citizens who hold this belief tend to vote more regularly. The recent increase in the turnout rate of younger adults is partly attributable to their growing sense that voting is a civic duty. In the past two decades, the percentage of young adults who think "it's my duty as a citizen always to vote" has nearly doubled.

Civic duty and apathy are attitudes that are usually acquired from one's parents. When parents vote regularly and take an active interest in politics, their children usually grow up thinking they have a duty to participate. When parents never vote and show no interest in public affairs, their children are likely to be politically apathetic. Alienation can be traced to childhood socialization but often has adult roots. For example, when the Democratic Party took the lead on civil rights issues in the 1960s, some working-class white Democrats felt left out, believing that gains for African Americans would come at their expense. Some of these Democrats switched parties, but a larger number simply stopped voting. Voter turnout among working-class whites dropped sharply in 1968 and in 1972—two presidential elections in which civil rights issues were paramount.[13]

Conventional Forms of Participation Other than Voting

No form of political participation is as widespread as voting. Nevertheless, voting is a restricted form of participation. Citizens have the opportunity to vote only at a particular time and only on the choices listed on the ballot. Fuller opportunities for participation exist, including contributing time and money to political and civic causes.

Campaign and Lobbying Activities

Compared with voting, working for a candidate is more time consuming. Not surprisingly, only a small percentage of citizens engage in such activities. Nevertheless, the number is substantially higher in the United States than in Europe (see Figure 7-3). One reason Americans are more active in campaigns, even though they vote less, is that the United States is a

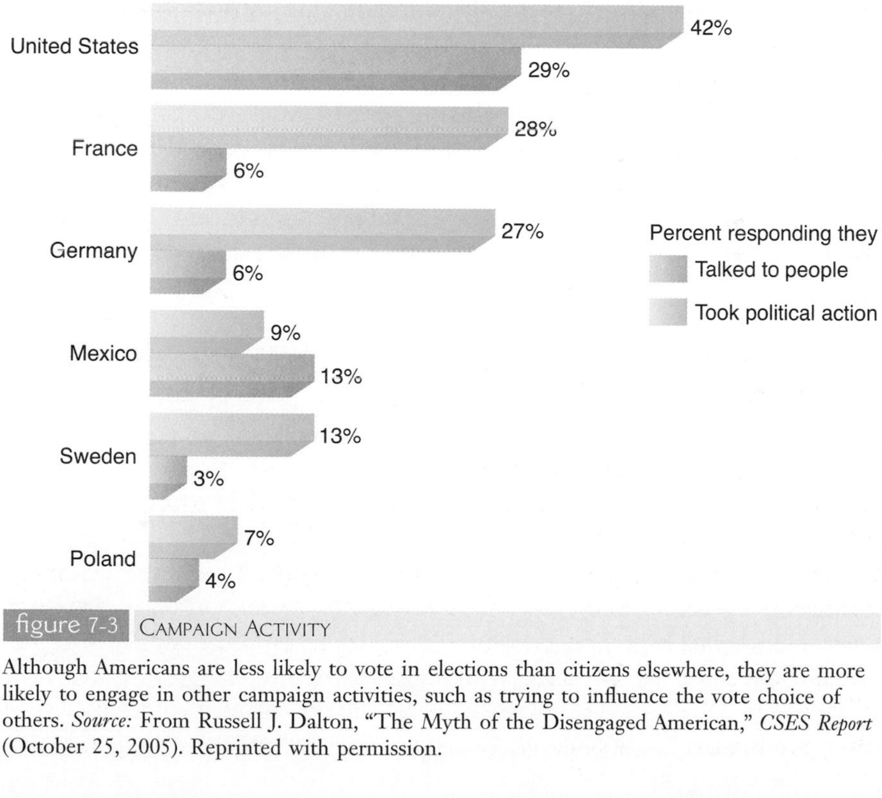

figure 7-3 CAMPAIGN ACTIVITY

Although Americans are less likely to vote in elections than citizens elsewhere, they are more likely to engage in other campaign activities, such as trying to influence the vote choice of others. *Source:* From Russell J. Dalton, "The Myth of the Disengaged American," *CSES Report* (October 25, 2005). Reprinted with permission.

federal system with campaigns for national, state, and local offices. A citizen who wants to participate can easily find an opportunity at one level of office or another. Most of the European governments are unitary in form (see Chapter 3), which means that there are fewer elective offices and thus fewer campaigns. (Election campaigns are discussed further in Chapter 8.)

Americans are also more likely than citizens elsewhere to support the activities of political groups. This support usually takes the form of a monetary contribution but also includes more active forms, such as contacting lawmakers or attending public rallies. Greenpeace, Common Cause, AARP (formerly known as the American Association of Retired Persons), the Christian Coalition of America, and the National Conservative Political Action Committee are among the many groups that depend on citizen activism. (Lobbying groups are discussed further in Chapter 9.)

Virtual Participation

The introduction of the World Wide Web in the 1990s opened up an entirely new venue for political participation—the Internet. Through e-mails, chat rooms, social networks, and the like, the Internet has created participation possibilities previously unimaginable. Although this participation is "virtual" rather than face-to-face, much of it involves contact with friends, acquaintances, and activists.

Internet participation peaks during presidential campaigns, during which virtual participation now far outweighs conventional participation (see Table 7-1). During the 2008 campaign, millions of Americans sent e-mails and text messages to family members, friends, and others in an attempt to promote their candidates. Internet fundraising also flourished.

table 7-1 Online Campaign Activities

Substantial numbers of Americans engaged in campaign-related activity online during the 2008 presidential campaign. Young adults had the highest engagement level.

Years of Age	**18–29**	**30–49**	**50–64**	**65+**
Engaged politically in a social networking site	35%	14%	4%	1
Posted original content related to campaign	29	14	9	2

Source: Pew Research Center for the People and the Press (2008). Reprinted with permission.

Roughly five million Americans contributed money through the Internet, usually in the amount of $100 or less.[14]

Political campaigns are not the only example of Internet-based citizen mobilization. Several groups have built extensive online organizations. MoveOn.org, for example, has a network of more than two million "online activists." When MoveOn's leaders make a concerted appeal—whether on behalf of a candidate, a cause, or a bill before Congress—it gets a swift response from the network. MoveOn was instrumental, for example, in helping Barack Obama defeat Hillary Clinton in their race for the 2008 Democratic presidential nomination. MoveOn's effort to shape the 2010 health care reform bill was less successful. MoveOn conducted a strenuous but failed lobbying campaign to convince Congress to adopt the so-called public option, which would have allowed the federal government to compete directly with private companies in providing health insurance.

The democratizing effect of the Web has been noted widely and, as Internet use and technology continue to advance, an era of unprecedented citizen involvement and influence could result.[15] Social networking is proving to be a powerful grassroots organizing force even in nondemocratic societies. Iranian citizens, for example, took to the streets in 2009 to protest their country's rigged presidential election, coordinating their actions through Twitter, Facebook, and other networking tools.

The outlook for Web-based politics is not entirely positive, however. Evidence is mounting that the Internet is contributing to political polarization. When citizens use the Internet for political purposes, most of them have a preference for sites and networks where they encounter people who think like they do. This tendency reinforces and intensifies their opinions; it also contributes to a belief that other opinions lack merit.[16] Interaction with like-minded people contributes to higher participation rates but can also lead to uncompromising views on political issues.[17] (The Internet is discussed further in Chapter 10.)

Community Activities

Political participation extends beyond campaigns and elections to involvement in the community. Citizens can join community groups, work to accomplish community goals, and let officials know their opinions on community matters. These forms of participation offer citizens a substantial degree of control over the timing and extent of their participation. The chief obstacle to participation is not opportunities, which are abundant, but the motivation to join in. Most people choose not to get involved, particularly when it comes to time-consuming activities.

Nevertheless, many Americans are involved in community affairs through local organizations such as parent-teacher associations, neighborhood groups, business clubs, church-affiliated groups, and hospital auxiliaries. The actual number of such participants is difficult to estimate, but it is surely in the tens of millions, reflecting in part a tradition of local participation that dates to colonial times. Moreover, compared with cities and towns in Europe, those in the United States have greater authority over local policies, giving their residents a motive to participate actively. Because of increased mobility and other factors, Americans may be less tied to their local communities than in the past and therefore less involved in community activity. Nevertheless, Americans are more than twice as likely as Europeans to work together in groups on issues of community concern.[18]

In a widely discussed book titled *Bowling Alone*, Harvard's Robert Putnam claims that America has been undergoing a long-term decline in its **social capital** (the sum of the face-to-face civic interactions among citizens in a society).[19] Putnam attributes the decline to television and other factors that pull people away from involvement in civic and political groups. Some scholars dispute Putnam's claim, but it appears to be true of older citizens. On the other hand, community participation among young adults has risen in the past two decades, partly because of high school and college internship programs.[20] According to a University of Maryland study, volunteering among young people has increased by roughly 20 percent since 1990.[21]

Unconventional Activism: Social Movements and Protest Politics

During the pre-democratic era, people resorted to protest as a way of expressing displeasure with their rulers. Tax and food riots were the typical forms of protest. When democratic governments came into existence, citizens had a regular and less disruptive way to express themselves—through their votes. Voting is double-edged, however. Although the vote gives citizens a degree of control over government, *the vote also gives government control over citizens.*[22] Elected officials can claim that their policies reflect the will of the electorate and therefore must be respected and obeyed.

Social movements, or **political movements** as they are sometimes called, are a way for citizens disenchanted with government to actively express their opposition.[23] These efforts are channeled through conventional forms of participation, such as political lobbying, but citizens sometimes take to the streets in protest against government. In 2003, for

HOW THE 50 STATES DIFFER
POLITICAL THINKING THROUGH COMPARISONS

Volunteer Activity

Volunteer work in the community is an American tradition and occurs through a variety of groups. At the top of the list are church groups, followed by education groups such as parent-teacher associations. Many Americans also get involved in their communities through social service, health, and civic groups. The volunteer rate varies considerably by state, however, as indicated by a recent study by the Corporation for National and Community Service, the government corporation that manages federally funded service programs such as AmeriCorps. Utah has the highest volunteer rate; 44 percent of its residents sixteen years of age or older are engaged yearly in community volunteer work of one

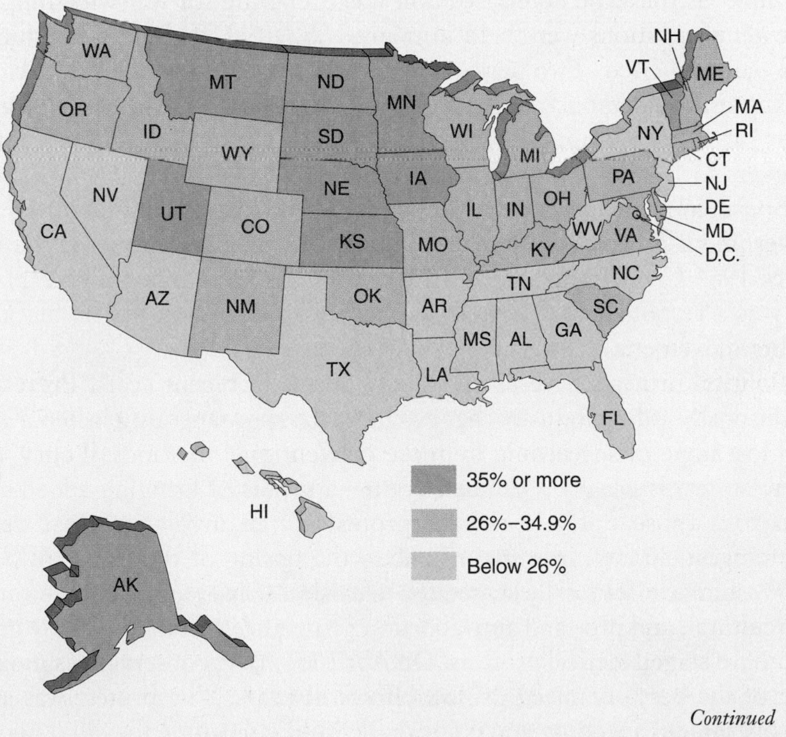

Continued

type or another. Nebraska (39 percent), Minnesota and Alaska (each at 38 percent), and Iowa (37 percent) are the other states in the top five.

Q: *Why does the Upper Midwest region (which includes Iowa, Minnesota, Nebraska, and the Dakotas) have the highest volunteer rate?*

A: *Political scientist Daniel Elazar found that states in the Upper Midwest have a strong community orientation, reflecting the values of the Scandinavians and others who settled in the region. In addition to their more active community life, states in the regions spend more heavily on community-centered policies, such as the public schools, than do most other states. Utah's high participation rate stems from a different tradition. A majority of its population is Mormon, a religious faith that emphasizes the individual's community responsibilities.*

Source: Corporation for National and Community Service, 2010

example, as the Bush administration was preparing for war with Iraq, protest demonstrations were held in many U.S. cities, including Washington and San Francisco. Two percent of adult Americans said they participated in an antiwar demonstration. Many of them were young adults. Participants in social movements are younger on average than nonparticipants, a reversal of the pattern for voting.[24]

Social movements do not always succeed, but they sometimes force government into action. For example, the timing and scope of the landmark 1964 Civil Rights Act and 1965 Voting Rights Act can be explained only as a response by Congress to the pressure created by the black civil rights movement.

Political protests have taken on new forms in recent years. Protest was traditionally a desperate act that began, often spontaneously, when a group had lost hope of succeeding by more conventional methods. Today, however, protest is usually a planned event—a means of bringing added attention to a cause.[25] These tactical protests often involve a great deal of planning, including, in some instances, the busing of thousands of people to Washington for a rally staged for television. Civil rights, environmental, agricultural, and pro- and anti-abortion groups are among the many groups that have staged tactical protests. On April 15, 2009, conservatives mounted one of the best organized protest efforts in years. The protest was aimed at government spending and coincided with the deadline for filing personal income taxes. The protests were labeled as "Tea Parties," a name derived

When Congress in 2006 seemed on the verge of enacting legislation that would crack down on illegal immigrants, most of whom are from Mexico, protest rallies were held in nearly every American city with a sizable Hispanic population. The rally in Los Angeles was the largest in the city's history. The scene here is of the rally in Lincoln, Nebraska, where the flags of the United States and Mexico were readily visible.

from the legendary Boston Tea Party. Several hundred thousand citizens participated in the Tea Parties, which were held in hundreds of cities and towns throughout the country. In Washington, D.C., the protesters hurled tea bags over the White House fence. Within the next year, the Tea Party movement had blossomed into a major force in American politics.

Protest politics has a long history in America. Indeed, the United States was founded on a protest movement that sparked a revolution against Britain. Despite this tradition, protest activity is less common today in the United States than in many Western democracies (see Figure 7-4). Spain, France, Germany, Sweden, and Mexico are among the countries that have higher rates of protest participation.

Public support for protest activity is also relatively low in the United States. The Vietnam War protests, which in some cases were accompanied by the burning of draft cards and the American flag, had only marginal public support. When unarmed student protesters at Kent State University and Jackson State University were shot to death in May 1970 by members of the National Guard, most Americans polls faulted the students. In a *Newsweek* poll, 58 percent of respondents blamed the Kent State killings on

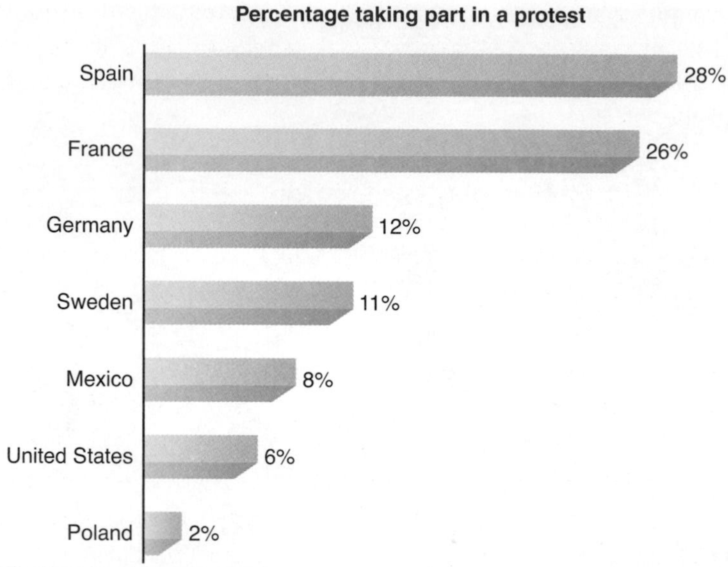

figure 7-4 PROTEST ACTIVITY

Despite the significance of protest activity in U.S. history, Americans are less likely to protest than are citizens of many other democracies. *Source:* From Russell J. Dalton, "The Myth of the Disengaged American," *CSES Report* (October 25, 2005). Reprinted with permission.

the student demonstrators, while only 11 percent said the guardsmen were at fault. The general public was more accepting of the Iraq war protest in 2003. Even after the fighting had begun, three in every five Americans said they saw the protests as "a sign of a healthy democracy." Still, almost two in five respondents felt that "opponents of the war should not hold antiwar demonstrations" and half of these respondents said that antiwar demonstrations should be outlawed. On the other hand, protesters are rarely assaulted by those who disagree with them, and most Americans recognize that protest is part of America's tradition of free expression. In that sense, protest is seen as something to be tolerated, if not widely admired.

Participation and the Potential for Influence

Most Americans are not highly active in politics. The emphasis that the American culture places on individualism is a reason. Most Americans under most conditions expect to solve their problems on their own rather than through political action. "In the United States, the country of individualism *par excellence*," William Watts and Lloyd Free write, "there is a sharp distinction in people's minds between their own personal lives and national life."[26]

POLITICAL THINKING

Is the Country Better Off?

Some writers claim that the country is better off if less interested and less knowledgeable citizens—most of whom are near the bottom of the economic ladder—stay home on election day. In a cover story in the December 1997 issue of The Atlantic Monthly, *Robert Kaplan wrote, "The last thing America needs is more voters—particularly badly educated and alienated ones." On the other hand, every citizen has the right to vote, and studies show that elected officials are truly responsive only to those who do go to the polls, which works to the disadvantage of the poor and less-well-educated. Where do you stand on the question of whether the country would be better off or worse off if nearly everyone voted?*

Paradoxically, given their greater need for government help, lower-income Americans are the least likely to vote or to otherwise engage in collective action. They lack the financial resources and communication skills that encourage participation in politics and make it personally rewarding.[27] As a consequence, their political influence is relatively limited. In *Unequal Democracy*, political scientist Larry Bartels demonstrates that elected officials are substantially more responsive to the concerns of their more affluent constituents than to those of their poorer constituents.[28] In other words, the pattern of individual political participation in the United States parallels the distribution of influence that prevails in the private sector. Those who have the most power in the marketplace also have the most power in the political arena. However, the issue of individual participation is only one piece of the larger puzzle of how power in America is distributed. Subsequent chapters will furnish additional pieces.

SUMMARY

Self-Test www.mhhe.com/pattersonwtp9e

Political participation is involvement in activities designed to influence public policy and leadership. A main issue of democratic government is the question of who participates in politics and how fully they participate.

Voting is the most widespread form of active political participation among Americans. Yet voter turnout is significantly lower in the United States than in other democratic nations. The requirement that Americans must personally register in order to establish their eligibility to vote is one reason for lower turnout among Americans; other democracies place the burden of registration on government officials rather than on individual citizens. The fact that the United States holds frequent elections also discourages some citizens from voting regularly.

Only a minority of citizens engage in the more demanding forms of political activity, such as work on community affairs or on behalf of a candidate during a political campaign. Nevertheless, the proportion of Americans who engage in these more demanding forms of activity exceeds the proportion of Europeans who do so. Most political activists are individuals of higher income and education; they have the skills and material resources to participate effectively and tend to take a greater interest in politics. More than in any other Western democracy, political participation in the United States is related to economic status.

Social movements are broad efforts to achieve change by citizens who feel that government is not properly responsive to their interests. These efforts sometimes take place outside established channels; demonstrations, picket lines, and marches are common means of protest. Protesters are younger and more idealistic on average than are other citizens, but they are a small proportion of the population. Despite America's tradition of free expression, protest activities do not have a high level of public support.

Overall, Americans are only moderately involved in politics. Although they are concerned with political affairs, they are mostly immersed in their private pursuits, a reflection in part of a cultural belief in individualism. The lower level of participation among low-income citizens has particular significance in that it works to reduce their influence on public policy and leadership.

Key Terms

alienation (*p. 234*)
apathy (*p. 233*)
civic duty (*p. 234*)
political participation (*p. 223*)
registration (*p. 228*)
social capital (*p. 238*)
social (political) movements (*p. 238*)
suffrage (*p. 224*)
voter turnout (*p. 226*)

Suggested Readings

Bartels, Larry. *Unequal Democracy*. Princeton, N.J.: Princeton University Press, 2008. An analysis that shows just how fully lower-income Americans are neglected by policymakers because of their low participation rates.

Burns, Nancy, Kay Lehman Schlozman, and Sidney Verba. *The Private Roots of Public Action: Gender, Equality, and Public Action*. Cambridge, MA.: Harvard University Press, 2001. An analysis of gender differences in political participation.

Dalton, Russell J. *The Good Citizen: How a Younger Generation Is Reshaping American Politics*, rev. ed. Washington, D.C.: CQ Press, 2008. A study of the recent increase in young people's civic and political participation.

Franklin, Mark N. *Voter Turnout and the Dynamics of Electoral Competition in Established Democracies since 1945*. New York: Cambridge University Press, 2004. A comparison of voter participation and its correlates in advanced democracies.

Leighley, Jan. *Strength in Numbers: The Political Mobilization of Racial and Ethnic Minorities*. Princeton, N.J.: Princeton University Press, 2001. A study of the factors that motivate blacks and Hispanics to participate.

Patterson, Thomas E. *The Vanishing Voter*. New York: Knopf, 2002. A study of the trends in electoral participation and what might be done to encourage higher participation levels.

Putnam, Robert. *Bowling Alone*. New York: Simon & Schuster, 2000. A provocative analysis of the trend in civic participation.

Sunstein, Cass R. *Going to Extremes: How Like Minds Unite and Divide*. New York: Oxford University Press, 2009. A study of the effect of social interaction, including Internet networking, on how people position themselves politically.

Zukin, Cliff, Scott Keeter, Molly Andolina, Krista Jenkins, and Michael X. Delli Carpini. *A New Engagement: Political Participation, Civic Life, and the Changing American Citizen*. New York: Oxford University Press, 2006. A comprehensive study concluding that young adults are finding ways other than election politics to exercise citizenship.

List of Websites

www.rockthevote.org The website of Rock the Vote, an organization dedicated to helping young people realize and utilize their power to affect the civic and political life of their communities.

www.electionstudies.org The University of Michigan's American National Election Studies site; provides survey data on voting, public opinion, and political participation.

www.civicyouth.org The website of a Tufts University institute dedicated to the study of young adults' civic engagement.

www.votesmart.org The website of Project Vote Smart; includes information on Republican and Democratic candidates and officials, as well as the latest in election news.

Politics in Theory and Practice

Thinking: Why does economic class—differences in people's incomes—make such a large difference in political participation levels? What are the policy consequences of this difference?

Participating: If you are not currently registered to vote, consider registering. You can obtain a registration form from the election board or clerk in your community of residence. There are several websites that contain state-by-state registration information. One such site is https://electionimpact.votenet.com/-declareyourself/voterreg. If you are already registered, consider participating in a registration or voting drive on your campus. Although students typically register and vote at relatively low rates, they will often participate if encouraged by other students to do so.

Extra Credit

For up-to-the-minute *New York Times* articles, interactive simulations, graphics, study tools, and more links and quizzes, visit the text's Online Learning Center at **www.mhhe.com/pattersonwtp9e**.

NATIONAL JOURNAL

Obama and Liberals: Can This Marriage Be Saved?

Long before Barack Obama became president, he expressed frustration with the partisan fireworks causing gridlock in Washington. As a youthful first-term senator, Obama seemed especially unhappy that his own party's internal warfare between ideological blocs on the left and in the center was preventing efforts to address big issues.

His governing style, Obama said in an interview with National Journal in 2006 just after his first year in the Senate, was all about looking for common ground to achieve progress rather than clinging inflexibly to a position. "My approach has been to try to be constant in terms of the values I care about . . . and then be as pragmatic in figuring out how to deliver on those goals as possible," he said.

True to his word, Obama in his first 20 months in the White House has been cutting legislative deals to win passage of big bills, from landmark health care reform to a sweeping overhaul of financial laws.

But the president's success in forging compromises may sting Democrats on the ballot. His style leaves the liberal activists in the Democratic Party cold. Outspoken liberals prefer a pugilist fighting for principle over a pragmatist agreeing to compromise.

These critics on the left have argued for months that Obama should have driven harder bargains. They say that he should have fought more for a public option in the health care reform package; rolled back more of the "excesses" on Wall Street in the financial reform legislation; and pushed for a bigger economic stimulus than the $787 billion package that he signed.

This dispiritedness poses a big question for the White House. Can the president reignite the enthusiasm of his party's core supporters so that they not only continue to vote Democrat but also take on the nitty-gritty grassroots work that campaigns need? Without the strong participation of these hard-chargers, the election results may be devastating for Obama.

"There is this relationship that people have to their political leadership, which is, they are willing to work hard for somebody who is perceived to be working very hard for them," said David Sirota, a liberal commentator and blogger. "Obama has not given the Democratic Party base a lot of things to point to as absolutely clear progressive policies."

Sirota, a former congressional aide who is now a party strategist and the host of a Denver-based radio show, frames the problem in stark language. "Either you are the guy who thinks we need real change immediately and in a fundamental way, and you are going to be the crusader for that and you are going to really use all the tools of the White House to move votes in the Congress for that agenda—or you are not. There is this problem when you are tacking back and forth. One day you are the crusader and the next day you are the guy who doesn't want to involve himself at all in legislative negotiations."

Presidential historian Richard Norton Smith faults the country's political dynamics for Obama's dilemma. "Obama is too rational for the current political climate. I mean, he's Woodrow Wilson and everyone else is Joe McCarthy."

When asked what the president might do to energize Democratic activists in time to make a difference in the midterm elections, more than a dozen strategists, academics, and pundits gave answers that covered the map. The only area of consensus was that Obama's efforts on the campaign trail to blame former President Bush for the country's economic woes and to urge voters not to "go back" to the days of Republican rule may not be enough to rally the Democratic troops.

"It is almost like he is reaching for another story [line]. It seems a little desperate," said Jeff Faux, who in 1986 founded the Economic Policy Institute, a liberal think tank. "For him to be blaming Bush would ring a lot truer than it does now, when it has a feeling of desperation, if he had been explaining to the public over the last two years. That would have built up credibility. What stopped him was Republican opposition and—this is where I think he blew it—his unwillingness to take them on early in the game. Taking them on with two and a half months to go before Election Day makes the whole thing just politics to most people."

Sirota agreed. "Look at the history of Ronald Reagan, who continued his campaign against Jimmy Carter for two and a half or three years after he got into office. Obama, right when he got in, basically just stopped talking about George Bush for a really long time. That was a tactical mistake, and I think, frankly, it was a substantive mistake. The idea that now, 20 months later, [the Democrats] will come back after effectively letting Bush off the hook seems to people kind of craven."

Faux doesn't see many good options at this late date. "It is 'Hail Mary pass' time," he said. "The only thing you can do is go after the Republicans, chapter and verse; drag out what [GOP Senate Leader Mitch] McConnell and those guys have been doing. Attack the obstructionism. Ridicule them for having held up unemployment compensation."

The sniping from liberal groups and commentators has created such heartburn in the White House that press secretary Robert Gibbs recently blasted "the professional Left" who, he told the newspaper The Hill, would not be happy even if liberal Rep. Dennis Kucinich of Ohio were president. Critics who contend that Obama is no different from Bush "ought to be drug-tested," Gibbs said.

The day that the Gibbs interview appeared, August 10, the president said at a fundraiser in Dallas, "I'll be honest with you. Sometimes, Democrats, we're our own worst enemies, because we can do great stuff and somehow still feel depressed. . . . Sometimes we do a little too much hand-wringing. Say, well, you know . . . I wish we had gotten that public option. Well, that's great, but we got 31 million people health insurance and we're reducing costs."

Frustrated or not, Obama has clearly hewed to that theme as he crisscrosses the country. Much of the president's message contrasts his policies with Bush's. He blames his predecessor and GOP lawmakers for driving the country into the ditch. "What they're counting on in this election is amnesia," Obama told the donors in Dallas. "They're counting on you not remembering the disastrous consequences of economic policies that, by the way, had caused problems for working-class families, for middle-class families, before the recession hit, before the crisis hit."

Howard Dean, former chairman of the Democratic National Committee, echoes the president's pitch. Sure, he concedes, Obama should have pushed a far more aggressive agenda on health care and other issues. But this is no time for activists to sit on the sidelines.

"Of course, the president could have done more and he should have done more," Dean said in an interview. "What I would say to my friends in the Democratic wing of the Democratic Party is, we never thought it would be easy. Just because you elect the guy you want doesn't mean you can stop working. Our job is to continue to hold their feet to the fire and get them to deliver on what they said they'd deliver on. But you don't get there by saying he's no different than Bush. He's obviously a great deal different than Bush."

Dean emphasized, however, that the onus is on Obama to reassure the faithful that his administration will not forgo "Democratic principles" to get to a Rose Garden signing ceremony. "He is going to have to be a fighter," Dean said. "If he isn't, you are not going to reinspire those who are disappointed. I am not pretending there weren't any huge mistakes. I have been pretty blunt. I said, if you come in as a reformer and your entire staff is insiders, it is not likely you are going to do much reforming.

"But that was then and this is now. Now we are in a fight to see who is going to control the country. We know what direction the Republicans are going to take us in—that is not acceptable."

Obama's strong advantage—better than 2-to-1—among Latino voters two years ago was a key to his victory over GOP nominee John McCain. After African-Americans, Hispanics were the group most likely to back the Democratic contender, support that was pivotal in his victories in Nevada and New Mexico, and very important in his wins in Pennsylvania and Virginia.

Yet since the beginning of this year, Latinos' attitudes toward the president have soured markedly. His favorability rating among Hispanics plunged 10 points between January and June, according to Gallup.

Obama's failure to make immigration reform the priority that he had promised during the campaign is mostly to blame, and fallout from the bleak economy has also hurt the president's support. The jobless rate for Hispanics jumped from 9.7 percent when Obama took office to 13 percent last October.

"Obama came in, and [Hispanics] fell in love with him," said Frank Sharry, founder and executive director of America's Voice, which supports immigration reform. "They saw themselves in him—a guy of color from an immigrant background who made good and spoke eloquently to their concerns and fears—not only about the economy but also about immigration.

"Like a lot of white progressives, they fell in love and are deeply disappointed," Sharry contended. "The economy is not getting better for them, and on immigration, a defining issue in which they see their very existence under threat, he has done precious little to deliver on his promises."

What's Your Opinion?

Based on the 2010 midterm election results, how do you rate President Obama as a party leader? What more could he do to hold Democrats together and assure the best possible results at the polls?

CHAPTER 8

Political Parties, Candidates, and Campaigns: Defining the Voter's Choice

> "Political parties created democracy and . . . modern democracy is unthinkable save in terms of the parties."
>
> E. E. Schattschneider[1]

Nine hundred miles and a week apart, they faced off, each offering its own plan for a better America.

The Democrats met first, in Denver, Colorado. Their 2008 platform included pledges to draw down U.S. forces in Iraq, bring health coverage to millions of uninsured Americans, combat global warming, and create more jobs and higher wages for working families. The Democrats chose Illinois senator Barack Obama, the first African American ever to be chosen for the position, as their presidential nominee. Their vice presidential nominee was Joe Biden, senator from Delaware.

The Republicans met in Minnesota's capital city, St. Paul. They selected Arizona senator John McCain as their presidential nominee and Sarah Palin, the governor of Alaska, as his running mate. The Republican platform included promises to keep taxes low, limit abortions, expand parental school choice, stimulate the business sector, and provide Iraq with a level of U.S. military support that would ensure its stability.

The political parties, as their 2008 presidential nominees and platforms illustrate, are in the business of offering the voting public a choice. A **political party** is an ongoing coalition of interests joined together in an effort to get its candidates for public office elected under a common label.[2] By offering a choice between policies and leaders, parties give voters a chance to influence the direction of government. "It is the competition of [parties] that provides the people with an opportunity to make a choice," political scientist E. E. Schattschneider wrote. "Without this opportunity popular sovereignty amounts to nothing."[3]

This chapter examines political parties and the candidates who run under their banners. U.S. campaigns are **party centered** in the sense that the Republican and Democratic parties compete across the country election after election. Yet campaigns are also **candidate centered** in the sense that individual candidates devise their own strategies, choose their own issues, and form their own campaign organizations. The following points are emphasized in this chapter:

- *Political competition in the United States has centered on two parties, a pattern that is explained by the nature of America's electoral system, political institutions, and political culture.* Minor parties exist in the United States but have been unable to compete successfully for governing power.
- *To win an electoral majority, candidates of the two major parties must appeal to a diverse set of interests.* This necessity has typically led them to advocate moderate and somewhat overlapping policies, although this tendency has weakened in recent years.
- *U.S. party organizations are decentralized and fragmented.* The national organization is a loose collection of state organizations, which in turn are loose associations of local organizations. This feature of U.S. parties can be traced to federalism and the nation's diversity, which have made it difficult for the parties to act as instruments of national power.
- *The ability of America's party organizations to control nominations and election to office is weak, which strengthens the candidates' role.*

- *Candidate-centered campaigns are based on money and media and utilize the skills of professional consultants.*

Party Competition and Majority Rule: The History of U.S. Parties

Through their numbers, citizens can exert influence, but it cannot be realized unless they act together. Parties give them that capacity. Parties are **linkage institutions**; they serve to connect citizens with government. When Americans go to the polls, they have a choice between candidates representing the Republican and Democratic parties. This **party competition** narrows voters' options to two and in the process enables people with different backgrounds and opinions to act together. In casting a majority of its votes for one party, the electorate chooses that party's candidates, philosophy, and policies over those of the opposing party.

The history of democratic government is synonymous with the history of parties. When the countries of Eastern Europe gained their freedom from the Soviet Union in the early 1990s, one of their first steps toward democracy was the legalization of parties. When the United States was founded over two centuries ago, the formation of parties was also a first step toward building its democracy. The reason is simple: it is the competition among parties that gives popular majorities a choice over how they will be governed.[4] If there were no mechanism like the party to enable citizens to act as one, they would be powerless—each too weak to influence government.

The First Parties

Many of America's early leaders mistrusted parties. George Washington in his farewell address warned the nation of the "baneful effects" of parties, and James Madison likened parties to special interests. However, Madison's misgivings about parties slowly gave way to grudging admiration as he came to realize that parties were a means of collective action.

America's first parties originated in the rivalry between Alexander Hamilton and Thomas Jefferson, who opposed Hamilton's attempts to strengthen the federal government through national commerce. To advance his goal, Hamilton organized his followers into the Federalist Party, taking the name from the faction that had spearheaded the ratification of the Constitution (see Figure 8-1). Jefferson responded by creating the Democratic-Republican Party. The name harkened to the spirit

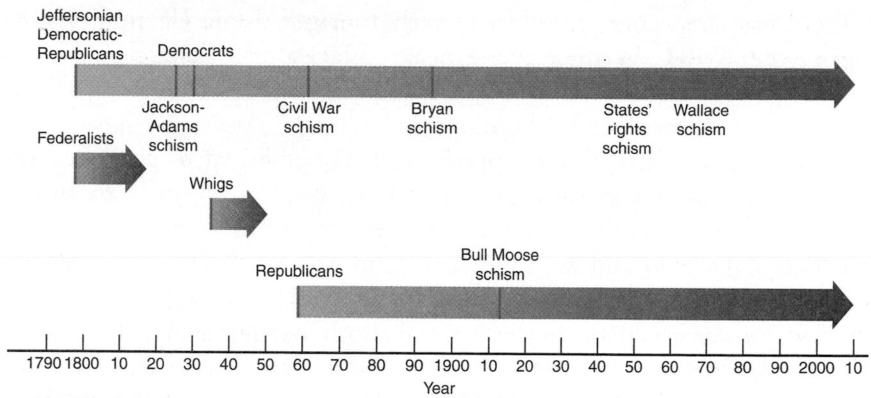

figure 8-1 A GRAPHIC HISTORY OF AMERICA'S MAJOR PARTIES

The U.S. party system has been remarkable for its continuity. Competition between two major parties has been a persistent feature of the system.

behind the Declaration of Independence and reflected the party's strength among small farmers and states' rights advocates. The Federalists' preoccupation with commercial and moneyed interests fueled Jefferson's claim that they were bent on establishing a government of the rich and wellborn. After Jefferson in the election of 1800 defeated John Adams, who had succeeded Washington as president, the Federalists never again controlled the White House or Congress.

During the so-called Era of Good Feeling, when James Monroe ran unopposed in 1820 for a second presidential term, it appeared as if the political system might operate without competing parties. Yet by the end of Monroe's second term, policy differences had split the Democratic-Republicans. The dominant faction, under the leadership of Andrew Jackson, embraced Jefferson's commitment to the common people and adopted the label "Democrats." Thus, the party of Jefferson is the forerunner of today's Democratic Party rather than of today's Republican Party.

Andrew Jackson and Grassroots Parties

Jackson's goal was to wrest political power from the established elite—the previous presidents had all come from old-line Virginia and Massachusetts families. Jackson saw a reorganized Democratic Party as the vehicle for change. Whereas Jefferson's party had operated largely at the leadership level, Jackson sought a **grassroots party**. As such, it was organized chiefly at the local level and was open to all citizens. The efforts of the local party organizations, along with the extension of voting rights to citizens without property, contributed to a nearly fourfold rise in election turnout during the 1830s.[5] Writing at the peak of Jacksonian democracy, Alexis de Tocqueville claimed that, "The People reign in the American political world as the Deity does in the universe."[6]

During this period, a new opposition party emerged to challenge the Democrats. The Whigs were a catchall party whose followers were united less by a coherent philosophy than by their opposition for one reason or another to Jackson and his followers. Competition between the Whigs and the Democrats was relatively short-lived, however. During the 1850s, the slavery issue began to tear both parties apart. The Whig Party disintegrated, and a northern-based new party, calling itself Republican, emerged as the Democrats' main challenger. In the 1860 presidential election, the Democratic Party's northern faction nominated Stephen A. Douglas, who held that the question of whether slavery would be allowed in a new state was for its voters to decide, while the southern faction nominated John C. Breckinridge, who called for legalized slavery in all states. The Democratic vote split sharply along regional lines between these two candidates—with the result that the Republican nominee, Abraham Lincoln, who had called for the gradual elimination of slavery, was able to win the presidency with only 40 percent of the popular vote. Lincoln's election prompted the southern states to secede from the Union.

The Civil War was the first and only time in the nation's history that the party system failed to peacefully settle Americans' political differences. The issue of slavery was simply too explosive to be settled through electoral competition.[7]

Republicans versus Democrats: Realignments and the Enduring Party System

After the Civil War, the nation settled into the pattern of competition between the Republican and Democratic parties that has lasted until today. The durability of the two parties is due not to their ideological consistency but to their remarkable ability to adapt during periods of crisis. By abandoning at these crucial times their old ways of doing things, the Republican and Democratic parties have reorganized themselves—with new bases of support, new policies, and new public philosophies.

These periods of extraordinary party change are known as *realignments*. A **party realignment** involves four basic elements:

1. The disruption of the existing political order because of the emergence of an unusually powerful and divisive issue.

2. An election contest in which the voters shift their support strongly toward one party
3. A major change in policy brought about by the newly dominant party
4. An enduring change in the party coalitions, which works to the lasting advantage of the newly dominant party

Realignments are rare. They do not occur simply because one party wrests control of government from the other in a single election. They involve deep and lasting change in the party system that affects subsequent elections as well. By this standard, there have been three clear-cut realignments since the 1850s.

The first of these, the Civil War realignment, brought about a wholesale change in the party system. The Republicans, called the "Union Party" by many, replaced the Democrats as the nation's majority party. The Republicans dominated the larger and more populous North, while the Democrats, who were widely blamed in the North for the Civil War, were left with a stronghold in what became known as "the Solid South." During the next three decades, the Republicans held the presidency except for Grover Cleveland's two terms in office and had a majority in Congress for all but four years.

The 1896 election also produced a realignment. Three years earlier, an economic panic following a bank collapse had resulted in a severe depression. The Democrat Cleveland was president when the crash happened, and people blamed him and his party. In the aftermath, the Republicans made additional gains in the Northeast and Midwest, solidifying

Abraham Lincoln had been a member of Congress from Illinois before he was elected to the presidency in 1860. In the view of many historians, Lincoln ranks as America's greatest president, a feat that is all the more remarkable in that Lincoln as a child was poor and largely self-taught. He was assassinated at Ford's Theater in the nation's capital shortly after the start of his second presidential term. Lincoln was the first Republican elected to the presidency, and his successful pursuit of victory in the Civil War led to a party realignment that solidified the GOP's status as the nation's majority party.

their position as the nation's dominant party. During the four decades between the 1890s realignment and the next one in the 1930s, the Republicans held the presidency except for Woodrow Wilson's two terms and had a majority in Congress for all but six years.

The Great Depression of the 1930s triggered yet another realignment of the American party system. The Republican Herbert Hoover was president when the stock market crashed in 1929, and many Americans blamed Hoover, his party, and its business allies for the economic catastrophe that followed. The Democrats became the country's majority party. Their political and policy agenda called for an expanded role for the national government. Franklin D. Roosevelt's presidency included unprecedented policy initiatives in the areas of business regulation and social welfare (see Chapter 3). Roosevelt's election in 1932 began a thirty-six-year period of Democratic presidencies that was interrupted only by Dwight D. Eisenhower's two terms in the 1950s. In this period, the Democrats also dominated Congress, losing control only in 1947–1948 and 1953–1954.

The reason realignments have such a substantial effect on future elections is that they affect voters' *party identification* (see Chapter 6). Young voters in particular tend to embrace the newly ascendant party, giving it a solid base of support for years to come. First-time voters in the 1930s came to identify with the Democratic Party by a two-to-one margin, establishing it as the nation's majority party and enabling it to dominate national politics for the next three decades.[8]

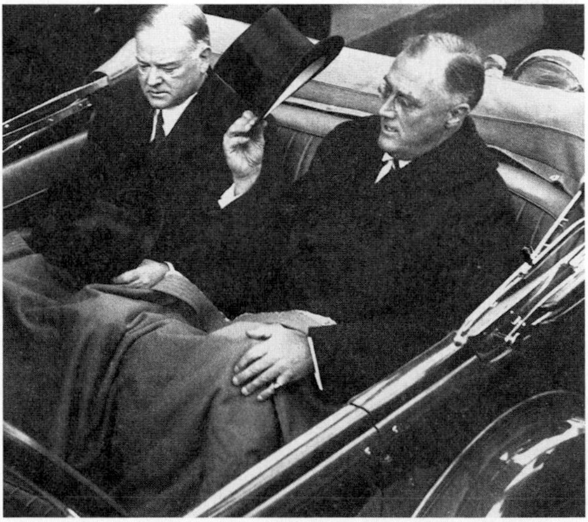

The new order begins: Franklin D. Roosevelt rides to his inauguration with outgoing president Herbert Hoover after the realigning election of 1932.

Today's Party Alignment and Its Origins

A party realignment gradually loses strength as the issues that gave rise to it decline in importance. By the late 1960s, with the Democratic Party divided over the Vietnam War and civil rights, it was apparent that the era of New Deal politics was ending.[9]

The change was most dramatic in the South. The region had been solidly Democratic at all levels since the Civil War, but the Democratic Party's leadership on civil rights alienated white conservatives. In the 1964 presidential election, five southern states voted Republican, an indicator of what was to come. Today, the Republican Party dominates presidential voting in the South and holds most of the region's top elected positions.

More slowly and less completely, the northeastern states have become increasingly Democratic. This shift is attributable in part to the declining influence of the Republican Party's moderate wing, which was concentrated in the region. As southern conservatives came to dominate Republican politics, the party's stands on social issues such as abortion and affirmative action tilted toward the right, reducing the party's appeal in the Northeast.[10]

The net result of these changes has been a remaking of the party landscape. Some analysts describe it as a realignment, albeit a slow and fitful one. Rather than occurring abruptly in response to a disruptive issue, as was the case in the 1860s, 1890s, and 1930s realignments, the change took place gradually and is the product of several issues rather than an overriding disruptive one. But the cumulative result—a reshuffling of the parties' coalitions and platforms—is like that of previous realignments. In effect, America's parties have realigned without going through the sudden shock of a realigning election.

Initially, the GOP (short for "Grand Old Party" and another name for the Republican Party) gained the most from the change. In the decades following the 1930s Great Depression, the GOP was decidedly the weaker party. Since 1968, however, Republicans have held the presidency for roughly twice as many years as the Democrats, and have controlled one or both houses of Congress more than a third of that time.

However, the Republican Party has not duplicated the success that the advantaged party had in the realignments of the 1860s, 1890s, and 1930s, partly because of missteps by two of its presidents. After winning the presidency in 1968 and 1972, Republican Richard Nixon became embroiled in the Watergate affair and was forced to resign, the first and only president to do so. The Republicans lost a huge number of congressional seats in the 1974 midterm election and did not recover the lost

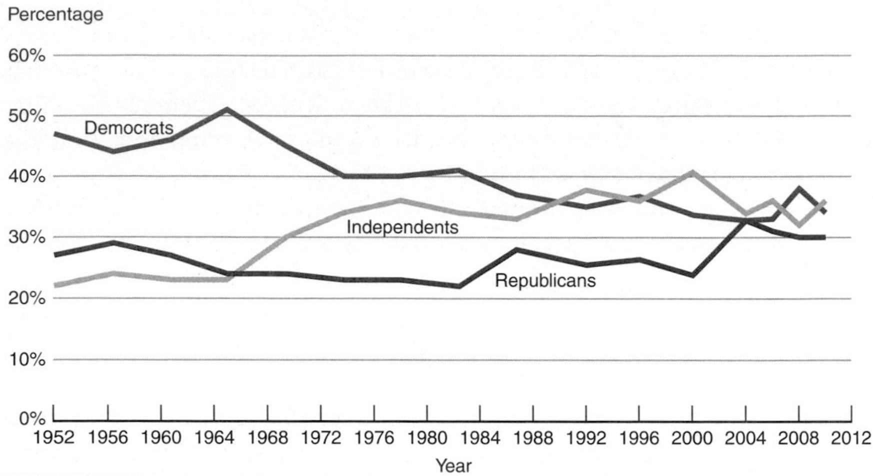

figure 8-2 PARTISAN IDENTIFICATION

Of the roughly one-third of voters who describe themselves as Independents, most say they "lean" toward one of the two major parties and tend to vote for that party's candidates. *Source:* American National Election Studies, 1952–2000; Gallup surveys, after 2000.

ground until the 1980s. After the 2000 election, the GOP for the first time in a half-century held the presidency and both houses of Congress. However, President George W. Bush's decision to invade Iraq in 2003 proved increasingly unpopular, contributing to his party's loss of the House and Senate in the 2006 midterm elections and its loss of the presidency in the 2008 election.

The Iraq conflict also undermined Republicans' hopes of capturing Americans' party loyalties. After trailing the Democrats for years, the Republicans by 2004 had narrowed the gap—Democratic party identifiers barely outnumbered Republican identifiers (see Figure 8-2). As discontent with Iraq grew, though, the trend toward the GOP reversed itself.[11] In 2010, however, Republicans gained ground as the public soured on the performance of President Obama and the Democratic Congress.

Analysts differ in their judgment on where the party system is heading in the long run. Some predict a period of Republican resurgence once the GOP is able to refocus the public's attention on the issues, such as taxes, that worked for it before the Iraq war derailed its momentum.[12] Others foresee a strong Democratic Party fueled by the increased voting power of Hispanics and young adults, who lean Democratic.[13] In the 2008 presidential election, the Democrats won about two-thirds of the Hispanic vote and nearly that proportion of the vote among those under thirty years of age.[14] If these groups remain loyal to the Democratic Party, it could achieve a lengthy period of dominance, although the party's setback in the 2010 congressional elections raises questions about the possibility. One thing about the future is virtually certain: as they have since 1860, Americans will continue to look to the Republican and Democratic parties for political leadership. The enduring strength and appeal of the two major parties is a constant feature of American politics.

Parties and the Vote

The power of party is at no time clearer than when, election after election, Republican and Democratic candidates reap the vote of their party's identifiers. In the 2008 presidential election, John McCain had the support of more than 85 percent of Republican Party identifiers, while Barack Obama garnered the votes of more than 85 percent of self-identified Democrats. Major-party candidates do not always do that well with party loyalists, but it is relatively rare—in congressional races as well as in the presidential race—for a party nominee to get less than 80 percent of the partisan vote.

Even "independent" voters are less independent than might be assumed. When Americans are asked in polls if they are a Republican, a Democrat, or an independent, about a third say they are independents. However, in the follow-up question that asks if they lean toward the Republican Party or toward the Democratic Party, about two in three independents say they lean toward one of the parties. Most of these independents vote in the direction they lean. In recent presidential elections, more than eight in ten leaners have backed the candidate of the party toward which they lean. Less than 15 percent of all voters are "true" independents in the sense that party loyalty plays little to no part in the votes they cast.

The power of party loyalties is evident in the extent to which *straight-ticket* voting occurs. Candidates for the presidency and Congress run separately, but voters do not treat them that way. Most voters who cast a ballot for the Republican presidential candidate also vote for the Republican congressional candidate in their district. The same is true on the Democratic side. Less than 20 percent of voters cast a *split-ticket*, voting for one party's presidential candidate and then voting for the other party's congressional candidate. For a period in the 1970s, when dissatisfaction with both parties was widespread, split-ticket voting occurred at nearly twice its current level. Analysts described this development as a

HOW THE U.S. DIFFERS
POLITICAL THINKING THROUGH COMPARISONS

Party Systems

Since 1860, electoral competition in the United States has centered on the Republican and Democratic parties. By comparison, most democracies have a multiparty system, in which three or more parties receive substantial support from voters. The difference is significant. In a two-party system, the parties tend to have overlapping coalitions and programs, because each party must appeal to the middle-of-the-road voters who provide the margin of victory. In multiparty systems, particularly those with four or more strong parties, the parties tend to separate themselves as each tries to secure the enduring loyalty of a particular set of voters.

Whether a country has a two-party or a multiparty system depends on several factors, but particularly the nature of its electoral system. The United States has a single-member, plurality district system in which only the top vote getter in a district is elected. This system is biased against smaller parties; even if they

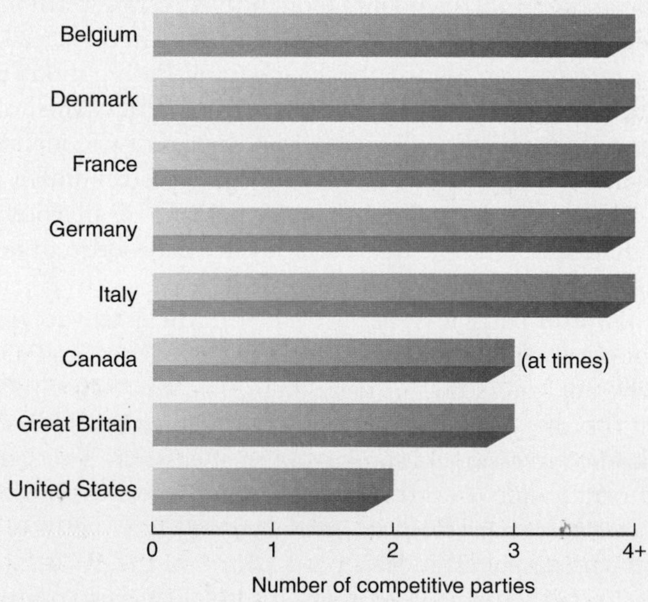

have some support in a great many races, they win nothing unless one of their candidates places first in an electoral district. By comparison, proportional representation systems enable smaller parties to compete; each party acquires legislative seats in proportion to its share of the total vote. All the countries in the chart that have four or more parties also have a proportional representation system of election.

Q: *Like the United States, Canada and Great Britain have the single-member district system of election. Yet, unlike the United States, they have more than two parties. Why?*

A: *Canada's third parties have stemmed from regional differences and resentments. French-speaking Quebec has a strong regional party, and from time to time, strong regional parties have appeared in the western provinces. Britain's third party (currently the Liberal Democrats) has been able to survive because the British House of Commons is much larger than the U.S. House of Representatives (659 seats versus 435 seats) and the population of Britain is much smaller than that of the United States. As a result, British election districts have only about a tenth as many voters as U.S. House districts. Britain's third party has enough concentrated strength in some of these districts to win the seat.*

dealignment—a movement of voters away from strong party attachments. The dealignment thesis has become less persuasive as a result of the increase in party-line voting in recent elections.

Electoral and Party Systems

Throughout nearly all of its history, the United States has had a **two-party system:** Federalists versus Jeffersonian Democratic-Republicans, Whigs versus Democrats, Republicans versus Democrats. A two-party system, however, is the exception rather than the rule (see "How the U.S. Differs"). Most democracies have a **multiparty system,** in which three or more parties have the capacity to gain control of government, separately or in coalition. Why the difference? Why are there three or more major parties in most democracies but only two major parties in the United States?

The Single-Member-District System of Election

America's two-party system is largely the result of the nation's choosing its officials through plurality voting in **single-member districts.** Each constituency elects a single member to a particular office, such as U.S. senator or state representative; the candidate with the most votes (a plurality) in a district wins the office. This system discourages minor parties. Assume, for example, that a minor party receives exactly 20 percent of the vote in each of the nation's 435 congressional races. Even though one in five voters nationwide backed the minor party, it would not win any seats in Congress because none of its candidates would have placed first in any of the 435 single-member-district races. The winning candidate in each race would be the major-party candidate with the larger share of the remaining 80 percent of the vote.

By comparison, most European democracies use some form of **proportional representation**, in which seats in the legislature are allocated according to a party's share of the popular vote. This type of electoral system enables smaller parties to compete for power. In the 2009 German elections, for example, the Green Party received nearly 11 percent of the national vote and thereby won more than 60 seats in the 603-seat Bundestag, the German parliament. If the Greens had been competing under American electoral rules, they would not have won any seats.

POLITICAL THINKING

Is Proportional Representation a Fairer System?

Politics is conducted by predetermined rules. Although these rules are often portrayed as neutral, they can affect who wins and who loses. An example is electoral systems. The United States has a single-member district system in which the election winners are the candidates who get the most votes in the district in which they run. Most European countries, by comparison, have proportional representation systems in which legislative seats are distributed to each party according to its share (proportion) of the popular vote. The European rule makes it possible for smaller parties to win legislative seats. In contrast, the American rule discourages smaller parties. A party that wins 15 percent of the national vote would end up with no seats in Congress if none of its candidates placed first in a congressional district. Which rule—proportional representation or the single-member district—do you think is the fairer one? Is one system inherently better suited than the other to the United States?

Politics and Coalitions in the Two-Party System

The overriding goal of a major American party is to gain power by getting its candidates elected to office. Because there are only two major parties, however, the Republicans or Democrats can win consistently only by attracting majority support. In Europe's multiparty systems, a party can hope for a share of power if it has the firm backing of a minority faction. In the United States, if either party confines its support to a narrow segment of society, it forfeits its chance of gaining control of government. The two parties usually take positions that have broad appeal or at least will not alienate significant blocs of voters.

Seeking the Center A two-party system usually compels the major parties to stay near the center of the political spectrum because of their need to win a majority of the votes. The **median voter theorem** holds that, if there are two parties, the parties can maximize their vote only if they position themselves at the location of the median voter—the voter whose preferences are exactly in the middle.[15]

Although the theorem is hypothetical, it helps explain what happens when a party makes a pronounced shift away from the center, leaving it open to the other party. In 1964, the Republican nominee, Barry Goldwater, proposed the elimination of mandatory social security and said he might consider the tactical use of small nuclear weapons in wars such as the Vietnam conflict—extreme positions that cost him many votes. Eight years later, the Democratic nominee, George McGovern, took positions on Vietnam and income security that alarmed many voters; like Goldwater, he was buried in one of the biggest landslides in presidential history.

It is impossible to understand the dynamics of the U.S. party system without recognizing that the balance of power in American elections usually rests with the moderate voters in the center rather than with those who hold more extreme positions. When congressional Republicans mistook their 1994 election victory as a mandate to trim assistance programs for the elderly, the poor, and children, they alienated many of the moderate voters who had contributed to their 1994 victory. These voters wanted "less" government but not a government that punished society's most vulnerable citizens. After weak showings in the 1996 and 1998 elections, congressional Republicans shifted course. They unseated Speaker Newt Gingrich, replacing him with a more pragmatic conservative, Dennis Hastert. "We still need to prove that we can be conservative without being mean," was how one Republican member of Congress described the change in strategy.[16] The adjustment reflects a basic truth about U.S. politics: party ideology is acceptable as long as it is tinged with moderation.

Nonetheless, the Republican and Democratic parties do offer somewhat different alternatives and, at times, a clear choice. When Roosevelt was elected president in 1932 and Ronald Reagan in 1980, for example, the parties were relatively far apart in their priorities and programs. Roosevelt's New Deal was a sharp move to the left, which Republicans fought bitterly. Reagan moved policy sharply to the right, opposed at each step by liberal Democrats. In both cases, the moderates shifted toward the president's direction. The lesson of these periods is that, although candidates risk a crushing defeat by straying too far from the center during normal times, they may do so with some success during turbulent times. The terrorist attacks of September 11, 2001, provided President George W. Bush with just such an opportunity. During his first term, Bush pushed major tax cuts through Congress and also sharply increased defense spending while pursuing an aggressive Middle East policy, backed at every step by congressional Republicans.

When he sought reelection in 2004, Bush pursued an unusual strategy, at least in American politics. He chose to mobilize his conservative base rather than reaching out to moderates. He won the election, though narrowly. His victory margin was the smallest for a seated president since Woodrow Wilson's reelection in 1916. But Bush's strategy haunted his second term when moderates and independents in increasing numbers turned away from his Iraq policy. When they then voted disproportionately Democratic in the 2006 midterm elections, the Republicans lost control of both the House and the Senate. The Bush presidency is a reminder that, although parties do not always govern toward the center, they risk defeat if they move too far from it.

Party Coalitions The groups and interests that support a party are collectively referred to as the **party coalition**. In multiparty systems, each party is supported by a relatively narrow range of interests. European parties tend to divide along class lines, with the center and right parties drawing most of their votes from the middle and upper classes and the left parties drawing most of theirs from the working class. By comparison, America's two-party system requires each party to accommodate a wide range of interests in order to gain the voting plurality necessary to win elections. The Republican and Democratic coalitions are therefore relatively broad. Each includes a substantial proportion of voters of nearly every ethnic, religious, regional, and economic grouping. Only a few groups are tightly aligned with a party. African

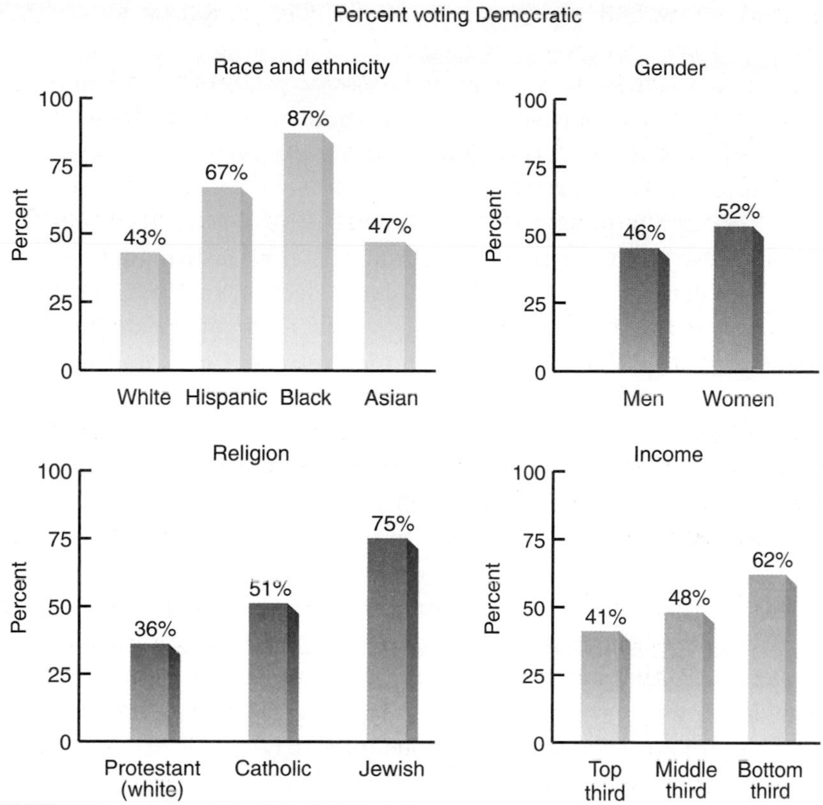

figure 8-3 THE VOTE OF SELECTED DEMOGRAPHIC GROUPS IN RECENT PRESIDENTIAL ELECTIONS

Although the Democratic and Republican coalitions overlap substantially, there are important differences, as illustrated by the Democratic Party's percentage of the two-party vote among some major demographic groups in recent elections. *Source:* Compiled by author from American National Election Studies and other surveys.

Americans are the clearest example; they vote about 85 percent Democratic in national elections.

Although the Republican and Democratic coalitions overlap, they are hardly identical (see Figure 8-3).[17] The party coalitions have been forged primarily through conflict over the federal government's role in solving social and economic problems. Each party has supported government action to promote economic security and social equality, but the Democrats have favored a greater level of government involvement. Virtually every major assistance program for the poor, the elderly, and low-wage workers since the 1930s has been initiated by the Democrats. Accordingly, the Democratic coalition draws support disproportionately from society's underdogs—blacks, union members, the poor, city dwellers, Hispanics, Jews, and other "minorities."[18] For a long period, the Democratic Party was also the choice of the nation's elderly as a result of its support for old-age assistance programs and because the basic political loyalties of the elderly were acquired during the New Deal era, a period favorable to the Democrats.

The Democratic Party's largest gains in recent decades have come from women, whose voting pattern at one time was barely distinguishable from men's. The pattern changed with Reagan's election in 1980, and today a substantial **gender gap** exists: women vote disproportionately for the Democratic Party. The tendency is policy related. Compared with men, women are more supportive of the Democratic Party's agenda of government assistance for the poor, minorities, children, and the elderly.[19]

The Republican coalition consists mainly of white middle-class Americans. The GOP has historically been the party of tax cuts and business incentives. It has also been more supportive of traditional values, as reflected, for example, in its opposition to abortion and to civil unions. Not surprisingly, the GOP is strongest in the suburbs and in regions where belief in traditional values and low taxes is prevalent, such as in the South, the Great Plains, and the Rocky Mountains. The Republican Party has made big gains in recent decades among white fundamentalist Christians, who are attracted by its positions on abortion, school prayer, same-sex marriage, stem cell research, and other social issues.[20] In recent presidential elections, the Republican nominee has garnered the votes of roughly three-fourths of fundamentalist Christians.

A key to the future of both parties is the Hispanic vote. With the exception of Cuban Americans, who are concentrated in southern Florida, Hispanics lean heavily Democratic. Hispanics who call themselves Democrats outnumber those who call themselves Republicans by more than two to one (see Figure 8-4). However, compared with African Americans, Hispanics are a less cohesive voting bloc. Whereas blacks of all income levels are solidly Democratic, lower-income Hispanics vote Democratic at substantially higher rates than do upper-income Hispanics. Polls show Hispanics to be relatively liberal on economic issues and relatively conservative on social issues, providing both parties a basis for appealing for their support.[21] In the short term, however, the advantage rests with the Democratic Party. The Republicans made inroads on the Hispanic vote in the 2004 presidential election. In late 2005, however, the Republican majority in the House of Representatives passed a bill that called for heavy penalties on employers who hire illegal immigrants and for a concerted

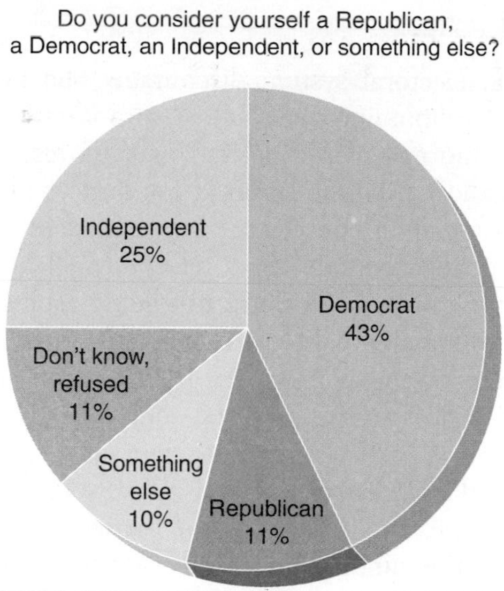

figure 8-4 HISPANICS' PARTY IDENTIFICATION

By a wide margin, Hispanics identify with the Democratic Party rather than the Republican Party. *Source:* From Pew Hispanic Center, a project of The Pew Research Center (2009). Reprinted with permission.

effort to apprehend and deport individuals who were in the country illegally. The Hispanic community responded with huge protest rallies—ones reminiscent of the 1960s civil rights movement. The rally in Los Angeles drew an estimated half million marchers, reputedly the largest such gathering in the city's history. The House Republican's bill had the effect of driving Hispanics toward the Democratic Party. Nearly 70 percent of Hispanics voted Democratic in the 2006 congressional races, a 10 percent increase from the 2004 level.

The Hispanic vote in the 2010 midterm election also went heavily Democratic, fueled in part by a recently enacted Arizona law that called for police to check for evidence of legal status whenever in the course of duty they stopped a person for another reason. If the individual was an illegal alien, he or she would be detained, charged with a state crime, and then turned over to federal authorities for deportation. Enacted by Arizona's Republican-controlled legislature, the law was praised by Republican officials elsewhere. For their part, Hispanics within and outside Arizona saw the law as targeted at their ethnic group, and they organized protest rallies in cities across the country. In the November election, the Hispanic vote went Democratic by a substantial margin.

Minor (Third) Parties

Although the U.S. electoral system discourages the formation of third parties (or, as they are more properly called, minor parties), the nation has always had them—more than a thousand over its history.[22] Most minor parties have been short lived, and only a few have had a lasting impact. Only one minor party, the Republican Party, has achieved majority status.

Minor parties in the United States have formed largely to promote policies that their followers believe are not being represented adequately by either of the two major parties. A major party is always somewhat captive to its past, which is the source of many of its ideas and most of its followers. When conditions change, major parties can be slow to respond, and a minor party can try to capitalize on neglected issues. Whatever success it achieves, however, is usually temporary. If a minor party gains a following, one or both major parties typically awaken to its issue, at which time the minor party begins to lose support. Nevertheless, the minor party will have served the purpose of making the major parties more responsive to the public's concerns.

Some minor parties have been virtually "antiparties" in the sense that they arose out of a belief that partisan politics is a corrupting influence. The most influential of these **reform parties** was the Progressive Party, which was as much a political movement as a political party. In the early 1900s, it succeeded in achieving its antiparty agenda in many states and localities. Primary elections, recall elections, nonpartisan elections, initiatives, and popular referendums, discussed in Chapter 2, were among the Progressives' contributions. A more recent reform party was titled just that, the Reform Party. It was created by Ross Perot after he ran as an independent on a balanced-budget platform and garnered 19 percent of the vote in the 1992 presidential election (second only to Theodore Roosevelt's 27 percent in 1912 among minor-party candidates). Perot ran again in 1996, this time as the Reform Party's nominee, and won 8 percent of the vote. When Perot chose not to run in 2000, a bitter fight for the Reform Party's presidential nomination virtually destroyed the party.

Minor parties were at their peak in the nineteenth century, when the party system was still in flux.[23] Many of these parties were **single-issue parties** formed around a lone issue of overriding interest to their followers. Examples are the Free Soil Party, which fought the extension of slavery into new territories, and the Greenback Party, which sought a currency system based on paper money rather than gold and silver. One nineteenth-century party, the Prohibition Party, persisted into the twentieth century and contributed to the ratification in 1919 of the Eighteenth

Amendment, which prohibited the manufacture, sale, and transportation of alcoholic beverages (but which was repealed in 1933). Although single-issue parties (for example, the Right to Life Party) exist today, they do not have large followings or much influence. The role that single-issue parties played in the nineteenth century is now played by single-issue interest groups (see Chapter 9).

Other minor parties have been characterized by their ideological commitment to a broad and noncentrist ideological position, such as redistribution of economic resources. The strongest ideological party was the Populists, whose 1892 presidential nominee, James B. Weaver, won 9 percent of the national vote and carried six western states on a radical platform that included a call for government takeover of the railroads. His strong showing was fueled by the anger of small farmers over low commodity prices, tight credit, and the high rates charged by railroad monopolies to transport their goods.[24] Modern-day **ideological parties** include the Socialist Workers Party and the Libertarian Party, each of which operates on the fringe of American politics.

If it were an actual political party, rather than a political movement, the recently formed Tea Party would easily be the strongest of the ideological parties. In 2010, determined to have an impact on the midterm election, the Tea Party issued a "Contract from America." "Our moral, political, and economic liberties are inherent, not granted by our government," the contract said. "It is essential to the practice of these liberties that we be free from restriction over our peaceful political expression and free from excessive control over our economic choices." The contract included ten planks, most of which aimed at reducing government spending and rolling back federal social programs. Although the Tea Party did not nominate its own slate of candidates in 2010, it actively backed primary and general election candidates whose policy positions were in accord with its philosophy.

The strongest minor party today on the liberal side of the political spectrum is the Green Party. Its 2000 presidential nominee, consumer rights advocate Ralph Nader, received 3 percent of the national vote. Nader got most of his support from voters who otherwise would have backed Democrat Al Gore, which tipped the election to the more conservative Republican nominee, George W. Bush. In 2004 and 2008, in an effort to reduce the likelihood of helping the Republican nominee a second time, the Green Party nominated low-profile presidential candidates.

The most important minor parties of the twentieth century were **factional parties** that resulted from a split within one of the major parties. Although the Republican and Democratic parties are typically adept at managing internal divisions, internal conflict has sometimes led dissidents to break away and form their own party. The most electorally successful of these factional parties was the Bull Moose Party in 1912.[25] Four years earlier, Theodore Roosevelt had declined to seek another presidential term, but he became disenchanted with the conservative policies of his handpicked successor, William Howard Taft, and challenged him for the 1912 Republican nomination. After losing out in the nominating race, Roosevelt proceeded to form the progressive Bull Moose Party (a reference to Roosevelt's claim that he was "as strong as a bull moose"). Roosevelt won 27 percent of the presidential vote to Taft's 25 percent, but the split within Republican ranks enabled the Democratic nominee, Woodrow Wilson, to win the 1912 presidential election. The States' Rights Party

Although the United States has long had a two-party system, numerous minor parties have surfaced. A few of them have been influential, including the Free Soil Party, which emerged before the Civil War with a platform that called for the abolition of slavery in new states and territories. Shown here is a Free Soil Party poster from the 1848 election. The party's presidential nominee was Martin Van Buren, who had been president from 1837 to 1841 as a member of the Democratic Party.

in 1948 and George Wallace's American Independent Party in 1968 are other examples of strong factional parties. They were formed by white southern Democrats angered by northern Democrats' support of black civil rights.

Party Organizations

The Democratic and Republican parties have organizational units at the national, state, and local levels. These **party organizations** concentrate on the contesting of elections.

The Weakening of Party Organizations

A century ago, party organizations enjoyed nearly complete control of elections. Although today's party organizations perform all the activities in which parties formerly engaged—candidate recruitment, fundraising, policy development, canvassing—they do not control these activities as fully as they once did. For the most part, the candidates now have the lead role.[26]

Nomination refers to the selection of the individual who will run as the party's candidate in the general election. Until the early twentieth century, the party organizations picked the nominees, who, if elected, were expected to share with it the spoils of office—government jobs and contracts. The party built its organization by giving the jobs to loyalists and by granting contracts to donors. Bribes and kickbacks were part of the process in some locations. New York City's legendary Boss Tweed once charged the city twenty times what a building had actually cost, amassing a personal fortune before winding up in prison. Reform-minded Progressives invented primary elections as a way to deprive party bosses of their power over nominations (see Chapter 2).

A **primary election** (or **direct primary**) gives control of nominations to the voters (see Chapters 2 and 12). The candidate who gets the most votes in a party's primary gets its nomination for the general election. In most states, the nominees are chosen in a *closed primary*, in which participation is limited to voters registered or declared at the polls as members of the party whose primary is being held. The logic of a closed primary is that a party's voters alone should have the power to choose its general election candidate. Some states, however, use an *open primary*, a form that allows independents and voters of either party to choose which primary they will vote in, though they can vote in only one of them. The logic of the open primary is that it gives all voters a say in the choices they will have in the general election. A few states use the blanket primary, in which voters get a single ballot listing both the Republican and Democratic candidates by office. Each voter can cast only one vote per office but can select a candidate of either party; the top finisher in each party becomes its nominee. Louisiana has a variation on this form in which all candidates are listed on the ballot without regard to party; the top two finishers, even if from the same party, become the general election candidates.

Primaries hinder the building of strong party organizations. If there were no primaries, candidates would have to seek nomination through the party organization, and they could be denied renomination if they were disloyal to the party's policy goals. Because of primaries, however, candidates can seek office on their own and create a personal following that places them beyond the party's direct control.

In the process of taking control of nominations, candidates also acquired control of most campaign money. At the turn of the twentieth century, when party machines were at their peak, most campaign funds passed through the hands of party leaders. Today, most of the money goes to the candidates directly, without first passing through the parties.

Party organizations were also weakened by the decline of patronage jobs. A century ago, when a party won control of government, it acquired control of nearly all public jobs, which were doled out to loyal party workers. However, as government jobs in the early twentieth century shifted from patronage to the merit system (see Chapter 13), the party organizations controlled many fewer positions. Today, because of the large size of government, thousands of patronage jobs still exist. These government employees help staff the party organizations (along with volunteers), but most patronage appointees are indebted to an individual politician rather than to a party organization. Congressional staff members, for example, are patronage employees, but they owe their jobs and their loyalty to their senator or representative, not to the party organization.

In Europe, where there are no primary elections, the parties are stronger. They control their nominations, and because of this, they also control campaign money and workers. A party's candidates are expected to support the national platform if elected. An officeholder who fails to do so is likely to be denied renomination in the next election.

The Structure and Role of Party Organizations

Although party organizations have lost influence, parties are in no danger of extinction. Candidates and activists need an organization through which to work, and the party meets that need. Moreover, certain activities, such

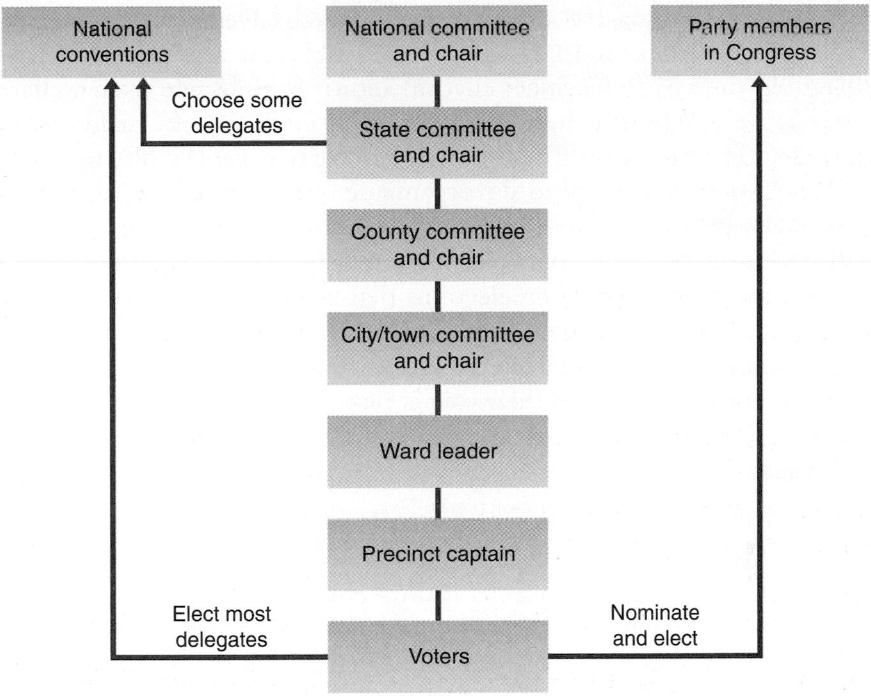

figure 8-5 FORMAL ORGANIZATION OF THE POLITICAL PARTY

U.S. parties are loosely structured alliances of national, state, and local organizations; most local parties are not as well organized as the chart implies.

as get-out-the-vote efforts on election day, affect all of a party's candidates and are done more efficiently through the party organization. Indeed, parties have staged a comeback of sorts.[27] National and state party organizations now assist candidates with fundraising, polling, research, and media production, all essential ingredients of a successful modern campaign.

Structurally, U.S. parties are loose associations of national, state, and local organizations (see Figure 8-5). The national party organizations cannot dictate the decisions made by the state organizations, which in turn do not control the activities of local organizations. However, the levels cooperate because they all have a shared stake in the party's success.[28]

Local Party Organizations In a sense, U.S. parties are organized from the bottom up, not the top down. Of the roughly 500,000 elective offices in the United States, fewer than 500 are contested statewide and only two—the presidency and vice presidency—are contested nationally. The rest are local offices; not surprisingly, at least 95 percent of party activists work within local organizations. Local parties vary greatly in their structure and activities. Only a few of them, including the Democratic organizations in Philadelphia and Chicago, bear even a faint resemblance to the fabled old-time party machines that, in return for jobs and even welfare services, were able to deliver the vote on election day. In many urban areas, and in most suburbs and towns, the party organizations today do not have enough activists to do organizing work outside the campaign period, at which time—to the extent their resources allow—they conduct registration drives, hand out leaflets, and help get out the vote. Local parties tend to concentrate on elections that coincide with local boundaries, such as races for mayor, city council, state legislature, and county offices. Local parties take part in congressional, statewide, and presidential contests, but in these cases, their role is typically secondary to that of the candidates' personal campaign organizations, which are discussed later in the chapter.

State Party Organizations At the state level, each party is headed by a central committee made up of members of local party organizations and local and state officeholders. State central committees do not meet regularly and provide only general policy guidance for the state organizations. Day-to-day operations are directed by a chairperson, who is a full-time, paid employee of the state party. The state party organizations engage in activities, such as fundraising and voter registration, that can improve their candidates' chances of success. State party organizations concentrate on statewide races, including those for governor and U.S. senator, and also focus on races for the state legislature. They play a smaller role in campaigns for national or local offices, and in most states, they do not endorse candidates in their statewide primaries.

National Party Organizations The national Republican and Democratic party organizations, which are located in Washington, D.C., are structured much like those at the state level: they have a national committee and a national party chairperson. Although the national parties in theory are run by their committees, neither the Democratic National Committee (DNC) nor the Republican National Committee (RNC) has great power. The RNC (with more than 150 members) and the DNC (with more than 300 members) are too cumbersome and meet too infrequently to oversee party activities. Their power is largely confined to setting organizational policy, such as determining the site of the party's presidential nominating convention and deciding the rules governing the selection of convention delegates. They have no power to pick nominees or to dictate candidates' policy positions. The national party's day-to-day operations are directed by a national chairperson chosen by the national committee, although the committee defers to the president's choice when the party controls the White House.

The RNC and DNC, among other things, run training programs for candidates and their staffs, raise money, seek media coverage of party positions and activities, conduct issue and group research, and send field representatives to help state and local parties with their operations. In some cases, the national parties also try to recruit potentially strong candidates to run in House and Senate races.

The national parties' major role in campaigns is the raising and spending of money. The RNC and the DNC are major sources of campaign funds, but they are not the only national-level party units involved in fundraising. There are also House and Senate party campaign committees, which raise funds and provide advice to the parties' congressional candidates. Altogether, the national party organizations raise in excess of $1 billion for each federal election, with the Republican Party usually in the lead (see Figure 8-6). Compared with the Democratic Party, the GOP has a wealthier constituency, although this advantage has been partially offset in recent election cycles by the Democrats' success with Internet-based fundraising.

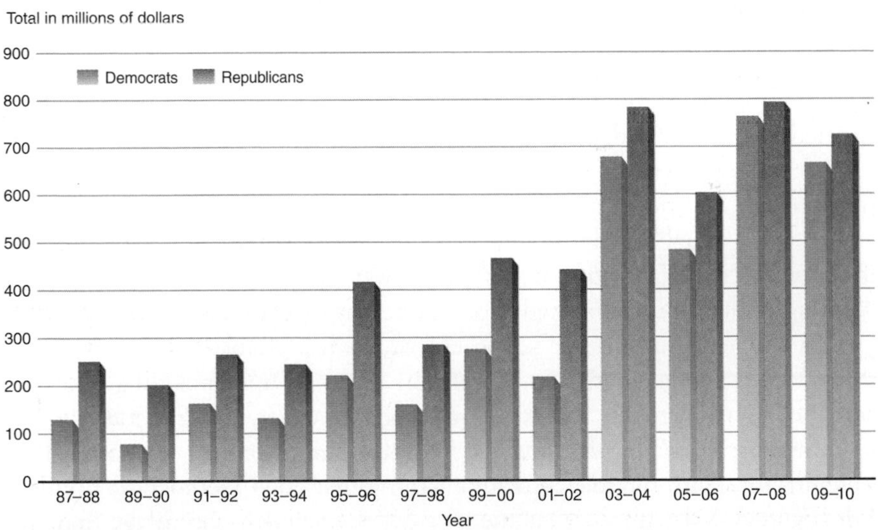

figure 8-6 NATIONAL PARTY FUNDRAISING, 1989–2010

Over the years, the Republican Party has raised significantly more money than has the Democratic Party, although the gap has narrowed in recent election cycles. *Source:* Center for Responsive Politics, 2010. Reprinted with permission. The figures include fundraising by the DNC and RNC, as well as the parties' Senate-based organizations (DSCC and NRSC) and House-based organizations (DCCC and NRCC). The 2009–2010 figures are based on author's projections from incomplete cycle.

Most of the money raised by the national party organizations is spent on their own activities, such as their get-out-the-vote, fundraising, and advertising efforts. Some of the money, however, is given directly to House or Senate candidates for their campaigns. The legal limit on these contributions is greater for Senate candidates than for House candidates, but, given the enormous cost of today's campaigns, the limit is not particularly high (about $40,000 in the case of Senate candidates). This funding, along with the money a candidate receives from individual contributors and interest groups, which is also subject to strict limits, is termed **hard money**—it goes directly to the candidate and can be spent as he or she chooses.

Limits on party contributions were established when the campaign finance laws were reformed in the 1970s after the Watergate scandal. However, a loophole in the laws developed when a court ruling allowed the parties to raise unlimited campaign funds provided the funds were not then given directly to their candidates. Thus, whereas a wealthy contributor could legally give a candidate only a limited amount, that same contributor could give an unlimited amount to the candidate's party. These so-called **soft money** contributions could be used to support party activities, such as voter registration efforts and party-centered television ads that could indirectly benefit its candidates.

In 2002, Congress closed the loophole through enactment of the Bipartisan Campaign Reform Act (BCRA), which prohibits the national parties from raising or spending soft money. The Supreme Court upheld these restrictions in a 2003 decision,[29] but a new loophole soon surfaced. The ban on soft money does not fully apply to so-called 527 groups. (Section 527 of the Internal Revenue Code defines the rules governing not-for-profit political groups.) Much of the money that previously would have been contributed to a party organization now finds its way into the hands of 527 groups. Although they are prohibited from attacking a candidate directly, these groups can engage in issue advocacy, which has enabled them to mount thinly veiled candidate attacks. Several of these groups, including MoveOn and Swift Boat Veterans for Truth, have been fined by the Federal Election Commission (FEC) for crossing the line into candidate advocacy. Swift Boat Veterans for Truth ran televised ads claiming that 2004 Democratic nominee John Kerry's Vietnam combat medals, which included the Silver Star and Purple Heart, were acquired fraudulently. The charges, which were shown to be false, were designed to hurt Kerry's candidacy and thus fell outside the realm of issue advocacy. Like all previous campaign finance legislation, BCRA has been only partially successful in regulating the flow of campaign money.[30]

In *Citizens United v. Federal Election Commission* (2010), the Supreme Court opened the flood gates even further by ruling that corporations and unions could not be banned from spending money on campaigns. In a ruling that overturned long-standing policy, the Court argued that corporations and unions have the same First Amendment free speech rights as individuals when it comes to campaign spending. The Court accepted limits on the amount that these organizations can contribute directly to a candidate or party but said corporations and unions could spend freely from their treasuries on independent efforts that might benefit a candidate or party.[31]

The Candidate-Centered Campaign

Party committees have more of a **service relationship** than a power relationship with their party's candidates. Because the party nominees are chosen through primaries, and because many of the potential candidates already have a power base at the local or state level, the national committees are unable to handpick the party nominees. Accordingly, the party organizations tend to back whichever candidate wins the primary. If the candidate then wins the general election, the party at least has denied the office to the opposing party.

Today's campaigns are largely controlled by the candidates, particularly in congressional, statewide, and presidential races. Each candidate has a personal organization, created especially for the campaign and disbanded once it is over. The candidates are entrepreneurs who play what political consultant Joe Napolitan labeled "the election game."[32] The game begins with money—lots of it.

Campaign Funds: The Money Chase

Campaigns for high office are expensive, and the costs keep rising. In 1980, about $250 million was spent by Senate and House candidates in the general election. The figure had jumped to $425 million by 1990. In 2010, the figure was roughly $1.5 billion—six times the 1980 level.[33] As might be expected, incumbents have a distinct advantage in fundraising. They have contributor lists from past campaigns and the policy influence that donors seek. House and Senate incumbents outspend their challengers by more than two to one.

Because of the high cost of campaigns, candidates spend much of their time raising funds, which come primarily from individual contributors, interest groups (through PACs, discussed in Chapter 9), and political parties. The **money chase** is relentless.[34] A U.S. senator must raise nearly $20,000 a week on average throughout the entire six-year term in order

HOW THE 50 STATES DIFFER
POLITICAL THINKING THROUGH COMPARISONS

Public Funding of State Elections

About half the states have public funding of election campaigns. Some of them give the money to political parties, which allocate it to candidates or spend it on party activities such as get-out-the-vote efforts. Other states give funds directly to candidates, although this funding typically is limited to candidates for designated offices, such as governor.

Q: *What might explain the fact that there is no clear-cut regional pattern to the public funding of state elections?*

A: *Public funding of elections is relatively new, so additional states may adopt it in the next decade or two, at which time a regional tendency could emerge. (If your state does not have public funding, do you think it is likely to adopt it anytime soon? Why or why not?)*

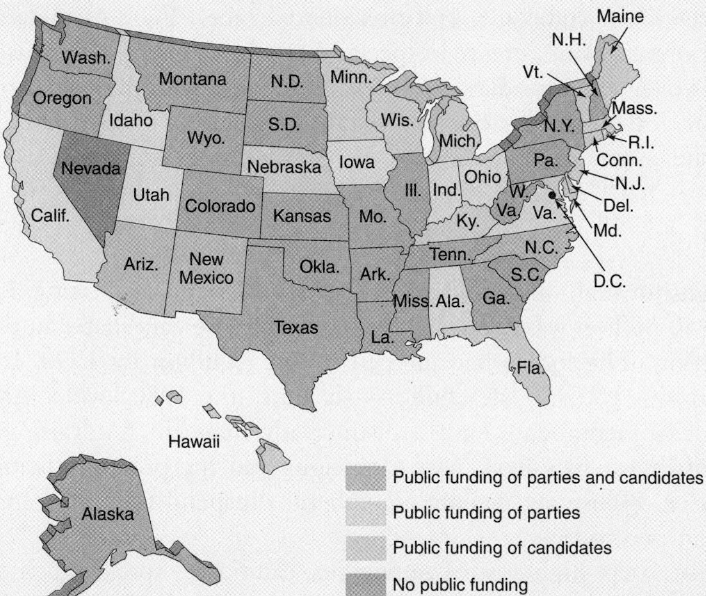

Source: © National Conference of State Legislatures (2008). Reprinted with permission.

to raise the minimum $5 million it takes to run a competitive Senate campaign in most states. A Senate campaign in one of the larger states can easily cost more than that amount. In the 2010 California Senate race, incumbent Barbara Boxer and her Republican challenger, former Hewlett-Packard CEO Carly Fiorina, spent more than $15 million each on their campaigns. House campaigns are less costly, but expenditures of $1 million or more have become commonplace. As for presidential elections, even the nominating race is expensive. In 2008, Barack Obama spent roughly $300 million during the competitive phase of his campaign for the Democratic nomination. (In presidential races, but not congressional ones, candidates are eligible to receive federal funds, a topic discussed in Chapter 12.)

Organization and Strategy: Political Consultants

The key operatives in today's campaigns—congressional as well as presidential—are highly paid **political consultants**: campaign strategists, pollsters, media producers, and fundraising and get-out-the-vote specialists. "The new king-makers" is the way writer David Chagall characterizes them.[35] They include campaign strategists who help the candidate to plot and execute a game plan. Over the years, some of these strategists, including James Carville, Dick Morris, and Roger Ailes, developed legendary reputations. Fundraising specialists are also part of the new politics. They know how to tap into the networks of large donors and interest groups that contribute to election campaigns and are adept at running targeted direct-mail fundraising campaigns. The consultant ranks also include experts on polling and focus groups (the latter are small groups of voters brought together to discuss at length their thoughts on the candidates and issues). Polls and focus groups are used to identify issues and messages that will resonate with voters.[36] Media consultants are another staple of the modern campaign. They are adept at producing televised political advertising, generating news coverage, and developing Internet-based strategies.

Campaign consultants are skilled at **packaging** a candidate—highlighting those aspects of the candidate's partisanship, policy positions, personal background, and personality that are thought most attractive to voters. Packaging is not new to politics. Andrew Jackson's self-portrayal in the nineteenth century as "the champion of the people" is an image that any modern candidate could appreciate. What is new is the need to fit the image to the requirements of a world of sound bites, thirty-second ads, televised debates, and Internet messages, and to do it in a persuasive way.

In the old days, it was sometimes enough for candidates to drive home the point that they were a Republican or a Democrat, playing on the tendency of voters to choose a candidate on that basis. Party appeals are still critical, but today's voters also want to know about a candidate's leadership ability and policy positions. In the 2008 presidential campaign, Barack Obama and John McCain sought to portray themselves as ideally suited to the demands of the moment, while portraying the opponent as unsuited to the nation's needs. At a campaign stop in Virginia, Obama said, "John McCain has provided honorable service to our country, but, when it comes to his economic policies, he is promising and proposing the same things we've been doing for the last eight years." That same day in New Mexico, McCain said that Obama lacked the experience to be commander-in-chief: "He has [taken these positions] not because he doesn't love America, but because he doesn't seem to understand the consequences of an American defeat in Iraq, how it would risk a wider war and threaten the security of American families."[37]

In some election campaigns, voters hear more about the candidates' faults than about their strengths.[38] Of course, negative campaigning is as old as American politics. Abraham Lincoln was ridiculed by opponents as "a baboon" for his gangly look and backwoods roots. But today's version of attack politics is unprecedented in its scale (see Figure 8-7). Negative television ads were once the exception, but they have increased to the point where they now constitute the largest share of political ads.[39] The attacks can be downright vicious. In 2002, for example, incumbent U.S. senator Max Cleland lost his bid for reelection when his lead in the polls withered in the face of blistering attacks on his patriotism, including an ad that showed his face alternately with those of Saddam Hussein and Osama bin Laden. Cleland's patriotism would have seemed above reproach; he had lost his legs and right arm in combat in Vietnam. Yet his opponent seized upon Cleland's vote against a Senate bill to create the Department of Homeland Security because the bill did not include the normal protections for civil service employees. The ad ignored the specifics of Cleland's objection to the bill, portraying him instead as "soft" on terrorism.

Voter Contacts: Pitched Battle

Today's elections for high office have no historical parallel in their length and penetration. Candidates start their active campaigning much earlier—often two years in advance of election day—than they did in times past. The modern campaign is relentless. Voters are bombarded with messages that arrive by air, by land, and by web.

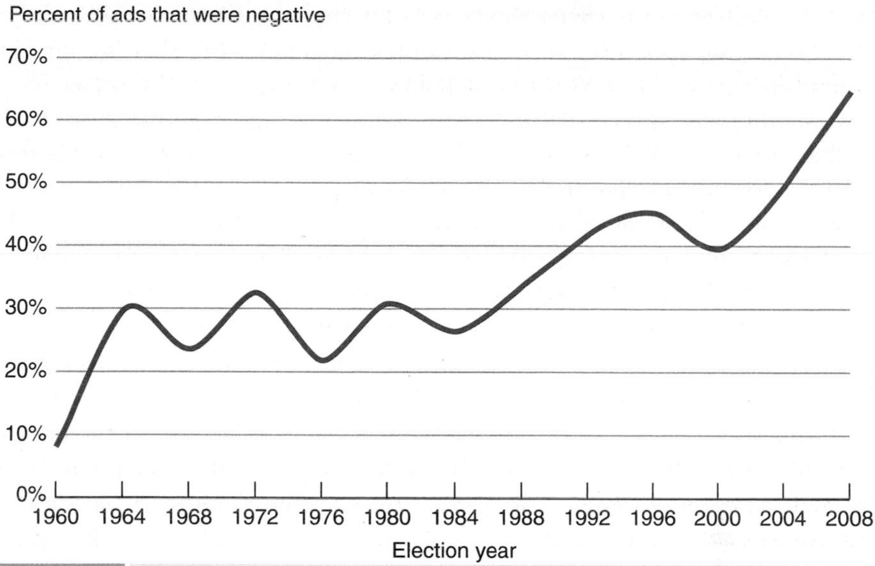

figure 8-7 THE RISE IN NEGATIVE CAMPAIGNING, 1960–2008

In the past half century, negative televised ads in presidential campaigns have increased to the point where they now constitute a majority of the televised ads. *Source:* John G. Geer, *Fanning the Flames: The News Media's Role in the Rise of Negativity in Presidential Campaigns*, Discusson Paper #D55, Joan Shorenstein Center on the Press, Politics, and Public Policy, Kennedy School of Government, Harvard University, February, 2010, p. 4. Reprinted with permission.

Air Wars The main battleground of the modern campaign is the mass media, particularly through the use of televised ads. **Air wars** is the term that political scientist Darrell West applies to this advertising.[40] Candidates increasingly play off each other's ads, seeking to gain the strategic advantage. Modern production techniques enable well-funded candidates to get new ads on the air within a few hours' time, which allows them to rebut attacks and exploit fast-breaking developments, a tactic known as *rapid response.* The airing of televised political ads accounts for roughly half of campaign spending. Indeed, televised ads are the main reason for the high cost of U.S. campaigns. In most democracies, televised campaigning takes place through parties, which receive free air time to make their pitch. Many democracies, including France and Great Britain, prohibit the purchase of televised advertising time by candidates.

Candidates also turn to journalists to get their messages across, although the amount of news coverage they can expect varies widely by location and office. Presidential candidates get daily coverage from the national and local media. Senate candidates always get some news coverage and, if their race is hotly contested, will get heavy local coverage. On the other hand, many

House candidates are virtually ignored by their local news media. The New York City media market, for example, includes more than a score of House districts in New York, New Jersey, Pennsylvania, and Connecticut, and candidates in these districts get little or no coverage from the New York media. They also get little exposure through televised ads because it is too expensive to buy ads in a metropolitan area where the congressional district is only a small fraction of the audience. Such candidates campaign the old-fashioned way, through leafleting, door-to-door canvassing, and the like.

Televised debates can be part of a modern media campaign. Although some House candidates find it impossible to convince local television stations to carry debates, they are commonplace in Senate and presidential races. Debates can be risky encounters, because they give viewers a chance to compare the candidates directly. Some analysts believe, for example, that Al Gore's performance in the first of the 2000 general election debates, when he grimaced and sighed loudly when George W. Bush was talking, cost him the election. Gore had been slightly ahead in the opinion polls but lost his lead following the debate.

Ground Wars Candidates' first priority in a close election is "swing voters"—those voters who conceivably could be persuaded to vote for either side. As election day nears, however, candidates concentrate on getting their supporters to the polls. Get-out-the-vote efforts traditionally have been conducted by the parties and other organizations, such as labor unions. Although these groups remain the cornerstone of the effort, the candidates are also involved, and increasingly so. As partisanship has intensified in recent years, candidates have found it more difficult to persuade voters to switch sides. It is therefore important for them to get as many of their supporters as possible to the polls on election day. Some campaign funds that formerly would have been spent on televised advertising are now spent on voter turnout efforts. In the final phase of the 2010 congressional election, millions of potential voters were contacted by phone or in person by the Republican and Democratic campaigns.

Web Wars New communication technology usually makes its way into campaign politics, and the Internet is no exception. All the candidates for the 2008 Democratic and Republican presidential nominations, for example, had websites dedicated to providing information, generating public support, attracting volunteers, and raising money. Barack Obama's website was easily the most successful. Among its features was a "Fight the Smears" section that provided immediate responses to what the campaign regarded as false or misleading charges, such as the claim that Obama was a Muslim or that his acquaintance Bill Ayers was a terrorist sympathizer.

More significantly, Obama used the Internet to raise tens of millions of dollars in campaign contributions and to create a nationwide network of several million supporters.

Although television is still the principal medium of election politics, some analysts believe that the Internet will eventually overtake it. Internet messaging is less expensive than television advertising. Because it is a targeted medium, the Internet could become the channel through which candidates reach identifiable voting groups. However, the Internet also has some disadvantages relative to television. The most important is that the individual user has greater control over Internet messages. With television, when a brief political ad appears during a favorite program, many viewers will sit through it. An unsolicited message on the Internet is more easily ignored or deleted. Future candidates may conclude that the Internet is the better medium for fundraising and mobilizing supporters and that television is the better medium for building name recognition and reaching less-interested voters.

In Retrospect: The Consequences of the Last War A strong campaign effort can be the difference between winning and losing.[41] In the end, however, nothing so tips the balance in close races as voters' satisfaction with the party that holds power as a result of the previous election. Although some voters are swayed by what candidates promise to do if elected (a form of voting known as *prospective voting*), a greater number respond to past performance (*retrospective voting*). National economic conditions are particularly important in voters' judgments about whether to support the party in power. A weak economy, in conjunction with an unpopular war in Iraq, contributed heavily to the GOP's loss of Congress in 2006 and its loss of the presidency in 2008. When Americans think the country is headed in the wrong direction, the in-party has nearly always lost support in the next election. When times are good, the in-party has less to fear. The 2010 congressional elections followed the typical pattern. Discontent with the performance of President Obama and the Democratic-controlled Congress contributed to the Democratic Party's loss of a large number of House and Senate seats.

Parties, Candidates, and the Public's Influence

Candidate-centered campaigns have some distinct advantages. First, they can infuse new blood into electoral politics. Candidate recruitment is typically a slow process in party-centered systems. Would-be officeholders pay their dues by working in the party and, in the process, tend

John McCain and Sarah Palin campaign during the 2008 presidential election. In America's candidate-centered system, party nominees have considerable latitude in deciding how they will conduct their campaigns. McCain had a nearly free hand in choosing the little-known Palin as his running mate, instantly making her a major political figure, which is a rare occurrence in a party-centered system.

to adopt the outlook of those already there. By comparison, a candidate-centered system is more open and provides opportunities for newcomers to gain office quickly. Barack Obama is a case in point. He had run unsuccessfully for the U.S. House of Representatives in 2000 before winning the 2004 U.S. Senate race in Illinois. Barely two years later, Obama announced his candidacy for president of the United States, winning his party's 2008 nomination against the more experienced U.S. senator Hillary Clinton and then beating the even more experienced U.S. senator John McCain in the general election. Obama's quick rise from political obscurity to the highest office in the country would be almost unthinkable in a party-centered democracy. Nor is he the only example. In 1976, Jimmy Carter went from being an obscure one-term governor of Georgia to winning the presidency two years later. In 2008, the same year that Obama won the presidency, Sarah Palin went from being a little-known small-state governor to one of the Republican Party's most prominent leaders.

Candidate-centered campaigns also lend flexibility to electoral politics. When political conditions and issues change, self-directed candidates adjust quickly, bringing new ideas into the political arena. Strong party organizations are rigid by comparison. Until the early 1990s, for example, the British Labour Party was controlled by old-line activists who refused to concede that changes in the British economy called for changes in the party's trade unionist and economic policies. The result was a series of humiliating defeats at the hands of the Conservative Party that ended only after Tony Blair and other proponents of "New Labour" successfully recast the party's image.

POLITICAL THINKING

Is It Smart to Vote for "the Person?"

It is sometimes said that it is better to "vote the person, not the party." Is that good advice, or bad advice? In voting for a president, for example, Americans are choosing more than the person who will sit behind the desk in the Oval Office. They are also selecting several hundred other executive officers, including the secretary of state, the attorney general of the United States, and the director of the Central Intelligence Agency. The president also nominates all federal judges and justices. Presidents almost invariably choose members of their party for these positions. The election of a senator or a representative is also more than a decision about which individual will occupy a seat in Congress. No single member of Congress has a decisive voice in legislation. Dozens of important legislative votes are cast in Congress each term, and typically, most Republicans are aligned on one side of the vote while most Democrats are aligned on the other side. Does it make more sense "to vote the party, not the person?"

Also, candidate-centered campaigns encourage national officeholders to be responsive to local interests. In building personal followings among their state or district constituents, members of Congress respond to local needs. Nearly every significant domestic program enacted by Congress is adjusted to accommodate the interests of states and localities that otherwise would be hurt by the policy. Where strong national parties exist, national interests take precedence over local concerns. In both France and Britain, for example, the pleas of legislators from underdeveloped regions have often gone unheeded by their party's majority.

In other respects, candidate-centered campaigns have distinct disadvantages. Often they degenerate into mudslinging contests, and they are fertile ground for powerful special-interest groups, which contribute much of the money that underwrites candidates' campaigns. Many groups give large sums of money to incumbents of both parties, which enables them to insulate themselves from an election's outcome. The contributors are assured of having friends in high places regardless of which party wins.

Candidate-centered campaigns also weaken accountability by making it easier for officeholders to deny personal responsibility for government's actions. If national policy goes awry, an incumbent can always say that he or she represents only one vote out of many and that the real problem resides with the president or with "others" in Congress. The problem of accountability is apparent from surveys that have asked Americans about their confidence in Congress. Most citizens have a low opinion of Congress as a whole but say they have confidence in their local representative in Congress. This paradoxical attitude prevails in so many districts that the net result in most elections is a Congress whose membership is not greatly different from the previous one (see Chapter 11). In contrast, party-centered campaigns are characterized by collective accountability. When problems occur, voters tend to hold the majority party responsible and invariably vote large numbers of its members out of office.

In sum, candidate-centered campaigns strengthen the relationship between the voters and their individual representatives while weakening the relationship between the full electorate and their representative institutions. Whether this arrangement serves the public's interest is debatable. Nevertheless, it is clear that Americans do not favor party-centered politics. Parties survived the shift to candidate-centered campaigns and will persist, but their organizational heyday has passed. (Congressional and presidential campaigns are discussed further in Chapters 11 and 12, respectively.)

SUMMARY Self-Test www.mhhe.com/pattersonwtp9e

Political parties serve to link the public with its elected leaders. In the United States, this linkage is provided by the two-party system; only the Republican and Democratic parties have any chance of winning control of government. The fact that the United States has only two major parties is explained by several factors: an electoral system—characterized by single-member districts—that makes it difficult for third parties to compete for power; each party's willingness to accept differing political views; and a political culture that stresses compromise and negotiation rather than ideological rigidity.

Because the United States has only two major parties, each of which seeks to gain majority support, their candidates typically avoid controversial or extreme political positions. Sometimes, Democratic and Republican candidates do offer sharply contrasting policy alternatives, particularly during times of crisis. Ordinarily, however, Republican and Democratic candidates pursue moderate and somewhat overlapping policies. Each party can count on its party loyalists, but U.S. elections can hinge on swing voters, who respond to the issues of the moment either prospectively, basing their vote on what the candidates promise to do if elected, or retrospectively, basing their vote on their satisfaction or dissatisfaction with what the party in power has already done.

America's parties are decentralized, fragmented organizations. The national party organization does not control the policies and activities of the state organizations, and these in turn do not control the local organizations. Traditionally, the local organizations have controlled most of the party's work force because most elections are contested at the local level. Local parties, however, vary markedly in their vitality. Whatever their level, America's party organizations are relatively weak. They lack control over nominations and elections. Candidates can bypass the party organization and win nomination through primary elections. Individual candidates also control most of the organizational structure and money necessary to win elections. The state and national party organizations have recently expanded their capacity to provide candidates with modern campaign services. Nevertheless, party organizations at all levels have few ways of controlling the candidates who run under their banners. They assist candidates with campaign technology, workers, and funds, but they cannot compel candidates to be loyal to organizational goals.

American political campaigns, particularly those for higher office, are candidate centered. Most candidates are self-starters who become adept at "the election game." They spend much of their time raising campaign funds, and they build their personal organizations around campaign consultants: pollsters, media producers, fundraisers, and election consultants. Strategy and image making are key components of the modern campaign, as is televised political advertising, which accounts for half or more of all spending in presidential and congressional races.

The advantages of candidate-centered politics include a responsiveness to new leadership, new ideas, and local concerns. Yet this form of politics can result in campaigns that are personality driven, that depend on powerful interest groups, and that blur responsibility for what government has done.

Key Terms

air wars (*p. 281*)
candidate-centered campaigns (*p. 251*)
factional (minor) party (*p. 269*)
gender gap (*p. 266*)
grassroots party (*p. 253*)
hard money (*p. 276*)
ideological (minor) party (*p. 269*)
linkage institution (*p. 252*)
median voter theorem (*p. 263*)
money chase (*p. 277*)
multiparty system (*p. 261*)
nomination (*p. 271*)
packaging (of a candidate) (*p. 279*)
party-centered campaigns (*p. 251*)
party coalition (*p. 264*)
party competition (*p. 252*)
party organizations (*p. 271*)
party realignment (*p. 254*)
political consultants (*p. 279*)
political party (*p. 251*)
primary election (direct primary) (*p. 271*)

proportional representation (*p. 262*)
reform (minor) party (*p. 268*)
service relationship (*p. 277*)
single-issue (minor) party (*p. 268*)
single-member districts (*p. 262*)
soft money (*p. 276*)
two-party system (*p. 261*)

Suggested Readings

Brewer, Mark D., and Jeffrey M. Stonecash. *Dynamics of American Political Parties.* New York: Cambridge University Press, 2009. A careful assessment of party change and its impact.

Buell, Emmett H., Jr., and Lee Sigelman. *Attack Politics: Negativity in Presidential Campaigns since 1960.* Lawrence: University Press of Kansas, 2008. A look at how negative politics has come to pervade campaigns.

Craig, Stephen C. *The Electoral Challenge: Theory Meets Practice.* Washington, D.C.: CQ Press, 2006. A comprehensive assessment of the impact of election campaigns.

Farrar-Myers, Victoria A., and Diana Dwyer. *Limits and Loopholes: The Quest for Money, Free Speech, and Fair Elections.* Washington, D.C.: CQ Press, 2008. A careful look at the development of campaign finance legislation.

Flanigan, William H., and Nancy H. Zingale. *Political Behavior of the American Electorate*, 12th ed. Washington, D.C.: CQ Press, 2009. A concise but insightful look at the American voter.

Geer, John. *In Defense of Negativity*. Chicago: University of Chicago Press, 2006. A provocative and award-winning analysis of televised political ads.

Hershey, Marjorie Randon. *Party Politics in America*, 14th ed. New York: Longman, 2010. A well-written and thorough analysis of U.S. political parties.

Hillygus, D. Sunshine, and Todd G. Shields. *The Persuadable Voter: Wedge Issues in Presidential Campaigns.* Princeton, N.J.: Princeton University Press, 2008. A careful analysis of the use of wedge issues, such as abortion, in campaign strategy.

Kaufmann, Karen M., John R. Petrocik, and Daron R. Shaw. *Unconventional Wisdom: Facts and Myths about American Voters.* New York: Oxford University Press, 2008. An illuminating assessment of how America's voters actually behave.

Mayhew, David R. *Parties and Policies: How the American Government Works.* New Haven, CT.: Yale University Press, 2008. An insightful analysis that digs deeply into the dynamics of American politics.

Trautman, Karl G. *The Underdog in American Politics: The Democratic Party and Liberal Values.* New York: Palgrave Macmillan, 2010. A careful analysis of the underdog's place in American politics.

West, Darrell M. *Air Wars: Television Advertising in Election Campaigns, 1952–2008*, 5th ed. Washington, D.C.: Congressional Quarterly Press, 2009. A leading study of the role of televised advertising in election campaigns.

List of Websites

www.democrats.org The Democratic National Committee's site; provides information on the party's platform, candidates, officials, and organization.

www.gp.org The Green Party's site; contains information on the party's philosophy and policy goals.

www.rnc.org Home page of the Republican National Committee; offers information on Republican leaders, policy positions, and organizations.

www.teapartypatriots.org The site of the Tea Party; contains information on the movement's policy positions and activities.

Politics in Theory and Practice

Thinking: Why are elections conducted so differently in the United States than in European democracies? Why are the campaigns so much longer, more expensive, and more candidate-centered?

Participating: Consider becoming a campaign or political party volunteer. The opportunities are numerous. Parties and candidates at every level from the national on down seek volunteers to assist in organizing, canvassing, fundraising, and other activities. As a college student, you have communication and knowledge skills that would be valuable to a campaign or party organization. You might be pleasantly surprised by the tasks you are assigned.

Extra Credit

For up-to-the-minute *New York Times* articles, interactive simulations, graphics, study tools, and more links and quizzes, visit the text's Online Learning Center at **www.mhhe.com/pattersonwtp9e**.

NATIONAL JOURNAL

The Curse of One-Party Government

Here is what you already know: President Obama's approval ratings are below 50 percent in most polls. Independents have swung against him, and Republicans loathe him. The Democratic Party is in the doghouse. The Republican Party, although gleeful over the Democrats' setbacks, is in worse shape institutionally, held captive by its most extreme partisans and lacking appeal beyond its base. Health care reform, deficit reduction, and global-warming legislation are going nowhere. Obama's campaign promises to change Washington's hyperpartisan ways look like a sad joke.

The question is, how could things have gone south so fast? The economy is clearly a factor, but the economy was even worse a year ago, when Obama was popular and hopes were high. He made mistakes, but politicians always do. Consider a further possibility: Unified government makes the country virtually ungovernable.

Like a lot of people, I have believed for quite some time that power-sharing (one party controls the White House, the other at least one chamber of Congress) works better. The voters prefer it, having split control in 23 of the past 30 years. The two most politically successful and popular recent presidents, Ronald Reagan and Bill Clinton, shared power for most or all of their terms; the most widely reviled of recent presidents, George W. Bush, saw his popularity collapse when Republicans won total control. Reforms win broader acceptance and are more durable when both parties' fingerprints are on them. The two great domestic reforms of their respective eras, tax reform in 1986 and welfare reform in 1996, were products of divided control.

All of that you have heard before from me and others. Recently, however, watching the neck-snapping speed with which a backlash has formed against Obama's all-Democratic government, I have become convinced of a stronger proposition: In practice, the difference between divided and unified control has become so stark that we should think of them as being, for practical purposes, two distinct systems of government—if you will, binary government. Though the country has only one Constitution, it has two governability settings. Call them Mode 1 (one-party control) and Mode 2 (two-party control). Power-sharing is the switch that toggles between them.

The root cause of binary government is that the two parties, once both broad coalitions with large ideological overlaps, sorted themselves in the 1970s and 1980s into two ideologically distinct entities with effectively no overlap. Their centers are well to the left and right, respectively, of the country's center, and even further from each other.

However, neither party, even if it holds a congressional majority (a majority in the House and Senate), can by itself command a governing majority (a majority of voters), because neither accounts for more than about a third of the electorate. Between them floats a sea of relatively centrist independents. The only way either party can govern sustainably is in coalition with a majority of independents. But moderates are severely underrepresented on Capitol Hill, where there is no Independent Party with which Republicans or Democrats could form a coalition.

So that's the arithmetic. What happens, then, in Mode 1, unified control? The out-party's members (Republicans, at the moment) have no incentive to help the in-party succeed and every incentive to help it fail. They walk away, taking their votes with them. To govern in the face of Republicans' boycott, Democrats need to hold almost every vote in their caucus. But that means governing from the center of their party, rather than from the center of the country—exactly what has happened with health care reform.

The trouble is that governing from off-center alienates independents, who are angry both because they feel, often correctly, that the system is ignoring them and because they hate the shrill noise emanating from Washington as the outs wage scorched-earth combat. Again, that is exactly what is happening now.

In Mode 1, the president can attempt to hold together a governing coalition by slaloming: veering from left or right to center and back. That is what Clinton struggled to do in his first two years, and it is what Obama is struggling to do now. It can work briefly but not for long. Every zig toward the center offends the party's base (too many compromises!), and every zag back toward the base upsets centrists (he's just too extreme!), and the president looks weak and inconsistent.

The whole system, now, has become dynamically unstable, toxic to itself. As the in-party's base grows restive and the out-party lobs stink bombs, the president bleeds support, Washington turns rancorous, partisans pump up the volume, and independents get disgusted with the president and both parties. Downstream from Washington, public opinion sours on the parties, the president, and government itself. Neither party commands support beyond its base. Neither has a mandate to govern. The country's governability quotient sinks. Doing everything becomes harder.

That is Mode 1. No wonder the voters prefer Mode 2: It runs the cycle in reverse. When the parties share power, the only way to pass legislation is to compromise. Forced to tug against each other, they drag policy toward the center, which makes independents feel included. Forced to work with the other party, the president can now position himself in the center ("triangulate," as the Clinton people called it) and impose centrism on his party's base. Neither party commands support beyond its base. Neither has a mandate to govern. The country's governability quotient sinks.

Not everyone will be pleased; far from it. Nonetheless, when the parties share power, it becomes arithmetically possible to find enough support among Democrats and Republicans and independents to form a sustainable governing coalition. The president's popularity improves. The country's governability quotient rises. Politicians, especially the president, have an easier job.

Modes 1 and 2 are tendencies, not inevitabilities. But they appear to be strong tendencies with fundamentally distinct political dynamics. Yes, they are related, but in the way that a bicycle is related to a unicycle: Both are rideable, but one is much more stable for the long haul.

I can't prove the binary-government theory, but it fits the facts. In all three recent extended Mode 1 periods (Clinton's first two years, Bush's middle four, and now Obama's first year), the cycle of events was eerily similar: Congress leaned too far left or right, the president was dragged off center, the country became bitterly polarized, independents grew disgusted, and the voters soon switched to Mode 2. Much the same thing happened in Reagan's first two years, when the defection of "Boll Weevil" Democrats gave Republicans effective one-party control.

For Reagan and Clinton, the switch back to Mode 2 in 1982 and 1994, respectively, proved a godsend. The majority party was forced to compromise, the minority party was forced to behave responsibly, policy swung toward the center, and the presidents regained their standing and left office with high approval ratings. Obviously, other factors were important, especially the economy. But I believe that in both cases the parties governed more successfully and sustainably together than either could have done separately, and the voters felt the same way.

Bush, of course, played the tape backward. His first two years, when Democrats mostly controlled the Senate, produced a series of mostly centrist reforms: No Child Left Behind, campaign finance reform, corporate-governance reform, the anti-terrorism USA PATRIOT Act. Then Republicans won the Senate and spent four years trying to run a one-party government, alienating not only Democrats but also independents and finally even many Republicans. When Democrats won back Congress in 2006, Bush moderated his policies, but it was too late. The public had written him off and was already focusing on 2008.

Obama, so far, is playing Bush's tape, not because he is a wild-eyed extremist or partisan (neither was Bush), but because he is cursed with a Democratic Congress. All the telltale symptoms of Mode 1 syndrome have appeared. The in-party is too far off center, the out-party is stymieing it at every turn, the president can't find stable ground, independents are disgusted, the public is angry. The Democrats cannot translate their congressional majority into a governing majority. Here we go again.

In a world of binary government, forcing the parties to share power is the only way to achieve sustainable bipartisanship in government; to ensure that moderate voters and policies are adequately represented in politics; and to give controversial reforms such as health care legislation the imprimatur of consensus. And there is nothing partisan about hoping that this year's election brings a return to Mode 2.

What's Your Opinion?

If you were president, would you rather your Congress be of the same or the opposite political party? Explain some of the reasons you think voters have become dissatisfied with the Obama administration. Do you think a Republican Congress has the potential to reverse some or all of this discontent?

CHAPTER 9

Interest Groups: Organizing for Influence

“The flaw in the pluralist heaven is that the heavenly chorus sings with a strong upper-class bias.”

E. E. Schattschneider[1]

The insurance companies began their effort to undermine the health care reform effort nearly as soon as the meeting ended. President Barack Obama had organized the meeting to hear what health industry groups had to say about reform of the nation's medical care system. Insurance industry representatives attended the meeting and spoke favorably about the need for change. Insurance companies were determined, however, to block any change that would erode their profits. They ran a national advertising campaign that claimed they were "supporting bipartisan reforms that Congress can build on." In that congressional Republicans were united in their opposition to a major overhaul of the health care system, "bipartisan reforms" could only mean something less than Obama had in mind. As the legislation worked its way through Congress, the insurance industry stepped up its attack. One day before a crucial Senate vote on the legislation, for instance, an industry trade group, America's Health Insurance Plans (AHIP), issued a report claiming the typical American family would wind up paying $4,000 more in premiums if the reform was enacted, a figure that was substantially higher than other projections.[2] All told, the insurance industry spent over $200 million on advertising and lobbying in its effort to derail legislation that would threaten its hold on America's health care system.[3]

The insurance industry's campaign against comprehensive health care reform suggests why interest groups are both admired and feared. Insurance companies have legitimate interests that are affected by public policy. It is perfectly appropriate for them to lobby on policy issues. The same can be said of farmers, consumers, minorities, college students—indeed, of virtually every interest in society. In fact, the *pluralist* theory of American politics (see Chapter 1) holds that society's interests are represented most effectively through group action.

Yet groups can wield too much power, getting their way at an unreasonable cost to the rest of society. When Obama launched his health care initiative, polls indicated that most Americans thought a major change in the nation's medical care system was needed. They were not necessarily behind Obama's plan. In fact, most of them were not exactly sure of what he had in mind, or what the leading alternatives might be. That said, the time was ripe for a fruitful public debate about the advantages, and the drawbacks, of an alternative health care system. Did the insurance industry, in pursuit of its self-interest, help to derail that debate?

Opinions would differ on the answer to this question, but there is no doubt that groups have considerable influence over public policy. Indeed, most observers believe that group influence has increased in recent decades. The situation has been described as the rise of **single-issue politics**: groups have organized around nearly every conceivable policy issue, with each group pressing its demands to the utmost through lobbying and other forms of political pressure.

An **interest group**—also called a "faction," "pressure group," "special interest," or "organized interest"—can be defined as any organization that actively seeks to influence public policy.[4] Interest groups are similar to political parties in some respects but differ from them in important ways.[5]

Like parties, groups are a linkage mechanism: they serve to connect citizens with government. However, political parties address a broad range of issues so as to appeal to diverse blocs of voters. Above all, parties are in the business of trying to win elections. Groups, on the other hand, concentrate on policies directly affecting their interests. A group may involve itself in elections, but its major purpose is to influence the policies that affect it.

This chapter examines the degree to which various interests in American society are represented by organized groups, the process by which interest groups exert influence, and the costs and benefits of group politics. The main points made in the chapter are these:

- *Although nearly all interests in American society are organized to some degree, those associated with economic activity, particularly business activity, are by far the most thoroughly organized.* Their advantage rests on their superior financial resources and on the private goods (such as wages and jobs) they provide to those in the organization.
- *Groups that do not have economic activity as their primary function often have organizational difficulties.* These groups pursue public or collective goods (such as a safer environment) that are available even to individuals who are not group members, so individuals may free ride, choosing not to pay the costs of membership.
- *Lobbying and electioneering are the traditional means by which groups communicate with and influence political leaders.* Recent developments, including grassroots lobbying and political action committees, have heightened interest groups' influence.
- *The interest-group system overrepresents business interests and fosters policies that serve a group's interest more than the society's broader interests.* Thus, although groups are an essential part of the policy process, they also distort that process.

The Interest-Group System

In the 1830s, the Frenchman Alexis de Tocqueville wrote that the "principle of association" was nowhere more evident than in America.[6] His description still holds. Americans are more likely than citizens of other nations to join organized groups (see "How the U.S. Differs"). However, not all of these organizations are interest groups. Book clubs, softball teams, social clubs, and most church groups are examples of groups that are not in the interest-group category because they do not seek to influence the policy process. Even so, no other nation has as many organized interest groups as does the United States. The country's tradition of free association makes it natural for Americans to join together for political

HOW THE U.S. DIFFERS

POLITICAL THINKING THROUGH COMPARISONS

Groups: "A Nation of Joiners"

"A nation of joiners" is how the Frenchman Alexis de Tocqueville described the United States during his visit to this country in the 1830s. Tocqueville was stunned by the group and community activity he saw, suggesting that Europeans would find it hard to comprehend. "The political activity that pervades the United States," said Tocqueville, "must be seen to be understood."

Today, Americans still are more actively involved in groups and community causes than are Europeans. Some observers, including Robert Putnam, believe that group activity in the United States is in decline (*Bowling Alone*, 2000). Even if that is true, Americans are more engaged in groups than citizens elsewhere. Among the reasons are the nation's tradition of free association, the openness of American society, and the prominence of religion and public education. Much of the nation's group life revolves around its churches and its schools.

Such differences are reflected in citizens' participation rates. Americans are more likely to belong to groups than are the French, Italians, British, or Germans, as the accompanying figures from the World Values Survey indicate.

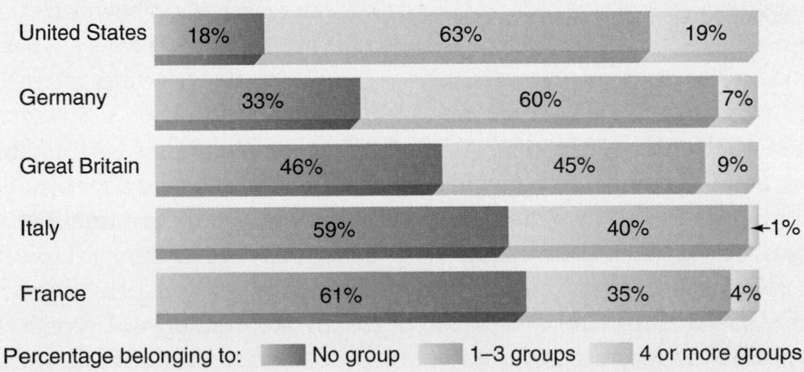

Source: World Values Survey Association, 2010.

Q: *How does the structure of the U.S. government contribute to the proliferation of interest groups in America?*

A: *Because of federalism and the separation of powers, the American system offers numerous points at which groups can try to influence public policy. If unsuccessful with legislators, groups can turn to executives or to the courts. If thwarted at the national level, groups can turn to state and local governments. By comparison, the governments of most other democratic nations are not organized in ways that facilitate group access and influence. Great Britain's unitary government, for example, concentrates power at the national level. Moreover, in the British House of Commons, power is concentrated in the top leadership to a far greater degree that it is in the U.S. Congress (see Chapter 11).*

purposes, and their diverse interests give them reason to pursue policy influence through group action.

The nation's political structure also contributes to group action. Because of federalism and the separation of powers, groups have multiple points of entry through which to influence policy. The structure of the American system even contributes to a type of lobbying that is sometimes overlooked. While the vast majority of organized interests represent private interests, some represent governments. Most states and major cities have at least one Washington lobbyist. Intergovernmental lobbying also occurs through groups such as the Council of State Governments, the National Governors Association, the National Association of Counties, the National League of Cities, and the U.S. Conference of Mayors. These organizations sometimes play a significant role in national policy debates. For example, as Congress was preparing in 2006 to renew and amend the antiterrorism legislation that had gone into effect in 2001, the National Governors Association and the U.S. Conference of Mayors lobbied heavily to ensure that the changes reflected their concerns. Even foreign governments lobby in Washington. Arms sales, foreign aid, immigration, and trade practices are among the U.S. policies they target.[7]

The extraordinary number of interest groups in the United States does not mean that the nation's various interests are equally well organized. Groups develop when people with a shared interest have the opportunity and the incentive to join together. Some individuals or organizations have the skills, money, contacts, or time to participate in group politics; others do not. Moreover, some groups are inherently more attractive to potential members than others and thus find it easier to organize. Groups also differ in their financial resources and thus in their capacity for political action.

Therefore, a first consideration in regard to group politics in America is the issue of how thoroughly various interests are organized. Interests that are highly organized stand a good chance of having their views heard by policymakers. Those that are poorly organized run the risk of being ignored.

Economic Groups

No interests are more fully or effectively organized than those that have economic activity as their primary purpose. Corporations, labor unions, farm groups, and professional associations, among others, exist primarily for economic purposes—to make profits, provide jobs, improve pay, or protect an occupation. For the sake of discussion, we will call such organizations **economic groups**. Almost all such organizations engage in political activity as a means of promoting and protecting their economic interests. An indicator of this is the fact that Washington lobbyists who represent economic groups outnumber those of all other groups by more than two to one.

Among economic groups, the most numerous are *business groups*. Writing in 1929, political scientist E. Pendleton Herring noted, "Of the many organized groups maintaining offices in [Washington], there are no interests more fully, more comprehensively, and more efficiently represented than those of American industry."[8] Although corporations do not dominate lobbying as thoroughly as they once did, Herring's general conclusion still holds: more than half of all groups formally registered to lobby Congress are business organizations. Virtually all large corporations and many smaller ones are politically active.

Business firms are also represented through associations. Some of these "organizations of organizations" seek to advance the broad interests of business. One of the oldest associations is the National Association of Manufacturers, which was formed in 1894, and today represents 14,000 manufacturers. Another large business association is the U.S. Chamber of Commerce, which represents nearly three million businesses of all sizes. Other business associations, such as the American Petroleum Institute and the National Association of Home Builders, are confined to a single trade or industry.

Economic groups also include those associated with organized labor. *Labor groups* seek to promote policies that benefit workers in general and union members in particular. Although there are some major independent unions, such as the United Mine Workers and the Teamsters, the dominant labor group is the AFL-CIO, which has its national headquarters in Washington, D.C. The AFL-CIO has 12 million members in its nearly sixty affiliated unions, which include the International Brotherhood of Electrical Workers, the Sheet Metal Workers, and the Communications Workers of America.

At an earlier time, about a third of the U.S. workforce was unionized. Today, only about one in eight workers is a union member. Historically, skilled and unskilled laborers constituted the bulk of organized labor, but their numbers have decreased as the economy has changed, while the number of professionals, technicians, and service workers has increased. Professionals have shown little interest in union organization, perhaps because they identify with management or consider themselves economically secure. Service workers and technicians can also be difficult for unions to organize because they work closely with managers and, often, in small offices. Nevertheless, unions have made inroads in their efforts to organize service and public employees.

In fact, most union members today work in the public sector, despite the fact that it has only a fifth of the number of workers as does the private sector (see Figure 9-1). The most heavily unionized employees are those who work for local government, such as teachers, police officers, and fire

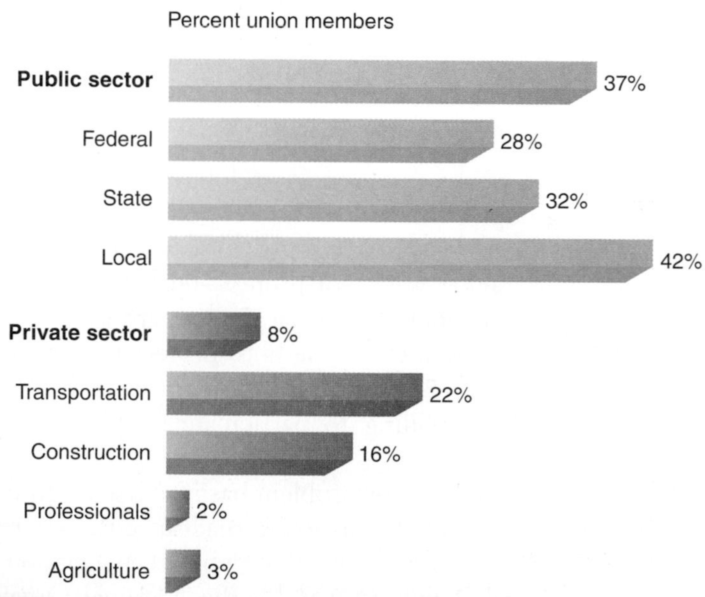

figure 9-1 PERCENTAGE OF UNION MEMBERS, BY SECTOR AND INDUSTRY

Historically, union membership was concentrated in the private sector, as in the case of factory and construction workers. Today, most union members work in the public sector, as in the case of teachers, police officers, and firefighters employed by local government. *Source:* U.S. Department of Labor, 2010. For the private sector, the figure includes selected industries only.

fighters. Many state and federal employees are also union members. The overall rate of unionization among public-sector workers is nearly 40 percent, compared with less than 10 percent for private-industry workers. Even the construction industry, which ranks high by comparison with most private-sector industries, has a unionization rate of only 16 percent.[9]

Farm groups represent another large economic lobby. The American Farm Bureau Federation is the largest of the farm groups, with more than four million members. The National Farmers Union, the National Grange, and the National Farmers Organization are smaller farm lobbies. Agricultural groups do not always agree on policy issues. For instance, the Farm Bureau sides with agribusiness and owners of large farms, while the Farmers Union promotes the interests of smaller "family" farms. There are also numerous specialty farm associations, including the Association of Wheat Growers, the American Soybean Association, and the Associated Milk Producers. Each association acts as a separate lobby, seeking to obtain policies that will serve its members' particular interests.

Most professions also have lobbying associations. Among the most powerful of these *professional groups* is the American Medical Association (AMA), which includes more than 200,000 physicians. Other professional groups include the American Bar Association (ABA) and the American Association of University Professors (AAUP).

Citizens' Groups

Economic groups do not have a monopoly on lobbying. There is another category of interest groups—**citizens' groups** (or **noneconomic groups**). Group members in this category are joined together not by a *material incentive*—such as jobs, higher wages, or profits—but by a *purposive incentive*, the satisfaction of contributing to what they regard as a worthy goal or purpose.[10] Whether a group's purpose is to protect the environment, return prayer to the public schools, or feed the poor at home or abroad, there are citizens who are willing to participate simply because they believe the cause is a worthy one.

Nearly every conceivable issue or problem has its citizens' group, often several of them. Some citizens' groups work to advance the interests of a particular social grouping; examples are the National Association for the Advancement of Colored People (NAACP), the National Organization for Women (NOW), and La Raza, which is the largest Hispanic American lobbying group. Other citizens' groups are dedicated to the promotion of a political ideology. Such groups have a broad agenda that derives from a philosophical or moral position. The American Conservative

Union (ACU) is the largest conservative organization and lobbies on issues like taxation and national defense. MoveOn is a liberal counterpart to the ACU, as is Americans for Democratic Action (ADA). Another example is the Christian Coalition of America, which describes itself as "America's leading grassroots organization defending our godly heritage." The group addresses a wide range of issues, including school prayer, abortion, and television programming. Ideology is also a component of the state-level Public Interest Research Groups (PIRGs), such as NYPIRG (New York), CALPIRG (California), and TexPIRG (Texas). Almost every state has a PIRG, which usually has chapters on college campuses. Drawing on their network of researchers, students, and advocates, they approach issues from a liberal perspective. Ideological groups on both the left and the right have increased substantially in number since the 1960s.

Most citizens' groups, however, have an issue-specific policy agenda. *Single-issue groups* have risen sharply in number in the past half century and now pressure government on almost every conceivable policy, from

This 1873 lithograph illustrates the benefits of membership in the National Grange, an agricultural interest group.

nuclear arms to drug abuse. Notable current examples are the National Rifle Association and the various right-to-life and pro-choice groups. Most environmental groups can also be seen as single-issue organizations in that they seek to influence public policy in a specific area, such as pollution reduction, wilderness preservation, or wildlife protection. The Sierra Club, one of the oldest environmental groups, was formed in the 1890s to promote the preservation of scenic areas. Also prominent are the National Audubon Society, the Wilderness Society, the Environmental Defense Fund, Greenpeace U.S.A., and the Izaak Walton League. Since 1960, membership in environmental groups has more than tripled in response to increased public concern about the environment.[11]

Citizens' groups are difficult to classify precisely because they differ so widely in their focus and goals. Some single-issue groups, for example, are ideological whereas others are pragmatic. A simple but precise way to describe citizens' groups is that they are "groups anyone can join." This does not mean that everyone would want to join a particular group. A conservative would not choose to join the ADA, just as a liberal would not join the ACU. But there is no barrier to joining a citizens' group if one is willing to contribute the required time or money. In this way, citizens' groups are distinct from business firms, which are closed to all but their employees, and distinct also from labor groups, farm groups, and professional associations, whose members have a particular type of training or vocation.[12]

POLITICAL THINKING

Parties or Groups?

Political parties and interest groups are linking organizations through which people connect to their government. How do groups differ from parties in terms of who they represent? Can either substitute for the other? Think of your own situation. Do you think you are represented more effectively through the party you identify with, or through the groups you are a part of?

The Organizational Edge: Economic Groups versus Citizens' Groups

Although the number of citizens' groups has mushroomed in recent decades, they are substantially outnumbered by economic groups. By most accounts, they also have less influence on government than do economic groups. The predominance of economic interests was predicted in *Federalist* No. 10, in which James Madison declared that property is "the most

table 9-1 ADVANTAGES AND DISADVANTAGES HELD BY ECONOMIC AND CITIZENS' GROUPS

Compared with economic groups, citizens' groups have fewer advantages and more disadvantages.

Economic Groups	**Citizens' Groups**
Advantages	*Advantages*
Economic activity provides the organization with the resources necessary for political action.	Members are likely to support leaders' political efforts because they joined the group in order to influence policy.
Individuals are encouraged to join the group because of economic benefits they individually receive (such as wages).	
In the case of firms within an industry, their small number encourages organization because the contribution of each firm can make a difference.	
Disadvantages	*Disadvantages*
Persons within the group may not support leaders' political efforts because they did not join the group for political reasons.	The group has to raise funds, especially for its political activities.
	Potential members may choose not to join the group because they get collective benefits even if they do not join (the free-rider problem).
	Potential members may choose not to join the group because their individual contribution may be too small to affect the group's success one way or the other.

common and durable source of factions." Stated differently, nothing seems to matter quite so much to people as their economic self-interest. Several factors (summarized in Table 9-1) give economic groups an organizational advantage, including their resources and their size.

Unequal Access to Resources One reason for the abundance of economic groups is their access to financial resources. Political lobbying does not come cheap. If a group is to make its views known, it typically must have a headquarters, an expert staff, and communication facilities. Economic groups pay for these things with money generated by their economic activity. Corporations have the greatest built-in advantage. They do not have to charge membership dues or conduct fundraisers to support their lobbying. Their political money comes from their business profits.

Some economic groups rely on dues rather than profits to support their lobbying, but they have something of economic value to offer in exchange. Labor unions, for example, provide their members access to higher-paying jobs in return for the dues they pay. Such groups offer what is called a

private (individual) good—a benefit, such as a job, that is given directly to a particular individual. An important feature of a private good is that it can be held back. If an individual is unwilling to pay organizational dues, the group can withhold the benefit.

Citizens' groups do not have these inherent advantages. They do not generate profits or fees as a result of economic activity. Moreover, the incentives they offer prospective members are not exclusive. As opposed to the private or individual goods provided by many economic groups, most non-economic groups offer **collective (public) goods** as an incentive for membership. Collective goods are, by definition, goods that belong to all; they cannot be granted or withheld on an individual basis. The air people breathe and the national forests people visit are examples of collective goods. They are available to one and all, those who do not pay dues to a clean-air group or a wilderness preservation group as well as those who do.

The shared characteristic of collective goods creates what is called the **free-rider problem**: individuals can obtain the good even if they do not contribute to the group's effort. Take the case of National Public Radio (NPR). Although NPR's programs are funded primarily through listeners' donations, those who do not contribute can listen to the programs. The non-contributors are free riders: they receive the benefit without paying for it. About 90 percent of regular listeners to NPR do not contribute to their local station.

In a purely economic sense, as economist Mancur Olson noted, it is not rational for an individual to contribute to a group when its benefit can be obtained for free.[13] Moreover, the dues paid by any single member are too small to affect the group's success one way or another. Why pay dues to an environmental group when any improvements in the air, water, or wildlife from its lobbying efforts are available to everyone and when one's individual contribution is too small to make a real difference? Although many people do join such groups anyway, the free-rider problem is one reason citizens' groups are organized less fully than economic groups.

The free-rider problem has been lessened, but not eliminated, in recent decades by communication technologies that enable citizens' groups to easily contact prospective members. Computer-assisted direct mail is one of these technologies. Group organizers buy mailing lists and flood the mails with computer-typed "personal" letters asking recipients to pay a small annual membership fee. For some individuals, a fee of $25–50 annually represents no great sacrifice and offers the satisfaction of supporting a cause in which they believe. "Checkbook membership" is how political scientist Theda Skocpol describes such contributions.[14] Until the computer era, citizens' groups had great difficulty identifying and contacting potential members.

The Internet has made it easier for citizens' groups to organize and increase their membership. One of the most successful examples is MoveOn. It was founded by a small group of liberal activists.

The Internet has also been a boon to citizens' groups. Virtually every such group of any size has its own website and e-mail list. MoveOn illustrates the Internet's organizing capacity. MoveOn was started by a handful of liberal activists working out of a garage. Its network now includes roughly five million members. In 2009–2010, during the fight over health care reform, MoveOn repeatedly mobilized its membership, including requests for help in correcting misunderstandings about the legislation. Among the misunderstandings that MoveOn members were asked to address were "President Obama wants to euthanize your grandmother" and "Democrats are going to outlaw private insurance and force you into a government plan."

The Advantages and Disadvantages of Size Although citizens' groups have proliferated in recent decades, the organizational muscle in American politics rests primarily with economic groups. Business interests in particular have an advantage that economist Mancur Olson calls "the size factor."[15] Although it might be thought that the interests of groups with large memberships would typically prevail over the interests of smaller groups, the reverse is more often true. Olson notes that small groups are ordinarily more united on policy issues and often have more resources, enabling them to win out against large groups. Business groups in a specific industry are usually few in number and have an incentive to work together to influence government on issues of joint interest. The U.S. automobile industry, for example, has its "Big Three"—General Motors, Ford, and Chrysler. Although they compete for car sales, they usually work together on policy issues. They have succeeded at times, for example, in persuading government to delay or reduce higher fuel efficiency and safety standards, which has meant billions in additional profits for them at an incalculable cost to car owners.

Business associations testify to the advantage of small size. The business sector is divided into numerous industries, most of which include only a small number of major firms. Virtually every one of these industries, from oil to cereals to bow ties, has its own trade association. More than one thousand trade associations are represented in Washington, and they spend hundreds of millions of dollars annually on lobbying.

Their situation is far different from that of, say, taxpayers, who number in the tens of millions. Although taxpayers would be enormously powerful if they all joined together in a single cohesive group, most taxpayers have no real interest in paying dues to a taxpayers' group that would lobby on their behalf. In 2008, these differences came together in ways that conceivably hurt taxpayers while helping leading financial institutions. At issue was a government bailout aimed at protecting major investment banks from bankruptcy as a result of their purchase of mortgage-backed securities, which had declined sharply in value as the U.S. housing market weakened. With the backing of policymakers in the Federal Reserve, the Treasury Department, the White House, and Congress, troubled financial institutions received $700 billion in taxpayers' money to rescue them from bankruptcy, even though their risky investments had brought them to that point. Getting millions of taxpayers to work together to influence policy is infinitely more difficult than getting top financial firms to collaborate. "[T]he larger the group," Olson wrote, "the less it will further its common interests."[16]

Nevertheless, there is strength in numbers. No group illustrates this better than AARP (formerly known as the American Association of Retired Persons). Although not every retired person belongs to AARP, its membership dues are so low (five dollars annually) that millions do. AARP has a staff of more than one thousand and is a formidable lobby on social security, Medicare, and other issues affecting retirees. A *Fortune* magazine survey of 2,200 Washington insiders, including members of Congress and their staffs, ranked AARP as the nation's most powerful lobbying group.[17] AARP is the only citizens' group that ranks among the top twenty groups in terms of lobbying expenditures; the others are business firms or business associations.[18]

INSIDE LOBBYING: SEEKING INFLUENCE THROUGH OFFICIAL CONTACTS

Modern government is involved in so many issues—business regulation, income maintenance, urban renewal, cancer research, and energy development, to name only a few—that hardly any interest in society could fail to benefit significantly from having influence over federal policies or programs. Moreover, modern government is action oriented. Officials are more inclined to solve problems than to let them fester. When forest fires in California destroyed property worth millions in 2010, the federal government granted large sums to meet the clean-up and other costs to the state and its residents.

Groups seek government's support through **lobbying**, a term that refers broadly to efforts by groups to influence public policy through contact with public officials.[19] Lobbying in America is a big business. An area of the nation's capital known as K Street is populated by lobbying firms. More than 20,000 lobbyists work in Washington. They are regulated by the Honest Leadership and Open Government Act of 2007 (which amended the Lobbying Disclosure Act of 1995). The legislation requires lobbyists to register and to file detailed reports on their lobbying activities and expenditures.

Interest groups rely on two main lobbying strategies, which have been called *inside lobbying* and *outside lobbying*.[20] Each strategy involves communication with public officials, but the strategies differ in what is communicated and who does the communicating. This section discusses **inside lobbying**, which is based on group efforts to develop and maintain close ("inside") contacts with policymakers. (Outside lobbying is described in the next section.)

Acquiring Access to Officials

Though inside lobbying groups seek to gain direct access to officials in order to influence their decisions. Lobbying once depended significantly on tangible inducements, sometimes including bribes. This old form of lobbying survives, but modern lobbying generally involves subtler methods than simply slipping a cash-filled envelope to a public official. Lobbyists concentrate on contacting policymakers to supply them with information that supports the group's position on pending policy.[21] "If I don't explain what we do . . . Congress will make uninformed decisions without understanding the consequences to the industry," said one lobbyist.[22] For the most part, inside lobbying is directed at policymakers who are inclined to support the group rather than at those who have opposed it in the past. This tendency reflects both the difficulty of persuading opponents to change long-held views and the advantage of working through trusted officials. Thus, union lobbyists work mainly with pro-labor officeholders, just as corporate lobbyists work mainly with policymakers who support business interests.

For lobbyists to be fully persuasive, they must understand the policy process as well as the issue under consideration. For this reason, a "revolving door" exists between lobbying firms and government. Many lobbyists worked previously in government, and some top officials were once lobbyists. Upon retirement, many members of Congress join lobbying firms. Although they are prohibited by law from lobbying Congress for a set period of time after leaving office, they are free to do so thereafter and they usually lobby for groups or on issues they handled during their time in Congress.[23]

Money is a key element in inside-lobbying efforts. The amount of money spent on lobbying is staggering—roughly $3.5 billion in 2009 alone (see Figure 9-2). The American Petroleum Institute, for example, with its abundant financial resources, can afford a downtown Washington office staffed by lobbyists, petroleum experts, and public relations specialists who help the oil companies maintain access to and influence with legislative and executive leaders. Many groups spend upward of $1 million annually

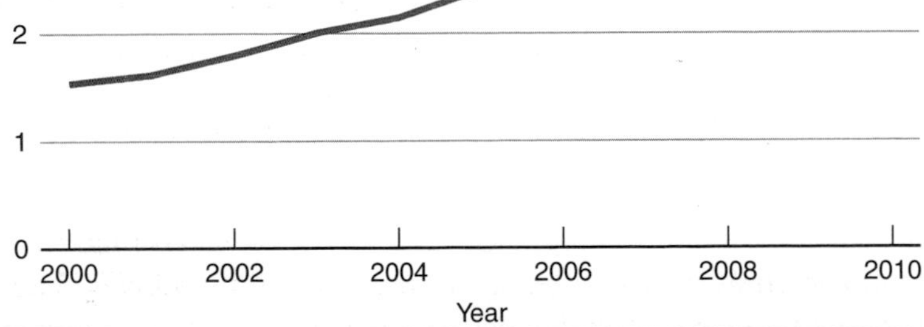

figure 9-2 TOTAL SPENDING ON LOBBYING OF FEDERAL GOVERNMENT

Lobbying of the federal government is a big business. There are more than 20,000 registered lobbyists in Washington, D.C., and the organizations they respresent spend over $3 billion annually to influence federal officials. *Source:* Center for Responsive Politics, 2010. Reprinted with permission.

table 9-2 THE TOP FIFTEEN SPENDING LOBBYING GROUPS, 2009

Some lobbying groups spend over $10 million annually to influence national policy. Nearly all of them are business firms or business associations.

Group	Lobbying Expenditure
U.S. Chamber of Commerce	$144,496,000
Exxon Mobil	27,430,000
Pharmaceutical Research and Manufacturers of America (PhRMA)	26,150,520
General Electric	25,520,000
Blue Cross/Blue Shield	22,715,439
Pfizer	21,930,000
AARP	21,010,000
American Medical Association	20,830,000
Chevron	20,815,000
National Association of Realtors	19,477,000
American Beverage Association	18,850,000
American Hospital Association	18,307,176
ConocoPhillips	18,069,858
Verizon Communications	17,820,000
Boeing	16,850,000

Source: Center for Responsive Politics, 2010. Reprinted with permission.

on lobbying. One of the top spenders, the American Hospital Association, spent more than $18 million on lobbying in 2009. Other groups get by on much less, but it is hard to lobby effectively on a tiny budget. Given the costs of maintaining a Washington lobby, the domination by corporations and trade associations is understandable (see Table 9-2). These economic groups have the money to retain high-priced lobbyists, while many other interests do not.

Lobbying Congress The targets of inside lobbying are officials of all three government branches—legislative, executive, and judicial. The benefits of a close relationship with members of Congress are the most obvious. With support in Congress, a group can obtain the legislative help it needs to achieve its policy goals. By the same token, members of Congress benefit from ties to lobbyists. The volume of legislation facing Congress is heavy, and members rely on trusted lobbyists to identify bills that deserve their attention. When Republican lawmakers took control of Congress in 1995, they invited corporate lobbyists to participate directly in drafting legislation affecting business. Congressional Democrats complained loudly, but Republicans said they were merely getting advice from those who best understood business's needs and noted that Democrats had worked closely with organized labor when they were in power.

Lobbyists' effectiveness depends in part on their reputation for fair play. Lobbyists are expected to play it straight. Said one congressman, "If any [lobbyist] gives me false or misleading information, that's it—I'll never see him again."[24] Bullying is also frowned upon. During the debate over the North American Free Trade Agreement in 1993, the AFL-CIO threatened to campaign against congressional Democrats who supported the legislation. The backlash from Democrats on both sides of the issue was so intense that the union withdrew its threat. The safe lobbying strategy is the aboveboard approach: provide information, rely on trusted allies in Congress, and push steadily but not too aggressively for favorable legislation.

Inside lobbying offers groups a chance to make their policy views known. Access to public officials is critical to the inside-lobbying strategy.

Lobbying the Executive As the range of federal policy has expanded, lobbying of the executive branch has grown in importance. Some of this lobbying is directed at the president and presidential staff, but they are less accessible than top officials in the federal agencies, who are the chief targets.

Group influence is particularly strong in the regulatory agencies that oversee the nation's business sectors. Pharmaceutical companies, for example, provide much of the scientific evidence used by the Food and Drug Administration (FDA) in deciding whether a new drug is safe to market. The potential for influence is high, as are the stakes. After the FDA approved the marketing of the arthritis drug Vioxx, it generated $2.5 billion a year in sales for Merck, the pharmaceutical company that invented and patented it. As it turned out, Vioxx was unsafe. Its users suffered an abnormally high number of strokes and heart attacks. A review panel concluded that the FDA had been lax in testing the drug's safety, bowing to pressure from Merck and its political friends to approve Vioxx for sale.[25]

The FDA is sometimes cited as an example of "agency capture." The capture theory holds that, over time, regulatory agencies side with the industries they are supposed to regulate rather than with the public, which they are supposed to protect. Studies have found that capture theory explains some group-agency relationships, but not all of them. Agency officials are aware that they can lose support in Congress, which controls agency funding and program authorization, if they show too much favoritism toward an interest group.[26] In response to the Vioxx controversy, as well as problems with other new drugs, Congress passed legislation in 2007 that forced the FDA to toughen its pre- and post-marketing safety tests.

Lobbying the Courts Judicial rulings in areas such as education and civil rights have made interest groups recognize that they may be able to achieve their policy goals through the courts.[27] Interest groups have several judicial lobbying options, including efforts to influence the selection of federal judges. Right-to-life groups have pressured Republican administrations to make opposition to abortion a prerequisite for nomination to the federal bench. Democratic administrations have in turn faced pressure from pro-choice groups in their judicial nominations.[28] Judicial lobbying also includes lawsuits. For some organizations, such as the American Civil Liberties Union (ACLU), legal action is the primary means of lobbying. The ACLU often takes on unpopular causes, such as the free-speech rights of fringe groups. Such causes have little chance of success in legislative bodies but may prevail in a courtroom.

As interest groups have increasingly resorted to legal action, they have often found themselves facing one another in court. Environmental litigation groups such as the Earthwise Legal Defense Fund and the Environmental Defense Fund have fought numerous court battles with oil, timber, and mining corporations. Even when groups are not a direct party to a lawsuit, they sometimes get involved through amicus curiae ("friend of the court") briefs. An amicus brief is a written document in which a group explains to a court its position on a legal dispute the court is handling.

Webs of Influence: Groups in the Policy Process

To get a fuller picture of how inside lobbying works, it is helpful to consider two policy processes—iron triangles and issue networks—in which many groups are enmeshed.

Iron Triangles An **iron triangle** consists of a small and informal but relatively stable set of bureaucrats, legislators, and lobbyists who seek to develop policies beneficial to a particular interest. The three "corners" of one such triangle are the Department of Agriculture (bureaucrats), the agriculture committees of Congress (legislators), and farm groups such as the Associated Milk Producers and the Association of Wheat Growers (lobbyists). Together they determine many of the policies affecting farmers. Although the support of the president and a majority in Congress is needed to enact new policies, they often defer to the judgment of the agricultural triangle, whose members are intimately familiar with farmers' needs.

Groups embedded in iron triangles have an inside track to well-positioned legislators and bureaucrats. They can count on getting a full hearing on issues affecting them. Moreover, because they have something to offer in return, the relationship tends to be clad in "iron." The groups provide lobbying support for agency programs and campaign contributions to members of Congress. Agricultural groups, for instance, donate millions of dollars to congressional campaigns during each election cycle. Most of the money goes to the campaigns of House and Senate incumbents who sit on the agriculture committees. Figure 9-3 summarizes the benefits that flow to each member of an iron triangle.

Issue Networks Iron triangles represent the pattern of influence in only certain policy areas and are less common now than in the past. A more frequent pattern of influence today is the **issue network**—an informal grouping of officials, lobbyists, and policy specialists (the "network") who come together *temporarily* around a policy problem (the "issue").

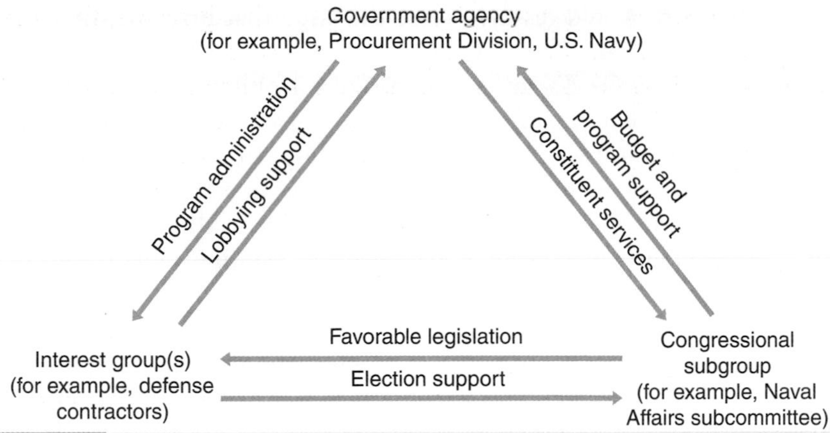

figure 9-3 HOW AN IRON TRIANGLE BENEFITS ITS PARTICIPANTS

An iron triangle works to the advantage of each of its participants: an interest group, a congressional subgroup, and a government agency.

Issue networks are a result of the increasing complexity of policy problems. Participants must have a precise knowledge of the issue at hand in order to address it effectively. Thus, unlike iron triangles, in which a participant's position is everything, an issue network is built around specialized interests and knowledge. On any given issue, the participants might come from a variety of executive agencies, congressional committees, interest groups, and institutions such as universities or think tanks. Compared to iron triangles, issue networks are less stable. As the issue develops, new participants may join the debate and old ones may drop out. Once the issue is resolved, the network disbands.[29]

An example of an issue network is the set of participants who would come together over the issue of whether a large tract of old forest should be opened to logging. A few decades ago, this issue would have been settled in an iron triangle consisting of the timber companies, the U.S. Forest Service, and relevant members of the House and Senate agriculture committees. But as forestlands have diminished and environmental concerns have grown, such issues can no longer be contained within the cozy confines of an iron triangle. Today, an issue network would form that included logging interests, the U.S. Forest Service, House and Senate agriculture committee members, research scientists, and representatives of environmental groups, the housing industry, and animal-rights groups. Unlike the old iron triangle, which was confined to like-minded interests, this issue network would include opposing interests (for example, the loggers and the environmentalists). And unlike an iron triangle, the issue network would dissolve once the issue that brought the parties together was resolved.

In sum, issue networks differ substantially from iron triangles. In an iron triangle, a common interest brings the participants together in a long-lasting and mutually beneficial relationship. In an issue network, an immediate issue brings together the participants in a temporary network that is based on their ability to knowledgeably address the issue and where they play out their separate interests before disbanding once the issue is settled. Despite these differences, iron triangles and issue networks do have one thing in common: they are arenas in which organized groups exercise influence. The interests of the general public may be taken into account in these webs of power, but the interests of the participating groups are foremost.

Outside Lobbying: Seeking Influence through Public Pressure

Although an interest group may rely solely on inside lobbying, this approach is not likely to be successful unless the group can demonstrate that it represents an important constituency. Accordingly, groups also engage in **outside lobbying**, which involves bringing constituency ("outside") pressure to bear on policymakers (see Table 9-3).[30]

table 9-3 Tactics Used in Inside and Outside Lobbying Strategies

Inside and outside lobbying are based on different tactics.

Inside Lobbying	Outside Lobbying
Developing contacts with legislators and executives	Encouraging group members to write, phone, or e-mail their representatives in Congress
Providing information and policy proposals to key officials	Seeking favorable coverage by news media
Forming coalitions with other groups	Encouraging members to support particular candidates in elections
	Targeting group resources on key election races
	Making political action committee (PAC) contributions to candidates

Constituency Advocacy: Grassroots Lobbying

One form of outside pressure is **grassroots lobbying**—that is, pressure designed to convince government officials that a group's policy position has popular support. Grassroots lobbying is a specialty, for example, of AARP. When major legislation affecting retirees is pending, AARP swings into action. Congress receives more mail from members of AARP than it does from members of any other group. AARP's support was instrumental, for example, in the enactment in 2003 of a controversial prescription drug program for the elderly. Until AARP's last-minute endorsement, the program seemed headed for a narrow defeat in Congress.

Grassroots lobbying seeks to get members of the public to take action—for example, by participating in a demonstration or sending an e-mail—that will get policymakers' attention and convince them that a policy position has broad support. A case in point is the 2000 legislation that resulted in the permanent normalization of trade relations with China. Most business lobbies supported the proposed legislation, and several of them launched grassroots lobbying efforts. Boeing Corporation, for example, asked its employees, subcontractors, and suppliers—more than 40,000 in all—to contact members of Congress. Motorola was among the other corporations that engaged in grassroots lobbying on the issue of trade with China. It spent more than $1 million on media advertising that highlighted a toll-free number through which people could contact members of Congress.[31]

Electoral Action: Votes and PAC Money

An "outside" strategy can also include election activity. "Reward your friends and punish your enemies" is a political adage that loosely describes how interest groups view elections. The possibility of campaign opposition from a powerful group can restrain an officeholder. Opposition from the three-million-member National Rifle Association, for example, is a major reason the United States has lagged behind other Western societies in its handgun control laws, despite polls indicating that a majority of Americans favor such laws.

Interest groups gain influence by contributing money to candidates' campaigns. As one lobbyist said, "Talking to politicians is fine, but with a little money they hear you better."[32] Members of Congress sometimes get into hot water by listening to lobbyists while also taking contributions from them. When it was alleged in 2005 that lobbyist Jack Abramoff had cheated some of his clients while also lavishing campaign donations on members of Congress in return for favorable legislation, it sent shock waves through Washington. Several members of Congress quickly returned Abramoff's campaign donations in the hope that doing so would insulate them from the corruption scandal. A casualty of the Abramoff affair was Representative Tom DeLay (R-Tex.), who lost his post as House majority leader for accepting hundreds of thousands of dollars from Abramoff, some of it of allegedly questionable legality.

A group's election contributions are funneled through its **political action committee (PAC)**. A group cannot give organizational funds (such as corporate profits or union dues) to candidates, but through its PAC, a group can solicit voluntary contributions from members or employees and then donate this money to candidates. A PAC can back as many candidates as it wants but is legally limited in the amount it can contribute to a single candidate. The ceiling is $10,000 per candidate—$5,000 in the primary campaign and $5,000 in the general election campaign. (These financial limits apply to candidates for federal office. State and local campaigns are regulated by state laws, and some states allow PACs to make unlimited contributions to individual candidates—see "How the 50 States Differ.")

There are more than four thousand PACs, and PAC contributions account for roughly a third of total contributions to congressional campaigns. Their role is less significant in presidential campaigns, which are bigger in scale and depend largely on individual contributors.

More than 60 percent of all PACs are associated with businesses (see Figure 9-4). Most of these are corporate PACs, such as the Ford Motor Company Civic Action Fund, the Sun Oil Company Political Action Committee, and the Coca-Cola PAC. The others are tied to trade associations, such as RPAC (National Association of Realtors). The next-largest set of PACs consists of those linked to citizens' groups (that is, public-interest, single-issue, and ideological groups), such as the liberal People for the American Way and the conservative National Conservative Political Action Committee. Labor unions, once the major source of group contributions, constitute less than 10 percent of PACs.

PACs contribute roughly eight times as much money to incumbents as to their challengers. PACs recognize that incumbents are likely to win and thus to remain in positions of power. One PAC director, expressing a common view, said, "We always stick with the incumbent when we agree with them both."[33] To some extent, the tendency of PACs to back incumbents has blurred long-standing partisan divisions in campaign funding. Business interests are especially pragmatic.

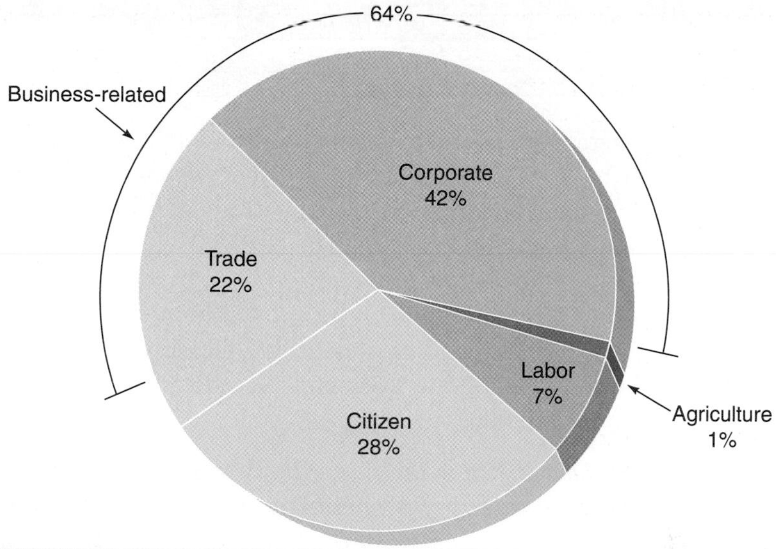

figure 9-4 PERCENTAGE OF PACs BY CATEGORY

Most PACs represent business. Corporate and trade association PACs make up 64 percent of the total. *Source:* Federal Election Commission, 2010.

Although they tend to favor Republican candidates, they are reluctant to anger Democratic incumbents. The result is that Democratic incumbents, particularly in House races, have received substantial support over the years from business-related PACs.[34] Other PACs, of course, are less pragmatic. The Christian Coalition of America, for example, backs only candidates who take conservative stands on issues such as school prayer and abortion.

PAC influence has been hotly debated. Critics complain that PACs give interest groups—economic groups particularly—far too much influence on Congress.[35] Advocates of PACs claim that groups have a right to be heard, including the right to express themselves with money. Advocates also note that PACs raise their money through contributions by small donors and therefore constitute a better system of campaign finance than one based on wealthy donors, although the recent Supreme Court decision in *Citizens United v. Federal Election Commission* (2010) undercuts that argument somewhat. The Court's ruling allows corporations and labor unions to spend unlimited amounts of funds on campaigns, as long as the spending is not coordinated directly with that of candidates and parties (see Chapter 8).[36]

Although members of Congress deny that they are unduly influenced by PACs, there is no question that PACs give interest groups a level of

HOW THE 50 STATES DIFFER

POLITICAL THINKING THROUGH COMPARISONS

Limits on PAC Contributions

Elections of state officials (such as governors and state legislators) are regulated by state law rather than by federal law. In federal elections, PACs can contribute to as many candidates as they like, but they cannot contribute more than $10,000 ($5,000 in the primary and $5,000 in the general election) to a particular candidate. Some states place no limits on how much money a PAC can contribute to a state or local candidate. Of the states that limit PAC contributions, only New York and Nevada allow contributions in excess of $10,000.

Q: *Why might states located to the west of the Mississippi River (which runs down the eastern borders of Minnesota, Iowa, Missouri, Arkansas, and Louisiana) place fewer limits on PAC contributions than other states?*

A: *A possible explanation is that the political cultures of the westernmost states, as a result of their frontier heritage, are less accepting of government regulation of any kind.*

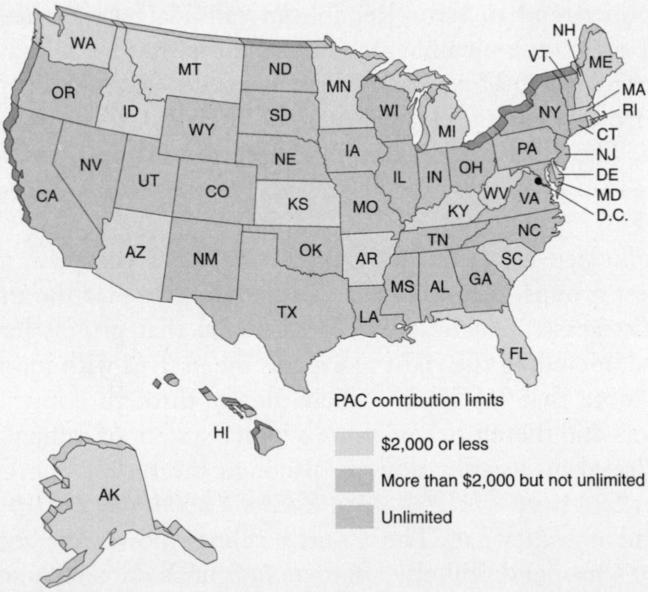

Source: National Conference of State Legislatures, 2010. If a state places different limits for statewide and state legislative races, the limit on contributions to state legislative candidates was the amount used in constructing the map.

access to lawmakers that ordinary citizens lack. Nevertheless, Congress is unlikely in the foreseeable future to pass legislation that would outlaw PACs. The fact is that most members of Congress are unwilling to eliminate a source of campaign funds that helps them to stay in office.

The Group System: Indispensable but Biased

As noted in the chapter's introduction, pluralist theory holds that organized groups are a source of sound governance. On one level, this claim is indisputable. Groups are a means of getting government to pay attention to people's needs and interests. Yet the issue of representation through groups is also a question of whether the various interests in society are fairly represented, and here the pluralist argument is less compelling.

The Contribution of Groups to Self-Government: Pluralism

Government does not exist simply to serve majority interests. The fact that most people are not retirees or union members or farmers or college students or Hispanics is not an indication that the interest of such "minorities" is unworthy of government's attention. And what better instrument exists for promoting their interest than lobbying groups working on their behalf?

Some pluralists even question the usefulness of terms such as the *public interest*. If people disagree on society's goals and priorities, as they always do, how can anyone claim that their goal or priority represents the public interest? As an alternative, pluralists say that society is best seen as a collection of separate interests and is best served by a process that serves a wide array of these interests. Thus, if manufacturing interests prevail on one issue, environmentalists on another, farmers on a third, minorities on a fourth, and so on until a great many interests are served, the "public interest" will have been served. Pluralists also note that the promotion of the special interest often benefits others as well. Tax incentives for corporations that encourage research and capital investment, for example, can result in job creation and improved goods and services.

Finally, interest groups address issues that the political parties neglect. Party leaders sometimes shy away from issues that are controversial and, in any case, concentrate on those that have broad impact, which leaves hundreds of issues unaddressed through the party system. As political scientist Jack Walker noted, the party and group systems together produce a more responsive and inclusive type of politics than would be the case if one of the systems somehow did not exist.[37]

Flaws in Pluralism: Interest-Group Liberalism and Economic Bias

Pluralist theory has questionable aspects. Political scientist Theodore Lowi points out that there is no concept of the public interest in a system that gives special interests the ability to determine the policies affecting them.[38] Nor can it be assumed that what a lobbying group receives is what the majority would also want. Consider the case of the federal law that required auto dealers to list the known defects of used cars on window stickers. The law was repealed after the National Association of Automobile Dealers contributed more than $1 million to the reelection campaigns of members of Congress. Auto dealers won another victory when their loans to car buyers were exempted from regulation by the new consumer protection agency that was created as part of the Restoring American Financial Stability Act of 2010.

Lowi uses the term **interest-group liberalism** to describe the tendency of officials to support the policy demands of the interest group or

Although Wall Street in New York City is the traditional symbol of financial power in the United States, business firms also dominate political lobbying in Washington. Pluralism theory has traditionally underestimated the power of the business lobby. As political scientist E.E, Schattschneider expressed it: "The flaw in the pluralist heaven is that the heavenly chorus sings with a strong upper-class bias."

groups that have a special stake in a policy. It is "liberal" in the sense that Republican and Democratic lawmakers alike are in the habit of using government to promote group interests. Each party has its favorites—for example, business groups usually do better when Republicans are in power, and labor groups usually do better when Democrats are in power. But neither party is "conservative" in the sense of being reluctant to use the power of government on behalf of groups. An effect is a weakening of majority rule. Rather than policymaking by the majority acting through its elected representatives, interest-group liberalism involves policymaking by narrow segments of society acting on their own behalf with the help of lawmakers. Another adverse effect is an inefficient use of society's resources: groups get what they want, whether or not their priorities match those of society as a whole.

Another flaw in the pluralist argument resides in its claim that the group system is representative. Although pluralists acknowledge that well-funded interests have more clout, they say that the group process is relatively open and few interests are entirely left out. This claim contains an element of truth, but it is not the full story. As this chapter has shown, organization is an unequally distributed resource. Economic interests, particularly corporations, are the most highly organized, and studies indicate that group politics works chiefly to the advantage of moneyed interests.[39] Of course, economic groups do not dominate everything, nor do they operate unchecked. Many of the citizens' groups formed since the 1960s were created as checks on the power of corporate lobbies. Most environmental groups, for example, work to shield the environment from threats posed by business activity. Activist government has also brought the group system into closer balance; the government's poverty programs have spawned groups that act to protect the programs. Nevertheless, the power of poverty-related groups is a pittance compared with the power of moneyed interests. Nearly two-thirds of all lobbying groups in Washington are business related, and their political clout is enormous.

A Madisonian Dilemma

James Madison recognized the dilemma inherent in group activity. Although he worried that interest groups would have too much political influence, he argued in *Federalist* No. 10 that a free society must allow the pursuit of self-interest. Unless people can promote the separate opinions that stem from differences in their needs, values, and possessions, they are not a free people.

POLITICAL THINKING

Can Group Power Be Limited?

"Liberty is to faction what air is to fire," wrote James Madison in Federalist *No. 10. Madison was lamenting the self-interested behavior of factions or, as they are called today, interest groups. Yet Madison recognized that the only way to suppress this behavior was to destroy the liberty that allows people to organize. Numerous efforts have been made to restrict the power of groups without infringing on free expression rights. Laws have been enacted that restrict group contributions to candidates and that require lobbyists to register and report their expenditures. Yet nothing in the end seems to be all that effective in harnessing the self-interested actions of groups. Do you think there is an answer to Madison's concern? Or are the excesses of group politics simply one of the costs of living in a free society?*

Ironically, Madison's constitutional solution to the problem of factions is now part of the problem. The American system of checks and balances, with a separation of powers at its core, was designed to prevent a majority faction from trampling on the interests of smaller groups. This same system, however, makes it relatively easy for minority factions—or, as they are called today, special-interest groups—to gain government support. If they can get the backing of even a small number of well-placed policymakers, as in the case of iron triangles, they are likely to get many of the benefits they seek. Because of the system's division of power, they have numerous points at which to gain access and exert influence. Often, they need only to find a single ally, whether it is a congressional committee or an executive agency or a federal court, to get at least some of what they seek. And once they obtain a government benefit, it is likely to endure. Benefits are hard to eliminate because concerted action by the executive branch and both houses of Congress is usually required. If a group has strong support in even a single institution, it can usually fend off attempts to eliminate a policy or program that serves its interest. Such support ordinarily is easy to acquire, because the group has resources—information, money, and votes—that officeholders want.

Economist Mancur Olson concluded that groups ultimately exercise too much power in the American system. When groups are examined individually, their influence is not all that significant. In the aggregate, however, groups receive a huge share of government benefits and have nearly an unbreakable hold on them. Any attempt to trim a group's benefits is met by strenuous political opposition that in nearly every case blocks the attempt. In the process, government loses its flexibility. Resources that might be used to meet new challenges are tied up in previous commitments to organized interests.[40] (Chapters 11 and 13 discuss further the issue of interest-group power.)

SUMMARY Self-Test www.mhhe.com/pattersonwtp9e

A political interest group is composed of a set of individuals organized to promote a shared concern. Most interest groups owe their existence to factors other than politics. These groups form for economic reasons, such as the pursuit of profit, and maintain themselves by making profits (in the case of corporations) or by providing their members with private goods, such as jobs and wages. Economic groups include corporations, trade associations, labor unions, farm organizations, and professional associations. Collectively, economic groups are by far the largest set of organized interests. The group system tends to favor interests that are already economically and socially advantaged.

Citizens' groups do not have the same organizational advantages as economic groups. They depend on voluntary contributions from potential members, who may lack interest and resources or who recognize that they will get the collective good from a group's activity even if they do not participate (the free-rider problem). Citizens' groups include public-interest, single-issue, and ideological groups. Their numbers have increased dramatically since the 1960s despite their organizational problems.

Organized interests seek influence largely by lobbying public officials and contributing to election campaigns. Using an inside strategy, lobbyists develop direct contacts with legislators, government bureaucrats, and members of the judiciary in order to persuade them to accept the group's perspective on policy. Groups also use an outside strategy, seeking to mobilize public support for their goals. This strategy relies in part on grassroots lobbying—encouraging group members and the public to communicate their policy views to officials. Outside lobbying also includes efforts to elect officeholders who will support group aims. Through political action committees (PACs), organized groups now provide nearly a third of all contributions received by congressional candidates.

The policies that emerge from the group system bring benefits to many of society's interests and often serve the collective interest as well. But when groups can essentially dictate policies, the common good is rarely served. The majority's interest is subordinated to group (minority) interests. In most instances, the minority consists of individuals who already enjoy a substantial share of society's benefits.

Key Terms

citizens' (noneconomic) groups (*p. 300*)
collective (public) goods (*p. 304*)
economic groups (*p. 298*)
free-rider problem (*p. 304*)
grassroots lobbying (*p. 315*)
inside lobbying (*p. 307*)
interest group (*p. 294*)
interest-group liberalism (*p. 320*)
iron triangle (*p. 312*)
issue network (*p. 312*)
lobbying (*p. 307*)
outside lobbying (*p. 314*)
political action committee (PAC) (*p. 316*)
private (individual) goods (*p. 303*)
single-issue politics (*p. 294*)

Suggested Readings

Baumgartner, Frank R., Jeffrey M. Berry, Marie Hojnacki, David C. Kimball, and Beth L. Leech, *Lobbying and Policy Change: Who Wins, Who Loses, and Why*. Chicago: University of Chicago Press, 2009. A thorough assessment of the impact of lobbying.

Grossman, Gene M., and Elhanan Helpman. *Interest Groups and Trade Policy*. Princeton, N.J.: Princeton University Press, 2002. An examination of the impact of groups' campaign and lobbying activities on trade policy.

Herrnson, Paul S., Ronald G. Shaiko, and Clyde Wilcox, eds. *The Interest Group Connection: Electioneering, Lobbying, and Policymaking in Washington*, 2d ed. Washington, D.C.: CQ Press, 2004. Essays and commentaries on groups and officials and the linkages between them.

Lowery, David, and Holly Brasher. *Organized Interests and American Government*. New York: McGraw-Hill, 2004. An overview of interest-group politics.

Lowi, Theodore J. *The End of Liberalism*, 2d ed. New York: Norton, 1979. A thorough critique of interest groups' influence on American politics.

Nownes, Anthony J. *Total Lobbying: What Lobbyists Want (and How They Try to Get It)*. New York: Cambridge University Press, 2006. An up-to-date, thoughtful assessment of the lobbying process.

Olson, Mancur, Jr. *The Logic of Collective Action*, rev. ed. Cambridge, MA.: Harvard University Press, 1971. A pioneering analysis of why some interests are more fully and easily organized than others.

Rozell, Mark J., Clyde Wilcox, and David Madland. *Interest Groups in American Campaigns*, 2d ed. Washington, D.C.: Congressional Quarterly Press, 2005. An assessment of the role of interest groups in elections.

List of Websites

www.opensecrets.org The Center for Responsive Politics site; offers information on elections, voting, campaign finance, parties, and PACs.

www.pirg.org The Public Interest Research Group (PIRG) site; PIRG has chapters on many college campuses, and the site provides state-by-state policy and other information.

www.sierraclub.org The website of the Sierra Club, one of the oldest environmental protection interest groups, which promotes conservation; provides information on its activities.

www.townhall.com The website of the American Conservative Union (ACU); includes policy and political information, and has a lively chat room.

Politics in Theory and Practice

Thinking: Why are there so many more organized interests in the United States than elsewhere? Why are so many of these groups organized around economic interests—particularly business interests?

Participating: Consider contributing to a citizens' interest group. Such groups depend on members' donations for operating funds. Citizens' groups cover the political spectrum from right to left and touch on nearly every conceivable public issue. You will not have difficulty locating a group through the Internet that has policy goals consistent with your beliefs and values. If you are interested in contributing your time instead, some citizens groups (for example, PIRG) have college chapters that might provide opportunities for you to work on issues of personal interest.

Extra Credit

For up-to-the-minute *New York Times* articles, interactive simulations, graphics, study tools, and more links and quizzes, visit the text's Online Learning Center at **www.mhhe.com/pattersonwtp9e**.

NATIONAL JOURNAL

K Street Paradox

"$1.3 million per hour."

That eye-popping number doesn't refer to the salary of a Wall Street banker, a health insurance CEO, or an oil company executive. It's what K Street reported in fees in 2009, according to a recent analysis by the Center for Responsive Politics. The center derives the provocative number by dividing the amount of money lobbyists and other entities received to influence Congress and the executive branch (a record $3.47 billion, up 5 percent from 2008) by the number of hours Congress was in session (2,668). Although the figure is somewhat hyperbolic—lobbyists work many hours when Congress isn't in session—the message is clear.

"The numbers just keep going up, up, up," the center's executive director, Sheila Krumholz, said. "I was surprised, given the state of the economy last year."

Although the year on K Street started off slowly, with many lobbying firms reporting cuts in their fee income during the first few months, the downturn flattened as the year went on. Ironically, the White House's ambitious policies fueled the boom, with Obama's "change" agenda effectively making Washington the center of the country as it tackled financial services reform, energy reform, health care reform, and the $819 billion stimulus package. Even as Obama clamped down on "special interests," corporations rushed to Washington and hired lobbyists to shape legislation in their favor. According to the center, 15,712 companies or entities reported that they lobbied the federal government in 2009, 663 more than in 2008.

"It's been one of the busiest years that I have seen in a long time," said John Castellani, president of the Business Roundtable, a trade group that reported spending $13.4 million on lobbying, as its 160 corporate members engaged on almost every major piece of legislation that Congress took up this year. "Depending upon the issue, we were playing offense and defense."

Wayne Berman, a Republican and a managing director of Ogilvy Government Relations, which raked in $21.7 million in lobbying fees in 2009, said, "The president and the Democratic congressional leadership have embarked on an all-out assault on a wide range of economic interests, and those interests have sought to protect themselves by dramatically increasing their lobbying budgets."

Health care-related lobbying, in particular, drove profits on K Street. The Center for Public Integrity reported that 4,525 lobbyists were working on health care reform last year—which works out to eight for every member of Congress. According to the Center for Responsive Politics, pharmaceutical and health products companies spent a total of $266.8 million on lobbying, making it the top-spending industry for the year.

Even amid the overall K Street boom, Obama has been on a possibly quixotic quest to change Washington by reining in lobbyists' interaction with government. He began with an executive order aimed at excluding recently registered lobbyists from political appointment posts, pledging to close the revolving door between government and lobbying.

In March of 2009, Obama set restrictions on communications between lobbyists and government officials relating to stimulus funds—a regime that the administration eventually extended to everyone seeking stimulus money during the grant application process. That September, Obama banned lobbyists from government advisory boards and commissions. He also put White House visitor logs online (which enabled anyone to see which representatives of special interests were entering the mansion), and he is pushing federal departments and agencies to develop plans for making their contacts with lobbyists more transparent to the public.

But insiders think that the rules may have had the unintended consequence of making lobbying less transparent. The administration has relied on the definition of "lobbyists" in the 1995 Lobbying Disclosure Act, which sought to impose uniform disclosure standards on the industry. The law has loopholes, however, that allow huge swaths of the influence industry—including grassroots advocacy and public-relations campaigns—to remain in the shadows.

Numerous regulations require lobbyists to register with the House and Senate; the key rule, however, applies to those who spend at least 20 percent of their time on lobbying activities and make at least two lobbying contacts during a calendar quarter. For many years, people registered "out of abundance of caution, or to show off their clients," Thomas Susman, director of government affairs at the American Bar Association, said. "There was no downside."

Now that lobbyists have become a punching bag for politicians, many people have been looking at ways to avoid registering—or to deregister from the official congressional roster.

The number of lobbyists dropped last year for the first time since 2001, to a total of 13,742, according to the Center for Responsive Politics. In 2008, 14,446 people were registered to lobby.

"People are trying to game it so they can show on a work spreadsheet that they are spending 19.99 percent of their time lobbying, rather than the 20 percent that requires you to register," said one corporate lobbyist who didn't want to be named. As Kelly Bingel, a partner with Mehlman Vogel Castagnetti, puts it, "I think we've moved backwards in terms of disclosure. I'm seeing heads of [Washington corporate] offices on the Hill, and they aren't registering."

Stefan Passantino, a partner at McKenna Long & Aldridge, and other lawyers are doing a brisk business in advising lobbyists on the registering and deregistering strictures. "Whenever you create rules," he says, "people will try to figure out how to modify their behavior so they aren't subject to it."

Some K Streeters think that the decision banning lobbyists from boards will do the opposite of what Obama intended. Stephen Lamar, executive vice president of the American Apparel & Footwear Association, who chaired one of the trade advisory panels, said, "We think rather than increasing the diversity of voices, it will decrease them. We represented many small businesses. And those small businesses don't have the money and time to participate in these panels, so now their voices won't be heard."

Meanwhile, Obama is now focusing his attention on lobbyists and Congress. In his State of the Union address, Obama called for new limits on lobbyists' campaign contributions and bundling activities, and for new requirements under the Lobbying Disclosure Act. Lobbyists, he said, should have to report every contact with lawmakers, staff, and members of the executive branch and the substance of the interaction. The president also wants to toughen the threshold that requires lobbyists to register, below the current 20 percent time regulation in the law.

"We face a deficit of trust—deep and corrosive doubts about how Washington works that have been growing for years," Obama said in his State of the Union speech. "To close that credibility gap, we have to take action on both ends of Pennsylvania Avenue to end the outsized influence of lobbyists, to do our work openly, and to give our people the government they deserve."

This latest proposal left some lobbyists reeling. "Some of us are joking that the next proposal will be to put RFD tracking chips in lobbyists necks so they know where we are at all times," said Rich Gold, a partner at Holland & Knight. "We are either just over, or significantly over, the line on the administration's approach on these issues. I don't think this is improving people's trust in government." Bob Maloney, founder of Maloney Government Relations said, "Requiring us to report every contact would be a nightmare. What if I run into a lawmaker or their staff in the elevator or cafeteria or socially? Would I have to report that? If I did, the staff would never talk to me again."

Obama's focus on lobbyists again leaves out the many special-interest influencers—such as lawyers and CEOs—who don't have to register. Gina Mahony, policy director at Brownstein Hyatt Farber Schreck, wrote on National Journal's Under the Influence blog: "Let's be honest about how lobbying really works. If you really want transparency and intellectual honesty about how this 'nefarious' industry works, then let's require 100 percent disclosure of all advocacy contacts."

Lawmakers haven't expressed much interest in embracing the lobbying reforms. Many members of Congress count lobbyists among their friends, and some even have aspirations to join the profession (witness the 318 former lawmakers who have registered to lobby since 1998, according to the Center for Responsive Politics).

Rep. Chellie Pingree, D-Maine, who formerly headed Common Cause, supports Obama's lobbying reforms but thinks that the president should put his second-year spotlight on campaign finance reform. "I would spend more time focusing on the influence of money, because I don't think it's about the time you spend with lobbyists; it's about the influence of money on the process," said Pingree, who has made passing a public financing bill, the Fair Elections Now Act, one of her top priorities. "When an interest with money comes in to lobby you, and after the meeting as they walk out the door, they say, 'Hey, I am happy to organize an event and help you with your campaign,' that is where things get confused." Pingree is a co-sponsor of the public financing proposal, which would provide matching payments for qualified small-dollar contributions; it has 140 backers in the House and 10 in the Senate.

She says, however, that Congress is missing an opportunity by not addressing public financing. "We have this level of awareness, like when you have a major scandal, everyone says, 'Oh, we have to clean this whole place up,' " she said. "I see this as an open door, and we may as well go in and try and change the whole system, not just a piece of it."

When asked whether Obama would support the Fair Elections Now Act, Eisen said, "The president supports public financing for presidential elections." Obama has not endorsed a similar system for congressional elections.

Pingree perhaps speaks for many both inside and outside the ranks of lobbyists when she concludes, "Without looking at the influence of money, there isn't really going to be change in Washington.

What's Your Opinion?

Based on the article and on this chapter, what recommendations would you give President Obama on how to improve transparency in the relationship between government and lobbyists? Why do you think money remains an influence in politics, despite efforts like those of the Obama administration to diminish the influence of lobbyists?

CHAPTER 10

The News Media: Communicating Political Images

> “The press in America . . . determines what people will think and talk about an authority that in other nations is reserved for tyrants, priests, parties, and mandarins.”
>
> Theodore H. White[1]

The news flashed across America. Mark Sanford, governor of South Carolina, was missing. Neither his wife nor the state troopers in charge of his security knew where he was. Repeated calls to his cell phone went unanswered. As concern mounted, Sanford’s press secretary announced that the governor was hiking the Appalachian Trail and would be out of contact until his return.

As it turned out, Sanford was in Argentina visiting a woman with whom he was having a relationship. At a press conference after his return, Sanford admitted to the extramarital affair, saying that it had begun years before as an innocent relationship, only to turn romantic a year earlier. He called her his "soul mate." His admission led state officials to demand his resignation, but Sanford refused. In turn, the South Carolina legislature appointed a committee, granting it the power to hold impeachment hearings. Although impeachment proceedings were eventually dropped, the committee unanimously passed a censure motion and ethics charges were filed against Sanford.

Sanford was elected after having first made a reputation as a tough-minded conservative in the U.S. House of Representatives. In early 2009, he had made headlines by announcing that he would reject the stimulus funds due to his state from the economic recovery bill that Congress had enacted. He was among a half-dozen Republicans whose name cropped up whenever discussion turned to possible 2012 GOP presidential nominees. Nevertheless, nothing that Sanford had done previously—not as a member of Congress, not as governor, and not as a potential presidential contender—generated anything like the headlines accompanying his extramarital affair. It was front-page news throughout the country, the lead story on television newscasts, and the leading topic of conversation on talk shows and Internet blogs. It was also grist for the late-night TV shows. David Letterman, after noting in his opening monologue that Sanford was having an affair with a woman from another country, quipped: "Once again, foreigners taking jobs that Americans won't do."

Although reporters sometimes compare the news to a mirror held up to reality, the news is described more accurately as a refracted version of reality. The **news** is mainly an account of obtruding events, particularly those that are *timely* (new or unfolding developments rather than old or static ones), *dramatic* (striking developments rather than commonplace ones), and *compelling* (developments that arouse people's emotions).[2] These tendencies have their origins in a number of factors, the most significant of which is that news organizations need to attract an audience in order to make a profit. Thus, compared with Sanford's sexual liaison, his work as a top public official was less newsworthy. It was part of the ongoing business of government and did not lend itself to the vivid storytelling of a sex scandal.

News and public affairs outlets are known collectively as the **press** or the **news media**. The news media include broadcast networks (such as ABC and National Public Radio [NPR]), cable networks (such as CNN and Fox), newspapers (such as the *Chicago Tribune* and *Dallas Morning News*), news

At a press conference, South Carolina governor Mark Sanford announces the real reason he had gone missing for several days. His office had claimed he was hiking the Appalachian Trail. As it turned out, Sanford was in Argentina to see a woman with whom he was having an affair. The news media, as their coverage of Sanford illustrates, presents a refracted version of reality, where sensational developments typically get more attention than the day-to-day problems affecting Americans' lives.

magazines (such as *Time* and *Newsweek*), and Internet sites that provide news and commentary (such as Instapundit and the Drudge Report).

This chapter examines the news media's role in American politics. The media are a key intermediary between Americans and their leaders, but they are a different kind of intermediary than political parties and interest groups. The latter seek influence in order to promote particular leaders or policies. Although some members of the press do the same, the media's basic goal is to inform the public about politics and government. Yet, because news organizations also seek to attract an audience in their pursuit of a profit, their news coverage often centers on events of secondary importance. The main ideas presented in the chapter are these:

- *The American press was initially tied to the nation's political party system (the partisan press) but gradually developed an independent position (the objective press).* In the process, the news shifted from a political orientation, which emphasizes political values and ideas, to a journalistic orientation, which stresses newsworthy information and events.
- *In recent years, traditional news organizations have faced increased competition for people's attention from cable and the Internet, which has contributed*

to audience fragmentation and an increase in opinionated and entertainment-laced journalism.

- *The news media have several functions—signaling (the press brings relevant events and problems into public view), common-carrier (the press serves as a channel through which leaders and citizens can communicate), watchdog (the press scrutinizes official behavior for evidence of deceitful, careless, or corrupt acts), and partisan (the press promotes particular interests and values).* The traditional media (print and broadcast) contribute mainly to the first three functions whereas the "new" news media (cable and the Internet) contribute mainly to the last one.
- *The news audience has been shrinking and fragmenting, partly as a result of new technology and partly because young adults are less likely than older ones to pay attention to news.* One consequence has been a widening gap in the information levels of America's more-attentive and less-attentive citizens.

Historical Development: From the Nation's Founding to Today

Democracy depends on a free flow of information,[3] a fact not lost on America's early leaders. Alexander Hamilton persuaded John Fenno to start a newspaper, the *Gazette of the United States*, as a means of publicizing the policies of George Washington's administration. To finance the paper, Hamilton, as secretary of the treasury, granted it the Treasury Department's printing contracts. Hamilton's political rival, Thomas Jefferson, dismissed the *Gazette*'s reporting as "pure Toryism" and convinced Philip Freneau to start the *National Gazette* as an opposition paper. Jefferson, as secretary of state, gave Freneau the authority to print State Department documents.

Early newspapers were printed a page at a time on flat presses, a process that limited production and kept the cost of each copy beyond the reach of the ordinary citizen. Leading papers such as the *Gazette of the United States* had fewer than fifteen hundred readers and could not have survived without party support. Not surprisingly, the "news" they printed was laced with partisanship.[4] In this era of the **partisan press**, publishers openly backed one party or the other.

Technological innovation in the early 1800s helped bring about the gradual decline of partisan newspapers. With the invention of the telegraph, editors had access to breaking news about events outside the local area, which led them to substitute news reports for opinion commentary. The invention of the hand-cranked rotary press was equally important; it enabled publishers to print their newspapers more cheaply and quickly. The *New York Sun* was the first paper to take full advantage of the new technology. The *Sun* reduced the price of its daily paper from six cents to a penny, and its daily circulation rose from one thousand to ten thousand in less than a year.[5] Increased circulation meant increased advertising revenue, which helped to free newspapers from their dependence on government printing contracts.

By the late nineteenth century, propelled by the invention of newsprint and power-driven presses, many American newspapers were printing fifty thousand or more copies a day. The period marked the height of newspapers' power and the low point in their civic contribution. A new style of reporting—"yellow journalism"—had emerged as a way of attracting readers. It was "a shrieking, gaudy, sensation-loving, devil-may-care kind of journalism which lured the reader by any possible means."[6] A circulation battle between William Randolph Hearst's *New York Journal* and Joseph Pulitzer's *New York World* may have contributed to the outbreak of the Spanish-American War through sensational (and largely inaccurate) reports on the cruelty of Spanish rule in Cuba. A young Frederic Remington (who later became a noted painter and sculptor), working as a news artist for Hearst, planned to return home because Cuba appeared calm and safe, but Hearst supposedly cabled back: "Please remain. You furnish the pictures and I'll furnish the war."[7]

The Objective-Journalism Era

The excesses of yellow journalism led some publishers to devise ways of reporting the news more responsibly. One step was to separate the newspaper's advertising department from its news department, thus reducing the influence of advertisers on news content. A second development was **objective journalism**, which is based on the reporting of "facts" rather than opinions and is "fair" in that it presents both sides of partisan debate. A chief advocate of this new model of reporting was Adolph Ochs of the *New York Times*. Ochs bought the *Times* in 1896, when its circulation was 9,000; four years later, its readership had grown to 82,000. Ochs told his reporters that he "wanted as little partisanship as possible . . . as few judgments as possible."[8] The *Times* gradually acquired a reputation as the country's best newspaper. Objective reporting was also promoted through newly formed journalism schools, such as those at Columbia University and the University of Missouri. Within a few decades, objective journalism had become the dominant reporting model.

Until the twentieth century, the print media were the only form of mass communication. By the 1920s, however, hundreds of radio stations were broadcasting throughout the nation. At first the government did not regulate radio broadcasting. The result was chaos. A common problem was that nearby stations often used the same or adjacent radio frequencies, interfering with each other's broadcasts. Finally, in 1934, Congress passed the Communications Act, which regulated broadcasting and created the Federal Communications Commission (FCC) to oversee the process. Broadcasters had to be licensed by the FCC, and because broadcasting frequencies are limited in number, licensees were required to be impartial in their political coverage. A further restriction was the "equal time" provision of Section 315 of the Communications Act, which prohibits broadcasters from selling or giving airtime to a political candidate without offering to sell or give an equal amount of airtime to other candidates for the same office. (An exception was later made for election debates; broadcasters can televise them even if third-party candidates are excluded.)

Television followed radio, and by the late 1950s, more than 90 percent of American homes had a TV set. In this period, the FCC imposed a second restriction—the Fairness Doctrine—on broadcasters. The Fairness Doctrine required broadcasters to "afford reasonable opportunity for the discussion of conflicting views of public importance." Broadcasters were prohibited from using their news coverage to promote one party or issue position at the expense of another. In effect, the objective-reporting model practiced voluntarily by the newspapers was imposed by law on broadcasters.

The Rise of the "New" News

During the era of objective journalism, the news was not entirely devoid of partisanship. Although broadcasters were prohibited by law from editorializing, newspapers were not. Most of them backed one political party or the other on their editorial and opinion (op-ed) pages. Nevertheless, it was usually difficult to tell from their news pages which party they backed editorially. Nearly all of them highlighted the same national stories each day, and if a high-ranking public official got embroiled in a scandal or policy blunder, they played it up, whether the official was a Republican or a Democrat.

The introduction of cable television did not at first change this pattern. Cable television is transmitted by privately owned wire rather than broadcast over the public airways and therefore was not required to comply with the Fairness Doctrine. Nevertheless, when media mogul Ted Turner started CNN in 1980, he chose to abide by it, instructing his correspondents to pursue a path of partisan neutrality. He sought to attract viewers through round-the-clock news and live on-the-scene reports. Turner's marketing plan was a success. CNN's audience and reputation ballooned whenever a major event occurred. In 1991, for example, Americans were riveted to CNN's live coverage from Baghdad as the first American bombs of the Persian Gulf War began falling on that city.

When CNN was launched in 1980, barely more than 10 percent of American homes had cable service. Within a decade, however, the number exceeded 50 percent, which led the FCC to rescind the Fairness Doctrine. Cable had greatly expanded the number of television channels, and the FCC felt that it was no longer necessary to force broadcast outlets to balance their political coverage.

Radio stations were the first to respond to the opportunity. They had previously been required to air a liberal talk show if they aired a conservative one. The reverse was also true. The elimination of the Fairness Doctrine freed broadcasters from this constraint, and scores of radio stations switched from playing music to airing political talk shows. These shows also sprung up on cable television, a trend that accelerated when billionaire media mogul Rupert Murdoch launched Fox News in 1996.

Elimination of the Fairness Doctrine opened the airwaves to partisan talk shows. Rush Limbaugh, a conservative talk show host, was the first to attract a huge following. During the 1990s, his daily radio program was heard by more than 20 million listeners each week. Even today, Limbaugh's show has the largest audience of any radio or television talk show.

He hired Roger Ailes, a Republican political consultant, to run Fox News, instructing him to devise a format appealing to political conservatives. Ailes hired several conservative talk show hosts, including Bill O'Reilly. Within a few years, buoyed by a largely Republican audience, Fox News had overtaken CNN as the most heavily watched cable news network.

In the 1990s, the Internet emerged as yet another source of news and political commentary. Unlike a newspaper, broadcast station, or cable company, where the capital investment can run into the tens or even hundreds of millions of dollars, the Internet has a low cost of entry. Anyone with a computer and technical savvy can create a website or blog devoted to news and public affairs. Thousands of such sites exist. Their sheer number and the stunning success of some of them—the Drudge Report, Instapundit, Daily Kos, and Boing Boing, to name a few—have created an important "new" news media. Such sites resemble political talk radio in that they freely mix news and partisanship.

The Politics of News

The news media are Americans' window onto the world of politics. For most people, politics is a second-hand experience, something they observe through the media rather than directly. People's mental pictures of events and policy problems, and even their images of political institutions and leaders, stem largely from what they see and hear through the media. Although the media are not the main source of citizens' political *opinions* (such as their opinion on gun control), they are the main source of people's political *perceptions* (such as their perception of the level of crime in their community).

The news media operate as *gatekeepers*. Out of the countless story possibilities each day, they determine which events will be covered and which ones will not. These selections, in turn, will influence what citizens are thinking and talking about. What determines these selections? What determines whether a story will make the news, and thus become known to the public, or will not make the news, and thus remain largely out of sight except to those affected directly? As it happens, journalists' selections are channeled by four functions—the signaling, common-carrier, watchdog, and partisan functions. We'll look first at the signaling function.

The Signaling Function

The media's responsibilities include a **signaling function**. The media seek to alert the public to important developments as soon as possible after they happen—a state visit to Washington by a foreign leader, a bill

HOW THE 50 STATES DIFFER:
POLITICAL THINKING THROUGH COMPARISONS

In the News, or Out?

Most of the news that reaches Americans, no matter where they live, originates with a handful of news outlets, such as NBC News. This coverage, however, concentrates on events in a few places. The map shows the relative frequency with which each of the fifty states was mentioned on NBC News during a one-year period.

Q: *Why do some states get more coverage than other states?*

A: *The heavily covered states are usually the more populous ones, which increases the likelihood that a newsworthy event will occur. In NBC's case, coverage is also heavier in states where its permanent correspondents are based. NBC has correspondents stationed in New York, Washington, Los Angeles, Miami, Houston, Atlanta, and Chicago.*

Source: Data compiled by the author from Nexis.

that Congress has just passed, a change in the nation's unemployment level, or a terrorist bombing in a foreign capital.

The U.S. media are well equipped to play a signaling role. They are poised to converge on any major news event anywhere in the nation and nearly anywhere in the world. The signaling function is performed largely by the traditional media—the wire services, the daily newspapers, and the television networks. These news organizations are staffed and organized to cover events and consequently are the source of most breaking news. Occasionally, an event enters the news stream through the Internet. It was bloggers who first recognized that a racially laden comment by Senate Republican leader Trent Lott in 2002 was big news—big enough that it would eventually force Lott to resign his leadership post. Nevertheless, hundreds of news stories enter the news stream daily, and the great bulk of them are generated by traditional news outlets.

A Common Version of Reality In their capacity as signalers, the media have the power to focus the public's attention. The term **agenda setting** has been used to describe the media's ability to influence what is on people's minds.[9] By covering the same events, problems, issues, and leaders—simply by giving them space or time in the news—the media place them on the public agenda. The press, as Bernard Cohen notes, "may not be successful much of the time in telling people what to think, but it is stunningly successful in telling them what to think about."[10]

Even when "media reality" does not match "objective reality," it can have a powerful effect on what people think is true. A classic example occurred in the early 1990s when local television stations, in an attempt to bolster sagging news ratings, upped their crime coverage. "If it bleeds it leads" became the mantra of local TV news. Meanwhile, the national media were playing up high-profile murder cases including the kidnap-murder of twelve-year-old Polly Klaas in California. Crime was the most heavily reported national issue, overshadowing even coverage of the nation's struggling economy. The effect on public opinion was dramatic. In the previous decade, no more than 5 percent of Americans had believed at any time that crime was the country's biggest problem. By 1994, however, more than 40 percent of Americans said that crime was the top issue facing the nation. Lawmakers got caught up in the public's anxiety by enacting tough new sentencing policies and building new prisons at the fastest rate in the nation's history. The irony was that the level of crime in America was actually *declining* during this period. According to U.S. Justice Department statistics, the rate of violent crime had dropped by 5 percent since 1990.[11]

The norms of objective journalism lead most U.S. news outlets to report the news in similar ways. Also contributing to this tendency is the fact that news organizations assign their reporters to cover many of the same stories. In some cases, there are more journalists on the scene of a news event than there are newsmakers.

The press is a powerful agenda setter in part because nearly all major news organizations focus on the same stories and interpret them in pretty much the same way. In view of the freedom and great number of news organizations—there are roughly fifteen hundred daily newspapers and a thousand local television outlets in the United States—it might be expected that Americans would be exposed to widely different versions of national news. The opposite is true. Each day, newspapers and broadcast outlets from coast to coast tend to highlight the same national issues and events.

Objective journalism is one reason the national news is everywhere pretty much the same. Unlike some European news systems, in which journalism norms allow and even encourage reporters to present the news through a partisan lens, American reporters are expected to treat the political parties and their leaders in a balanced way. They do not always do so, but in their quest for balance, American reporters tend toward a common interpretation of political developments, as opposed to a Republican version or a Democratic version.

Another reason the news everywhere in the United States is pretty much the same is that news outlets depend on the wire services for most of their national coverage. Most U.S. news organizations lack the resources to gather news outside their own location and rely for this coverage on the wire services, particularly the Associated Press (AP), which has three thousand reporters stationed throughout the country and the world to gather news stories and transmit them to subscribing news organizations. More than 95 percent of the nation's dailies (as well as most broadcast news stations) subscribe to the AP, which, because it serves the full range of American news outlets, studiously avoids partisanship in preparing its stories. Even the top U.S. newspapers—including the *New York Times, Wall Street Journal, Los Angeles Times, Washington Post*, and *Chicago Tribune* give similar coverage to the same top stories each day. They differ mostly in their feature and follow-up reports, which usually appear on the inside pages rather than the front page.

Local television stations also depend on outside sources for their national news coverage. Television production is hugely expensive, which limits the ability of local stations to produce anything except local news. For their national coverage, they rely on video feeds from the leading television networks—ABC, CBS, NBC, CNN, Fox, and MSNBC. Even the national networks have a similar lineup of stories. Most network newscasts are a half hour in length, with ten minutes devoted to advertising. With so little time for news, the day's top stories tend to dominate the newscasts of all networks. Moreover, network correspondents cover the same beats and rely on many of the same sources, which lead them to report more or less the same things. After filming a congressional hearing, for example, network correspondents are likely to agree on what was most newsworthy about it—often a testy exchange between a witness and one of the committee members.

Informing the Public, or Attracting an Audience? The signaling function of the press is sometimes called its informing function, but the latter is a less accurate description. Although news organizations take seriously their responsibility to inform the public, the more pressing concern is a need "to attract and hold a large audience for advertisers."[12] Without ad revenue, nearly all U.S. news organizations would go out of business. Only a few news outlets—an example is NPR, which depends on listener contributions—support themselves through something other than commercial advertising.

The very definition of news—what it is and what it is not—is built around the need to attract an audience.[13] The news is intentionally shortsighted. Each day, journalists must have new stories to tell, ones that are different from yesterday's stories. The continuing need for fresh news leads journalists to cover what they call "hard events"—developments that have taken a clear and definable shape within the past twenty-four hours.[14] Without a hard event to lend it form and immediacy, an issue is likely to go unreported. For example, although few developments in the post–World War II era had a bigger impact on U.S. politics than the northward trek of southern blacks, it was rarely mentioned in the news. As African Americans in the late 1940s and 1950s moved into the northern cities by the hundreds each day, white people, pushed by racial fears and pulled by the lure of the suburbs, moved out in equally large numbers. Within a few decades, the political, social, and economic landscape of urban America had been altered substantially—a transformation that was rarely the subject of news coverage. Columnist George Will noted wryly that a ribbon should have been stretched across the Mason-Dixon line as the one-millionth African American crossed it on the way north; the breaking of the ribbon would have given the media a "peg" on which to hang the story of urban America's extraordinary transformation.[15]

Policy issues and problems do not change much from day to day, and thus are not considered particularly newsworthy. The first time that a top politician talks about a major policy issue, it is likely to be reported, and it may even make the front page. Thereafter, it loses its news value because journalists look upon it as "old news." Although the 2008 presidential campaign, for example, was waged against the backdrop of the weak economy, the Iraq conflict, and other issues, these were not the main focus of the news coverage. Journalists focused instead on the latest poll results, accusations, missteps, and the like. These were the "new" developments in the presidential race and therefore what journalists saw as "news."[16] The press's need for novelty also explains why sensational crimes and wayward celebrities get so much attention. In 2009, police were called to the home of the golfer Tiger Woods, who had crashed his car just outside the entrance to his driveway after an argument with his wife. It was the start of a months-long story about Woods's personal life, including numerous extramarital affairs.

Of course, serious issues also get coverage. But the mix of news stories is designed as much to attract an audience as to inform it.[17] An example is the relative scarcity of international coverage. Market research has found that American audiences are not all that interested in world news, and most U.S. news organizations make no real effort to provide it.[18] Not surprisingly, Americans are relatively uninformed about world affairs. A study of seven Western countries found, for example, that Americans ranked next to last (ahead only of Spaniards) in their ability to identify prominent world leaders and developments.[19]

HOW THE U.S. DIFFERS
POLITICAL THINKING THROUGH COMPARISONS

Public Broadcasting

Public broadcasting got off to a slow start in the United States. Unlike the case in Europe, where public broadcasting networks (such as Britain's BBC) were created at the start of the radio age, the U.S. government in the 1930s handed control of broadcasting to commercial networks, such as NBC and CBS. By the time Congress decided in the 1960s that public broadcasting was needed, the commercial networks were so powerful that they convinced Congress to assign it second-class status. Public broadcasting was poorly funded and was denied access to the most powerful broadcast frequencies. In fact, most television sets in the 1960s had tuners that could not dial in the stations on which public broadcast programs were aired. Not surprisingly, public broadcasting faltered at the beginning and still operates in the shadow of commercial broadcasting.

Nevertheless, public broadcasting does have a success story—NPR. Since the early 1990s, NPR's audience has more than tripled. Each week, more than 20 million Americans listen to NPR, many of them on a regular basis. NPR's growth is a stark contrast to what has happened to commercial newscasts during the same period. The combined audience of the ABC, CBS, and NBC evening newscasts is now half that of the early 1980s. NPR has built its audience through a strategy opposite to that of the commercial networks. As the news audiences of these networks declined in the face of widening competition from cable television, they "softened" their newscasts—boosting entertainment content in the hope of luring viewers away from cable programs. Former FCC chairman Newton Minow derided the change as "pretty close to tabloid." In contrast, NPR has held to the notion that news is news and not also entertainment. Although NPR carries features, they are typically tied to news developments. Studies indicate that NPR's audience is more politically interested and informed than any other broadcast news audience. Many of its listeners are refugees from the broadcast network news they used to watch but now find to be lacking in substance.

Q: *What effect on public information might have resulted from the U.S. government's decision in the 1930s to base the nation's broadcasting system on commercial stations rather than public stations?*

A: *In countries like Britain, where public broadcasting has been well funded from the start, it has set a standard for high-quality news that conditions the public to prefer it and to expect it from other news providers as well. In the United States, public broadcasting depends on stories reported first by commercial outlets, where the profit motive can lead to news based more on its audience appeal than its social relevance. Accordingly, many Americans have become accustomed to, and even prefer, news that has an entertainment component.*

The Common-Carrier Function

The press at times has as a **common-carrier function**, serving as a conduit through which political leaders communicate with the public. The justification for this role is straight forward. Citizens cannot support or oppose a leader's plans and actions if they do not know about them, and leaders require news coverage if they are to get the public's attention and support.

Indeed, national news focuses largely on the words and actions of top political leaders, particularly the president (see Chapter 12). Presidents pursue what has come to be known as the "Rose Garden strategy"—so-called because many of their pronouncements are delivered in the flower garden just outside the Oval Office. More than two hundred reporters are assigned to cover the White House, where they are inundated with press releases and briefings. In fact, the presidency gets substantially more coverage in the national press than does Congress.[20]

Although officials sometimes succeed in getting favorable coverage, two things blunt their efforts to manage the news. One is journalists' norm of partisan neutrality. Although reporters depend heavily on official sources, they often present the positions of leaders of both parties—the "he said, she said" style of reporting. If the president, secretary of defense, Senate majority leader, or other high-ranking official says or does something newsworthy, the news report often includes a contrary statement or action by another individual, usually of the opposite party.

Second, although news typically originates in the words and actions of political leaders, they do not monopolize the news, particularly on

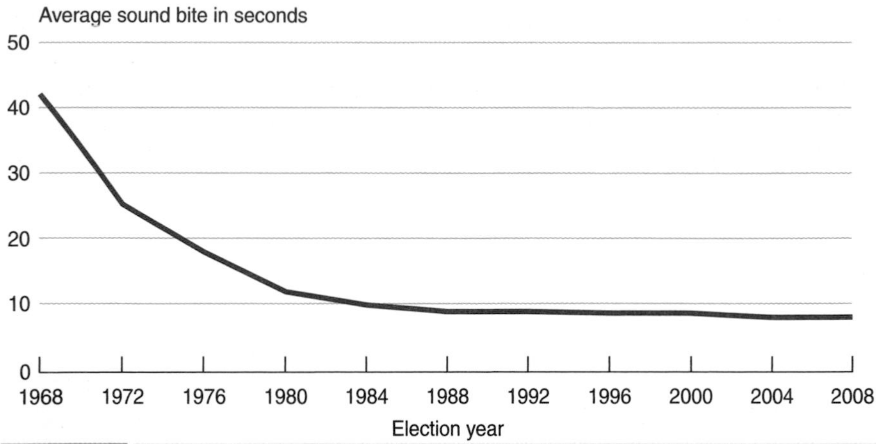

figure 10-1 THE SHRINKING SOUND BITE OF TELEVISION CAMPAIGN COVERAGE

The average length of time that presidential candidates are shown speaking without interruption on broadcast television newscasts has declined sharply in recent elections. *Source:* Adapted from Daniel C. Hallin, "Sound Bite News Television Coverage of Elections 1968–1988" from *Journal of Communication* 42 (Spring 1992): 6. Reprinted with the permission of Blackwell Publishers, Ltd. The 1992–2008 data are from the Center for Media and Public Affairs.

television. TV news is now more journalist centered than it is newsmaker centered.[21] In an effort to keep their viewers tuned in, television newscasts use a fast-paced format in which each story has multiple pieces woven together in story form, with the journalist acting as the storyteller. One indicator of this format is the "shrinking sound bite" in presidential campaigns. In the 1960s, a candidate's sound bite (the length of time within a television story that a candidate speaks without interruption) was more than forty seconds on average.[22] In recent campaigns, the average sound bite has been less than ten seconds, barely enough time for the candidate to utter a long sentence (see Figure 10-1). It is the journalists, not the candidates, who do most of the talking. For every minute that Barack Obama and John McCain spoke on the network evening newscasts during the 2008 presidential campaigns, the journalists who were covering them spoke for more than five minutes.[23] Most of the time that Obama and McCain could be seen on the evening news with their mouths moving, their voices could not be heard; the journalist's voice was the audible one.

Journalists also say different things than public officials do. Whereas officials talk mainly about policy problems and issues, journalists talk mainly about the "game" of politics. They focus on political strategy and infighting, portraying politics as a struggle for personal power and competitive advantage. Journalists could present politics in the context of policy problems and debates, but they choose instead to present it in the context of its strategic aspects. For the journalist, the strategic context has two advantages over the policy frame. First, the give-and-take among political leaders is more easily observed and reported than are policy positions and conditions. Second, the political game is a reliable source of fresh material. Policy problems and issues do not change much from day to day, but the political game is in constant motion.[24]

POLITICAL THINKING

Who's at Fault?

Survey after survey has demonstrated that Americans as a whole are not well informed about politics and public affairs. Some analysts place most of the blame on the press, which, they say, is more concerned with entertaining its audience than informing it. Other observers place most of the blame on the public. They point out that there is almost no vital piece of information about a policy issue that is not reported by the media at one time or another. From this perspective, the problem rests with the public's failure to pay close attention to the news. In your opinion, is the press or the public primarily to blame for the citizenry's low level of political awareness? What changes in news coverage might improve the public's level of awareness?

Communication scholars use the term **framing** to describe the way in which events are cast. Framing is a process of selecting certain aspects of reality and making them the most salient part of the communication.[25] Although the strategic game is a natural part of politics, it is an ever larger part of the news about politics because it is the frame through which journalists construct most of their political stories.[26] This emphasis "primes" the audience to view politicians more as strategists than as leaders. **Priming** refers to the process by which a communicated message, because of its content, activates certain opinions but not others. Given the media's emphasis on the strategic game, it is not altogether surprising that most Americans believe that politicians spend too much time fighting among themselves and think that politicians will say almost anything to get elected or to hold on to power.[27]

The Watchdog Function

The American press has assumed responsibility for exposing incompetent, hypocritical, and corrupt officials. In this **watchdog function**, the press stands ready to expose officials who violate accepted legal, ethical, or performance standards. The American news media have rightfully been called a fourth branch of government—part of the political system's checks on abuses by those in power.

The norms of objective journalism foster watchdog reporting. Although journalists are expected to fairly treat opposing political views, no norm exists that would limit criticism of officials who abuse the public trust. American journalists also operate within a system that provides substantial protection from libel judgments (see Chapter 4). It is nearly impossible for a U.S. official to win a libel suit against a newspaper, magazine, or broadcast organization even if his or her reputation has been harmed by false allegations. In Britain, where libel judgments are obtained more easily, journalists have to be more judicious in alleging that officials have been guilty of misconduct.

American journalists have not always vigorously fulfilled their watchdog function. After the terrorist attacks of September 11, 2001, the news media stepped back from their watchdog role. Press criticism of political leaders and institutions fell sharply, as journalists sought to contribute to a newfound sense of national unity and purpose. NBC News outfitted its peacock logo with stars and stripes after the World Trade Center and Pentagon attacks, and computer-generated flags festooned the other networks. Although there was some critical reporting during the lead-up to the 2003 invasion of Iraq, news organizations did not vigorously scrutinize the Bush administration's arguments in favor of war.[28]

The Iraq invasion was an exception, however. Journalists are typically skeptical of politicians' motives and actions, an outlook that deepened during the Vietnam War. A turning point was the *New York Times*'s publication in 1970 of the so-called Pentagon Papers—classified documents revealing that government had deceived the public by claiming that the war in Vietnam was going well when in fact it was going badly. The Nixon administration tried to block publication of the documents but was overruled by the Supreme Court (see Chapter 4). The Watergate scandal gave journalists further reason to believe that they should not take politicians at their word. Led by investigative reporting of the *Washington Post*, the press uncovered evidence that high-ranking officials in the Nixon administration had lied about their role in the 1972 burglary of the Democratic National Committee's headquarters and the subsequent cover-up. President Richard Nixon was forced to resign, as was his attorney general, John Mitchell.

Ever since Watergate, the press usually has been quick to pounce on any sign of public wrongdoing. An example is the *Washington Post* exposé of neglect at the Walter Reed Army Hospital in the handling of wounded

U.S. soldiers from the Iraq and Afghanistan conflicts. The *Post*'s reporters conducted stakeouts at the hospital, talked with dozens of patients and staff, and secured hundreds of documents in the course of their investigation. The *Post*'s stories led to congressional hearings and eventually forced the Department of Veterans Affairs to change health care practices at its medical facilities.

The Internet, with citizens acting in the role of journalists, has expanded the media's watchdog capacity. Virtually any public event involving a major politician today is likely to be filmed or taped by someone in attendance, which can land a politician in trouble. At a closed-door campaign fundraiser in San Francisco on April 11, 2008, for example, Barack Obama was asked about his difficulty in making inroads with Pennsylvania's primary election voters. "You go into these small towns in Pennsylvania and, like a lot of small towns in the Midwest, the jobs have been gone now for 25 years and nothing's replaced them," Obama said. "And it's not surprising then they get bitter, they cling to guns or religion or antipathy to people who aren't like them or anti-immigrant sentiment or anti-trade sentiment as a way to explain their frustrations." Obama was unaware that someone at the fundraiser had taped his remark, which ended up in the hands of the news media. Pundits and talk show hosts had a field day, asking whether the Harvard-educated Obama was completely out of touch with the concerns of ordinary people. Hillary Clinton, his chief rival for the Democratic nomination, went on the attack: "The people of faith I know don't 'cling to' religion because they're bitter. People embrace faith not because they are materially poor, but because they are spiritually rich." Obama tried to contain the damage by claiming that he was only trying to voice the frustrations of workers in economically depressed communities. "I didn't say it as well as I should have," he said. A week later, Obama lost the Pennsylvania primary to Clinton by a margin of 55–45 percent.

The Partisan Function

Traditionally, the **partisan function**—acting as an advocate for a particular viewpoint or interest—has been the responsibility of political leaders, institutions, and organizations. Today, however, the news media—particularly the newer of these media—also function in that capacity.

Traditional Media: Mostly Neutral During the era of the partisan press, newspapers sought to guide their readers' opinions. In the presidential election campaign of 1896, for example, the *San Francisco Call*, a Republican newspaper, devoted 1,075 column-inches of photographs to the Republican ticket of McKinley-Hobart and only 11 inches to their Democratic opponents, Bryan and Sewell.[29] San Francisco Democrats had their own oracle, the Hearst-owned *Examiner*, which touted William Jennings Bryan as the savior of working men. The emergence of objective journalism brought an end to that style of reporting. Rather than slanting the news to favor the Republican or Democratic side, journalists sought to give their audience both sides, leaving it to them to decide which one was better.

The traditional media—the daily newspapers and broadcast networks—still operate largely in this way. Even their editorial pages, though slanted toward one party or the other, carry at least some opposing opinions so as not to alienate a portion of their readers. Most newspapers also make the safe choice in elections; they endorse incumbents of both parties with much greater frequency than they endorse their challengers.[30]

The traditional broadcast television networks—ABC, CBS, and NBC—do not endorse candidates and claim to be unbiased, although conservatives dispute the claim. In a best-selling book, a former network correspondent, Bernard Goldberg, accused the networks of having a liberal agenda.[31] Such allegations are not completely baseless. Until recently, for example, the concerns of evangelical Christians were rarely a subject of broadcast news except in the context of conflict-ridden issues like creationism and abortion. Also, most broadcast news journalists, as well as most journalists generally, lean Democratic in their personal beliefs.[32]

Nevertheless, scholarly research does not support the allegation that the traditional media have a substantial and systematic liberal bias. Communication scholars David D'Alessio and Mike Allen examined fifty-nine academic studies of media bias and found almost no pattern of bias in newspapers, a slight but insignificant bias in the Democratic direction on television news, and a slight but insignificant bias in the Republican direction in news magazines.[33] In fact, the television-age president with the worst press coverage was a Democrat, Bill Clinton. The Center for Media and Public Affairs found that Clinton's negative coverage exceeded his positive coverage in every quarter of every year of his two-term presidency—a dubious record that no president before or since has equaled.[34]

Instead of a strong partisan bias, scholars have highlighted a different kind of network bias—the networks' preference for the negative. Michael Robinson concluded that broadcast journalists have a "negativist, contentious" outlook on politics.[35] The networks' preference for "bad news" can be seen, for example, in their coverage of presidential candidates. Nearly all nominees since the 1980s have received mostly negative coverage during the course of the campaign. "Bad news" has characterized network coverage of Democratic and Republican nominees alike.[36]

The news turned negative after Vietnam and Watergate—developments that convinced journalists that politicians could not be trusted—and has largely stayed that way. Studies of news coverage in the 1990s found, for example, that every high-profile agency except the Department of Defense had received more negative than positive coverage. The State Department's coverage was only 13 percent positive, and the Justice Department's coverage was just 10 percent favorable.[37] The legislative branch has fared no better. Press coverage of Congress has been steadily negative since the 1970s, regardless of which party controlled Congress or how much or little was accomplished. "Over the years," concluded scholar Mark Rozell, "press coverage of Congress has moved from healthy skepticism to outright cynicism."[38]

The networks' negativity helps to explain why they are widely perceived as biased. Research indicates that negative news is perceived differently by those who support and those who oppose the politician being attacked. Opponents tend to see the criticism as valid whereas supporters tend to see it as unjustified and therefore biased.[39] It is not surprising, then, that Democrats during Bill Clinton's presidency thought that the networks favored the Republicans while Republicans during George W. Bush's presidency thought that the networks favored the Democrats. Such findings do not mean that the networks are completely unbiased, for they are not. The findings do indicate, however, that much of the perceived bias is in the eye of the beholder.[40]

Scholars have found a correlation between the tone of news coverage and Americans' trust and confidence in political leaders and institutions. The University of Pennsylvania's Joseph Cappella and Kathleen Hall Jamieson demonstrated, for example, that negative messages bring out feelings of mistrust of politicians and political institutions. "The effect," Cappella and Jamieson write, "occurs for broadcast as well as print news."[41] For their part, journalists acknowledge a negative slant but say that Americans are best served when the press errs on the side of criticism, even if that criticism is sometimes unfair or exaggerated. As CNN correspondent Bob Franken put it, "We historically are not supposed to be popular, and it's almost our role to be the bearer of bad news."[42]

Talk Shows: Mostly Conservative The broadcast networks' partisan bias—real and perceived—has been an issue for conservatives at least since 1970 when Republican vice president Spiro Agnew called the networks "nattering nabobs of negativism." Nevertheless, Republicans could only pressure the networks to cover politics differently in that there was no ready alternative. Cable television and the rescinding of the Fairness

Broadcast news dominated television until the advent of cable. Today, the ABC, CBS, and NBC newscasts compete for viewers with those of Fox News, CNN, and MSNBC. Cable news organizations have also developed new models of journalism. For example, CNN specializes in live coverage of events whereas Fox News pursues a politically conservative news agenda. Shown here is Bill O'Reilly of Fox News, who has the largest audience among the TV talk show hosts.

Doctrine changed that situation by providing a host of new options, including partisan talk shows.

On both radio and television, most of the successful partisan talk shows have been hosted by conservatives. The host with the largest audience is radio's Rush Limbaugh. In the top twenty-five radio markets, Limbaugh's show has more listeners, in all age groups, than the listenership of all the top liberal talk shows combined. Limbaugh built his following in the early 1990s with attacks on Bill Clinton, whom Limbaugh variously characterized as a draft-dodger, womanizer, and wimp. When Republicans in the 1994 midterm elections won control of both the House and Senate for the first time in four decades, Limbaugh's contribution was widely heralded. "Operation Restore Democracy" was Limbaugh's label for his months-long radio campaign to get GOP candidates elected, and political conservatives went to the polls in unusually high numbers, prompting analysts to call Limbaugh the Republicans' "electronic precinct captain."

The success of Limbaugh's radio show led Roger Ailes, a Republican political consultant, to create a television version. However, Limbaugh's television talk show never caught on, and it folded in 1996 after a four-year run. Rupert Murdoch then hired Ailes to run a new television network, Fox

News. Murdoch reasoned that conservatives, because of their discontent with the established networks, would embrace a conservative alternative. Fox's newscasts concentrate on top stories but give them a conservative slant. For example, although Fox did not ignore the post-debate polls in 2004 indicating that most Americans thought John Kerry had outdebated George W. Bush each time, Fox carried fewer debate-related stories than the other networks and was the only network to portray Bush more favorably than Kerry during the debate period.[43] Fox's talk show hosts—including Glenn Beck, Sean Hannity, and Bill O'Reilly, who has the highest-rated political talk show on cable television—tilt toward the conservative side. Like the audience for political talk radio, the Fox News television audience is disproportionately Republican. CNN's audience, which was roughly balanced between Republicans and Democrats until Fox News came along, now tilts Democratic, as does the audience of MSNBC, the third cable network. These differences are reflected in how partisans view the three networks. Republicans have the more favorable view of Fox whereas Democrats have the more favorable view of CNN and MSNBC (see Figure 10-2).

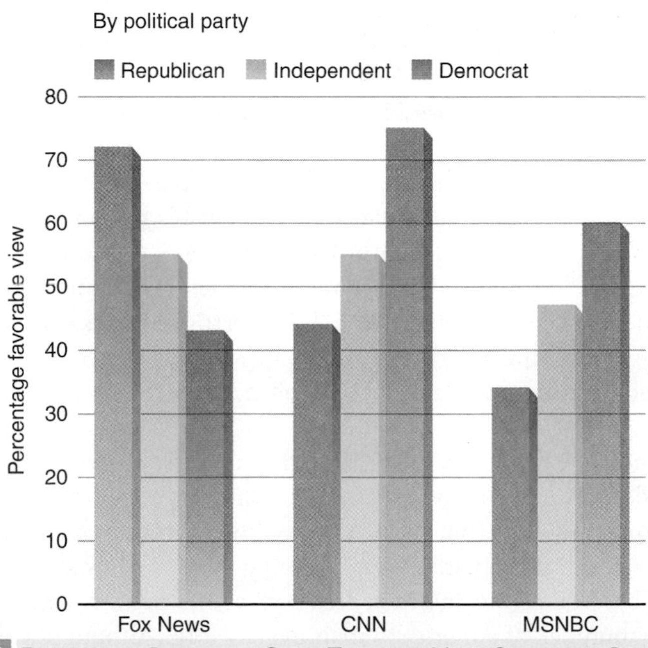

figure 10-2 FAVORABILITY RATING OF CABLE TELEVISION NEWS OUTLETS, BY PARTY IDENTIFICATION

Republicans think more highly of Fox News whereas Democrats think more highly of CNN and MSNBC. *Source:* From Pew Research Center for the People and the Press, September 13, 2009. Reprinted with permission.

CNN and MSNBC have responded to Fox's ratings success by installing talk show hosts who also lure their audiences through partisan or hard-edged appeals. MSNBC's lineup is liberal, featuring Keith Olbermann and Rachel Maddow, as well as Chris Matthews, a former Democratic congressional staffer who is critical of both parties but aims his sharpest barbs at the Republicans. CNN has a more diverse set of talk show hosts, a marketing formula that has been less successful than Fox's.

The news outlet with the largest liberal following is NPR. Its weekly audience of 20 million listeners rivals Limbaugh's, although its format is different. NPR's newscasts are based on breaking stories from AP and other news outlets, and NPR presents a balanced view of the two parties. NPR's appeal to liberals is based on its talk shows, which, though neutral in tone, usually touch on issues of particular concern to liberals, such as global warming.

The most popular of the stridently liberal talk shows employ political humor to make their point. In fact, the most prominent of these shows—*The Daily Show*, *The Colbert Report*, and *Real Time with Bill Maher*—are televised on entertainment channels (Comedy Central and HBO) rather than news channels. Jon Stewart's *Daily Show*, seen by more than a million viewers each night, has the largest following. Like Limbaugh's radio talk show, which soared in the 1990s when Limbaugh was attacking Democratic president Bill Clinton, Stewart's show rose in popularity as his attacks on the policies of Republican president George W. Bush sharpened. In a telling episode, Stewart looked blankly at the television screen for seemingly endless seconds before blurting out "Please say, please say, you're kidding me." This comment followed a videotape of Bush's national security advisor, Condoleezza Rice, admitting to Congress that she had read a classified document titled "Bin Laden Determined to Attack Inside the United States" a month before the September 11, 2001, terrorist attacks on the World Trade Center and the Pentagon. Rice had earlier asserted that no one in the Bush administration could possibly have foreseen the attacks.

The Internet: Mostly Liberal Although the First Amendment protects each individual's right to press freedom, this right in practice was once reserved for a tiny few. Journalist A. J. Liebling wrote that freedom of the press belonged to those with enough money to own a news organization.[44]

Today, because of the Internet, freedom of the press is actively enjoyed by a larger number of Americans than ever before. Although access to the Internet is no substitute for owning a newspaper or a television station, it does provide the ordinary citizen with an opportunity to be part of the news system. Through their websites, citizens can post news and information about public affairs, harangue officials, and argue for public policies. The

Unlike talk shows, where conservative viewpoints dominate, Internet blogs and comedy-based shows are bastions of liberal sentiment. Shown in this photo is *The Colbert Report*'s Stephen Colbert, who hosts a news and comedy program that satirizes conservative talk show hosts.

Internet has reduced the barriers to public communication to a level not seen since colonial days, when pamphleteers like Thomas Paine dominated political communication. Thomas Paine's pamphlet, *Common Sense*, sold over a hundred thousand copies and mobilized American opposition to British rule. "We have the power to begin the world over again," wrote Paine, who also penned the famous line "These are the times that try men's souls."

The Internet has been a boon to political activists. During the 2008 presidential campaign, Barack Obama used his opposition to the Iraq war, his oratorical skill, and the power of the Internet to go from relative obscurity to the White House. Obama's campaign raised roughly $600 million, much of it through Internet contributions of less than $250. The Internet was also the medium for one of the most successful citizen-led efforts in history—a global movement that succeeded in getting nearly one hundred countries to sign an international treaty banning the use of land mines. Its organizer, Jody Williams, was awarded the Nobel Peace Prize.

When it comes to news, however, the Internet's significance is harder to pinpoint. Because the cost of entry is low, there are literally thousands of websites where news is regularly posted and examined. However, Internet news is characterized by what analysts call "the long tail." When news-based websites are arrayed by the number of visitors to each site, there are a few heavily visited sites on one end and many lightly visited sites on the other end—the long tail. As it happens, most of the heavily visited sites are those of the traditional media, including CNN.com and nytimes.com. In addition, most of the other heavily visited sites, such as Google News, carry news that was gathered and reported first by the established media. In other words, most Americans who go to the Internet for news are seeing news generated by the same sources they otherwise tap.

Occasionally, a major story will originate on the Internet. Bloggers were the first to identify as forgeries the government documents that Dan Rather, CBS news anchor, presented during the 2004 presidential campaign as proof that George W. Bush had shirked his National Guard duties in the early 1970s. Within months, Rather was forced into early retirement. Rather's departure was a source of glee for many in the blogging community. Whether liberal or conservative, bloggers tend to share a disdain for the mainstream press, which they accuse of everything from bias to irrelevance.

Unlike most of the successful talk-radio programs, most of the successful blogs have a liberal bias.[45] An example is the Huffington Post, which was started in 2005 by liberal activist Arianna Huffington. The site has more unique visitors each month than the news sites of several major news organizations, including CBS and the *Los Angeles Times*.

The Internet is in its early years as a news medium, so it is hazardous to guess whether initial tendencies will continue. Since their defeat in the 2008 elections, for example, conservatives have established a stronger presence on the Internet. In any case, as Americans increasingly look to the Internet for information, including news, it is safe to say that the Internet's importance will continue to grow.[46]

POLITICAL THINKING

Are the "New" Media the Reason?

Research suggests that the level of public "misinformation" is rising. It appears that Americans increasingly believe things that are untrue. During the 2009–2010 health care debate, for example, polls indicated that about a third of Americans erroneously believed that the legislation included "death panels"—committees that could deny medical care to ailing elderly patients. "The Case for Killing Granny" is how Newsweek *magazine satirically described the situation. Do you think the "new" media—political talk shows, blogs, social networks, and the like—are contributing to the increase in misinformation? If not, what do you think might explain this recent development?*

Attention to News

The U.S. news system now has more outlets—including newspapers, television stations, talk shows, and bloggers—than at any time in its history. The news system also provides a wider variety of content—everything from straight news to partisan harangues. Although it might be assumed that Americans are therefore more attentive and more informed about public affairs than ever before, that is not the case. The same media system that makes news available on demand at any time also makes it easy for people to choose other content. America today has many citizens who consume copious amounts of news. It also has many citizens who consume almost none.

The Shrinking Audience for News

The 1980s were the turning point in the shape of the news audience. Until then, and for nearly two centuries, the news audience had been growing. Rising literacy rates, increased urbanization, and low-cost newspapers had widened the audience during the nineteenth century. The introduction of radio and television news in the twentieth century widened it further.

Television was the critical element in the last phase of this expansion. Americans were nearly obsessed with television in its early years and would watch most anything available. In most television markets at the dinner hour, the only choices available to viewers were the ABC newscast, the CBS newscast, and the NBC newscast. Viewers who were intent on watching television in this time period had no alternative but to sit through the news. They constituted an "inadvertent news audience"—brought to the news less by a strong preference for it than by an addiction to television.[47]

The television news audience at its peak was enormous. At the dinner hour, most television sets in America were turned on, and 85 percent of these sets were tuned to the news. This exposure rubbed off on the children. The evening news was a ritual in many families, and though the children might have preferred something else, they, too, watched it. By the time many of these children finished school, many of them had acquired a television news habit of their own.

Television's capacity to generate an interest in news declined sharply in the 1980s with the rapid spread of cable. Viewers no longer had to sit through the news while waiting for entertainment programming to appear. Television news did not lose most of its regular viewers, but it did lose its ability to develop an interest in news among adults who preferred

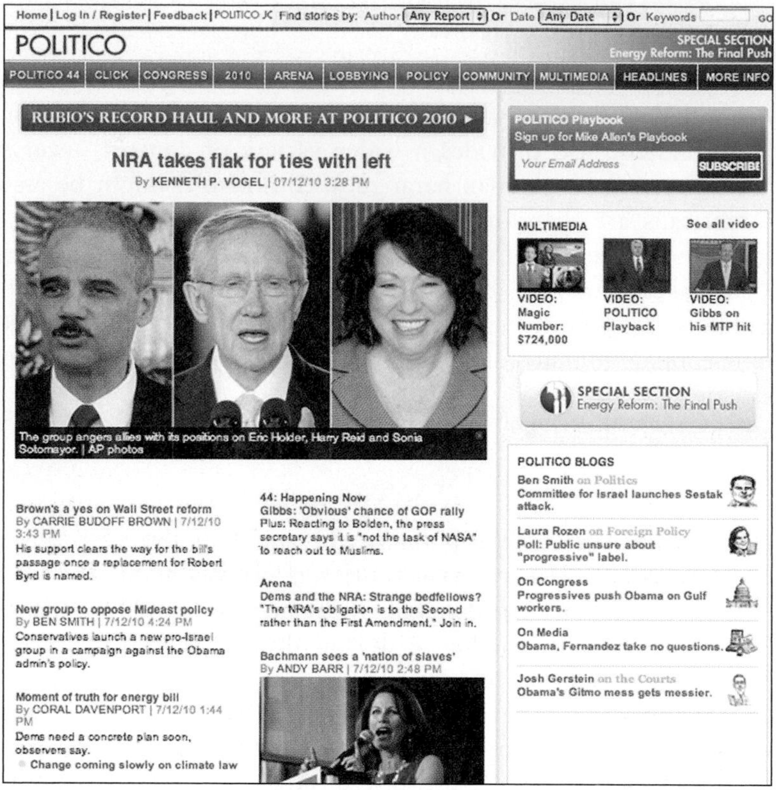

The Internet has opened up the media system, allowing citizens, groups, and leaders to communicate more powerfully than was possible during the not-so-distant era when news organizations almost totally controlled the instruments of mass communication. Shown here is a web page from Politico, a nonpartisan site that is followed closely by political insiders and outsiders alike.

entertainment programming. And its capacity to generate news interest in children was greatly diminished. Fewer of their parents were watching the dinner-hour news, and even if they were watching, the children, as a Kaiser Family Foundation study revealed, were usually in another room watching entertainment shows.[48]

To be sure, some Americans were getting more news than was possible in earlier times. Round-the-clock news was available to anyone with cable TV. Yet cable also made it possible for people to avoid the news with ease. And large numbers of Americans, mostly younger adults, abandoned news for movies, sitcoms, comedy shows, and other cable programs.[49] The result was a steady decline in the broadcast news audience. Some of the drop was attributable to viewers who shifted to cable news. Even when they are accounted for, however, the absolute proportion of Americans watching television news on a daily basis dropped significantly. Newspaper circulation also declined, partly because cable TV was taking up more and more of people's media time and partly because fewer people had a daily news habit.

Age and Attention to News

Today, the daily audience for news consists disproportionately of older adults. Compared with adults thirty years of age or younger, those over fifty are three times more likely to follow public affairs closely through a newspaper—meaning they read a newspaper nearly every day and pay reasonably close attention to the news pages while doing so. The disparity is not as great with television news, but it is still a substantial one. Older adults are roughly twice as likely as young adults to watch television news almost daily and to sit through most of the newscast while doing so. Age differences shrink for Internet-based news but do not disappear. Even though older adults are somewhat less likely than young adults to access the web, they are more likely to access news content when doing so. In fact, about 40 percent of young adults pay little or no attention on a regular basis to any news source.[50]

Young adults differ also from older ones in a preference for partisan information. A recent Pew Research Center study found that, among those who rely on the Internet for news, individuals under thirty years of age, but not older ones, prefer outlets with a partisan slant. Young adults are also more likely than older adults to turn to nontraditional television outlets, such as *The Daily Show*, and to see them as bona fide news sources. This perception is not groundless. These programs occasionally dig more deeply into an issue than do the mainstream news outlets. On the other hand, these nontraditional programs make no effort to provide comprehensive news coverage or to convey information that might contradict the host's point of view.[51]

A few decades ago, the news habits of younger and older adults were similar, as political scientist Martin Wattenberg has shown. In the late 1950s, for example, 53 percent of those in the 21–29 age group regularly read news coverage of national politics, compared with 61 percent in the 30–44 age group, 60 percent in the 45–60 age group, and 57 percent of those over 60. Wattenberg found a similar pattern for television news. "There was little variation in news viewing habits by age," Wattenberg writes. "TV news producers could hardly write off young adults, given that two out of three said they had watched such broadcasts every night."[52]

The widening age gap in news consumption has been accompanied by a widening age "information gap." Wattenberg found that, until the early 1970s, young adults were more knowledgeable about current events and leaders than senior citizens, which he attributed largely to differences in education. Most older citizens of the time had not graduated from high school. Since the 1980s, and increasingly so, young adults have been less informed than older ones. In 2004, for example, whereas adults sixty-five years of age and older could answer correctly 55 percent of factual questions about politics contained in the American National Election Studies (ANES) survey, adults under thirty years of age could answer only 36 percent of the questions accurately. In fact, young adults scored lower than all other age groups on every ANES question, whether it was identification of current political leaders, information about the presidential candidates, knowledge of which party controlled Congress, or basic civic facts. The chapter of Wattenberg's book in which these findings are presented is titled pointedly, "Don't Ask Anyone Under 30."[53]

Media and the Public in the Internet Age

The news media today are a greatly different political intermediary than they were only a few decades ago, and the political consequences are substantial.

The old media system was dominated by a few powerful news organizations—the broadcast networks, in particular. They had a huge daily audience, enabling them to alert Americans of all ages and classes to the same events. They also provided a platform for political leaders who, through a single statement or event, could reach tens of millions of citizens. And because these media reported developments in a largely nonpartisan way, the political translation of these developments rested largely with political parties and interest groups, enhancing their political roles.

Today's media system is markedly different. The traditional media are still major players, but their audiences are smaller and their influence is diminished. The audience for news and public affairs is fragmented in a way unimaginable a few decades ago. The audience is now spread across hundreds of outlets that vary widely in how they present politics, how they portray political leaders, and what aspects of politics they highlight. In this sense, Americans now have less in common when their thoughts turn to politics.

This development, as political scientist Marcus Prior shows in *Post-Broadcast Democracy*, has contributed to partisan polarization.[54] Many of the new media outlets play up partisan differences, praising their side while tearing down the other, contributing to the widening split in the opinions of liberals and conservatives. The new media system also contributes to another widening divide—the information gap between America's more-attentive and less-attentive citizens. Although the information gap is not new, the gap is widening because today's news system makes it easier for citizens without an interest in news to avoid it. When using the media, people can easily bypass the news if it holds little or no appeal.

SUMMARY

Self-Test www.mhhe.com/pattersonwtp9e

In the nation's first century, the press was allied closely with the political parties and helped the parties mobilize public opinion. Gradually, the press freed itself from this partisan relationship and developed a form of reporting known as objective journalism, which emphasizes fair and accurate accounts of newsworthy developments. That model still governs the news reporting of the traditional media—daily newspapers and broadcasters—but does not hold for the newer media—radio talk shows, cable TV talk shows, and Internet blogs. Although some of them cover politics in the traditional way, many of them transmit news through a partisan lens.

The press performs four basic functions. First, in their signaling function, journalists communicate information to the public about breaking events and new developments. This information makes citizens aware of developments that affect their lives. However, because of the media's need to attract an audience, breaking news stories often focus on developments, such as celebrity scandals, that have little to do with issues of politics and government. Second, the press functions as a common carrier in that it provides political leaders with a channel for addressing the public. Increasingly, however, the news has centered nearly as much on the journalists themselves as on the newsmakers they cover. In a third function, that of watchdog, the press acts to protect the public by exposing deceitful, careless, or corrupt officials. Finally, the press functions as a partisan advocate. Although the traditional media perform this function to a degree, the newer media—the talk shows and blogs—specialize in it. Their influence has contributed to a rising level of political polarization in the United States.

The news audience has changed substantially in the past few decades. Daily newspapers and broadcast news have lost audiences to cable television and the Internet. At the same time, the emergence of cable television and the Internet has made it easier for citizens to avoid news when using the media. Although some citizens today consume more news than was possible at an earlier time, other citizens—young adults, in particular—consume less news than was previously typical. A consequence is that young adults are less informed politically relative to both older adults and to earlier generations of young adults.

Key Terms

agenda setting (*p. 338*)
common-carrier function (*p. 343*)
framing (*p. 345*)
news (*p. 330*)
objective journalism (*p. 333*)
partisan function (*p. 347*)
partisan press (*p. 332*)
press (news media) (*p. 330*)
priming (*p. 345*)
signaling (signaler) function (*p. 336*)
watchdog function (*p. 345*)

Suggested Readings

Baum, Matthew A., and Tim J. Groeling. *War Stories: The Causes and Consequences of Public Views of War*. Princeton, N.J.: Princeton University Press, 2009. A study of the public's perceptions of war that includes an examination of the media's role.

Bennett, W. Lance, Regina G. Lawrence, and Steven Livingston. *When the Press Fails: Political Power and the News Media from Iraq to Katrina*. Chicago: University of Chicago Press, 2008. A revealing account of news coverage, particularly during the buildup to the Iraq conflict.

Bimber, Bruce A., and Richard Davis. *Campaigning Online: The Internet in U.S. Elections*. New York: Oxford University Press, 2003. A careful study of Internet use in election campaigns.

Farnsworth, Stephen J., and S. Robert Lichter. *The Nightly News Nightmare: Media Coverage of U.S. Presidential Elections*. Lanham, MD.: Rowman & Littlefield, 2010. An empirical study of television coverage of elections.

Hamilton, James T. *All the News That's Fit to Sell*. Princeton, N.J.: Princeton University Press, 2004. A careful study of the economic influences on news content.

Jones, Alex. *Losing the News: The Future of the News That Feeds Democracy*. New York: Oxford University Press, 2009. A thoughtful commentary on why the decline of the newspaper and its reporting values will weaken democracy.

Kerbel, Matthew R. *Netroots: Online Progressives and the Transformation of American Politics*. Boulder, CO.: Paradigm Publishers, 2009. A look at how the Internet is changing politics in the United States.

McChesney, Robert. *The Political Economy of Media*. New York: Monthly Review Press, 2008. A look at the economic factors driving the media and the resulting political effects.

Overholser, Geneva, and Kathleen Hall Jamieson. *The Press*. New York: Oxford University Press, 2005. A comprehensive survey of U.S. journalism and news.

Prior, Markus. *Post-Broadcast Democracy: How Media Choice Increases Inequality in Political Involvement and Polarizes Elections*. New York: Cambridge University Press, 2007. A thoughtful assessment of how the new media system is widening the information and partisan divides.

Wattenberg, Martin. *Is Voting for Young People?* 2d ed. New York: Longman, 2007. A careful look at how young adults' political attention and information have changed.

List of Websites

www.drudgereport.com The website through which Matt Drudge (The Drudge Report) has challenged the traditional media's control of the news.

www.fcc.gov The Federal Communications Commission website; provides information on broadcasting regulations and current issues.

www.mediatenor.com The website for Media Tenor, a nonpartisan organization that analyzes news coverage on a continuing basis; useful to anyone interested in the media's political coverage.

www.newslink.org A website that provides access to more than a thousand news organizations, including most U.S. daily newspapers.

Politics in Theory and Practice

Thinking: Why does almost every U.S. news outlet, despite having the freedom to say nearly anything it wants, cover virtually the same national stories in virtually the same way as other news organizations?

Participating: Before the Internet opened new channels of communication, freedom of the press, which is granted by the First Amendment to all Americans, was enjoyed for the most part only by the very few who owned or worked in the news media. With the Internet, the opportunity for citizen communication, though not unlimited, is greater than at any time in the nation's history. Take advantage of the opportunity. Meetup.com is one of literally thousands of Internet sites where you can participate in discussion forums about politics and issues. A more ambitious alternative is to start your own web log. Blogging is time consuming but allows you to create an agenda of news, information, and opinion—an activity previously reserved for newspaper editors and broadcast producers. Either of these options will enable you to make your voice heard and also help you to hone your citizenship skills—the ability to communicate, to defend your own views, and to learn what others think.

Extra Credit

For up-to-the-minute *New York Times* articles, interactive simulations, graphics, study tools, and more links and quizzes, visit the text's Online Learning Center at **www.mhhe.com/pattersonwtp9e**.

NATIONAL JOURNAL

Lobbying for Media Diversity

Conservatives and free-market advocates are trying to derail a campaign by federal officials and progressive groups to boost the role of minorities and local activists in the nation's media.

"This is ultimately a battle about content in our electronic communications," said Craig Parshall, general counsel for the National Religious Broadcasters, based in Manassas, Va. "It's about who controls the message."

The effort has several components, including at least three projects at the Federal Communications Commission and the Federal Trade Commission. The FCC hopes to complete a review of media-industry ownership and consolidation by the spring of 2011, and the two agencies are conducting two other far-ranging surveys of the media.

Liberal advocates and some federal officials, such as FCC Commissioner Michael Copps, have long campaigned for diversity regulations that would raise the media visibility of ethnic and racial groups. Activists have also pressed for "localism" regulations that would give community organizers a greater role in shaping broadcasters' programming and content, and for ownership rules that would increase racial and ethnic minorities' access to broadcast licenses.

"You won't have true diversity of viewpoint until you have diversity of ownership," Copps told National Journal. Minority groups are "stereotyped" today, he said. "If Hispanic, the [media] story will likely be about crossing the border, or [it will be] a crime story for other groups; and all the positive contributions these communities are making don't get picked up and don't get covered." Media license-holders, Copps said, should "have an obligation to work for localism and diversity. I'm trying to get the principle established."

These efforts are now combined with a Future of Media project intended to aid the hard-hit profession. In October, FCC Chairman Julius Genachowski hired Internet entrepreneur Steven Waldman to run the project. "The American people are skimming perilously close to not having the breadth and depth of information they need to make intelligent decisions for the future of the country," Copps said. "This is one of the major problems facing the country."

A medley of liberal advocacy organizations, informally led by the Washington-based nonprofit group Free Press, are backing these efforts. On May 11, Free Press held an event to rally support for regulations that would give citizen activists a greater role in shaping media content and would increase taxpayer subsidies for media outlets.

Susan DeSanti, director of the policy planning office at the Federal Trade Commission, told the audience that the FTC may issue a report offering recommendations to aid the financially distressed media sector. These measures could include revised rules on copyrights, taxes, and business alliances, she said. On May 24, the FTC released a "discussion draft" that prompted cheers from liberal groups and raspberries from conservatives, but agency officials said they had not decided to back any of the draft proposals.

At the event, Bill Freedman, associate chief of the FCC's media bureau, which is responsible for the Future of Media project, encouraged Free Press's members to pursue their case for regulatory changes. The project "is unique, in that everything is on the table," including potential new rules to govern companies' use of "the people's airwaves," he said. The FCC will likely release recommendations early next year, setting the stage for regulatory or congressional action.

The agency's priorities closely match the agenda proffered by Free Press, whose cofounder, Josh Silver, told National Journal that the group's progressive funders "are after universal access to communications; they're after critical fact-based journalism [and] health care for every American, [plus] clean air and clear water."

The coalition includes many groups that are seeking increased federal support. More funding is "our last best hope . . . [especially for] people of color," Maxie Jackson, president of the National Federation of Community Broadcasters, told the Free Press meeting.

Jessica Gonzalez, the policy and legal affairs chief at the National Hispanic Media Coalition, said that new licensing regulations should help community activists persuade broadcasters to curb what she calls "hate speech." Gonzalez's group is a member of the National Latino Media Council, which also includes the Congressional Hispanic Caucus Institute and the National Association of Latino Elected Officials.

Additional regulations governing the TV industry and Internet firms are needed because "at the heart of the idea of America is a diversity of voices, and not letting a humongously rich and controlling group [of companies] crowd out the voices of the many," said Marcy Carsey, who developed and sold several successful TV series, including The Cosby Show, Roseanne, and That '70s Show to the networks. "Having worked in the industry since I got out of school, I know for a fact that a lot of the most wonderful and just interesting and full-of-voice television shows would not have gotten on [the air] if not for the fact that they were produced by independents," Carsey said. She donated $150,000 to Free Press in 2008 and sits on its board.

Few, if any, conservative or free-market groups have aligned themselves with the diversity campaign. When asked how nonliberal media outlets might gain from the various proposals, an FCC official hesitated before responding, "I'd have to think about that."

The effort offers risks and potential benefits to the corporate broadcast industry. "We would like to see more diversity of ownership of broadcast properties," Dennis Wharton, a spokesman for the National Association of Broadcasters, said. But "it's an issue of financing, and that's why we supported minority tax credits." He added, "The best way to serve a community with broadcast programming is to allow the local TV and radio stations to not have one-size-fits-all Washington mandates."

Minority-owned stations sometimes oppose government mandates themselves. Regulations can be expensive to implement, and "the minority broadcasters who are the new entrants [would be] less able to carry that expense," said Amador Bustos, chairman of Bustos Media, which buys and sells Spanish-language stations. "Conservative talkers are popular. We need to compete better . . . instead of manipulating the industry."

The agencies' focus on the future of journalism also causes concern, the NAB's Wharton said. "We're watching that very carefully. . . . It always scares us when you have government involved in 'saving journalism.'"

Regulation intended to promote diversity of content is unnecessary, said Richard Wiley, owner of Wiley Rein, Washington's leading telecommunications law firm. "If people want to listen to Rush Limbaugh, it's because he has something interesting to say. . . . [And liberal Rachel Maddow] is making a place on the airwaves" by attracting TV viewers to MSNBC, he said.

"The view of the clients I represent is that the broadcasters have been hit hard by the economic recession . . . [and by] more and more competition," Wiley said. "Probably the last thing these folks need is more regulation." The broadcast industry would welcome new tax rules that encourage investment by racial and ethnic minorities, he added.

Media-industry lobbyists have repeatedly used the courts to stymie regulation. In

April, the U.S. Court of Appeals for the District of Columbia Circuit ruled that FCC officials had overreached when they sought to regulate Comcast's management of Internet traffic. Efforts by agency officials to mandate content diversity would not "be a legitimate use of government regulation," Wiley contended. "I don't anticipate [FCC officials] putting their thumb on the scale."

Parshall, the National Religious Broadcasters general counsel, said that proposals to give community organizers more influence over broadcasters' content would result in abortion-rights or non-Christian religious groups gaining government-enforced influence over Christian broadcasters' programming. "If that is not the heavy hand of government on content, I don't know what is," he said.

For progressives, he said, diversity means the inclusion of their allies, and "making sure there are a suitable number of liberals on the air," while conservatives favor the ideal of free markets, which produce a range of content to match the variety of consumers. Conservatives want a free market "open to all comers . . . [and] we're against federal bailouts for conservative or liberal outlets," Parshall said.

The FCC could help the marketplace by allowing religious stations to accept small-scale donations from outside groups and to receive contributions in exchange for brief sponsorship mentions, similar to those on National Public Radio, he said. "We aren't asking for tax breaks."

Parshall has allies on Capitol Hill whose clout could well increase in November. Rep. Mike Pence of Indiana, chairman of the House Republican Conference, has repeatedly pushed back against government efforts to increase media diversity and localism.

Yet at least until January, Democratic activists "have all the pieces on the chessboard," Parshall said. The White House appoints top officials at the FTC and three of the five FCC commissioners. Democrats, some of whom strongly support stricter media regulation, control both chambers of Congress. But "if we are able to frame the argument so that the American public can understand," he contended, "we can stop this from happening."

Advocates for the federal overhaul aren't promising imminent victory amid the disjointed business and conservative opposition. This "is not going to be easy," the FCC official said, "and we've never talked about it being so."

What's Your Opinion?

Do you think the federal government should have a hand in assuring the media represents a diversity of viewpoints and opinions? If so, how? If not, why not?

Is the argument for media diversity irrelevant for new media, like Internet news, where everyone is free to speak out as they like? Why or why not?

CHAPTER 11

Congress: Balancing National Goals and Local Interests

> "There are two Congresses. . . . The tight-knit complex world of Capitol Hill is a long way from [the member's district], in perspective and outlook as well as in miles."
>
> ROGER DAVIDSON AND WALTER OLESZEK[1]

In September 2005, Congress faced the question of how to come up with the billions of dollars that would be required to rebuild New Orleans and the other Gulf Coast communities devastated by hurricane Katrina.

One option was to trim the $286-billion transportation bill that Congress had enacted a little more than a month earlier. In it were hundreds of pork-barrel projects that members of Congress had secured for their home states and districts. One such project was a bridge that came to be known as "the bridge to nowhere." Nearly the length of the Golden Gate Bridge, it would link the town of Ketchikan, Alaska (population 9,000) to Gravina Island (population 50). Its inclusion in the transportation bill was due to the power of its sponsor, Representative Don Young (R-Alaska), who chaired the House Transportation and Infrastructure Committee that oversaw the legislation. Congressman Young's project was only the most salient example. Virtually every member of Congress, House and Senate alike, had put something into the transportation bill that served constituent interests.

When commentators proposed that the projects be canceled and the money spent instead on Katrina relief, the response from many members of Congress was a deafening no. Some members stepped forward to say that the transportation bill should be trimmed. A much larger number said nothing at all, or rejected the idea outright. When a reporter asked Representative Young whether he was willing to cancel the Ketchikan-Gravina bridge, he replied, "They can kiss my ear! That's the dumbest thing I've ever heard." Young later relented, but the money for the bridge, rather than being spent in the Gulf Coast area, was given to Alaska transportation officials to use on other projects in their state.

The story of Katrina and the 2005 transportation bill illustrates the dual nature of Congress. It is both a lawmaking institution for the country and a representative assembly for states and districts.[2] Members of Congress have a duty to serve both the interests of their constituencies and the interests of the nation as a whole. The nation's needs sometimes come first, but not always, because the support of the voters back home is necessary to members' reelection.[3]

The framers of the Constitution regarded Congress as the preeminent branch of the federal government and granted it the most important of all the powers of government: the power to make the laws: "All legislative powers herein granted shall be invested in a Congress, which shall consist of a Senate and House of Representatives." Congress is granted the authority even to decide the form and function of the executive departments and the lower courts. No executive agency or lower court can exist unless authorized by Congress.

The positioning of Congress as the first among equals in a system of divided powers reflected the framers' trust in representative institutions. Congress was to be the branch where the interests of the people, through the House of Representatives, and the interests of the states, through the Senate, would find their fullest expression. Of course, the framers had an innate mistrust of political power and were not about to give Congress free rein. The Congress was to be subject to checks by the president and the courts (see Chapter 2). Yet the government's most important functions—lawmaking and representation—were granted largely to Congress. The framers' vision of a preeminent Congress has not fully met the test of time, however. Developments in the twentieth century served to shift power from Congress to the presidency and, today, both institutions have a central role in lawmaking. The points emphasized in the chapter are these:

- *Congressional elections have a local orientation and usually result in the reelection of the incumbent.* Congressional office provides incumbents with substantial resources (free publicity, staff, and legislative influence) that give them (particularly House members) a major advantage in election campaigns.
- *Leadership in Congress is provided by party leaders, including the Speaker of the House and the Senate majority leader.* Party leaders are in a more powerful position today than a few decades ago because the party caucuses in Congress are more cohesive than in the past.
- *The work of Congress is done mainly through its committees and subcommittees, each of which has its own leadership and its designated policy jurisdiction.*
- *Congress lacks the central direction and hierarchical organization required to provide consistent leadership on major national policies, which has allowed the president to assume this role. On the other hand, Congress is well organized to handle policies of narrower scope.*
- *Congress's policymaking role is based on three major functions: lawmaking, representation, and oversight.*

Congress as a Career: Election to Congress

In the nation's first century, service in Congress was not a career for most of its members. Before 1900, at least a third of the seats in Congress changed hands at each election. Most members left voluntarily. Because travel was slow and arduous, serving in the nation's capital meant spending months away from one's family. Moreover, the national government was not the center of power that it is today; many politicians preferred to serve in state capitals.

The modern Congress is a different kind of institution. Most of its members are professional politicians, and a seat in the U.S. Senate or House is as high as most of them can expect to rise in politics. The pay (about $170,000 a year) is reasonably good, and the prestige of their office is substantial, particularly if they serve in the Senate. A lengthy career in Congress is what most of its members seek, and they stand a good chance of achieving it. Getting elected to Congress in the first place is much harder than staying there (see Figure 11-1). **Incumbents** (as officeholders are called) have a roughly 90 percent probability of winning reelection.

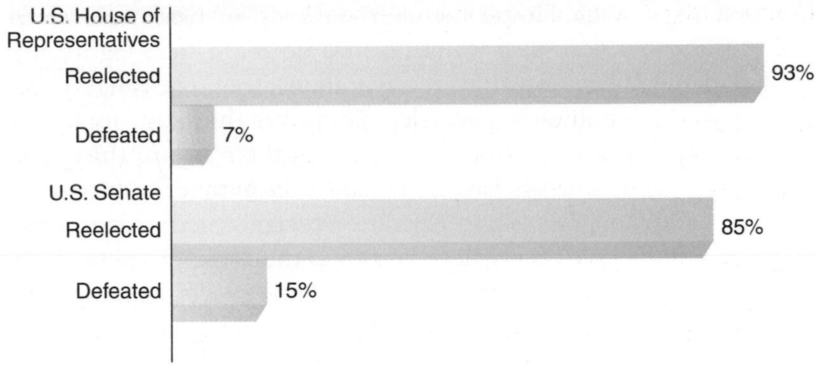

figure 11-1 RECENT REELECTION RATES OF HOUSE AND SENATE INCUMBENTS

Congressional incumbents have a very good chance of winning another term, as indicated by the reelection rates of U.S. representatives and senators who sought reelection during the past five congressional elections.

Most of them win easily—in 2010, for example, roughly three-fourths of House incumbents seeking reelection won by a margin of 20 percentage points or higher.

Using Incumbency to Stay in Congress

The main reason incumbents run so strongly is that many congressional districts and some states are so lopsidedly Democratic or Republican that candidates of the stronger party seldom lose. However, whether their constituency is lopsided or competitive, incumbents have several built-in advantages over their challengers.

The Service Strategy: Taking Care of Constituents An incumbent promotes his or her reelection prospects by catering to the **constituency**: the people residing in the incumbent's state or district. Members of Congress pay attention to constituency opinions when choosing positions on legislation, and they work hard to get their share of federal spending projects. Such projects are often derided as **pork** (or **pork-barrel spending**) by outsiders but are embraced by those who live in the state or district that gets a federally funded project, such as a new hospital, research center, or highway. Incumbents also respond to their constituents' individual requests, a practice known as the **service strategy**. Whether a constituent is seeking information about a government program or looking for help in obtaining a federal benefit, the representative's staff is ready to assist.

Congressional staffers spend most of their time not on legislative matters but on constituency service and public relations—efforts that pay off on election day.[4] Each House member receives an office allowance of roughly $800,000 a year with which to hire no more than eighteen permanent staff members.[5] Senators receive allowances that range between $2 million and $4 million a year, depending on the population size of their state. Smaller-state senators have staffs in the range of thirty people whereas larger-state senators have staffs closer in number to fifty people.[6] Each member of Congress is also permitted several free mailings annually to constituent households, a privilege known as the "frank." These mailings, along with press releases and other public relations efforts, help incumbents build name recognition and constituent support—major advantages in their reelection campaigns.

Campaign Fundraising: Raking in the Money Incumbents also have a decided advantage when it comes to raising campaign funds. Congressional elections are expensive because of the high cost of TV advertising, polling, and other modern campaign techniques (see Figure 11-2). Today a successful House campaign in a competitive district costs more than a million dollars. The price of victory in competitive Senate races is much higher, ranging from several million dollars in small states to $20 million or more in larger states. Rarely do incumbents say they had trouble raising

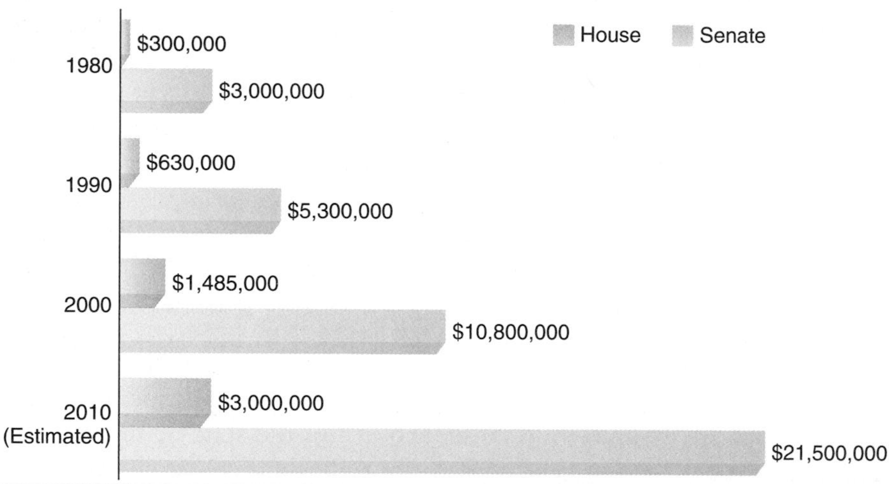

figure 11-2 CONGRESSIONAL CAMPAIGN EXPENDITURES, BY DECADE

Each decade, the cost of running for congressional office has risen sharply as campaign techniques—TV advertising, opinion polling, and so on—have become more elaborate and sophisticated. The increase in spending can be seen from a comparison of the approximate average spending by both candidates per House or Senate seat at ten-year intervals, beginning in 1980. Roughly speaking, the cost has doubled each decade, which is the basis for the 2010 estimate. *Source:* Federal Election Commission.

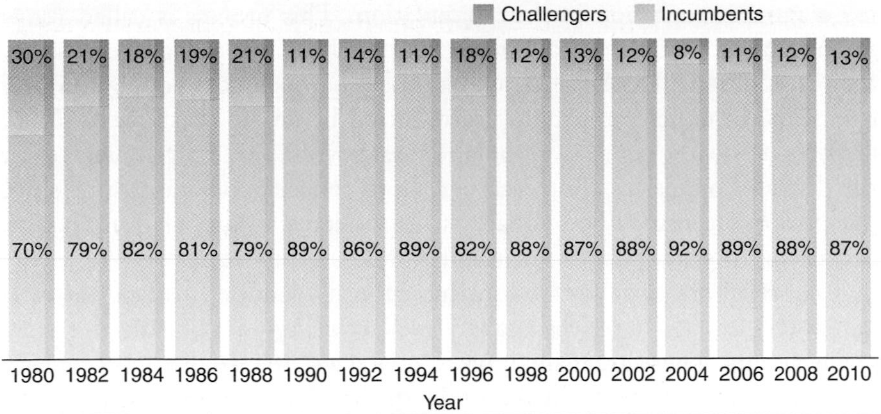

figure 11-3 ALLOCATION OF PAC CONTRIBUTIONS BETWEEN INCUMBENTS AND CHALLENGERS IN CONGRESSIONAL RACES THAT INCLUDED AN INCUMBENT, 1980–2010.

In allocating campaign contributions, PACs favor incumbent members of Congress over their challengers by a wide margin. *Source:* Federal Elections Commission. Figures for 2010 based on preliminary data.

enough money to conduct an effective campaign, whereas challengers usually complain that their fundraising fell far short of their needs.[7]

Incumbents' past campaigns and constituent service enable them to develop mailing lists of potential contributors. Individual contributions, most of which are $100 or less, account for about 60 percent of all funds raised by congressional candidates and are obtained mainly through fundraising events, websites, and direct-mail solicitation. Incumbents also have an edge with political action committees (PACs), which are the fundraising arm of interest groups (see Chapter 9). Most PACs are reluctant to oppose an incumbent unless the candidate appears beatable. Nearly 90 percent of PAC contributions in recent elections have gone to incumbents (see Figure 11-3). "Anytime you go against an incumbent, you take a minute and think long and hard about what your rationale is," said Desiree Anderson, director of the Realtors PAC.[8] (A race without an incumbent—called an **open-seat election**—often brings out a strong candidate from each party and involves heavy spending, especially when the parties are rather evenly matched in the state or district.)

Redistricting: Favorable Boundaries for House Incumbents House members, but not senators, have a final electoral advantage. Because incumbents are hard to unseat, they are always a force to be reckoned with, a fact that is apparent during redistricting. Every ten years, after each population census, the 435 seats in the House of Representatives are reallocated among the states in proportion to their population. This process is called **reapportionment.** States that have gained population since the last census may acquire additional House seats, while those that have lost population may lose seats. In either case, states are required by law to make their House districts as nearly equal in population as possible, so they must redraw the district boundaries after each census to reflect population shifts since the previous census. (The Senate is not affected by population change, because each state has two senators regardless of its size.)

The responsibility for redrawing House election districts after a reapportionment—a process called **redistricting**—rests with the state governments. There are many ways to divide a state into districts of nearly equal size, and the party in power in the state legislature will draw the boundaries in a way that favors candidates of its party—a process called **gerrymandering**. One of the few exceptions to this practice is Iowa, which entrusts redistricting to a nonpartisan commission.

Incumbents are the chief beneficiaries of gerrymandering. When redistricting, the majority party in the state legislature places enough of its party's voters in its incumbents' districts to ensure their reelection. Most of the minority party's incumbents are also given a safe district. Because they have a solid base of support, and are difficult to defeat, the optimal strategy is to pack their districts with as many voters of their party as possible, so that in effect the party "wastes" votes, reducing its competitiveness elsewhere in the state.

For a few House incumbents, redistricting is a threat to reelection. When a state loses a congressional seat or seats, there may be fewer seats than there are incumbents, who end up running against each other. Moreover, the party in control of the state legislature might conclude that a particular incumbent of the opposite party is vulnerable and will redraw the boundaries of the incumbent's district to the incumbent's disadvantage. By and large, however, incumbents do not suffer greatly from redistricting, and the large majority of them wind up in districts that nearly assure their reelection. After the 2000 census, no more than 75 of the 435 House districts were competitive in the sense that they had a reasonably close balance of Republican and Democratic voters. The rest were heavily Republican or heavily Democratic.

Pitfalls of Incumbency

Incumbency is not without its risks. Potential pitfalls for Senate and House incumbents alike include disruptive issues, personal misconduct, and variation in turnout, as well as strong challengers.

When Massachusetts was redistricted in 1812, Governor Elbridge Gerry had the lines of one district redrawn in order to ensure that a candidate of his party would be elected. Cartoonist Elkanah Tinsdale, noting that the strangely shaped district resembled a salamander, called it a "Gerry-mander."

Disruptive Issues Most elections are not waged in the context of disruptive issues, but when they are, incumbents are at greater risk. When voters are angry about existing political conditions, they are more likely to believe that those in power should be tossed out of office. The 2006 congressional election, which was waged in the context of Republican president George W. Bush's leadership of an unpopular war in Iraq, saw the defeat of more than twice the usual number of incumbents. Virtually all of them were Republicans, enabling the Democrats to seize control of both chambers. The parties' fortunes swung the other way in the 2010 congressional elections when public anger over economic conditions and the mushrooming federal deficit contributed to the defeat of an unusually high number of incumbents, nearly all of them Democrats.

Personal Misconduct Members of Congress can also fall prey to scandal. Life in Washington can be fast paced, glamorous, and expensive, and some members of Congress get caught up in influence peddling, sex scandals, and other forms of misconduct. Roughly a fourth of House incumbents who lost their bid for reelection in the past two decades were shadowed by ethical questions. In 2005, for example, Representative William Jefferson demanded $100,000 in cash from a firm in return for helping it obtain government contracts. The firm alerted authorities to Jefferson's acceptance of the money, and the FBI raided Jefferson's congressional office, finding $90,000 hidden in a small freezer. In the 2008 election, Jefferson lost to his Republican opponent, even though his Louisiana district was heavily Democratic. "The first thing to being reelected is to stay away from scandal, even minor scandal," says political scientist John Hibbing.[9]

Turnout Variation: The Midterm Election Problem In only four of the last twenty-five **midterm elections** has the president's party gained House seats. The 2010 midterm election, when the Democrats lost House seats, fit the normal pattern.

The tendency is attributable partly to the drop-off in turnout that accompanies a midterm election. The electorate in a presidential election is substantially larger than the midterm electorate. People who vote only in the presidential election tend to have weaker party ties and are more responsive to the issues of the moment. These issues are likely to favor one party, which contributes to the success not only of its presidential candidate but also of its congressional candidates. In the subsequent midterm election, many of these voters stay home while those who do go the polls vote largely along party lines. Accordingly, the congressional candidates of the president's party do not get the boost they enjoyed in the previous election, and House seats are lost as a result.[10] The pattern also can be explained by the tendency of voters to frame their view of national politics in terms of their opinion of the president's performance. Presidents usually lose popularity after taking office as a result of tough policy choices or the emergence of new problems. As the president's support declines, so does voters' inclination to support congressional candidates from the president's party.[11]

Primary Election Challengers The widening ideological gap between the parties (see Chapter 8) has made primary elections a riskier time for incumbents with moderate views. If they break with their party on key congressional votes or otherwise alienate party activists, they may find themselves in a primary election against a strong challenger who represents the party's extreme wing. They stand a chance of losing because intense partisans are more likely than moderate ones to vote in primary elections. Although moderate incumbents prevail, they have fared less well in primary elections than they did a few decades ago.[12] In the 2010 Arizona Republican primary for the U.S. Senate, incumbent John McCain, who had been the GOP presidential nominee two years earlier, faced a tough challenge from J. D. Hayworth, a conservative talk show host and former congressman. McCain had angered many of the state's conservatives with his moderate positions on key policies. To counter Hayworth's challenge,

McCain moved to the right on several issues, including immigration. Although McCain won the Republican primary, there was a point in the race at which Hayworth drew almost even with him in the polls.

General Election Challengers: A Problem for Senators Incumbents, particularly those in the Senate, are also vulnerable to strong challengers. Behind the presidency, the Senate is the highest rung of the political ladder. Governors and House members are frequent challengers for Senate seats, and they have the voter base, campaign organization, fundraising ability, public recognition, and credentials. The U.S. Senate lures wealthy challengers. Maria Cantwell spent $10 million of her own money to defeat Senator Slade Gorton in the state of Washington's Senate race in 2000. Cantwell made her fortune as an executive with RealNetworks, a high-tech company. Running again in 2006, Cantwell found herself in a tighter-than-expected race, partly because her opponent, Mike McGavick, was himself a millionaire executive.

House incumbents have less reason to fear strong challengers. A House seat often is not attractive enough to induce prominent local politicians, such as mayors or state legislators, to risk their political careers in a challenge to an incumbent.[13] As a result, House incumbents typically face weak opponents with little or no government or political experience. However, the situation changes when the electorate is disgruntled. Then, the party out of power has an easier time convincing potentially strong challengers to run. In 2006, when the political mood favored the Democrats, the Democrats fielded a relatively strong slate of challengers, which contributed to the party's success in unseating Republican incumbents. In 2010, with the parties' roles reversed, the Republican Party fielded an unusually strong group of challengers and picked up House seats.

Safe Incumbency and Representation

Safe incumbency reduces Congress's responsiveness to changes in public opinion. Studies show that incumbents tend to hold relatively stable policy positions during their congressional careers.[14] As a result, Congress does not change its policy direction all that much from one election to the next, unless majority control switches from one party to the other.

In European democracies, incumbents tend to win or lose depending on their political party's popularity, which can change markedly from one election to the next. Such shifts can produce large changes in the number of legislative seats controlled by each party and held by incumbents. In the 2010 British elections, the Labour Party went into the campaign with 356 seats in the House of Commons and emerged with 258 seats. About half of the candidates elected to the House of Commons in 2010 were newcomers. There is no comparable example in the modern history of U.S. elections. Congressional incumbents have built-in advantages that allow the large majority of them to hold on to their seats even when the public is seeking change.

It is worth noting that national legislators in other democracies do not have the large personal staffs or the travel and publicity budgets that members of Congress have. Nor do national legislators elsewhere enjoy anywhere near the inside track to campaign funding that members of Congress enjoy.

Who Are the Winners in Congressional Elections?

The Constitution places a few restrictions on who can be elected to Congress. House members must be at least twenty-five years of age and have been a citizen for at least seven years. For senators, the age and citizenship requirements are thirty years and nine years, respectively. Senators and representatives alike must be residents of the state from which they are elected.

But if the formal restrictions are minimal, the informal limits are substantial. Congress is not a microcosm of the population. Although lawyers constitute less than 1 percent of the population, they make up a third of Congress. Attorneys enter politics in large numbers in part because knowledge of the law is an asset in Congress and also because campaign publicity—even if a candidate loses—is a good way to build up a law practice. Along with lawyers, professionals such as business executives, educators, bankers, and journalists account for roughly 90 percent of congressional membership.[15] Blue-collar workers, clerical employees, and homemakers are seldom elected to Congress. Farmers and ranchers are less rare; a fair number of House members from rural districts have agricultural backgrounds.

Finally, members of Congress are disproportionately white and male. Although the number of women in Congress is twice that of two decades ago, they account for only about 15 percent of the membership (see Chapter 5). The same is true of minorities. Women and minorities occupy fewer seats than white men in part because they are less likely to have the personal wealth that is sometimes required to run a successful congressional campaign. They are also less likely to attempt a run for Congress, even though the winning percentage of those who do is roughly the same as that of nonincumbent white males.[16] In local and state legislative elections, where money is less important and where the holding of office is less likely to be a full-time occupation, women and minority candidates have made greater inroads.[17]

HOW THE 50 STATES DIFFER

POLITICAL THINKING THROUGH COMPARISONS

Women in the State Legislatures

Women have had more success in gaining election to state legislatures than to Congress, partly because there is more turnover and less incumbency advantage at the state level, which creates more opportunities for newcomers to run and to win. More than one in five state legislators are women, a fourfold increase since 1970. The state of Vermont, with 38 percent, has the highest proportion of women legislators. South Carolina, with 10 percent, has the lowest.

Q: *Why do the northeastern and western regions have the most women legislators?*

A: *The northeastern and western regions have a higher proportion of college-educated women in the workforce than do other regions. College-educated women are more likely to run for public office and to actively support those who do run.*

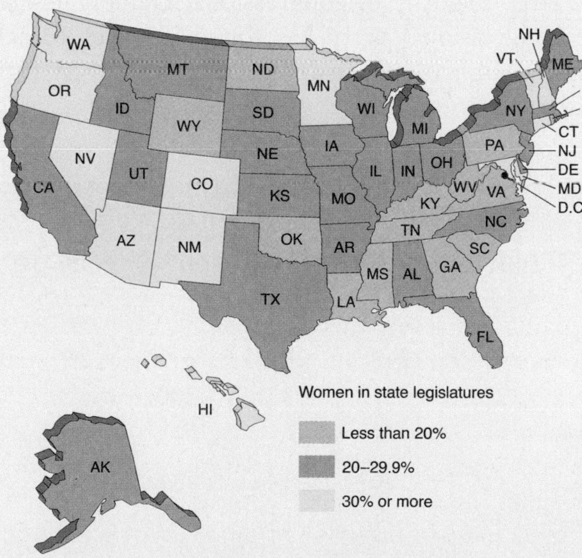

Source: Created from data gathered by the Center for the American Woman and Politics (CAWP); National Information Bank on Women in Public Office; and Eagleton Institute of Politics, Rutgers University, 2010.

Parties and Party Leadership

The House and Senate are organized along party lines. At the start of each two-year congressional term, party members in each chamber meet to elect their **party leaders**—the individuals who will lead their party's efforts in the chamber. Party members also meet periodically in closed session, which is called a **party caucus**, to plan strategy, develop issues, and resolve policy differences. (Table 11-1 shows the party composition in Congress during the past two decades.)

Party Unity in Congress

Political parties are the strongest forces within Congress. The parties are the greatest source of unity among members of Congress, as well as the greatest source of division.

The partisan divide in Congress has intensified since the mid-1980s, partly as a result of changes in the composition of the parties. At an earlier time, congressional Republicans were divided almost evenly between the party's conservative and progressive wings, and congressional Democrats consisted of a liberal northern wing and a conservative southern wing. Today, the large majority of congressional Republicans are conservative and the large majority of congressional Democrats are liberal. As a result, each congressional party has found it easier to achieve **party unity**—in which members of a party band together on legislation and stand against the opposite party.[18]

table 11-1 The Number of Democrats and Republicans in the House of Representatives and the Senate, 2001–2012

	2001–2	2003–4	2005–6	2007–8	2009–10	2011–12
House						
Democrats	213	208	203	235*	257	191
Republicans	222	227	232	200	178	244*
Senate						
Democrats	51*	49	45	51*	60	53
Republicans	49	51	55	49	40	47

*Chamber not controlled by the president's party. Senate and House members who are independents are included in the total for the party with which they caucused. Figures based on party totals that result from the congressional elections as opposed to subsequent totals that result from the death or resignation of seated members.

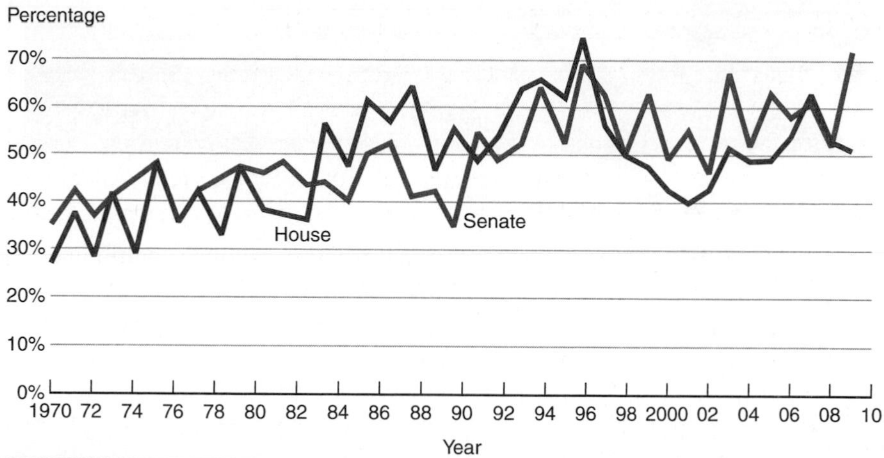

figure 11-4 PERCENTAGE OF ROLL-CALL VOTES IN HOUSE AND SENATE IN WHICH A MAJORITY OF DEMOCRATS VOTED AGAINST A MAJORITY OF REPUBLICANS

Democrats and Republicans in Congress are often on opposite sides of issues; party-line voting has been relatively high since the 1980s. *Source: CQ Weekly*, various dates.

The heightened level of party unity in Congress can be seen from an examination of *roll-call votes* (votes on which each member's vote is officially recorded, as opposed to voice votes, where the members simply say "aye" or "nay" in unison and the presiding officer indicates which side prevails without tallying individual members' positions). Since the mid-1980s, party-line voting on roll calls has increased considerably (see Figure 11-4). In the 1970s, roll-call votes generally did not pit most Republicans against most Democrats. More recently, most roll-call votes have divided along party lines. The ideological split in the congressional parties is most pronounced on major domestic legislation. When the $787 billion economic stimulus bill went through Congress in 2009, it did so almost entirely on Democratic votes. No House Republican and only three Senate Republicans voted for the bill. The health care reform bill enacted in 2010 was passed without a single Republican vote in the House or Senate. (The effect of heightened partisanship on the congressional process is discussed later in the chapter.)

Party Leadership in Congress

Party leaders in Congress are usually chosen for their demonstrated leadership ability, as well as their ability to work effectively with other members. In European parliaments, party leaders can count on the backing of party members (see "How the U.S. Differs"). The members

HOW THE U.S. DIFFERS
POLITICAL THINKING THROUGH COMPARISONS

Legislative Structure

The U.S. House and Senate are separate and coequal chambers, each with its own leadership and rules. This type of legislative structure is not found in most democracies. Many democracies, for example, have a single legislative chamber, which is apportioned by population. If the United States had an equivalent legislature, it would consist only of the House of Representatives.

Even democracies that have bicameral (two-chamber) legislatures tend to structure them differently than the U.S. Congress is structured. The U.S. Senate is apportioned strictly by geography: there are two senators from each state. Germany is among the democracies that have a chamber organized along geographical lines, but Germany's upper house (the Bundesrat) differs from the U.S. Senate. Each of the German states (known as Länder) has at least three representatives in the Bundesrat, but the more populous states have more than three representatives. Moreover, in most bicameral legislatures, one legislative chamber has substantially less power than the other. In the British Parliament, for example, the House of Lords in some instances can slow down legislation that is passed by the House of Commons but cannot stop it from becoming law. In the German Parliament, the Bundesrat has a voice on constitutional policy issues but not on most other issues, and its vote can in some cases be overridden by the population-based chamber (the Bundestag). In the United States, the Senate and House are equal in their legislative powers; without their joint agreement, no law can be enacted.

The U.S. Congress is fragmented in other ways as well: it has elected leaders with limited formal powers, a network of relatively independent and powerful committees, and members who are free to follow or ignore other members of their party. It is not uncommon for a fourth or more of a party's legislators to vote against their party's position on legislative issues. In contrast, European legislatures have a centralized power structure. Top leaders have substantial authority, the committees are weak, and the parties are

Country	*Form of Legislature*
Canada	One house dominant
France	One house dominant
Germany	One house dominant (except on certain issues)
Great Britain	One house dominant
Israel	One house only
Japan	One house dominant
Mexico	Two equal houses
Sweden	One house only
United States	Two equal houses

unified. European legislators are expected to support their party unless granted permission to vote otherwise on a particular bill.

Q: *In terms of the enactment of legislation, what is the relative advantage and disadvantage of the way in which Congress is structured, compared with a national legislature that has a single dominant chamber in which the majority party can count on its members to support its legislative agenda?*

A: *Congress is structured in a way that slows the passage of legislation, which can be a safeguard against hastily prepared, ill-considered, or weakly supported laws. On the other hand, the structure of Congress can permit a determined minority to block legislation that has majority support within and outside Congress.*

depend on the party for nomination to office and can be denied nomination in the next election if they fail to support the party on key legislative votes. In contrast, members of the U.S. Congress depend on themselves for reelection, which gives them the freedom to selectively back or oppose the party's position on key votes. Accordingly, the power of party leaders in Congress depends to a considerable extent on their ability to gain the trust of party members and to forge positions that bridge their policy views.

House Leaders The Constitution specifies that the House of Representatives will be presided over by a Speaker, elected by the vote of its members. Since the majority party has the largest number of members, it also has the most votes, and the Speaker is invariably a member of the majority party. Thus, when the Republicans took control of the House after the 2010 election, John Boehner, the Republicans' leader in the chamber, replaced Democrat Nancy Pelosi as Speaker. Boehner, an Ohio representative, was first elected to the House in 1991.

Next to the president, the Speaker of the House is sometimes said to be the most powerful federal official. The Speaker is active in developing the party's positions on issues and in persuading party members in the House to support them. Although the Speaker cannot require party members to support the party's program, they look to the Speaker for leadership. The Speaker also has certain formal powers, including the right to speak first during House debate on legislation and the power to recognize members—that is, to grant them permission to speak from the floor. Because the House places a time limit on floor debate, not everyone has a chance to speak on a given bill, and the Speaker can sometimes influence legislation simply by exercising the power to decide who will speak and when. The Speaker also chooses the chairperson and the majority-party members of the powerful House Rules Committee, which controls the scheduling of bills. Those that the Speaker wants passed are likely to reach the floor under conditions favorable to their enactment; for example, the Speaker may ask the Rules Committee to delay sending a bill to the floor until there is sufficient support for its passage. The Speaker also has other ways of influencing the work of the House. The Speaker assigns bills to committees, places time limits on the reporting of bills out of committees, and assigns members to conference committees. (The importance of these committee-related powers will become apparent later in this chapter.)

The Speaker is assisted by the House majority leader and the House majority whip, who are also chosen by the majority party's members. The majority leader acts as the party's floor leader, organizing the debate on bills and lining up legislative support. The whip has the job of informing party members when critical votes are scheduled. As voting is getting under way on the House floor, the whip will sometimes stand at a location that is easily seen by party members and let them know where the leadership stands on the bill by giving them a thumbs-up or thumbs-down signal.

The minority party also has its House leaders. The House minority leader heads the party's caucus and its policy committee and plays the leading role in developing the party's legislative positions. The minority leader is assisted by a minority whip.

Nancy Pelosi became the first woman in U.S. history to lead a major party in Congress when she was chosen as Speaker of the House in 2007. First elected to Congress in 1987 from a northern California district, Pelosi quickly made a reputation for herself as a diligent legislator and tenacious bargainer. Her father also served in the House of Representatives and later served five terms as mayor of Baltimore, where she grew up. Pelosi is shown here with other House Democratic leaders to highlight a bill that had just been passed by the House of Representatives.

Senate Leaders In the Senate, the most important party leadership position is that of the majority leader, who heads the majority-party caucus. The majority leader's role resembles that of the Speaker of the House in that the Senate majority leader formulates the majority party's legislative agenda and encourages party members to support it. Like the Speaker, the Senate majority leader chairs the party's policy committee and acts as the party's voice in the chamber. The majority leader is assisted by the majority whip, who sees to it that members know when important votes are scheduled. The minority party in the Senate also has its leaders. The minority leader and minority whip have roles comparable to those of their House counterparts.

For several reasons, the Senate majority leader's position is less powerful than that of the Speaker. Because of the Senate's smaller size, its members tend to view themselves as equals and are less inclined than House members to take direction from their leadership. In addition, the Senate majority leader, unlike the Speaker of the House, is not the chamber's presiding officer. The Constitution assigns this position to the vice president of the United States, who is allowed to vote only in case of a tie. For this reason, the vice president rarely attends Senate sessions except when there is a chance of a tie. In the absence of the vice president, the president pro tempore has the right to preside over the Senate. By tradition, the majority party's most senior member serves as president pro tempore. The position is largely honorary because the Senate's presiding officer has no real power. Unlike the House, where the Speaker has a degree of control over floor debate, the Senate has a tradition of unlimited debate. Ordinarily, any senator who wishes to speak on a bill can do so.

Committees and Committee Leadership

Most of the work in Congress is conducted through **standing committees**, which are permanent committees with responsibility for particular areas of public policy. At present there are twenty standing committees in the House and sixteen in the Senate (see Table 11-2). Each chamber has, for example, a standing committee that handles foreign policy issues. Other important standing committees are those that deal with agriculture, commerce, the interior (natural resources and public lands), defense, government spending, labor, the judiciary, and taxation. House committees, which average about thirty-five to forty members each, are about twice the size of Senate committees. Each standing committee has legislative authority in that it can draft and rewrite proposed legislation and can recommend to the full chamber the passage or defeat of the bills it handles.

Most of the standing committees have subcommittees, each of which has a defined jurisdiction. The House Foreign Affairs Committee, for instance, has seven subcommittees: Africa and Global Health; Asia, the Pacific, and the Global Environment; Europe; International Organizations, Human Rights, and Oversight; Middle East and South Asia; Terrorism, Nonproliferation, and Trade; and Western Hemisphere. Each House and Senate subcommittee has about a dozen members. These few individuals do most of the work and have a leading voice in the disposition of bills in their policy area.

Congress could not manage its workload without the help of its committee system. About ten thousand bills are introduced during each two-year session of Congress. This amount of legislation would overwhelm the institution if it did not divide the work among its standing committees, each of which has its own staff. Unlike the members' personal staffs, which concentrate on constituency relations, the committee staffs perform table 11-2 THE STANDING COMMITTEES OF CONGRESS

House of Representatives	Senate
Agriculture	Agriculture, Nutrition, and Forestry
Appropriations	Appropriations
Armed Services	Armed Services
Budget	Banking, Housing, and Urban Affairs
Education and Labor	Budget
Energy and Commerce	Commerce, Science, and Transportation
Financial Services	Energy and Natural Resources
Foreign Affairs	Environment and Public Works
Homeland Security	Finance
House Administration	Foreign Relations
Judiciary	Health, Education, Labor, and Pensions
Natural Resources	Homeland Security and Governmental Affairs
Oversight and Government Reform	Judiciary
Rules	Rules and Administration
Science and Technology	Small Business and Entrepreneurship
Small Business	Veterans' Affairs
Standards of Official Conduct	
Transportation and Infrastructure	
Veterans' Affairs	
Ways and Means	

an almost entirely legislative function. They help draft legislation, gather information, and organize hearings.

In addition to its permanent standing committees, Congress also has a number of *select committees*, which are created for a specific time period and purpose. An example is the Senate Select Committee on Intelligence, which oversees the work of intelligence agencies, such as the CIA. Congress also has *joint committees*, composed of members of both houses, which perform advisory functions. The Joint Committee on the Library, for example, oversees the Library of Congress, the largest library in the world. Finally, Congress has *conference committees*—joint committees formed temporarily to work out differences in House and Senate versions of a particular bill. The role of conference committees is discussed more fully later in the chapter.

Committee Jurisdiction

The 1946 Legislative Reorganization Act requires that each bill introduced in Congress be referred to the proper committee. An agricultural bill introduced in the Senate must be assigned to the Senate Agriculture Committee, a bill dealing with foreign affairs must be sent to the Senate Foreign Relations Committee, and so on. This requirement is a source of each committee's power. Even if a committee's members are known to oppose certain types of legislation, bills clearly within its **jurisdiction**—the policy area in which it is authorized to act—must be sent to it for deliberation.

Jurisdiction is not always clear cut, however. Which House committee, for example, should handle a major bill addressing the role of financial institutions in global trade? The Financial Services Committee? The Energy and Commerce Committee? The Foreign Affairs Committee? All committees seek legislative influence, and each is jealous of its jurisdiction, so a bill that overlaps committee boundaries can provoke a "turf war" over which committee will handle it.[19] Party leaders can take advantage of these situations by assigning the bill to the committee that is most likely to handle it in the way they would like. But because party leaders depend on the committees for support, they cannot regularly ignore a committee that has a strong claim to a bill. At times, party leaders have responded by dividing up a bill, handing over some of its provisions to one committee and other provisions to a second committee.

Committee Membership

Each committee has a fixed number of seats, with the majority party holding most of them. The ratio of Democrats to Republicans on each committee is approximately the same as the ratio in the full House or Senate, but there is no fixed rule on this matter, and the majority party determines the ratio (mindful that at the next election it could become the chamber's minority party). Members of the House typically serve on only two committees. Senators often serve on four, although they can sit on only two major committees, such as the Finance Committee or the Foreign Relations Committee. Once appointed to a committee, the member can usually choose to stay on it indefinitely.

Each committee has a fixed number of seats, and a committee must have a vacancy before a new member can be appointed. Most vacancies occur after an election as a result of the retirement or defeat of committee members. Each party has a special committee in each chamber that decides who will fill the vacancies. A variety of factors influence these decisions, including members' preferences. Most newly elected members of Congress ask for and receive assignment to a committee on which they can serve their constituents' interests and at the same time enhance their reelection prospects. For example, when Amy Klobuchar was elected to the Senate in 2006 from Minnesota, a state that depends heavily on the farm sector, she asked for and received an appointment to the Senate Agriculture Committee, which oversees this sector.

Some members of Congress prefer a seat on the most prestigious committees, such as the Senate Foreign Relations Committee or the House Ways and Means (taxation) Committee. Although these committees do not align closely with constituency interests, they have responsibility for prominent policy issues. Factors such as party loyalty, level of knowledge, willingness to work hard, and length of congressional service determine whether a member is granted a seat on one of these committees.[20]

Subcommittee assignments are handled differently. The members of each party on a committee decide who among them will serve on each of its subcommittees. The members' preferences and seniority, as well as the interests of their constituencies, are key factors in subcommittee assignments.

Committee Chairs

Each committee (as well as each subcommittee) is headed by a chairperson. The position of committee chair is a powerful one. The chair schedules committee meetings, determines the order in which committee bills are considered, presides over committee discussions, directs the committee's majority staff, and can choose to lead the debate when a committee bill goes to the floor of the chamber for a vote.

Committee chairs are always members of the majority party and usually the party member with the most **seniority** (consecutive years of service) on the committee. Seniority is based strictly on time served on a committee, not on time spent in Congress. Thus, if a member switches committees, the years spent on the first committee do not count toward seniority on the new one. The seniority system has advantages: it reduces the number of power struggles that would occur if the chairs were decided each time by open competition, it places committee leadership in the hands of experienced members, and it enables members to look forward to the reward of a position as chair after years of service on the same committee.

The seniority system is not absolute, however, and is applied less strictly than in the past. There was a period when seniority was a strict rule, which led to abuses. Although most chairs were responsive to the concerns of other members, some were dictatorial. Howard Smith, an arch segregationist, chaired the House Rules Committee from 1955 to 1965 and used his position to keep civil rights legislation from reaching the House floor for a vote. During that era, a committee could not meet unless its chair called it into session, and Smith would leave Washington for his Virginia farm when a civil rights bill came to the Rules Committee, returning only if committee members agreed to withdraw the bill from consideration. Abuses by Smith and other chairs led to reforms in the 1970s that reduced the power of committee chairs. Seniority was no longer an absolute rule, and a committee majority was given the power to call a committee into session if the chair refused to do so.

Committees and Parties: Which Is in Control?

In one sense, committees are an instrument of the majority party, in that it controls most of each committee's seats and appoints its chair. In another sense, each committee is powerful in its own right. Committees have been described as "little legislatures," each secure in its jurisdiction

Republican Olympia Snowe was elected to the U.S. Senate from Maine in 1994. Snowe is among the growing number of women who sit in the U.S. Congress. Snowe easily won her race for a third Senate term in 2006.

and membership, and each wielding considerable control over the legislation it handles.

Committees decentralize power in Congress and serve individual members' power and reelection needs. Less than a dozen members hold a party leadership position, but several hundred serve as committee or subcommittee chairs or are *ranking members*, the term for the minority party's committee and subcommittee leaders. In these positions, they exercise authority, often in ways that serve local constituencies or personal policy agendas—actions that may or may not coincide with the party leadership's goals. The result is an institution very different from European parliaments, where party leaders hold nearly all the power (an arrangement reflected even in the name for rank-and-file members: "backbenchers").

When Republicans took control of Congress in 1995, they sought to reduce the power of committees and their chairs, in an effort to strengthen the party's role. The Republicans passed over some senior party members in selecting the committee chairs and placed term limits on the rest. After six years, a chair or ranking member must relinquish the post. Each chair was to use the position's power to promote the goals of the party as opposed to those of individual committee members. When the Democrats took over Congress in 2007, they left the term limits in place. In fact, during the past dozen or so years, as is discussed later in the chapter, the political parties have had unusually strong control over the legislative agenda, though less than that of the parties in European legislatures.

Although the party is ascendant currently, the balance between party power and committee power is an ongoing issue. The institution is at once a place for conducting the nation's business and a venue for promoting constituency interests. At times, the balance has tipped toward the committees and their leadership. At other times, it has tipped toward the parties and their leadership. At all times, there has been an attempt to achieve a workable balance of the two. The distinguishing feature of congressional power is its division among the membership, with provision for added power—sometimes more and sometimes less—in the hands of the top party leaders.

How a Bill Becomes Law

Parties, party leaders, and committees are critical actors in the legislative process. Their roles and influence, however, vary with the nature of the legislation under consideration. The formal process by which bills become law is shown in Figure 11-5. A **bill** is a proposed legislative act. Many bills are prepared by executive agencies, interest groups, or other

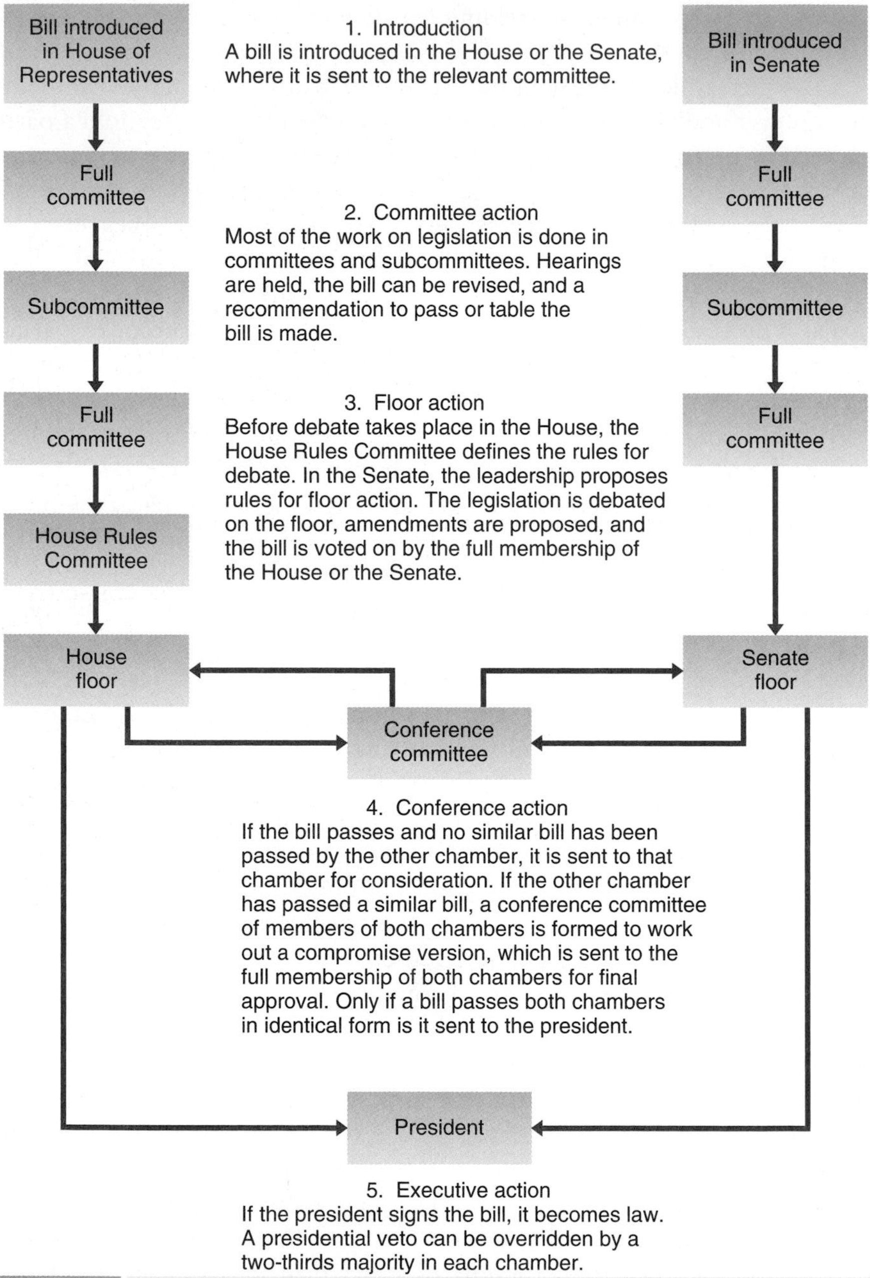

figure 11-5 HOW A BILL BECOMES LAW

Although the legislative process can be short-circuited in many ways, this diagram describes a normal way a bill becomes law.

outside parties, but members of Congress also draft bills, and they alone can formally submit a bill for consideration by their chamber.

Committee Hearings and Decisions

When a bill is introduced in the House or Senate, it receives a bill number and is sent to the relevant committee, which assigns it to one of its subcommittees. Less than 10 percent of the bills referred to committee will get to the floor for a vote; the others are "killed" when committees decide they lack merit. The full House or Senate can overrule such decisions, but this rarely occurs. Most bills die in committee because they are poorly conceived or of little interest to anyone other than a few members of Congress. Some bills are not even supported by the members who introduce them. A member may submit a bill to appease a powerful constituent group and then quietly inform the committee to ignore it.

The fact that committees kill more than 90 percent of the bills submitted in Congress does not mean that they exercise 90 percent of the power in Congress. Committees do not operate in a vacuum. They rarely decide the fate of major bills that are of keen interest to other members. They also have to take into account the fact that their decisions can be reversed by the full chamber, just as subcommittees must recognize that the full committee can override their decisions.[21]

If a bill appears to have merit, the subcommittee will schedule hearings on it. After the hearings, if the subcommittee still feels that the legislation is needed, members will recommend the bill to the full committee, which might hold additional hearings. In the House, both the full committee and a subcommittee can "mark up," or revise, a bill. In the Senate, mark up usually is reserved for the full committee.

From Committee to the Floor

If a majority of the committee vote to recommend passage of the bill, it is referred to the full chamber for action. In the House, the Rules Committee has the power to determine when the bill will be voted on, and how long the debate on it will last. On most House bills, only a small number of legislators are granted the opportunity to speak on the floor; in most cases, the bill's chief sponsor and one of the bill's leading opponents will choose speakers. The Rules Committee also decides whether a bill will receive a "closed rule" (no amendments will be permitted), an "open rule" (members can propose amendments relevant to any of the bill's sections), or something in between (for example, only certain sections of the bill will be subject to amendment). The rules are a means by which the majority party controls legislation. When they had a majority in the House in the period before 1995, Democrats employed closed rules to prevent Republicans from proposing amendments to major bills, a tactic House Republicans said they would forgo when they took control in 1995. Once in control, however, the Republicans applied closed rules to a number of major bills. The tactic was too effective to ignore.

The Senate also has a rules committee, but it is less important than its House counterpart. In the Senate, the majority leader, usually in consultation with the minority leader, schedules bills. All Senate bills are subject to unlimited debate unless a three-fifths majority (60 of the 100 senators) vote for **cloture**, which limits debate to thirty hours. Cloture is a way of defeating a Senate **filibuster**, which is a procedural tactic whereby a minority of senators can block a bill by talking until other senators give in and the bill is withdrawn from consideration or altered to fit opponents' demands. In 2010, for example, Senate Republicans twice used the filibuster to block a bill that would tighten the regulations governing financial institutions. The bill passed only after Democrats granted enough concessions to get the Republican votes they needed to break the filibuster.

POLITICAL THINKING

Eliminate the Filibuster?

Of all the impediments to congressional action, perhaps none is more imposing than a Senate filibuster, which can be ended only if three-fifths of the senators agree to end it. In effect, a minority of Senators has the power to kill legislation, even if it is backed by the president and the House of Representatives. No other democratic legislature has a rule that allows the minority so much power. Should the filibuster be eliminated? Why or why not?

In the House, proposed amendments must directly relate to the bill's contents. In the Senate, however, members can propose any amendment to any bill. For example, a senator may propose an antiabortion amendment to a bill dealing with defense expenditures. Such amendments are called **riders**.

Leadership and Floor Action

A bill that emerges from committee with the support of all or nearly all of its members is usually passed by an overwhelming majority of the full chamber. On the other hand, when the committee vote is closely divided, other members may conclude that they need to give the bill a close look before deciding whether to support it. Other members are also less deferential to committee action on major bills and on those that affect their constituents.

On major bills, the majority party's leaders (particularly in the House) have increasingly assumed the lead.[22] They shape the bill's broad content and work closely with the relevant committee during the committee phase. Once the bill clears the committee, they often direct the floor debate. In these efforts, they depend on the ongoing support of their party's members. To obtain it, they consult their members informally and through the party caucus. (The role of parties in Congress is discussed further in the section on Congress's representation function.)

Conference Committees and the President

For a bill to pass, it must have the support of a simple majority (50 percent plus one) of the House or Senate members voting on it. To become law, however, a bill must be passed in identical form by both the House and the Senate. About 10 percent of the bills that pass both chambers differ in important respects in their House and Senate versions. These bills are referred to conference committees to resolve the differences. Each **conference committee** is formed temporarily for the sole purpose of handling a particular bill; its members are usually appointed from the House and Senate standing committees that drafted the bill. The conference committee's job is to develop a compromise version, which then goes back to the House and Senate floors for a vote. There it can be passed, defeated, or returned to conference, but not amended.

A bill that is passed in identical form by the House and the Senate is not yet a law. The president also has a say. If the president signs the bill, it becomes a **law**. If the president rejects the bill through use of the **veto**, the bill is sent back to Congress with the president's reasons for not signing it. Congress can override a veto by a two-thirds vote of each chamber; the bill then becomes law without the president's signature. A bill also becomes law if Congress is in session and the president fails to sign or veto the bill within ten days (Sundays excepted). However, if Congress has concluded its term and the president fails to sign a bill within ten days, the bill does not become law. This last situation, called a *pocket veto*, forces Congress in its next term to start over from the beginning: the bill again must pass both chambers and again is subject to presidential veto.

Congress's Policymaking Role

The framers of the Constitution expected that Congress, as the embodiment of representative government, would be the institution to which the people looked for policy leadership. During most of the nineteenth century, Congress had that stature. Aside from a few strong leaders such as Andrew Jackson and Abraham Lincoln, presidents did not play a major legislative role (see Chapter 12). However, as national and international forces combined to place greater policy demands on the federal government, the president assumed a central role in the legislative process. Today Congress and the president share the legislative effort, although their roles differ.[23]

Congress's policymaking role revolves around its three major functions: lawmaking, representation, and oversight (see Table 11-3). In practice, the three functions overlap, but they are conceptually distinct.

The Lawmaking Function of Congress

Under the Constitution, Congress is granted the **lawmaking function:** the authority to make the laws necessary to carry out the powers granted to the national government. The constitutional powers of Congress are substantial; they include the power to tax, to spend, to regulate commerce, and to declare war. However, whether Congress takes the lead in the making of laws usually depends on the type of policy at issue.

table 11-3 The Major Functions of Congress

Function	Basis and Activity
Lawmaking	Through its constitutional grant to enact law, Congress makes the laws authorizing federal programs and appropriating the funds necessary to carry them out.
Representation	Through its elected constitutional officers—U.S. senators and representatives—Congress represents the interests of constituents and the nation in its deliberations and its lawmaking.
Oversight	Through its constitutional responsibility to see that the executive branch carries out the laws faithfully and spends appropriations properly, Congress oversees and sometimes investigates executive action.

Broad Issues: Fragmentation as a Limit on Congress's Role Congress is structured in a way that can make agreement on large issues difficult to obtain. Congress is not one house but two, each with its own authority and constituency base. Neither the House nor the Senate can enact legislation without the other's approval, and the two chambers are hardly identical. California and North Dakota have exactly the same representation in the Senate, but in the House, which is apportioned by population, California has fifty-three seats compared to North Dakota's one.

Congress also includes a lot of lawmakers: 100 members of the Senate and 435 members of the House. They come from different constituencies and represent different and sometimes opposing interests, which leads to disagreements. Nearly every member of Congress, for example, supports the principle of global free trade. Yet when it comes to specific trade provisions, members often disagree. Foreign competition means different things to manufacturers who produce automobiles, computer chips, or underwear; it means different things to farmers who produce corn, sugar, or grapes; and it means different things to firms that deal in international finance, home insurance, or student loans. And because it means different things to different people in different areas of the country, members of Congress who represent these various areas have conflicting views on when free trade makes sense.

For such reasons, Congress often has difficulty taking the lead on broad issues of national policy. Although an increase in party unity in Congress has strengthened the role of the chamber's majority party and its leaders, the fact remains that House and Senate members are largely free to vote as they please. As a result, Congress sometimes struggles when faced with the task of crafting major legislation. In 2009, for example, Congress thrashed about for months in the process of trying to draft a comprehensive health care reform bill. Even though the Democrats had substantial majorities in both chambers, the Senate's filibuster rule and a set of divisive issues, including whether federal health care funds could be used for abortions, kept the Democrats from mustering the necessary votes. Both the House and the Senate eventually passed a health care bill, although the House and Senate versions differed substantially on key provisions. At that point, because Senate Democrats could not garner the three-fifths majority necessary to hold a vote on a compromise version of the legislation, the House passed the Senate version, even though it was widely acknowledged to have significant flaws.

As an institution, the presidency is better suited to the task of providing leadership on major national issues. First, whereas Congress's authority is divided, executive power is vested constitutionally in the hands of a single individual—the president. Unlike congressional leaders, who must bargain with their party's members when taking a stand on legislation, the president has less need to negotiate with other executive officials in taking a position. Second, whereas members of Congress often see issues from the perspective of their state or constituency, presidents have a national constituency and tend to look at policy from that perspective. Third, news coverage tilts national policy leadership toward the presidency and away from Congress. In the national press, the presidency gets roughly twice as much news coverage as does the Congress.

Presidential leadership means that Congress will pay attention to White House proposals, not that it will adopt them. It may reject a proposal outright—particularly when the president is from the opposing party. However, if a proposal is at all close to what a congressional majority would regard as acceptable, Congress will normally use it as a starting point for negotiations. (The legislative roles of Congress and the president are discussed further in Chapter 12.)

In its lawmaking activities, Congress has the support of three congressional agencies. One is the Congressional Budget Office, which was created as part of the Budget Impoundment and Control Act of 1974. Its 250 employees provide Congress with general economic projections, overall estimates of government expenditures and revenues, and specific estimates of the costs of proposed programs. A second congressional agency is the Government Accountability Office (GAO). With three thousand

Surrounded by Democratic lawmakers, President Obama signs into law the 2010 health care reform bill. The legislation provoked an intensely partisan fight in Congress. In the end, the bill was enacted without the support of a single Republican senator or representative.

employees, the GAO is the largest congressional agency. Formed in 1921, it has primary responsibility for overseeing executive agencies' spending of money that has been appropriated by Congress. The programs that the executive agencies administer are authorized and funded by Congress. The GAO's responsibility is to ensure that executive agencies operate in the manner prescribed by Congress. The third and oldest congressional agency is the Congressional Research Service, which has a staff of one thousand employees and operates as a nonpartisan reference agency. It conducts research and responds to information requests from congressional committees and members.

Congress in the Lead: Fragmentation as a Policymaking Strength Congress occasionally takes the lead on major issues. Labor legislation, environmental law, federal aid to education, and urban development are policy areas in which Congress has taken an initiating role.[24] Nevertheless, Congress does not routinely develop broad policy programs and carry them through to passage. "Congress remains organized," James Sundquist notes, "to deal with narrow problems but not with broad ones."[25]

Not surprisingly, then, the great majority of the hundreds of bills that Congress considers each session deal with narrow issues. Congress takes the lead on these bills, which are handled largely through the standing committees. The same fragmentation that makes it difficult for Congress to lead on broad issues enables Congress to tackle scores of smaller issues simultaneously. Most of the legislation passed by Congress is "distributive"—that is, it confers a benefit on a particular group while spreading the cost across the taxpaying public, as in the case of veterans' benefits. Distributive policies have a clear political advantage. The benefit is large enough that members of the recipient group will recognize and appreciate it, while the cost to each taxpayer is barely noticeable. Such policies are also the type that Congress, through its committee system, is organizationally best suited to handle. Most committees parallel a major constituent interest, such as agriculture, commerce, labor, or veterans.

The Representation Function of Congress

In the process of making laws, the members of Congress represent various interests within American society, giving them a voice in the national legislature. The proper approach to the **representation function** has been debated since the nation's founding. A recurrent issue is whether the representative should respond to the interests of the nation as a whole or those of the constituency. These interests overlap to some degree but do not coincide exactly. Policies that have broad benefits are not necessarily advantageous to particular localities. Free trade in steel is an example. Although U.S. manufacturers as a whole benefit from access to low-priced steel from abroad, domestic steel producers and the communities where they are located are hurt by it.

Representation of States and Districts The choice between national and local interests is not a simple one, even for a legislator who is inclined toward one or the other orientation. To be fully effective, members of Congress must be reelected time and again, a necessity that compels them to pay attention to local demands. Yet, they serve in the nation's legislative body and cannot ignore national needs. In making the choice, most members of Congress, on narrow issues at least, vote in a way that will not antagonize local interests.[26] Opposition to gun control legislation, for example, is stronger among members of Congress representing rural areas where hunting is prevalent than it is among those from urban areas where guns are more likely to be perceived as a threat to public safety.

Local representation occurs in part through the committee system. Although studies indicate that the preferences of most committees are not radically different from those of the full House or Senate,[27] committee memberships roughly coincide with constituency interests. For example, farm-state legislators dominate the membership of the House and Senate Agriculture Committees, and westerners dominate the Interior Committees (which deal with federal lands and natural resources, most of which are concentrated in the West). Committees are also the site of most **logrolling**—the practice of trading one's vote with another member's so that both get what they want. For example, it is not uncommon in the agricultural committees for members from livestock-producing states of the North to trade votes with members from the cotton- and peanut-producing states of the South.

Nevertheless, representation of constituency interests has its limits. Constituents have little awareness of most issues that come before Congress. Whether Congress appropriates a few million dollars in foreign aid to Chad or Bolivia is not the sort of issue that local residents will hear about. Moreover, members of Congress often have no choice but to go against the wishes of a significant portion of their constituency. The interests of workers and employers in a district or state, for example, can differ considerably. In the case of conflicting interests within their constituencies, members of Congress typically side with those that align with their party. When local business and labor groups take opposing sides on issues before Congress, for example, Republican members tend to back business's position, whereas Democratic members tend to line up with labor.

Moreover, constituent groups are not the only groups that get legislators' support. The nation's capital is filled with powerful lobbies that contribute funds to congressional campaigns. Some of these lobbies represent interests that coincide with those of the legislator's state or district but many of them do not—for example, American Crystal Sugar, a firm that produces sugar from sugar beets grown in the Red River Valley between Minnesota and the Dakotas, contributed money during 2009–2010 to dozens of congressional candidates, most of whom were from states and districts outside American Crystal Sugar's home area.

POLITICAL THINKING

Local, or National?

Members of Congress represent both the nation and *a particular state or district. These representational roles often complement each other but sometimes conflict. When should a representative place the interest of the nation ahead of that of the particular state or district? When should the local interest dominate? Try to place your answer in the context of specific policy issues, such as energy, trade, immigration, or defense spending?*

Representation of the Nation through Parties When a clear-cut and vital national interest is at stake, members of Congress can be expected to respond to that interest. With the economy showing signs of a recession in early 2008, Congress enacted legislation that provided most taxpayers a rebate of several hundred dollars in the hope that they would spend it, thereby giving the economy a boost. The House voted 380–34 in favor of the tax rebate; the Senate vote was 81–16.

In most cases, however, members of Congress, though agreeing on a need for national action, disagree on the course of action. Most Americans believe, for example, that the nation's education system requires strengthening. The test scores of American schoolchildren on standardized reading, math, and science examinations are substantially below those of children in many other industrial democracies. This situation creates pressure for political action. But what action is necessary and desirable? Does more money have to be funneled into public schools, and if so, which level of government—federal, state, or local—should provide it? Or does the problem rest with teachers? Should they be subject to higher performance standards? Or is the problem a lack of competition for excellence? Should schools be required to compete for students and the tax dollars they represent? Should private schools be part of any such competition, or would their participation wreck the public school system? There is no general agreement on such issues.

In Congress, disagreements over national goals occur primarily along party lines. Republican and Democratic lawmakers have different perspectives on national issues because their parties differ philosophically and politically. Differences in the parties' approach to education policy, for example, played out in the legislative debate on No Child Left Behind (NCLB), which President George W. Bush was pushing. NCLB would tie federal education grants to public schools to their students' performance on standardized national tests. Republicans stressed a need for tough testing standards. Democrats stressed a need to provide schools, particularly those in poorer communities, with the financial support necessary for them to meet NCLB testing requirements.

Partisan divisions have increasingly defined congressional action. In the past, the diversity of the congressional parties—the presence of a large number of conservatives within Democratic ranks and a large number of progressives within Republican ranks—was a barrier to legislation rooted in party ideology. Neither party could muster the support of enough of its members to pursue such legislation on a regular basis. Democratic lawmakers from the South, for example, did not share the liberal outlook of Democratic lawmakers from the North. Today, as was discussed earlier, the large majority of congressional Democrats are liberal and the large majority of congressional Republicans are conservative, which has enabled each group to pursue a legislative agenda rooted in its ideology. Local differences still matter in Congress but less so, as national party ideologies have taken center stage. On small and large issues alike, Republican and Democratic lawmakers have been deeply split.

A positive aspect of this development is that party differences are increasingly apparent to voters. At times in the past, many voters believed that the parties did not offer a clear choice. In the view of some political scientists, this situation was a barrier to accountability. They argued that America's voters deserve to have the choice between "responsible parties"—parties that take clear-cut and opposing policy positions and seek to enact them when in office so that voters can more easily hold them to account for their actions.

The major concern today is a sense that partisanship has gotten out of hand in Congress, contributing to unnecessary legislative deadlock and acrimony. In *Beyond Ideology*, political scientist Frances Lee shows that, even on low-stake issues, lawmakers exploit negotiation and floor debate to attack opponents and promote their party's image. Lee also notes that the congressional agenda is increasingly shaped by partisan considerations rather than policy priorities; the parties elevate issues on the basis of what they think will give them a political edge.[28] In *The Broken Branch*, congressional scholars Thomas Mann and Norman Ornstein argue that the deep partisan division in Congress has kept it from devising thoughtful, workable responses to major problems and has embroiled it in debates over incendiary issues like stem-cell research. Mann and Ornstein blame both parties for the problem—the Democrats for starting it in the 1980s and the Republicans for institutionalizing it during the decade after they took control of Congress in 1994.[29]

As congressional partisanship has intensified, the public's image of Congress has plummeted. In a 2010 Pew Research Center poll, three-fourths of the respondents said that elected officials in Washington care only about reelection and tearing each other down. The same poll revealed that only one in four Americans had confidence in Congress—the lowest level recorded in a quarter century of Pew Research Center surveys (see Figure 11-6).

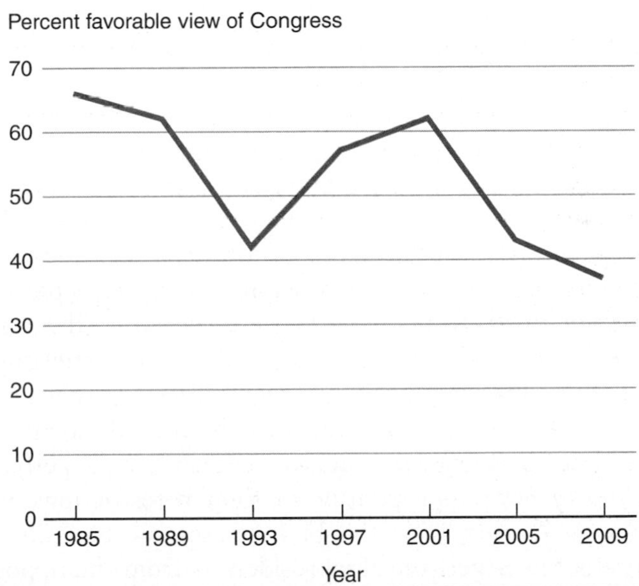

figure 11-6 PUBLIC CONFIDENCE IN CONGRESS

Partisan polarization in Congress has been accompanied by declining public confidence in Congress. *Source:* Pew Research Center for the People and the Press surveys.

The Oversight Function of Congress

Although Congress enacts the nation's laws, their administration is entrusted to the executive branch. Congress has the responsibility to see that the executive branch carries out the laws faithfully, a supervisory activity referred to as the **oversight function** of Congress.[30]

Oversight is carried out largely through the committee system of Congress and is facilitated by the parallel structure of the committees and the executive bureaucracy: the House and Senate judiciary committees oversee the work of the Department of Justice, the House and Senate Agriculture Committees monitor the Department of Agriculture, and so on. The Legislative Reorganization Act of 1970 spells out each committee's responsibility for overseeing its parallel agency:

> Each standing committee shall review and study, on a continuing basis, the application, administration, and execution of those laws, or parts of laws, the subject matter of which is within the jurisdiction of that committee.

Oversight is a demanding task. The bureaucracy has hundreds of agencies and thousands of programs. Congress gets some leverage from the fact that federal agencies have their funding renewed each year, which provides an opportunity for congressional committees to review agency activities. Congress also gets leverage from its committee staffs, which interact regularly with the top bureaucrats in the agencies within their committee's jurisdiction.[31] Nevertheless, because the task is so large, oversight is not pursued vigorously unless members of Congress are annoyed with an agency, have discovered that a legislative authorization is being abused, or are intending to modify an agency program. When an agency is suspected of abuses, a committee is likely to hold hearings. Congress's investigative power is not listed in the Constitution, but the judiciary has upheld this power as a reasonable extension of Congress's power to make the laws. Except in cases involving *executive privilege* (the right of the executive branch to withhold confidential information affecting national security), executive branch officials are required to testify when called to do so. If they refuse, they can be cited for contempt of Congress, a criminal offense. When an agency is found to have acted improperly, Congress can reduce the agency's appropriation or tighten restrictions on its use.

Congressional interest in oversight increases substantially when the White House is the target, and the president is from the opposite party. Until they gained control of the House and Senate in the 2006 congressional elections, Democratic lawmakers were unable to probe deeply into the Bush administration's handling of the Iraq war. After they gained control, they held scores of hearings, examining everything from the administration's justification for the war to its treatment of enemy prisoners. Through their oversight hearings, they exposed activities that were politically damaging to Bush and the Republicans.

Congress: Too Fragmented?

Of all U.S. political institutions, Congress most closely reflects aspects of American culture. The individualism that pervades American society is evident in the independence of members of Congress. They are self-reliant politicians who are both part of and apart from the institution they serve. This characteristic is especially evident when candidates for Congress attack the institution for its failings and then, once in office, use the institution's resources to keep themselves there.

The diversity of American society is also reflected in Congress. This is not to say that the members of Congress are a microcosm of the U.S. population. Far from it. But Congress is diverse in the sense that it is a vast network of power centers. Each committee has its separate leaders and members and has jurisdiction over an area of American life; agriculture, labor, education, commerce, and other economic sectors have their own committees. It is hard to conceive of a national legislature structured to parallel the economic sectors of society more closely than the Congress of the United States. There is also the fact that individual representatives and senators are keenly attuned to the interests of their separate districts and states.

Congress is not an institution where majorities rule easily. Separate majorities in the two chambers, and sometimes within the relevant committees, are required for enactment of significant legislation. For this reason Congress is sometimes portrayed as a weak institution. However, the power to prevent change can be as powerful as the power to accomplish change. This was the intention of the framers of the Constitution. They designed the institution in a way that the majority could rule but only if that majority was exceptionally strong.

What the writers of the Constitution did not clearly anticipate was the degree to which members of Congress, out of self-interest and because of their local base, would cater to the demands of special interests. The framers were intent on designing an institution that would forestall majority tyranny; in doing so, they created an institution that facilitates access and influence by special interests. The writers of the Constitution also did not clearly anticipate how intense partisanship would interact with the structure of Congress. Party unity is the clearest way for the majority to overcome the obstacles to action inherent in Congress's fragmented structure.

At the same time, party unity is the most direct way for the minority to block action. And because Congress's structure makes it easier to block legislation than to enact it, a determined minority party can act in ways that foster deadlock and delay, even in the face of urgent national problems.

Conflicting opinions on Congress are inevitable. The strength of Congress is its representativeness, its attention to local interests, and its function as an arena in which compromise is normally an ingredient of legislative accomplishment. The weakness of Congress lies in the fact that the minority—whether acting on behalf of a special interest or to block the majority from acting—has disproportionate influence. Thus, in a sense, the source of Congress's strength is also the source of its weakness. Congress could not at once be structured as an institution where power is concentrated in the hands of the majority and an institution where power is divided.

SUMMARY Self-Test www.mhhe.com/pattersonwtp9e

Members of Congress, once elected, are likely to be reelected. Members of Congress can use their office to publicize themselves, pursue a service strategy of responding to the needs of individual constituents, and secure pork-barrel projects for their states or districts. House members gain a greater advantage from these activities than do senators, whose larger constituencies make it harder for them to build close personal relations with voters and whose office is more likely to attract strong challengers. Incumbency does have some disadvantages. Members of Congress must take positions on controversial issues, may blunder into political scandal or indiscretion, must deal with changes in the electorate, or may face strong challengers; any of these conditions can reduce members' reelection chances. By and large, however, the advantages of incumbency far outweigh the disadvantages. Incumbents' advantages extend into their reelection campaigns: their influential positions in Congress make it easier for them to raise campaign funds from PACs and individual contributors.

Congress is a fragmented institution. It has no single leader; rather, the House and Senate have separate leaders, neither of whom can presume to speak for the other chamber. The principal party leaders of Congress are the Speaker of the House and the Senate majority leader. They share leadership power with committee and subcommittee chairpersons, who have influence on the policy decisions of their committee or subcommittee.

It is in the committees that most of the day-to-day work of Congress is conducted. Each standing committee of the House or the Senate has jurisdiction over congressional policy in a particular area (such as agriculture or foreign relations), as does each of its subcommittees. In most cases, the full House and Senate accept committee recommendations about the passage of bills, although amendments to bills are quite common and committees are careful to take other members of Congress into account when making legislative decisions. Congress is a legislative system in which influence is widely dispersed, an arrangement that suits the power and reelection needs of its individual members. However, partisanship is a strong and binding force in Congress. It is the basis on which party leaders are able to build support for major legislative initiatives. On this type of legislation, party leaders and caucuses, rather than committees, are the central actors.

The major function of Congress is to enact legislation. Yet the role it plays in developing legislation depends on the type of policy involved. Because of its divided chambers and committee structure, as well as the concern of its members with state and district interests, Congress, through its party leaders and caucuses, only occasionally takes the lead on broad national issues. Congress instead typically looks to the president for this leadership. Nevertheless, presidential initiatives are passed by Congress only if they meet its members' expectations and usually only after a lengthy process of compromise and negotiation. Congress is more adept at handling legislation that deals with problems of narrow interest. Legislation of this sort is decided mainly in congressional committees, where interested legislators, bureaucrats, and groups concentrate their efforts on issues of mutual concern.

A second function of Congress is the representation of various interests. Members of Congress are highly sensitive to the state or district on which they depend for reelection. They do respond to overriding national interests, but for most of them local concerns generally come first. National or local representation often operates through party representation, particularly on issues that divide the Democratic and Republican parties and their constituent groups, which is increasingly the case.

Congress's third function is oversight—the supervision and investigation of the way the bureaucracy is implementing legislatively mandated programs. Although oversight is a difficult process, it is an important means of legislative control over the actions of the executive branch.

Key Terms

bill (*p. 389*)
cloture (*p. 392*)
conference committees (*p. 385*)
constituency (*p. 369*)
filibuster (*p. 392*)
gerrymandering (*p. 372*)
incumbent (*p. 368*)
jurisdiction (of a congressional committee) (*p. 386*)
law (as enacted by Congress) (*p. 393*)
lawmaking function (*p. 394*)
logrolling (*p. 398*)
midterm election (*p. 374*)
open-seat election (*p. 371*)
oversight function (*p. 402*)
party caucus (*p. 378*)
party leaders (*p. 378*)
party unity (*p. 378*)
pork (pork-barrel spending) (*p. 369*)
reapportionment (*p. 372*)
redistricting (*p. 372*)
representation function (*p. 397*)
rider (*p. 392*)
seniority (*p. 387*)
service strategy (*p. 369*)
standing committees (*p. 384*)
veto (*p. 393*)

Suggested Readings

Burden, Barry C. *Personal Roots of Representation.* Princeton, N.J.: Princeton University Press, 2007. An analysis that reveals how representatives' personal preferences affect their legislative votes.

Dwyre, Diana, and Victoria Farrar-Myers. *Legislative Labyrinth: Congress and Campaign Finance Reform.* Washington, D.C.: CQ Press, 2001. An inside look at the mix of Congress and campaign money.

Herrnson, Paul S. *Congressional Elections: Campaigning at Home and in Washington,* 5th ed. Washington, D.C.: CQ Press, 2008. A study arguing that members of Congress run two campaigns, one at home and one in Washington.

Lee, Frances E. *Beyond Ideology: Politics, Principles, and Partisanship in the U.S. Senate.* Chicago: University of Chicago Press, 2009. A careful account of the sources of discord in the U.S. Senate.

Mann, Thomas E., and Norman J. Ornstein. *The Broken Branch: How Congress Is Failing America and How to Get It Back on Track.* New York: Oxford University Press, 2008. An assessment of how excessive partisanship is weakening Congress's lawmaking capacity.

Sidlow, Edward. *Challenging the Incumbent: An Underdog's Undertaking.* Washington, D.C.: CQ Press, 2003. A fascinating case study of the difficulties faced by those who dare to challenge an incumbent.

Sinclair, Barbara. *Unorthodox Lawmaking: New Legislative Processes in the U.S. Congress,* 2d ed. Washington, D.C.: CQ Press, 2000. A detailed analysis of the American legislative process.

Smith, Steven S., Jason M. Roberts, and Ryan J. Vander Wielen. *The American Congress,* 6th ed. New York: Cambridge University Press, 2009. An insightful and comprehensive examination of Congress.

Strahan, Randall. *Leading Representatives: The Agency of Leaders in the Politics of the U.S. House.* Baltimore, MD.: Johns Hopkins University Press, 2007. A study arguing that congressional leaders are powerful in their own right.

Theirault, Sean M. *Party Polarization in Congress.* New York: Cambridge University Press, 2008. A careful accounting of the various sources of the increased level of party polarization in Congress.

List of Websites

www.usafmc.org/default.asp?pagenumber=8 The website of the United States Association of Former Members of Congress, which has a "Congress to Campus" program that upon request brings former congressional members to campuses for talks.

http://thomas.loc.gov/ The Library of Congress site, named after Thomas Jefferson; provides information about the congressional process, including the status of pending legislation.

www.house.gov The U.S. House of Representatives' website; has information on party leaders, pending legislation, and committee hearings, as well as links to each House member's office and website.

www.senate.gov The U.S. Senate's website; similar to that of the House and provides links to each senator's website.

Politics in Theory and Practice

Thinking: How does the structure of Congress (for example, its two chambers and its committee system) affect its policymaking role?

Participating: Each year, thousands of college students serve as interns in Congress or a state legislature. Many internships are unpaid, but students can ordinarily receive college credit for the experience. Internships are not always a great adventure. Many legislative interns envision themselves contributing ideas and research that might influence public policy only to find that they are answering letters, developing mailing lists, or duplicating materials. Nevertheless, few interns conclude that their experience has been a waste of time. Most find it rewarding and, ultimately, memorable. Information about internships can be obtained from the American Political Science Association (www.apsa.org). In addition, there are organizations in Washington that arrange internships in Congress and the executive agencies. These organizations frequently charge a fee for their services, so you might want to contact a legislative office or executive agency directly. It is important to make your request as early as possible in the college year, because some internship programs have deadlines and nearly all offices receive more requests than they can accommodate. You could also check with the student services office at your college or university. Some of these offices have information on internship programs and can be of assistance.

Extra Credit

For up-to-the-minute *New York Times* articles, interactive simulations, graphics, study tools, and more links and quizzes, visit the text's Online Learning Center at **www.mhhe.com/pattersonwtp9e**.

NATIONAL JOURNAL

Blanche Lincoln Faces Double Jeopardy

A stone's throw from the Texas state line, Democratic Sen. Blanche Lincoln spent a warm afternoon early last week practicing the handshake-to-handshake retail politicking her state admires. Before flying back to Washington to rejoin the Senate's efforts to clamp down on big banks, Lincoln visited the paneled boardroom of a small community bank and gingerly tried to elicit support from five influential representatives of the African-American community. She is up against a well-financed challenger, Lt. Gov. Bill Halter, in the May 18 Democratic primary.

Lincoln's Texarkana campaign representatives arranged the meeting here. And the 10 people in the room, including her campaign staff members, were well aware of the senator's re-election problems. Political analysts say that a third Senate term may well elude Lincoln in a conservative state that backed Republican John McCain for president in 2008 and has been unimpressed with the Democrats' expansion of government since Barack Obama won the White House.

Black voters in Arkansas are disenchanted with Lincoln's centrist sensibilities, particularly her reluctant, holdout voting record on the health care reform law that President Obama struggled to enact. But Lincoln needs African-American Democrats to mobilize for her in the primary and, if she gets that far, in November's general election. Organized labor and the liberal group MoveOn.org are spending millions of dollars on advertising and grassroots activities to defeat an incumbent they view as an unreliable Democrat.

"The national unions—there's no doubt there are some awful ads on TV about me right now," Lincoln told the Texarkana group, most of whom listened quietly as the senator recounted her record of support for health care and child nutrition programs, help for Arkansas's aging population and for the state's timber and agriculture interests, and advocacy on behalf of black farmers.

"You should know that those outside groups can come in and they've spent a little over $4 million just in the last four or five weeks, just running negative ads against me," she complained in her Southern Delta twang. "They want to tell us what to do."

In a small, poor, right-to-work state where union influence is weak, Lincoln may be smart to depict herself as defending Arkansas against bullying by Big Labor, and to portray Halter as labor's puppet. In this city, Lincoln insisted that she has "a good voting record with the unions" but added, "I'm not with them 100 percent of the time." Lincoln opposed the Employee Free Choice Act, a key union goal that would make it easier to organize workplaces, after she originally supported it. Her change of heart on the "card-check" bill helped make her a target.

"With the national group, if you're not with them 100 percent of the time, they're going to get angry with you," she said, teeing up a joke that she knew would get laughs from the men gathered in the boardroom. "But you know, I don't even agree with my husband 100 percent of the time, but that doesn't mean he's going to leave me!"

After some bantering about Razorback football, local churches that she had visited, and the well-being of various children of the assembled supporters, Lincoln made a relaxed exit to catch a plane back to the nation's capital.

Watching her leave, Londell Williams, 62, a member of the elected city board of directors, told National Journal that resistance to Lincoln among some African-Americans—about 16 percent of Arkansas's population—stems from "misguided information" that he, among others here, will work hard to refute. Williams said he had distributed 442 Lincoln campaign fliers—ones showcasing a photo of the senator with Obama—at his church the previous morning. All but six of the fliers made their way out of the church, and Williams predicts that his backing for Lincoln will spread "like gangrene" within his community.

Obama and native son Bill Clinton have recorded radio ads for Lincoln. Their support, however, is not an unmixed blessing for her. When she tacks a bit left—for example, by attacking big banks and talking up her A grade from the NAACP—in hopes of winning the Democratic primary, the senator muddies her campaign boast that she votes "with Arkansas," not in lockstep with the national party. Lincoln does, in fact, side with the Senate's conservative Republicans as often as she does with her own party. In a political climate that strongly encourages party discipline, she stands out in the Senate like a party of one. This year, Lincoln is finding little refuge in the middle.

National Journal's analysis of lawmakers' 2009 voting records placed Lincoln smack in the middle of the embattled Senate centrists, elbow-to-elbow with Connecticut's independent Democrat, Joe Lieberman. Anticipating a battle for re-election but apparently not imagining a primary challenge, Lincoln voted quite a bit more conservatively in 2009 than in previous years. Her average composite liberal score in the first four years of her term was 64.8. In 2009, it was 50.3, meaning she had drifted 14.5 points to the right.

Now, Lincoln's touting of Obama's endorsement ties her more closely to the liberal image of the Senate Democratic Conference. She will be battling uphill for re-election and will almost certainly try to distance herself from Obama and her party.

Wherever Lincoln speaks in her home state, she is pressed about her complicated health care reform positions, which angered liberals and conservatives alike, and which suggested to some observers that she may have more spin than spine. Lincoln ended up opposing a public insurance option she initially warmed to, and it was dropped. She maneuvered to gain attention by being among the last senators to line up to give the Democrats the filibuster-proof 60 votes needed to move their bill forward in December. But then in March she was one of only three Democrats to vote with 40 Republicans against the budget reconciliation measure that finally got the health insurance reforms to the president's desk.

Lincoln's campaign team in Little Rock accuses outside groups and opponents who are footing the bill for expensive ads around the state of distorting the senator's record on health care—by, for example, saying she was responsible for the demise of the public option. Asked whether Lincoln should have better anticipated her vulnerabilities when she made herself a holdout vote on health care, her team responded that Republicans were always going to paint her as the key 60th vote for passage and that liberals were just as determined to cast her as the villain who blocked a public option. "In any other environment in any other time, her typical M.O. works out pretty well," campaign manager Steve Patterson told National Journal last week.

"This is the way she rolls, and people can assign various motives to what she was doing, and how it all worked out, and whether she made a mistake. But, look, that's just who she is. She works these issues," he said. "She represents a small, rural state, with four congressional districts, that routinely ranks low among the 50 states in terms of the poverty rate, the teen pregnancy rate, education. And on all these issues she's fighting to increase resources and opportunities in the state."

Lincoln, who was first elected to the Senate in 1998 and re-elected in 2004 with 56 percent of the vote, has been a familiar and popular figure in Arkansas. She talks about herself as the just-folks daughter of an east Arkansas rice farmer who instilled in her the "rock-solid" values of the state.

Lincoln's biggest challenge, Patterson said, is attempting to respond simultaneously to attacks from the Right and Left. "That's been a pretty potent combination. And not very many incumbents can withstand that," he added. "We think it will be a tough, close election, but we still think we're going to win."

In an interview at his campaign headquarters, Halter predicted that he will defeat Lincoln. "People just want change," he said.

A 73-year-old Little Rock retiree named Rosemary said as she exited the courthouse that she had voted for Halter in protest, although she believes that Lincoln can win the primary and perhaps shape up to be a better candidate by November. "Both campaigns have been ghastly, full of things that are untrue and unfair, just throwing mud," she complained. "I'm sending Blanche a message."

Voting began on May 3 at designated polling places. In Texarkana, 125 people of the nearly 24,000 registered to vote in the county cast ballots that day. That number was "about average," according to a deputy clerk. About 1,000 voters showed up in the first two days at nine Little Rock polling places.

Among them were 88-year-old William Nelson, walking carefully with the aid of a crutch, and his smiling wife of eight years, Hazel Nelson, 87. The Nelsons of North Little Rock are African-Americans who proudly voted for Obama for president and decided to cast their ballots for Lincoln. "She's doing what she's supposed to be doing," William Nelson explained. "Everyone makes mistakes," he continued, referring to her handling of health care reform. "She'll do more for Arkansas than anyone else."

What's Your Opinion?

What tensions does Lincoln's reelection campaign reveal that are specific to congressional races? What are the issues a congressional candidate faces in appealing to his or her state or district to which a presidential candidate or local office-seeker is more immune? Do you think it's a plus or a minus to be a centrist in today's electoral climate?

CHAPTER 12

The Presidency: Leading the Nation

"[The president's] is the only voice in national affairs. Let him once win the admiration and confidence of the people, and no other single voice will easily overpower him."

Woodrow Wilson[1]

Barack Obama was sinking in the polls. Unemployment remained high, and the federal deficit was mounting. The mood in the White House was downcast compared with the first months of his presidency when his public approval rating topped 70 percent and pundits were comparing him to Franklin D. Roosevelt. His election as the first African-American president had been historic, and he had campaigned on the promise of change. "We are the ones we've been waiting for," he exclaimed. "We are the change we seek."

He successfully steered his first major presidential initiative, a nearly $800 billion economic stimulus bill, through Congress. It was a legislative triumph, but it came at a price. The stimulus bill had contributed to the ballooning federal deficit, which increased the likelihood of a tax hike. The stimulus bill was followed by knock-down, drag-out partisan battle over health care reform. Although Obama was able in the end to get a health bill through Congress, it, too, came at a price. Many Americans had doubts about the legislation's content and cost, and were confused and angered by the partisan bickering that accompanied its passage. By early 2010, Obama's approval rating had sunk below 50 percent. In a widely cited *New Yorker* article, George Packer wrote about "Obama's Lost Year." His first year in office, Packer said, bore little resemblance to the fabled "One Hundred Days" that had marked the start of Franklin D. Roosevelt's presidency.[2]

The Obama story is but one in the saga of the ups and downs of the modern presidency. Lyndon Johnson's and Richard Nixon's dogged pursuit of the Vietnam War led to talk of "the imperial presidency," an office so powerful that constitutional checks and balances were no longer an effective constraint on it. Within a few years, because of the Watergate scandal and intractable international problems during the Ford and Carter presidencies, the watchword became "the imperiled presidency," an office too weak to meet the nation's need for executive leadership. Ronald Reagan's policy successes prior to 1986 renewed talk heard in the Roosevelt and Kennedy years of "a heroic presidency," an office that is the inspirational center of American politics. After the Iran-Contra scandal in 1986, Reagan was more often called a lame duck. George H. W. Bush's handling of the Gulf crisis—leading the nation in 1991 into a major war and emerging from it with a stratospheric public approval rating—bolstered the heroic conception of the office. A year later, Bush was defeated in his campaign for a second term. Bill Clinton overcame a fitful start to his presidency to become the first Democrat since Franklin D. Roosevelt in the 1930s to win reelection. As Clinton was launching an aggressive second-term policy agenda, however, he got entangled in an affair with a White House intern, Monica Lewinsky, which led to his impeachment by the House of Representatives and weakened his claim to national leadership. After the terrorist attacks of September 11, 2001, George W. Bush's job approval rating soared to a record high. By the time he left office, Americans had turned against his economic and war policies and only a third of the public had a positive view of his leadership.

No other political institution has been subject to such varying characterizations as the modern presidency. One reason is that the formal powers of the office are relatively modest and so presidential power changes with political conditions and the personal capacity of the office's occupant. The American presidency is always a central office in that its occupant is a focus of national attention. Yet the presidency operates in a system of divided powers, which means that presidential power is conditional. It depends on the president's own abilities but even more on circumstances—on whether the situation demands strong leadership and whether there is public and congressional support for that leadership. When circumstances

President Barack Obama speaks at a press conference. Like all recent presidencies, the Obama presidency illustrates the fact that the power of the office can change dramatically when conditions change.

are favorable, the president exercises considerable power. When circumstances are unfavorable, the president struggles to exercise power effectively.

This chapter examines the roots of presidential power, and the factors associated with the success and failure of presidential leadership. The main ideas of this chapter are these:

- *Over time, the presidency has become a powerful office.* This development owes largely to the legacy of strong presidents and to domestic and international developments that have increased the need for executive leadership.
- *The modern presidential campaign is a marathon affair in which self-selected candidates seek a strong start in the nominating contests and a well-run media campaign in the general election.*
- *The president could not control the executive branch without a large number of presidential appointees—advisors, experts, and skilled managers—but the sheer number of these appointees is itself a challenge to presidential control.*

- *The president's election by national vote and position as sole chief executive make the presidency the focal point of national politics.* Nevertheless, whether presidents are able to accomplish their goals depends on their personal capacity for leadership, national and international conditions, the stage of their presidency, the partisan composition of Congress, and whether the issue is foreign or domestic.

FOUNDATIONS OF THE MODERN PRESIDENCY

The framers of the Constitution knew what they wanted from the presidency—national leadership, statesmanship in foreign affairs, command in time of war, enforcement of the laws—but they did not have a precise sense of how the office would work in practice. Accordingly, they chose to describe the powers of the president in general terms. Compared with Article I of the Constitution, which contains a precise listing of Congress's powers, Article II defines the president's powers in general terms (see Table 12-1).[3]

Over the course of American history, each of the president's constitutional powers has been expanded in practice beyond the framers' expectation. For example, the Constitution grants the president command of the nation's military, but only Congress can declare war. In *Federalist* No. 69, Alexander Hamilton wrote that a surprise attack on the United States was the only justification for war by presidential action. Nevertheless, presidents on their own authority have launched military attacks abroad on more than two hundred occasions. Of the roughly fifteen major wars included in that figure, only five were formally declared by Congress.[4] None of America's most recent major conflicts—the Korean, Vietnam, Persian Gulf, Balkans, Afghanistan, and Iraq wars—have been waged on the basis of a congressional declaration of war.

The Constitution also empowers the president to act as diplomatic leader with the authority to appoint ambassadors and to negotiate treaties with other countries, subject to approval by a two-thirds vote of the Senate. The framers anticipated that Congress would define the nation's foreign policy objectives, while the president would oversee their implementation. However, presidents gradually took charge of U.S. foreign policy and have even acquired the power to make treaty-like arrangements with other nations. In 1937, the Supreme Court ruled that *executive agreements*—which are formal agreements that presidents make on their own with foreign nations—are legally binding in the same way that treaties are.[5] Since World War II, presidents have negotiated over 15,000 executive agreements—more than ten times the number of treaties ratified by the Senate during the same period.[6]

table 12-1 The Constitutional Authority for the President's Roles

Unlike Congress's powers, which are specifically enumerated in the Constitution, the president's powers are provided through relatively general clauses. This openness has facilitated an expansion of presidential power over the course of the nation's history.

Commander in chief: Article II, Section 2: "The President shall be commander in chief of the Army and Navy of the United States, and of the militia of the several states."

Chief executive: Article II, Section 2: "He may require the opinion, in writing, of the principal officer in each of the executive departments, upon any subject relating to the duties of their respective offices, and he shall have power to grant reprieves and pardons for offences against the United States, except in cases of impeachment."

Article II, Section 2: "He shall have power, by and with the advice and consent of the Senate, to make treaties, provided two thirds of the senators present concur; and he shall nominate, and by and with the advice and consent of the Senate, shall appoint ambassadors, other public ministers and consuls, judges of the Supreme Court, and all other officers of the United States, whose appointments are not herein otherwise provided for, and which shall be established by law."

Article II, Section 2: "The President shall have power to fill up all vacancies that may happen during the recess of the Senate, by granting commissions which shall expire at the end of their next session."

Article II, Section 3: "He shall take care that the laws be faithfully executed, and shall commission all the officers of the United States."

Chief diplomat: Article II, Section 2: "He shall have power, and with the advice and consent of the Senate, to make treaties, provided two thirds of the senators present concur."

Article II, Section 3: "He shall receive ambassadors and other public ministers."

Legislative leader: Article II, Section 3: "He shall from time to time give to the Congress information of the state of the Union, and recommend to their consideration such measures as he shall judge necessary and expedient; he may, on extraordinary occasions, convene both houses, or either of them, and in case of disagreement between them, with respect to the time of adjournment, he may adjourn them to such time as he shall think proper." (Article I, Section 7, which defines the president's veto power, is also part of his legislative authority.)

Knowing that his presidency would define future ones, George Washington wrote, "It is devoutly wished on my part that these precedents may be fixed on true principles." Washington sought a national government strong enough to keep the nation from disintegrating over sectional rivalries. Washington retired after two terms, saying that the presidency was a citizen's office and not a monarchy. The two-term precedent is now institutionalized through the Constitution's Twenty-second Amendment.

The Constitution also vests "executive power" in the president. This power includes the responsibility to execute the laws faithfully and to appoint major administrators, such as the heads of federal agencies. In *Federalist* No. 76, Hamilton indicated that the president's real authority as chief executive was to be found in this appointive capacity. Presidents have indeed exercised power through their appointments, but they have also found their administrative authority—the power to execute the laws—to be significant, because it enables them to decide how laws will be implemented. President George W. Bush used his executive power to *prohibit* the use of federal funds by family-planning clinics that offered abortion counseling. President Barack Obama exerted the same power to *permit* the use of federal funds for this purpose. The same act of Congress was the basis for each of these decisions. The act authorizes the use of federal funds for family-planning services, but it neither requires nor prohibits their use for abortion counseling, enabling the president to decide the issue.

Finally, the Constitution provides the president with legislative authority, including use of the veto and the ability to propose legislation to Congress. The framers expected this authority to be used in a limited way. George Washington acted as the framers anticipated: he proposed only three legislative measures and vetoed only two acts of Congress. Modern presidents have assumed a more active legislative role. They regularly submit proposals to Congress and do not hesitate to veto legislation they dislike.

The Changing Conception of the Presidency

The presidency, for many reasons, is a more powerful office than the framers envisioned. But two features of the office in particular—*national election* and *singular authority*—have enabled presidents to make use of changing demands on government to claim national policy leadership. It is a claim that no other elected official can routinely make. Unlike the president, who is elected by nationwide vote and is the sole chief executive, members of Congress are elected from separate states or districts and operate in an institution where they share power with the other members. Unlike the president, no member of Congress can fully claim to be the nation's leader.

The first president to forcefully assert a broad claim to national policy leadership was Andrew Jackson, who was elected in 1828 on a tide of popular support that broke the upper class's hold on the presidency (see Chapter 2). Jackson used his popular backing to challenge Congress's claim to national policy leadership, contending that he was "the people's tribune." This view, however, was not shared by his immediate successors. The nation's major issues were of a sectional nature (especially the North-South split over slavery) and were suited to action by Congress, which represented state interests. In fact, throughout most of the nineteenth century (the Civil War presidency of Abraham Lincoln was an exception), Congress jealously guarded its constitutional authority over national policy. James Bryce wrote in the 1880s that Congress paid no more attention to the president's policy pronunciations than it did to the editorial stands of newspaper publishers.[7]

The nineteenth-century conception of the presidency was expressed in the **Whig theory**, which holds that the presidency is a limited or constrained office whose occupant is empowered to act only within the confines of expressly granted constitutional authority. According to this "weak presidency" theory, the president is primarily an administrator, charged with carrying out the will of Congress. "My duty," said President James Buchanan, a Whig adherent, "is to execute the laws . . . and not my individual opinions."[8]

Upon taking office in 1901, Theodore Roosevelt cast aside the Whig tradition.[9] He embraced what he called the **stewardship theory**, which calls for a "strong presidency" that is limited, not by what the Constitution allows, but by what it prohibits. In his autobiography, Roosevelt wrote: "I declined to adopt the view that what was imperatively necessary for the nation could not be done by the President unless he could find some specific authorization for it. My belief was that it was not only his right but his duty to do anything that the needs of the nation demanded unless such action was forbidden by the Constitution or by the laws."[10] Acting on this belief, Roosevelt challenged the power of business monopolies. When coal mine owners refused to bargain with miners, he threatened to seize the mines, forcing owners to improve mine safety and increase miners' wages. He also opened world markets to American goods, using the navy and marines to project U.S. influence southward into the Caribbean and Latin America and westward toward Hawaii, the Philippines, and China (the "Open Door" policy). When congressional leaders objected, he forced a showdown, knowing that the American people would support the troops. Roosevelt said: "I have the money to send [the navy's ships] halfway around the world—let Congress bring them back."

Theodore Roosevelt's conception of a strong presidency was not shared by most of his immediate successors.[11] Herbert Hoover was slow to respond to the human misery caused by the Great Depression, saying that he lacked the constitutional authority to act decisively. However, Hoover's successor, Franklin D. Roosevelt (FDR), shared the stewardship theory of his distant cousin Theodore Roosevelt. FDR's New Deal included unprecedented public works projects, social welfare programs, and economic regulatory actions (see Chapter 3). The New Deal marked the end of the limited presidency. FDR's successor, Harry S. Truman, wrote in his memoirs: "The power of the President should be used in the interest of the people and in order to do that the President must use whatever power the Constitution does not expressly deny him."[12]

The Need for a Strong Presidency

Today the presidency is an inherently strong office, made so by the federal government's increased policy responsibilities. Although individual presidents differ in their capacity for leadership, the office they hold is one that requires active involvement in a broad range of policy areas.

Modern government consists of thousands of programs and hundreds of agencies. Congress is ill suited to directing and coordinating them. Congress is a fragmented institution that acts through negotiation, bargaining, and compromise. It is simply not structured in a way that would enable it to easily and regularly oversee government activity and develop comprehensive approaches to policy. The presidency is structured in a way that enables it to do so. Final authority rests with a single individual, the president, who is thereby able to direct the actions of others and to undertake large-scale planning.[13] As a result, major domestic policy initiatives since the New Deal era have usually come from the White House, as exemplified by Lyndon Johnson's Great Society and Ronald Reagan's New Federalism (see Chapter 3). In fact, as the size of government has increased, all democracies have seen a shift in power from their legislature to their executive. In Britain, for example, the prime minister has taken on policy responsibilities that once belonged to the cabinet or the Parliament.

The presidency has also been strengthened by the expanded scope of foreign policy. World War II fundamentally changed the nation's international role and the president's role in foreign policy. The United States emerged from the war as a global superpower, a giant in world trade, and the recognized leader of the non-communist world—a development that had a one-sided effect on America's institutions.[14] Because of the president's constitutional authority as chief diplomat and military commander and the special demands of foreign policy leadership, the president, not Congress, assumed the dominant role.[15] Foreign policy requires singleness of purpose and, at times, fast action. Congress—a large, divided, and often unwieldy institution—is poorly suited to such a response. In contrast, the president, as sole head of the executive branch, can act quickly and speak authoritatively for the nation as a whole in its relations with other nations. After the terrorist attacks of September 11, 2001, for example, President Bush took the lead in obtaining international support for U.S. military, intelligence, and diplomatic initiatives. Although Congress backed these

Harry S. Truman's presidency was characterized by bold foreign policy initiatives. He authorized the use of nuclear weapons against Japan in 1945, created the Marshall Plan as the basis for the economic reconstruction of postwar Europe, and sent U.S. troops to fight in Korea in 1950. Truman is shown here greeting British prime minister Winston Churchill at a Washington airport in early 1952.

actions, it had little choice but to support Bush's decision. Americans wanted decisive action and looked to the president, not to Congress, for leadership in combating terrorism. (The changing shape of the world and its implications for presidential power and leadership are discussed more fully later in the chapter.)

Choosing the President

As the president's policy and leadership responsibilities changed during the nation's history, so did the process of electing presidents. The public's role in selecting the president has grown ever more direct.[16] The United States in its history has had four systems of presidential selection, each more "democratic" than its predecessor (see Table 12-2).

The delegates to the constitutional convention of 1787 feared that popular election of the president would make the office too powerful and accordingly devised an electoral vote system (the so-called Electoral

table 12-2 The Four Systems of Presidential Selection

Selection System	Period	Features
1. Original	1788–1828	Party nominees are chosen in congressional caucuses. Electoral College members act somewhat independently in their presidential voting.
2. Party convention	1832–1900	Party nominees are chosen in national party conventions by delegates selected by state and local party organizations. Electoral College members cast their ballots for the popular-vote winner in their respective states.
3. Party convention, primary	1904–1968	As in system 2, except that a *minority* of national convention delegates are chosen through primary elections (the majority still being chosen by party organizations).
4. Party primary, open caucus	1972–present	As in system 2, except that a *majority* of national convention delegates are chosen through primary elections.

College). The president was to be chosen by electors picked by the states, with each state entitled to one elector for each of its members of Congress (House and Senate combined). This system was modified after the election in 1828 of Andrew Jackson, who believed that the people's will had been denied four years earlier when he got the most popular votes but failed to receive an electoral majority. Although Jackson was unable to persuade Congress to support a constitutional amendment to eliminate the Electoral College, he championed the next-best alternative. Under Jackson's reform, which is still in effect today, the candidate who wins a state's popular vote is awarded its electoral votes (see Chapter 2). Thus, the popular vote for the candidates directly affects their electoral vote, and one candidate is likely to win both forms of the presidential vote. Since Jackson's time, only Rutherford B. Hayes (in 1876), Benjamin Harrison (in 1888), and George W. Bush (in 2000) have won the presidency after having lost the popular vote.

Jackson also championed the national party convention as a means of nominating the party's presidential candidate (before this time, nominations were made by party caucuses in Congress and in state legislatures). Jackson saw the national convention—where each state is represented by delegates who select the party nominee—as a means of strengthening the link between the presidency and the people. Since Jackson's time, all presidential nominees have been formally chosen at national party conventions.

Jackson's system of presidential nomination remained intact until the early twentieth century, when the Progressives devised the primary election as a means of curbing the power of the party bosses (see Chapter 2). State party leaders had taken control of the nominating process by handpicking their states' convention delegates. The Progressives sought to give voters the power to select the delegates. Such a process is called an *indirect primary*, because the voters are not choosing the nominees directly (as they do in House and Senate races) but rather are choosing delegates who in turn select the nominees. However, the Progressives were unable to persuade most states to adopt presidential primaries, which meant that party leaders continued to control a majority of the convention delegates.

That arrangement held until 1968 when Democratic Party leaders ignored the strength of anti–Vietnam War sentiment in the primaries and nominated Vice President Hubert Humphrey, who had not entered a single primary and was closely identified with the Johnson administration's Vietnam policy. After Humphrey narrowly lost the 1968 general election to Richard Nixon, reform-minded Democrats forced changes in the nominating process. The new rules gave the party's voters more control by requiring states to select their delegates through either primary elections or **open party caucuses** (meetings open to any registered party voter who wants to attend). Although the Democrats initiated the change, the Republicans also adopted it. Today it is the voters in state primaries and open caucuses who choose the Democratic and Republican presidential nominees.[17] (About forty states choose their delegates through a primary election; the others use the caucus system.)

In sum, the presidential election system has changed from an elite-dominated process to one based on voter support. This arrangement has strengthened the presidency by providing the office with the added power that popular election confers on the president.

The Nominating Campaign: Primaries and Caucuses

The fact that voters pick the party nominees has opened the nominating races to nearly any prominent politician with the energy, resources, and desire to run. The competition is intense, except in the case of an incumbent president seeking renomination. The list of possible candidates is always much longer than is the number who run, as the 2012 Republican contest illustrates. Among those mentioned as possible contenders for the GOP nomination were Haley Barbour, Scott Brown, Jeb Bush, Chris Christie, John Cornyn, Mitch Daniels, Jim DeMint, Newt Gingrich, Mike Huckabee, Bobby Jindal, Bob McDonnell, Sarah Palin, George Pataki, Ron Paul, Tim Pawlenty, Mike Pence, David Petraeus, Rick Perry, Mitt Romney, Marco Rubio, Rick Santorum, and John Thune.

Candidates for nomination have no choice but to start early and campaign hard. A key to success is **momentum**—a strong showing in the early contests that contributes to voter support in subsequent ones. Nobody—not the press, not donors, not the voters—has an interest in candidates who are at the back of the pack. No candidate in recent decades has got off to a lousy start in the first few contests and then picked up enough steam to win nomination. The advantage rests with the fast starters. They get more attention from the press, more money from contributors, and more consideration by the voters. Not surprisingly, presidential contenders strive to do well in the early contests, particularly the first caucus in Iowa and the first primary in New Hampshire. In 2008, Barack Obama's successful quest for the Democratic presidential nomination began with a victory in Iowa. John McCain, the eventual Republican nominee, lost there but placed first a few days later in New Hampshire's primary.

POLITICAL THINKING

Should There Be a National Primary?

The nomination of presidential candidates is a marathon affair. The campaign goes from state to state until the voters of each state have had their turn to cast a ballot. An alternative system would be a national primary in which, on a single day, voters throughout the nation cast their ballots. What would be the advantages and disadvantages of a national primary? Why do you think the political parties have opposed the adoption of a national primary? Would you personally prefer a national primary to the current state-by-state system?

Money is a critical factor in presidential nominating races. Observers estimate that it takes upwards of $50 million to run a truly strong nominating campaign, particularly for a candidate who lacks name recognition and public support at the start of the campaign. In nearly every nominating race in the past three decades, the winner has been the candidate who raised the most money in advance of the first contest in Iowa.

Candidates in primary elections are eligible to receive federal funding if they meet certain eligibility criteria. The Federal Election Campaign Act of 1974 (as amended in 1979) provides for federal matching funds. Under the program, the government matches the first $250 of each private donation received by a primary election candidate if the candidate raises at least $5,000 in individual contributions of up to $250 in at least twenty states. This provision is designed to restrict matching funds to candidates who can demonstrate that they have a reasonable level of public support. In addition, any candidate who receives matching funds must agree to limit expenditures for the nominating phase to a set amount overall (roughly $50 million in 2012) and in particular states (the limits in Iowa and New Hampshire, for example, are roughly $1.4 million and $800,000, respectively). The limits are adjusted upward each election year to account for inflation.

Until the 2000 election, when George W. Bush declined matching funds so that he could raise an unrestricted amount of money, candidates for nomination had routinely accepted matching funds, which required them to abide by the spending limits. In 2004, Bush again turned down matching funds, as did the two leading Democratic contenders, Howard Dean and John Kerry. In 2008, an even larger number of candidates declined public funds. Obama was easily the leading fundraiser, garnering in excess of $300 million for his nominating campaign—more than four times the amount allowed if he had accepted matching funds.

Some observers have proposed raising the allowable spending limit under public financing, perhaps to $100 million. Otherwise, they say, the only candidates who will accept matching funds are those with no chance of victory. This development would defeat the purpose of public funding, which is to free the nominees from the obligations that come from accepting contributions from private groups and individuals.

The National Party Conventions

The summertime national party conventions mark the end of the nominating campaign. In an earlier era, the delegates from the various states actually bargained and negotiated over the choice of a presidential nominee. However, after the delegate selection process was changed in 1972, the strongest candidate in every case has acquired enough delegates through the primaries and caucuses to secure nomination in advance of the convention. Despite the lack of suspense, the convention remains a major event. It brings together the delegates elected in the state caucuses and primaries, who approve a party platform and formally nominate the party's presidential and vice presidential candidates.

Although the national party conventions are not the tumultuous and decisive events they once were, they offer the parties a showcase for their candidates and platforms. Shown here is a scene from the 2008 Republican convention, which selected John McCain and Sarah Palin as the party's presidential and vice presidential nominees.

By tradition, the choice of the vice presidential nominee rests with the presidential nominee. In 2008, Obama selected Delaware senator Joe Biden, who had the foreign policy experience that Obama lacked. For his part, McCain picked little-known Alaska governor Sarah Palin, whose forceful acceptance speech at the Republican convention propelled her to national prominence.

The General Election Campaign

The winner in the November general election is certain to be the Republican or the Democratic candidate. Two-thirds of the nation's voters identify with the Republican or Democratic Party, and most independents lean toward one or the other party. As a result, the major-party presidential nominees have a reservoir of votes. Even Democrat George McGovern, whose level of party support was the lowest in the past half-century, was backed in 1972 by 60 percent of his party's identifiers. Because the Democratic and Republican nominees have this built-in advantage, a third-party candidate has no realistic hope of victory. Even Ross Perot, who in 1992 ran the most successful third-party campaign in nearly a century, attracted only a fifth of the vote. On the other hand, a third-party candidate can create problems for a major party by drawing votes away from its nominee. In 2000, third-party candidate Ralph Nader received 3 percent of the popular vote, most of it from voters who otherwise preferred Al Gore, the Democratic nominee. If Nader had not been in the race, Gore, rather than George W. Bush, would have won the 2000 presidential election.

Election Strategy The candidates' strategies in the general election are shaped by several considerations, none more so than the Electoral College (see Chapter 2). Each state has two electoral votes for its Senate representation and a varying number of electoral votes depending on its House representation. Altogether, there are 538 electoral votes, including 3 for the District of Columbia, even though it has no voting representatives in Congress. To win the presidency, a candidate must receive at least 270 votes, an electoral majority. (If no candidate receives a majority, the election is decided in the House of Representatives. No president since John Quincy Adams in 1824 has been elected in this way.)

The importance of electoral votes is magnified by the **unit rule:** all the states except Maine and Nebraska grant all their electoral votes as a unit to the candidate who wins the state's popular vote. For this reason, candidates are concerned with winning the most populous states, such as Arizona, California, Florida, Georgia, Illinois, Indiana, Massachusetts,

Michigan, New Jersey, New York, North Carolina, Ohio, Pennsylvania, Tennessee, Texas, Virginia, and Washington.

A larger strategic factor than a state's size is its competitiveness. Because of the unit rule, the candidates have no incentive to campaign in lopsidedly Republican or Democratic states where the electoral votes are not in doubt. As a result, the fall campaign becomes a battle for the toss-up states (see "How the 50 States Differ"). In 2008, no more than a third of the states were seen by the Obama and McCain campaigns as states that could realistically be won by either candidate. During the general election phase, the two candidates spent nearly all their money and time in these so-called battleground states. Other states might just as well have been located in Canada for the amount of attention they received.

Media and Money At an earlier time, candidates based their campaigns on the party organizations. Today, they rely on the media, particularly the Internet and television. The Internet is used mostly for fundraising and organizing. Obama raised more than $200 million through the Internet for his 2008 general election campaign and had a web-based organization of 10 million supporters. Television is used mostly as a way to persuade undecided voters. Through appearances on news and interview programs, as well as through their televised advertising (which accounts for most of their spending), the nominees try to win over those voters who are undecided or wavering in their choice (see Chapter 8).[18] The televised presidential debates are part of this effort, although the debates usually do not have a large impact on the candidates' support. The 2008 Obama-McCain debates were typical in this respect. Although the polls revealed that most Americans judged Obama to have won all three debates, the polls also indicated that few viewers changed their minds about the candidates as a result of watching the debates.

The Republican and Democratic nominees are eligible for federal funding of their general election campaigns even if they do not accept it during the primaries. The amount was set at $20 million when the policy was instituted in 1976 and has been adjusted for inflation in succeeding elections—the figure for the 2012 election is roughly $90 million. The only string attached to this money is that a nominee who accepts it cannot spend additional funds on the general election campaign (although each party is allowed to spend some money—in 2012, roughly $5 million—on behalf of its nominee). In 2008, Barack Obama declined public funding, becoming the first major-party nominee to do so. Obama had promised to run on public funds but went back on his promise upon realizing that he could raise a much larger sum on his own. John McCain accepted

HOW THE 50 STATES DIFFER
POLITICAL THINKING THROUGH COMPARISONS

Electoral Vote Strategy in the 2012 Election

The Constitution of the United States specifies that the president is to be chosen by electoral votes. The candidate receiving a majority of the electoral vote, even if receiving fewer popular votes than the opponent, becomes president. The Constitution further specifies that states have authority to determine how their electors will be chosen. Today, all states except two (Maine and Nebraska, which give one electoral vote to the winner of each congressional district and two electoral votes to the statewide winner), give all their electoral votes to the popular-vote winner in the state—the

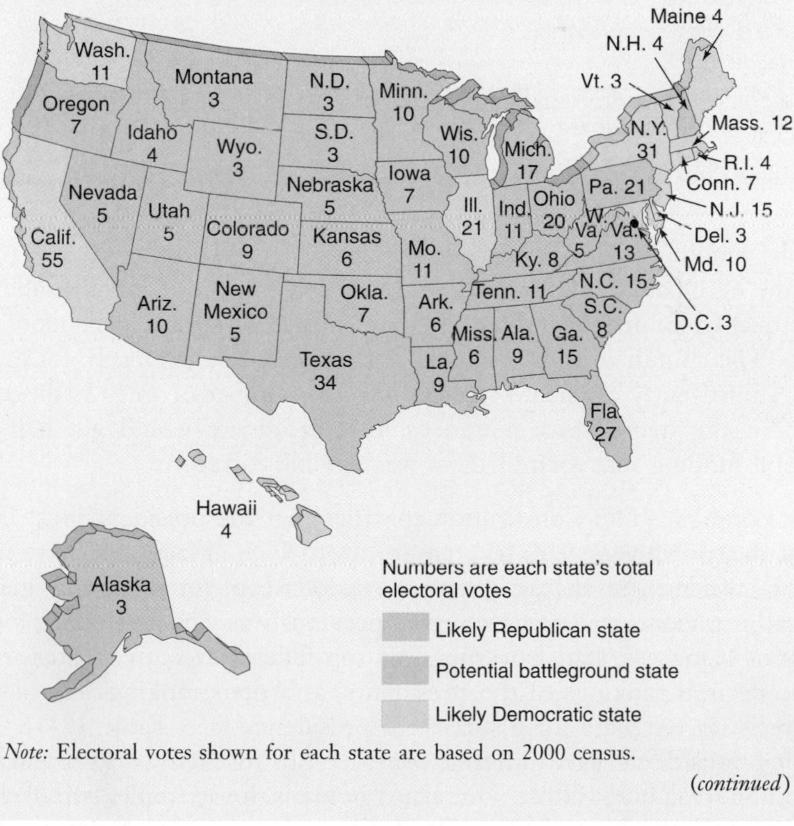

Note: Electoral votes shown for each state are based on 2000 census.

(*continued*)

so-called unit rule. This winner-take-all feature of the electoral vote system leads presidential candidates to focus on toss-up states—those that conceivably could be won by either party. These so-called battleground states are the only ones where the candidates spend any appreciable amount of time and money during the general election. One-sided states—those that are solidly Republican or Democratic—are more or less ignored during the fall campaign.

The map on page 427 identifies the potential battleground states in the 2012 presidential race, based on the closeness of the vote in the three most recent presidential elections. A state is classified as a battleground state if each party has won or nearly won the state at least once in this period.

Q: *The unit rule is only one of the possible ways of allocating electoral votes. As indicated above, Maine and Nebraska use a different method. Some state legislatures are considering yet a third method: allocating their state's electoral votes among the candidates in proportion to the popular votes they each receive. What's your view? Do you think the unit rule is a fair way for states to distribute their electoral votes, or do you prefer one of the alternatives?*

public funding for his general election campaign and was outspent three to one by Obama. (Minor-party and independent presidential candidates can qualify for federal funding if they receive at least 5 percent of the vote. Their funding is proportional to the votes they attract. If, for example, a third-party candidate receives half the number of votes as the average for the major-party nominees, that candidate would get half the federal funding that each of them was eligible to receive.)

The Winners The Constitution specifies that the president must be at least thirty-five years old, be a natural-born U.S. citizen, and have been a U.S. resident for at least fourteen years. Except for four army generals, all presidents to date have served previously as vice presidents, members of Congress, state governors, or top federal executives. Historians have devised rankings of the presidents, and their rankings reveal that there is no template for a successful presidency (see Table 12-3). The strong presidents have differed considerably in their backgrounds, as have the weak ones. Of the four army generals, for example, two of them (George Washington and Dwight D. Eisenhower) are in the upper ranks table 12-3 The Path to the White House

President	Years in Office	Highest Previous Office	Second Highest Office
Theodore Roosevelt	1901–1908	Vice president*	Governor
William Howard Taft	1909–1912	Secretary of war	Federal judge
Woodrow Wilson	1913–1920	Governor	None
Warren G. Harding	1921–1924	U.S. senator	Lieutenant governor
Calvin Coolidge	1925–1928	Vice president*	Governor
Herbert Hoover	1929–1932	Secretary of commerce	War relief administrator
Franklin D. Roosevelt	1933–1945	Governor	Assistant secretary of Navy
Harry S Truman	1945–1952	Vice president*	U.S. senator
Dwight D. Eisenhower	1953–1960	None (Army general)	None
John F. Kennedy	1961–1963	U.S. senator	U.S. representative
Lyndon Johnson	1963–1968	Vice president*	U.S. senator
Richard Nixon	1969–1974	Vice president	U.S. senator
Gerald Ford	1974–1976	Vice president*	U.S. representative
Jimmy Carter	1977–1980	Governor	State senator
Ronald Reagan	1981–1988	Governor	None
George H. W. Bush	1989–1992	Vice president	Director, CIA
Bill Clinton	1993–2000	Governor	State attorney general
George W. Bush	2001–2008	Governor	None
Barack Obama	2009–	U.S. senator	State senator

*Became president on death or resignation of incumbent.

while the other two (Ulysses S. Grant and Zachary Taylor) are in the lower ranks.

Until Obama's election in 2008, all presidents had been white. No woman has won the presidency, though it is only a matter of time before the nation elects its first woman president. Until the early 1950s, a majority of Americans polled said they would not vote for a woman for president. Today, fewer than 5 percent hold this view. A similar change of opinion preceded John F. Kennedy's election to the presidency in 1960. Kennedy was the nation's first Catholic president and only the second Catholic to receive a major party's nomination. By the time of Kennedy's candidacy, anti-Catholic sentiment had declined to the point where it did not block his election.

Staffing the Presidency

When Americans go to the polls on election day, they are electing more than a president. They are also picking a secretary of state, the director of the FBI, and hundreds of other federal executives. Each of these is a presidential appointee, and each of these is an extension of the president's authority. Although the president cannot be in a hundred places at once, the president's appointees collectively can be. Not surprisingly, presidents typically appoint party loyalists who are committed to the administration's policy goals.

Even the vice presidency can be seen as an extension of the president's authority. Although the vice president holds a separate elective office, the Constitution assigns no executive authority to the vice president. His or her influence within the administration depends entirely on the president's desires. At an earlier time, presidents more or less ignored their vice presidents, who did not even have an office in the White House. Nomination to the vice presidency was declined by several leading politicians, including Daniel Webster and Henry Clay. Said Webster, "I do not propose to be buried until I am really dead."[19] When Jimmy Carter assumed the presidency in 1977, he redefined the office by assigning important policy duties to his vice president and relocating him to an office in the White House. The vice president is now entrenched in the White House and is supported by a staff of policy advisors (the Office of the Vice President). Some observers believe that George W. Bush gave his vice president, Dick Cheney, too much power.[20] Cheney was a vigorous proponent of the Iraq invasion and other policies that ultimately weakened Bush's public and congressional support.

The Executive Office of the President (EOP)

The key staff organization is the Executive Office of the President (EOP), created by Congress in 1939 to provide the president with the staff necessary to coordinate the activities of the executive branch.[21] The EOP has since become the command center of the presidency. Its exact configuration is determined by the president, but some of its organizational units have carried over from one president to the next. These include the White House Office (WHO), which consists of the president's closest personal advisers; the Office of Management and Budget (OMB), which consists of experts who formulate and administer the federal budget; and the National Security Council (NSC), which advises the president on foreign and military affairs.

Of the EOP's organizational units, the **White House Office (WHO)** serves the president most directly. The WHO includes the Communications Office, the Office of the Press Secretary, the Office of the Counsel to the President, and the Office of Legislative Affairs. As these labels suggest, the WHO consists of the president's personal assistants, including top advisers, press agents, legislative and group liaison aides, and special assistants for domestic and international policy. These individuals do much of the legwork for the president and are a main source of advice. They tend to be skilled at developing political strategy and communicating with the public, the media, and other officials. They are among the most powerful individuals in Washington because of their closeness to the president.

Most of the EOP's other organizational units are staffed by policy experts. These include economists, legal analysts, national security specialists, and others. The president is advised on economic issues, for example, by the National Economic Council (NEC).

Cabinet and Agency Appointees

The heads of the fifteen executive departments, such as the Department of Defense and the Department of Agriculture, constitute the president's **cabinet**. They are appointed by the president, subject to confirmation by the Senate. Although the cabinet once served as the president's main advisory group, it has not played this role since Herbert Hoover's administration. As issues have become increasingly complex, presidents have increasingly relied on presidential advisors and individual cabinet members rather than on the cabinet as a whole. Cabinet meetings are no longer the scene of lengthy debates over policy. Nevertheless, cabinet members, as individuals who head major departments, are important figures in any administration. The president selects them for their prominence in politics, business, government, or the professions.[22] The office of secretary of state, currently held by Hillary Clinton, is widely regarded as the most prestigious cabinet post.

In addition to cabinet secretaries, the president appoints the heads and top deputies of federal agencies and commissions, as well as the nearly two hundred ambassadors. There are more than a thousand full-time presidential appointees, a much larger number than are appointed by the chief executive of any other democracy.[23]

The Problem of Control

Although the president's appointees are a major asset, their large number poses a control problem for the president. President Truman kept a wall chart in the Oval Office that listed the more than one hundred officials who reported directly to him. He often told visitors, "I cannot even see all of these men, let alone actually study what they are doing."[24] Since Truman's time, the number of bureaucratic agencies has more than doubled, compounding the problem of presidential control over subordinates.[25]

The president's problem is most severe in the case of appointees who work in the departments and agencies. Their offices are located outside the White House, and their loyalty is sometimes split between a desire to promote the president's goals and an interest in promoting themselves or the agencies they lead. In 2005, when Hurricane Katrina devastated New Orleans, FEMA director Michael Brown, a Bush appointee, took control even though he had no appreciable experience with disaster relief. Intent on taking the lead, Brown ignored the chain of command, withholding information from his immediate superior, the Homeland Security

Presidents rely on trusted advisers in making critical policy decisions. During the Cuban missile crisis in 1962, this group of advisers to President John F. Kennedy helped him decide on a naval blockade as a means of forcing the Soviet Union to withdraw its missiles from Cuba.

secretary, thereby making a coordinated relief effort harder to achieve. Brown's incompetence was initially obscured by the scale of the disaster. Two days into the relief effort, President Bush said publicly, "Brownie, you're doing a heck of a job." Several days later, however, Brown's missteps had become headline news, leading the White House to force him to resign.

Lower-level appointees within the departments and agencies pose a different type of problem. The president rarely, if ever, sees them, and many of them are political novices (most have less than two years of government or policy experience). They are sometimes "captured" by the agency in which they work because they depend on the agency's career bureaucrats for advice and information (see Chapter 13).

In short, the modern presidential office is a mixed benefit. Although presidential appointees enable presidents to extend their influence into every executive agency, these appointees do not always act in ways that serve the president's interest. (The subject of presidential control of the executive branch is discussed further in Chapter 13.)

Factors in Presidential Leadership

All presidents are expected to provide national leadership, but not all presidents are equally adept as leaders.[26] Presidents lead by motivating others to support their goals. Strong presidents, as political scientist Stephen Skowronek notes, have usually had a strategic vision of where they want to lead the country, as well as a clear sense of how their ideas intersect with Americans' aspirations.[27] As a result, they have been able to explain their goals in a way that generates public support and confidence. Ronald Reagan had this capacity, which enabled him to alter the direction of domestic and foreign policy. Jimmy Carter lacked it. In what was arguably the most important speech of his presidency, Carter lamented "the malaise" that he said was infecting American life. At a time when Americans were struggling with rising inflation and unemployment and were seeking strong leadership, Carter lectured them on their lack of confidence.

Although effective leadership is a key to presidential success, it is only one component. The president operates within a system of separate institutions that share power (see "How the U.S. Differs"). Significant presidential action typically depends on the approval of Congress, the cooperation of the bureaucracy, and sometimes the acceptance of the judiciary. Because other officials have their own priorities, presidents do not always get their way. Congress in particular—more than the courts or the bureaucracy—holds the key to presidential success. Without congressional

HOW THE U.S. DIFFERS
POLITICAL THINKING THROUGH COMPARISONS

Systems of Executive Leadership

The United States instituted a presidential system in 1789 as part of its constitutional checks and balances. This form of executive leadership was copied in Latin America but not in Europe. European democracies adopted parliamentary systems, in which executive leadership is provided by a prime minister, who is a member of the legislature. In recent years, some European prime ministers have campaigned and governed as if they were a singular authority rather than the head of a collective institution. In the 2010 British election, the three main parties' candidates for prime minister even engaged in televised debates, almost as if they were running against each other rather than as heads of their respective parties.

The policy leadership of a president can differ substantially from that of a prime minister. As a singular head of an independent branch of government, a president does not have to share executive authority but nevertheless depends on the legislative branch for support. By comparison, a prime minister shares executive leadership with a cabinet, but once agreement within the cabinet is reached, he or she is almost assured of the legislative support necessary to carry out policy initiatives.

On the other hand, the American president has the advantage of being both the head of state and the head of government. Most democracies divide the executive office between a head of state, who is the ceremonial leader, and the head of government, who is the policy leader. In Great Britain, these positions are filled by the queen and the prime minister, respectively. In democracies without a hereditary monarchy, the position of head of state is usually held by an individual chosen by the legislature. Germany's head of state, for example, is the president, who is elected by the Federal Assembly. The head of government is the chancellor, who is chosen by the majority party in the lower house (Bundestag) of the Federal Assembly. A disadvantage of the American system is that the president must devote considerable time to ceremonial functions, such as hosting visiting heads of state. An offsetting advantage is that the president alone is the center of national attention.

Q: *Which type of executive leadership do you think is better? Do you prefer a presidential system, in which the chief executive heads only the executive branch, or a parliamentary system, in which the chief executive heads both the executive and the legislative branches? Why? Then, do you prefer a system in which the positions of head of state and head of government are combined in a single individual, as in the American case, or a system that divides the executive office between a head of state and a head of government, as in the British or German case? Why?*

authorization and funding, most presidential proposals are nothing but ideas, empty of action. Dwight D. Eisenhower, whose personal integrity made him perhaps the most trusted president of the twentieth century, had a keen awareness of the need to win over Congress. "I'll tell you what leadership is," he said. "It's persuasion, and conciliation, and education, and patience. It's long, slow, tough work."[28]

Whether a president's initiatives succeed depends substantially on several factors, including the force of circumstance, the stage of the president's term, the nature of the particular issue, the president's support in Congress, and the president's standing with the American people. The remainder of this chapter discusses the importance of these factors.

The Force of Circumstance

During his first months in office and in the midst of the Great Depression, Franklin D. Roosevelt accomplished the most sweeping changes in domestic policy in the nation's history. Congress moved quickly to pass nearly every New Deal initiative he proposed. In 1964 and 1965, Lyndon Johnson pushed landmark civil rights and social welfare legislation through Congress on the strength of the civil rights movement, the legacy of the assassinated President Kennedy, and large Democratic majorities in the House and Senate. When Ronald Reagan assumed the presidency in 1981, inflation and high unemployment had greatly weakened the national economy and created a mood for change, enabling Reagan to persuade Congress to enact some of the most substantial taxing and spending changes in history.

From such presidencies has come the popular impression that presidents single-handedly decide national policy. However, each of these periods of presidential dominance was marked by a special set of circumstances—a decisive election victory that gave added force to the president's leadership, a compelling national problem that convinced Congress and the public that bold presidential action was needed, and a president who was mindful of what was expected and championed policies consistent with expectations.

When conditions are favorable, the power of the presidency is remarkable. The problem for most presidents is that they serve at a time when conditions are not conducive to ambitious goals. Political scientist Erwin Hargrove suggests that presidential influence depends largely on circumstance.[29] Some presidents serve in periods when resources are scarce or when important problems are surfacing in American society but have not yet reached a critical stage. Such situations, Hargrove notes, work against the president's efforts to accomplish significant policy changes. In 1994, reflecting on the constraints of budget deficits and other factors beyond his control, President Clinton said he had no choice but "to play the hand that history had dealt" him. Stark reality also confronted President Obama's determination in his early months in office to address global warming by requiring firms to take steps to curb their carbon emissions. The weakness of the American economy precluded action that would impose a costly new requirement on corporations.

The Stage of the President's Term

If conditions conducive to great accomplishments occur irregularly, it is nonetheless the case that nearly every president has favorable moments. Such moments often come during the first months in office. Most newly elected presidents enjoy a **honeymoon period** during which Congress, the press, and the public anticipate initiatives from the Oval Office and are more predisposed than usual to support them. Most presidents propose more new programs in their first year in office than in any subsequent year.[30] Later in their terms, presidents may have run out of good ideas or depleted their political resources; meanwhile, the momentum of their election is gone, and sources of opposition have emerged. Even successful presidents like Johnson and Reagan had weak records in their final years. Franklin D. Roosevelt began his presidency with a remarkable period of achievement—the celebrated "Hundred Days"—that he was unable to duplicate later in his presidency.

An irony of the presidency, then, is that presidents are often most powerful when they are least experienced—during their first months in office. These months can, as a result, be times of risk as well as times of opportunity. An example is the Bay of Pigs fiasco during the first year of John F. Kennedy's presidency, in which a U.S.-backed invasion force of anticommunist Cubans was easily defeated by Fidel Castro's army.

The Nature of the Issue: Foreign or Domestic

In the 1960s, political scientist Aaron Wildavsky wrote that the nation has only one president but two presidencies: one domestic and one foreign.[31] Wildavsky was referring to Congress's greater deference to presidential leadership on foreign policy than on domestic policy. He had in mind the broad leeway Congress had granted Truman, Eisenhower, Kennedy, and Johnson in their foreign policies. Wildavsky's thesis is now regarded as a somewhat time-bound conception of presidential influence. Today, many of the same factors that affect a president's domestic policy success, such as the partisan composition of Congress, also affect foreign policy success.

Nevertheless, presidents still have an edge when the issue is foreign policy, because they have more authority to act on their own and are more likely to have congressional support.[32] The president is recognized by other nations as America's voice in world affairs, and members of Congress will sometimes defer to the president in order to maintain America's credibility abroad. In some cases, presidents can literally dictate the direction of foreign policy. In 2009, Obama delayed for weeks a decision on a new strategy for the war in Afghanistan, saying that "it is a matter of making certain . . . that it's making us safer." When he finally announced his strategy, which included an increase in troop levels and a timetable for withdrawal, there was some dissent in Congress, but it did not materially affect Obama's war plans.

Presidents also acquire leverage in foreign and defense policy because of their special relationship with the defense, diplomatic, and intelligence agencies. Other agencies are sometimes more responsive to Congress than to the president. The Department of Agriculture, for example, relies more heavily on the support of farm-state senators and representatives than on the president's backing. The defense, diplomatic, and intelligence agencies are a different matter. Their missions closely parallel the president's constitutional authority as commander in chief and chief diplomat. In the period before the Iraq invasion in 2003, for example, U.S. intelligence

Additional U.S. troops were deployed to Afghanistan by order of President Obama. The military escalation was decided solely by the president after consultation with his advisers and military commanders.

agencies provided assessments that bolstered President Bush's assertion that Iraq's weapons systems threatened American interests. Only later did Congress discover that some of the assessments were tailored to fit Bush's claims about Iraq's capabilities.

A president's domestic policy initiatives usually encounter stiffer opposition than their foreign policy efforts. The Republican and Democratic parties differ sharply in their domestic policy philosophies, and there are strong interest groups on each side of nearly every important domestic issue. Attempts at significant action in the domestic policy realm invariably activate contending forces. A case in point is President Obama's promise to reform the nation's immigration system. Obama said he would take up the issue in early 2010, but as opposition intensified, it became clear that he had little chance of getting a reform bill through Congress. Although Hispanic groups and liberal Democrats in Congress urged him to make the push anyway, believing it would mobilize the Hispanic vote in the 2010 midterm election, Obama chose not to take on the fight.

Relations with Congress

Although the power of the presidency is not nearly as substantial as some Americans assume, the president's ability to set the national agenda is unrivaled. Whenever the president directs attention to a particular issue, members of Congress take notice. But will they take action? The answer is sometimes yes and sometimes no, depending in part on whether the president takes their interests into account.

Seeking Cooperation from Congress As the center of national attention, presidents can start to believe that their ideas should prevail over those of Congress. This reasoning invariably gets the president into trouble. Jimmy Carter had not held national office before he was elected president in 1976 and lacked a sense of how Washington operates.[33] Soon after taking office, Carter cut from his budget nineteen public works projects that he regarded as a waste of taxpayers' money, ignoring the determination of members of Congress to obtain federally funded projects for their constituents. Carter's action set the tone for a conflict-ridden relationship with Congress.

To get the help of members of Congress, the president must respond to their interests.[34] The most basic fact about presidential leadership is that it takes place in the context of a system of divided powers. Although the president gets most of the attention, Congress has lawmaking authority, and presidents need its cooperation to achieve their legislative goals.

Even the president's most direct legislative tool, the veto, has limits. Congress can seldom muster the two-thirds majority in each chamber required to override a presidential veto, so the threat of a veto can make Congress bend to the president's demands. Yet, as presidential scholar Richard Neustadt argued, the veto is as much a sign of presidential weakness as it is a sign of strength, because it arises when Congress refuses to accept the president's ideas.[35] An example is the first veto cast by George W. Bush. Until then, Bush was on track to join Thomas Jefferson as the only two-term president not to veto a bill. In 2006, however, Bush vetoed a bill that would have expanded federal support for embryonic-stem-cell research. He had announced his opposition to such research early in his presidency and succeeded for a time in getting congressional Republicans to back him. As Bush's popularity plummeted in 2005, however, some congressional Republicans separated themselves from the president out of concern for their reelection chances. Enough Republicans defected on the stem-cell bill to get it through Congress, setting the stage for Bush's first veto. Bush was weakened further when his party lost control of the House and Senate in the 2006 midterm elections. He increasingly resorted to actual and threatened vetoes in dealing with Congress.

Congress is a constituency that all presidents must serve if they expect to have its support. Neustadt concluded that presidential power, at base, is "the power to persuade."[36] Like any singular notion of presidential power, Neustadt's has limitations. Presidents at times have the power to command and to threaten. They can also appeal directly to the American people as a means of pressuring Congress. But Congress can never be taken for granted. Theodore Roosevelt expressed the wish that he could "be the president and Congress too for just ten minutes." Roosevelt would then have had the power to enact as well as to propose legislation.

Benefiting from Partisan Support in Congress For most presidents, the next best thing to being "Congress, too" is to have a Congress filled with members of their own party. The sources of division within Congress are many. Legislators from urban and rural areas, wealthier and poorer constituencies, and different regions of the country often have conflicting policy views. To obtain majority support in Congress, the president must find ways to overcome these divisions.

No source of unity is more important to presidential success than partisanship. Presidents are more likely to succeed when their own party controls Congress (see Figure 12-1). Between 1954 and 1992, each Republican president—Eisenhower, Nixon, Ford, Reagan, and Bush—had to contend with a Democratic majority in one or both houses of Congress. Congress

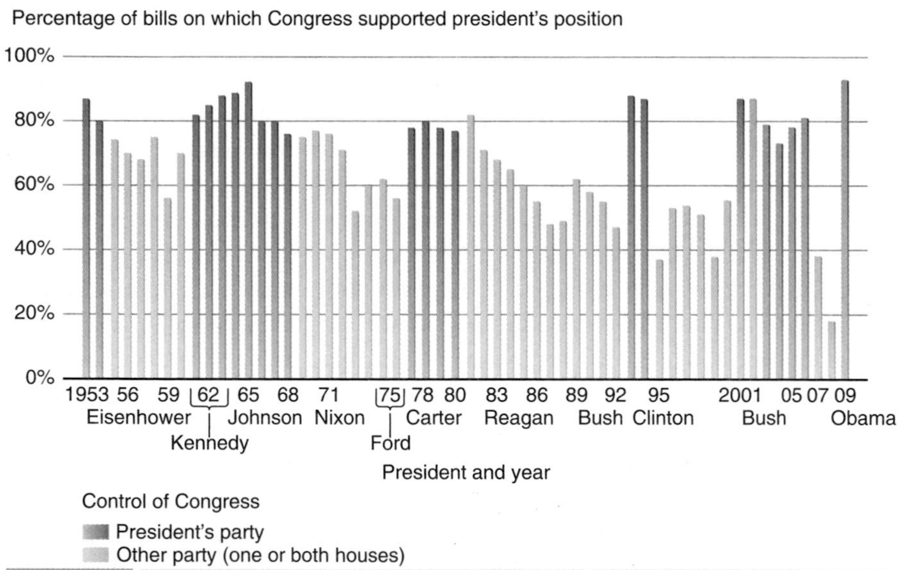

figure 12-1 PERCENTAGE OF BILLS PASSED BY CONGRESS ON WHICH THE PRESIDENT ANNOUNCED A POSITION, 1953–2009

In most years, presidents have been supported by Congress on a majority of policy issues on which they have taken a stand. Presidents fare better when their party controls Congress.
Source: CQ Weekly, various dates.

passed a smaller percentage of the initiatives backed by each of these presidents than those supported by any Democratic president of the period: Kennedy, Johnson, or Carter. In Clinton's first two years in office, backed by Democratic majorities in the House and Senate, more than 85 percent of the bills that he supported were enacted into law. After Republicans took control of Congress in 1995, Clinton's legislative success rate sank below 40 percent. George W. Bush suffered a similar fate. He had a legislative success rate of 81 percent in 2006, but when control of Congress shifted from the Republicans to the Democrats in 2007, it fell to 38 percent—a sharp illustration of how presidential power depends on which party controls Congress.

Few recent policies illustrate the importance of partisan support than does the major health care bill that Congress enacted in 2010. President Obama had sought the legislation for nearly a year, seeking at least some Republican support for the bill. In the end, not a single Republican senator or representative voted for it. In the House of Representative, the bill passed by a narrow 219–212 margin, and it did so only because 86 percent of Democratic lawmakers backed the president's position.

Colliding with Congress On rare occasions, presidents have pursued their goals so zealously that Congress has taken steps to curb their use of power.

Congress's ultimate sanction is its constitutional authority to impeach and remove the president from office. The House of Representatives decides by majority vote whether the president should be impeached (placed on trial), and the Senate conducts the trial and then votes on the president's case, with a two-thirds vote required for removal from office. In 1868, Andrew Johnson came within one Senate vote of being removed from office for his opposition to Congress's harsh Reconstruction policies after the Civil War. In 1974, Richard Nixon's resignation halted congressional proceedings on the Watergate affair that almost certainly would have ended in his impeachment and removal from office. In 1998, the House of Representatives impeached President Clinton on grounds he had lied under oath about a sexual relationship with intern Monica Lewinsky and had obstructed justice by trying to conceal the affair. The Senate acquitted Clinton, partly because polls indicated that most Americans did not think Clinton's behavior constituted "treason, bribery, or other high crimes and misdemeanors," which is what the Constitution specifies as the grounds for removing a president from office.

The gravity of impeachment action makes it an unsuitable basis for curbing presidential action except in rare instances. More often, Congress has responded legislatively to what it sees as unwarranted assertions of executive power. An example is the Budget Impoundment and Control Act of 1974, which prohibits a president from indefinitely withholding funds that have been appropriated by Congress. The legislation grew out of President Nixon's practice of withholding funds from programs he disliked. A similar controversy erupted in 2006 when it was revealed that President Bush had used so-called signing statements to challenge the constitutionality of more than seven hundred bills. These statements, appended to a bill when the president signs it, are meant to indicate that the president does not necessarily intend to abide by particular provisions of a law. Although Bush was not the first president to use this device, he had attached signing statements to more bills than all his predecessors combined and had done so in secrecy. Even congressional Republicans expressed concern about the practice. At Senate Judiciary Committee hearings, Senator Arlen Specter (R-Penn.), chair of the committee, argued that presidents do not have the authority to pick and choose among legislative provisions, accepting those they like and disregarding the rest. The president's choice is to accept or reject a bill in its entirety. Said Specter, "The president has the option under the Constitution to veto or not."[37]

Congress's most ambitious effort to curb presidential power is the War Powers Act. During the Vietnam War, Presidents Johnson and Nixon misled Congress, supplying it with intelligence estimates that painted a falsely optimistic picture of the military situation. Believing the war was being won, Congress regularly voted to provide the money to keep it going. However, congressional support changed abruptly in 1971 with publication in the *New York Times* of classified documents (the so-called Pentagon Papers) that revealed the Vietnam situation to be more perilous than Johnson and Nixon claimed.

In an effort to prevent future presidential wars, Congress in 1973 passed the War Powers Act. Nixon vetoed the measure, but Congress overrode his veto. The act does not prohibit the president from sending troops into combat, but it does require the president to consult with Congress whenever feasible before doing so and requires the president to inform Congress within forty-eight hours of the reason for the military action. The War Powers Act also requires hostilities to end within sixty days unless Congress extends the period. The act gives the president an additional thirty days to withdraw the troops from hostile territory, although Congress can shorten the thirty-day period. Presidents have claimed that the War Powers Act infringes on their constitutional power as commander in chief, but the Supreme Court has not ruled on the issue, leaving open the question of whether it constrains the president's war-making powers.

POLITICAL THINKING

Can the President's War Power Be Checked?

U.S. government is based on a system of checks and balances. In practice, there is an area where the system is deficient—the president's power to wage war. As commander in chief of the armed forces, the president has the authority to order troops into combat. Once this action occurs, Congress is almost powerless to reverse it. Congress could conceivably withhold funding for the conflict but in doing so might risk the lives of the troops. Moreover, even if a war is going badly, the president is unlikely to withdraw the troops. To do so would be an admission that the decision to go to war was a mistake. The War Powers Act of 1973 is an attempt by Congress to assert more control over America's wars. Do you think Congress should have more say in this area? How do you think the Supreme Court would rule if Congress invoked the War Powers Act and the president defied it, citing as the basis the constitutional provision that establishes the president as commander in chief of the armed forces?

In sum, the effect of presidential efforts to circumvent congressional authority has been to heighten congressional opposition. Even if presidents gain in the short run by acting on their own, they undermine their capacity to lead in the long run if they fail to keep in mind that Congress is a coequal branch of the American governing system.

Public Support

Presidential power rests in part on a claim to national leadership, and the strength of that claim is roughly proportional to the president's public support. **Presidential approval ratings** are predictably high at the start of the president's time in office. When asked in polls whether they "approve or disapprove of how the president is doing his job," most Americans express approval during a president's first months in office. The honeymoon rarely lasts long, however. Difficult issues and adverse developments inevitably cut away at the president's public support, and more than half of post–World War II presidents have left office with an approval rating of less than 50 percent (see Table 12-4).

With public backing, the president's leadership cannot be dismissed easily by other Washington officials. When the president's public support table 12-4 PERCENTAGE OF PUBLIC EXPRESSING APPROVAL OF PRESIDENT'S PERFORMANCE

Presidential approval ratings generally are higher at the beginning of the term than at the end.

	Years in Office	Average During Presidency	First-Year Average	Final-Year Average
Harry S Truman	1945–1952	41%	63%	35%
Dwight D. Eisenhower	1953–1960	64	74	62
John F. Kennedy	1961–1963	70	76	62
Lyndon Johnson	1963–1968	55	78	40
Richard Nixon	1969–1974	49	63	24
Gerald Ford	1974–1976	46	75	48
Jimmy Carter	1977–1980	47	68	46
Ronald Reagan	1981–1988	53	58	57
George H. W. Bush	1989–1992	61	65	40
Bill Clinton	1993–2000	57	50	60
George W. Bush	2001–2008	51	68	33
Barack Obama	2009–	—	58	—

Source: Averages compiled from Gallup polls.

sinks, however, officials are less inclined to accept that leadership. In the early years of his presidency, for example, Congress gave George W. Bush most of what he asked for, which is the main reason that five years elapsed before his first veto. During Bush's first two years, Congress enacted seventeen major legislative acts, the second highest for this period among postwar presidents.[38] However, as Bush's popularity slipped as a result of a deteriorating economy and a worsening of the Iraq conflict, congressional opposition increased. Among the Bush initiatives defeated in Congress were his social security and immigration reform proposals.

Events and Issues Public support for the president is conditioned by developments at home and abroad. International crises tend to produce a patriotic "rally 'round the flag" reaction that builds support for the president. Virtually every foreign policy crisis of the past four decades has followed this pattern. Although Americans were divided in 2003 over the wisdom of war with Iraq, for example, President Bush's approval rating rose when the fighting began. On the other hand, public support tends to erode if the crisis is not resolved successfully or in a relatively short period. Bush's support fell steadily as U.S. casualties mounted in Iraq. By 2006, his approval rating had dropped below 40 percent, contributing to his party's heavy losses in that year's midterm election.

Economic conditions play a large part in a president's public support. Economic downturns invariably reduce public confidence in the president.[39] Ford, Carter, and the first President Bush lost their reelection bids when their popularity plummeted after the economy dipped. In contrast, Clinton's popularity rose in 1995 and 1996 as the economy strengthened, contributing to his 1996 reelection. The irony, of course, is that presidents do not have all that much control over the economy. If they did, it would always be strong.

The Televised Presidency An advantage that presidents have in their efforts to nurture public support is their access to the media, particularly television. Only the president can expect the networks to provide free air time to address the nation, and in terms of the amount of news coverage, the presidency receives twice as much news coverage as Congress.

Political scientist Samuel Kernell calls it "going public" when the president bypasses bargaining with Congress and promotes "his policies by appealing to the American public for support."[40] Such appeals are at least as old as Theodore Roosevelt's use of the presidency as a "bully pulpit," but they have increased substantially in recent decades. Television has made it easier for presidents to go public with their programs, though the public's response depends partly on the president's rhetorical skill. President Reagan was so adept at the use of television that he was labeled the "Great Communicator."

Nevertheless, presidents are unable to control everything that reporters say about them.[41] Journalists are adept at putting their own spin on what political leaders say and tend to play up adverse developments. For example, although journalists give the president some credit when the economy is doing well, they heap blame on him when it is doing poorly. Presidents also get blamed for misconduct within the administration. In 2004, informed sources claimed that the Bush administration had targeted Iraq long before it ordered an invasion of that country. Even though there was no evidence linking Iraq to the terrorist attacks of September 11, 2001, Secretary of Defense Donald Rumsfeld reportedly wanted to bomb Iraq immediately thereafter. Rumsfeld was quoted by a White House insider

President Ronald Reagan became known as the "Great Communicator" because of his adept use of television. Reagan acquired many of his on-camera skills during his years as a movie and television actor.

as saying "There aren't any good targets in Afghanistan and there are lots of good targets in Iraq." The allegation was front-page news for days on end, putting the Bush administration on the defensive.

The Illusion of Presidential Government Presidents have no choice but to try to counter negative press portrayals by putting their own spin on developments. Such efforts can carry a president only so far, however. No president can fully control his communicated image, and national conditions ultimately have the largest impact on a president's public support. No amount of public relations can disguise adverse developments at home or abroad. Indeed, presidents run a risk by building up their images through public relations. By thrusting themselves into the limelight, presidents contribute to the public's belief that the president is in charge of the national government, a perception political scientist Hugh Heclo calls "the illusion of presidential government."[42] If they are as powerful as they project themselves to be, they will be held responsible for policy failures as well as policy successes.

Because the public's expectations are high, presidents get too much credit when things go well and too much blame when things go badly. Therein rests an irony of the presidential office. More than from any constitutional grant, more than from any statute, and more than from any crisis, presidential power derives from the president's position as the sole official who can claim to represent the entire American public. Yet because presidential power rests on a popular base, it erodes when public support declines. The irony is that the presidential office typically grows weaker as problems mount, which is the time when strong presidential leadership is needed most.[43]

SUMMARY Self-Test www.mhhe.com/pattersonwtp9e

The presidency has become a much stronger office than the framers envisioned. The Constitution grants the president substantial military, diplomatic, legislative, and executive powers, and in each case the president's authority has increased measurably over the nation's history. Underlying this change is the president's position as the one leader chosen by the whole nation and as the sole head of the executive branch. These features of the office have enabled presidents to claim broad authority in response to the increased demands placed on the federal government by changing global and national conditions.

During the course of American history, the presidential selection process has been altered in ways intended to make it more responsive to the preferences of ordinary people. Today, the electorate has a vote not only in the general election but also in the selection of party nominees. To gain nomination, a presidential hopeful must win the support of the electorate in state primaries and open caucuses. Once nominated, the candidates are eligible to receive federal funds for their general election campaigns, which today are based on Internet and televised appeals.

Although the campaign tends to personalize the presidency, the responsibilities of the modern presidency far exceed any president's personal capacities. To meet their obligations, presidents have surrounded themselves with large staffs of advisers, policy experts, and managers. These staff members enable the president to extend control over the executive branch while at the same time providing the information necessary for policymaking. All recent presidents have discovered, however, that their control of staff resources is incomplete and that some things that others do on their behalf can work against what they are trying to accomplish.

As sole chief executive and the nation's top elected leader, presidents can always expect that their policy and leadership efforts will receive attention. However, other institutions, particularly Congress, have the authority to make presidential leadership effective. No president has come close to winning approval of all the programs he has placed before Congress, and presidents' records of success have varied considerably. The factors in a president's success include whether national conditions that require strong leadership from the White House are present and whether the president's party has a majority in Congress.

Presidential success stems from the backing of the American people. Recent presidents have made extensive use of the media to build public support for their programs, yet they have had difficulty maintaining that support throughout their terms of office. A major reason is that the public expects far more from its presidents than they can deliver.

Key Terms

cabinet (*p. 431*)
honeymoon period (*p. 436*)
momentum (in campaigns) (*p. 422*)
open party caucuses (*p. 422*)
presidential approval ratings (*p. 443*)
stewardship theory (*p. 417*)
unit rule (*p. 425*)
Whig theory (*p. 417*)
White House Office (WHO) (*p. 431*)

Suggested Readings

Campbell, James E. *The American Campaign: U.S. Presidential Campaigns and the National Vote*. College Station: Texas A&M University Press, 2008. An analysis that reveals the predictability of presidential campaign outcomes.

Cohen, Jeffrey E. *The Presidency in the Era of 24-Hour News*. Princeton, N.J.: Princeton University Press, 2008. A look at how changes in the media have affected presidential communication and politics.

Hargrove, Erwin C. *The Effective Presidency*. Boulder, CO.: Paradigm Publishers, 2008. An assessment of presidential leadership through an examination of the Kennedy through George W. Bush presidencies.

Jones, Charles O. *The Presidency in a Separated System*. Washington, D.C.: Brookings Institution Press, 2005. A careful analysis of president-Congress relations.

Milkis, Sidney, and Michael Nelson. *The American Presidency: Origins and Development, 1776–2002*, 5th ed. Washington, D.C.: CQ Press, 2007. A thoughtful assessment of the factors and conditions that have molded the presidential office.

Neustadt, Richard E. *Presidential Power and the Modern Presidents: The Politics of Leadership from Roosevelt to Reagan*. New York: Free Press, 1990. The classic analysis of the limitations on presidential power.

Norrander, Barbara. *The Imperfect Primary: Oddities, Biases, and Strengths in U.S. Presidential Nomination Politics*. New York: Routledge, 2010. A thoughtful analysis of the nominating process.

Pika, Joseph A., and John Anthony Maltese. *The Politics of the Presidency*, 7th ed. Washington, D.C.: CQ Press, 2008. An insightful look at the leadership skills demanded of presidents.

Skowronek, Stephen. *Presidential Leadership in Political Time: Reprise and Reappraisal*. Lawrence: University of Kansas Press, 2008. An assessment of how conditions of the time have affected presidents' role and power.

List of Websites

www.ibiblio.org/lia/president A site with general information on specific presidents and links to the presidential libraries.

www.ipl.org/div/potus A site that profiles the nation's presidents, their cabinet officers, and key events during their time in office.

www.usa.gov A site that gives information on the presidency and the Executive Office of the President, as well as links to key executive agencies and organizations.

www.whitehouse.gov The White House's home page; has an e-mail guest book and includes information on the president, the vice president, and current White House activities.

Politics in Theory and Practice

Thinking: Why is presidential power "conditional"—that is, why is it affected so substantially by circumstance, the makeup of Congress, and popular support? (The separation of powers should be part of your answer.)

Participating: Consider writing a letter or sending an email to the president or a top presidential appointee that expresses your opinion on an issue that is currently the object of executive action. You can inform yourself about the administration's policy or stance on the issue through the website of the White House (www.whitehouse.gov) or of the agency in question (for example, the State Department's site, www.state.gov).

Extra Credit

For up-to-the-minute *New York Times* articles, interactive simulations, graphics, study tools, and more links and quizzes, visit the text's Online Learning Center at **www.mhhe.com/pattersonwtp9e**.

NATIONAL JOURNAL

Obama Finds Reality Is Messy

Audacious. Barack Obama would change the way politics happens in America. Youthful. He would usher in the temperament of a new generation. Smart. He would lead the country out of the thicket it had wandered into with such distressing results.

Have hope, Obama said. Change is coming.

Yeah, well. It hasn't been the finest of first years. But nor has it been, by any means, the worst. As a candidate, Obama said that people projected onto him what they wanted to see—they invested their hopes and expectations in this unusually cool and appealing politician. And now, as 2010 gets under way, they are still projecting because there has yet to be a climactic moment, a turn in the road, a major victory, a historic accomplishment. Or, to be sure, an abject failure.

A good number of Americans are now thrusting their worries and fears onto President Obama, rather than their hopes and dreams, but what everyone is doing is waiting to see how this turns out. The health care bill—pummeled and shaken up and overhauled and practically waterboarded in Congress—will be trumpeted as a signature achievement of the new administration. But does it inspire hope? Does the final product of such a gruesome sausage-making process hold the promise of more and better change to come?

"There isn't a sense of singular accomplishment," said Lee Miringoff, director of the Marist Poll. "What Obama needs is a few big wins. He needs to put some points on the board."

Obama's approval ratings in his first year have closely tracked those of Ronald Reagan, who also held out the promise of novelty and invigoration. Support for Obama soared after his election, particularly among people who hadn't voted for him. "A lot of people were kind of kicking the tires: Maybe this is a new day, maybe this is pretty amazing," said Ruy Teixeira, a senior fellow at the Center for American Progress. Now that support has fallen away again.

That's not a precarious situation to be in, especially when, like Reagan, Obama is personally more popular than his policies are. "This is someone who people want to succeed," Miringoff said. But Democrats, waiting for success, are growing restive. Some are dismayed by the escalation in Afghanistan, some by the compromises over health care, some by the way the administration has enabled Wall Street to flourish again.

"I think there is disappointment, particularly among young people, because things just don't seem all that different," Miringoff said. "Young people really thought they were going to get a shake-up of the system."

One possible counterargument is that real change takes time, especially if it is to include new voices. "Early on, people didn't understand the political process," Jeremy Bird, deputy national director of Organizing for America, the Obama volunteer group that now works for the Democratic National Committee, said of the rank-and-file Democrats who have been coming to meetings around the country. "People not in Washington have been shut out of that."

So part of his group's mission in 2009 was educational, he said: Here's the sausage, and this is how it got made. Bird predicted that his advocacy group will become an increasingly important player and an usher for change. "We're building a lasting infrastructure," he said, but he acknowledged that organizing to support a president's agenda is a lot harder than organizing a campaign.

The crucial turf lies in the suburbs, according to Teixeira. Obama will rise or fall depending on how he can do among America's biggest, and in many ways most skeptical, voting bloc. He won't win over the rural areas. And he has the cities locked up.

Away from the press's klieg lights, the administration has in fact been accomplishing quite a lot. Obama's team has taken dramatic steps to rewrite administrative regulations to take climate change into account. The Education Department has been promoting charter schools (not a traditional Democratic objective) and pushing a whole slew of reforms under the Race to the Top rubric. The Interior Department has been setting aside fairly vast amounts of federal land for habitat protection. The administration expanded the State Children's Health Insurance Program. It reformed student loans. It unleashed the Environmental Protection Agency to take action against greenhouse gases.

"We have a ton of hope," Bird said. "A lot of change has happened, and there's a lot of hope that more change is going to be able to happen."

Obama made one very big move directly in the glare of the spotlight when he took over Chrysler and General Motors to rescue them from bankruptcy. Then he fired GM's chief executive, Rick Wagoner. That bailout was change, no doubt about it. But it was change that didn't sit well with a lot of Americans. Today, Obama says that if he hadn't done something dramatic the auto industry would have died, but as Teixeira points out, "You just don't get enough credit for keeping things from falling off the shelf."

Everybody knows about Franklin Roosevelt's first 100 days in office and the passage of 15 major pieces of legislation that became the foundation of the New Deal. Everybody also knows that neither Obama nor any other contemporary president could ever hope to match that record. The good news of 1933 didn't end with that first 100 days, however.

Roosevelt had the advantage of taking office just as the country's economic collapse was bottoming out. Millions of Americans earnestly believed that desperate measures were called for, and they understood how much was at stake. In spring 1933, unemployment was 25 percent; Roosevelt immediately began putting people back to work. On October 22, William Green, the president of the American Federation of Labor, reported that 3.6 million jobs had been added since the inauguration.

Obama can only wish for such a welcome string of events.

Not only is the economy still in pretty bad shape, relatively speaking, but people are starting to lose faith in its stewards, whatever the statistics might say. A year ago there was general alarm, but as Obama took office, polls showed that a strong majority of Americans approved of his handling of the economy. In October, public disapproval outpaced approval for the first time, and the gap has continued to widen since then as unemployment remains high. These aren't desperate times, like 1933, but they're bad enough to make folks pretty cranky. At some point, the improvements already under way in the economy are bound to show. But how soon and how dramatically, no one knows.

FDR enjoyed outfoxing the Republicans. Of course, he had substantial majorities in both chambers of Congress. But in the undiluted partisanship of modern-day Washington, Obama seems less able, or less inclined, to engage in give-and-take with the other party. And this leads to a conundrum: If Obama is to change the way Washington does business, what does that mean? Steamrolling the Republicans? Or working with them?

As opposed to domestic politics, foreign policy provides presidents more leeway to act and less chance of harming their image. An administration's approach to Burma isn't going to sway too many voters on Election Day. But a cumulative impression can build—of competence, or of the reverse. Obama might be maneuvering patiently toward a resolution of the disputes with Iran or North Korea, or of the Middle East troubles. Or he might be pursuing false leads. So far, not much to point to. The Republicans are trying to portray him as naive and outwitted by foreign adversaries, but it's a minor complaint amid joblessness, a mortgage crisis, mounting debt, and health care reform.

All but forgotten today is that Jimmy Carter began his presidency with a string of foreign-policy successes, James Lindsay of the Council on Foreign Relations said. He sponsored the Camp David Accords, concluded the Panama Canal Treaty, and opened formal ties to China. The economy, however, made him unpopular—and then came 1979, bringing the Iranian revolution and the Soviet invasion of Afghanistan, two events largely out of Carter's control, but both helping to doom his re-election effort.

Thirty years later, Iran and Afghanistan are still giant headaches for the White House, and the Middle East and China remain major concerns. Only Panama is quiet today.

"These are problems that have been going on for a long time because we don't know how to solve them," Lindsay said. "Obama's misfortune is that they might come to a head on his watch." And it's quite clear, Lindsay continued, that despite support for the Afghanistan troop surge, Americans otherwise don't have an appetite for any more foreign adventures.

In a way, it's part of the usual chasm between running for office and then actually governing, a chasm that stems from the delightful reality that candidates don't have to make hard decisions. And in Obama's case, that chasm is just a bit wider than for most, Miringoff said. "Running against a failed incumbent's policy by promising change doesn't necessarily tell you what it's going to look like," he said. Americans turn to Obama and see too much change, too little change, or perhaps the wrong kind of change. They're still looking for the definitive moment of change.

One day in December, Robert Gibbs, the White House press secretary, defended at his daily briefing Obama's meeting with bankers and promised that it would help lead to financial reform in 2010.

"Did all the world's problems get solved today?" Gibbs asked. "I can tell you guys, no. But I can tell you this: The president is going to get financial reform."

The fact is, change is hard. A study of presidential Inaugural Addresses by the Miller Center of Public Affairs at the University of Virginia found that "hope" is Republican and "change" is Democratic. That is, William Howard Taft talked a lot about hope when he was sworn in, and so did Dwight Eisenhower and George H.W. Bush and Calvin Coolidge. Bill Clinton and Lyndon Johnson mentioned change more than any other 20th-century presidents. They got some—Johnson a lot more than Clinton—but it was a tough slog all the way. Republicans sought to inspire. Democrats sought to transform.

Obama dwelt on neither hope nor change in his Inaugural Address, judging by literal word count. His handful of scattered references to those concepts put him on a par with another Democrat—none other than Franklin Roosevelt, in that dark spring of 1933. So maybe it's not the rhetoric or the sloganeering that counts in the end. Maybe it's the results.

What's Your Opinion?

How would you rate President Obama's first two years in office? What impact does his domestic and foreign policy have on this overall grade?

Explain the analogy the article makes between the health care bill and a sausage. What is the author saying about the legislative process?

CHAPTER 13

The Federal Bureaucracy: Administering the Government

> "From a purely technical point of view, a bureaucracy is capable of attaining the highest degree of efficiency, and is in this sense formally the most rational known means of exercising authority over human beings."
>
> Max Weber[1]

On April 20, 2010, as the *Deepwater Horizon* was drilling an exploratory oil well nearly a mile deep in the Gulf of Mexico, methane gas shot out from the drilling pipe and exploded, engulfing the oil platform in flames, killing eleven workers and forcing the rest to jump into the rig's lifeboats. Two days later, still aflame, the *Deepwater Horizon* sank, collapsing the drilling pipe, which sent oil from the well gushing into the Gulf. Nearly three months elapsed before the oil well could be capped, resulting in the worst environmental disaster in the nation's history. The resulting oil spill forced closure of much of the Gulf to

The Gulf of Mexico oil spill in 2010 was caused primarily by carelessness and corner cutting on the part of the oil firm BP, but a government agency, the Minerals Management Service (MMS), had a hand in the disaster. MMS had failed in its responsibility to closely regulate offshore drilling operations.

fishing, damaged hundreds of miles of beaches and wetlands, and killed unknown quantities of marine life.

The U.S. government blamed the disaster on the oil firm BP, which owned the drilling rights and was supervising the ill-fated drilling operation. But the government itself had a hand in the disaster. Oversight of offshore drilling was the responsibility of the Minerals Management Service (MMS), a bureau within the Department of the Interior. MMS had been lax, or worse, in its responsibilities. Rather than closely regulating offshore drilling, top MMS managers had given oil companies wide latitude in meeting safety and environmental standards. When this information became known in the days following the sinking of the *Deepwater Horizon*, MMS's top officials were forced to resign and a reorganization of MMS was undertaken. In announcing this action, President Barack Obama said: "For a decade or more, the cozy relationship between the oil companies and the federal agency was allowed to go unchecked. That allowed drilling permits to be issued in exchange not for safety plans, but assurances of safety from oil companies. That cannot and will not happen anymore."

Government agencies are seldom in the headlines unless they slip up, as in the case of MMS. Indeed, no federal institution ranks lower in public esteem than the bureaucracy. Even though most Americans have a favorable impression of their most recent encounter with the federal bureaucracy (as, for example, when a senior citizen applies for social security), they have a low opinion of the bureaucracy as a whole. A Pew Research Center poll found, for example, that roughly two-thirds of Americans believe that government programs are "usually inefficient and wasteful."

Yet, ambitious programs like space exploration, social security, interstate highways, and universal postal service would not be possible if the federal government lacked a bureaucracy. Bureaucracy is found wherever there is a need to manage large numbers of people and tasks. The usefulness of the bureaucratic form is clear from the fact that virtually every large private organization is also a bureaucracy, although such organizations typically operate by a different standard than do most public organizations. Efficiency is the chief goal of private organizations but is only sometimes the goal of public organizations. The most efficient way to administer government loans to college students, for instance, would be to give money to the first students who apply and then shut down the program when the money runs out. College loan programs, like many other government programs, operate on the principles of fairness and need, which require that each application be judged on its merit.

In formal terms, **bureaucracy** is a system of organization and control that is based on three principles: hierarchical authority, job specialization, and formalized rules. These features are the reason bureaucracy, as a form of organization, is the most efficient means of getting people to work together on tasks of large magnitude. **Hierarchical authority** refers to a chain of command whereby the officials and units at the top of a bureaucracy have authority over those in the middle, who in turn control those at the bottom. Hierarchy speeds action by reducing conflict over the power to make decisions: those higher in the organization have authority over those below them. **Job specialization** refers to explicitly defined duties for each job position and to a precise division of labor within the organization. Specialization yields efficiency because each individual concentrates on a particular job and becomes proficient at the tasks it involves. **Formalized rules** are the established procedures and regulations by which a bureaucracy conducts its operations. Formalized rules enable workers to make quick and consistent judgments because decisions are based on preset rules rather than on a case-by-case basis.

The noted German sociologist Max Weber (1864–1920) was the first scholar to systematically analyze the bureaucratic form of organization. Weber concluded that bureaucratic efficiency is achieved at a high price. He noted that bureaucracy forces employees to behave as rational actors. Their behavior is dictated by position, specialty, and rule. In the process, they become insensitive to circumstance, as anyone who has applied for a driver's license knows all too well. "Specialists without spirit," was Weber's unflattering description of the bureaucratic mindset.[2]

This chapter examines both the need for bureaucracy and the problems associated with it. The chapter describes the bureaucracy's responsibilities, organizational structure, and management practices. The chapter also explains the "politics" of the bureaucracy. Although the three constitutional branches of government impose a degree of accountability on the bureaucracy, its sheer size confounds their efforts to control it fully. The main points discussed in this chapter are these:

- *Bureaucracy is an inevitable consequence of complexity and scale.* Modern government could not function without a large bureaucracy. Through authority, specialization, and rules, bureaucracy provides a means of managing thousands of tasks and employees.
- *Bureaucrats naturally take an "agency point of view," seeking to promote their agency's programs and power.* They do this through their expert knowledge, support from clientele groups, and backing by Congress or the president.
- *Although agencies are subject to oversight by the president, Congress, and the judiciary, bureaucrats exercise considerable power in their own right.*

Origin and Structure of the Federal Bureaucracy

The federal bureaucracy was initially small (three thousand employees in 1800, for instance). The federal government's role was confined largely to defense and foreign affairs, currency and interstate commerce, and the delivery of the mail. In the latter part of the 1800s, the bureaucracy began to grow rapidly in size (see Figure 13-1), largely because economic growth was generating new demands on government. Farmers were among the groups clamoring for help, and Congress in 1889 created the Department of Agriculture. Business and labor interests also pressed their claims, and Congress in 1903 established the Department of Commerce and Labor. (A decade later, the department was split into separate commerce and labor departments.) The biggest spurt in the bureaucracy's growth, however, took place in the 1930s. Franklin D. Roosevelt's New Deal included creation of the Securities and Exchange Commission (SEC), the Social Security Administration (SSA), the Federal Deposit Insurance Corporation (FDIC), the Tennessee Valley Authority (TVA), and numerous other federal agencies. Three decades later, Lyndon Johnson's Great Society initiatives, which thrust the federal government into policy areas traditionally

figure 13-1 NUMBER OF FULL-TIME FEDERAL EMPLOYEES

The federal bureaucracy grew slowly until the 1930s, when an explosive growth began in the number of programs that required ongoing administration by the federal government. *Source: Historical Statistics of the United States and Statistical Abstract of the United States, 1986*, 322; recent figures from U.S. Office of Personnel Management. Figure excludes uniformed military personnel.

dominated by the states, resulted in the creation of additional federal agencies, including the Department of Transportation and the Department of Housing and Urban Development.

Federal employment has not changed markedly since the 1960s. This fact is deceiving, however, in that the federal government has increasingly contracted some of its work to privately owned firms. At an earlier time, for example, the U.S. armed forces operated their own food services. Today, these services are operated primarily by private firms.

Types of Federal Agencies

At present, the U.S. federal bureaucracy has about 2.5 million employees, who have responsibility for administering thousands of programs. The president and Congress get far more attention in the news, but the federal bureaucracy has a more direct impact on Americans' everyday lives. It performs a wide range of functions; for example, it delivers the daily mail, oversees the national forests, administers social security, enforces environmental protection laws, maintains the country's defense systems, provides foodstuffs for school lunch programs, operates the airport flight-control systems, and regulates the stock markets.

The U.S. federal bureaucracy is organized along policy lines. One agency handles veterans' affairs, another specializes in education, a third is responsible for agriculture, and so on. No two units are exactly alike.

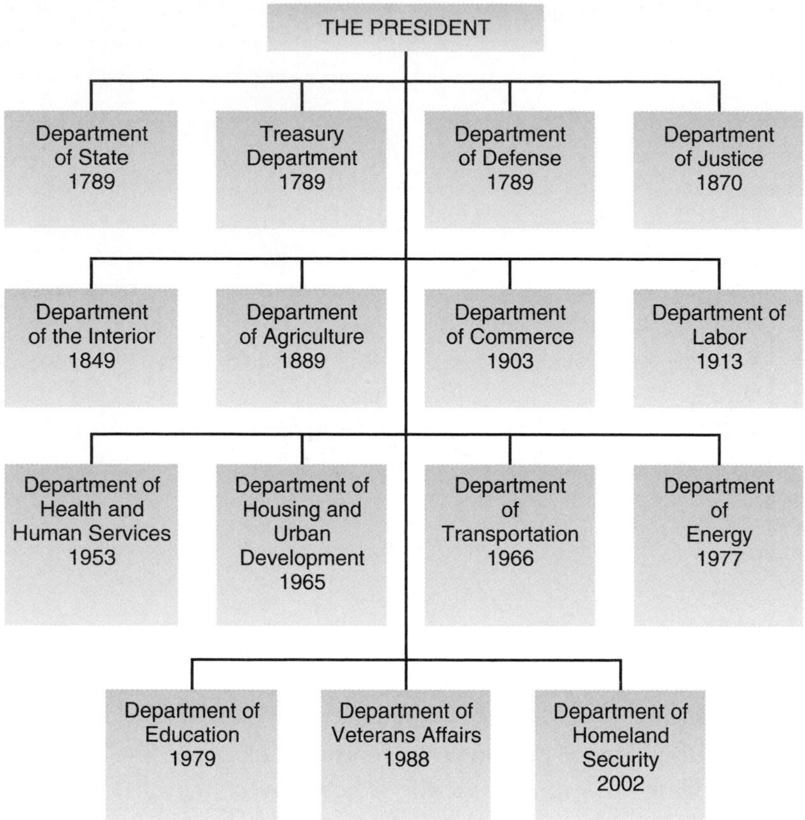

figure 13-2 CABINET (EXECUTIVE) DEPARTMENTS

Each executive department is responsible for a general policy area and is headed by a secretary or, in the case of Justice, the attorney general, who serves as a member of the president's cabinet. Shown is each department's year of origin. (The Office of the Attorney General was created in 1789 and became the Justice Department in 1870.)

Nevertheless, most of them take one of five forms: cabinet department, independent agency, regulatory agency, government corporation, or presidential commission.

The leading administrative units are the fifteen **cabinet (executive) departments** (see Figure 13-2). Except for the Department of Justice, which is led by the attorney general, the head of each department is its secretary (for example, the secretary of defense), who also serves as a member of the president's cabinet. Cabinet departments vary greatly in their visibility, size, and importance. The Department of State, one of the oldest and most prestigious departments, is also one of the smallest, with approximately 25,000 employees. The Department of Defense has the largest workforce, with more than 600,000 civilian employees (apart from the more than 1.4 million uniformed active service members). The Department of Health and Human Services has the largest budget; its activities account for more than a fourth of all federal spending, much of it in the form of social security and Medicaid payments. The Department of Homeland Security is the newest department, dating from 2002.

Each cabinet department has responsibility for a general policy area, such as defense or law enforcement. This responsibility is carried out within each department by semiautonomous operating units that typically carry the label "bureau," "agency," "division," or "service." The Department of Justice, for example, has thirteen such operating units, including the Federal Bureau of Investigation (FBI), the Civil Rights Division, the Tax Division, and the Drug Enforcement Administration (DEA).

Independent agencies resemble the cabinet departments but typically have a narrower area of responsibility. They include organizations such as the Central Intelligence Agency (CIA) and the National Aeronautics and Space Administration (NASA). The heads of these agencies are appointed by and report to the president but are not members of the cabinet. In general, the independent agencies exist apart from cabinet departments because their placement within a department would pose symbolic or practical problems. NASA, for example, could conceivably be located in the Department of Defense, but such positioning would suggest that the space program exists solely for military purposes and not also for civilian purposes, such as space exploration and satellite communication.

Regulatory agencies are created when Congress recognizes the need for ongoing regulation of a particular economic activity. Examples of such agencies are the Securities and Exchange Commission (SEC), which oversees the stock and bond markets, and the Environmental Protection Agency (EPA), which regulates industrial pollution. In addition to their administrative function, regulatory agencies have a legislative function and a judicial function. They develop law-like regulations and then judge whether individuals or organizations are complying with them. The EPA, for example, can impose fines and other penalties on business firms that violate environmental regulations.

Government corporations are similar to private corporations in that they charge clients for their services and are governed by a board of directors. However, government corporations receive federal funding to help defray operating expenses, and their directors are appointed by the president with Senate approval. Government corporations include the Federal Deposit Insurance Corporation (FDIC), which insures individuals' savings accounts against bank failures, and the National Railroad

Passenger Corporation (Amtrak), which provides passenger rail service. The largest government corporation is the U.S. Postal Service, with roughly 700,000 employees. The postal service was established when the nation was founded, making it one of the oldest federal agencies. It delivers a first-class letter for the same low price to any postal address in the United States, a policy made possible by its status as a government corporation. If the postal service were privatized, the price of a first-class stamp would be much higher and would vary by location, with sparsely populated rural areas paying extremely high rates.

Presidential commissions provide advice to the president. Some of them are permanent bodies; examples include the Commission on Civil Rights and the Commission on Fine Arts. Other presidential commissions are temporary and disband after making recommendations on specific issues. An example is the President's Commission to Strengthen Social Security, which was created by President George W. Bush in 2001 to study ways of reforming social security.

Federal Employment

The roughly 2.5 million full-time civilian employees of the federal government include professionals who bring their expertise to the problems involved in governing a large and complex society, service workers who perform such tasks as the typing of correspondence and the delivery of mail, and middle and top managers who supervise the work of the various federal agencies. Most civil servants are hired through the government's **merit system**, whereby they have to score high on a competitive exam (as in the case of postal service, civil service, and foreign service employees) or have specialized training (as in the case of lawyers, engineers, and scientists). The merit system is overseen by two independent agencies. The Office of Personnel Management supervises the hiring and job classification of federal employees. The Merit Service Protection Board hears appeals from career civil servants who have been fired or face other disciplinary action.

The merit system is an alternative to the **patronage system** that governed federal employment during much of the nineteenth century. Patronage was the post-election practice of filling administrative offices with people who had supported the winning party. In the view of President Andrew Jackson, its chief advocate, the patronage system was a way to tie the administration of government to the people it served. Later presidents extended patronage to all levels of administration without much regard for its impact on the quality of administration, which led critics to label

HOW THE 50 STATES DIFFER
POLITICAL THINKING THROUGH COMPARISONS

The Size of State Bureaucracies

Although the federal bureaucracy is often criticized as being "too big," it is actually smaller on a per-capita basis than even the smallest state bureaucracy. There are 83 federal employees for every 1,000 Americans. Illinois, with 103 state employees for every 1,000 residents, has the smallest state bureaucracy on a per-capita basis. Hawaii has the largest—428 state employees per 1,000 residents.

Q: *What do the states with larger per-capita bureaucracies have in common?*

A: *In general, the less populous states, especially those that cover a large geographical area, have larger bureaucracies on a per-capita basis. This pattern reflects the fact that a state, whatever its population or area, must perform basic functions (such as highway maintenance and policing).*

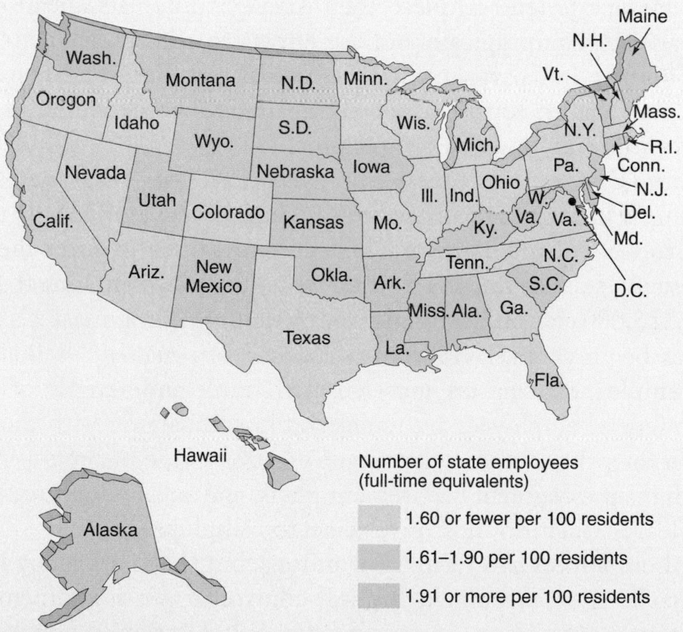

Source: U.S. Census Bureau, 2010.

it a **spoils system**—a device for the awarding of government jobs to friends and party hacks. In any case, as the federal government grew in size and complexity, the need for a more skilled workforce emerged. In 1883, Congress passed the Pendleton Act, which established a merit system for certain positions. By 1885, roughly 10 percent of federal positions were filled on a merit basis. The proportion increased sharply when the Progressives championed the merit system as a way of eliminating partisan corruption (see Chapter 2). By 1920, as the Progressive Era was concluding, more than 70 percent of federal employees were merit appointees. Today, they make up more than 90 percent of the federal workforce.[3] (Among the nonmerit employees are patronage appointees, who include those holding presidential and congressional staff positions—see Chapters 11 and 12.)

The administrative objective of the merit system is **neutral competence.**[4] A merit-based bureaucracy is "competent" in the sense that employees are hired and retained on the basis of their skills, and it is "neutral" in the sense that employees are not partisan appointees and are expected to be of service to everyone, not just those who support the incumbent president. Although the merit system contributes to impartial and proficient administration, it has its own biases and inefficiencies. Career bureaucrats tend to place their agency's interests ahead of those of other agencies and typically oppose efforts to trim their agency's programs. They are not partisans in a Democratic or Republican sense, but they are partisans in terms of protecting their own agencies, as will be explained more fully later in the chapter.

The large majority of federal employees have a GS (Graded Service) job ranking. The regular civil service rankings range from GS-1 (the lowest rank) to GS-15 (the highest). College graduates who enter the federal service usually start at the GS-5 level, which provides an annual salary of roughly $27,000 for a beginning employee. With a master's degree, employees begin at level GS-9 with a salary of roughly $40,000 a year. Federal employees' salaries increase with rank and length of service. Although federal employees are underpaid in comparison with their counterparts in the private sector, they receive better fringe benefits—including full health insurance, secure retirement plans, and substantial vacation time and sick leave—than do most private-sector employees.

Federal employees can form labor unions, but their unions by law have limited scope; the government has full control of job assignments, compensation, and promotion. Moreover, the Taft-Hartley Act of 1947 prohibits strikes by federal employees and permits the firing of striking workers. When federal air traffic controllers went on strike anyway in

1981, President Reagan fired them. There are also limits on the partisan activities of civil servants. The Hatch Act of 1939 prohibited them from holding key jobs in election campaigns. Congress relaxed this prohibition in 1993, although some high-ranking administrators are still barred from taking such positions.

The Budgetary Process

The Constitution mentions executive agencies but does not grant them authority. Their authority derives from grants of power to the three constitutional branches: Congress, the president, and the courts.

Particularly important for executive agencies is the **budgetary process**, which is the process through which annual federal spending and revenue determinations are made. It is no exaggeration to say that agencies live and die by the outcome of the budgetary process. No agency or program can exist without funding. Although agencies play an active role in the budgetary process, the elected branches have final authority over the budget. The Constitution grants Congress the power to tax and spend, but the president, as chief executive, also helps shape the budget (see Chapter 12). In reality, the budgetary process involves give-and-take between Congress and the president as each tries to influence how federal funding will be distributed among various agencies and programs.[5] From beginning to end, the budgetary process lasts a year and a half (see Figure 13-3).

The President and Agency Budgets

The budgetary process begins in the executive branch when the president, in consultation with the Office of Management and Budget (OMB), establishes general budget guidelines. OMB is part of the Executive Office of the President (see Chapter 12) and takes its directives from the president. Hundreds of agencies are covered by the budget, and OMB uses the president's directives to issue guidelines for each agency's budget preparations. Each agency, for example, is assigned a budget ceiling that it cannot exceed in developing its budget proposal.

The agencies receive their guidelines in the spring and then work through the summer to create a detailed agency budget, taking into account their existing programs and new proposals. Agency budgets are then submitted to OMB in September for a full review that invariably includes further consultation with each agency and the White House. OMB then finalizes the agency budgets and combines them into the president's budget proposal.

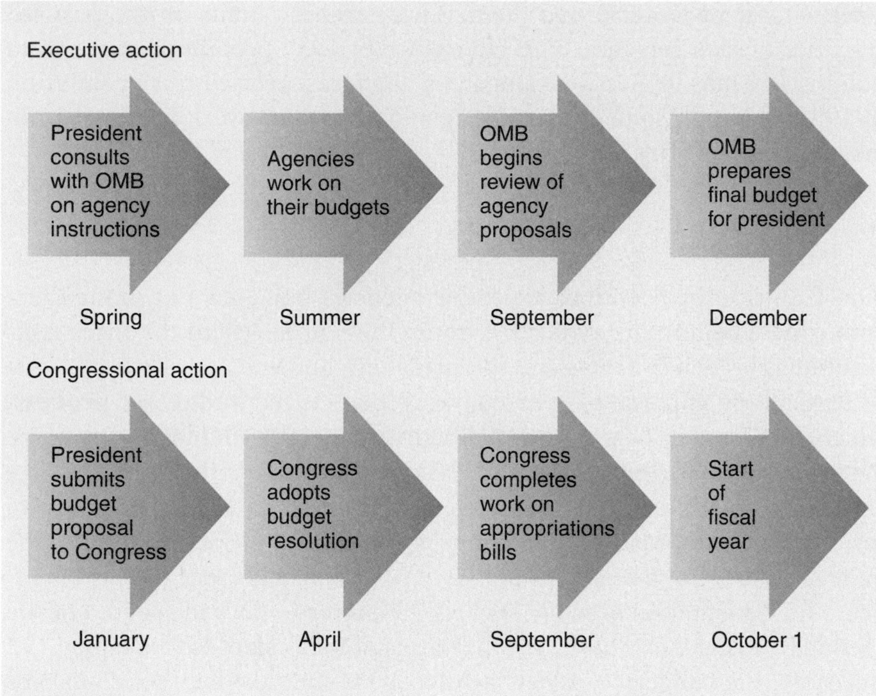

figure 13-3 FEDERAL BUDGETARY PROCESS

The budget begins with the president's instructions to the agencies and ends when Congress enacts the budget. The entire process spans about eighteen months.

The agencies naturally seek additional funding for their programs, whereas OMB has the job of matching the budget to the president's priorities. However, the president does not have any real say over most of the budget, about two-thirds of which involves mandatory spending. This spending is required by law, as in the case of social security payments to retirees. The president has no authority to suspend or reduce such payments. Accordingly, OMB focuses on the one-third of the budget that involves discretionary spending, which includes spending on defense, foreign aid, education, national parks, space exploration, and highways. In reality, even a large part of this spending is not truly discretionary. No president would slash defense spending to almost nothing or cut off funding for the national parks.

The president, then, works on the margins of the budget. In most policy areas, the president will propose a modest spending increase or decrease over the previous year. There are always a few areas, however, where the president will seek a substantial adjustment. In his 2010 budget, for example, President Barack Obama requested an additional $45 billion in defense spending to support a troop increase in Afghanistan.

Congress and the Agency Budgets

In January, the president's budget is submitted to Congress. During its work on the budget, the president's recommendations undergo varying degrees of change. Congress has constitutional authority over government spending and its priorities are never exactly the same as the president's, even when the congressional majority is of the same political party. When it is of the opposite party, its priorities will differ substantially from those of the president.

Upon reaching Congress, the president's budget proposal goes to the House and Senate budget committees. Their job is to recommend overall spending and revenue levels. Once approved by the full House and Senate, the levels are a constraint on the rest of Congress's work on the budget.

The House and Senate appropriations committees take over at this point. The House Appropriations Committee through its thirteen subcommittees reviews the budget, which includes hearings with officials from each federal agency. Each subcommittee has responsibility for a particular substantive area, such as defense or agriculture. A subcommittee may cut an agency's budget if it concludes that the agency is overfunded or may increase the budget if it concludes that the agency is underfunded. The subcommittees' recommendations are then reviewed by the House Appropriations Committee as a whole. The budget is also reviewed by the Senate Appropriations Committee and its subcommittees. However, the Senate is a smaller body, and its review of agency requests is less exacting than that of the House. To a degree, the Senate Appropriations Committee serves as a "court of last resort" for agencies that have had their funding requests cut by OMB or by the House Appropriations Committee.

Throughout this process, members of the House and Senate rely on the Congressional Budget Office, which, as discussed in Chapter 11, is the congressional equivalent of OMB. If the Congressional Budget Office believes that OMB or an agency has miscalculated the amount of money needed to carry out its mandated programs, it will alert Congress to the discrepancy.

After the House and Senate appropriations committees have completed their work, they submit their recommendations to the full chambers for a vote. If approved by a majority in the House and in the Senate, differences in the Senate and House versions are then reconciled in conference committee (see Chapter 11). The reconciled version of the budget is then voted upon in the House and Senate and, if approved, is sent to the president to sign or veto. The threat of a presidential veto can be enough to persuade Congress to accept many of the president's recommendations. In the end, the budget inevitably reflects both presidential and congressional priorities. Neither branch gets everything it wants, but each branch always gets some of what it seeks.

POLITICAL THINKING

Balanced Budget, Good Idea or Bad Idea?

A constitutional amendment to require a balanced federal budget has been proposed from time to time. The amendment would force lawmakers to bring spending and revenues into line each year. Do you think a balanced budget amendment is a good idea? Would you make an exception in time of war or economic recession? If such an amendment were enacted, what spending cuts and tax increases would you like to see in order to balance the budget?

After the budget has been signed by the president, it takes effect on October 1, the starting date of the federal government's fiscal year. If agreement on the budget has not been reached by October 1, temporary funding legislation is required in order to maintain government operations. In late 1995, President Clinton and the Republican Congress deadlocked on budgetary issues to such an extent that they could not even agree on temporary funding. Their standoff twice forced a brief shutdown of nonessential government activities, such as the national parks.

Policy and Power in the Bureaucracy

Administrative agencies' main task is **policy implementation**—that is, the carrying out of decisions made by Congress, the president, and the courts. This task occurs for the most part within the confines of the federal budget; agencies are limited to the level of funding that has been appropriated for particular activities. Implementation is relatively straightforward in the case of agencies that are charged with the delivery of services—carrying the mail, processing welfare applications, approving government loans, and the like. Such activities are governed by rules, and in most instances the rules determine what gets done.

Nevertheless, agency employees have discretionary authority in many areas. The bureaucracy is far more than an administrative extension of the three branches. Administrative agencies make policy in the process of determining how to implement congressional, presidential, and judicial decisions. FBI agents, for example, pursue organized crime more vigorously than they pursue white-collar crime, even though the law does not say that white-collar crime should be pursued less aggressively.[6] The U.S. Forest Service provides another example. It is required by law to employ a "dual use" policy of forest land—preserving the forests as an environmental heritage while also opening up the forests for harvesting by lumber companies. The Forest Service's decisions have sometimes favored environmental interests and at other times have favored logging interests. The Federal Communications Commission (FCC) provides a third example.

The U.S. Postal Service is regarded by analysts as the best entity of its kind anywhere. It delivers more mail to more addresses than any other postal administration in the world, and does so inexpensively and without undue delay. Yet, like many other government agencies, it is often criticized for its inefficiency and ineptness.

It has a broad mandate under the Federal Communication Act to regulate various forms of communication. On its own authority, it has developed different regulatory regimes for telephones, broadcast television, cable television, and the Internet. For a lengthy period, for example, the FCC required broadcasters to adhere to a fairness standard; if they aired one side of a political issue, they were also required to air opposing sides. The FCC later rescinded this doctrine. Both of these FCC rulings were based on the same legislative act. Such *rulemaking*—determining how a law will work in practice—is the chief way administrative agencies exercise control over policy.[7]

In the course of their work, administrators also develop policy ideas that they then propose to the White House or Congress. The origin of the Occupational Safety and Health Act is an example. A bureaucrat believed that worker safety was not receiving enough attention and encouraged his brother, a presidential speechwriter, to bring it to the attention of the White House. Department of Labor officials then picked up the issue, as did some labor unions and members of Congress. When the legislation was under consideration by congressional committees, bureaucrats who had pressed for the creation of an occupational safety and health program were among those invited to testify.[8]

In sum, administrators initiate policy, develop it, evaluate it, apply it, and decide whether others are complying with it. The bureaucracy does not simply administer policy. It also *makes* policy.

The Agency Point of View

A key issue about bureaucratic policymaking is the perspective that bureaucrats bring to their decisions. Do they operate from the perspective of the president? Or do they operate from the perspective of Congress? The answer is that, although bureaucrats are responsive to both of them, they are even more responsive to the needs of the agency in which they work, a perspective called the **agency point of view**. This outlook comes naturally to most high-ranking civil servants. More than 80 percent of top bureaucrats reach their high-level positions by rising through the ranks of the same agency.[9] As one top administrator said when testifying before the House Appropriations Committee, "Mr. Chairman, you would not think it proper for me to be in charge of this work and not be enthusiastic about it . . . would you? I have been in it for thirty years, and I believe in it."[10] One study found, for example, that social welfare administrators are three times as likely as other civil servants to believe that social welfare programs should be a top spending priority.[11]

Professionalism also cements agency loyalties. High-level administrative positions have increasingly been filled by scientists, engineers, lawyers, educators, physicians, and other professionals. Most of them take a job in an agency whose mission they support, as in the case of the aeronautical engineers who work for NASA or the doctors who work for the National Institutes of Health (NIH).

Although the agency point of view distorts government priorities, bureaucrats have little choice but to look out for their agency's interests. The president and members of Congress differ in their constituencies and thus in the agencies to which they are most responsive. Republican and Democratic officials also differ in their priorities. If an agency is to operate successfully in this partisan system of divided power, it must seek support wherever it can find it. If the agency is a low priority for the president, it needs to find backing in Congress. If Republican lawmakers want to cut the agency's programs, it must turn to Democratic lawmakers for support. In other words, agencies are forced to play politics if they want to protect their programs.[12] An agency that sits on the sidelines while other agencies seek support from the White House and Congress is likely to lose out in budget negotiations.

Sources of Bureaucratic Power

In promoting their agency's interests, bureaucrats rely on their specialized knowledge, the support of interests that benefit from their programs, and the backing of the president and Congress.

The Power of Expertise Most of the policy problems confronting the federal government are extraordinarily complex. Whether the problem relates to space travel or hunger in America, a solution requires deep knowledge of the problem. Much of this expertise is provided by bureaucrats. They spend their careers working in a particular policy area, and many of them have had scientific, technical, or other specialized training (see "How the U.S. Differs").[13] Elected officials, on the other hand, are generalists, none more so than the president, who must deal with dozens of issues. Members of Congress acquire some expertise through their committee work, but most of them lack the time, training, or inclination to become deeply knowledgeable of the issues they handle. Not surprisingly, Congress and the president rely heavily on career administrators for policy advice.

All agencies acquire some influence over policy through their careerists' expertise. No matter how simple a policy issue may appear at first, it nearly always has layers of complexity. The recognition that the United

HOW THE U.S. DIFFERS

POLITICAL THINKING THROUGH COMPARISONS

Educational Backgrounds of Bureaucrats

To staff its bureaucracy, the U.S. government tends to hire persons with specialized educations to hold specialized jobs. This approach heightens the tendency of bureaucrats to take the agency point of view. By comparison, Great Britain tends to recruit its bureaucrats from the arts and humanities, on the assumption that general aptitude is the best qualification for detached professionalism. The continental European democracies also emphasize detached professionalism, but in the context of the supposedly impartial application of rules. As a consequence, high-ranking civil servants in Europe tend to have legal educations. The college majors of senior civil servants in the United States and other democracies reflect these tendencies.

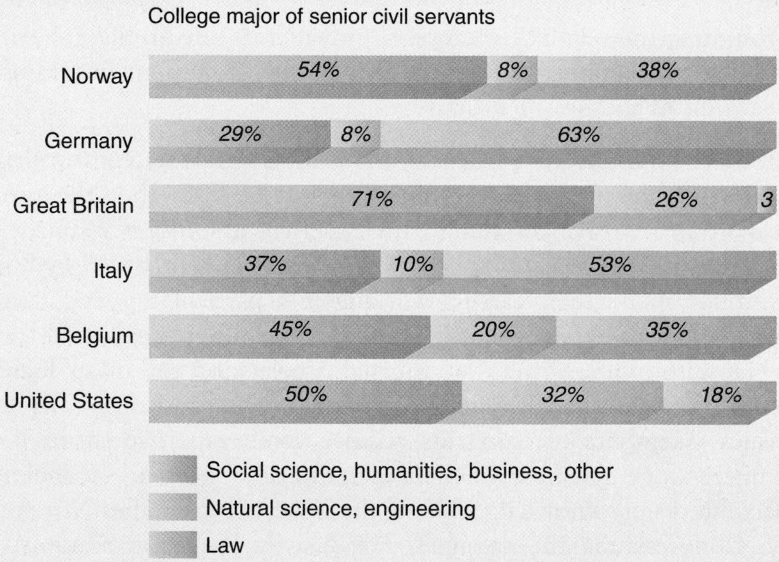

Source: Adapted from *The Politics of Bureaucracy*, 5th ed., by B. Guy Peters. Copyright 2001 by Routledge. Reprinted by permission of International Thomson Publishing Services.

Q: *Why might the hiring pattern for the U.S. bureaucracy make it more likely that civil servants in the United States will take an agency point of view than will civil servants in some other democracies?*

A: *Compared with the bureaucracies of other western democracies, the U.S. bureaucracy has a higher proportion of employees with a specialized education. They tend to take jobs in agencies where their specialty is particularly desirable, as in the case of the aeronautical engineers who work at NASA. Accordingly, their training would incline them to support their agency's mission—the agency point of view. European civil servants are more likely to have a type of education, as in the case of law or the humanities, that is less specific to the work of a particular agency, which presumably would make them less likely to deeply embrace their agency's mission.*

States has a trade deficit with China, for example, can be the premise for policy change, but this recognition does not begin to address basic issues such as the form the new policy might take, its probable cost and effectiveness, and its links to other issues, such as America's standing in Asia. Among the officials most likely to understand these issues are the career bureaucrats in the Treasury Department, the Department of State, the Commerce Department, and the Federal Trade Commission.

The Power of Clientele Groups Most federal agencies were created for the purpose of promoting, protecting, or regulating a particular interest. Indeed, nearly every major interest in society—commerce, labor, agriculture, banking, and so on—has a corresponding federal agency. In most cases, these interests are **clientele groups** in the sense that they benefit directly from the agency's programs. As a result, clientele groups can be counted on to lobby Congress and the president on behalf of the agency when its programs and funding are being reviewed.[14] Even a relatively weak or loosely organized clientele group can be of help to an agency if its programs—and therefore, the group's benefits—are threatened with cuts or elimination. When House Speaker Newt Gingrich threatened in 1995 to "zero out" funding for the Corporation for Public Broadcasting, Congress was inundated by complaints from the listeners of National Public Radio (NPR) and the viewers of the Public Broadcasting System (PBS). They claimed that programs like *Sesame Street* and *All Things Considered* were irreplaceable. Within a few weeks, Gingrich had retreated from his position, saying that a total funding cut was not what he had in mind.

The popular children's program *Sesame Street* is produced through the Corporation for Public Broadcasting, a government agency that gains leverage in budgetary deliberations from its public support. Shown here in a photo of a display at the Smithsonian National Museum of American History is Oscar the Grouch, a *Sesame Street* puppet whose home is a garbage can.

The relationship between an agency and its clientele group is a reciprocal one. Just as a clientele group can be expected to protect its agency, the agency will work to protect the group.[15] The Department of Agriculture, for instance, is a dependable ally of farm interests year after year. The same cannot be said of the president or Congress as a whole, which must balance farmers' demands against those of other groups.

The Power of Friends in High Places Although the goals of the president or Congress can conflict with those of the bureaucracy, they need it as much as it needs them. An agency's resources—its programs, expertise, and group support—can help elected officials achieve their policy goals. When President Obama early in his presidency announced the goal of making the United States less dependent on foreign oil, he needed the help of the Department of Energy's experts to develop programs that would further that objective. At a time when other agencies were feeling the pinch of a tight federal budget, the Department of Energy's budget nearly doubled.

Agencies also have allies in Congress. Agencies with programs that benefit important key voting blocs are particularly likely to have congressional support. A prime example is the Department of Agriculture. Although the agricultural sector is just one of the president's many concerns, it is a primary concern of farm-state senators and representatives. They can be counted on to support Department of Agriculture funding and programs.

Democracy and Bureaucratic Accountability

Studies have found that the U.S. federal bureaucracy compares favorably to government bureaucracies elsewhere. "Some international bureaucracies," Charles Goodsell writes, "may be roughly the same [as the U.S. bureaucracy] in quality of performance, but they are few in number."[16] The U.S. Postal Service, for example, has an on-time and low-cost record that few national postal services can match.

Nevertheless, the federal bureaucracy's policy influence is at odds with democratic principles. The bureaucratic form of governing is the antithesis of the democratic form. Bureaucracy entails hierarchy, command, permanence of office, appointment to office, and fixed rules, whereas self-government involves equality, consent, rotation of office, election to office, and open decision making. The president and members of Congress are accountable to the people through elections. Bureaucrats are not elected and yet exercise a significant degree of independent power.

Their influence raises the question of **bureaucratic accountability**—the degree to which bureaucrats are held accountable for the power they exercise. To a small degree, they are accountable directly to the public. In some instances, for example, agencies are required to hold public hearings before issuing new regulations. For the most part, however, bureaucratic accountability occurs largely through the president, Congress, and the courts.[17]

Accountability through the Presidency

Periodically, presidents have launched broad initiatives aimed at making the bureaucracy more responsive. The most recent was the National Performance Review, which Bill Clinton began when he assumed the presidency in 1993. He had campaigned on the issue of "reinventing government" and assembled "reinventing teams" that produced 384 specific recommendations grouped into four broad imperatives: reducing red tape, putting customers first, empowering administrators, and eliminating wasteful spending.[18] Although different in its particulars, the National Performance

Review was like earlier reform panels, including the Brownlow, Hoover, and Volcker commissions,[19] which sought with some success to improve the bureaucracy's efficiency, responsiveness, and accountability.

Presidents can also intervene more directly through *executive orders* to force agencies to pursue particular administrative actions. In the closing days of his presidency, for example, Bill Clinton ordered federal agencies to take the steps necessary to ensure that eligible individuals with limited English proficiency obtained full access to federal assistance programs.

Nevertheless, presidents do not have the time or knowledge to exercise personal oversight of the federal bureaucracy. It is far too big and diverse. Presidents rely instead on management tools that include reorganization, presidential appointees, and the executive budget.[20]

Reorganization The bureaucracy's size—its hundreds of separate agencies—makes it difficult for presidents to coordinate its activities. Agencies pursue independent and even conflicting paths. For example, the United States spends more than $50 billion annually to gather intelligence on threats to the nation's security and does so through several agencies, which sometimes fail to cooperate. A lack of communication between the CIA and the FBI contributed to the failure to prevent the terrorist attacks on the World Trade Center and the Pentagon on September 11, 2001. Each agency had information that might have disrupted the attack if the information had been shared with the other agency.

Presidents have sought to streamline the bureaucracy in an attempt to make it more accountable. After the intelligence breakdown in 2001, for example, President Bush commissioned a study of the intelligence agencies that resulted in the creation of the Office of the Director of National Intelligence in 2004. Fifteen intelligence agencies, including the CIA and the FBI, now report directly to the director of national intelligence, who has responsibility for coordinating their activities.

Such reorganization efforts usually improve the bureaucracy's performance, but only marginally.[21] On Christmas Day 2009, for example, Umar Farouk Abdulmutallab boarded a plane in Amsterdam that was headed for Detroit. As the plane prepared to land in Detroit, Abdulmutallab attempted to detonate plastic explosives hidden in his underwear. Quick action by other passengers might have been all that prevented him from blowing up the plane and killing all aboard. After his arrest, it was revealed that his father had contacted CIA officials to tell them of his son's extremism and that U.S. intelligence officials had earlier obtained information tying Abdulmutallab to terrorist groups. Nevertheless, U.S. intelligence officers had failed to revoke his visa to enter the United States and had failed to enter his name on the "no-fly list," enabling him to escape detection when he went through airport security in Amsterdam. The episode led to presidential and congressional investigations that sought to discover how America's reorganized intelligence system could have performed so poorly.

Presidential Appointments For day-to-day oversight of the bureaucracy, presidents rely on their political appointees. The top positions in every agency are held by presidential appointees. Their influence is greatest in agencies that have substantial discretionary authority. Some agencies, like the Social Security Administration (SSA), operate within guidelines that limit what agency heads can do. Although the SSA has a huge budget and makes monthly payments to more than 40 million Americans, recipient eligibility is determined by fixed rules. The head of the SSA does not have the option, say, of granting a retiree an extra $100 a month because the retiree is facing financial hardship. At the other extreme are the regulatory agencies, which have considerable latitude in their decisions. For example, Republican Ronald Reagan's appointee to chair the Federal Trade Commission (FTC), James Miller III, shared Reagan's belief that consumer protection policy had gone too far and was hurting business interests. In Miller's first year as head of the FTC, it dropped one-fourth of its pending cases against business firms. During Miller's full tenure at the FTC, it pursued only half as many cases as it had under his predecessor, who was appointed by a Democratic president, Jimmy Carter.[22]

Nevertheless, as was noted in Chapter 12, there are limits to what presidents can accomplish through their appointees. They number in the hundreds, and many of them lack detailed knowledge of the agencies they head, making them dependent on agency careerists. By the time they acquire a reasonable understanding of the agency's programs, most of them leave. The typical presidential appointee stays on the job for less than two years before moving on to other employment.[23]

OMB: Budgets, Regulations, and Legislative Proposals Of the management tools available to the president, few are more direct than the Office of Management and Budget. Funding and policy are the mainstays of every agency, and OMB has substantial control over each. In addition to OMB's role in overseeing the preparation of agency budgets, it acts as a review board for agency regulations and policy proposals. No agency can issue a major regulation without OMB's verification that the benefits of the regulation outweigh its costs, and no agency can propose legislation to Congress without OMB's approval. In making these decisions, OMB operates from a presidential perspective. A proposed regulation or bill that conflicts with the president's policies is unlikely to be approved.

Accountability through Congress

A common misperception is that the president, as the chief executive, has sole authority over executive agencies. In fact, Congress also claims ownership because it is the source of each agency's programs and funding. One presidential appointee asked a congressional committee whether it had a problem with his plans to reduce an agency's programs. The committee chairman replied, "No, you have the problem, because if you touch that bureau I'll cut your job out of the budget."[24]

The most substantial control that Congress exerts over the bureaucracy is through its "power of the purse." Congress has constitutional authority over spending; it decides how much money will be appropriated for agency programs. Without funding, a program simply does not exist, regardless of how important the agency believes it is. Congress can also void an administrative decision through legislation that instructs the agency to follow a different course of action.

POLITICAL THINKING

Who Is the Problem?

No institution is an easier target for politicians than the bureaucracy. In election campaigns, politicians often run against government, saying it is wasteful. Yet it is the politicians themselves who create and fund the programs that administrative agencies run. On the other hand, once a program is created, the bureaucrats in charge of it try to protect it. Where would you place most of the blame for government waste and duplication? Does it rest with the administrators who run the programs or with the lawmakers who create them?

Congress also has control through its oversight function, which involves monitoring the bureaucracy's work to ensure its compliance with legislative intent.[25] If any agency steps out of line, Congress can call hearings to ask tough questions and, if necessary, take legislative action to correct the problem. Bureaucrats are required by law to appear before Congress when asked to do so, and the mere possibility of being grilled by a congressional panel can lead administrators to stay in line. The effect is not altogether positive. Bureaucrats are sometimes reluctant to try innovative approaches out of a fear that particular members of Congress will disapprove.[26]

Nevertheless, Congress lacks the time and expertise to define in detail how programs should be run.[27] Accordingly, Congress has delegated much of its oversight responsibility to the Government Accountability Office (GAO).

At an earlier time, the GAO's role was limited largely to keeping track of agency spending. The GAO now also monitors whether agencies are implementing policies in the way that Congress intended. When the GAO finds a problem with an agency's handling of a program, it notifies the appropriate congressional committees, which can then take corrective action.

Oversight cannot correct mistakes or abuses that have already occurred. Recognizing this limit, Congress has devised ways to constrain the bureaucracy *before* it acts. The simplest method is to draft more detailed laws. Legislation typically contains *enabling provisions* that give administrators the authority to implement the law. By including specific instructions in these provisions, Congress limits bureaucrats' options. *Sunset provisions* are another restrictive device. These provisions establish specific dates when all or part of a law will expire unless it is extended by Congress. Sunset provisions are a method of countering the bureaucracy's reluctance to give up outdated programs. However, because members of Congress usually want the programs they create to last into the future, most legislation does not include a sunset provision.

Accountability through the Courts

The bureaucracy is also overseen by the judiciary. Legally, the bureaucracy derives its authority from acts of Congress, and an injured party can bring suit against an agency on the grounds that it has failed to carry out a law properly. If the court agrees, the agency must change its policy.[28] In 1999, for example, a federal court approved a settlement in favor of African

As one of thousands of services provided by the federal bureaucracy, the National Oceanic and Atmospheric Association monitors hurricane activity and provides early warning to affected coastal areas.

American farmers who demonstrated that the Department of Agriculture had systematically favored white farmers in granting federal farm loans.[29]

Nevertheless, the courts tend to support administrators if their actions are at least somewhat consistent with the law they are administering. The Supreme Court has held that agencies can apply any reasonable interpretation of statutes unless Congress has stipulated something to the contrary and that agencies in some instances have discretion in deciding whether to enforce statutes.[30] These rulings reflect the judiciary's recognition that administrators must have flexibility if they are to operate effectively. The bureaucracy and the courts would both grind to a crunching halt if judges routinely intervened in agency decisions.

Accountability within the Bureaucracy Itself

The recognition of the difficulty of ensuring adequate accountability of the bureaucracy through the presidency, Congress, and the courts has led to the development of mechanisms of accountability within the bureaucracy itself. Four of these mechanisms—the Senior Executive Service, administrative law judges, whistleblowing, and demographic representativeness—are particularly noteworthy.

Senior Executive Service The agency point of view within the bureaucracy is partly a result of career patterns. Most civil servants work in the same agency throughout their time in government service. As they acquire the skills and knowledge associated with a particular agency, they rise through its ranks and derive job satisfaction and security from supporting its mission.

Recognizing that the bureaucracy's employment system encourages an agency point of view, Congress in 1978 established the **Senior Executive Service (SES)**. Enacted at the urging of President Jimmy Carter, the SES represents a compromise between a president-led bureaucracy and an expert one.[31] The SES consists of roughly seven thousand top-level career civil servants who qualify through a competitive process to receive a higher salary than their peers but, in return, can be assigned by the president to any position within the bureaucracy. They are intended to be the intermediaries between the regular presidential appointees at the top of federal agencies and the regular civil servants who work in these agencies. Unlike the president's regular appointees, SES bureaucrats cannot be fired; if the president relieves them of their jobs, they have "fallback rights" to their former rank in the regular civil service.

The SES has been less successful in practice than its proponents anticipated. A 2009 study found that most senior executives are assigned to work within their original agency. The study concluded that most SES employees "have been viewed primarily as agency-specific assets, not federal or national assets." The major obstacle to moving SES members from one agency to another is that much of their value rests on their knowledge of a particular agency's programs. Although SES employees undergo development training designed to strengthen their leadership ability, their real strength is their intimate knowledge of an agency and its programs. "Part of the reason that people don't move is they get comfortable in a particular agency, they learn the policy issues and the policy challenges in a particular area, and they feel like that's their comfort zone," a former senior executive said. "I got promoted because I became an expert in the policies in that area, not because I'm such a great executive who can go anywhere and do anything."[32]

Administrative Law Judges Every day, bureaucrats make tens of thousands of decisions affecting individuals. Occasionally, an individual will believe that he or she was unfairly disadvantaged by a bureaucrat's decision and will contest it. Such disputes are usually handled by an **administrative law judge**. These judges are empowered to administer oaths, seek evidence, take testimony, make factual and legal determinations, and render decisions. However, they operate through a less formal process than do regular federal judges. Administrative law hearings usually take place in an office or meeting room rather than a courtroom, and administrative law judges do not wear a robe or sit on a high bench. The system is designed to provide a less formal, less expensive, and faster method of resolving administrative disputes than would be the case if they were handled through the regular federal courts. Under some circumstances, the decision of an administrative law judge can be appealed to such a court, although this seldom occurs.

Administrative law judges typically work within the confines of a particular agency and specialize in the laws and regulations governing its activities. Although they are employees of their agency, they are charged with protecting individuals from arbitrary, prejudicial, or incorrect decisions by the agency. Accordingly, their positions are insulated from agency pressure. Administrative law judges are not subject to performance or salary review by agency heads, and their superiors are prohibited from interfering with their hearings or undermining their rulings.

Whistleblowing Although the bureaucratic corruption that is commonplace in some countries is rare in the United States, a certain amount of fraud and abuse is inevitable in any large bureaucracy. One way to stop these prohibited practices is **whistleblowing**—the act of reporting instances of official mismanagement. To encourage whistleblowers to come forward with their information, Congress enacted the Whistleblower Protection

Act. It protects whistleblowers from retaliation by their superiors and gives them a financial reward in cases where their information results in a savings to government.

Nevertheless, whistleblowing is not for the faint-hearted. Many federal employees are reluctant to report instances of mismanagement because they fear retaliation. Their superiors might claim that they are malcontents or liars and find ways to ruin their careers. As a result, whistleblowing often does not occur until an employee has moved to another agency or quit government service entirely. A case in point is former CIA intelligence official John Kiriakou, who said in 2007 that the CIA had used waterboarding to interrogate Abu Zubaydah, a high-ranking leader of al Qaeda. It was the first such admission by a CIA operative and prompted some CIA officials to demand an FBI investigation of Kiriakou. They withdrew the request upon realizing that an investigation might result in additional embarrassing disclosures. (Waterboarding is an interrogation technique in which the person is strapped down with the head inclined downward. Water is then poured over the face, leading to inhalation and a sense of drowning and impending death. The technique was once considered a war crime by the U.S. government and violates the Geneva Conventions on the treatment of detainees.)

Demographic Representativeness Although the bureaucracy is an unrepresentative institution in the sense that its officials are unelected, it can be representative in the demographic sense. The concept of a demographically representative civil service was endorsed in 1961 by the President's Commission on Equal Employment Opportunity, which was created by President John F. Kennedy. The commission concluded that, if civil servants were a demographic microcosm of the general public, they would treat the various groups and interests in society more responsibly.[33]

The federal government has made progress in improving the employment status of women and, to a lesser extent, minorities. If all employees are taken into account, the federal bureaucracy comes reasonably close to being representative of the nation's population (see Table 13-1). Moreover, women and minorities are better represented among the top ranks of administrators than they are in Congress or the judiciary. Nevertheless, the bureaucracy is not demographically representative at the top levels. About three in every five managerial and professional positions are held by white males, a marked improvement over earlier periods but less than fully representative.

In any case, **demographic representativeness** is only a partial answer to the problem of bureaucratic accountability. The careerists in the defense and welfare agencies, for example, have similar demographic backgrounds, table 13-1 FEDERAL JOB RANKINGS (GS) OF VARIOUS DEMOGRAPHIC GROUPS

Women and minority-group members are underrepresented in the top jobs of the federal bureaucracy, but their representation has been increasing.

	Women's Share		Blacks' Share		Hispanics' Share	
Grade Level*	**1982**	**2002**	**1982**	**2002**	**1982**	**2002**
GS 13–15 (highest ranks)	5%	32%	5%	10%	2%	4%
GS 9–12	20	46	10	16	4	7
GS 5–8	60	67	19	26	4	9
GS 1–4 (lowest ranks)	78	69	23	28	5	8

*In general, the higher-numbered grades are managerial and professional positions, and the lower-numbered grades are clerical and manual labor positions.
Source: Office of Personnel Management, 2010.

but they differ markedly in their opinions about policy. Each group believes that the goals of its agency should be a top priority. In this sense, agency loyalty trumps demographics. Once in an agency, civil servants—whatever their demographic background—become advocates for its programs.

SUMMARY Self-Test www.mhhe.com/pattersonwtp9e

Bureaucracy is a method of organizing people and work, based on the principles of hierarchical authority, job specialization, and formalized rules. As a form of organization, bureaucracy is the most efficient means of getting people to work together on tasks of great magnitude and complexity. It is also a form of organization that is prone to waste and rigidity, which is why efforts are always being made to reform it.

The United States could not be governed without a large federal bureaucracy. The day-to-day work of the federal government, from mail delivery to provision of social security to international diplomacy, is done by federal agencies. Federal employees work in roughly four hundred major agencies, including cabinet departments, independent agencies, regulatory agencies, government corporations, and presidential commissions. Yet the bureaucracy is more than simply an administrative giant. Administrators have discretion when making policy decisions. In the process of implementing policy, they make important policy and political choices.

Administrative agencies operate within budgets established by the president and Congress, and they participate in the budgetary process. The process begins with the president's budget instructions, conveyed through OMB, to the agencies. They then develop their budgets, which are consolidated and sent by the president to Congress, where the House and Senate budget and appropriations committees do the bulk of the work, including holding hearings involving agency heads. Throughout, Congress, the president, and the agencies seek to promote their respective budgetary goals. Once the annual budget has been passed by the House and Senate and signed by the president, it takes effect on October 1, the starting date of the federal government's fiscal year.

Administrators are actively engaged in politics and policymaking. The fragmentation of power and the pluralism of the American political system result in a contentious policy process, which leads government agencies to compete for power and resources. Accordingly, civil servants tend to have an agency point of view: they seek to advance their agency's programs and to repel attempts by others to weaken them. In promoting their agencies, civil servants rely on their policy expertise, the backing of their clientele groups, and the support of the president and Congress.

Administrators are not elected by the people they serve, yet they wield substantial independent power. Because of this, the bureaucracy's accountability is a central issue. The major checks on the bureaucracy occur through the president, Congress, and the courts. The president has some power to reorganize the bureaucracy and the authority to appoint the political head of each agency. The president also has management tools (such as the executive budget) that can be used to limit administrators' discretion. Congress has influence on bureaucratic agencies through its authorization and funding powers and through various devices (including enabling provisions, sunset provisions, and oversight hearings) that can increase administrators' accountability. The judiciary's role in ensuring the bureaucracy's accountability is smaller than that of the elected branches, but the courts have the authority to force agencies to act in accordance with legislative intent, established procedures, and constitutionally guaranteed rights. Internal checks on the bureaucracy—the Senior Executive Service, administrative law judges, whistleblowing, and demographic representativeness—are also mechanisms for holding the bureaucracy accountable.

Key Terms

administrative law judge (*p. 479*)
agency point of view (*p. 468*)
budgetary process (*p. 463*)
bureaucracy (*p. 455*)
bureaucratic accountability (*p. 473*)
cabinet (executive) departments (*p. 458*)
clientele groups (*p. 471*)
demographic representativeness (*p. 480*)
formalized rules (*p. 455*)
government corporations (*p. 459*)
hierarchical authority (*p. 455*)
independent agencies (*p. 459*)

job specialization (*p. 455*)
merit system (*p. 460*)
neutral competence (*p. 462*)
patronage system (*p. 460*)
policy implementation (*p. 466*)
presidential commissions (*p. 460*)
regulatory agencies (*p. 459*)
senior executive service (*p. 478*)
spoils system (*p. 462*)
whistleblowing (*p. 479*)

Suggested Readings

Aberbach, Joel D., and Bert A. Rockman. *In the Web of Politics: Two Decades of the U.S. Federal Executive.* Washington, D.C.: Brookings Institution, 2000. An evaluation of the federal bureaucracy and its evolving nature.

Du Gay, Paul. *The Values of Bureaucracy.* New York: Oxford University Press, 2005. An insightful analysis of how bureaucracies work and the values they embody.

Huber, Gregory A. *The Craft of Bureaucratic Neutrality: Interests and Influence in Governmental Regulation of Occupational Safety.* New York: Cambridge University Press, 2007. An argument that claims political neutrality is the best political strategy, as well as the proper administrative approach, for agencies.

Ketti, Donald F. *System under Stress: Homeland Security and American Politics.* Washington, D.C.: CQ Press, 2007. An award-winning study of executive reorganization that focuses on the Department of Homeland Security.

Lewis, David E. *The Politics of Presidential Appointments: Political Control and Bureaucratic Performance.* Princeton, N.J.: Princeton University Press, 2008. An assessment of the trade-off between competency and loyalty in presidential appointments.

Meier, Kenneth J., and Laurence J. O'Toole Jr. *Bureaucracy in a Democratic State.* Baltimore, MD.: Johns Hopkins University Press, 2006. A careful assessment of the relationship between bureaucracy and democracy.

Osborne, David, and Ted Gaebler. *Reinventing Government: How the Entrepreneurial Spirit Is Transforming the Public Sector.* New York: Addison-Wesley, 1992. The book that Washington policymakers in the 1990s regarded as the guide to transforming the bureaucracy.

Page, Edward C., and Bill Jenkins. *Policy Bureaucracy: Government with a Cast of Thousands.* New York: Oxford University Press, 2005. An assessment of the bureaucracy as a policymaking institution.

Sagini, Meshack M. *Organizational Behavior: The Challenges of the New Millennium.* Lanham, MD.: University Press of America, 2001. A comprehensive assessment of bureaucratic structures and behaviors.

List of Websites

www.census.gov The website of the U.S. Census Bureau, the best source of statistical information on Americans and the government agencies that administer programs affecting them.

www.whistleblower.org The Government Accountability Project's website; designed to protect and encourage whistleblowers by providing information and support to federal employees.

www.whitehouse.gov/government/cabinet.html A website that lists the cabinet secretaries and provides links to each cabinet-level department.

Politics in Theory and Practice

Thinking: What are the major sources of bureaucrats' power? What mechanisms for controlling that power are available to the president and Congress?

Participating: If you are considering a semester or summer internship, you might want to look into working for a federal, state, or local agency. Compared with legislative interns, executive interns are more likely to get paid and to be given significant duties. (Many legislative interns spend the bulk of their time answering phones or responding to mail.) Internship information can often be obtained through an agency's website. You should apply as early as possible; some agencies have application deadlines. You might even consider a career in government. President John F. Kennedy said that government is "the highest calling." Although this view is not widely shared today, government service can be a satisfying career. A 2002 study by Harvard's Kennedy School of Government found that public-sector managers get more intrinsic satisfaction from their work, which focuses on improving public life, than do private-sector managers. For people who want to pursue a government career, a first step is often a master's degree program in public administration or public policy. Many of these programs require only a year of study after the bachelor's degree. For an entry-level employee with a master's degree rather than a bachelor's degree, the initial salary is 40 percent higher. Appointees with master's degrees enter the civil service at a higher rank (GS-9 rather than GS-5) and are placed in positions that entail greater responsibility than those assigned to newly hired appointees with bachelor's degrees. Those who enter the civil service at the higher rank also are more likely to advance to top positions as their careers develop.

Extra Credit

For up-to-the-minute *New York Times* articles, interactive simulations, graphics, study tools, and more links and quizzes, visit the text's Online Learning Center at **www.mhhe.com/pattersonwtp9e**.

NATIONAL JOURNAL

Too Much Information

When the news reached Washington that a Northwest Airlines passenger had been taken into custody in Detroit after, authorities alleged, he tried to set off a bomb aboard the plane, the staff at the National Counterterrorism Center outside Washington quickly huddled. During any critical terrorist incident, the NCTC becomes the central clearinghouse for information and updates across the government.

Within hours of the Christmas Day attack, officials organized a secure video teleconference that included more than 20 agencies that would have to respond to the incident. They began sharing what they knew and asking what they needed to find out. Using established protocols, the NCTC's staffers—experts drawn from the CIA, the FBI, and other intelligence agencies—tried to get their hands around the rapidly developing story line.

According to an official with knowledge of the day's events, once the NCTC analysts had a name, they began looking for whatever information they had in their databases on Umar Farouk Abdulmutallab, a young Nigerian man who would later assert he had been trained by Al Qaeda in Yemen to blow up the plane with a bomb hidden in his underwear. The analysts hunted for links to reporting on terrorist activity, which the center routinely collects. They first had to determine whether this was an isolated event or a part of a larger plot.

The White House directed the dozens of agencies participating in the secure teleconference, and soon they began reporting in. The FBI would start an investigation. The Homeland Security Department would step up airline passenger screening. The Federal Aviation Administration would have to adjust to the disruption in air travel schedules. The NCTC analysts began working the plot, just as they had after the July 2005 bombing of the London subway and bus system and the 2006 plan to sneak liquid bombs onto trans-Atlantic airliners. They searched for connections, leads, and clues, those notorious "dots" that made up the full narrative of an attack that, until that moment, had not been fully understood.

Crisis control is not the center's usual routine. It also has a portfolio of longer-term duties, including helping plan global counterterrorism strategy and keeping track of terrorism trends. Director Michael Leiter has said that the task that has grown the most in the past two years involves deep analysis of the root causes of radicalization. Academics have praised the NCTC for its terrorism research. If the government had a think tank for terrorism, this would be it.

The center's most immediate role, though, is in defending against attacks. It is a data hub, the one place in the government where streams of terrorist reports—and warnings—from dozens of agencies are supposed to come together. Since the Christmas Day attempt, many critics have questioned why the NCTC's analysts, who examine this information every day, failed to detect Abdulmutallab's plan. According to an Obama administration review, the analysts had received or were privy to intelligence about him from at least three agencies. They were also aware, more broadly, about a burgeoning terrorist threat in Yemen.

Last April, in a speech at the Aspen Institute, Leiter described a "resurgence of Al Qaeda in the Arabian Peninsula which is quite worrisome . . . and a stated desire in their propaganda to expand their reach beyond Yemen into the Kingdom of Saudi Arabia and elsewhere." Last year, the National

Security Agency intercepted phone traffic of Qaeda operatives in Yemen talking about a "Nigerian" who was engaged in a new plot. And, as most of the country now knows, in November, Abdulmutallab's father, a prominent Nigerian banker, walked into the U.S. Embassy in Abuja and told officials he was afraid that his son had gone to Yemen and had become an Islamic radical.

In hindsight, if any one outfit was in a position to put all of these pieces together, it was the NCTC. That is, after all, why federal officials set it up in 2004, to be a "fusion center" for the intelligence community. But to describe the center as the place where all the dots are connected—implying, as some unnamed officials have in recent press reports, that its staff are supposed to be able to predict the next attack—is at best a misunderstanding of the NCTC's capabilities and at worst an attempt to pin the intelligence failures of Christmas Day on a single organization.

In the global fight against terrorism, the NCTC is mostly a passive participant. It cannot investigate terrorist suspects in the United States. (That's the FBI's job.) It cannot legally conduct covert operations overseas. (That's the CIA's domain.) It cannot intercept foreign communications. (That's the NSA's bailiwick.) And it cannot revoke visas. (That's up to the State Department.)

"NCTC, it's important to remember, is just an aggregator of information," said Rick (Ozzie) Nelson, who worked in the center's strategic operational planning directorate and is now at the Center for Strategic and International Studies. "Certainly, some criticism can be leveled that they didn't connect all the dots. But that can't fall all on NCTC's shoulders."

In his Aspen Institute speech, Leiter said that every threat report that his analysts write is available to more than 17,000 people at the federal, state, and local government levels. But even many in that vast network of colleagues, he said, don't always understand the NCTC's role. "I think it's important to remind people what we do, because, frankly, even the people with whom I work on a daily basis aren't always sure."

So what does the NCTC do? For starters, it tries to keep up. From within their headquarters at a new secure facility in Northern Virginia, the center's analysts can access at least 28 computer networks maintained by other agencies. They're supposed to pan these streams of dots for clues. But, according to former NCTC employees and current intelligence officials, that is a mostly manual process, and a time-consuming one.

In a 2006 interview with CBS News, Russell Travers, a deputy director responsible for the center's major database of terrorist names, said that most NCTC analysts need six or seven computers on their desks to plug into the different systems around the government. A Defense Department analyst at the center, for example, can read raw data from the CIA or the FBI. The NCTC is the only place where that kind of cross-agency sharing, a key recommendation of the 9/11 commission, actually happens, Travers said.

The data come into the center in huge floods, however. After the 9/11 attacks, the FBI, the CIA, and electronic spies such as the National Security Agency went into collection overdrive. If there was a way to get more information, they found it—from interrogations, from computers, from the pocket detritus of Qaeda fighters killed in battle. After the NCTC was established, the intelligence agencies turned their data streams on the center with the ferocity of a rushing river. From 2004 to 2005, the master database of known or suspected terrorists doubled in size, Travers said. Then, it doubled again in 2006. Today, officials estimate that the system contains half a million names, all of which were poured in by other agencies.

"Right now, we are getting on a daily basis many thousands of names," Travers told CBS. (Outside experts have put the number between 4,000 and 8,000.) "Lots of them are undoubtedly duplicates. Some of them aren't really terrorists." Just to keep up with the names, Travers said, he employed "about 80 analysts," who spent their days sifting through "fragmentary," "ambiguous," and "conflicting" information. That is the nature of intelligence, but American analysts have never had to manage data on this scale. Travers seemed to be "drowning" in information, the CBS reporter commented.

"It's probably the single biggest challenge that the community's got right now," Travers replied. "The information that's out there is coming in a deluge."

Another senior intelligence official concurred. Ron Sanders, the top personnel official for the national intelligence director, told reporters this month, "The amount of information, the amount of dots that need to be connected, the needles in the haystack, it's just mind-numbing."

Obama seemed to grasp the underlying problem when he said that the Christmas attack "was not a failure to collect intelligence; it was a failure to integrate and understand the intelligence that we already had." But why the failure? It's not because the analysts are incapable of fusing different pieces of a story. It's just that it is exceedingly difficult to do so using the tools now at their disposal. Compounding this problem, current and former officials say, is the lack of an auditing system. Agencies are throwing information into databases at a dizzying rate, but no one is keeping track of who uses the data and how, or whether proper follow-through takes place.

It's not clear whether the immediate corrections that the president has called for involve a new tool for keeping track of where those dots are in the system and who is looking at them. But Leiter told the Senate Homeland Security and Governmental Affairs Committee that technology improvements—including the ability to simultaneously search multiple databases—is one of the areas on which Obama wants the center to direct its attention.

What's Your Opinion?

Do you think America's national security interests would be better or worse off if the agencies responsible for collecting and analyzing counterterrorism information were condensed and reduced? When was the last time you interacted with the bureaucracy? Did you leave with a positive or negative impression of the agency?

CHAPTER 14

THE FEDERAL JUDICIAL SYSTEM: APPLYING THE LAW

> "It is emphatically the province and duty of the judicial department to say what the law is. Those who apply the rule to particular cases, must of necessity expound and interpret that rule. If two laws conflict with each other, the courts must decide on the operation of each."
>
> JOHN MARSHALL[1]

Through its ruling in *Citizens United v. Federal Election Commission* (2010), the Supreme Court opened the door to unrestricted corporate and union spending in federal election campaigns. At issue was a provision of the 2002 Bipartisan Campaign Reform Act that banned corporations and unions from using organization funds to pay for broadcasts or other advertisements that were designed to promote a political candidate. The ban applied thirty days before a primary and sixty days before the general election and extended a century-old policy of limiting election contributions by economic organizations on grounds that such spending would give them undue influence with lawmakers.

A majority of the Supreme Court justices saw the issue differently than Congress had, concluding that the spending restriction infringed on the free speech rights of corporations and unions. Writing for the five justices in the majority, Justice Anthony Kennedy said: "If the First Amendment has any force, it prohibits Congress from fining or jailing citizens, or associations of citizens, for simply engaging in political speech." Kennedy went on to say: "When government seeks to use its full power . . . to command where a person may get his or her information or what distrusted source he or she may not hear, it uses censorship to control thought. This is unlawful." The four justices in the minority took issue with this argument, saying that allowing powerful organizations to spend freely on elections could corrupt the political process. "While American democracy is imperfect," Justice John Paul Stevens wrote, "few outside the majority of this court would have thought its flaws included a dearth of corporate money in politics. The court's ruling threatens to undermine the integrity of elected institutions across the nation." Stevens added that the First Amendment was intended to protect the free speech rights of individuals and not of corporations or unions.[2]

The Court's campaign finance ruling illustrates three key points about court decisions. First, the judiciary is an important policymaking body. Some of its rulings are as consequential as a law of Congress or an executive order of the president. Second, the judiciary has considerable discretion in its rulings. The *Citizens United* decision was not based on any literal reading of the law or else the justices would have been in full agreement on the proper ruling. Third, the judiciary is a political as well as legal institution. The campaign finance ruling was a product of contending political forces, had political content, and was decided by political appointees.

This chapter describes the federal judiciary. Like the executive and legislative branches, the judiciary is an independent branch of the U.S. government, but unlike the other two branches, its top officials are not elected by the people. The judiciary is not a democratic institution, and its role is different from and, in some ways, more controversial than the roles of the executive and legislative branches. This chapter explores this issue in the process of discussing the following main points:

- *The federal judiciary includes the Supreme Court of the United States, which functions mainly as an appellate court; courts of appeals, which hear appeals; and the district courts, which hold trials.* Each state has a court system of its own, which for the most part is independent of supervision by the federal courts.

- *Judicial decisions are constrained by applicable constitutional law, statutory and administrative law, and precedent.* Nevertheless, political factors have a major influence on judicial appointments and decisions; judges are political officials as well as legal ones.
- *The judiciary has become an increasingly powerful policymaking body in recent decades, raising the question of the judiciary's proper role in a democracy.* The philosophies of judicial restraint and judicial activism provide different answers to this question.

THE FEDERAL JUDICIAL SYSTEM

The Constitution establishes the judiciary as a separate and independent branch of the federal government. The Constitution provides for the Supreme Court of the United States but gives Congress the power to determine the number and types of lower federal courts.

All federal judges are nominated and appointed to office by the president, subject to confirmation by majority vote in the Senate. Unlike the office of president, senator, or representative, the Constitution places no age, residency, or citizenship requirements on the office of federal judge. Nor does the Constitution require judges to have legal training, though by tradition they do. Once seated on the bench, as specified in the Constitution, they "hold their offices during good behavior." This has meant, in effect, that federal judges serve until they die or retire voluntarily. No Supreme Court justice and only a handful of lower-court judges have been removed through impeachment and conviction by Congress, the method of early removal specified by the Constitution.

Alexander Hamilton argued forcefully for life tenure for federal judges in *Federalist* No. 78. Responding to arguments by anti-Federalists that unelected, life-appointed judges would be a threat to the republic, Hamilton argued that the judicial branch would be the weakest of the three branches. Whereas congressional power rests on spending authority ("the power of the purse") and presidential power rests on control of military force ("the power of the sword"), judicial power rests on what Hamilton called "judgment"—the reasonableness and fairness of its decisions. The best way to ensure that judicial decisions meet this standard, Hamilton claimed, is to grant life tenure to federal judges so that they are free of all allegiances except to the rule of law.

The Supreme Court of the United States

The Supreme Court of the United States is the nation's highest court. It has nine members—the chief justice and eight associate justices. The chief justice presides over the Court but has the same voting power as each of the other justices.

Article III of the Constitution grants the Supreme Court both original and appellate jurisdiction. A court's **jurisdiction** is its authority to hear cases of a particular type. **Original jurisdiction** is the authority to be the first court to hear a case. The Supreme Court's original jurisdiction includes legal disputes involving foreign diplomats and cases in which the opposing parties are state governments. The Court in its history has convened as a court of original jurisdiction only a few hundred times and has rarely done so in recent decades.

The Supreme Court does its most important work as an appellate court. **Appellate jurisdiction** is the authority to review cases that have already been heard in lower courts and are appealed to a higher court by the losing party. These higher courts are called *appeals courts* or *appellate courts*. Appellate courts do not retry cases; rather, they determine whether a trial court in hearing a case has acted in accord with applicable law. The Supreme Court's appellate jurisdiction extends to cases arising under the

The Supreme Court's campaign finance decision in 2010 effectively overturned a century-old policy of limits on campaign spending by corporations. Shown here is a cartoon depicting the effect of the Court's decision.
Source: Reprinted by permission of Dwayne Powell and Creators Syndicate, Inc.

Constitution, federal law and regulations, and treaties. The Court also hears appeals involving legal controversies that cross state or national boundaries. Article III of the Constitution gives Congress the power to create "exceptions" to the Supreme Court's appellate jurisdiction, whereas its original jurisdiction is unalterable by Congress.

Selecting and Deciding Cases The Supreme Court's power is most apparent when it declares another institution's action to be unconstitutional. This power, called **judicial review**, was first asserted by the Supreme Court in *Marbury v. Madison* (1803), when the Court rebuked both Congress and the president (see Chapter 2). It is a power that the Supreme Court has used sparingly; it has usually deferred to Congress and the president when there is reasonable doubt as to whether their actions fall inside or outside the bounds of the Constitution.[3]

Although judicial review is its most dramatic power, the Supreme Court's primary responsibility is to establish legal precedents that will guide the decisions of lower courts. A **precedent** is a judicial decision that serves as a rule for settling subsequent cases of a similar nature. Lower courts are expected to follow precedent—that is, to resolve cases in ways consistent with upper-court rulings.

Nearly all cases that reach the Supreme Court do so after the losing party in a lower-court case requests that it hear the case. If at least four of the justices agree to do so, the Court issues a **writ of certiorari**, which is a request to the lower court to submit to the Supreme Court a record of the case. Each year roughly eight thousand parties apply for certiorari, but the Court grants certiorari to fewer than a hundred cases.

The Supreme Court is most likely to grant certiorari when the U.S. government through the solicitor general (the high-ranking Justice Department official who serves as the government's lawyer in Supreme Court cases) requests it.[4] When the government loses a case in a lower court, the solicitor general decides whether to appeal it. Such cases often make up half or more of the cases the Supreme Court hears in a term.

The Supreme Court seldom accepts a routine case, even if the justices believe that a lower court has made a mistake. The Court's job is not to correct the errors of other courts but to resolve substantial legal issues. The Court's own guidelines say that there must be "compelling reasons" for accepting a case, which include resolving issues that are being decided inconsistently by the lower courts, correcting serious departures from accepted standards of justice, settling key questions of federal law, and reviewing lower-court rulings that conflict with a previous Supreme Court decision. When the Court does accept a case, chances are that most of the justices disagree with the lower court's ruling. About three-fourths of Supreme Court decisions reverse the lower court's judgment.[5]

During a Supreme Court hearing, the attorneys for the two sides present their oral arguments, which typically are limited to thirty minutes for each side.[6] Each side also provides the Court a written **brief**, which contains its full argument. The oral session is followed by the **judicial conference**, which is attended only by the nine justices and in which they discuss and vote on the case. The chief justice has the option of speaking first on the case and can sometimes influence the decision by framing the choice in a persuasive way. Regardless, the conference's proceedings are secret, which allows the justices to speak freely about a case and to change their positions as the discussion progresses.[7]

Issuing Decisions and Opinions After a case has been decided, the Court issues its ruling, which consists of a decision and one or more opinions. The **decision** indicates which party the Court supports and by how large a margin. The most important part of the ruling, however, is the **opinion**, which explains the legal basis for the decision. In the landmark *Brown* opinion, for instance, the Court held that government-sponsored school segregation was unconstitutional because it violated the Fourteenth Amendment provision that guarantees equal protection under the law to all citizens. This opinion became the legal basis by which public schools throughout the South were ordered by lower courts to end their policy of racial segregation.

When a majority of the justices agree on the legal basis of a decision, the result is a **majority opinion**. In some cases there is no majority opinion because, although a majority of the justices agree on the decision, they disagree on the legal basis for it. The result in such cases is a **plurality opinion**, which presents the view held by most of the justices who vote with the winning side. Another type of opinion is a **concurring opinion**, a separate view written by a justice who votes with the majority but disagrees with its reasoning. The final type is a **dissenting opinion**; in it, a justice on the losing side explains the reasons for disagreeing with the majority position.

When part of the majority, the chief justice decides which justice will write the majority opinion. Otherwise, the senior justice in the majority picks the opinion author. The justice who writes the Court's majority opinion has the responsibility to express accurately the majority's reasoning. The vote on a case is not considered final until the opinion is written and agreed upon, so give-and-take can occur during the writing stage. In rare instances, the writing stage has produced a change in the Court's decision. In *Lee v. Weisman* (1992), a case involving prayer at a public school graduation, Justice Anthony Kennedy originally sided with the four justices who said the prayer was permissible. While writing the 5-4 majority opinion, Kennedy found that he could not make a persuasive case for allowing it. He switched sides, resulting in a 5-4 majority the other way. Kennedy's switch was dramatic in its effect, but strategic considerations are a component of the workings of the Court. Justices have been known, for example, to vote with the majority even when disagreeing with it in order to have a say in the draft opinion that circulates during preparation of the final version.[8]

Other Federal Courts

The Supreme Court's position at the top of the judicial system gives it unrivaled importance. Nevertheless, the Supreme Court is not the only court that matters. Judge Jerome Frank once wrote of the "upper-court myth," which is the view that lower courts dutifully follow the rulings handed down by the courts above them.[9] The reality is different, as the following discussion explains.

U.S. District Courts The lowest federal courts are the district courts (see Figure 14-1). There are ninety-four federal district courts altogether—at least one in every state and as many as four in some states. Each district includes several judges, who number roughly seven hundred in all. The federal district courts are the chief trial courts of the federal system. Virtually all criminal and civil cases arising under federal law are argued first in the district courts. They are the only courts in the federal system where the two sides present their case to a jury for a verdict. Cases at this level are usually presided over by a single judge.

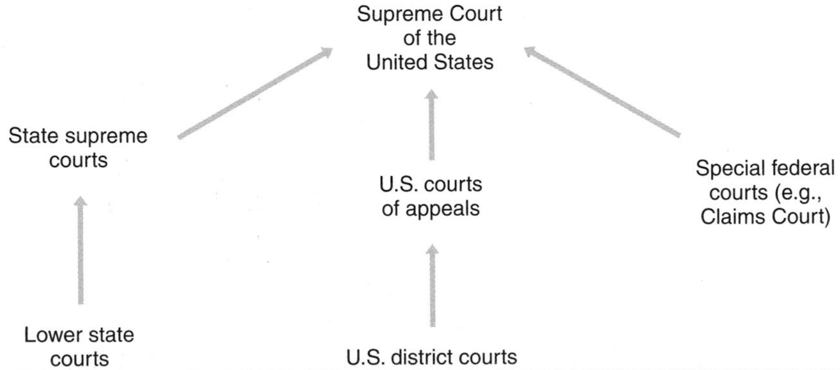

figure 14-1 THE FEDERAL JUDICIAL SYSTEM

The simplified diagram shows the relationships among the various levels of federal courts and between state and federal courts. The losing party in a case can appeal a lower-court decision to the court at the next-highest level, as the arrows indicate. Decisions normally can be moved from state courts to federal courts only if they raise a constitutional question.

Lower federal courts rely on and follow Supreme Court decisions in their own rulings. The Supreme Court reiterated this requirement in a 1982 case, *Hutto v. Davis:* "Unless we wish anarchy to prevail within the federal judicial system, a precedent of this Court must be followed by the lower federal courts no matter how misguided the judges of those courts may think it to be."[10] However, the idea that lower courts are rigidly bound to Supreme Court rulings is part of the upper-court myth. District court judges might misunderstand the Supreme Court's position and deviate from it for that reason. In addition, the facts of a case before a district court are seldom identical to those of a case settled by the Supreme Court. The lower-court judge must decide whether a different legal judgment is appropriate. Finally, ambiguities or unaddressed issues in Supreme Court rulings give lower courts some flexibility in deciding cases.

Another indication of the significant role of district court judges is that most federal cases end with the district court's decision. Typically, the losing party decides not to appeal the decision to a higher court.

U.S. Courts of Appeals Cases appealed from district courts go to federal courts of appeals, which are the second level of the federal court system. Courts of appeals do not use juries. Ordinarily, no new evidence is submitted in an appealed case; rather, appellate courts base their decision on a review of the lower court's records. Appellate judges act as supervisors in the legal system, reviewing trial court decisions and correcting what they consider to be legal errors. Facts (that is, the circumstances of a case) found by district courts are ordinarily presumed to be correct.

The United States has thirteen courts of appeals. Eleven of them have jurisdiction over a "circuit" comprised of the district courts in anywhere from three to nine states (see Figure 14-2). Of the remaining two, one has jurisdiction over appeals arising in the District of Columbia and the other (the U.S. Court of Appeals for the Federal Circuit) has jurisdiction over appeals involving patents and international trade, regardless of the circuit in which it arises. Between four and twenty-six judges sit on each court of appeals, but each case usually is heard by a panel of three judges. On rare occasions, all the judges of a court of appeals sit as a body (*en banc*) in order to resolve difficult controversies, typically ones that have resulted in conflicting decisions within the same circuit. Each circuit is monitored by a Supreme Court justice, who typically takes the lead in reviewing appeals originating in that circuit. Conflict or inconsistency in how the different circuits are applying a law can lead the Supreme Court to review such cases.

Courts of appeals offer the only real hope of reversal for many appellants, because the Supreme Court hears so few cases. The Supreme

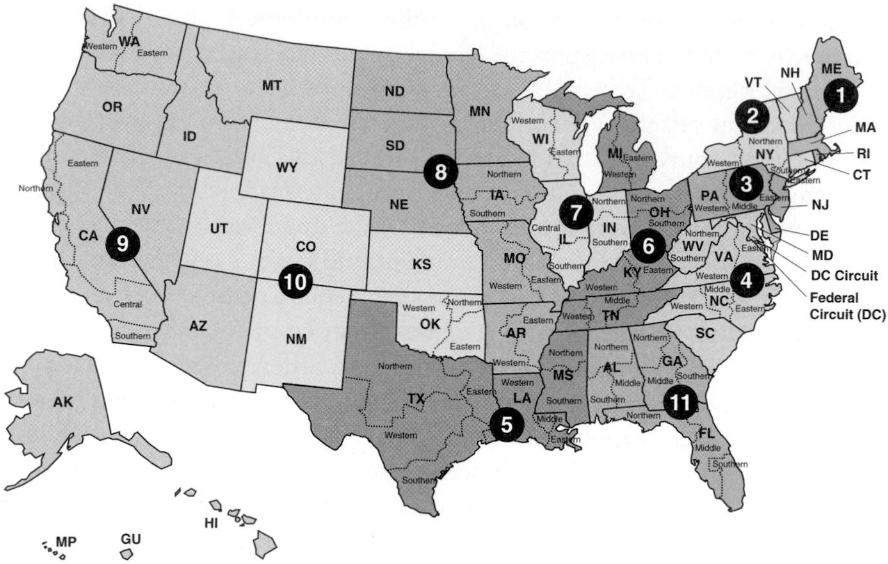

figure 14-2 GEOGRAPHIC BOUNDARIES OF U.S. COURTS OF APPEALS

The United States has thirteen courts of appeals, each of which serves a "circuit." Eleven of these circuit courts serve anywhere from three to nine states, as the map shows. The other two are located in the District of Columbia: the Court of Appeals for the District of Columbia and the Court of Appeals for the Federal Circuit, which specializes in appeals involving patents and international trade. Within each circuit are federal trial courts, most of which are district courts. Each state has at least one district court within its boundaries. Larger states like California (which has four district courts, as can be seen on the map) have more than one. *Source:* Administrative Office of the U.S. Courts.

Court reviews less than 1 percent of the cases heard by federal appeals courts.

Special U.S. Courts In addition to the Supreme Court, the courts of appeals, and the district courts, the federal judiciary includes a few specialty courts. Among them are the U.S. Claims Court, which hears cases in which the U.S. government is being sued for damages; the U.S. Court of International Trade, which handles cases involving appeals of U.S. Customs Office rulings; and the U.S. Court of Military Appeals, which hears appeals of military courts-martial. Some federal agencies and commissions also have judicial powers (for example, the issuing of fines), and their decisions can be appealed to a federal court of appeals.

The State Courts

The American states are separate governments within the U.S. political system. The Tenth Amendment protects each state in its sovereignty, and each state has its own court system. Like the federal courts, state court systems have trial courts at the bottom level and appellate courts at the top.

Each state decides for itself the structure of its courts and the method of selecting judges. In some states the governor appoints judges, but in most states judges are elected to office. The most common form involves competitive elections of either a partisan or a nonpartisan nature. Other states use a mixed system called the *merit plan* (also called the "Missouri Plan" because Missouri was the first state to use it), under which the governor appoints a judge from a short list of acceptable candidates provided by a judicial selection commission. The selected judge must then be reviewed periodically by the voters, who, rather than choosing between the judge and an opponent, simply decide by a "yes" or "no" vote whether the judge should be allowed to stay in office (see "How the 50 States Differ").

Besides the upper-court myth, there exists a "federal court myth," which holds that the federal judiciary is the most significant part of the judicial system and that state courts play a subordinate role. This view is also inaccurate. More than 95 percent of the nation's legal cases are decided by state or local courts. Most cases arising under *criminal law* (from shoplifting to murder) and most cases arising under *civil law* (such as divorces and business disputes) are defined by state laws or by local ordinances, which are derived from state laws.[1]

Moreover, nearly all cases that originate in state or local courts also end there. The federal courts do not come into the picture because the case does not involve a federal issue. The losing party in a divorce suit, for example, cannot appeal the decision to federal court because no federal law is involved. In most state criminal cases, there is also no federal

---

[1]Laws fall into three broad categories—procedural, civil, and criminal. *Procedural law* refers to rules that govern the legal process. In some cases, these rules apply to government, as in the example of the obligation of police to inform suspects of their right to an attorney. In other cases, the rules apply to private parties. For example, in some states, a homeowner cannot take an insurance company to court over a policy claim without first having that claim heard, and possibly resolved, by an arbitration board. *Civil law* governs relations with and between private parties. Marriage, divorce, business contracts, and property ownership are examples of relations covered by civil law. The losing party in a civil suit might be ordered to pay or otherwise compensate the other party but would not face jail unless he or she refuses to comply with a court order, which can be a punishable offense. Government can also be a party to a civil suit, as when the IRS sues a taxpayer in a dispute over how much the taxpayer owes the government. *Criminal law* deals with acts that government defines as illegal and which can result in a fine, imprisonment, or other punishment. Murder, assault, and drunk driving are examples of acts covered by criminal law. The government is always a party to a criminal law case; the other party is the individual alleged to have broken the law. (Legal relationships between government and private parties, whether criminal or civil, are defined as *public law*. The term *private law* is used to refer to the legal rights and relationships between private parties.)

HOW THE 50 STATES DIFFER

POLITICAL THINKING THROUGH COMPARISONS

Principal Methods of Selecting State Judges

The states use a variety of methods for selecting the judges on their highest court, including the merit plan, election, and political appointment. The states that appoint judges grant this power to the governor, except in Virginia, Connecticut, and South Carolina, where the legislature makes the choice.

Q: *What might explain why several states in the middle of the nation use the merit plan for selecting judges?*

A: *The merit plan originated in the state of Missouri. Innovations in one state sometimes spread to adjacent states with similar political cultures.*

Source: From the Council of State Governments. In the case of states that use more than one method, the most widely used method is shown on the map.

issue, unless state authorities are alleged to have violated a right protected by the U.S. Constitution, such as the right of the accused to remain silent (see Chapter 4). In such instances, an individual convicted in a state court can, after exhausting the avenues of appeal in the state system, appeal to a federal court. If the federal court accepts such an appeal, it ordinarily confines itself to the federal aspects of the matter, such as whether the defendant's constitutional rights were violated. In addition, the federal court accepts the facts determined by the state court unless such findings are clearly in error. Federal courts are also disinclined, when a provision of federal law does not clearly resolve a case, to substitute their own interpretation of a state's law for that applied by the state court. In short, legal and factual determinations of state courts can bind the federal courts—a clear contradiction of the federal court myth.

However, issues traditionally within the jurisdiction of the states can become federal issues through the rulings of federal courts. In its *Lawrence v. Texas* decision in 2003, for example, the Supreme Court invalidated state laws that had made it illegal for consenting adults of the same sex to engage in private sexual relations.[11] John Lawrence had been convicted under a Texas sodomy law and appealed his conviction on grounds that it violated his Fourteenth Amendment due process rights. By grounding his appeal in federal law, Lawrence was able to have his case heard in federal court. When the Supreme Court then decided in his favor, federal law became the governing authority in such cases. Until its *Lawrence* decision, the Court had held that states could decide whether to prohibit sexual relations among same-sex partners.[12]

Federal Court Appointees

Appointments to the Supreme Court and the lower federal courts are controlled by the president, who selects the nominees, and the Senate, which confirms or rejects them. The quiet dignity of the courtroom and the lack of fanfare with which a court delivers its decisions give the impression that the judiciary is as far removed from the world of politics as a governmental institution can possibly be. In reality, federal judges and justices bring their political views with them to the courtroom and have opportunities to promote their political beliefs through the cases they decide. Not surprisingly, the process by which federal judges are appointed is a partisan one.

Supreme Court Nominees

A Supreme Court appointment is a significant opportunity for a president.[13] Most justices retain their positions for many years, enabling presidents to influence judicial policy through their appointments long after they have left office. The careers of some Supreme Court justices provide dramatic testimony to the enduring nature of judicial appointments. For example, Franklin D. Roosevelt appointed William O. Douglas to the Supreme Court in 1939, and for thirty years after Roosevelt's death in 1945, Douglas remained a strong liberal influence on the Court.

Presidents usually appoint jurists who have a compatible political philosophy. Although Supreme Court justices are free to make their own decisions, their legal positions can usually be predicted from their background. A study by judicial scholar Robert Scigliano found that about three of every four appointees have behaved on the Supreme Court approximately as presidents could have expected.[14] Of course, a president has no guarantee that a nominee will actually do so. Justices Earl Warren and William Brennan, for example, proved to be more liberal than President Dwight D. Eisenhower had anticipated. Asked whether he had made any mistakes as president, Eisenhower replied, "Yes, two, and they are both sitting on the Supreme Court."[15]

Although presidents seek nominees who share their political philosophy, they also must take into account a nominee's acceptability to others. Every nominee is scrutinized closely by the legal community, interested groups, and the media; must undergo an extensive background check by the FBI; and then must gain the approval of a Senate majority. Within the Senate, the key body is the Judiciary Committee, whose members have responsibility for conducting hearings on judicial nominees and recommending their confirmation or rejection by the full Senate.

Nearly 20 percent of presidential nominees to the Supreme Court have been rejected by the Senate on grounds of judicial qualification, political views, personal ethics, or partisanship. Most of these rejections occurred before 1900, and partisan politics was the usual reason. Today a nominee with strong professional and ethical credentials is less likely to be blocked for partisan reasons alone. On the other hand, nominees can expect confirmation if they have a clean personal record and a strong professional record, and are able to demonstrate during Senate confirmation hearings that they have the temperament and intellect expected of a Supreme Court justice. President Bush's nomination of John Roberts in 2005 to be chief justice is a case in point. Roberts faced tough questioning during Senate hearings, but nothing startlingly new or disturbing came out, and he was confirmed by a 78-22 vote. The Senate vote in 2010 on Elena Kagan, who was nominated by President Obama, was closer, even though the Senate hearings went smoothly. Although Kagan was confirmed by a 63-37 vote, only five GOP senators voted for her. Expressing a view held

In 2010, President Barack Obama nominated Elena Kagan to replace the retiring John Paul Stevens on the Supreme Court. Kagan is shown here testifying before the Senate Judiciary Committee during her confirmation hearings.

by many Republicans, Orrin Hatch of Utah said she lacked an "appropriate judicial philosophy," which was his way of saying that some of her decisions would be at odds with his view of how the Court should rule.

Lower-Court Nominees

The president typically delegates to the deputy attorney general the task of identifying potential nominees for lower-court judgeships, a process that includes seeking recommendations from U.S. senators of the president's party, and sometimes House members as well. **Senatorial courtesy,** a tradition that dates back to the 1840s, holds that a senator from the state in which a vacancy has arisen should be consulted on the choice of the nominee if the senator is of the same party as the president.[16] If not consulted, the senator can request that confirmation be denied. Other senators usually grant the request as a "courtesy" to their colleague.

Although presidents are not as personally involved in selecting lower-court nominees as in naming potential Supreme Court justices, lower-court appointments are collectively significant. A president who serves two terms can shape the federal judiciary for years to come. By the time he left office, George W. Bush had appointed more than a third of the seated federal judges. Bill Clinton appointed a similar number during his two terms.

Presidents typically select members of their own party for lower-court judgeships. More than 90 percent of recent district and appeals court nominees have been members of the president's political party.[17] This fact does not mean that federal judges engage in blatant partisanship while on the bench. They are officers of a separate branch of government and prize their judicial independence. All Republican appointees do not vote the same way on cases, nor do all Democratic appointees. Nevertheless, partisanship influences judicial decisions. A study of the voting records of appellate court judges, for example, found that Democratic appointees were more likely than Republican appointees to side with parties who claim the government has violated their civil liberties.[18]

Personal Backgrounds of Judicial Appointees

In recent years, increasing numbers of federal justices and judges have had prior judicial experience on the assumption that such individuals are best qualified for appointment to the federal bench.[19] Elective office (particularly a seat in the U.S. Senate) was once a common route to the Supreme Court,[20] but recent appointees, with the exception of Elena Kagan, who was solicitor general, have come from the appellate courts (see Table 14-1).

table 14-1 Justices of the Supreme Court

Most recent appointees held an appellate court position before being nominated to the Supreme Court.

Justice	Year of Appointment	Nominating President	Position before Appointment
Antonin Scalia	1986	Reagan	Judge, D.C. Circuit Court of Appeals
Anthony Kennedy	1988	Reagan	Judge, 9th Circuit Court of Appeals
Clarence Thomas	1991	G. H. W. Bush	Judge, D.C. Circuit Court of Appeals
Ruth Bader Ginsburg	1993	Clinton	Judge, D.C. Circuit Court of Appeals
Stephen Breyer	1994	Clinton	Judge, 1st Circuit Court of Appeals
John Roberts Jr.*	2005	G. W. Bush	Judge, D.C. Circuit Court of Appeals
Samuel Alito Jr.	2006	G. W. Bush	Judge, 3rd Circuit Court of Appeals
Sonia Sotomayor	2009	Obama	Judge, 2nd Circuit Court of Appeals
Elena Kagan	2010	Obama	Solicitor general of the United States

*Chief justice.

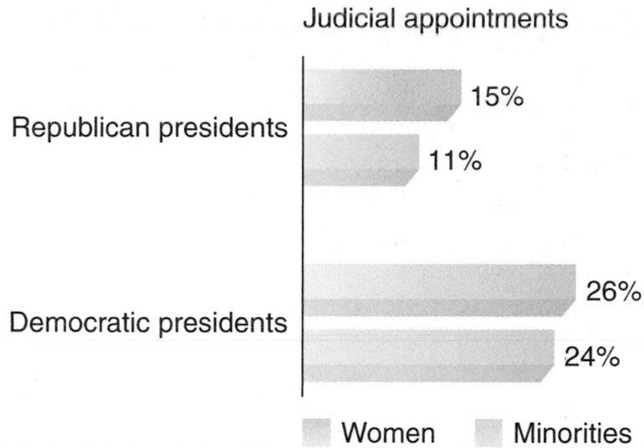

figure 14-3 POLITICAL PARTIES, PRESIDENTS, AND WOMEN AND MINORITY JUDICIAL APPOINTEES

Reflecting differences in their parties' coalitions, recent Republican and Democratic presidents have quite different records in terms of the percentage of their judicial appointees who have been women or minority-group members. *Source:* Various sources. Data based on appointees of Presidents Carter, Reagan, G. H. W. Bush, Clinton, and G. W. Bush.

White males are overrepresented on the federal bench, just as they dominate in Congress and at the top levels of the executive branch. However, the number of women and minority-group members appointed to federal judgeships has increased significantly in recent decades. The number of such appointees has varied according to which party controls the presidency. Women and minority-group members are key constituencies of the Democratic Party, and Democratic presidents have appointed more judges from these groups than have Republican presidents (see Figure 14-3). Of President Bill Clinton's appointees, for example, roughly 30 percent were women and 25 percent were members of racial or ethnic minority groups, compared with 20 percent in each category for George W. Bush.

The Supreme Court has a degree of diversity. Of the nine current justices, three are women (Ruth Bader Ginsburg, Sonia Sotomayor, and Elena Kagan) and two are minority-group members (Clarence Thomas and Sotomayor). The historical pattern is more one-sided. Until 1916, when Louis D. Brandeis was appointed to the Court, no Jewish justice had ever served. Prior to the twentieth century, only one Catholic, Roger Taney, had served on the Court. Six of the current justices are Catholic and three are Jewish, marking the first time the Court has been without a Protestant member. Thurgood Marshall in 1967 was the first black justice, and Sandra Day O'Connor in 1981 was the first woman justice. Antonin Scalia in 1986 was the Court's first justice of Italian descent. Sotomayor, who was appointed in 2009, is the first Hispanic justice. No person of Asian descent has been appointed to the Supreme Court.

The Nature of Judicial Decision Making

Unlike the president or members of Congress, federal judges make their decisions within the context of a legal system. Yet, they are also political officials: they constitute one of three coequal branches of the national government. As a result, their decisions, though rooted in law, also have a political component.

Legal Influences on Judicial Decisions

Article III of the Constitution bars a federal court from issuing a decision except in response to a case presented to it. This restriction is a substantial one. For one thing, it limits judges to issues that arise from actual legal disputes. As federal judge David Bazelon noted, a judge "can't wake up one morning and simply decide to give a helpful little push to a school system, a mental hospital, or the local housing agency."[21]

The facts of a particular case also limit judicial action. The **facts** of a case are the relevant circumstances of a legal dispute or offense. In the case of a person accused of murder, for example, key facts would include evidence about the crime and whether the rights of the accused had been upheld by police. A judge must treat a murder case as a murder case, applying to it the laws that define murder and the penalties for it. A murder case cannot be used as an occasion for a judge to pronounce judgment on free speech rights or campaign finance laws.

Judicial decisions are also restricted in their breadth. Technically, a court ruling is binding only on the parties involved. Its broader impact depends on the willingness of others to accept it. If a court were to decide, for example, that a school was bound by law to spend more on programs for the learning disabled, the ruling would extend to other schools in the same situation only if those schools voluntarily complied or were forced by subsequent court action to do so. By comparison, if Congress were to pass legislation granting funds to schools for programs for the learning disabled, all eligible schools would receive the funding.

The major constraint on the courts is the law itself. Although a president or Congress can make almost any decision that is politically acceptable, the judiciary must work within the confines of the law. When asked by a friend to "do justice," Justice Oliver Wendell Holmes Jr. said that he was bound to follow the law rather than his personal desires.[22]

The judiciary works within the context of three main sources of law: the Constitution, legislative statutes, and legal precedents (see Table 14-2).

table 14-2 Sources of Law That Constrain the Decisions of the Federal Judiciary

Federal judges make their decisions in the context of law, which limits their discretion. The Constitution, statutes, and precedents are major constraints on the judiciary.

U.S. Constitution: The federal courts are bound by the provisions of the U.S. Constitution. The sparseness of its wording, however, requires the Constitution to be applied in the light of present circumstances. Thus, judges are accorded some degree of discretion in their constitutional judgments.

Statutory law: The federal courts are constrained by statutes and by administrative regulations derived from the provisions of statutes. Many laws, however, are somewhat vague in their provisions and often have unanticipated applications. As a result, judges have some freedom in deciding cases based on statutes.

Precedent: Federal courts tend to follow precedent (or stare decisis), which is a legal principle developed through earlier court decisions. Because times change and not all cases have a clear precedent, judges have some discretion in their evaluation of the way earlier cases apply to a current case.

The Constitution of the United States is the nation's highest law, and judges and justices are sworn to uphold it. When a case raises a constitutional issue, a court has the duty to apply the Constitution to it. For example, the Constitution prohibits the states from printing their own currency. If a state decided that it would do so anyway, a federal judge would be obligated to rule against the practice.

The large majority of cases that arise in courts involve issues of statutory and administrative law rather than constitutional law. *Statutory law* is legislative (statute) law. *Administrative law* is based on statutory law but is set by government agencies rather than by legislatures. Administrative law consists of the rules, regulations, and judgments that agencies make in the process of implementing and enforcing statutory law. All federal courts are bound by federal statutory and administrative laws, as well as by treaties, and judges must work within the confines of these laws. A company that is charged with violating an air pollution law, for example, will be judged within the context of that law—what it permits and what it prohibits, and what penalties apply if the company is found to have broken the law. When hearing such a case, a judge will typically try to determine whether the meaning of the statute or regulation can be determined by common sense (the "plain meaning rule"). The question for the judge is what the law or regulation was intended to safeguard (such as clean air). In most cases, the law or regulation is clear enough that when the facts of the case are determined, the decision is fairly straightforward.

The U.S. legal system developed from the English common-law tradition, which includes the principle that a court's decision on a case should be consistent with previous judicial rulings. This principle, known as precedent, reflects the philosophy of stare decisis (Latin for "to stand by things that have been decided"). Precedent holds that principles of law, once established, should be applied in subsequent similar cases. Judges and justices often cite past rulings as justification for their decisions in the cases before them. Deference to precedent gives predictability to the application of law. Government has an obligation to make clear what its laws are and how they are being applied. If courts routinely ignored how similar cases had been decided in the past, they would create confusion and uncertainty about what is lawful and what is not. A business firm that is seeking to comply with environmental protection laws, for example, can develop company policies that will keep the company safely within the

The Supreme Court's power is never more evident than when its strikes down a law passed by Congress or a state legislature on grounds that it violates the Constitution. Over the years, the Court has invalidated a number of state laws that have sought to promote religion in public schools. The Court considers the issue of religion in the schools to be an issue of individual rights rather than of majority rule.

law if court decisions in this area are consistent. If courts routinely ignored precedent, a firm could unintentionally engage in an activity that a court might conclude was unlawful.

Political Influences on Judicial Decisions

Adherence to the law in the judging of cases is what gives substance to the claim that the United States is governed by "the rule of law." If judges were to ignore or downplay their obligation to uphold the law, the public's respect for the law and willingness to comply with it would diminish accordingly.

Nevertheless, the law is not always a precise guide to judicial decisions, with the result that judges often have some have leeway in their rulings.[23] The Constitution, for example, is a sparsely worded document and must be adapted to new and changing situations. The judiciary also has no choice at times but to impose meaning on statutory law. Statutes are typically more detailed in their provisions than is the Constitution, but Congress cannot always anticipate the specific applications of a legislative act and often defines statutory provisions in general terms. The judiciary is then required to determine what the language means in the context of a specific case. Precedent is even less precise as a guide to decisions in that it is specific to particular cases. A new case may differ in important ways from its closest precedent or rest at the intersection of competing precedents. In such instances, a judge must determine which precedent, if any, applies to the case at hand.

The Supreme Court's ruling in *Faragher v. City of Boca Raton* (1998), involving sexual harassment in the workplace, illustrates the ambiguity that can exist in the law. The Court developed its ruling in the context of the antidiscrimination provisions of the Civil Rights Act of 1964. However, the act itself contains no description of, or even reference to, job-related sexual harassment. Yet the act does prohibit workplace discrimination, and the Court was unwilling to dismiss sexual harassment as an irrelevant form of job-related discrimination. In this sense, the Court was "making" law; it was deciding how legislation enacted by Congress applied to behavior that Congress had not specifically addressed when it wrote the legislation. In the end, the Court decided that sexual harassment on the job is among the types of job-related discrimination prohibited by the Civil Rights Act.[24]

Political influences affect how judges decide cases in which they have leeway. These influences come from both inside and outside the judicial system.

Inside the Court: Judges' Political Beliefs Although the judiciary symbolizes John Adams's description of the U.S. political system as "a government of laws, and not of men," court rulings are not simply an extension of the laws. They are also influenced by the political beliefs of the men and women who sit on the federal bench.[25] Changes in the Supreme Court's membership, for example, can bring about a change in its position. Samuel Alito's appointment to the Court in 2006 produced that kind of change. Although the justice he replaced, Sandra Day O'Connor, usually voted with the Court's four most conservative justices, she sometimes switched sides. Voting with the Court's four most liberal justices, she cast the deciding vote, for example, in the 2000 Nebraska case that upheld the use of partial-birth abortion when the mother's life is endangered. In contrast, Alito cast the deciding vote in the 2007 decision to uphold a congressional ban on the use of partial-birth abortion. Alito's decision in this case and others prompted observers to say that the Supreme Court had swung to the right. Even one of the Supreme Court justices admitted as much. "It is not often in the law," wrote Justice Stephen Breyer, "that so few have so quickly changed so much."[26]

Studies by Jeffrey Segal and Harold Spaeth show that justices tend to vote in line with their political attitudes. Segal and Spaeth examined thousands of non-unanimous Court decisions, looking at the extent to which each justice voted on the same side or the opposite side from each of the other justices. Clear patterns emerged, such as the tendency of Antonin Scalia and Clarence Thomas, who are Republican appointees, to vote the same way and opposite that of Stephen Breyer and Ruth Bader Ginsburg, who are Democratic appointees. Segal and Spaeth concluded that the "[policy] preferences of the justices go a long way toward explaining their decisions."[27]

It is true, of course, that disputes that reach the Supreme Court are anything but clear-cut. If they were, they would have been settled in the lower federal courts. Nevertheless, Supreme Court decisions are a mix of law and politics. Arguably, partisanship was never more evident than in the Supreme Court's *Bush v. Gore* (2000) decision that blocked a manual recount of the Florida presidential vote in 2000, thereby assuring the election of the Republican nominee, George W. Bush.[28] The five justices in the majority—Chief Justice William Rehnquist and associate justices Sandra Day O'Connor, Anthony Kennedy, Antonin Scalia, and Clarence Thomas—were Republican appointees and were the same justices who in previous decisions had deferred to state authority and had opposed new applications of the Fourteenth Amendment's equal protection clause. Yet they rejected the authority of Florida's highest court, which had ordered a statewide manual recount of the vote. They also devised a never-before-used application of the equal protection clause, concluding that the recount could not go forward because no uniform standard for counting the ballots existed. Justice John Paul Stevens, who thought the Florida high court had acted properly in ordering a recount, accused the Court's majority of devising a ruling based on their partisanship rather than on the law, saying the majority had ignored "the basic principle, inherent in our Constitution and our democracy, that every legal vote should be counted."[29] Stevens noted that different standards for casting and counting ballots are used throughout the country, even within the same state.

Outside the Court: The Public, Groups, and Elected Officials The courts can and do make unpopular decisions. In the long run, however, judicial decisions must be seen as fair if they are to be obeyed. In other words, the judiciary cannot routinely ignore the expectations of the general public, interest groups, and elected officials.

Judges are less responsive to public opinion than are elected officials. Nevertheless, the Supreme Court in some instances has tempered its rulings in an effort to get public support or reduce public resistance. The Supreme Court usually stays close enough to public opinion to reduce the likelihood of outright defiance of its decisions.[30] In the 1954 *Brown* case, for example, the justices, recognizing that school desegregation would be an explosive issue in the South, required only that desegregation take place "with all deliberate speed" rather than immediately or on a fixed timetable. After its *Swann v. Charlotte-Mecklenburg Board of Education* (1971) school busing decision led to riots in several cities, the Court held in *Milliken v. Bradley* (1974) that busing across school district lines would not be permitted. The *Milliken* decision effectively insulated suburban school districts from busing, which served to reduce white suburbanites' opposition to the policy.[31]

Interest groups also have an influence on the judiciary. Groups petition the White House and Congress to appoint judges and justices who share their outlook on legal disputes. More directly, they submit amicus curiae ("friend of the court") briefs to make their positions known on court cases (see Chapters 5 and 9) and file lawsuits to advance their policy goals. Some groups, in fact, rely almost entirely on legal action, knowing they have a better chance of success in the courts than in Congress or the White House. The American Civil Liberties Union (ACLU), for example, has filed hundreds of lawsuits over the years on issues of individual rights. In 2010, for instance, the ACLU filed suit to force federal agents to meet

Even though the Supreme Court tried to temper the public response to its 1954 *Brown v. Board of Education* decision by ruling that desegregation of public schools should proceed with "all deliberate speed" rather than immediately or on a fixed timetable, the delay in implementation did little to quell the anger of many white southerners. Shown here is one of the many billboards in the South that called for the impeachment of Chief Justice Earl Warren.

constitutional requirements for search and seizure before they could examine documents stored on travelers' laptop computers. Groups that rely on a judicial strategy pick their cases carefully, choosing those that offer the greatest chance of success. They also carefully pick the courts in which they file their lawsuits, knowing that some judges are more sympathetic than others to their argument.

Elected officials also have ways of influencing the courts. Congress can rewrite legislation that it feels the judiciary has misinterpreted. Meanwhile, the president is responsible for enforcing court decisions and has some influence over the cases that come before the courts. Under President Reagan, for example, the Justice Department vigorously pursued lawsuits that challenged the legality of affirmative action, a strategy consistent with Reagan's determination to limit its use.

Judicial appointments offer the president and Congress their biggest opportunity to influence the courts. In 2008, when it became clear that their party was likely to win the presidency, Senate Democrats slowed action on the confirmation of President Bush's judicial nominees. When

Barack Obama took office in 2009, scores of judgeships were vacant, which he filled with loyal Democrats. It was a tactic Senate Republicans had employed in 2000. They had delayed action on President Clinton's nominees, enabling Bush to appoint Republicans to existing vacancies when he took office in 2001.

POLITICAL THINKING

Partisanship, or Merit?

Partisan considerations have increasingly influenced the selection of federal judges. Interest groups on the right and the left have insisted on the appointment of judges who hold compatible views. Presidents and members of Congress have also increasingly sought appointees who will decide issues in ways of their liking. What is your view? Should politics play such a large role in judicial appointments? Or should merit be given greater weight?

As a result of heightened partisanship in Congress (see Chapter 11), the judicial appointment process has become increasingly contentious. Democratic and Republican lawmakers alike recognize the power of the courts to determine policy in areas such as affirmative action and environmental protection, and each party's lawmakers have been determined to confirm judicial appointees whose policy views align with their own. Nevertheless, the influence of elected officials on the judiciary is never total. Judges prize their independence, and their lifetime appointment insulates them from political pressures. In 2004, for example, the Republican-laden Supreme Court rejected the Bush administration's claim that it had the authority to jail suspected terrorists indefinitely without a court hearing (see Chapter 4).

Judicial Power and Democratic Government

Federal judges are unelected officials with lifetime appointments, which places them beyond the reach of the voters. Because the United States has a constitutional system that places limits on the power of the majority, the judiciary has a legitimate role in the system. Yet court decisions reflect in part the personal political beliefs of the judges. A basic question is how far judges should go in substituting their judgments for those of elected officials.

HOW THE U.S. DIFFERS
POLITICAL THINKING THROUGH COMPARISONS

Judicial Power

U.S. courts are highly political compared to the courts of most other democracies. First, U.S. courts operate within a common-law tradition, in which judge-made law becomes (through precedent) a part of the legal code. Many democracies have a civil-law tradition, in which nearly all law is defined by legislative statutes. Second, because U.S. courts operate in a constitutional system of divided powers, they are required to rule on conflicts between state and nation or between the executive and the legislative branches, which thrusts the judiciary into the middle of political conflicts. Not surprisingly, then, federal judges and justices are appointed through an overtly political process in which partisan views and activities are major considerations. Many federal judges, particularly at the district level, have no significant prior judicial experience. In fact, the United States is one of the few countries that does not require formal training for judges.

The pattern is different in most European democracies, where judgeships tend to be career positions. Individuals are appointed to the judiciary at an early age and then work their way up the judicial ladder largely on the basis of seniority. Partisan politics does not play a large role in appointment and promotion. By tradition, European judges see their job as the strict interpretation of statutes, not the creative application of them.

The power of U.S. courts is nowhere more evident than in the exercise of judicial review—the voiding of a legislative or executive action on the grounds that it violates the Constitution. Judicial review had its origins in European experience and thought, but it was first formally applied in the United States at the federal level when, in *Marbury v. Madison* (1803), the Supreme Court declared an act of Congress unconstitutional. Some democracies, including Great Britain, still do not allow broad-scale judicial review, but most democracies now provide for it.

In the so-called American system of judicial review, all judges can evaluate the applicability of constitutional law to particular cases and can declare ordinary law invalid when it conflicts with constitutional law. By comparison, the so-called Austrian system restricts judicial review to a special constitutional court. Judges in other courts cannot declare a law void on the grounds that it is unconstitutional; they must apply ordinary law as it is written. In the Austrian system, moreover, constitutional decisions can be made in response to requests for judicial review by elected officials when they are considering legislation. In the American case, judges can act only within the framework of actual legal cases; thus, their rulings are made only after laws have been enacted.

Q: *Do you think it would be advantageous if the U.S. Supreme Court, in response to queries by Congress or the president, could issue advisory opinions on the constitutionality of policies under consideration? Or do you prefer the current American system, whereby the Supreme Court can issue opinions only in the context of an actual court case, which means that legislative or executive action must take place in advance of any court ruling?*

This power is most dramatically evident when courts declare laws enacted by Congress to be unconstitutional. In such instances, unelected judges are substituting their decision for that of the people's elected representatives. The difficult process of amending the Constitution (two-thirds majorities in the House and Senate and approval by three-fourths of the states are required) makes such amendments an impracticable means of reversing the Supreme Court. During the past century, only one constitutional amendment—the Sixteenth, which provides for a federal income tax—has been adopted in reaction to a Supreme Court decision.

The judiciary's power has been a source of controversy throughout the nation's history, but the debate has seldom been livelier than during recent decades. The judiciary at times has acted almost legislatively by addressing broad social issues, such as abortion, busing, affirmative action, church-state relations, campaign finance, and prison reform. During the 1990s, for example, the prison systems in forty-two states were operating under federal court orders that mandated improvements in health care or reductions in overcrowding. Through such actions the judiciary has restricted the policymaking authority of the states, has narrowed legislative discretion, and has made judicial action an effective political strategy for certain interests.[32]

The judiciary has become more extensively involved in policymaking for many of the same reasons that Congress and the president have been thrust into new policy areas and become more deeply involved in old ones. Social and economic changes have required government to play a larger role in society, and this development has generated a seemingly endless series of new legal controversies. Environmental pollution, for example, was not a major issue until the 1960s; since then, it has been the subject of innumerable court cases.

How far should judges go in asserting their interpretations of the law, as opposed to those put into effect by the people's elected representatives? What is the proper role of an unelected judiciary in a system rooted in the principle of majority rule? There are competing schools of thought on this issue, none of which is definitive. The Constitution is silent on the question of how it should be interpreted, which has left the judiciary's proper role open to dispute. Nevertheless, a brief review of the major competing theories is instructive.

Originalism Theory vs. Living Constitution Theory

Originalism theory, a prominent philosophy of conservatives, holds that the Constitution should be interpreted in the way that a reasonable person would have interpreted it at the time it was written.[33] Originalists emphasize the wording of the law, arguing that the words of the framers are the only reliable indicator of how the law should be interpreted. As Supreme Court justice Antonin Scalia, an avowed originalist, has said: "You figure out what [the Constitution] was understood to mean when it was adopted and that's the end of it." The difficult part, Scalia claims, is trying to figure out what the words meant to those who wrote and ratified them. "It requires immersing oneself in the political and intellectual atmosphere of the time—somehow placing out of mind knowledge that we have which an earlier age did not."[34]

An opposing theory, embraced more often by liberals, holds that the Constitution is a living document that should be interpreted in light of changing circumstances. Proponents of the **living constitution theory** claim that the framers, through the use of broad language and basic principles, intended the Constitution to be an adaptable instrument. They cite the preamble of the 1787 Constitutional Convention's Committee of Detail, which says the Constitution "ought to be accommodated to times and events." Supreme Court justice Stephen Breyer embraces this view, saying that the judiciary should promote in today's world the kind of government the Constitution was meant to establish. "The Constitution," Breyer argues, "provides a

John Marshall served thirty-four years as chief justice of the Supreme Court, the longest tenure in that position in U.S. history. An ardent nationalist, Marshall led the Court to a series of activist rulings that established it as a powerful institution and helped lay the foundation for a strong Union.

framework for the creation of democratically determined solutions, which protect each individual's basic liberties . . . while securing a democratic form of government."[35]

Critics of the living constitution theory argue that, in practice, it allows judges to promote their personal views by enabling them to devise arguments that support the rulings they prefer. Such judges are said to turn the law into what they want it to say, rather than what it actually says. On the other hand, critics of originalism theory say that the framers in using broad terms such as "search and seizure" could not possibly have had the practices of their time solely in mind. If that is what the framers intended, it is said, they would have expressed the provisions in specific terms. The only plausible reason for why the framers used general phrases and invoked broad principles was their recognition that society and the law necessarily evolve.

Judicial Restraint vs. Judicial Activism

A longer standing debate over the judiciary's proper role has pitted the advocates of judicial restraint against the advocates of judicial activism. This debate centers on the degree to which judges should defer to precedent and elected officials.

The doctrine of **judicial restraint** holds that judges should generally defer to precedent and to decisions made by legislatures. The restraint doctrine holds that in nearly every instance policy issues should be decided by elected lawmakers and not by appointed judges. The role of the judge is to apply the law rather than determine it. Advocates of judicial restraint say that when judges substitute their views for those of elected representatives, they undermine the fundamental principle of self-government—the right of the majority, through its elected representatives, to determine how they will be governed.[36] Underlying this argument is the idea that policy is the result of conflicts between contending interests and that elected representatives, because they deal with these interests regularly, are in a better position than judges to determine how the conflicts should be resolved.[37]

In contrast, the doctrine of **judicial activism** holds that judges should actively interpret the Constitution, statutes, and precedents in light of fundamental principles and should intervene when elected representatives fail to act in accord with these principles. Although advocates of judicial activism acknowledge the importance of majority rule, they claim that the courts should not bow to precedent or the decisions of elected officials when core principles—such as liberty, equality, and self-government—are threatened. In such instances, judges should not hesitate to reverse precedent or to override executive or legislative action.

Over its history, the Supreme Court has had strong proponents of each doctrine. Chief Justice John Marshall was an avowed activist who used the Court to enlarge the judiciary's power and to promote the national government (see Chapters 2 and 3). Judicial review—the most substantial form of judicial power—is not granted explicitly by the Constitution but was claimed through Marshall's opinion in *Marbury v. Madison*. Associate Justice Oliver Wendell Holmes Jr. was Marshall's philosophical opposite. One of the nation's most influential jurists, Holmes argued that the judiciary should defer to the elected branches unless they blatantly overstepped their authority.[38] Holmes wrote the opinion in *Schenck v. United States* (1919) that upheld a congressional restriction on free speech, despite the First Amendment admonition that Congress shall pass "no law . . . abridging the freedom of speech." Holmes argued that the First Amendment does not prevent Congress from enacting laws prohibiting speech that results in "substantive evils," such as rioting or loss of life (see Chapter 4).[39]

Although judicial activism is sometimes associated with liberal justices, history indicates it has also been practiced by conservative justices. During the period between the Civil War and the Great Depression, the Supreme Court was dominated by conservatives and had an activist agenda, striking down most state and congressional legislation aimed at economic regulation (see Chapter 3). In the period after World War II, the Court was again in an activist mode, but this time in a different direction. Dominated by liberal justices, the Court struck down numerous state statutes in the course of expanding fair-trial rights and civil rights (see Chapters 4 and 5).

In recent years, the conservative-dominated Supreme Court has also been an activist court. In the past fifteen years or so, the Supreme Court has struck down more acts of Congress than were invalidated during the previous half-century.[40] A case in point is the Court's recent ruling on campaign spending. In deciding that corporations and unions could spend freely on election campaigns, the Court overturned congressional action and also overturned precedent. The Court had previously held that Congress could regulate corporate and union spending during elections.

POLITICAL THINKING

Judicial Activism, or Judicial Restraint?

Which philosophy—judicial activism or judicial restraint—comes closer to your own thinking about the proper role of the courts? Does your support for restraint or activism depend on whether a judicial decision conforms to your own preference on the issue in question?

What Is the Judiciary's Proper Role?

Like the debate between originalism and living Constitution theorists, the debate between advocates of judicial restraint and activism is a normative one. There is no conclusive way of settling the issue because the Constitution does not specify the method by which judges should arrive at their decisions.

Nevertheless, the debates are important because they address the fundamental question of the role of judges in a governing system based on the often-conflicting concepts of majority rule and individual rights. The United States is a constitutional democracy that recognizes both the power of the majority to rule and the claim of the minority to protection of its rights and interests. The judiciary was not established as the nation's final authority on all things relating to the use of political power. Yet the judiciary was established as a coequal branch of government charged with responsibility for protecting individual rights and constraining political authority. The question of how far the courts should go in asserting their authority is one that every student of government should ponder.

SUMMARY Self-Test www.mhhe.com/pattersonwtp9e

At the lowest level of the federal judicial system are the district courts, where most federal cases begin. Above them are the federal courts of appeals, which review cases appealed from the lower courts. The U.S. Supreme Court is the nation's highest court. Each state has its own court system, consisting of trial courts at the bottom and one or two appellate levels at the top. Cases originating in state courts ordinarily cannot be appealed to the federal courts unless a federal issue is involved, and then the federal courts can choose to rule only on the federal aspects of the case. Federal judges at all levels are nominated by the president, and if confirmed by the Senate, they are appointed by the president to the office. Once on the federal bench, they serve until they die, retire, or are removed by impeachment and conviction.

The Supreme Court is unquestionably the most important court in the country. The legal principles it establishes are binding on lower courts, and its capacity to define the law is enhanced by the control it exercises over the cases it hears. However, it is inaccurate to assume that lower courts are inconsequential (the upper-court myth). Lower courts have considerable discretion, and the great majority of their decisions are not reviewed by a higher court. It is also inaccurate to assume that federal courts are far more significant than state courts (the federal court myth).

The courts have less discretionary authority than elected institutions do. The judiciary's positions are constrained by the facts of a case and by the laws as defined through the Constitution, legal precedent, and statutes (and government regulations derived from statutes). Yet existing legal guidelines are seldom so precise that judges have no choice in their decisions. As a result, political influences have a strong impact on the judiciary. It responds to national conditions, public opinion, interest groups, and elected officials, particularly the president and members of Congress. Another political influence on the judiciary is the personal beliefs of judges, who have individual preferences that affect how they decide issues that come before the courts. Not surprisingly, partisan politics plays a significant role in judicial appointments.

In recent decades, as the Supreme Court has crossed into areas traditionally left to lawmaking majorities, the issue of judicial power has become more pressing, which has prompted claims and counter-claims about the judiciary's proper role. Advocates of originalism theory argue that judges should apply the law in terms of the words of the law as they were understood at the time of enactment. Advocates of the living constitution theory hold that the law should be interpreted in light of changing circumstances. Judicial restraint and activism are two additional theories of the judiciary's proper role. Advocates of judicial restraint claim that the justices' personal values are inadequate justification for exceeding the proper judicial role; they argue that the Constitution entrusts broad issues of the public good to elective institutions and that the courts should ordinarily defer to the judgment of elected officials. Judicial activists counter that the courts were established as an independent branch and should not hesitate to promote general principles when necessary, even if this action brings them into conflict with elected officials.

Key Terms

appellate jurisdiction (*p. 491*)
brief (*p. 493*)
concurring opinion (*p. 493*)
decision (*p. 493*)
dissenting opinion (*p. 493*)
facts (of a court case) (*p. 504*)
judicial activism (*p. 516*)
judicial conference (*p. 493*)
judicial restraint (*p. 515*)
judicial review (*p. 492*)
jurisdiction (of a court) (*p. 491*)
living constitution theory (*p. 514*)
majority opinion (*p. 493*)
opinion (of a court) (*p. 493*)
original jurisdiction (*p. 491*)
originalism theory (*p. 514*)
plurality opinion (*p. 493*)
precedent (*p. 492*)
senatorial courtesy (*p. 501*)
writ of certiorari (*p. 492*)

Suggested Readings

Breyer, Stephen. *Active Liberty: Interpreting the Democratic Constitution*. New York: Vintage, 2006. A treatise on constitutional interpretation by one of the Supreme Court's most liberal justices.

Davis, Richard. *Electing Justices: Fixing the Supreme Court Nomination Process*. New York: Oxford University Press, 2005. An examination of the now-contentious process through which Supreme Court justices are nominated and confirmed.

Hansford, Thomas G., and James F. Spriggs II. *The Politics of Precedent on the Supreme Court*. Princeton, N.J.: Princeton University Press, 2006. An examination of how the Court interprets precedent to suit new situations and goals.

Maltzman, Forest, Paul Wahlbeck, and James Spriggs. *The Collegial Game: Crafting Law on the U.S. Supreme Court*. New York: Cambridge University Press, 2000. A fascinating look at the strategic considerations that go into Supreme Court justices' interactions and decisions.

McGuire, Kevin T. *Understanding the Supreme Court: Cases and Controversies*. New York: McGraw-Hill, 2002. An overview of Supreme Court decisions and approaches to legal disputes.

O'Brien, David M. *Storm Center: The Supreme Court in American Politics*, 8th ed. New York: Norton, 2008. A thorough assessment of the Supreme Court.

Sandler, Ross, and David Schoenbord. *Democracy by Decree: What Happens When Courts Run Government*. New Haven, CT.: Yale University Press, 2003. A critical evaluation of the courts' widening policy role.

Scalia, Antonin. *A Matter of Interpretation: Federal Courts and the Law*. Princeton, N.J.: Princeton University Press, 1998. A treatise on constitutional interpretation by one of the Supreme Court's most conservative justices.

Segal, Jeffrey A., and Harold J. Spaeth. *The Supreme Court and the Attitudinal Model Revisited.* New York: Cambridge University Press, 2002. A study of inter-justice agreement on Supreme Court decisions that reveals the influence of political attitudes.

List of Websites

www.supremecourt.gov The website of the U.S. Supreme Court; it includes information on the Court, as well as on its previous and pending cases.

www.fjc.gov The home page of the Federal Judicial Center, an agency created by Congress to conduct research and provide education on the federal judicial system.

www.lib.umich.edu/govdocs/fedjudi.html A University of Michigan web page that provides detailed information on the federal judicial system.

www.law.cornell.edu The Cornell University Legal Information Institute's website; includes full-text versions of historic and recent Supreme Court decisions, as well as links to state constitutions and other subjects.

Politics in Theory and Practice

Thinking: Which philosophy—judicial restraint or judicial activism—comes closer to your own thinking about the proper role of the courts? Does your support for restraint or activism depend on whether a judicial decision conforms to your own preference on the issue in question?

Participating: The right to a jury trial is one of the oldest features—dating to the colonial period—of the American political experience. Jury trials also offer the average citizen a rare opportunity to be part of the governing structure. Yet Americans increasingly shirk jury duty. When summoned, many of them find all sorts of reasons why they should be excused from jury duty. In some areas of the country, the avoidance rate exceeds 50 percent. Some citizens even give up their right to vote because they know that jurors in their area are selected from names on voter registration lists. There are reasons, however, to look upon jury duty as an opportunity as well as a responsibility. Studies indicate that citizens come away from the jury experience with a fuller appreciation of the justice system. Jurors acquire an understanding of the serious responsibility handed to them when asked to decide upon someone's guilt or innocence. The legal standard in American courts—"guilty beyond a reasonable doubt"—is a solemn one. The fairness of the jury system also requires full participation by the community. Studies show that jurors' life experiences can affect the decisions they reach. If everyone on a jury is from the same background and one that is different from the defendant's, the odds of a wrongful verdict increase. "A jury of one's peers" should mean just that—a jury of individuals who, collectively, represent the range of groups in the community.

If you are called to serve on a jury, you should answer the call. You would want nothing less from others than if you, a family member, or a friend were the person on trial.

EXTRA CREDIT

For up-to-the-minute *New York Times* articles, interactive simulations, graphics, study tools, and more links and quizzes, visit the text's Online Learning Center at **www.mhhe.com/pattersonwtp9e**.

NATIONAL JOURNAL

Supreme Court Nominations: Is There a Better Way?

Long before he became exasperated by Supreme Court nominee Elena Kagan dodging his pointed questions, Sen. Arlen Specter, D-Pa., had teed up a surefire way for the Senate to improve the process for considering judicial nominations. The prickly Pennsylvanian said that the Senate should reject those hoping to sit on the nation's highest court if they are not forthright about their judicial philosophy. Nominees would have to be more responsive, he figured, if they knew they might otherwise get shot down.

"In my judgment, the Senate should resist, if not refuse to confirm, Supreme Court nominees who refuse to answer questions on fundamental issues," Specter wrote in his 2000 autobiography, Passion for Truth. "Senators should not have to gamble or guess about a candidate's philosophy but should be able to judge on the basis of the candidate's expressed views."

The irascible former district attorney, who was defeated in a May primary, might just follow through on that opinion as he nears the end of his 30-year Senate career. He appears to be the only Democrat on the Judiciary Committee who might vote against Kagan. "I'm thinking about it," he told reporters on June 30, after he repeatedly took issue with Kagan ducking questions, such as whether she would vote to take up certain cases if she were on the Supreme Court. She demurred, saying that she needed to read the briefs or hear arguments before taking a position.

Specter, who chaired the Judiciary Committee for two years as a Republican, has plenty of company in the academic community—and some among his Senate colleagues—who agree that the confirmation process for Supreme Court justices is in need of repair. Frustration over proceedings in which nominees have ducked and dodged questions and past instances in which nominees say one thing to senators and then act quite differently on the Court have convinced some observers that it is time to change certain aspects of the confirmation process. But if the process is broken, no consensus has emerged on how it might be fixed—and some senators argue that flawed or not, there is no good alternative.

"It used to be the case that the nominee didn't come to the hearing," said Geoffrey Stone, a law professor at the University of Chicago School of Law. "It may be that that was a more sensible approach. What's happened is that the hearing has become a kind of theater, particularly with it being televised and the media so focused on it. Everybody plays to the camera, and nobody really wants to watch anything but the candidate being grilled. That is sort of the highlight reel. The problem is that it is very hard for it to remain a serious process, given the fact that it has become kind of a circus because of the media."

"Everybody is playing for different stakes," Stone added. "Almost nobody is playing for the actual question of, who is this candidate and do I think she should be confirmed? They are all playing for the TV screen and their constituents."

Sen. Jon Kyl, R-Ariz., agreed that klieg lights in the hearing room sometimes inspire showboating, but he does not see it as a major issue. "Sure, senators always play to the cameras, but I don't know that that is the problem," he said in an interview. "The problem is witnesses who are schooled to avoid saying anything controversial. It's hard to make somebody say something. If you are really clever in your cross-examination, sometimes you can get some useful things out of it. But if you have a really clever nominee, he or she can avoid giving up very much. And [Kagan], for example, is a very clever nominee."

Senators repeatedly reminded Kagan during her three days of testimony this week that she had written an article in 1995 severely criticizing the confirmation process. She had singled out the hearings of Supreme Court nominees Ruth Bader Ginsburg and Stephen Breyer, who, she wrote, "felt free to decline to disclose their views on controversial issues and cases. They stonewalled the Judiciary Committee to great effect." She chided senators for not engaging in "meaningful discussion of legal issues," so that the process took on an "air of vacuity and farce" and rendered the lawmakers "incapable of either properly evaluating nominees or appropriately educating the public."

Now that she found herself sitting in the nominee's chair, Kagan backpedaled, saying that the article was "a little bit off." Some veteran observers of judicial nominations, however, see much merit in her critique and suggest that one way to get more-responsive answers would be to have more-skilled questioners who know how to follow up systematically in a way that gives the nominee less wiggle room.

The Judiciary Committee ought to follow the model that Congress used in the Iran-Contra investigation in 1987, Sanford Levinson, a law professor at the University of Texas, said. "Look at the Iran-Contra hearings. The Joint Committee hired [prominent lawyer] Arthur Liman and other first-rate attorneys to ask questions. It is not that the senators and representatives completely restrained themselves; but they recognized they were really dealing with serious stuff. In the Senate, it is much more amateur hour even for those [senators] who have been around for a while, because they have so many things to do."

"It really is the senators who make it such an unfortunate process," Levinson continued. "Let each of them bloviate for a few minutes, and then I'd like to see questions directed by well-trained lawyers or legal academics or, for that matter, journalists who follow the Court and have a very sophisticated understanding."

Tom Goldstein, co-creator of Scotus blog, a widely read site that focuses on the Supreme Court, agreed. "While senators have their own distinct role and should ask some questions, if you really want answers, you need to put it in the hands of a professional. So I do think that that would help, and help a lot, actually."

"The nominees have been preparing for this for months, and they are highly trained lawyers. You can't do this by asking a question; you have to ask five questions on a topic," Goldstein added. "Having an outside counsel who prepares exclusively for the hearing would make it easier to elicit information—or more difficult for the nominee to duck."

But some lawmakers see their job in the confirmation process as far more circumscribed, and certainly not one that requires a high-powered outsider. "We have a more limited role than people think," said Sen. Amy Klobuchar, D-Minn., a Judiciary Committee member. "We are trying to figure out if the nominees are qualified or competent. [Senators] grandstand, that's going to happen. But what we are asking to see is if [Kagan] knows these Court cases. Is she smart enough to handle all these senators? Seems to me she is."

Levinson, however, says that approach makes the committee a rubber stamp and marginalizes the Senate's role. "That is, frankly, a silly standard, because no smart president is going to nominate somebody who doesn't have a sterling resume," he said. "Look at [George W. Bush's nominees, John] Roberts and [Samuel] Alito. You can't challenge their resume."

Mark Kende, who teaches constitutional law at Drake Law School, agrees that the process is broken but insists that bringing in outside lawyers is not the answer. "All of these senators have staff people who are trained and very excellent attorneys who spend [lots of] time on it," he said. "And some senators are former prosecutors—like Specter. I think that [outside counsel] would only make a marginal difference."

Instead, Kende proposes taking a page from South Africa, where top-notch jurists are selected without the polarization that occurs in the U.S. Using that country's proceedings as a model, potential nominees would emerge from a process that begins with establishing a highly respected judicial service commission comprising the chief justice, other judges and lawyers, a number of bipartisan lawmakers and academics, and the attorney general. The commission would choose several possible candidates for an opening, interview them in a public hearing, and forward a list to the president with three more names than the number of openings.

"With this process, the months-long character assassinations of U.S. high court nominees don't happen," Kende recently wrote in The Christian Science Monitor. "There are still political disputes, but they are reduced. Moreover, nominees are viewed as esteemed lawyers or judges, not simply as political allies."

But when pressed on why a president would willingly relinquish some of his power to make Supreme Court selections, Kende acknowledged the political obstacles. "I am not unaware that the proposal has elements that at this point wouldn't have political traction," he said. "But if you view the system as fundamentally broken and you are trying to think of what are some solutions that are workable and have been used elsewhere, this is one."

Kyl says he is open to suggestions to making the hearings work better, but he seems resigned to the status quo. "I don't know what to do," he said. "I am not one for being a nasty questioner. Whereas somebody might be able to bore in and finally get something from a witness by just sheer, brute force, I am not suggesting that that is a good technique."

Then, reflecting a bit more, the Republican whip concluded, "If somebody can figure it out, let me know."

What's Your Opinion?

Do you think nominees to the federal bench should have to answer questions about how they would decide cases that might come before the courts to which they've been nominated? Explain the arguments for and against this confirmation practice.

What phrase(s) in the Constitution are at the basis of our modern Supreme Court confirmation hearings?

CHAPTER 15

Economic and Environmental Policy: Contributing to Prosperity

"We the people of the United States, in order to . . . insure domestic tranquility . . ."
PREAMBLE, U.S. CONSTITUTION

The financial markets were downright scary. The housing market was in turmoil. Foreclosures were on the rise as homeowners with subprime adjustable rate mortgages were unable to make their monthly payments. Then, on September 15, 2008, after its stock had dropped precipitously, Lehman Brothers, one of the nation's oldest and largest commercial banks, filed for bankruptcy, sending shock waves through the stock markets. Was the United States headed for an economic meltdown that would rival the Great Depression of the 1930s?

Although some pundits suggested another Great Depression might be in the offing, few economists predicted as much, and for understandable reasons. When the Great Depression began in 1929, there were no government programs in place to stabilize and stimulate the economy. Back then, panic had swept through society, worsening the downturn. Businesses cut back on production, investors fled the stock market, depositors withdrew their bank savings, and consumers slowed their spending—all of which accelerated the downward spiral. In 2008, by contrast, government programs were in place to protect depositors' savings, slow the drop in home and stock prices, and steady the economy through adjustments in interest rates and government spending. Among the government initiatives were the Troubled Asset Relief Program (TARP) of 2008 that made $700 billion available to bolster shaky financial institutions and the American Recovery and Reinvestment Act of 2009 that allocated $787 billion to stimulate the economy. By 2010, job loss had lessened, the financial markets were beginning to stabilize, and businesses were starting to recover. The turnaround was slower and more fitful than many economists had predicted, but government intervention had helped prevent a repeat of the 1930s, a decade when unemployment rose as high as 25 percent and never dropped below 10 percent.

This chapter examines economic and environmental policy. As was discussed in Chapter 1, public policy is a decision by government to follow a course of action designed to produce a particular result (see "The Public Policy Process"). In this vein, economic policy aims to promote and regulate economic interests and, through fiscal and monetary actions, to foster economic growth and stability. The main ideas presented in this chapter are these:

- *Through regulation, the U.S. government imposes restraints on business activity for the purpose of promoting economic efficiency and equity.*
- *Through regulatory and conservation policies, the U.S. government seeks to protect and preserve the environment from the actions of business firms and consumers.*
- *Through promotion, the U.S. government helps private interests achieve their economic goals.* Business in particular benefits from the government's promotional efforts, including, for example, tax breaks and loans.
- *Through its taxing and spending decisions (fiscal policy), the U.S. government seeks to generate a level of economic supply and demand that will maintain economic prosperity.*
- *Through its money supply decisions (monetary policy), the U.S. government—through the Federal Reserve System (the "Fed")—seeks to maintain a level of inflation consistent with sustained, controllable economic growth.*

The Public Policy Process

Government action in the economic sector is part of the public policy process—the political interactions that lead to the emergence and resolution of public policy issues. Political scientists have identified three stages that together make up the policy process. The first stage—problem recognition—refers to the emergence of issues. The second stage—policy formulation—refers to the formulation and enactment of a policy response to the problem. The third stage—policy implementation—refers to the carrying out of policy.

Policy problems stem from conditions of society—the employment rate, the quality of the schools, the security of the nation, the safety of the streets, and so on. Yet only certain conditions will be seen as problems of a public nature. Only recently, after research studies revealed the scope of the problem, have Americans begun to think of obesity as a public policy problem. In some cases problem recognition happens suddenly, even shockingly, as in the case of the terrorist attacks of September 11, 2001, when hatred of the United States by extremist elements abroad—a condition—erupted into a threat to America's long-term security—a policy problem. Policy problems come to public attention in a variety of ways. The president, interest groups, members of Congress, political parties, and the news media are among the actors that set the policy agenda. By highlighting a problem day after day, for example, the news media can convince people that it needs to be addressed.

After a policy problem is recognized, the question of how to address it arises. What is the proper policy response? Policy formulation—the development of a policy for dealing with the problem—is seldom easy. For one thing, an array of actors will want a say in what gets done. Such actors will include elected officials but could also include interest groups, citizens, and civic organizations. In addition, because society is complex, most policy problems are connected to other problems and cannot be resolved effectively without also taking them into account. The complexity of modern policymaking has created an entire industry—that of the policy analyst. Thousands of scholars, consultants, and policy specialists are engaged in policy development. Trained economists, for example, develop the particulars of most economic policies. Politicians also formulate policy. They lack the analytic skill of the policy specialists but have their own strength—a sense of what other politicians might be willing to support.

Once a policy is adopted, it has to be put into effect. This stage is the policy implementation phase. Responsibility for implementation rests mainly with bureaucrats, who are charged with carrying out policy (see Chapter 13). In doing so, they often work in consultation with the interests

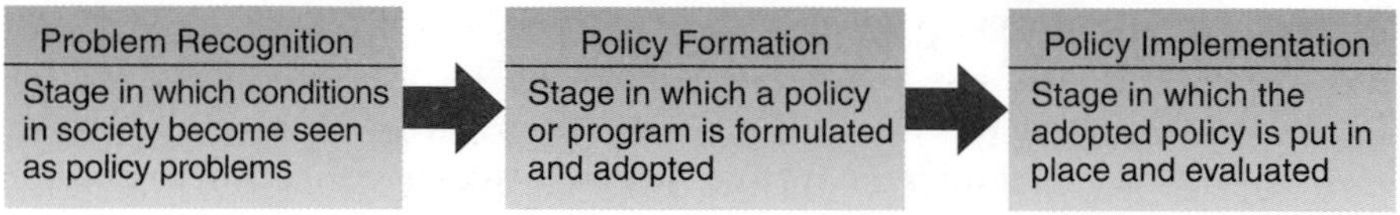

that are most directly affected by a policy. Agencies also have to take into account local differences when implementing some policies. Legislation aimed at improving roadways poses different implementation problems in Manhattan than in rural Mississippi. Policy evaluation is also part of the implementation stage. It is not enough simply to carry out policy. It is necessary also to determine whether it is having the expected effect. If not, adjustments in the policy or its implementation may be necessary.

In summary, the public policy process is a set of analytically distinct stages that problems go through on their way to some sort of resolution. The problem recognition stage is when conditions in society become seen as public policy problems; the policy formulation stage is when a solution is settled upon in the form of a policy or program; and the policy implementation stage is when the adopted policy is put into place and its effectiveness assessed.

Government as Regulator of the Economy

An **economy** is a system of production and consumption of goods and services that are allocated through exchange. When a shopper selects an item at a store, and pays for it with cash or credit card, the transaction is one of the millions upon millions of exchanges that make up the economy.

In *The Wealth of Nations* (1776), Adam Smith advanced the doctrine of **laissez-faire economics**, which holds that private firms should be free to make their own production and distribution decisions. Smith reasoned that firms will supply a good when there is a demand for it (that is, when people are willing and able to buy it). Smith argued that the profit motive is the "invisible hand" that guides supply decisions in a capitalist system. He acknowledged that laissez-faire capitalism had limits. Certain areas of the economy, such as roadways, are natural monopolies and are better handled by government than by private firms. Government is also needed to impose order on private transactions by regulating banking, currency, and contracts. Otherwise, Smith argued, the economy should be left largely in private hands.

Although laissez-faire economics prevailed in the United States during the nineteenth century, government was not sidelined completely. Through the Pacific Railways Act of 1862, for example, Congress authorized the issuance of government bonds and the use of public lands to build the transcontinental railroad, which, though operated by private firms, was subject to government regulation. Nevertheless, it was not until the Great Depression of the 1930s that government assumed a large economic role. Today, the United States has what is described as a *mixed economy*. Although the economy operates mainly through private transactions, government plays a substantial role. The U.S. government even owns some industry (for example, the Tennessee Valley Authority, which produces electricity). Nevertheless, in comparison, say, with the Scandinavian countries, where government provides health care to all citizens and controls a number of major industries, including the airlines, the United States relies more heavily on free-market mechanisms to make its production, distribution, and consumption decisions.

One way the U.S. government participates in the economy is through the **regulation** of privately owned businesses.[1] U.S. firms are not free to act as they please but instead operate within the limit of government regulation, which is designed to promote economic *efficiency* and *equity* (see Table 15-1).

Efficiency through Government Intervention

Economic efficiency results when the output of goods and services is the highest possible given the amount of input (such as labor and material) that is used to produce them.[2] Efficiency is desirable. It means that society is getting as many goods and services as possible from the resources expended on their production.

table 15-1 THE MAIN OBJECTIVES OF REGULATORY POLICY

The government intervenes in the economy to promote efficiency and equity.

Objective	**Definition**	**Representative Actions by Government**
Efficiency	Fulfillment of as many of society's needs as possible at the cost of as few of its resources as possible. The greater the output for a given input, the more efficient the process.	Preventing restraint of trade; requiring producers to pay the costs of damage to the environment; reducing restrictions on business that cannot be justified on a cost-benefit basis.
Equity	When the outcome of an economic transaction is fair to each party.	Requiring firms to bargain in good faith with labor; protecting consumers in their purchases; protecting workers' safety and health.

Promoting Competition Adam Smith and other classical economists argued that the free market is the optimal means of achieving efficiency. In producing goods and services, firms will try to use as few resources as possible in order to keep their prices low, which will make their products more attractive to consumers. To compete, less efficient producers will have to cut their production costs or face the loss of customers to their lower-priced rivals.

Markets are not always competitive, however. If a producer can acquire a monopoly on a particular product or can successfully conspire with other producers to fix the price of the product at an artificially high level, the producer does not have to be concerned with efficiency. Consumers who need or want a good have no choice but to pay the seller's price. Price fixing was prevalent in the United States in the late nineteenth century when large trusts came to dominate many areas of the economy, including the oil, steel, railroad, and sugar industries. Railroad companies, for example, had no competition on short routes and charged such high rates that many farmers went broke because they could not afford to ship their crops to markets. In 1887, Congress enacted the Interstate Commerce Act, which created the Interstate Commerce Commission (ICC) and assigned it responsibility for regulating railroad practices, including shipping rates.

The goal of such regulatory activity is to improve efficiency by restoring market competition or by limiting what producers are permitted to charge for goods and services. Business competition today is overseen by a wide range of federal agencies, including, for example, the Federal Trade Commission and the Antitrust Division of the Justice Department. These agencies are charged with preserving market competition. The Federal Trade Commission, for example, blocked the attempted merger of Office Depot and Staples, on grounds that it would undermine competition in the sale of office supplies. On the other hand, the government does allow concentrated ownership in industries, such as oil and automobiles, where the capital costs are so high that small firms cannot thrive.[3] Government acceptance of corporate giants also reflects the realization that market competition is no longer simply an issue of domestic firms. For example, the major U.S. automakers—Chrysler, Ford, and General Motors—compete for customers not only with each other but also with Asian and European auto manufacturers, such as Honda and BMW.

Making Business Pay for Indirect Costs Economic inefficiencies also result when businesses or consumers fail to pay the full costs of resources used in production. Consider companies whose industrial wastes seep into nearby lakes and rivers. The price of these companies' products does not reflect the cost to society of the resulting water pollution. Economists label these unpaid costs **externalities.**

Until the 1960s, the federal government did not require firms to pay such costs. The impetus to begin doing so came from the scientific community and environmental groups. The Clean Air Act of 1963 and the Water Quality Act of 1965 required firms to install antipollution devices designed to keep the discharge of air and water pollutants within specified limits. In 1970, Congress created the Environmental Protection Agency to monitor firms and ensure their compliance with federal regulations governing air and water quality and the disposal of toxic wastes. (Environmental policy is discussed more fully later in the chapter.)

Deregulation and Underregulation Although government regulation is intended to increase economic efficiency, it can have the opposite effect if it unnecessarily increases the cost of doing business.[4] Firms have to devote work hours to monitor and implement government regulations, which in some instances (for example, pollution control) also require companies to buy and install expensive equipment. These costs are efficient to the degree that they produce commensurate benefits. Yet if government places excessive regulatory burdens on firms, they waste resources in the process of complying. The result of overregulation is higher-priced goods that are more expensive for consumers and less competitive in the domestic and global markets.

To curb overregulation, Congress in 1995 enacted legislation that prohibits administrators in some instances from issuing a regulation unless they can show that its benefits outweigh its costs. A more concerted response is **deregulation**—the rescinding of regulations already in force for the purpose of improving efficiency. This process began in 1977 with passage of the Airlines Deregulation Act, which eliminated government-set airfares and the requirement that airlines provide service to smaller-sized cities. The change had the intended effect. Competition between airlines increased on routes between larger-sized cities, resulting in cheaper airfares on these routes. Congress followed airline deregulation with partial deregulation of the trucking, banking, energy, and communications industries, among others.

Deregulation can be carried too far.[5] Freed of regulatory restrictions, firms can engage in reckless or unethical behavior out of a belief that they can get away with it. Such was the case with the recent subprime mortgage crisis. Mortgage firms lured marginally qualified homebuyers by offering low interest rates and small down payments. When the economy

A meltdown in the subprime mortgage sector contributed to falling home prices and a rise in foreclosures. This development rippled through the economy and the financial markets, contributing to an economic downturn in 2008.

weakened, many homeowners defaulted on their mortgages. The resulting financial crisis required a government bailout of banking and investment firms, including Bank of America and Citigroup. Expressing a view held by political leaders of both parties, Barack Obama said that government had failed to regulate mortgage lenders closely enough. "The free market," said Obama, "was never meant to be a free license to take whatever you can get." In 2010, Congress enacted the most substantial regulation of financial institutions since the New Deal. Designed to curb some of the abuses that contributed to the financial crisis, the legislation requires closer monitoring of risky financial activities and makes it easier to liquidate poorly performing financial firms. It also created a new consumer protection agency to protect individuals from exploitation by creditors.

The crisis in America's financial system demonstrates that the issue of business regulation is not a simple question of whether or not to regulate. Too much regulation can burden firms with excessive implementation costs, whereas too little regulation can give firms the leeway to engage in risky or unethical practices. Either too little or too much regulation can result in economic inefficiency. The challenge for policymakers is to strike the proper balance between regulatory and free-market mechanisms.

Equity through Government Intervention

The government intervenes in the economy to bring equity as well as efficiency to the marketplace. **Economic equity** occurs when an economic transaction is fair to each party.[6] A transaction can be considered fair if each party enters into it freely and ethically (for example, if the seller knows a product is defective, equity requires that the buyer also know of the defect).

The Progressive Era was marked by some equity efforts, including the creation of the Food and Drug Administration (FDA) in 1907. Unsafe food and drugs were being widely marketed, and the FDA was charged with keeping adulterated food and dangerous or worthless drugs off the market. The New Deal era produced another wave of equity measures, including financial regulation. The Securities and Exchange Act of 1934, for example, was designed in part to protect investors from dishonest or imprudent stock and bond brokers. The New Deal also provided greater equity for organized labor, which had been in a weak position in dealing with management. The Fair Labor Standards Act of 1938, for example, required employers to pay workers a minimum wage and placed limits on the use of child labor.

The 1960s and 1970s produced the greatest number of equity reforms. Ten federal agencies, including the Consumer Product Safety Commission, were established to protect consumers, workers, and the public from harmful business activity. Among the products declared to be unsafe in the 1960s and 1970s were cigarettes and leaded paint, and gasoline. This regulatory activity has produced remarkable improvements in public health. Brain damage in children from lead poisoning, for example, has declined sharply in the past few decades.[7]

The Politics of Regulatory Policy

Economic regulation has come in waves, as changes in national conditions have created social awareness. The first wave came during the Progressive Era, when reformers sought to stop the unfair business practices of the new monopolies, such as the railroads. The second wave came during the Great Depression, when reformers sought to regulate troubled economic sectors, such as banking.

Although business firms fought the Progressive Era and New Deal reforms, their opposition diminished gradually as they adapted to the idea that the new regulatory agencies were charged with overseeing particular industries, such as banking or pharmaceuticals. This arrangement enabled a regulated industry to develop a close relationship with the agency overseeing its activities. Pharmaceutical firms, for example, established a working relationship with the FDA that at times has served their interest. In the 1990s, for instance, drug companies convinced the FDA to streamline its drug-safety reviews in order to speed the marketing of new drugs.[8] In some cases, the FDA's fast-track reviews were harmful to consumers. One fast-tracked drug, Vioxx, had to be taken off the market in 2004 after it was found to cause strokes and heart attacks.

The third wave of regulatory reform, in the 1960s and 1970s, differed from the Progressive and New Deal phases in both its form and its politics. This third wave has been called the era of "new social regulation" because of the broad social goals it addressed in three policy areas: environmental protection, consumer protection, and worker safety. Most of the regulatory agencies established during the third wave were granted a broader mandate than those created earlier. They have responsibility not for a single industry but for firms of all types, and their policy scope covers a wide range of activities. The Environmental Protection Agency (EPA), for example, is charged with regulating environmental pollution of almost any kind by almost any firm.

Because newer agencies such as the EPA have a broad mandate, no one firm or industry can easily influence agency decisions. Group competition also exists within the newer regulatory spheres. For example, environmental groups such as the Sierra Club and Greenpeace compete with business lobbies for influence with the EPA.[9] Business lobbies face much less competition when it comes to the older regulatory agencies. For example, although patients have a stake in the FDA's decisions, they are not an organized group, which limits their ability to counter the influence of the pharmaceutical lobby on the FDA.

Most of the older agencies, including the Federal Communications Commission (FCC) and the Securities and Exchange Commission (SEC), are run by a commission whose members are nominated by the president and serve fixed terms but cannot be removed by the president during their term of office. Most of the newer agencies, including the EPA, are headed by a single director who can be removed from office at the president's discretion. As a result, the newer agencies tend to be more responsive to the president than to the firms they regulate.

Government as Protector of the Environment

Few changes in public opinion and policy during recent decades have been as dramatic as those relating to the environment. Most Americans today recycle some of their garbage, and roughly two-thirds say they are either an active environmentalist or sympathetic to environmental concerns. In the 1960s, few Americans sorted their trash, and few could have answered a polling question that asked them whether they were an "environmentalist." The term was not widely used, and most people would not have understood its meaning.

The publication in 1962 of Rachel Carson's *The Silent Spring* helped launch the environmental movement.[10] Written at a time when the author was dying of breast cancer, *Silent Spring* revealed the threat to birds and animals of pesticides such as DDT. Carson's appearance at a Senate hearing contributed to legislative action that produced the 1963 Clean Air Act and the 1965 Water Quality Act. They were the first major federal laws designed to protect the nation's air, water, and ground from pollution. Today, environmental protection extends to nearly two hundred harmful forms of emission.

Conservationism: The Older Wave

Although antipollution policy is relatively new, the government has been involved in land conservation for more than a century.[11] The first national park was created at Yellowstone in 1872 and, like the later ones, was established to preserve the nation's natural heritage for generations to come.

The Silent Spring brought lasting fame to Rachel Carson. Even before the book was published in 1962, chemical companies were threatening lawsuits and portraying her as mentally unstable and scientifically untrained. Despite the attacks, *The Silent Spring* became a huge best-seller and contributed to passage of the first federal safe air and water legislation.

The national park system serves more than 100 million visitors each year and includes a total of 80 million acres, an area larger than every state except Alaska, Texas, California, and Montana. The national parks are run by the National Park Service, an agency within the Department of the Interior. Another agency, the U.S. Forest Service, located within the Department of Agriculture, manages the national forests, which cover an area more than twice the size of the national parks. They too have been established in order to protect America's natural heritage.

The nation's parks and forests are subject to a "dual use" policy. They are nature preserves and recreation areas, but they are also rich in natural resources—minerals, timber, and grazing lands. The federal government sells permits to ranchers, logging companies, and mining firms that authorize them to take some of these resources, which can bring them into conflict with conservationists. A case in point is Alaska's Arctic National Wildlife Refuge (ANWR). The refuge is home to numerous species, including caribou and moose, but it also contains substantial oil and natural gas reserves. Oil companies have long wanted to drill in ANWR, whereas environmental groups have sought to prohibit drilling. Over the past few decades, ANWR has periodically been the focus of intense political debate and lobbying. President George W. Bush sought to open ANWR to drilling as a means of increasing the nation's energy supply. President Obama has blocked new drilling in the area.

As the debate over ANWR reveals, conservation is more than an issue of protecting nature's unspoiled beauty. Also involved is the protection of species that cannot survive outside their natural habitat. Some species, such as the deer and the raccoon, adapt easily to human encroachment. Other species are harmed by it. These species are covered by the Endangered Species Act (ESA) of 1973, which requires federal agencies to protect threatened and endangered species. Hundreds of mammals, birds, fishes, insects, and plants are currently on the ESA's protection list.

Not surprisingly, ESA administrators have clashed frequently with business firms that extract natural resources. The northern spotted owl, which inhabits the forests of Oregon and Washington, was the focus of one of these disputes. The spotted owl nests in old-growth trees that are coveted by the logging industry. Federal administrators, invoking the ESA, banned logging in the owl's habitat. The ensuing legal battle ended with a compromise in which logging was permitted in some old-growth timber areas and prohibited in others. Although the outcome left neither side fully satisfied, it is typical of how most such disputes are settled. More recently, federal officials have emphasized cooperative relationships with

The federal government's environmental efforts include programs designed to conserve nature through the protection of forests and other natural assets. Shown here is a scene from Yellowstone National Park.

private parties, who can receive grants that promote the protection of threatened and endangered species. A Wyoming wildlife association, for example, obtained a $120,000 federal grant to improve a creek inhabited by a rare species of trout.

Environmentalism: The Newer Wave

The 1960s were pivotal to the federal government's realization of the harmful effects of air, water, and ground pollutants. The period was capped by the first Earth Day. Held in the spring of 1970, it was the brainchild of Senator Gaylord Nelson (D-Wis.), who had devoted nearly ten years to finding ways to create public interest in environmental issues. With Earth Day, Nelson succeeded to a degree not even he could have imagined: ten thousand grade and high schools, two thousand colleges, and one thousand communities participated in the event, which included public rallies and environmental cleanup efforts. Earth Day has been held every year since 1970 and is now a worldwide event.

Environmental Protection The year 1970 also marked the creation of the Environmental Protection Agency. Within a few months, the EPA was issuing new regulations at such a rapid pace that business firms had difficulty implementing them. Corporations eventually found an ally in President Gerald Ford, who in a 1975 speech claimed that business regulation was costing $150 billion annually, or $2,000 for every American family.[12] Although Ford's estimate was disputed by economic analysts, his point was not lost on policymakers or the public. The economy was in a slump, and the costs of complying with the new regulations were slowing the recovery. Polls indicated declining public support for regulatory action.

Since then, environmental protection policy has not greatly expanded, nor has it greatly contracted. The emphasis has been on implementation of laws put into effect in the 1960s and 1970s. In a 2001 decision, for example, the Supreme Court ruled unanimously that public health is the only thing that the EPA should take into account in establishing air quality standards; the costs to industry are not to be considered.[13] The Court went further in 2007 by ordering the EPA to act on carbon emissions. The Court held that the EPA had to comply with its legislative mandate: "Under the clear terms of the Clean Air Act, EPA can avoid taking further action only if it determines that greenhouse gases do not contribute to climate change. . . ."[14]

Environmental regulation has led to dramatic improvements in air and water quality. Pollution levels today are far below their levels of the 1960s, when yellowish-gray fog ("smog") hung over cities like Los Angeles and New York and when bodies of water like the Potomac River and Lake Erie were open sewers. In the past four decades, toxic waste emissions have been halved, hundreds of polluted lakes and rivers have been revitalized, energy efficiency has increased, food supplies have been made safer, and urban air pollution has declined by 60 percent.[15]

However, a regulatory lapse contributed to one of the most damaging ecological disasters in recent U.S. history—a huge oil discharge in the Gulf of Mexico in 2010 that resulted from the collapse of an offshore drilling platform. The agency in charge of overseeing offshore drilling—the Minerals Management Service (MMS)—was lax in regulating petroleum companies. It allowed them to drill without complying fully with safety regulations, which contributed to the explosion that sunk the drilling platform. Several months elapsed before British Petroleum, the company in charge of the well, was able to stem the flow of oil into the Gulf. Enormous damage to the environment ensued, and the adverse effect on marine life and coastal areas is projected to last for more than a decade. Shortly after the disaster, Congress divided MMS into three agencies in an effort to improve the regulation of oil companies.

POLITICAL THINKING

Should Offshore Drilling Be Expanded?

In 2010, President Obama announced a plan to expand the areas open to offshore drilling as part of a comprehensive energy plan that also included increased use of non-fossil energy sources, such as wind power. A few weeks later, a massive oil spill in the Gulf of Mexico produced billions of dollars in damage to the region's fishing and tourism industries, as well as incalculable damage to the environment. What's your opinion on expanded offshore drilling? Is it a necessary part of the answer to America's future energy needs? Or are the environmental risks too great to allow it?

Badly contaminated toxic waste sites are also a problem. These sites pollute local water supplies, resulting in increased rates of cancer and other illnesses. Although Congress in the 1980s established the so-called Superfund program to rid these sites of their contaminants, the cleanup process has been slow and contentious. Firms that caused the pollution are liable for some of the cleanup costs, but many of these firms are no longer in business, have since been purchased by other companies, or lack the funds. Firms that could pay the costs have often chosen to fight the issue in court, further delaying the cleanup. According to EPA figures, more than a third of the most dangerous sites are still contaminated.

Global Warming and Energy Policy No environmental issue receives more attention than global warming. Scientific evidence indicates that emissions from carbon-based fuels, such as oil and coal, are creating a "greenhouse effect" (the trapping of heat in the atmosphere). The effects include a melting of the polar ice caps and a rise in ocean levels that threatens low-lying coastal areas.

Polls indicate that some Americans regard global warming as a myth. This mistaken belief owes to several factors, including a tendency to confuse changes in the weather with climate change. An unusually cold winter can lead people in the affected location to conclude that global warming is not happening. In fact, however, changes in the weather and changes in the climate are not the same. The weather refers to conditions in a particular location over a relatively short period, such as whether Los Angeles is having an unusually wet spring. Climate change refers to broad

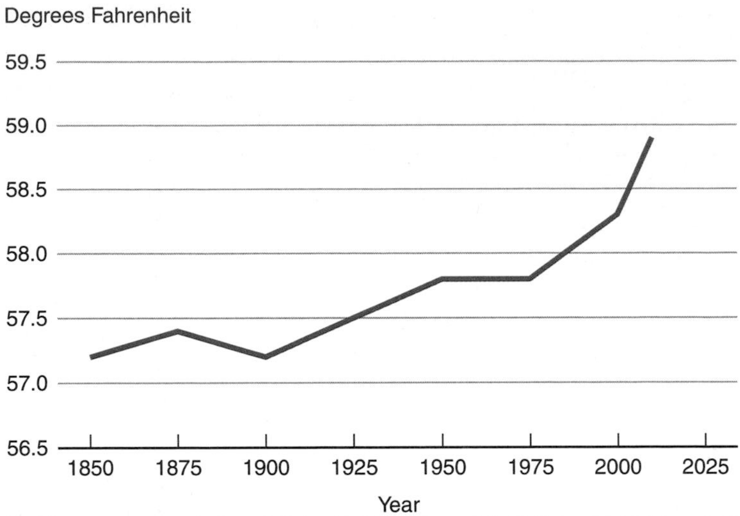

figure 15-1 AVERAGE TEMPERATURE OF THE EARTH'S SURFACE, 1850–2010

The average surface temperature of the earth has risen substantially in the past century and has done so at an accelerating pace in the past three decades. *Source:* National Weather Service, Great Britain, 2010.

long-term trends such as a gradual change in the average temperature of the earth. By this standard, global warming is hardly a myth. Over the past century, the earth has warmed considerably and the rate of increase has accelerated. Most of the warmest years in recorded history have occurred within the past two decades (see Figure 15-1).

In late 2009 at the United Nations Climate Change Conference held in Copenhagen, Denmark, representatives from the world's nations gathered to address the problem of global warming. They came away without a binding agreement. President Obama negotiated a last-minute accord that said nations should aim to reduce carbon-based emissions by 50 percent over a period of four decades. The accord also proposed that the United States and other wealthier nations give $130 billion to poorer nations to help them mitigate the effects of climate change and reduce their emissions. Environmentalists criticized the accord, saying it was nothing more than a set of unenforceable promises. The executive director of Greenpeace International said there is "nothing to cheer about Copenhagen." Disputes between and within the developed and developing countries blocked a more substantial agreement.

The burden of addressing the global warming problem will fall unevenly on nations, which complicates efforts to reach a global agreement on reducing carbon-based emissions. Global warming can be retarded only by controlling carbon-based emissions, which can be accomplished only through the implementation of costly measures, such as forcing coal-based energy producers to install equipment to reduce or capture their carbon emissions. The issue is complicated further by the fact that no single nation can solve the problem on its own. When carbon emissions get into the atmosphere, they affect conditions elsewhere. The problem is also compounded by the rapid expansion of the economies of China, India, and other developing nations, resulting in increased use of carbon-based fuels. Yet the less-developed countries claim they should not bear primary responsibility for curbing global warming because the problem is the result of decades-long carbon emissions by the industrialized nations, including the United States (see "How the U.S. Differs").

The United States lags behind most Western countries, including Germany, France, and Great Britain, in reducing its greenhouse gas emissions. The reasons are several, including the structure of the U.S. political system. The division of power between the president, the House, and the Senate makes it difficult to garner the support necessary to implement policies that impose economic costs. In 1997, after helping to negotiate an international agreement on carbon emissions (the Kyoto Protocol), President Clinton was unable to persuade the Senate to ratify it. When George W. Bush assumed office in 2001, he explicitly rejected the agreement, saying that it would blunt economic growth. A congressional effort in 2010 to reduce greenhouse gases also failed to muster the necessary support. Although Democrats in the House of Representatives passed a bill that capped carbon emissions, the legislation died in the Senate.

U.S. policymakers have preferred to look to alternative energy sources and energy conservation as the answers to global warming. In 2007, a

Global warming is shrinking the polar ice caps, as can be seen from these two photos of the Arctic ice cap taken in 1979 (left) and 2003 (right). Within the foreseeable future and for the first time in recorded history, ships are expected to be able to travel in summer between Europe and Asia via the Arctic Ocean.

HOW THE U.S. DIFFERS
POLITICAL THINKING THROUGH COMPARISONS

Carbon-fuel Emissions and Global Warming

The United States, as the chart on p. 543 indicates, is the world's single largest source of carbon-fuel emissions on a per-capita basis. The United States emits about 20 percent of the world total. Carbon-fuel emissions have been linked to global warming and have increasingly drawn the attention of the international community. Although the rising land and water temperatures resulting from global warming have not yet created substantial problems, they are projected to do so within a few decades. Low-lying coastal areas, for example, will be submerged if ocean levels continue to rise. There is general agreement among scientists that global warming can be reduced only by curbing greenhouse gas emissions. Politics stands in the way of such action. Curbs on emissions would slow a country's economic growth, and no country by itself has the capacity to reduce global warming significantly. These realities have blocked full-scale international agreement on how to address the problem. The United Nations Framework Convention on Climate Change, which met in Copenhagen in 2009, broke down when the nearly two hundred participating nations could not agree on a binding method for allocating the costs associated with reducing carbon-based emissions. The United States and other advanced industrialized countries argued that global warming can be reduced only by significant action on the part of rapidly developing countries, China and India particularly. For their part, China and India argued that the largest burden should be borne by the United States and other advanced industrialized countries because they have been the largest source of carbon-fuel emissions.

Q: *Why might it make sense to place most of the burden for reducing carbon fuel emissions on nations with developing economies such as China and India? How might advanced industrialized nations such as the United States and Germany contribute to this effort?*

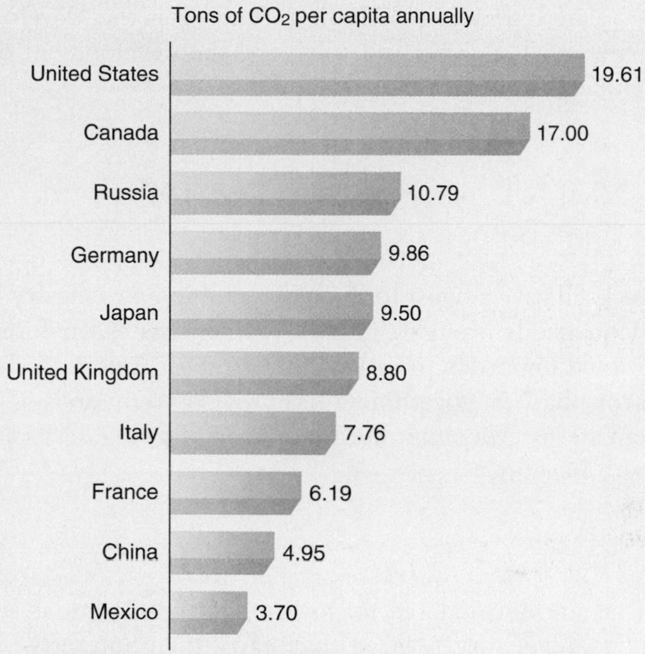

Source: From Organization for Economic Cooperation and Development, 2010. Reprinted with permission.

A: *An argument for placing the burden on developing economies is that their carbon emissions are increasing at the fastest rate. Advanced industrialized nations such as the United States and Germany could then provide developing countries with clean-energy technology that can be used, for example, when they install new power plants, which are a major source of carbon emissions. Developed countries could also provide monetary assistance to ease the economic burden that would fall on developing countries as a result of implementing costly carbon-reduction measures.*

bipartisan majority in Congress enacted the Energy Independence and Security Act, which established higher fuel-efficiency standards for vehicles and set a goal of eliminating incandescent light bulbs within a decade. House Speaker Nancy Pelosi (D-Calif.) described the bill as "a moment of change." President Bush said the legislation was a "major step . . . toward confronting global climate change." Some provisions of the American Recovery and Reinvestment Act of 2009 were also designed to address the problem of global warming. Roughly $40 billion was appropriated for energy-related projects, including funds for the development of renewable fuels such as wind and solar and the development of alternative fuel vehicles.

Government as Promoter of Economic Interests

Congress in 1789 gave a boost to the nation's shipping industry by imposing a tariff on goods brought into the United States on foreign ships, which prompted importers to make greater use of American ships. Since that first favor, the U.S. government has provided thousands of direct and indirect benefits to economic interests. The following sections describe some of these benefits.

Promoting Business

Business firms are not opposed to government regulation as such. They object only to regulatory policies that harm their interests. At various times and in different ways, as in the case of the FCC and broadcasters, some regulatory agencies have sided with the very industries they are supposed to regulate in the public interest.

Loans and tax breaks are other ways that government promotes business interests. Firms receive loan guarantees, direct loans, tax credits for capital investments, and tax deductions for capital depreciation. Since the 1970s, the burden of federal taxation has shifted from corporations to individuals. A few decades ago, the revenue from corporate income taxes was roughly the same as the revenue from individual income taxes. Today, individual taxpayers carry a substantially heavier burden. However, some economists do not regard the change as particularly significant, claiming that higher corporate taxes would be passed along to consumers in the form of higher prices for goods and services.

The most significant contribution that government makes to business is in the traditional services it provides, such as education, transportation, and defense. Colleges and universities, which are funded primarily by government, furnish business with most of its professional and technical workforce and with much of the basic research that goes into product development. The nation's roadways, waterways, and airports are other public-sector contributions without which business could not function. In short, America's business has no bigger booster than government.

Promoting Labor

Laissez-faire thinking dominated government's approach to labor well into the twentieth century. Union activity was held by the courts to be illegal because it interfered with the rights of business. Government hostility toward labor included the use of police and soldiers to break up strikes. In 1914 in Ludlow, Colorado, state militia attacked a tent colony of striking miners and their families, killing nineteen, including eleven children.

The 1930s Great Depression brought about a change in labor's position. The National Labor Relations Act of 1935, for example, gave workers the right to bargain collectively and prohibited business from disrupting union activities or discriminating against union employees. Government support for labor now also includes minimum-wage and maximum-work-hour guarantees, unemployment benefits, safer and more healthful working conditions, and nondiscriminatory hiring practices. Although the federal government's support of labor extends beyond these examples, its support is much less extensive than its support of business.

Promoting Agriculture

Government support for agriculture has a long history. The Homestead Act of 1862, for example, opened government-owned lands to settlement. The federal government provided 160 acres of land free to any family that staked a claim, built a house, and farmed the land for five years.

Government programs today provide billions of dollars of assistance annually to farmers, small and large. Some of this spending is designed to reduce the market risks associated with farming. Weather, global conditions, and other factors can radically affect crop and livestock prices, and federal subsidies lend stability to farm incomes. Efforts to wean U.S. farmers from government assistance have been difficult to achieve, practically and politically. A congressional attempt in 1996 to let the market determine the price and supply of agricultural commodities ended badly. Farm prices fell sharply because of surplus production of particular crops. In 2002, Congress abandoned the free-market approach; crop subsidies were increased and expanded to include more crops. Then, in 2008, Congress passed a five-year, $300-billion farm bill that would put farmers in line for hefty government assistance in future years. President Bush vetoed it, but Congress overrode his veto. An appeal by President Obama in 2009 to cut subsidies for large farms also was rejected by Congress. At present, federal payments account for more than a fourth of net agricultural income, making America's farmers among the most heavily subsidized in the world.

Fiscal Policy as an Economic Tool

Before the 1930s, prevailing economic theory held that the economy was self-regulating, that it would correct itself after a downturn. The greatest economic collapse in the nation's history—the Great Depression of the 1930s—shattered that idea. The economy did not recover on its own, but instead continued to decline. President Franklin D. Roosevelt's spending and job programs, which stimulated the economy and put Americans back to work, ushered in the modern era.[16] Today, government is expected to intervene when the economy dips.

The government's efforts to maintain a thriving economy occur in part through its taxing and spending decisions (see Figure 15-2), which together are referred to as its **fiscal policy**. Through changes in its level of spending and taxation, government can stimulate or slow the economy (see Table 15-2).

Demand-Side Policy

Fiscal policy has origins in the economic theories of John Maynard Keynes. Noting that employers tend to cut their production and workforce when the economy begins to weaken, Keynes challenged the traditional idea that government should also cut back on its spending. Keynes claimed that a downturn could be shortened only if government compensates for the slowdown in private spending by increasing its spending level. In doing so, the government pumps money into the economy, which stimulates

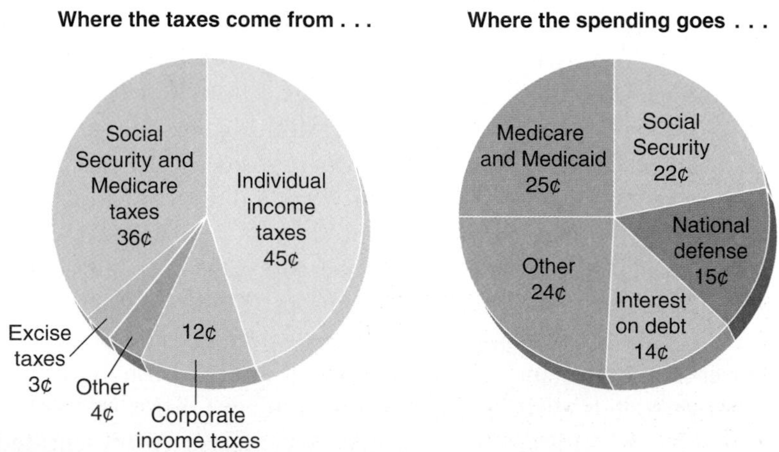

figure 15-2 The Federal Budget Dollar, Fiscal Year 2009

Source: Congressional Budget Office.

table 15-2 FISCAL POLICY: A SUMMARY OF THE GOVERNMENT'S ROLE

The federal government's taxing and spending levels can be adjusted as a means of influencing economic conditions.

Problem	Fiscal Policy Actions
Low productivity and high unemployment	Demand side: increase spending Supply side: cut business taxes
Excess production and high inflation	Decrease spending Increase taxes

consumer spending, which in turn stimulates business production and creates jobs, thereby hastening the economic recovery.[17]

Keynesian theory holds that the level of the government's response should be commensurate with the severity of the downturn. During an **economic depression**—an exceptionally steep and sustained decline in the economy—the government should engage in massive new spending programs to speed the recovery. During an **economic recession**, which is a less severe downturn, government spending should also be increased but by a lesser amount.

Keynes's theory is based on **demand-side economics**. It emphasizes the consumer "demand" component of the supply–demand equation. When the economy is sluggish, the government, by increasing its spending, places additional money in consumers' hands. With more money in their pockets, consumers spend more, which boosts economic activity. The theory is that if more goods and services are being purchased, whether for groceries or for new construction projects, firms will have to retain or hire workers to produce the goods and services, which will lessen the severity of the downturn. This line of reasoning was behind the $787 billion American Economic Recovery and Reinvestment Act that Congress passed in 2009 as a means of combating the steep economic slide precipitated by the near collapse of the financial markets. The legislation included, for example, funding for construction projects and enhanced unemployment benefits, as well as funding that enabled state and local governments to retain employees.

Although increased government spending can promote economic recovery, it is a tool that needs to be applied sensibly. Excessive spending results in a **budget deficit**—in which the federal government spends more in a year than it receives in tax and other revenues. The shortfall

HOW THE 50 STATES DIFFER
POLITICAL THINKING THROUGH COMPARISONS

Federal Taxing and Spending: Winners and Losers

Fiscal policy (the federal government's taxing and spending policies) varies in its effect on the states. The residents of some states pay a lot more in federal taxes than they receive in benefits. The biggest loser is New Jersey, whose taxpayers get back in federal spending in their state only $0.61 for every dollar they pay in federal taxes. Nevada taxpayers ($0.65 for every dollar) are the next-biggest losers. In contrast, the residents of some states get back more from federal spending programs than they contribute in taxes. The biggest winners are New Mexico and Mississippi, whose taxpayers get back $2.03 and $2.02, respectively, in federal spending in their states for every dollar they pay in federal taxes.

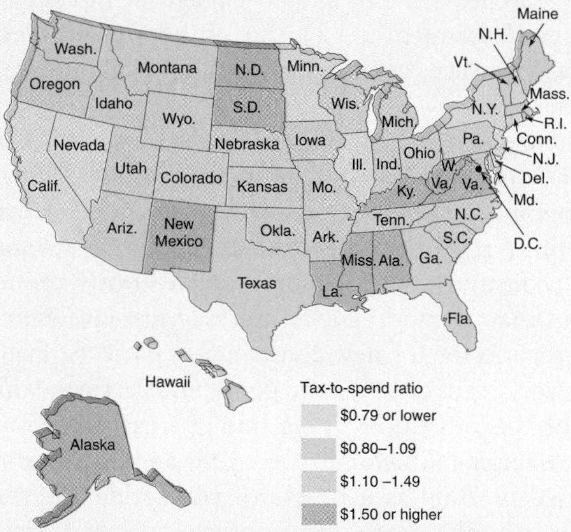

Source: Adapted from Tax Foundation Calculations, 2007.

Q: *Why are most of the "losers" in the northeastern section of the country?*

A: *The federal taxes that originate in a state reflect its wealth, and the northeastern states are generally the wealthier ones. Because they are wealthier, they also get less federal assistance for programs designed to help lower-income people and areas. Finally, most federal lands and military installations—sources of federal money—lie outside the northeastern region.*

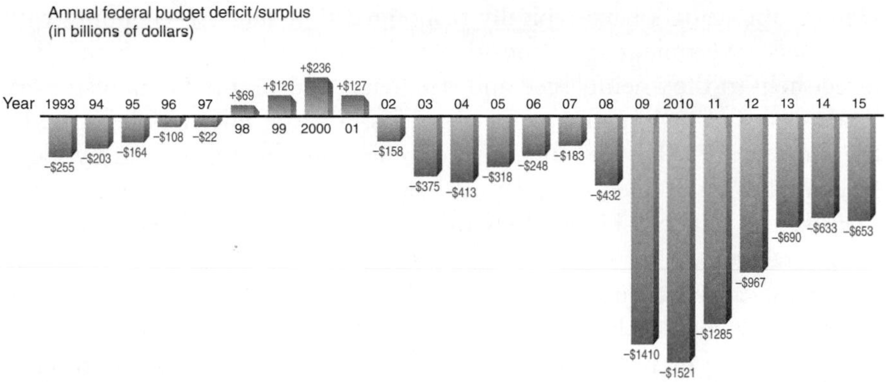

figure 15-3 THE FEDERAL BUDGET DEFICIT/SURPLUS

The federal government ran a budget deficit until 1998, at which time a surplus that was expected to last for years emerged. In 2001, however, the surplus quickly disappeared as a result of an economic downturn, costs associated with the war on terrorism, and a cut in federal taxes. *Source:* Office of Management and Budget, 2010. The 2010–2015 figures are projections.

increases the **national debt**, which is the total cumulative amount the federal government owes to its creditors. The government pays interest on the debt, which consumes money that would otherwise remain in taxpayers' pockets.

It is widely agreed that the United States faces a looming fiscal crisis because of a combination of high spending and low taxation. In 2010, the federal government's budget deficit was roughly $1.5 trillion, an all-time high. Projections indicate that deficits will continue into the future (see Figure 15-3), which will add to the national debt, which already exceeds $13 trillion. The U.S. government spends an enormous amount each year just to pay the interest on the debt. In fact, interest on the national debt accounts for nearly 15 percent of the federal budget. The interest payments are roughly the total of all federal income taxes paid by Americans living west of the Mississippi. Only rarely in recent decades has the U.S. government had a **balanced budget** (in which revenues are equal to government expenditures) or a **budget surplus** (in which the federal government receives more in tax and other revenues than it spends).

Supply-Side Policy

Demand-side stimulation has been the preferred policy of Democratic lawmakers. Lower-income Americans are a core Democratic constituency and are usually the most deeply affected by rising unemployment. Accordingly,

Democratic leaders have typically responded to a sluggish economy with increased government spending (demand-side fiscal policy), which offers direct help to the unemployed and stimulates consumption. Almost every increase in federal unemployment benefits, for example, was initiated by the Democrats. The $787 billion economic stimulus bill passed by Congress in 2009 was filled with demand-side programs and was ostensibly a Democratic bill. No House Republican and only three Senate Republicans voted for it.

Republican Party leaders are more likely to see an economic downturn through the lens of business firms. Republicans have typically resisted large spending increases because government has to borrow the money, which creates upward pressure on interest rates, including the rates that business firms have to pay for their loans.

A fiscal policy alternative to demand-side stimulation is **supply-side economics**, which emphasizes the business (supply) component of the supply-demand equation. Supply-side theory was a cornerstone of President Ronald Reagan's response to the economic downturn that began before he took office in 1981. Rather than relying on government spending programs to boost consumer spending, Reagan turned to tax cuts as a means of stimulating business activity. "Reaganomics" included large tax breaks for firms and upper-income individuals.[18] These supply-side measures were intended to encourage business investment with resulting increases in employment and income. As jobs and wages increased, consumer spending was also expected to increase, fostering economic growth.

Supply-side theory was also the basis of President George W. Bush's economic initiatives, which included reductions in the personal income tax and in the **capital-gains tax** (the tax that individuals pay on gains in capital investments such as property and stocks). Claiming that taxes on the wealthy were stunting economic growth, Bush persuaded Congress to reduce the capital-gains tax rate from 28 percent to 15 percent and to cut the highest marginal tax rate on personal income from 39 percent to 35 percent. The savings to Americans in the top 1 percent of income was $54,493 per year, compared with an average of $67 for those in the bottom 20 percent and $611 for those in the middle 20 percent.[19] (In contrast to the philosophy behind the Bush tax cuts, Democratic policymakers have pursued tax policies that favor working-class and lower-middle-class Americans. Democrats typically advocate a **graduated**, or **progressive, personal income tax**, in which the tax rate increases significantly as income rises, thus shifting more of the tax burden to wealthier individuals.)

POLITICAL THINKING

Who Should Get the Tax Cuts?

Few issues spark more controversy than taxes. When a tax cut is being debated, the argument usually centers on how the cut should be divided. Supply-side economists have one answer to the question: the taxpayers who are personally least in need of tax relief are the ones who should get the biggest share of the cut. Supply-side theory holds that high-income taxpayers will invest the extra income, which gives the economy a boost and thereby helps others. Warren Buffett, one of America's richest individuals, has a different answer to the question. He argues that tax cuts should be targeted for the less well off, because they have less income, which means they spend nearly every dollar they receive through a tax cut, thereby giving the economy a boost. Which of the two views is closer to your own?

As with demand-side stimulation, supply-side policy has its costs. President Bush argued that his tax cut would boost economic activity to such an extent that government revenue would actually increase. This prediction proved faulty. The loss in revenue from the tax cut exceeded the gain in revenue from heightened economic activity. In combination with the costs of the Iraq war, the Bush tax cut led to a ballooning of the budget deficit and the national debt.[20] When Bush took office, the budget was balanced and the national debt stood at $5.7 trillion. By the time he left office, the budget deficit had reached a record-high $432 billion and the national debt had risen to more than $10 trillion.[21]

Like demand-side policy, supply-side policy is intensely partisan. Whereas Republican lawmakers tend to balk at demand-side measures, Democratic lawmakers tend to balk at supply-side measures. Bush's supply-side tax cuts had the support of 90 percent of congressional Republicans and only 20 percent of congressional Democrats.[22]

Controlling Inflation

High unemployment and low productivity are not the only economic problems that government is called on to solve. Another is **inflation**—an increase in the average level of prices of goods and services. Before the late 1960s, inflation was a minor problem; it rose by less than 4 percent annually. But inflation jumped during the last years of the Vietnam War and remained high throughout the 1970s, reaching a postwar high of 13 percent in 1979. The effects were substantial. Prices were rising but personal income was stagnant. Many Americans were forced to cut back on basics, such as food purchases and medical care. Personal and business bankruptcies increased as a result of rising costs and skyrocketing borrowing rates. The interest rate on business loans and home mortgages topped 15 percent—up from 5 percent a few years earlier.

To fight inflation, government applies policies exactly the opposite of those used to fight an economic downturn. By cutting its spending or raising taxes, government takes money from consumers, thus reducing demand. The theory is that as demand weakens the price of goods and services will drop, thereby easing inflationary pressures. (The main policy tool for addressing inflation is monetary policy, which is discussed in the next section.)

Since the early 1980s, inflation has been kept in check. The inflation rate has not topped 5 percent in any year during the past two decades. Nevertheless, recent developments, including the growing national debt, have weakened the U.S. dollar, which could trigger an inflationary spiral. Some economists believe that the high level of government borrowing has flooded the world market with dollars, which will eventually depreciate their value with a resulting increase in inflation. Other economists believe that the risk of inflation is low; they foresee a sluggish economic

The unemployment office is an all-too-familiar scene for jobless Americans during an economic downturn. Through demand-side or supply-side policies, U.S. policymakers seek to stimulate the economy in order to reduce the unemployment rate.

recovery, which will dampen consumer spending and keep inflation at bay. Neither projection is a rosy one. Doomsayers suggest that America's fiscal crisis could be the harbinger of its decline as a world leader. "That's how empires decline," economic historian Niall Ferguson writes. "It begins with a debt explosion."[23]

Monetary Policy as an Economic Tool

Fiscal policy is not the only instrument of economic management available to government. A second is **monetary policy**, which is based on adjustments in the amount of money in circulation (see Table 15-3). Monetarists, as economists who emphasize monetary policy are called, contend that the money supply is the key to sustaining a healthy economy. Their leading theorist, the American economist Milton Friedman, held that supply and demand are best controlled by manipulating the money supply.[24] Too much money in circulation contributes to inflation because too many dollars are chasing too few goods, which drives up prices. Too little money in circulation results in a slowing economy and rising unemployment, because consumers lack the ready cash and easy credit required to maintain spending levels. Monetarists believe in increasing the money supply when the economy needs a boost and decreasing the supply when it needs to be slowed down.

The Fed

Control over the money supply rests not with the president or Congress but with the Federal Reserve Board (known as "the Fed"). Created by the Federal Reserve Act of 1913, the Fed has a board of governors whose seven members serve for fourteen years, except for the chair and vice chair, who serve for four years. All members are appointed by the president, subject to Senate approval. The Fed regulates all national banks and those state banks that meet certain standards and choose to become members of the Federal Reserve System.

The Fed decides how much money to add to or subtract from the economy, seeking a balance that will permit steady growth without causing an unacceptable level of inflation (see Table 15-3). One method the Fed uses to control the money supply is to raise or lower the cash reserve that member banks are required to deposit with the Federal Reserve. The cash reserve is the proportion of a member bank's total deposits that the bank must keep on hand, meaning that the bank cannot loan it out. By increasing table 15-3 MONETARY POLICY: A SUMMARY OF THE FED'S ROLE

The money supply can be adjusted in order to affect economic conditions.

Problem	**Monetary Policy Actions by Federal Reserve**
Low productivity and high unemployment (requiring an increase in the money supply)	Decrease interest rate on loans to member banks Decrease cash reserve that member banks must deposit in Federal Reserve System
Excess productivity and high inflation (requiring a decrease in the money supply)	Increase interest rate on loans to member banks Increase cash reserve that member banks must deposit in Federal Reserve System

the reserve rate, the Fed requires member banks to keep more of their money out of circulation, thereby reducing the money supply. By lowering the reserve rate, the Fed allows banks to use more of their money for loans to consumers and firms.

A second and more visible way in which the Fed affects the money supply is by lowering or raising the interest rate that member banks pay when they borrow money from the Federal Reserve. When the Fed raises the interest rate for banks, they in turn will raise the rate they charge their customers for new loans, which discourages borrowing, thereby reducing the amount of money entering the economy. Conversely, when the Fed lowers the interest rate on its loans to member banks, they are able to lower the rate they charge for their loans, which leads to additional borrowing by firms and consumers, resulting in an increase in the money supply. As the economy slowed down in 2008, for example, the Fed began a series of adjustments that dropped the interest rate by several percentage points, enabling member banks to lower their rates, making loans more affordable for firms and consumers.

Economists debate the relative effectiveness of monetary policy and fiscal policy, but monetary policy has one obvious advantage: it can be implemented more quickly. The Fed can adjust interest and reserve rates on short notice, thus providing the economy with a psychological boost to go along with the actual effect of a change in the money supply. In contrast, changes in fiscal policy usually take months to implement.

Congressional action is relatively slow, and new taxing and spending programs ordinarily require a preparation period before they can be put into effect. In early 2010, a full year after Congress passed the $787 billion economic stimulus bill, half of the money had not yet been spent.

The Politics of the Fed

The greater flexibility of monetary policy has positioned the Fed as the institution with primary policy responsibility for keeping the U.S. economy on a steady course. The Fed's power can easily be exaggerated. The U.S. economy is subject to a lot of influences, of which the money supply is only one. Nevertheless, the Fed is a vital component of U.S. economic policy.[25]

When the Fed was created in 1913, economists had not yet "invented" the theory of monetary policy, and the Fed had no role in the management of the nation's economy. It now plays a large role, which has raised questions about the power it wields. One concern is the issue of representation: whose interest should the Fed serve, that of the public as a whole or that of the banking sector? The Fed is not a wholly impartial body. Although it makes decisions in the context of economic theories and projections, it is "the bankers' bank" and as such tends to be protective of financial institutions. In 2008, the Fed provided emergency loans to keep banking institutions, including Citibank and JPMorgan Chase, from bankruptcy. The Fed justified its intervention by saying that the financial markets might otherwise have collapsed, adversely affecting every American. Many taxpayers saw it differently. A Pew Research Center national poll found that 87 percent of Americans opposed the use of taxpayer money to bail out the banks.

Another question about the Fed is the issue of its accountability. Should the Fed, an unelected body, have so much power? Though appointed by the president, members of the Federal Reserve Board are not subject to removal. They serve for fixed terms and are relatively insulated from political pressure. Of course, the Fed, as a banking institution, has a vested interest in a healthy economy (too much inflation erodes banks' returns on loans; too much unemployment decreases demand for loans) and thus operates within its own system of checks and balances. Nevertheless, the checks on the Fed's power are weaker than those on other policymaking institutions. The Fed, for example, refused a congressional request for the names of the banks that received emergency loans in 2008.

Regardless, the Fed is part of the new way of thinking about the federal government and the economy that emerged during the Great Depression of the 1930s. Prior to that time, the federal government's economic role was confined largely to the provision of a limited number of public services, such as the currency and mail delivery. Roosevelt's New Deal permanently changed the government's role. Through its economic management and regulatory activities, the government has assumed an ongoing role in the economy, contributing to its stability and efficiency. The overall results are fairly impressive. Although the American economy has suffered from economic downturns during the roughly three-quarters of a century in which the U.S. government has played a significant policy role, none of them has matched the severity of the depressions of earlier times. (The economic policies of the federal government in the areas of social welfare and national security are discussed in the next two chapters.)

SUMMARY Self-Test www.mhhe.com/pattersonwtp9e

Although private enterprise is the main force in the American economic system, the federal government plays a significant role through its policies to regulate, promote, and stimulate the economy.

Regulatory policy is designed to achieve efficiency and equity, which require the government to intervene, for example, to maintain competitive trade practices (an efficiency goal) and to protect vulnerable parties in economic transactions (an equity goal). Many of the regulatory decisions of the federal government, particularly those of older agencies (such as the Food and Drug Administration), are made largely in the context of group politics. Business lobbies have an especially strong influence on the regulatory policies that affect them. In general, newer regulatory agencies (such as the Environmental Protection Agency) have policy responsibilities that are broader in scope and apply to a larger number of firms than those of the older agencies. As a result, the policy decisions of the newer agencies are more often made in the context of party politics. Republican administrations are less vigorous in their regulation of business than are Democratic administrations.

Business is the major beneficiary of the federal government's efforts to promote economic interests. A large number of these programs, including those that provide loans and research grants, are designed to assist business firms, which are also protected from failure through measures such as tariffs and favorable tax laws. Labor, for its part, obtains government assistance through laws covering areas such as worker safety, the minimum wage, and collective bargaining. Yet America's individualistic culture tends to put labor at a disadvantage, keeping it less powerful than business in its dealings with the government. Agriculture is another economic sector that depends substantially on government's help, particularly in the form of income stabilization programs such as crop subsidies.

The U.S. government pursues policies that are designed to protect and conserve the environment. A few decades ago, the environment was not a policy priority. Today, there are many programs in this area, and the public has become an active participant in efforts to conserve resources and prevent exploitation of the environment. The continuing challenge is to find a proper balance between the nation's natural environment, its economic growth, and its energy needs.

Through its fiscal and monetary policies, Washington attempts to maintain a strong and stable economy—one characterized by high productivity, high employment, and low inflation. Fiscal policy is based on government decisions in regard to spending and taxing, which are aimed at either stimulating a weak economy or dampening an overheated (inflationary) economy. Fiscal policy is worked out through Congress and the president and consequently is responsive to political pressures. However, because it is difficult to raise taxes or cut programs, the government's ability to apply fiscal policy as an economic remedy is somewhat limited. Monetary policy is based on the money supply and works through the Federal Reserve, which is headed by a board whose members hold office for fixed terms. The Fed is a relatively independent body, a fact that has given rise to questions as to whether it should play such a large role in influencing national economic policy.

Key Terms

balanced budget (*p. 549*)
budget deficit (*p. 547*)
budget surplus (*p. 549*)
capital-gains tax (*p. 550*)
demand-side economics (*p. 547*)
deregulation (*p. 531*)
economic depression (*p. 547*)
economic recession (*p. 547*)
economy (*p. 528*)
economic efficiency (*p. 529*)
economic equity (*p. 533*)
externalities (*p. 531*)
fiscal policy (*p. 546*)
graduated (progressive) personal income tax (*p. 550*)
inflation (*p. 551*)
laissez-faire economics (*p. 528*)
monetary policy (*p. 553*)
national debt (*p. 549*)
regulation (*p. 529*)
supply-side economics (*p. 550*)

Suggested Readings

Duncan, Richard. *The Dollar Crisis: Causes, Consequences, Cures*, rev. ed. New York: John Wiley, 2005. A look at the problem of budget and trade deficits.

Fisher, Patrick. *The Politics of Taxing and Spending*. Boulder, CO.: Lynne Rienner Publishers, 2009. An assessment of the policies of taxing, spending, and the federal budget.

Jones, Bryan D., and Walter Williams. *The Politics of Bad Ideas: The Great Tax-Cut Delusion and the Decline of Good Government in America*. New York: Longman, 2008. A critique of the idea that tax cuts are the key to economic prosperity.

Lindbloom, Charles E. *The Market System: What It Is, How It Works, and What to Make of It*. New Haven, CT.: Yale University Press, 2001. A clear analysis of the advantages and disadvantages of the market system.

Mayer, Martin. *Fed: The Inside Story of How the World's Most Powerful Financial Institution Drives the Markets.* New York: Free Press, 2001. A look at the Fed's impact on the economy and politics.

Miller, Norman. *Environmental Politics: Stakeholders, Interests, and Policymakers.* New York: Routledge, 2008. A careful look at the politics of environmental policymaking.

Rosenbaum, Walter A. *Environmental Politics and Policy*, 7th ed. Washington, D.C.: CQ Press, 2007. A comprehensive examination of the politics of environmental policy.

Sheingate, Adam D. *The Rise of the Agricultural Welfare State.* Princeton, N.J.: Princeton University Press, 2003. A penetrating analysis of farm policy in the United States, France, and Japan.

List of Websites

www.federalreserve.gov/default.htm The Federal Reserve System website; describes the Fed, provides information about its current activities, and has links to some of the Fed's national and international information sources.

www.epa.gov The Environmental Protection Agency website; provides information on environmental policy and regulations, EPA projects, and related subjects.

www.ftc.gov The website of the Federal Trade Commission, one of the older regulatory agencies; describes the range of the FTC's activities.

www.whitehouse.gov/omb The home page of the Office of Management and Budget; contains a summary of the level of federal taxing, borrowing, and spending.

Politics in Theory and Practice

Thinking: What are the tools of fiscal policy and monetary policy? What are the advantages and disadvantages of each of these two approaches to managing the economy?

Participating: The environment is a policy area where individual citizens can make a difference by reducing waste and pollution. If you have a car, you will burn significantly less fuel if you accelerate and drive more slowly. Choosing a fuel-efficient car, keeping your car properly tuned, walking rather than driving short distances to stores, and living closer to work or school are other ways to cut gas consumption. In your residence, the simplest steps are to use lights sparingly and keep the thermostat lower during cold periods and higher during hot periods. Smaller but meaningful savings can be achieved through simple things such as using low-flow shower heads and replacing incandescent bulbs with fluorescent lights, which require less energy and last longer. Even a change in eating habits can make a difference. Frozen convenience foods are wasteful of energy. They are cooked, frozen, and then cooked again—not to mention the resources used up in packaging. Fresh foods are more nutritious and less wasteful. And if you prefer bottled water to tap water, consider using a water filter system instead. Nearly all of the cost of bottled water is due to the plastic container, which is a non-biodegradable petroleum product. The recycling of paper, plastics, and bottles also conserves natural resources. However, the recycling process itself requires the use of energy. By cutting back on your use of recyclables and by recycling those you do use, you will contribute twice over to a cleaner environment.

Extra Credit

For up-to-the-minute *New York Times* articles, interactive simulations, graphics, study tools, and more links and quizzes, visit the text's Online Learning Center at **www.mhhe.com/pattersonwtp9e**.

NATIONAL JOURNAL

Is Stability a Realistic Goal?

In many ways, Congress' major 2010 financial reform bill resembles other landmark pieces of legislation. Like health care reform, it tackles a pernicious side effect of America's free-market economy and treats it with a typically light touch by offering a package of incentives and disincentives for businesses and consumers. Instead of forcing banks to become smaller, the bill encourages them to do so. Instead of banning the kinds of home loans that contributed to the housing crisis, the legislation sets up a consumer protection agency that will rely mainly on disclosure to prompt Americans to make smarter financial decisions.

In at least one way, though, the financial reform plan represents a new approach. Grafted onto the largely familiar array of agencies that regulate banks is a council of top economic officials tasked with counteracting instability in the financial system before it becomes a critical threat. The council will look beyond individual institutions and practices to anticipate bubbles and spot potentially destabilizing financial innovations—such as the bonanzas that subprime lending and collateralized debt obligations seemed to be a few years ago.

The proposed Financial Stability Oversight Council, as the Senate legislation calls it, is an interagency group of nine people chaired by the Treasury secretary; it would include the chairman of the Federal Reserve Board, the heads of other financial agencies, and one or two other appointees. Some of its functions approximate the emergency powers that the Federal Reserve and Treasury have traditionally kept for themselves. But giving the council the job of foreseeing problems and acting to preserve stability in the nation's vast and complex financial system is an audacious undertaking, even for the U.S. government.

To put this commitment into perspective, consider the scope of the health care reform package enacted this year. Imagine for a moment that Washington had empowered a council to guarantee the stability of the U.S. health care system. If medical care, like credit, was scarce or too expensive, the council could intervene to make sure it was affordable and readily available, by acting wherever it chose to head off, say, shocking rate increases, or by guaranteeing medical care to everyone, with or without insurance. This sounds far-fetched because the epic health debate revealed that Americans are hardly eager to embrace government intervention to guarantee such ambitious outcomes.

Compared with many other countries, the U.S. government has tended to take a laissez-faire approach to regulating such essential services as transportation, electricity, and telecommunications. Washington does attempt to preserve the stability of agricultural supply and prices, with only mixed results. Most economists say that the current system of farm subsidies and price controls exists more to boost the farmers' income than to protect consumers.

But even these examples involve industries much smaller and simpler than the financial system, which extends beyond banks to include insurance, mortgage lending, and consumer credit—sectors that will remain relatively free of federal regulation, even after the regulatory reform package becomes law. The most comparable example of the government ambitiously trying to maintain the stability of markets was World War II and the extensive system of rationing and price controls that the Roosevelt administration used to prevent inflation, hoarding, and profiteering. That intervention was arguably successful, but a more recent iteration wasn't.

President Nixon imposed wage and price controls from 1971 to 1973 to combat inflation and escalating wage demands by labor unions. The move triggered runaway inflation, slow growth, food and commodity shortages, and an era of declining living standards. Economists consider the controls one of the most disastrous economic policy decisions ever by a U.S. president.

Oddly, the debate over financial reform hasn't focused much on the question of whether government can or should try to assume responsibility for stabilizing the financial system. Neither party in Congress has drawn attention to the goals of the systemic risk council or to the very notion that a government body would try to head off instability throughout the financial system before it causes a crisis.

In one form or another, the federal government has always taken emergency action to stem financial panics and other crises that threaten the economy, according to banking expert Liaquat Ahamed. Congress established the Federal Reserve Board in 1913 to coordinate emergency action, using the power to make emergency loans to counter bank runs and otherwise manipulate interest-rate policy to maintain liquidity in the banking system. Although the Fed and Treasury took actions during the recent crisis that were messy and in some ways unprecedented in size and scope, the interventions essentially followed past patterns, Ahamed says.

In Ahamed's view, the earliest days of the crisis made it clear that the United States had to do three things to minimize the risk of a plunge that could wreck the financial system. First, the government needed to bolster the capital reserves of banks, which had used holes in the accounting rules to evade reserve requirements; second, Washington needed to take on increased oversight to prevent excessive risk-taking and leveraging; and third, if the first two requirements weren't met, government would need a more streamlined and effective process to handle emergencies.

The first and final functions were already important government responsibilities, according to Ahamed, but the middle role—seeking to guarantee the stability of the financial system—is different. The Fed has been responsible for auditing many of the largest banks, and it has important duties to keep interests rates and inflation low and employment and the economy growing.

The Fed's responsibility for maintaining the overall stability of the financial system has been more ambiguous, especially in recent decades. Although regulators have stepped up its efforts to stabilize the financial system, "it is also true that the financial system is more complex" than a decade or two ago, Ahamed said.

The Federal Reserve has long had close relations with large bank holding companies such as Citigroup and Bank of America (where Fed examiners actually showed up for work every day). Until recently, though, Fed accountants were not as involved in the day-to-day operations of Wall Street banks—such as Bear Stearns, Goldman Sachs, and Lehman Brothers—that were some of the biggest customers for the Fed's Treasury bills. The chaos of the financial crisis revealed just how little attention the Fed paid to ensuring their stability and how limited were its powers to help them.

A hallmark of the era of Fed Chairman Alan Greenspan, from 1987 to 2006, was the Fed's unwillingness to serve as the kind of guarantor of financial stability envisioned in the plan for the Financial Stability Oversight Council. At the same moment that Long Term Capital Management's derivatives trades were souring, Greenspan was otherwise engaged in killing off an effort by Brooksley Born, then the chairwoman of the Commodities Futures Trading Commission, to regulate derivatives. At multiple congressional hearings, Greenspan argued successfully that no oversight was needed—because the self-interest of big banks and investors would be more effective than any government agency in controlling risk and maintaining stability.

Since then, Greenspan has expressed wonderment at the failures of such market discipline during the financial crisis, but he has not admitted that he might have been mistaken about unregulated trading in derivatives. Ten years after his tidy and privately financed rescue of Long Term Capital Management, one type of unregulated derivative was at the center of the subprime mortgage meltdown, and a related derivative underlay the $182 billion bailout of AIG, which at last count is expected to cost taxpayers $50 billion.

Vincent Reinhart has low expectations for the systemic risk council and the rest of the regulatory overhaul because he thinks that Congress is aiming at the wrong target—preventing banks from becoming "too big to fail." Reinhart, a former director of the Fed's Division of Monetary Affairs, believes that in the 24 years since the government made major changes to the tax code, banks have exploited weaknesses in accounting rules. Banks' "splintering" of their balance sheets, he says, made it impossible for regulators to understand what was going on, for the market to exercise the discipline that Greenspan was depending on, and even for managers of the banks to understand the risks that had accumulated.

Would the risk council use such countercyclical means to try to head off the next financial bubble? Goldstein thinks it is possible, but Reinhart is doubtful. When Greenspan issued his famous warning in late 1996 about "irrational exuberance" in the stock market, Reinhart said, no one wanted to listen. The market doubled in the next four years, until the dot-com crash, and Greenspan, according to his memoirs, concluded that even Fed chairmen are powerless to puncture a financial bubble.

No elected or appointed official would risk the political fallout from taking action against a possible bubble, Reinhart argues. At best, a lot of people will be poorer. At worst, he said, government officials risk destabilizing rather than stabilizing the situation.

If we are lucky, former investment banker Elliot says, the risk council's existence will be enough to deter excessive risk-taking. More likely though, Reinhart warns, it will take another crisis to move government to directly address the complexity of large banks that is at the root of systemic risk. "I fully expect it," he said.

What's Your Opinion?

What do you think government's role should be in controlling risk in the markets? What are the advantages and liabilities of government intervention? Is it possible for America to have an economy without large banks that risk becoming "too big to fail"? Why or why not?

CHAPTER 16

Welfare and Education Policy: Providing for Personal Security and Need

"We the people of the United States, in order to . . . promote the general welfare . . ."

Preamble, U.S. Constitution

President Barack Obama had been in office only a few weeks when he proposed a plan to change the nation's health care system. Obama vowed to cut rising medical costs and to increase Americans' access to health insurance. He had plenty of eager Democrats in the House and Senate on his side. The idea of extending health coverage to the millions of uninsured Americans had long been a Democratic Party goal. A half-century earlier, President Harry S Truman had tried but failed to create a universal health insurance system.

Congressional Republicans agreed with Obama that the nation's health care system has flaws. The agreement stopped at that point, however. Republican lawmakers were dead-set against any reform that would give the federal government substantially greater control over health insurance. They were willing to countenance a few restrictions on insurance companies but wanted to leave the rules and rates of health insurance largely in the hands of private companies. They were also concerned

The health care reform legislation that was passed by Congress in 2010 was bitterly contested. No Senate or House Republican voted for the bill. The dispute was not confined to the halls of Congress. Shown here is a rally held in protest of the recently enacted bill.

about increases in federal health care spending. For their part, Democrats expressed dismay that anyone could look at how insurance companies operate and conclude that the status quo was acceptable. They pointed to such industry practices as voiding the insurance of policyholders after they became sick. According to Democrats, insurance industry profits and practices are the primary reason the United States has the most expensive health care system in the world and yet by statistical indicators ranks below many other countries in quality of health care.

At several points in the months-long policy debate, a majority of Americans sided with Obama and Democratic lawmakers on the desirability of comprehensive health care reform. At other times, a majority sided with congressional Republicans. Throughout the debate, however, confirmed liberals were strongly in favor of having the federal government play a larger role in health care insurance whereas confirmed conservatives were strongly opposed to it.

Health policy issues, like other social welfare policy issues, activate opposing philosophies of government. Some Americans hold that government should intervene in the marketplace to assist disadvantaged individuals. Others hold that government assistance discourages personal effort and creates dependency. America's federal system of government also fuels conflict over welfare policies. Welfare was traditionally a responsibility of state governments. Only since the 1930s has the federal government also played a major role, which has sometimes brought it into conflict with the states over the best course of action.

This chapter examines the problems that federal social welfare programs are designed to alleviate and describes how these programs operate. It also addresses public education policies. This chapter seeks to provide an informed basis for understanding issues of social welfare and education and to show why disagreements in these areas are so substantial. The issues involve hard choices that inevitably require trade-offs between federal and state power and between the values of individual self-reliance and egalitarian compassion. The main points of the chapter are these:

- *Poverty is a large and persistent problem in America, affecting about one in eight Americans, including many of the country's most vulnerable—children, female-headed families, and minority-group members.*
- *Welfare policy has been a partisan issue, with Democrats taking the lead on government programs to alleviate economic insecurity and Republicans acting to slow down or restrict these initiatives.*
- *Social welfare programs are designed to reward and foster self-reliance or, when this is not possible, to provide benefits only to those individuals who*

are truly in need. U.S. welfare policy is not based on the assumption that every citizen has a right to material security.

- *Americans favor social insurance programs (such as social security) over public assistance programs (such as food stamps).* As a result, most social welfare expenditures are not targeted toward the nation's neediest citizens.
- *A prevailing principle in the United States is equality of opportunity, which in terms of policy is most evident in the area of public education.* America invests heavily in its public schools and colleges.

Poverty in America: The Nature of the Problem

In the broadest sense, social welfare policy includes any effort by government to improve social conditions. In a narrower sense, which is the way the term generally is used in this chapter, social welfare policy refers to government programs that help individuals meet basic needs, including food, clothing, and shelter. Social welfare policy can differ markedly even among countries that are similar in many other respects. As this chapter shows, U.S. social welfare policy is distinctive, even by comparison with Canada and other Western industrialized nations.

The Poor: Who and How Many?

Americans' social welfare needs are substantial. Although Americans are far better off economically than most of the world's peoples, poverty is a significant and persistent problem in the United States. The government defines the **poverty line** as the annual cost of a thrifty food budget for an urban family of four, multiplied by three to include the cost of housing, clothes, and other necessities. Families whose incomes fall below that line are officially considered poor. In 2010, the poverty line was set at an annual income of roughly $22,000 for a family of four. One in seven Americans—roughly 40 million people—live below the poverty line. If they could all join hands, they would form a line stretching from New York to Los Angeles and back again.

America's poor include individuals of all ages, races, religions, and regions (see "How the 50 States Differ"), but poverty is concentrated among certain groups. Children are one of the largest groups of poor Americans. One in every five children—more than 10 million in total—live in poverty. Most poor children live in families with a single parent, usually the mother. Single-parent, female-headed families are roughly five times as likely as two-income families to fall below the poverty line, a situation referred to as "the feminization of poverty."[1]

HOW THE 50 STATES DIFFER
POLITICAL THINKING THROUGH COMPARISON

Poverty Rates

Relative to other Western democracies, the United States has an unusually high proportion of poor people. Based on the government-defined poverty line, about one in eight Americans live in poverty. However, poverty is spread unevenly among the states. At one extreme are Louisiana, Mississippi, and New Mexico, each of which has a poverty rate above 18 percent. New Mexico has the highest rate—19.3 percent. At the other extreme are New Hampshire and Utah, which have poverty rates that are less than half that of the highest states. New Hampshire has the lowest rate, with 7.0 percent living in poverty. Utah's poverty rate is 7.6 percent.

Q: *What might explain the difference in poverty levels between the states?*

A: *States differ considerably in their natural wealth, level and type of economic activity, level of education, number of newer immigrants, and percentage of minority-group members. Each of these factors is correlated with level of poverty.*

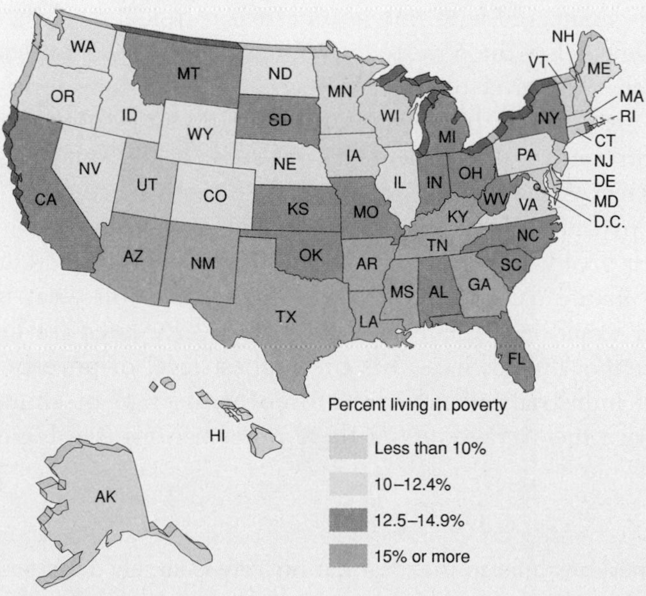

Source: U.S. Census Bureau, 2010.

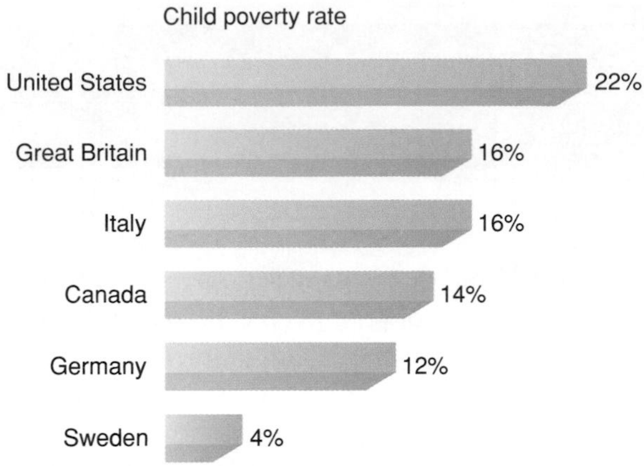

figure 16-1 CHILD POVERTY RATES

The United States has the highest child poverty rate among Western democracies. One in five American children lives in poverty; in most other Western democracies, the number is fewer than one in seven. *Source:* United Nations Children's Fund, 2010. Households with incomes less than half that of the median household are classified as living in poverty.

Poverty is also widespread among minority-group members. Compared with whites, African Americans and Hispanics are more than twice as likely to live below the poverty line. Poverty is also geographically concentrated. Although poverty is often portrayed as an urban problem, it is somewhat more prevalent in rural areas. About one in seven rural residents—compared with one in nine urban residents—lives in a family with income below the poverty line. The urban figure is misleading, however, in that the level of poverty is very high in some inner-city areas. Suburbs are the safe haven from poverty. Because suburbanites are far removed from it, many of them have no sense of the impoverished condition of what Michael Harrington called "the other America."[2]

The "invisibility" of poverty is evident in polls showing that most Americans greatly underestimate the level of poverty in the United States. Nothing in the daily lives of many Americans or in what they see on television would lead them to think that poverty rates are uncommonly high. Yet the United States has the highest level of poverty among the advanced industrialized nations. Moreover, its rate of child poverty is nearly twice the average rate of these other nations (see Figure 16-1).

Living in Poverty: By Choice or Chance?

Many Americans hold to the idea that poverty is largely a matter of choice—that most low-income Americans are unwilling to make the effort to hold a responsible job and get ahead in life. In his book *Losing Ground*, Charles Murray argues that America has a permanent underclass of unproductive citizens who prefer to live on welfare and whose children receive little educational encouragement at home and grow up to be copies of their parents.[3] There are, indeed, many such people in America. They number in the millions. They are the toughest challenge for policymakers because almost nothing about their lives equips them to escape from poverty and its attendant ills.

Yet most poor Americans are in their situation as a result of circumstance rather than choice. Economists Signe-Mary McKernan and Caroline Ratcliffe found that most of the poor are poor only for a while, and then for reasons largely beyond individual control—such as a job layoff or desertion by the father—rather than because they prefer not to work.[4] When the U.S. economy goes into a tailspin, the impact devastates many families. According to U.S. Department of Labor figures, more than seven million Americans lost their jobs during the recent economic downtown. The unemployment rate doubled between 2007 and 2011.

The Politics and Policies of Social Welfare

At one time in the nation's history, the federal government was not involved in social welfare policy. Poverty and other welfare problems were deemed to fall within the powers reserved to the states by the Tenth Amendment and to be adequately addressed by them, even though they offered few welfare services. Individuals were expected to fend for themselves, and those unable to do so were usually supported by relatives and friends. This approach reflected the idea of **negative government**, which holds that government governs best by staying out of people's lives, so that they can determine their own pursuits and become self-reliant.

The Great Depression changed that outlook. The unemployment level reached 25 percent, and many of those with jobs were working for pennies an hour. Americans looked to the federal government for help. Franklin D. Roosevelt's New Deal brought economic relief in the form of public jobs and assistance programs and altered Americans' view of the federal government's welfare role.[5] The new attitude was a belief in **positive government**—the idea that government intervention is necessary in order to enhance personal liberty and security when individuals are buffeted by economic and social forces beyond their control.

Not all Americans of the 1930s embraced the new philosophy. Many Republican leaders clung to traditional ideas about self-reliance and free markets. A key vote in the House of Representatives on the Social Security Act of 1935, for example, had 85 percent of Democrats voting in favor of it and 99 percent of Republicans voting against it.[6] Republicans gradually accepted the idea that the federal government has a social welfare role but argued that it should be kept as small as practicable. Thus, in the 1960s, Republican opposition to President Lyndon Johnson's Great Society was substantial. His programs included federal initiatives in health care, education, public housing, nutrition, and other areas traditionally dominated by state and local governments. More than 70 percent of congressional Republicans voted against the 1965 Medicare and Medicaid programs, which provide government-paid medical assistance for the elderly and the poor, respectively. In contrast, the 1996 Welfare Reform Act, which was designed to cut welfare rolls and costs, had the overwhelming support of congressional Republicans, whereas a majority of congressional Democrats voted against it.

Although the Republican and Democratic parties have been at odds on social welfare issues, they have also had reason to work together.

With the exception of Franklin D. Roosevelt, no American president had a greater impact on social welfare policy than Lyndon B. Johnson. LBJ's Great Society programs included Medicare and Medicaid, as well as increased federal spending in areas such as education, childhood nutrition, and poverty allevation. Johnson was also instrumental in passage of the 1964 Civil Rights Act and the 1965 Voting Rights Act.

Millions of Americans depend on the federal government to provide benefits to ease the loss of income caused by retirement, disability, unemployment, and the like. Some social welfare programs, such as federal grants for health research, benefit all of society. Other spending is aimed at helping particular individuals. *Transfer payments* are government benefits given directly to individual recipients, such as retirees' monthly social security checks. Most programs that support individuals are **entitlement programs**, meaning that any individual who meets the eligibility criteria is entitled to the benefit. For example, upon reaching the legal retirement age, any senior citizen who has paid social security taxes for the required amount of time is entitled to receive social security benefits. In this sense, entitlement programs have the same force of law as taxes. Just as individuals are required by law to pay taxes on the income they earn, they are entitled by law to receive government benefits for which they qualify.

Individual-benefit programs fall into two broad groups: social insurance programs and public assistance programs. Social insurance programs enjoy broader public support, are more heavily funded, and provide benefits to individuals of all income levels. Public assistance programs have less public support, receive less funding, and are restricted to people of low income. The next sections discuss these two types of programs.

Social Insurance Programs

More than 50 million Americans receive monthly benefits from social insurance programs—including social security, Medicare, unemployment insurance, and workers' compensation. The cost of the two major programs, social security and Medicare, exceeds one trillion dollars a year. Such programs are labeled **social insurance** because eligibility is restricted to individuals who paid special payroll taxes during their working years.

Social Security The main social insurance program is social security for retirees. Social security is one of the few welfare programs run entirely by the federal government. Washington collects the payroll taxes that fund the program and sends monthly checks directly to social security recipients, who receive on average about $1,000 a month.

The program began with passage of the Social Security Act of 1935 and is funded through payroll taxes on employees and employers (currently set at 6.2 percent). Franklin D. Roosevelt emphasized that retiring workers would receive an insurance benefit they had earned through their payroll taxes, not a handout from the government. This method of financing has resulted in broad public support for the social security program.[7]

Polls indicate that a large majority of Americans favor current or higher levels of social security benefits for the elderly.

Although people qualify for social security by paying payroll taxes during their working years, the money they receive upon retirement is funded by payroll taxes on current workers' salaries. This arrangement poses a threat to the long-term viability of the social security program because people are living longer than they once did. As a result, there will be fewer workers relative to the number of retirees, and the inflow of payroll taxes from workers will be less than the outflow of social security benefits to retirees. There is broad agreement among policymakers that adjustments in the social security program will be necessary in the near future in order to ensure its solvency. The year 2010 provided a look into the future if no action is taken. As a result of the economic recession, fewer people than normal were employed and the revenue from their payroll taxes was temporarily insufficient to cover the cost of social security payments to retirees.

POLITICAL THINKING

What's the Future of Social Security?

Social security for retirees is paid through payroll taxes on the current workforce. However, because retirees are living longer and increasing in number, the inflow of payroll tax revenue from workers at some point will be insufficient to fund the outflow of social security payments. One solution to the problem would be to increase taxes on workers. Another solution would be to reduce retiree benefits and require workers to wait longer before they become eligible for social security benefits (the earliest eligibility is currently 62 years of age). If you were asked to solve the problem, what would you propose?

Unemployment Insurance The 1935 Social Security Act provides for unemployment benefits for workers who lose their jobs involuntarily. Unemployment insurance is a joint federal-state program. The federal government collects the payroll taxes that fund unemployment benefits, but states have the option of deciding whether the taxes will be paid by both employees and employers or by employers only (most states use the latter option). Individual states also set the tax rate, conditions of eligibility, and benefit level, subject to minimum standards established by the federal government. Although unemployment benefits vary widely among states, they average about $300 a week, roughly a fourth of what an average worker makes while employed. The benefits are usually terminated after twenty-six weeks, but Congress, as it did in the recent economic downturn, sometimes extends the eligibility period in recessionary periods.

The unemployment program does not have the broad public support that social security enjoys. This situation reflects the widespread assumption that the loss of a job, or the failure to find a new one right away, is often a personal failing. Unemployment statistics indicate otherwise. A U.S. Bureau of Labor study found that only about one in seven workers who lost their jobs were fired or quit voluntarily. The rest became unemployed because of either a temporary layoff or the permanent elimination of a job position.

Medicare After World War II, most European democracies created government-paid health care systems, and Democratic president Harry S Truman proposed a similar program for Americans. The American Medical Association (AMA) called Truman's plan "un-American" and vowed to mobilize local physicians to campaign against members of Congress who supported "socialized medicine." Truman's proposal never came to a vote in Congress. In 1961, President John F. Kennedy, also a Democrat, proposed a health care program restricted to social security recipients, but the AMA, the insurance industry, and congressional conservatives succeeded in blocking the plan.[8]

The 1964 elections swept a tide of liberal Democrats into Congress, and the result was Medicare. Enacted in 1965, the program provides medical assistance to retirees and is funded primarily through payroll taxes. Medicare is based on the insurance principle, and because of this, it has gained as much public support as social security. Medicare does not cover all hospital, nursing home, or physicians' fees, but enrollees in the program have the option of paying an insurance premium for fuller coverage of these fees. Enrollees who cannot afford the additional premium can apply to have the government pay it. In 2006, a prescription drug benefit was added to the Medicare program, though it included restrictions on eligibility and the amount of the benefit. The health care reform bill that Congress enacted in 2010 reduced the restrictions but did not eliminate them entirely. The reform bill also included provisions designed to increase the solvency of the Medicare program, which was otherwise projected to run out of money within a few years.

Public Assistance Programs

Unlike social insurance programs, **public assistance** programs are funded through general tax revenues and are available only to the financially needy. Eligibility for these programs is established by a **means test**; that is, applicants must prove that they are poor enough to qualify for the benefit. Once they have done so, they are entitled to the benefit, unless their personal situation changes or government changes the eligibility criteria. These programs often are referred to as "welfare," and the recipients as "welfare cases."

Americans are far less supportive of public assistance programs than they are of social insurance programs. Americans tend to look upon social insurance benefits as having been earned by the recipient, whereas they see public assistance benefits as handouts. Support for public assistance programs is weakened further by Americans' perception that the government is already spending vast amounts on welfare. A poll found that Americans believe public assistance programs to be the second costliest item in the federal budget. These programs actually rank much farther down the list. In fact, the federal government spends hundreds of billions more on its two major social insurance programs—social security and Medicare—than it does on all public assistance programs combined.

Supplemental Security Income (SSI) is a combined federal-state program that provides public assistance to blind and disabled people.

Supplemental Security Income (SSI) Supplemental Security Income (SSI) is a major public assistance program that originated as federal assistance to the blind and elderly poor as part of the Social Security Act of 1935. Although SSI is primarily a federal program, the states have retained some control over benefits and eligibility and provide some of the funding. Because SSI recipients (who now include the disabled in addition to the blind and elderly poor) have physical limitations on their ability to provide fully for themselves, SSI is not widely criticized.

Temporary Assistance for Needy Families (TANF) Before passage of the 1996 Welfare Reform Act, needy American families had an open-ended guarantee of cash assistance. As long as their income was below a certain level, they were assured of government support. The program (Aid for Families with Dependent Children, or AFDC for short) was created in the 1930s as survivors' insurance to assist children whose fathers had died prematurely. Relatively small at the outset, the program became controversial as Americans increasingly linked it to welfare dependency and irresponsibility. AFDC was an entitlement program, which meant that any single parent (and in some states two parents) living in poverty could claim the benefit and keep it for as long as a dependent child was in the household. Some AFDC recipients were content to live on this assistance, and in some cases their children also grew up to become AFDC recipients, creating what was called "a vicious cycle of poverty." By 1995, AFDC was supporting 14 million Americans.

The 1996 Welfare Reform Act abolished AFDC, replacing it with the program titled Temporary Assistance for Needy Families (TANF). TANF's goal is to reduce long-term welfare dependency by limiting the length of time recipients can receive assistance and by giving the states an incentive to place welfare recipients into jobs. Each state is given an annual federal block grant that it uses to help poor families meet their subsistence needs and to develop programs that will help the parents find employment. The state programs operate within strict federal guidelines, including the following:

- Americans' eligibility for federal cash assistance is limited to no more than five years in their lifetime.
- Within two years, the head of most families on welfare must find work or risk the loss of benefits.
- Unmarried teenage mothers qualify for welfare benefits only if they remain in school and live with a parent or legal guardian.
- Single mothers lose a portion of their benefits if they refuse to cooperate in identifying for child support purposes the father of their children.

Although states can grant exceptions to some of the rules (for example, an unmarried teenage mother who faces sexual abuse at home is permitted to live elsewhere), the exceptions are limited. States can even choose to impose more restrictive rules in some areas. For example, states have the option of denying increased benefits to unwed mothers who give birth to another child. The biggest challenge facing the states, however, has been the creation of welfare-to-work programs that are effective enough to qualify people for secure jobs. Most welfare recipients who have found employment since 1996 had enough skills that they required little or no job training from the state. In contrast, most of those who have been unable to find stable long-term employment have limited education and few job-related skills.[9]

TANF has dramatically reduced the size of the welfare rolls (see Figure 16-2). Within five years of its enactment, the number of people on welfare had dropped by 50 percent. In only three states—Hawaii, Rhode Island, and New Mexico—was the drop less than 20 percent. However, the decline was not simply the result of TANF. The American economy expanded at a rapid rate in the late 1990s, which created millions of new jobs. Nevertheless, even as the economy weakened in 2000, the number of welfare recipients continued to decline.

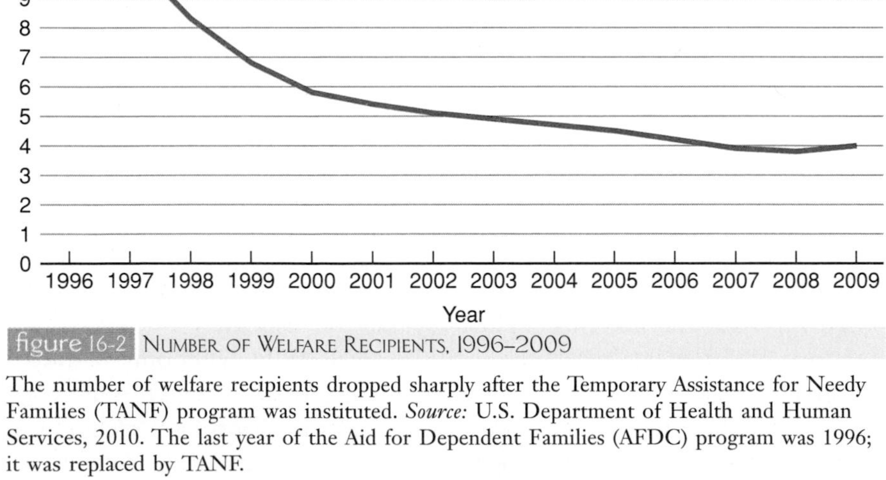

figure 16-2 NUMBER OF WELFARE RECIPIENTS, 1996–2009

The number of welfare recipients dropped sharply after the Temporary Assistance for Needy Families (TANF) program was instituted. *Source:* U.S. Department of Health and Human Services, 2010. The last year of the Aid for Dependent Families (AFDC) program was 1996; it was replaced by TANF.

Head Start Education programs for the poor are not limited to job training. In the 1960s, as part of Lyndon Johnson's Great Society, the federal government started an education program, Head Start, aimed at helping poor children at an early age. Head Start provides free preschool education to low-income children in order to help them succeed when they begin kindergarten. Nearly a million children are currently enrolled in Head Start, at an average annual cost of about $7,500 per child.

At no time in its history has the Head Start program been funded at a level that would allow all eligible children to participate. The low point was reached in the 1980s, when there was only enough money to enroll one in ten of those eligible. Today, less than half of all eligible children get to participate. In addition, Head Start has not met the performance goals expected when it was founded. Because many of the enrolled children have a home environment that is not conducive to educational achievement, their academic performance in primary school is not substantially higher than that of other poor children. Proponents of Head Start argue that its real contribution is a less tangible one: it places poor children, for part of the day, in an environment where their nutritional and social needs receive attention.

Earned Income Tax Credit (EITC) A full-time job does not guarantee that a family will rise above the poverty line. A family of four with one employed adult who works forty hours a week at $7 an hour (roughly the federal minimum wage) has an annual income of about $14,000, which is $8,000 below the poverty line. Millions of Americans—mostly household workers, service workers, unskilled laborers, and farm workers—are in this position. The U.S. Bureau of Labor Statistics estimates that roughly 10 percent of full-time workers, the so-called "working poor," do not earn enough to lift their family above the poverty line.[10]

Some of these workers are eligible to receive the Earned Income Tax Credit (EITC). Enacted in 1975 under President Gerald Ford and expanded during the presidencies of Ronald Reagan and Bill Clinton, EITC now covers about 10 million low-income American families. The maximum yearly payment to any family is roughly $4,500, and eligibility is limited to families that include a wage earner. EITC payments occur when the wage earner files a personal income tax return. Those whose incomes are sufficiently low receive an EITC payment, the amount of which depends on the level of their income and whether they have dependents. The EITC program is now the federal government's largest means-tested cash assistance program. According to U.S. Census Bureau calculations, the EITC lifts about a third of low-income Americans above the poverty line.

Although the EITC is subject to budgetary and political pressures, it has more public support than most assistance programs. The reason is simple: EITC is tied to employment. Only those who work are eligible to receive the payment. Polls that span more than a half-century reveal that Americans have consistently favored work-based assistance to welfare payments as the answer to poverty. Work is widely believed to foster initiative and accountability; welfare is widely held to breed dependency and irresponsibility.

In-Kind Benefits: Food Stamps and Housing Vouchers The Food Stamps program, which took its present form in 1961, is fully funded by the federal government. The program provides an **in-kind benefit**—not cash, but food stamps that can be spent only on grocery items. Food stamps are available only to people who qualify on the basis of low income. The program is intended to improve the nutrition of poor families by enabling them to purchase qualified items—mainly foodstuffs—with food stamps. Some critics say that food stamps stigmatize their users by making it obvious to onlookers in the checkout line that they are "welfare cases." More prevalent criticisms are that the program is too costly and that too many undeserving people receive food stamps.

Low-income persons are also eligible for subsidized housing. Most of the federal spending in this area is on rent vouchers, an in-kind benefit. The government gives the individual a monthly rent payment voucher, which the individual gives in lieu of cash to the landlord, who then hands the voucher over to the government in exchange for cash. About five million households annually receive a federal housing subsidy.

Like other public assistance programs, housing subsidies are criticized as being too costly. Nevertheless, the federal government spends less on public housing for the poor than it gives in tax breaks to homeowners, most of whom are middle- and upper-income Americans. Homeowners are allowed tax deductions for their mortgage interest payments and their local property tax payments. The total of these tax concessions is three times as much as is spent by the federal government on low-income housing. In many European democracies, there is no tax deduction for home mortgage payments.

Medicaid When Medicare was created for retirees in 1965, Congress also established Medicaid, which provides health care for the poor. It is a public assistance program, rather than a social insurance program like

Medicare, because it is based on need and funded by general tax revenues. Roughly 60 percent of Medicaid funding is provided by the federal government and about 40 percent by the states. More than 30 million Americans receive Medicaid assistance. The figure will increase as a result of the health care reform bill that Congress enacted in 2010. The legislation expanded the eligibility criteria for Medicaid recipients. Most single adults without children, for example, were not eligible under the old rules but are eligible under the new ones. (In addition, beginning in 2014, the new law will provide a subsidy to individuals and families with incomes below four times the poverty rate to help them pay for health insurance premiums, although in most cases they will have to bear the larger share of the cost.)

As health care costs have spiraled far ahead of the inflation rate, so have the costs of Medicaid. It absorbs roughly half of all public assistance dollars spent by the U.S. government and has forced state and local governments to cut other services to meet their share of the costs. "It's killing us" is how one local official described the impact of Medicaid on his community's budget.[11] As is true of other public assistance programs, Medicaid has been criticized for supposedly helping too many people who could take care of themselves.

Culture and Social Welfare

Surveys repeatedly show that most Americans are convinced that people on welfare could get along without it if they tried. As a consequence, there is constant political pressure to reduce welfare expenditures and to weed out undeserving recipients. The unwritten principle of social welfare in America, reflecting the country's individualistic culture, is that the individual must somehow earn a social welfare benefit or, barring that, demonstrate a convincing need for it. The result is a welfare system that is both inefficient, in that much of the money spent on welfare never reaches the intended recipients, and inequitable, in that less than half of social welfare spending goes to the people most in need.[12]

Inefficiency The United States has the most inefficient welfare system in the Western world. Scores of separate programs have been established to address different, often overlapping needs. A single individual in need of public assistance may qualify for many, one, or none of these programs, and the eligibility criteria can be mystifying. For some programs, there is no sliding eligibility scale. A person who makes $495 a month in wages

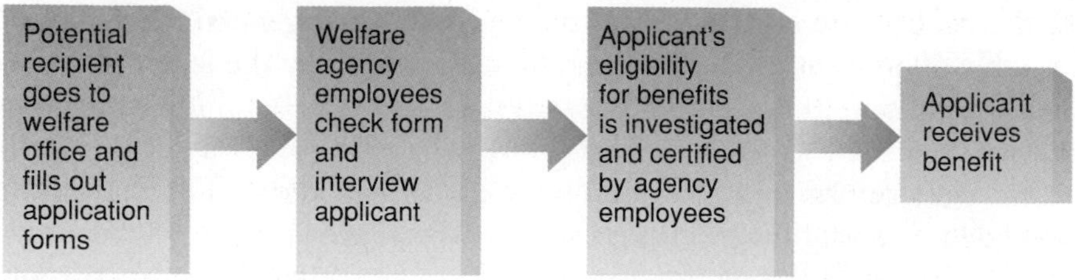

figure 16-3 THE CUMBERSOME ADMINISTRATIVE PROCESS BY WHICH WELFARE RECIPIENTS GET THEIR BENEFITS

might be eligible to receive a particular benefit, whereas a person making $500 might be ineligible.

Beyond the question of the fairness of such rules is the issue of their efficiency. The unwritten principle that the individual must somehow earn or be in absolute need of assistance makes the U.S. welfare system heavily bureaucratic. For example, the 1996 Welfare Reform Act—which limits eligibility to families with incomes below a certain level and, in most instances, to families with a single parent living in the home—requires that the eligibility of each applicant be checked periodically by a caseworker. This procedure makes such programs doubly expensive; in addition to making payments to recipients, the programs must pay local caseworkers, supervisors, and support staffs (see Figure 16-3). These costs do not include the administrative costs of the state and federal agencies that oversee the programs.

The bureaucratic costs of welfare are substantially lower in Europe because most European countries have unitary rather than federal systems, which eliminates a layer of government, and also because eligibility is often universal, as in the case of government-paid health care. Caseworkers do not have to pore over records to determine who is and who is not eligible for government-provided medical treatment—everyone is.[13]

Inequity European welfare programs are also more equitable in the sense that the major beneficiaries are those individuals most in need. In contrast, the United States spends as much, or more, on assistance programs for the nonpoor than it does for the poor.

Social security and Medicare provide an example. Spending on these programs, which assist rich and poor alike, exceeds the total of all spending of public assistance programs, which help only the needy. Many social security recipients are in the higher-income categories, and thus have no absolute economic need for the benefit. In fact, their monthly social security income is substantially higher than that of those in the lower-income categories as a result of the formula for determining social security payouts—the higher your income while working, the larger your social security benefit upon retirement. To be sure, social security recipients, regardless of their wealth, have a claim to the benefit as a result of having paid payroll taxes during their working years. Nevertheless, most retirees receive more in social security benefits than they contributed in payroll taxes while working. The excess payment could be regarded as public assistance and has been increasing as a result of lengthening life spans. The prime beneficiaries of the extra years on social security assistance are the more affluent. Poverty takes a toll on people's health and cuts short their retirement years. The poorest 10 percent of Americans live five fewer years on average than the wealthiest 10 percent.

Of course, social insurance programs do help many who are needy. Monthly social security checks keep millions of Americans, mostly widows, out of poverty. About one-fourth of America's elderly have no significant monthly income aside from what they receive from social security. Nevertheless, families in the top fifth of the income population receive more in social security and Medicare benefits than the government spends in total on TANF, SSI, food stamps, and housing subsidies for the poor.

Education as Equality of Opportunity

Although few Americans would support economic equality for all, most Americans endorse the principle of **equality of opportunity**—the idea that people should have a reasonable chance to succeed if they make the effort. The concept includes a commitment to equality in the narrow sense that everyone should have a fair chance to get ahead. But it is a form of equality shaped by liberty because the outcome—personal success or personal failure—depends on what individuals do with that opportunity. The expectation is that people will end up differently—some will make a good living and some will be poor. It is sometimes said that equality of opportunity gives individuals an equal chance to become unequal.

Equality of opportunity is an ideal. Americans do not start life on an equal footing. It was said of one successful American politician, whose father before him was a successful politician and a millionaire, that "he was born on third base and thought he hit a triple."[14] Some Americans are born into privilege, and others start life in such abject poverty that few of them escape it. Nonetheless, equality of opportunity is more than a catchphrase. It is the philosophical basis for a number of government programs, none more so than public education.

Until the 1960s, the federal government's role in education was relatively small. Education was largely the responsibility of state and local governments, and they continue to provide more than 90 percent of school funding and to determine the bulk of school policies, from the length of the academic year to teachers' qualifications. However, the federal government also has an ongoing role in education policy, largely as a result of legislation enacted in the 1960s. The 1964 Higher Education Act is the foundation for Pell Grants, federal loans to college students, and federally subsidized college work-study programs. The 1964 Elementary and Secondary Education Act provides funding for items such as school construction, textbooks, special education, and teacher training. Federal funding is split almost evenly between support for colleges and support for elementary and secondary schools.

Public Education: Leveling through the Schools

During the nation's first century, the question of a free education for all children was a divisive issue. Wealthy interests feared that an educated public would challenge their power. Egalitarians, on the other hand, saw education as a means of enabling ordinary citizens to get ahead. The egalitarians won out. Public schools sprang up in nearly every community and were free of charge.[15]

Equality continues to be a guiding principle of public education. Unlike the situation in countries that divide children even at the grade school level into different tracks that lead ultimately to different occupations, the curriculum in U.S. schools is relatively standardized. Of course, public education has never been a uniform experience for American children. Cities in the late nineteenth century neglected the education of many immigrant children, who were thereby placed at a permanent disadvantage. During the first half of the twentieth century, southern public schools for black children were designed to keep them down, not lift them up. Today, many children in poorer neighborhoods attend overcrowded, understaffed, and underfunded public schools. The quality of education depends significantly on the wealth of the community in which a child resides. The Supreme Court has upheld this arrangement, saying that the states are obliged to give all children an "adequate" education as opposed to one that is "equal" across communities.

POLITICAL THINKING

Education—American-Style Socialism?

Leon Sampson, a nineteenth-century socialist, noted the stark difference between the philosophy of public education in the United States and that in Europe. "The European ruling classes," he wrote, "were open in their contempt for the proletariat. But in the United States equality, and even classlessness, the creation of wealth for all and political liberty were extolled in the public schools." Sampson concluded that American schools embodied a unique conception of equality. Everyone was being trained in much the same way so that each person would have the opportunity to succeed. "It is," he said, "a socialist conception of capitalism." Would you agree with Sampson that public schools have done more than any other institution to foster equality in America? Are there ways today to improve public education as a means of promoting equality of opportunity?

Nevertheless, the United States through its public schools seeks to broadly educate its children. Public education in America was labeled "the great leveler" when it began in the early nineteenth century and the tradition has been maintained. Arguably, no country makes an equivalent effort to give children, whatever their parents' background, an equal opportunity in life through education. Per-pupil spending on public elementary and secondary schools is substantially higher in the United States than it is in Europe. America's commitment to broad-based education extends to college. The United States is easily the world leader in terms of the percentage of adults with a college education.[16]

The nation's education system preserves both the myth and the reality of an equal-opportunity society. The belief that success is within the reach of anyone who works for it could not be sustained if the public education system was designed to serve the privileged few. Moreover, educational attainment is related to personal success, at least as measured by income. In fact, the gap in income between those with and those without a college degree is greater now than at any time in the country's history. On average during their lifetime, college graduates will earn about 65 percent more than those without a college degree. This difference is greater than in European democracies; workers without college

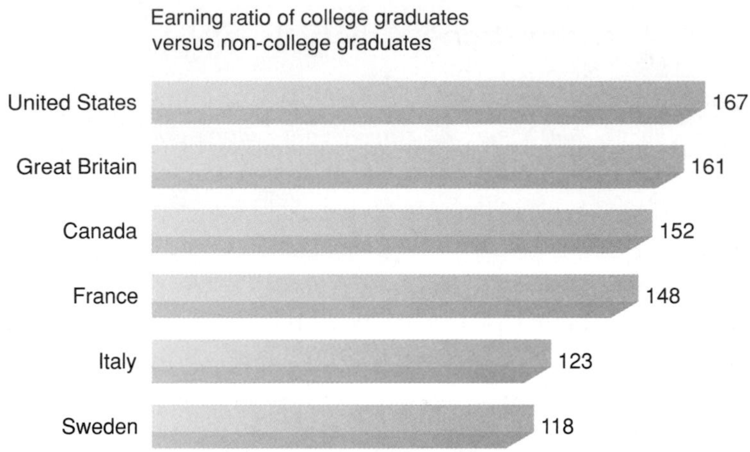

figure 16-4 THE EARNING POWER OF A COLLEGE DEGREE

College graduates in every Western democracy earn more on average than non-college graduates. The difference is more pronounced in the United States than elsewhere. *Source:* Organization for Economic Development and Cooperation, 2010. Average earning ratio of non-college graduate is indexed to 100 for each country.

degrees in those countries receive higher wages than their American counterparts because they have the benefit of higher minimum-wage laws and stronger labor unions (see Figure 16-4).

Improving America's Schools

Because America's public schools play such a key role in creating an equal-opportunity society, they are scrutinized closely. Parents of schoolchildren are not shy about saying what they think of their local schools. Interestingly, parents tend to rate their own children's schools more highly than they rate other schools. A national survey found that most parents gave their children's schools a grade of A or B while giving schools as a whole a grade of C or lower.[17]

By objective indicators, America's students are not high performers. U.S. students rank below students in Canada and most European countries on standardized reading, math, and science tests (see "How the U.S. Differs"). One reason is that the United States has a larger portion of non-native-speaking children. American students for whom English is a second language have lower standardized test scores on average than do other students.[18] The United States is also more segregated residentially by income than are European countries. As a result, poor children are more likely to go to schools where most of the other students are also poor. Moreover, because the wealth of a community affects the level of

HOW THE U.S. DIFFERS
POLITICAL THINKING THROUGH COMPARISON

Education Performance

Although the United States spends more heavily on its public schools than do nearly all other advanced industrialized democracies, its students perform less well on standardized tests than do students in most of these countries. In fact, American students do not rank even in the top ten countries in terms of academic performance. Some of the cross-national surveys have been conducted by the Organization for Economic Cooperation and Development (OECD). Its surveys are administered periodically in more than three dozen countries. The surveys in each case are given to a sample of fifteen-year-olds, by which age students in most countries are nearing the end of their compulsory time in school. Every OECD survey covers reading, mathematical and scientific literacy in terms of general competencies—that is, how well students can apply the knowledge and skills they have learned

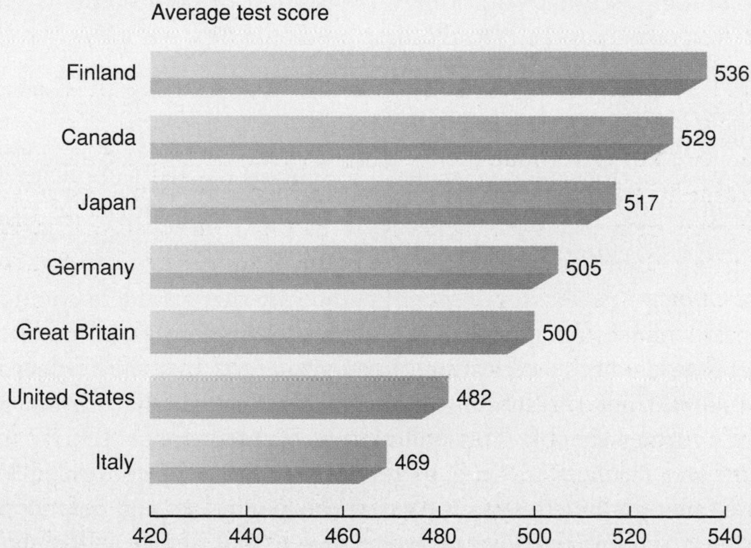

Source: Organization for Economic Development and Cooperation, 2010.

(*continued*)

at school to real-life situations. Only those questions that are approved unanimously by the participating countries are used in the survey. The chart on page 585 is based on the most recent OECD survey and shows the average test scores in selected countries.

Q: *Why might the United States lag behind other advanced industrialized democracies in student performance, even though it spends more heavily on public education?*

A: *Although the blame for the relatively poor performance of U.S. students on standardized tests is often directed at teachers, other factors have been found to be more important. Compared with most Western democracies, the United States has a relatively high proportion of non-native-speaking children, who on average do less well in school than other students. In addition, the United States has more residential segregation by income and more poor children than do other Western democracies. Poor children, particularly those residing in poor neighborhoods or communities, tend to perform less well in school than do their peers.*

school funding, schools with a high proportion of poor students tend to have fewer resources. In fact, the best predictor of a school's overall performance on standardized tests is the wealth of the community in which it is located; schools in poorer areas have much lower scores on average than do schools in more affluent areas.[19]

The weak performance of many U.S. schools has led to policies aimed at strengthening education in America. The most contentious of these policies are school choice and mandatory high-stakes testing.

School Choice Advocates of school choice say that a student should have the option of leaving a poorly performing school in favor of one that might provide a better education. They also argue that the student's new school should get the funding that otherwise would have gone to the student's former school. This policy, it is claimed, forces school administrators and teachers to do a better job, or face the continued loss of students and funding.[20] Opponents of the policy do not defend poorly performing schools but instead argue that school choice will only serve to weaken these schools further. They claim that the policy benefits middle- and upper-income students because the parents of poor children lack the means to transport them to a better but more distant school.[21]

School choice has gained momentum in recent years. The emergence of charter schools is a case in point. Although charter schools are publicly funded, they operate by different standards than other public schools. They have greater freedom, for example, in determining their curricula and in picking their students. In return, they must meet specified accountability criteria in order to remain open. Promoted primarily by conservatives, charter schools have faced substantial opposition from public school teachers and administrators on grounds that these schools drain the regular public schools of funding and top students. In 2009, President Obama broke with some Democratic policymakers by endorsing charter schools. Obama said charter schools are leaders in innovation and argued that state-imposed limits on the number of charter schools are not "good for our children, our economy, and our country."

School vouchers are another method for expanding students' options. Parents receive a voucher from the government that they can give to a private or parochial school to cover part of the cost of their child's tuition. Proponents say that vouchers force failing public schools to improve their instructional programs or face a permanent loss of revenue. For their part, opponents argue that vouchers weaken the public schools by siphoning off revenue and say that vouchers subsidize many families that would have sent their children to private or parochial schools anyway. They also note

The Supreme Court has held that American children are entitled to an "adequate" education but do not have a right to an "equal" education. America's public schools differ greatly in quality primarily as a result of differences in the wealth of the communities they serve. Some public schools are overcrowded and have few facilities and little equipment. Others are very well equipped, have spacious facilities, and offer small class sizes.

that vouchers are of little use to students from poor families because vouchers cover only part of the tuition costs at a private or parochial school and poor families do not have the money to pay the rest.

Although the courts have upheld the constitutionality of vouchers in some circumstances, polls indicate that Americans are divided over the issue of school vouchers.[22] The question gets majority support when it is framed in the context of giving students a choice among public schools but is opposed by the majority when private and parochial schools are included among the choices. The issue of vouchers reflects the tensions inherent in the concept of equal opportunity. Vouchers expand opportunity by increasing the number of choices available to students. Yet not all students are able to take advantage of the choices, and not all taxpayers want their tax dollars used to support private and parochial schools.

Mandatory High-Stakes Testing During his presidency, Bill Clinton opposed the idea of unrestricted school choice, arguing that it would devastate the nation's weaker public schools and make them a repository of America's poorest children. As an alternative, Clinton persuaded Congress to appropriate billions of dollars in new funding to enable overcrowded schools to hire tens of thousands of new teachers.[23]

President George W. Bush brought a different education agenda to the White House, persuading Congress in 2001 to pass the No Child Left Behind Act (NCLB). The legislation requires national testing in reading, math, and science and ties federal funding to the test results. Schools that show no improvement in students' test scores after two years receive an increased amount of federal aid. If these schools show no improvement by the end of the third year, however, their students become eligible to transfer elsewhere, and their school's federal assistance is reduced.

NCLB has been a source of dispute since its inception.[24] The National Education Association (NEA) claims that the law forces teachers to teach to the national tests and thereby undermines classroom learning. Congressional Democrats say that the program has failed to provide struggling schools with enough funds to improve the quality of classroom education. For their part, congressional Republicans have generally supported the law, saying that it holds teachers and schools accountable for student performance. Congressman John Boehner (R-Ohio) said, "Money alone is not the answer to the problems facing our children's schools. High standards and accountability for results—not just spending—are the key to erasing the achievement gap in education."[25] Opinion polls show that Americans are divided over the issue of whether NCLB is an effective program, with Republicans being somewhat more supportive of NCLB than are Democrats.[26]

Thus, many of the partisan and philosophical differences that affect federal welfare policy also affect federal education policy. Democrats are more inclined to find the answer to how to improve schools in increased federal spending on education, particularly in less affluent communities, whereas Republicans are more inclined to look to market-like mechanisms such as school choice and achievement tests.

The American Way of Promoting the General Welfare

All democratic societies promote economic security, but they do so in different ways and to different degrees. Economic security has a higher priority in European democracies than in the United States. European democracies have instituted programs such as government-paid health care for all citizens, compensation for all unemployed workers, and retirement benefits for all elderly citizens. As this chapter shows, the United States provides these benefits only to some citizens in each category. On the other hand, the American system of higher education dwarfs those in Europe.

The differences between the European and American approaches to welfare stem from historical and cultural differences. Democracy in Europe developed in reaction to centuries of aristocratic rule, which brought the issue of economic privilege to the forefront. European democracies initiated sweeping social welfare programs designed to bring about greater economic equality. Social inequality was harder to root out because it was thoroughly embedded in European society, shaping everything from social manners to education. Private schools and university training were the preserve of the elite, a tradition that, though now in the past, continues to affect how Europeans think about educational opportunity.

The American experience was a different one. Democracy in America grew out of a tradition of limited government that emphasized personal liberty, which included a belief in self-reliance. This belief contributed to Americans' strong support for public education, their weak support for public assistance, and their persistent preference for low tax rates. Unlike political equality, the idea of economic equality has never captured Americans' imagination. Political scientists Stanley Feldman and John Zaller found that Americans' support for public assistance programs rests more on compassion for the poor than on an ideological belief in economic sharing.[27] Or, as the political scientist Robert Lane expressed it, Americans have a preference for market justice, meaning that they prefer that society's material benefits be allocated through the economic marketplace

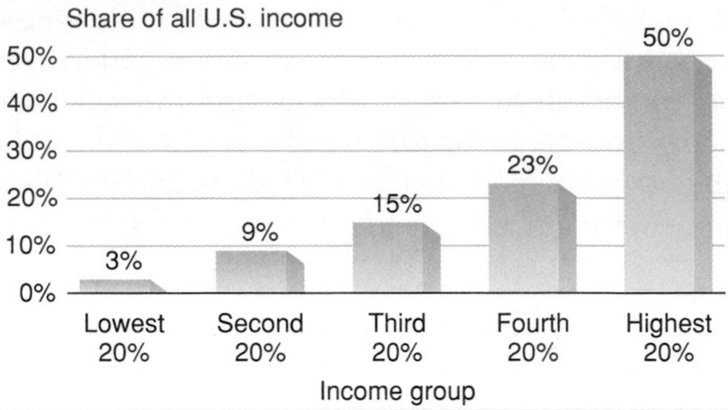

figure 16-5 INCOME INEQUALITY IN THE UNITED STATES

The United States has the highest degree of income inequality of any industrialized democracy. Citizens in the top fifth by income get half of all income: those in the bottom fifth get less than a twentieth of all income. *Source:* U.S. Census Bureau, 2008.

rather than through government policies.[28] Not surprisingly, the United States has a high level of income inequality (see Figure 16-5). Americans in the top fifth by income receive half of the total U.S. income, whereas those in the bottom fifth get less than a twentieth. This 10-to-1 income difference between the top earners and the bottom earners is easily the highest among Western democracies.

SUMMARY Self-Test www.mhhe.com/pattersonwtp9e

The United States has a complex social welfare system of multiple programs addressing specific welfare needs. Each program applies only to those individuals who qualify for benefits by meeting the specific eligibility criteria. In general, these criteria are designed to encourage self-reliance or, when help is necessary, to ensure that laziness is not rewarded or fostered. This approach to social welfare reflects Americans' traditional belief in individualism.

Poverty is a large and persistent problem in the United States. About one in nine Americans falls below the government-defined poverty line, including a disproportionate number of children, female-headed families, minority-group members, and rural and inner-city dwellers. The ranks of the poor are increased by economic recessions and are reduced through government assistance programs.

Welfare policy has been a partisan issue, with Democrats taking the lead on government programs to alleviate economic insecurity and Republicans acting to slow down or decentralize these initiatives. Changes in social welfare have usually resulted from presidential leadership in the context of public support for the change. Welfare policy traditionally has involved programs to provide jobs and job training, education programs, income measures, and especially individual-benefit programs.

Individual-benefit programs fall into two broad categories: social insurance and public assistance. The former includes programs such as social security for retired workers and Medicare for the elderly. Social insurance programs are funded by payroll taxes paid by potential recipients, who, in this sense, earn the benefits they later receive. Because of this arrangement, social insurance programs have broad public support. Public assistance programs, in contrast, are funded by general tax revenues and are targeted toward needy individuals and families. These programs are not controversial in principle; most Americans believe that government should assist the truly needy. However, because of a widespread belief that most welfare recipients could get along without assistance if they tried, these programs do not have universal public support, receive only modest funding, and are politically divisive.

Social welfare is a contentious issue. In one view, social welfare is too costly and assists too many people who could help themselves; another view holds that social welfare is not broad enough and that too many disadvantaged Americans live in poverty. Because of these irreconcilable beliefs and because of federalism and the widely shared view that welfare programs should target specific problems, the existing system of multiple programs, despite its administrative complexity and inefficiency, has been the only politically feasible solution.

The balance between economic equality and individualism tilts more heavily toward individualism in the United States than in other advanced industrialized democracies. Other democracies, for example, have government-paid health care for all citizens. The United States does not, although the recently enacted health care reform bill provides coverage to many of the previously uninsured.

Compared to other democracies, the United States attempts to more equally educate its children, a policy consistent with its cultural emphasis on equality of opportunity. Like social welfare, however, education is a partisan issue involving disputes over the federal government's role, school choice, spending levels, and mandatory high-stakes testing.

Key Terms

entitlement programs (*p. 571*)
equality of opportunity (*p. 581*)
in-kind benefit (*p. 578*)
means test (*p. 574*)
negative government (*p. 569*)
positive government (*p. 569*)
poverty line (*p. 566*)
public assistance (*p. 573*)
social insurance (*p. 571*)

Suggested Readings

Alesina, Alberto, and Edward Glaeser. *Fighting Poverty in the U.S. and Europe: A World of Difference.* New York: Oxford University Press, 2006. A comparison of poverty policies in the United States and Europe.

Howard, Christopher. *The Welfare State Nobody Knows: Debunking Myths about U.S. Social Policy*. Princeton, N.J.: Princeton University Press, 2006. A critical assessment of the U.S. social welfare system.

Koretz, Daniel. *Measuring Up: What Educational Testing Really Tells Us*. Cambridge, MA.: Harvard University Press, 2009. A comprehensive look at standardized testing performance and its correlates.

Kornbluh, Felicia Ann. *The Battle for Welfare Rights: Politics and Poverty in Modern America*. Philadelphia: University of Pennsylvania Press, 2007. An analysis of welfare rights and conditions, with particular attention to the feminization of poverty.

Patterson, James T. *America's Struggle against Poverty in the Twentieth Century*. Cambridge, MA.: Harvard University Press, 2000. A careful study of poverty and its history.

Quadagno, Jill. *One Nation, Uninsured: Why the United States Has No National Health Insurance*. New York: Oxford University Press, 2005. A look at the politics of U.S. health care policy.

Reed, Douglas S. *On Equal Terms: The Constitutional Politics of Educational Opportunity*. Princeton, N.J.: Princeton University Press, 2003. An insightful analysis of school reform issues.

Spring, Joel H. *The American School 1642–2004: From the Puritans to No Child Left Behind*. New York: McGraw-Hill, 2008. A history of U.S. public schools.

Van Dunk, Emily, and Anneliese M. Dickman. *School Choice and the Question of Accountability*. New Haven, CT.: Yale University Press, 2003. A careful look at the voucher system as applied in the Milwaukee school system.

List of Websites

www.doleta.gov The U.S. Department of Labor's website on the status of the welfare-to-work program, including state-by-state assessments.

www.nea.org The home page of the National Education Association; provides information on the organization's membership and policy goals.

www.dhhs.gov The website of the Department of Health and Human Services—the agency responsible for most federal social welfare programs.

www.npc.umich.edu The website of the University of Michigan's National Poverty Center, which seeks to stimulate interest in policy issues and to transmit research findings to policymakers.

Politics in Theory and Practice

Thinking: How has U.S. policy on welfare and education been influenced by Americans' belief in individualism? By America's federal system of government?

Participating: When it comes to partisan politics, poverty is a contentious issue. Republicans and Democrats disagree mightily on the question of how far government should go in helping the poor. On the other hand, virtually all Americans—on the right and on the left—support private efforts to help the poor. Numerous local religious, civic, social, and economic groups run programs for the poor, such as food kitchens and clothing drives. Also, many national organizations work locally to assist the poor. An example is Habitat for Humanity, which builds modest houses with volunteer labor and then makes them available to low-income families, which assist in the construction and receive low-interest or no-interest mortgages to pay for the cost of construction materials. Consider volunteering some of your time to a group that gives a helping hand to those in need—whether a church or a community group or a nonprofit organization like Habitat for Humanity. Habitat for Humanity has a website that makes it easy for you to volunteer.

Extra Credit

For up-to-the-minute *New York Times* articles, interactive simulations, graphics, study tools, and more links and quizzes, visit the text's Online Learning Center at **www.mhhe.com/pattersonwtp9e**.

NATIONAL JOURNAL

Any Public Support for an Energy Bill?

Although President Obama believes that the Gulf oil drilling disaster offers Congress a compelling rationale to pass comprehensive energy legislation in an election year, senators aren't sure the public has made that linkage. Even the most enthusiastic proponents of various energy bills in the Senate suggest that, instead of Obama's nod to preserving the environment and kicking the U.S. petroleum addiction, a more persuasive sales pitch might be the lure of jobs that new energy initiatives could create.

"The biggest rationale for doing this right now is the economic rationale, the jobs," Sen. John Kerry, D-Mass., said last week after a closed-door briefing among his fellow Democrats about pending energy bill options. "You have to create [economic] demand in the United States," he added. "The only way to create demand is to price carbon."

"I think it's pretty clear that we have to do something," Senate Majority Leader Harry Reid, D-Nev., told reporters. "The question is, what do we do? And a lot of that depends on what the White House is going to do to help us get something done."

Kerry and Sen. Joe Lieberman, ID-Conn., co-sponsored energy-plus-carbon-pricing legislation this spring, hoping that their alternative to the House energy and carbon cap-and-trade bill passed a year ago might attract 60 votes to break a certain Republican filibuster in the Senate. As the president and Reid continue to pursue possible compromises, Kerry, Lieberman, and other senators who back rival alternatives are poring over public polling, searching for footing that might reassure nervous lawmakers who worry about inviting any new voter wrath before November.

"There are two things going on," Sen. Maria Cantwell, D-Wash., said last week after she, too, briefed her colleagues about her competing "cap-and-dividend" approach to controlling carbon emissions. Her Democratic peers, she said, are worried in the near term about the federal response to the Gulf oil spill and the ongoing cleanup, and feel uncertain how energy legislation might fit in.

"I think we have a lot of work to do, but I think there is a big economic opportunity to create jobs, and a lot of passion about energy," Cantwell continued. "But I think we're so new in this process that every day the Gulf presents another challenge to us."

Focusing on employment opportunities—new "green" jobs, including production and manufacturing tied to energy—appeals to energy bill advocates at a time when unemployment remains stuck near 10 percent. However, analysts across the ideological spectrum who have looked at options for energy legislation cannot predict with any precision how many or what kind of jobs might be created, or how soon those jobs might come online.

And just as quickly as Democrats pivoted back to the comfort of their jobs message, Republicans have been eager to pull it apart.

"The action in the Democratic Congress seems to be too often about fewer jobs," Sen. Lamar Alexander, R-Tenn., a member of the GOP leadership, said this week in front of a bank of TV cameras. He cited higher taxes, rising fees, and expanded debt under the Democrats, plus a legislative crackdown on the financial industry that is working its way through a conference committee, as examples of policies that have cost workers their jobs during an economic downturn.

"My suggestion is that we use the oil spillcrisis as an excuse to clean up the oil spill with the minimum amount of impact on Gulf Coast jobs," Alexander said.

His reference to job losses because of the Deepwater Horizon catastrophe sought to hit a nerve. The minority party would like to widen the majority's divisions over energy, which existed well before the oil rig exploded and sank. The BP disaster looked initially to Obama like a catalyst for congressional momentum, but it has instead scrambled Democratic lawmakers' confidence about taking on another giant legislative task akin to health care before the elections.

The Obama administration's six-month moratorium on deepwater drilling imposed after the rig accident put an estimated 100,000 petroleum-related jobs in limbo in the Gulf region. The president is in the uncomfortable position of arguing for legislation tied to energy that could create jobs in the future, while he takes emergency steps in the near term that jeopardize jobs for the sake of the environment and safer drilling.

Many Democratic lawmakers from the Gulf states, given the choice between jobs lost before an election and jobs that might be created after their possible defeat, are keen to embrace reasonable alternatives to the president's suspension of drilling on 33 exploratory wells and his ban on new drilling permits. Three major oil companies have moved to escape rig leases in the Gulf on the grounds that the president's moratorium voided those contracts, The Wall Street Journal reports.

A Louisiana federal judge, setting up a potential clash over executive authority, recently struck down the administration's ban, asserting that the government went too far. The White House plans to issue a new ban order and promised that the government would appeal U.S. District Judge Martin Feldman's decision.

Recent polling finds public opinion divided and somewhat inconsistent across questions dealing with energy policy. If lawmakers are looking for clear direction from voters, polls are not finding it. In fact, opinions since the April 20 BP spill may have wandered in a direction the president initially did not foresee.

Asked three years ago whether protecting the environment or developing new sources of energy should be the higher government priority, 62 percent of Americans favored new sources of energy, followed by protecting the environment at 21 percent. Since 2008, Obama has been arguing for new sources of energy, and in January he spoke favorably about offshore drilling and nuclear power. After the BP accident, citing safety, Obama retreated on both stances.

This month, Americans said they found the appeal of new energy development—perhaps interpreted as drilling for petroleum in riskier locations—less attractive as a government priority; support dropped to 49 percent, while "protecting the environment" climbed 8 points compared with 2007, according to a recent New York Times/CBS News poll.

Twenty percent of Americans said that both energy and the environment should be important, up from 14 percent in 2007, the survey found. The same pollsters asked a smaller subgroup of Gulf state residents, where the BP spill is closer to home, the same questions: 48 percent responded that protecting the environment should be the government's higher priority, compared with 37 percent who chose new energy development. A majority of Americans—58 percent—said that there are "good things" in the nation's energy policy, but that "fundamental changes" are needed, while a higher percentage of respondents from the Gulf region (62 percent) said they would favor seeing "fundamental" changes, rather than minor adjustments, on the one hand, or a complete overhaul of energy policies on the other.

What's Your Opinion?

Do you think the economy is an issue more worthy of legislators' attention than a comprehensive energy policy in general? What could be done to persuade Americans to look more seriously at energy and climate change?

CHAPTER 17

Foreign Policy: Protecting the American Way

“We the people of the United States, in order to . . . provide for the common defense . . .”

Preamble, U.S. Constitution

In announcing on national television his decision to send 30,000 additional troops to Afghanistan, President Barack Obama declared the action to be “in our vital national interest.” Terrorism, he said, cannot be quelled without stopping it in Afghanistan. “I make this decision,” he declared, “because I am convinced our national security is at stake. . . . Afghanistan is the epicenter of violent extremism.” Yet Obama went on to say that America’s commitment in Afghanistan was not open ended. He announced that American troops would train Afghan military forces at an accelerated pace so that U.S. forces could begin withdrawing in 2011. In justifying the timetable, Obama spoke of America’s other pressing needs. “I must weigh all the challenges that our nation faces,” he said. “Over the past several years we have lost that balance. We’ve failed to appreciate the connection between national security and our economy. . . . So we can’t simply afford to ignore the price of these wars.”

The cornerstone of foreign policy is the **national interest**—what is best for the nation in terms of protecting its physical security and way of life. Americans may disagree on the specific policies that will serve the national interest. President Obama's decision to escalate the war in Afghanistan was praised by many, but it was also criticized widely. Nonetheless, though the national interest is difficult to define in practice, it is the underlying objective of foreign policy. The national interest is promoted through adequate military preparedness and through productive trade relations.

Foreign policy, unlike other areas of government policy, rests on relations with actors outside rather than within the country. As a result, the chief instruments of national security policy differ from those of domestic policy. One of these instruments is diplomacy—the process of negotiation between countries. The lead agency in U.S. diplomatic efforts is the Department of State, which is headed by the secretary of state and coordinates the efforts of U.S. embassies abroad, each of which is directed by a U.S. ambassador. American diplomacy also takes place through international organizations—such as the United Nations—to which the United States belongs. A second instrument of foreign policy is military power. The lead agency in military affairs is the Department of Defense, which is headed by the secretary of defense and oversees the military services—the Army, Air Force, Navy, and Marines. Here, too, the United States sometimes works through alliances, the most important of which is the North Atlantic Treaty Organization (NATO). NATO has nearly thirty member nations, including the United States, Canada, and most Western and Eastern European countries. A third instrument of world politics is intelligence gathering, or the process of monitoring other countries' activities. For many reasons, but primarily because all countries pursue their self-interest, each nation keeps a watchful eye on other nations. In the United States, the task of intelligence gathering falls to specialized federal agencies including the Central Intelligence Agency (CIA) and the National Security Agency (NSA). Economic exchange, the fourth instrument of foreign affairs, involves both international trade and foreign aid. U.S. interests in this area are promoted by a range of U.S. agencies, such as the Agriculture, Commerce, Labor, and Treasury Departments, as well as specialty agencies such as the Federal Trade Commission. The United States also pursues its economic goals through international organizations of which it is a member, including the World Trade Organization, the World Bank, and the International Monetary Fund.

The national security policies of the United States include an extraordinary array of activities—so many, in fact, that they could not possibly be addressed adequately in an entire book, much less a single chapter. There are roughly two hundred countries in the world, and the United States has relations of one kind or another—military, diplomatic, economic—with all of them. This chapter narrows the subject by concentrating on a few main ideas:

- *Since World War II, the United States has acted in the role of world leader, which has substantially affected its military, diplomatic, and economic policies.*
- *The United States maintains a high degree of defense preparedness, which requires a substantial level of defense spending and a worldwide deployment of U.S. conventional and strategic forces.*
- *Changes in the international marketplace have led to increased economic interdependence among nations, which has had a marked influence on the U.S. economy and on America's security planning.*

The Roots of U.S. Foreign and Defense Policy

Before World War II, except within its own hemisphere, the United States was a mostly **isolationist** country. It was preoccupied with its internal development and intent on avoiding European entanglements. A different America emerged from the devastation of World War II. It had more land, sea, and air power than any other country; a huge armaments industry; and more than a hundred military installations overseas. The United States had become a fully **internationalist** country—a nation deeply involved in world affairs.[1]

The United States was also a nation not fully at peace. It was locked in a wide-reaching conflict with the Soviet Union, which, after World War II, had engineered the communist takeover of Poland, Hungary, Czechoslovakia, Hungary, and other Eastern European nations. President Harry S Truman and other American leaders regarded communist Russia as an implacable foe, a view that led to adoption of the doctrine of **containment**—the notion that Soviet aggression could be stopped only by the determined use of American power.[2] This doctrine had roots in the failed efforts to appease Germany's Adolf Hitler in the years leading up to World War II. At the 1938 Munich conference, Germany was allowed to annex Czechoslovakia's Sudetenland, which had a substantial German population. The annexation whetted Hitler's expansionist goals. The "Lesson of Munich" was that totalitarian leaders could not be appeased; they had to be confronted.

The Cold War Era

Developments in the late 1940s embroiled the United States in a **cold war** with the Soviet Union.[3] The term refers to the fact that the two

Cold war propaganda, like this poster warning of the danger of communism, contributed to a climate of opinion in the United States that led to public support for efforts to contain Soviet power.

countries were not directly engaged in actual combat (a "hot war") but were locked in deep-seated hostilities that lasted forty-five years. The structure of international power was **bipolar**—the United States versus the Soviet Union. Each side was supreme in its sphere and was blocked by the power of the other from expanding its influence. A first application of containment policy was a massive aid program for Greece, where communists were gaining headway. President Truman believed that if Greece went communist, Turkey would be the next "domino" to fall, which would give control of the eastern Mediterranean to the Soviets. Then, in June 1950, when the Soviet-backed North Koreans invaded South Korea, Truman sent U.S. forces into the conflict in an attempt to stop the spread of communism in Northeast Asia. Nearly 35,000 U.S. troops lost their lives in the Korean War, which ended in stalemate.

The turning point in U.S. foreign policy was the Vietnam War. Responding to the threat of a communist takeover in Vietnam, the United States became ever more deeply involved. Washington policymakers were driven by the "domino theory"—the claim that if Vietnam fell to the communists, so too would Laos, Cambodia, and the rest of Southeast

Asia. By the late 1960s, 550,000 Americans were fighting in South Vietnam. Although U.S. forces were technically superior in combat to the communist fighters, Vietnam was a guerrilla war, with no front lines and few set battles.[4] U.S. public opinion, most visibly among the young, gradually turned against the war, contributing to President Lyndon Johnson's decision not to seek reelection in 1968. Public opinion also forced Richard Nixon, who became president in 1969, to aim not for victory but for a gradual disengagement. U.S. combat troops left Vietnam in 1973, and two years later North Vietnamese forces completed their takeover of the country. Vietnam was the most painful and costly application of the containment doctrine: 58,000 Americans lost their lives in the fighting.

POLITICAL THINKING

What's the Threat?

During the 1950s when the cold war was at its peak, President Dwight D. Eisenhower warned that threats originating abroad could lead Americans to compromise the nation's ideals. "The problem in defense," Eisenhower said, "is how far you can go without destroying from within what you are trying to defend from without." Eisenhower believed that excessive government secrecy—justified in the name of national security—threatened liberty. He also worried that a huge permanent military and the industrial firms that profit from it would incline the United States to rely too heavily on military force in its relations with other countries. Do you think Eisenhower's concerns were justified, given what you know of post-1950s U.S. foreign policy?

America's failure in Vietnam led U.S. policymakers to reconsider the country's international role. The "Lesson of Vietnam" was that there were limits to the country's ability to assert its will in the world. Nixon proclaimed that the United States could no longer act as the free world's "Lone Ranger" and sought to reduce tensions with communist countries. In 1972, Nixon visited the People's Republic of China, the first official contact with that country since the communists seized power in 1949. Nixon also initiated the Strategic Arms Limitation Talks (SALT), which resulted in reductions in the nuclear arsenals of the United States and the Soviet Union. This spirit of cooperation lasted until the Soviets' ill-fated invasion of Afghanistan in 1979, which convinced U.S. leaders that the Soviet Union was bent on expanding its influence into the oil-rich Middle

East. Ronald Reagan, elected president in 1980, called for a renewed hard line toward the Soviet Union, which he described as the "evil empire."

Although U.S. policymakers did not realize it, the Soviet Union was collapsing under the weight of its heavy defense expenditures, its isolation from Western technology, and its inefficient centralized economy. In 1985, Soviet leader Mikhail Gorbachev undertook a restructuring of Soviet society, an initiative known as *perestroika*. Gorbachev's reforms came too late to prevent the Soviet Union's collapse. In 1989, the Soviet Union withdrew its troops from Eastern Europe. Within the next two years, nearly all of the Soviet republics declared their independence, marking the end of the Soviet Union as a governing entity. The bipolar power structure that had defined world politics since the end of World War II was finished. The new structure was **unipolar**—the United States was now the world's unrivaled military superpower.

A New World Order

The end of the cold war prompted the first President Bush in 1990 to call for a "new world order." George H. W. Bush advocated **multilateralism**—the idea that major nations should act together in response to problems and crises. Included in Bush's plan was a stronger role for multinational organizations such as the United Nations and NATO.

Multilateralism defined America's response to the Iraqi invasion of Kuwait in August 1990. President Bush secured UN resolutions ordering Iraq to withdraw from Kuwait and authorizing the use of force if it failed to do so. Five months later, a half million troops, mostly American but including contingents from nearly two dozen nations, attacked Iraq, first with an aerial bombardment and then with combat troops. Four days into the ground fighting, Iraqi units fled the battlefield, ending the war.

The Gulf operation was a military triumph, prompting President Bush to declare that the United States had "kicked the Vietnam syndrome [the legacy of America's defeat in Vietnam] once and for all." The Gulf War, however, was less successful in another way. Believing that an overthrow of Hussein's regime would destabilize Iraq, President Bush ordered a halt to the hostilities after Iraqi forces retreated. Hussein remained in power but was ordered by a UN resolution to dismantle his weapons programs, subject to UN inspections. However, Hussein repeatedly interfered with the inspectors' attempts to verify the status of his weapons programs, raising concern about his intentions.

Multilateralism carried over into the Clinton administration. Confronting Serb atrocities in Bosnia—where tens of thousands of Muslims and

Croats were murdered, raped, or driven from their homes—President Bill Clinton pursued UN economic sanctions as a means of halting Serb aggression. When sanctions failed, the United States and its NATO allies attacked Serb forces with air power in 1995, which culminated in a U.S.-negotiated peace agreement (the Dayton Accords) that included the deployment to Bosnia of nearly 60,000 peacekeeping troops, including 20,000 Americans. War in the Balkans flared again in 1999 when the Serbs undertook a campaign of "ethnic cleansing" in the Serbian province of Kosovo, whose population was 90 percent Albanian. When attempts at a negotiated settlement failed, NATO planes, including U.S. aircraft, attacked Serbia.[5] After weeks of intensive bombing, Serb president Slobodan Milosevic (who died in 2006 while on trial for war crimes) pulled his troops out of Kosovo. Ethnic Albanians moved back in and, despite the presence of UN peacekeeping troops, launched revenge attacks on Serbs who remained. (In 2008, Kosovo became an independent state.)

As these examples indicate, multilateralism was not a wholly successful strategy for resolving international conflicts. With the deployment of enough resources, the world's major powers showed that they could act together with some success. However, these interventions offered no guarantee of long-term success. Regional and internal conflicts typically stem from enduring ethnic, religious, factional, or national hatreds or from chronic problems such as famine, overcrowding, or government corruption. Even if these hatreds or problems can be eased momentarily, they are often too deep-seated to be settled permanently.

The War on Terrorism

Upon assuming the presidency in 2001, George W. Bush rejected his father's multilateral approach to foreign policy. Declaring that he would reduce America's military presence abroad, Bush also announced that the United States would not participate in either the Kyoto Protocol (a global climate treaty) or the International Criminal Court (the ICC, a permanent international tribunal with jurisdiction over war crimes). Bush altered his stance after the terrorist attacks on the World Trade Center and the Pentagon on September 11, 2001. Although he continued to oppose the ICC and the Kyoto Protocol, Bush urged other nations to join the United States in a multilateral "war on terrorism."

The war on terrorism resulted in the first major reorganization of the U.S. national security bureaucracy since the Department of Defense was formed from the War and Navy Departments after World War II. This time, the new agency was the Department of Homeland Security (DHS), which was created in 2002 to coordinate domestic anti-terrorism efforts. The DHS's responsibilities include securing the nation's borders, enhancing defenses against biological attacks, preparing emergency personnel (police, firefighters, and rescue workers) for their roles in responding to terrorist attacks, and coordinating efforts to stop domestic terrorism.[6]

The first U.S. military action in the war on terrorism was an attack on Afghanistan, which commenced barely a month after the September 11 attacks. Afghanistan's Taliban-led government had granted sanctuary and training sites to the al Qaeda terrorists who carried out the attacks. Supported by troops from other NATO countries, U.S. forces quickly toppled the Taliban government, but failed to capture al Qaeda leader Osama bin Laden and his top lieutenants.

The Iraq War

In 2002, President Bush labeled Iraq, Iran, and North Korea "the axis of evil." A few months later, he announced a new national security doctrine: the **preemptive war doctrine**.[7] Speaking at West Point, Bush asserted that the United States would not wait until it was attacked by hostile nations. Instead, America would take "preemptive action."[8] The concept was not entirely new—U.S. officials had long maintained a right to strike first if faced with an imminent attack. What was new in the Bush Doctrine was its embrace of a first-strike option before a threat became imminent. Bush's words were chosen carefully. In some circumstances, *preemptive war*—a first strike in the face of a dangerous threat—is legal under international law, whereas *preventive war*—a first strike to forestall a remote threat—is illegal. In his speech, Bush employed the term for a legal war but set forth a doctrine that, in the minds of critics, met the definition of an illegal one.[9]

In the summer of 2002, Bush targeted the regime of Iraq's Saddam Hussein, claiming that it had weapons of mass destruction (WMDs)—chemical and biological weapons, and possibly nuclear weapons. That October, Congress authorized the use of military force against Iraq if it did not disarm voluntarily. Facing the possibility of an unwanted war in Iraq, America's European allies urged UN weapons inspectors to undertake the disarmament of Iraq, which had blocked earlier UN attempts to verify its weapon stockpiles. In late 2002, the United Nations passed a resolution requiring Iraq to accept weapons inspections. A two-track policy ensued. UN weapons inspectors entered Iraq in search of WMDs, while the United States deployed combat units to Iraq's borders.

Despite the UN's refusal to authorize a military attack and in the face of strenuous opposition from France, Germany, and Russia, President Bush in March 2003 ordered U.S. forces to invade Iraq. British troops were also involved, but the attack was essentially an act of **unilateralism**—the situation in which one nation takes action against another state or states.[10] The Iraqi regime collapsed quickly, but the postcombat phase proved costlier than the Bush administration had anticipated. Age-old animosities between Sunni, Shiite, and Kurdish groups within Iraq blocked political compromise and fueled internal violence. Improvised explosive devices and suicide bombers took a heavy toll on U.S. troops. Moreover, weapons inspectors did not find the WMDs that the Bush administration had claimed were in Iraq's possession. In early 2004, the chief U.S. weapons inspector, David Kay, testified before Congress that U.S. intelligence agencies had greatly exaggerated the extent of Iraq's weapons program.

The American public, which had backed the invasion of Iraq, came to question the war. Opinions elsewhere were less favorable. A year before the war, two-thirds of Western Europeans had expressed a positive opinion of the United States. After the invasion, less than half did so, which

After Saddam Hussein's regime in Iraq was toppled, the United States began the task of reconstructing Iraqi oil operations, schools, hospitals, roads, and other facilities. Internal violence among Iraq's opposing factions made the reconstruction effort more difficult than U.S. policymakers had anticipated.

contributed to America's inability to persuade European governments to play a large part in Iraq's reconstruction. The United States bore 90 percent of the troop casualties and the financial costs of the Iraq conflict.

In 2007, President Bush authorized a "surge" to give the struggling Iraqi government an opportunity to govern more effectively. Some 30,000 U.S. combat troops were added to the 130,000 military personnel already there. The surge contributed to a significant reduction in the violence, leading Bush to announce a phased withdrawal of U.S. combat forces by 2010. Upon taking office, President Obama chose to abide by Bush's timetable.

The Afghanistan Escalation

When the United States shifted its main theater of military operations to Iraq in 2003, the situation in Afghanistan began to deteriorate. The newly installed Afghan government, headed by Hamid Karzai, proved to be ineffective and corrupt, and the Taliban regrouped, slowly reasserting control over parts of the country, while using neighboring Pakistan as a safe haven.

During the 2008 presidential campaign, Obama argued that Afghanistan was America's "war of necessity." A month after taking office, he ordered 20,000 additional troops to be deployed to Afghanistan. Nine months later, after a months-long series of meetings with top advisors, he ordered the deployment of 30,000 more troops, while urging America's NATO allies to also increase their troop levels. The escalation had a threefold purpose: to disrupt the Taliban resurgence, to speed the training of Afghan army and police, and to provide a level of security that would strengthen Afghans' confidence in their government. At the same time, Obama rejected an open-ended commitment in Afghanistan, announcing that American troops would begin to withdraw in 2011. Many analysts thought the Afghan situation could not be stabilized in such a short period and questioned the wisdom of a troop escalation that was accompanied by a preannounced withdrawal date. It was suggested that Obama's withdrawal timetable was politically motivated, aimed at pacifying an American public that was increasingly leery of the costs of the war and the prospects for success.

Thus, as is true of multilateralism, unilateralism has limits. Even with the world's most powerful military, the United States has found it difficult to bear the brunt of the Afghan and Iraq conflicts. Wars of this type do not lend themselves to quick and tidy battlefield solutions. It is one thing to defeat a conventional army in open warfare and quite another to prevail in a conflict in which the fight is not so much a battle for territory as it is a struggle for people's loyalties, especially when they distrust each other, as in the case of Iraq's Sunnis, Shiites, and Kurds and Afghanistan's Pashtun, Tajik, Hazara, and Uzbek tribes. Moreover, Iraq and Afghanistan are not the only worrying foreign developments facing U.S. policymakers. In the decade since the terrorist attacks on American soil in 2001, for example, North Korea has developed nuclear weapons and Iran is acquiring the technology necessary to build them.

The Military Dimension of National Security Policy

Defense spending by the United States is far higher than that of any other nation. In fact, the United States accounts for more than 40 percent of all military spending worldwide (see "How the U.S. Differs"). The U.S. defense budget exceeded $600 billion in 2010, a level of military spending that is five times that of China and more than eight times that of Russia.

Military Power, Uses, and Capabilities

U.S. military forces are trained for different types of military action, ranging from nuclear conflict to terrorism.

Nuclear War Although the possibility of all-out nuclear war declined dramatically with the collapse of the Soviet Union, the United States retains a nuclear arsenal designed to prevent such a war. **Deterrence policy** is based on the concept of mutually assured destruction (MAD). The assumption is that any nation would be deterred from launching a full-scale nuclear attack by the knowledge that, even if it destroyed the United States, it too would be obliterated.

America's nuclear weapons are deployed in what is called the "nuclear triad." This term refers to the three ways—by land-based missiles, submarine-based missiles, and bombers—that nuclear weapons can be launched. The triad provides a second-strike capability—that is, the ability to absorb a first-strike nuclear attack and survive with enough nuclear capacity for a massive retaliation (second strike). Since the end of the cold war, the United States and Russia have negotiated substantial reductions in their nuclear arsenals and have established monitoring systems designed to reduce the possibility that either side could launch an effective surprise attack. In 2010, for example, the two countries signed a pact reducing their nuclear weapons and tightening the monitoring systems.

A greater fear today than nuclear war with Russia is the possibility that a terrorist group or rogue nation will smuggle a nuclear device into the

HOW THE U.S. DIFFERS
POLITICAL THINKING THROUGH COMPARISONS

Worldwide Military Spending

The United States spends more than 40 percent of all the money spent worldwide on the military. The U.S. military establishment is huge and deployed across the globe. More than half a trillion dollars each year are spent on national defense. China is second in military spending, but its expenditures are only a fifth of those of the United States. Russia spends about an eighth of what the United States spends. Even on a per-capita basis, the United States ranks far ahead of other nations in military spending.

The United States has pressured its Western allies to carry a larger share of the defense burden, but many of them have resisted, contending that the cost would be too high and that their security would not improve substantially. Of America's European allies, Britain and France spend the most on their military.

Q: *What do you make of the disparity in military spending between the United States and its military allies? Do you think they spend too little on defense, relying too heavily on the United States for their security? Or do you think the United States spends too much on defense, placing too much emphasis on military force as an instrument of foreign policy?*

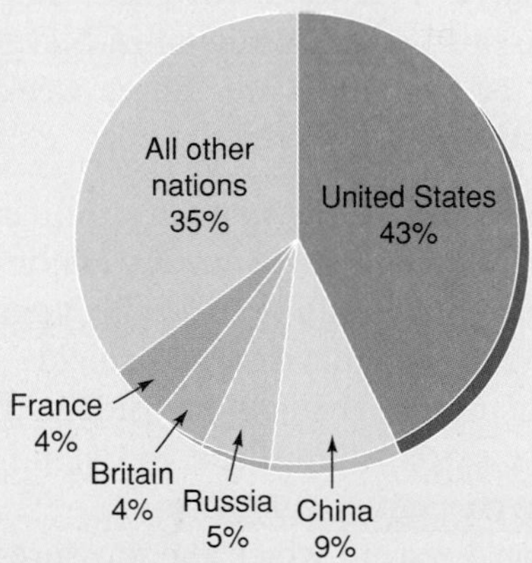

Source: Center for Arms Control and Non-Proliferation, 2010. Reprinted with permission.

United States and detonate it. The technology and materials necessary to build a nuclear weapon (or to buy one clandestinely) are more readily available than ever before. Accordingly, the United States, Russia, and other nations are cooperating to halt the spread of nuclear weapons, although, as the weapons programs of North Korea and Iran illustrate, the effort has had only limited success.

Conventional War Not since World War II has the United States fought an all-out conventional war, nor at present does it have the capacity to do so. Such a war would require the reinstatement of the military draft and the full mobilization of the nation's industrial capacity. Instead, the U.S. armed forces are structured to be capable of fighting two medium-sized wars simultaneously if necessary.

The United States today relies on an all-volunteer military force (see "How the 50 States Differ") that is second to none in its destructive power. The U.S. Navy has a dozen aircraft carriers, scores of attack submarines, and hundreds of fighting and supply ships. The U.S. Air Force has thousands of high-performance aircraft, ranging from fighter jets to jumbo transport planes. The U.S. Army has roughly 500,000 regular troops and more than 300,000 Reserve and National Guard soldiers, who are supplied with tanks, artillery pieces, armored personnel carriers, and attack helicopters. This armament is doubly lethal because it is linked to sophisticated surveillance, targeting, and communication systems. No other nation has anywhere near the advanced weapons systems that the United States possesses.

The U.S. military has shown itself to be effective in fighting a limited conventional war. When U.S. forces invaded Iraq in 2003, they were outnumbered three to one by Iraqi army units. Nevertheless, U.S. ground forces seized control of Baghdad within three weeks, at which time the remaining Iraqi military units quit the field.

Unconventional (Guerrilla) War America's military firepower is not a large advantage in so-called unconventional wars of the type taking place in Afghanistan. The insurgents employ guerrilla tactics including hit-and-run attacks, roadside explosive devices, and suicide bombings, as well as the killing and intimidation of civilians who side with the Afghan government. Such tactics are extremely difficult to defend against and virtually impossible to stop by conventional means.

Unlike a conventional war, in which the measures of success are territory gained, casualties inflicted, and combat units destroyed, an unconventional war requires winning the support of the people or, as it is described, "winning their hearts and minds." Insurgents depend on the

HOW THE 50 STATES DIFFER
POLITICAL THINKING THROUGH COMPARISONS

The All-Volunteer Military's Recruits

Until 1973, the United States had an active military draft. Upon reaching age eighteen, males were required to register for the draft. Local draft boards would then pick the draftees based on quotas that varied with the size of the local population. Accordingly, each state contributed equally to the military's manpower needs relative to its population size. Today's military is an all-volunteer force, and the states' contributions vary significantly. The map below indicates the degree to which each state is over-

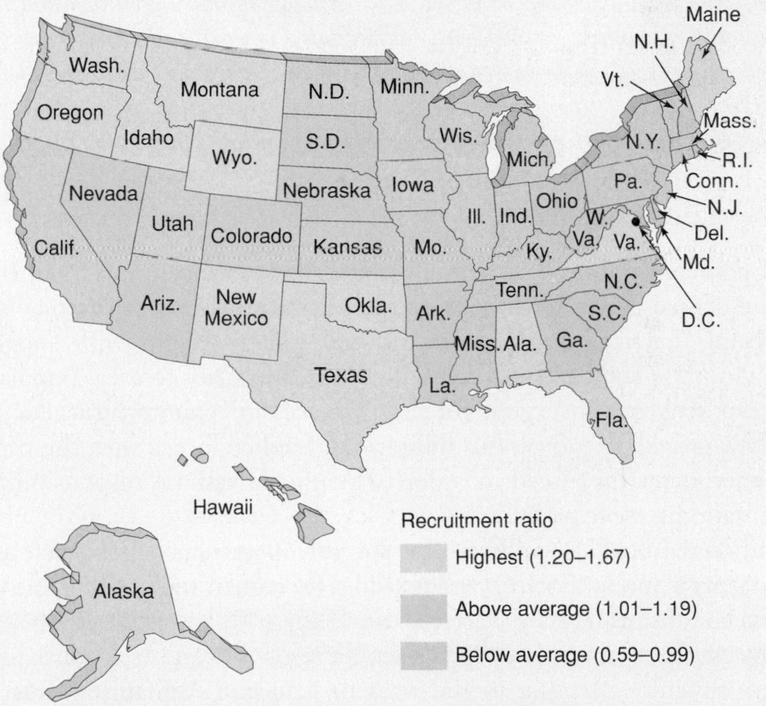

Source: Adapted from Tim Kane, "Who Bears the Burden? Demographic Characteristics of U.S. Military Recruits before and after 9/11," Heritage Foundation, Center for Data Analysis Report #05-08, November 7, 2005. Reprinted by permission of the Heritage Foundation.

(*continued*)

and underrepresented in the military, as indicated by the ratio of military recruits from a state to the number of males aged eighteen to thirty-four in that state's population. Montana has the largest number of recruits relative to its population, followed in order by Alaska, Wyoming, and Maine. Utah, Rhode Island, and Massachusetts rank lowest, in that order.

Q: *What might explain why military recruits come disproportionately from states like Montana, Alaska, Wyoming, and Maine, as well as from the southern states?*

A: *According to Department of Defense data, recruits are more likely to come from rural areas, particularly areas where few well-paying jobs are available to young adults. The four states with the highest recruitment ratios have these characteristics. As for the South, higher recruitment levels have been explained in terms of its stronger military tradition and its numerous military installations. Individuals from areas near these installations, as well as the sons and daughters of military personnel, are more likely to enlist in the military. (Mississippi and Tennessee, with the South's lowest recruitment rates, have relatively few military installations.)*

local population for recruits, intelligence, hiding places, and food. If they can be denied access to these resources, their military capability falls dramatically. Tactically, an unconventional war is fought with small and highly mobile combat units that can provide security to local populations and can seek out insurgent forces. A successful counterinsurgency also involves providing indigenous military and police forces with the training and equipment they need in order to gradually assume responsibility for their nation's security.[11]

Although the U.S. military has special operations units (such as the U.S. Army's Special Forces), and provides its regular units with some training in counterinsurgency warfare, the U.S. military for the most part is not designed or trained to fight unconventional wars. As a consequence, it had difficulty adapting to the wars in Iraq and Afghanistan, just as it struggled to adapt to the war in Vietnam four decades earlier. Moreover, an outside country like the United States is at the disadvantage in a counterinsurgency because of its unfamiliarity with the local terrain and because many in the local population will see it as an invading army. If the insurgents have the will and capacity to continue the fight indefinitely,

Shown here is the deadly result of a suicide bombing. Such tactics are difficult for the U.S. military to counter. Most of its units are not designed and equipped for this type of combat.

as was the case in Vietnam and could be the situation in Afghanistan, they can win by outlasting the occupying power.

Transnational Terrorism The terrorist attacks of September 11, 2001, thrust the U.S. military into a new kind of war—a war on terrorism. The United States was not prepared for a terrorist war when it was attacked in 2001. Its intelligence agencies had not focused their efforts on terrorist activity, and its military units had few linguists who spoke the terrorists' languages.

Terrorism is not by itself a new form of warfare. It has been employed in many places over the centuries, but it has become a broader threat in recent years. Historically, terrorism was a domestic problem, employed by disgruntled groups against their own government. Terrorism today has an international dimension. **Transnational terrorism** is terrorism that transcends national borders and includes attacks on nonmilitary targets.[12] When terrorists attacked the United States in 2001, or bombed the Madrid commuter system in 2004, they were not seeking to take over the United States or Spain. They were seeking to alter the balance of power in the Middle East by forcing Western nations to rethink their presence in the region.

America's war on terrorism is aimed at groups, such as al Qaeda, rather than nations. Al Qaeda is a nonstate actor without clearly defined borders, which complicates the task of locating and destroying it. Moreover, transnational terrorists have become adept at waging "asymmetric war," so called because they lack the strength to directly engage opposing military forces. In fighting their wars, terrorists resort to improvised weapons, including suicide bombers.

The war on terrorism lacks sharply defined battlefronts and is being waged through a variety of instruments, including military force, intelligence gathering, law enforcement, foreign aid, international cooperation, and immigration control. In reality, the main responsibility for rooting out terrorist cells rests with law enforcement and intelligence agencies in the United States and abroad rather than with military units. Recent arrests of suspected terrorists in the United States, Europe, Africa, Asia, and South America have usually been the result of the work of nonmilitary agencies. Some analysts argue that the United States erred in 2001 in assigning the main role in the war on terrorism to the military. Some European countries saw it from the start as primarily a mission for their law-enforcement and intelligence agencies.

The Politics of National Defense

Policy elites, public opinion, and special interests all play significant roles in national defense policy. The American public usually backs the judgment of its political leaders on the use of military force. In nearly all military initiatives of the past half-century, Americans have supported the action at the outset. When President Bush ordered U.S. forces to invade Iraq in 2003,[13] two-thirds of Americans supported his decision. The rest were split between those who opposed the war and those who were unsure about the proper course of action.

On the other hand, if a war begins to seem endless, public support inevitably erodes. A swing in public opinion against the Vietnam War forced U.S. policymakers to withdraw American troops in 1973. Public opinion on the Iraq war soured more quickly, partly because the stated reason for the war—the threat of Iraq's WMDs—proved faulty. Public support for the Afghanistan war has been steadier but is substantially below its peak, which suggests that Americans will not back it indefinitely. Studies of the Korean and Vietnam wars found that public support is difficult to recapture once it is lost.[14]

Although the public has an influence on war policy, it is not informed enough or involved enough to affect most national security polices, which are decided largely by the president and Congress in consultation with top experts and military officers. Of these various actors, the president has the most say. Eight months into his presidency, for instance, Barack Obama unilaterally scrapped President Bush's plan to build a land-based missile shield in Eastern Europe, proposing instead to rely on a ship-based missile shield. Bush had argued that a land-based shield would protect Europe from a possible missile attack from Iran or elsewhere in the Middle East. Russia had protested Bush's plan, saying it was designed to increase America's influence in Eastern Europe. Observers suggested that Obama's decision was based in part on a desire to improve relations with Russia.

The defense industry also has a say in national security policy. In his 1961 farewell address, President Dwight D. Eisenhower, who had commanded U.S. forces in Europe during World War II, warned Americans against "the unwarranted influence" and "misplaced power" of what he termed "the military-industrial complex." Eisenhower was referring to the fact that national defense is big business, involving the annual expenditure of hundreds of billions of dollars.[15] As Eisenhower described it, the **military-industrial complex** has three main components: the military establishment, the arms industry, and the members of Congress from states and districts that depend heavily on the arms industry. All three benefit from a high level of defense spending, whether needed or not. The defense industry suffered a rare defeat in 2009 when Congress, backed by President Obama and Defense Secretary Robert Gates, refused to appropriate funds for building additional F-22 fighter jets. The F-22 is the world's most sophisticated fighter jet, but it is hugely expensive and excels at air-to-air combat, a type of warfare that the United States has not fought on any scale since the Korean War. Secretary Gates said the military would be better served by less expensive aircraft suited to wars of the type fought in Iraq and Afghanistan. Nevertheless, forty-two senators voted to continue production of the F-22. Some of them were less concerned with the F-22's cost and capabilities than with the fact that tens of thousands of jobs in more than forty states would be lost if production was stopped.

Dwight D. Eisenhower was Supreme Commander of Allied Forces in Europe during World War II and was elected president in 1952. Though trained in the art of war, Eisenhower sought throughout his presidency to reduce cold war tensions. As his presidency was ending, he used his farewell address to warn of the dangers of the military-industrial complex, arguing that sustained high levels of military expenditure and secrecy would weaken America in the long run.

THE ECONOMIC DIMENSION OF NATIONAL SECURITY POLICY

National security is more than an issue of military might. It is also a question of maintaining a strong position in the global economy. Geographically, the world has three major economic centers. One is the United States, which produces roughly 25 percent of the world's goods and services. Another center, also responsible for about 25 percent of the world's economy, is the European Union (EU), which includes most European countries. The EU is dominated by Germany, Britain, and France, which together account for roughly half its economy. The third center is the Pacific Rim, anchored by the economies of Japan and China, which together account for more than 15 percent of the world's economy.

By some indicators, the United States is the weakest of the three economic centers. Its trade deficit is easily the world's largest. The United States imports substantially more goods and services than it exports. In fact, the United States has not had a trade surplus since 1975 and over the past decade its deficit has exceeded $300 billion annually (see Figure 17-1).

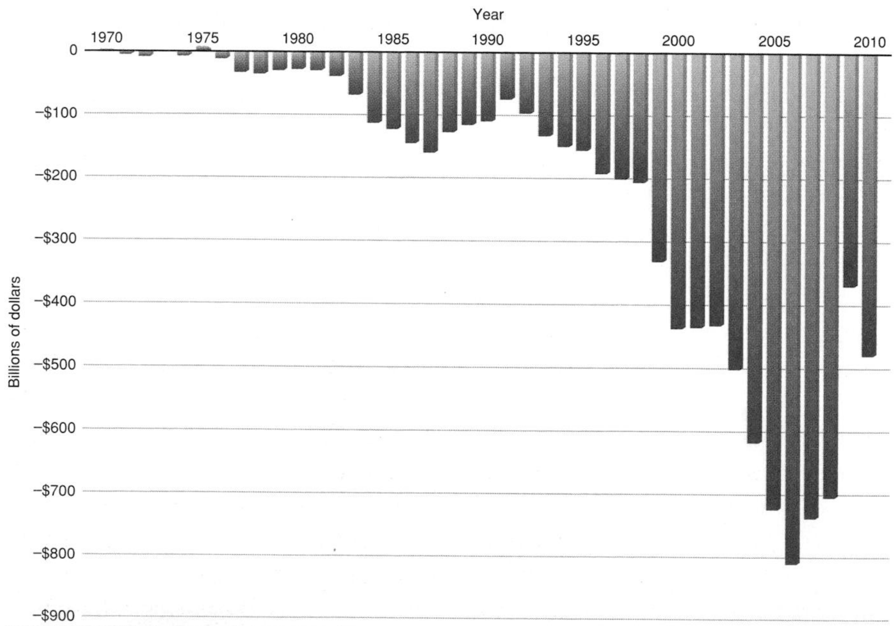

figure 17-1 THE U.S. TRADE DEFICIT

The United States has not had a trade surplus since 1975. The deficit has reached record highs in recent years. *Source:* U.S. Bureau of Economic Analysis, 2010.

In other ways, however, the United States is the strongest of the three centers. According to the Switzerland-based World Economic Forum, the United States is economically more competitive than its major rivals. The United States owes this position to several factors, including its technological innovation, financial institutions, and extensive higher education system.[16] The U.S. economy is also the most diversified of the three. In addition to its industrial base, the United States has a strong agricultural sector and abundant natural resources. Its vast fertile plains and advanced farming methods have made it the world's leading agricultural producer. The United States ranks among the top three countries worldwide in production of wheat, corn, soybeans, peanuts, cotton, eggs, cattle, and pigs. As for natural resources, the United States ranks among the top five nations in deposits of copper, uranium, lead, sulfur, zinc, coal, gold, iron ore, natural gas, silver, and magnesium.[17]

Nevertheless, the United States does not have the option of "going it alone" economically. To meet Americans' production and consumption needs, the country depends on other countries' raw materials, finished goods, markets, and capital. This imperative requires the United States to exert global economic influence. The broad goals of the United States in the world economy include the following:[18]

- Sustaining a stable and open system of trade that will promote prosperity at home
- Maintaining access to oil and other natural resources vital to the strength of the U.S. economy
- Preventing the widening gap between rich and poor countries from destabilizing the world economy

Promoting Global Trade

After World War II, the United States helped enact a global trading system with itself at the center. The U.S. dollar had become the leading currency of international trade, replacing the English pound, which held that position for more than a century. World War II had weakened Britain's global economic position and elevated that of the United States, which quickly asserted its dominance. A key initiative was the European Recovery Plan, better known as the Marshall Plan. It included an unprecedented amount of aid (more than $100 billion in today's dollars) for the postwar rebuilding of Europe. Apart from enabling the countries of Western Europe to better confront the perceived Soviet threat, the Marshall Plan served America's economic needs. Wartime production had lifted the United States out of the Great Depression, but the immediate postwar period was marked by a recession and renewed fears of hard times. A rebuilt Western Europe would become a much-needed market for American products.

Since then, major shifts have taken place in the world economy. Germany is now a trading rival of the United States, as is Japan, which also received substantial postwar reconstruction aid from the United States. More recently, China and the European Union have taken their place as trading giants, and Russia, propelled by its huge oil and gas reserves, has the potential to become one.

Today, the American economy depends more heavily on international commerce than in any period in history. The domestic manufacturing sector that at one time was the source of most jobs has shrunk. Most of the nonagricultural goods that Americans now buy, from television sets to automobiles, are produced by foreign firms. Indeed, nearly all large U.S. firms are themselves **multinational corporations** (or **transnational corporations**), with operations in more than one country. From a headquarters in New York City, a firm has no difficulty managing a production facility in Thailand that is filling orders for markets in Europe and South America. Money, goods, and services today flow freely and rapidly across national borders, and large U.S. firms increasingly think about markets in global terms. As a result, they sometimes engage in activities that conflict with America's foreign policy goals. In Africa, for example, U.S. oil companies have sometimes supported dictatorial regimes in order to maintain access to oil fields.

Economic globalization is a term that describes the increased interdependence of nations' economies. This development is both an opportunity for and a threat to U.S. economic interests. The opportunity rests with the possibility of increased demand abroad for U.S. products and lower prices to U.S. consumers as a result of inexpensive imports. The threat lies in the fact that foreign firms also compete in the global marketplace and may use their competitive advantages, such as cheaper labor, to outposition U.S. firms.

In general, international commerce works best when countries trade freely with one another. This situation keeps the price of traded items, whether finished goods or raw materials, at their lowest level, resulting in economic efficiency (see Chapter 15). However, global trade is a political issue as well as an economic one, and there are conflicting views on international trade. **Free trade** holds that barriers to international trade should be kept to a minimum. Proponents of free trade claim that the long-term economic interests of all countries are advanced when tariffs (taxes on imported goods) and other trade barriers are kept to a minimum.

Most free-trade advocates couple their advocacy with fair-trade demands, but they are committed, philosophically and practically, to the idea that free trade results in a net gain for firms and consumers. The 1993 North American Free Trade Agreement (NAFTA) was a product of this thinking. It created a largely free market between the United States, Canada, and Mexico.

For the most part, the United States has been a leading proponent of free trade.[19] Its effort to strengthen the World Trade Organization (WTO) is an example. Created in 1995, the WTO is the formal international institution through which most nations negotiate general rules of trade.[20] The WTO's mission is to promote global free trade through reductions in tariffs, protections for intellectual property (copyrights and patents), and other policies. Trade disputes among WTO members are settled by arbitration panels, which consist of representatives from the member nations.

Not all U.S. policymakers support free trade. Some argue for **protectionism**, which holds that domestic producers should be protected from foreign competitors. The classic protectionist measure is a tariff on a particular import, which raises the market price of the product, thereby giving domestic producers of the same product a competitive advantage. For some protectionists, the issue is a simple matter of defending domestic firms against their foreign competitors. For others, the issue is one of fair trade. They are protectionists in those instances where foreign firms have an unfair competitive advantage as a result, for example, of a subsidy from their government that enables them to market their goods at an artificially low price.

Protectionist sentiment is usually stronger in Congress than in the White House. Although most members of Congress say they support free trade, many of them act differently when a key economic interest in their state or district is threatened by foreign competition. In such cases, they seek protective measures, such as a tariff on the competitor's products.

Economists argue that economic disruption is an inevitable result of market change and that firms should try to adapt to the change rather than turn to government for protection. Elected officials, however, cannot take the long-range view so easily because they face immediate pressures from constituents who have lost jobs and from communities that have lost firms. In response to such pressures, U.S. officials have insisted that foreign governments halt practices that put American firms at an unfair disadvantage. In 2009, for example, President Obama placed a 35 percent tariff on the import of Chinese tires on the grounds that the Chinese government was subsidizing their production. However, other countries are not convinced that the United States itself always plays fair. In 2006, international trade talks collapsed in part because the United States refused to reduce its hefty farm subsidies, which enable U.S. agricultural producers to sell their products at a low price in world markets, thereby giving them a competitive advantage.

POLITICAL THINKING

Is Free Trade Good for America?

Although the United States pursues a largely free trade policy, the American people have had conflicting opinions on the issue. During the 1990s, when the economy was booming, polls indicated that most Americans thought free trade was beneficial. Since then, the economy has been weaker and so has support for free trade. A 2010 Gallup poll, for example, found that as many Americans saw free trade as a threat to the U.S. firms and workers as saw it as an opportunity for economic growth. What's your opinion of free trade policy?

Trade with China is a particularly vexing issue.[21] In the past decade, America's trade deficit with China has increased more than thirtyfold, surpassing $250 billion annually. The United States has provided China with a marketplace for its goods, which has helped fuel China's economic growth. In turn, China has provided the United States with inexpensive goods, which has satisfied the demands of America's consumers and kept inflation in check. Nevertheless, the trade deficit with China is a growing concern. The United States has pressured China to increase the value of its currency (the yuan), which would increase the price of the goods it exports for sale, thereby making American goods more competitive with those produced in China.

China is also a key to the future of the U.S. dollar as the world's preferred reserve currency. Because of its trade advantage with the United States, China holds more than $1 trillion in U.S. treasury bonds—the largest such holding in the world. The value of China's holding declines as the dollar declines in value, which is a realistic prospect given America's huge national debt (see Chapter 15). China and other countries, including Russia and Japan, have threatened to reduce their holdings in dollars, which would put additional pressure on the value of the dollar. "We have lent a huge amount of money to the U.S.," Chinese premier Wen Jiabao

Although the Chinese yuan will not rival the American dollar as the dominant international currency anytime soon, it has become a symbol of China's rise to global economic prominence.

said in 2009. "Of course we are concerned about the safety of our assets." If the dollar should decline sharply in value, the United States would be forced to pay a higher rate of interest to get other countries to buy its bonds, which would raise the cost of borrowing and add to America's debt problem.

Maintaining Access to Oil and Other Natural Resources

For decades, America has used its economic and military power to protect its access to natural resources, particularly oil. Although the United States produces a significant amount of oil domestically, it provides only a third of what the nation consumes. The United States gets most of its oil imports from Canada and Latin America, but the price of oil is determined by worldwide production and demand. The demand for oil has risen as a result of rapid economic growth in China, India, Brazil, and other developing countries, which has created upward pressure on oil prices and has intensified efforts to increase oil production.[22]

The key oil-producing region is the Middle East, which has substantially larger oil reserves than elsewhere in the world. After World War II, the United States acquired a foothold in the region when its oil companies, with their technical capacity and huge amounts of capital, acquired a stake in Middle Eastern oil fields. Since then, U.S. firms have been leaders in worldwide oil exploration and production. Underpinning their activities is the military might of the United States. For example, the U.S. Navy patrols the world's shipping routes to ensure that oil tankers reach their destinations safely.

The influence of oil on U.S. foreign policy is undeniable. The 1991 Gulf War was driven by a concern with oil. Iraq's invasion of Kuwait threatened access not only to Kuwait's oil fields but also to those of its neighbors. Protection of the oil supply may also have contributed to President Bush's decision in 2003 to invade Iraq, which has oil reserves of more than 100 billion barrels, second only to those of Saudi Arabia. Oil has also limited U.S. actions. When Iranian militants in 1979 overthrew their country's pro-Western ruler and seized U.S. embassy personnel as hostages, the United States refrained from a military response in part out of fear of disrupting the flow of Iranian oil. In 2008, when Russia invaded parts of neighboring Georgia, the relatively restrained response of the United States and its European allies stemmed in part from Europe's dependence on Russian oil and natural gas.

Assisting Developing Nations

Industrialized nations have a stake in helping developing nations to grow. With growth comes greater political stability as well as markets for the goods and services that industrialized nations produce. For such reasons, the United States provides developmental assistance to poorer countries. Contributions include direct foreign aid and also indirect assistance through international organizations, such as the International Monetary Fund (IMF) and the World Bank, which were created by the United States and Great Britain at the Bretton Woods Conference near the end of World War II. The IMF makes short-term loans to keep countries experiencing temporary problems from collapsing economically or resorting to destructive practices such as the unrestricted printing of paper money. For its part, the World Bank makes long-term development loans to poor countries for capital investment projects such as dams, highways, and factories.

Since World War II, the United States has been the leading source of aid to developing countries. Although the United States still contributes the

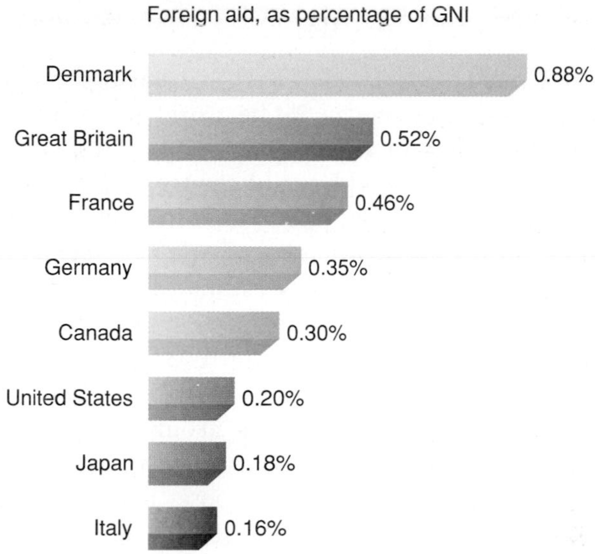

figure 17-2 ASSISTANCE TO DEVELOPING COUNTRIES, AS A PERCENTAGE OF GROSS NATIONAL INCOME

The United States ranks highest in terms of total amount spent on foreign aid to developing countries but ranks lower in terms of percentage of gross national income (GNI).
Source: Organization for Economic Cooperation and Development, 2010. Reprinted with permission.

most in terms of total dollars, Canada and European countries now spend more on a per-capita basis than does the United States (see Figure 17-2). America's fiscal problems, and its costly wars in Iraq and Afghanistan, have weakened it ability to strengthen its position in the world through the use of foreign aid. China, with its huge monetary reserves, has begun to fill the gap. Through loans and grants, China is spending heavily on infrastructure, mining, and commercial projects in Africa, South America, and Asia.

Foreign aid does not have strong popular support in the United States. Polls show that most Americans believe the United States is already spending huge amounts on foreign aid. In a poll that asked Americans to name the largest federal programs, foreign aid topped the list, with 27 percent identifying it as the most expensive program.[23] In reality, foreign aid is far from the top. Nevertheless, Americans' perception makes foreign aid a potent issue for politicians who would prefer to see less foreign aid spending. Jesse Helms (R-N.C.), a past chair of the Senate Foreign Relations Committee, liked to say that foreign aid was nothing more than pouring billions of dollars "down foreign ratholes."[24]

A Challenging World

Seldom has the United States faced as wide an array of foreign and defense policy challenges as it faces today. "The world will never again be the same" was a common refrain after September 11, 2001, but few analysts foresaw just how much the world would change in a few short years, let alone the difficulties the United States would have in adapting to it.

The terrorist threat has grown beyond what policymakers expected. According to U.S. intelligence agency estimates, international terrorism is a larger problem today than it was when the al Qaeda network attacked American soil in 2001. Although U.S. military intervention in Afghanistan and Iraq disrupted terrorist activity, it had the unintended effect of mobilizing Islamic extremists around the globe. There is, today, hardly any part of the world where terrorist cells are not operating, though they vary greatly in the threat they pose. The duration of America's fight with radical Islamists is uncertain. Some analysts believe the conflict will unwind within a decade or so, as a result of the withdrawal of U.S. combat forces from the Middle East. Other analysts see it stretching across a far longer period, much like the religiously motivated Thirty Years' War that consumed the first half of the seventeenth century in Europe.

No less daunting is the challenge of the global economy. A decade or so ago, the U.S. economy was the envy of the world, but it has been weakened by adverse developments at home and abroad. Even the U.S. dollar—long the symbol of America's global preeminence—has lost strength. Some analysts believe the United States will recapture its global momentum through its advanced technology and innovative markets. Other analysts foresee a long-term decline, driven by America's financial excesses and oil dependency and by surging economies elsewhere, particularly China's.

Summary Self-Test www.mhhe.com/pattersonwtp9e

The chief instruments of national security policy are diplomacy, military force, economic exchange, and intelligence gathering. These are exercised through specialized agencies of the U.S. government, such as the Departments of State and Defense that are largely responsive to presidential leadership. National security policy has also relied on international organizations, such as the United Nations and the World Trade Organization, that are responsive to the global concerns of major nations.

From 1945 to 1990, U.S. foreign and defense policies were dominated by a concern with the Soviet Union. During most of this period, the United States pursued a policy of containment based on the premise that the Soviet Union was an aggressor nation bent on global conquest. Containment policy led the United States to enter into wars in Korea and Vietnam and to maintain a large defense establishment.

A first response to the end of the cold war period was multilateralism—the idea that major nations could achieve common goals by working together, including the use of force to restrain regional conflicts. The interventions in the Persian Gulf and the Balkans during the 1990s are examples. They demonstrated that major nations can intervene with some success in global hot spots but also showed that the ethnic, religious, and national conflicts that fuel these conflicts are not easily resolved. The terrorist attacks on the World Trade Center and the Pentagon in 2001 led to broad changes in national security organization and strategy. Increased defense and homeland security spending has been coupled with a partial reorganization of U.S. intelligence, law enforcement, and immigration agencies, as well as new laws affecting the scope of their activities. However, the defining moment of the post–September 11 period was America's invasion of Iraq in 2003, which was rooted in President George W. Bush's preemptive war doctrine and his willingness to commit the United States to unilateral action. The locus of Middle East conflict has shifted recently to Afghanistan.

In recent decades, the United States has increasingly taken economic factors into account in its national security considerations, which has meant, for example, that trade has played a larger part in defining its relationships with other countries. The trading system that the United States helped erect after World War II has given way to one that is global in scale and more competitive. Changes in communication, transportation, and computing have altered the way large corporations operate, and as businesses have changed their practices, nations have had to adapt. The changes include the emergence of regional and international economic structures, such as the European Union, NAFTA, and the WTO. Nevertheless, nations naturally compete for economic advantage, including access to natural resources; accordingly, trade is a source of conflict as well as a source of cooperation. In the coming years, oil and trade balances are likely to be at the center of the conflict.

Key Terms

bipolar (power structure) (*p. 599*)
cold war (*p. 598*)
containment (*p. 598*)
deterrence policy (*p. 606*)
economic globalization (*p. 616*)
free trade (*p. 616*)
internationalist (*p. 598*)
isolationist (*p. 598*)
military-industrial complex (*p. 613*)
multilateralism (*p. 601*)
multinational (transnational) corporations (*p. 616*)
national interest (*p. 596*)
preemptive war doctrine (*p. 603*)
protectionism (*p. 617*)
transnational terrorism (*p. 611*)
unilateralism (*p. 604*)
unipolar (power structure) (*p. 601*)

Suggested Readings

Clarke, Richard A. *Against All Enemies: Inside America's War on Terror*. New York: Free Press, 2004. A best-selling book by the nation's former top-ranking presidential advisor on terrorism.

Deese, David A. *World Trade Politics: Power, Principles, and Leadership*. New York: Routledge, 2007. A meticulous study of the politics of international trade negotiations.

Fishman, Ted C. *China, Inc.: How the Rise of the Next Superpower Challenges America and the World*. New York: Scribner, 2005. A look at China's rapid economic growth and its implications.

Hixson, Walter L. *The Myth of American Diplomacy: National Identity and U.S. Foreign Policy*. New Haven, CT.: Yale University Press, 2008. An analysis of the influence of America's cultural ideals on its foreign policy.

Klare, Michael T. *Rising Powers, Shrinking Planet: The New Geopolitics of Energy*. New York: Holt, 2009. An assessment of the energy and environmental challenges posed by global economic development.

Nye, Joseph S. *Soft Power: The Means to Success in World Politics*. New York: PublicAffairs, 2004. An argument for making diplomacy, assistance, and other forms of "soft power" the basis of U.S. foreign policy.

Odom, William E. *Fixing Intelligence*. New Haven, CT.: Yale University Press, 2003. A detailed critique of U.S. intelligence efforts by a former military intelligence officer.

Pearlstein, Richard. *Fatal Future? Transnational Terrorism and the New Global Disorder*. Austin: University of Texas Press, 2004. A penetrating look at the dangers posed by transnational terrorism.

Sobel, Richard. *The Impact of Public Opinion on U.S. Foreign Policy since Vietnam*. New York: Oxford University Press, 2001. An account of public opinion's impact on foreign policy.

List of Websites

www.defenselink.mil The U.S. Department of Defense website; provides information on each of the armed services, daily news from the American Forces Information Service, and other material.

www.cfr.org A website that includes reports and assessments of the Council of Foreign Relations and transcripts of speeches by U.S. and world political leaders on topics of international interest.

www.igc.org/igc The website of the Institute for Global Communications (IGC); provides information and services to organizations and activists on a broad range of international issues, including human rights.

www.wto.org The World Trade Organization (WTO) website; contains information on the organization's activities and has links to related sites.

Politics in Theory and Practice

Thinking: What are the major objectives of U.S. foreign and defense policy? What are the mechanisms for pursuing those objectives?

Participating: In his 1961 inaugural address, President John F. Kennedy said, "Ask not what your country can do for you. Ask what you can do for your country." Kennedy called America's young people to service on behalf of their country. His call was not just a call to military service. One of Kennedy's early initiatives, the Peace Corps, offered Americans the opportunity to apply their skills to development projects in other countries. Under Kennedy's successor, President Lyndon Johnson, a domestic version of the Peace Corps—Volunteers in Service to America (VISTA)—was established. Before the military draft ended in 1973, male Americans expected to serve their country. Not all did so, but millions served in the Army, Navy, Air Force, or Marines. Since the end of the draft, Congress has from time to time considered establishing a National Service that would require every young American man and woman to serve the country in one way or another for a set period of time. However, you do not need an act of Congress if you want to serve your country. A range of alternatives are available, including the all-volunteer military, the Peace Corps, and AmeriCorps (a network of local, state, and national service programs).

Extra Credit

For up-to-the-minute *New York Times* articles, interactive simulations, graphics, study tools, and more links and quizzes, visit the text's Online Learning Center at **www.mhhe.com/pattersonwtp9e**.

NATIONAL JOURNAL

Obama and China: Year Two

The first generation of American leadership after World War II dealt with China by ignoring it. The second generation of postwar U.S. presidents embraced the new giant panda on the world stage and occasionally sparred with it. Now a third generation is recognizing that it will have to engage the growing panda, which has never been cuddly, as an equal on a broad range of issues—reforming the global financial system and responding to climate change, among others.

The premise of the Obama administration's China policy, which the president outlined last summer, is that "the United States and China share mutual interests" and that "our ability to partner with each other is a prerequisite for progress on many of the most pressing global challenges."

To that end, U.S. Ambassador to China Jon Huntsman said at a press briefing in Beijing earlier this month, "We spent the last year building bridges, getting to know each other, ensuring that the new administration was able to frame our relationship going forward with China in ways meaningful to both countries."

So, after a year of effort, how is that outreach working for America? "Are we getting a return on that investment?" asked Jonathan Pollack, director of the strategic research department at the Naval War College. "Certainly what we have seen lately creates concern."

China policy in the first year of any administration is often fraught with uncertainty, and the Obama presidency, like its predecessors, made initial missteps. But on the positive side, Washington worked closely with Beijing to keep the global recession from devolving into a depression. A backdoor dialogue on North Korea was re-established. And confrontations were avoided over historically difficult issues such as human rights.

But 2009 ended on some sour notes, with the Chinese stiffing President Obama at a bilateral summit in China in November and snubbing him at the Copenhagen climate gathering in December. And 2010 opened with controversy: allegations of Chinese cyber-espionage against Google; a long-promised U.S. arms sale to Taiwan followed by Chinese threats of retaliation against U.S. firms; and a presidential meeting with the Tibetan religious leader, the Dalai Lama, in defiance of Chinese warnings.

"The challenges coming in the relationship are extremely deep and profound," an administration official warned.

The White House spent its first year building personal bonds between Obama and Chinese President Hu Jintao and Prime Minister Wen Jiabao, scheduling frequent meetings, encounters, and phone calls. If all went as planned, it was hoped, Obama's November trip to China would cement a new working relationship that could serve the administration well in the years ahead.

Administration efforts got off to an inauspicious start, however, when Secretary of State Hillary Rodham Clinton remarked, en route to her first official visit to China, that human-rights concerns would not interfere with Washington's dealings with Beijing on the global economic crisis or climate or security. That statement, coupled with her plea that Beijing continue to buy U.S. Treasury bonds, made Washington sound more like a supplicant than a superpower.

International affairs often follow Newton's third law of motion: For every action, there is an equal and opposite reaction. As Beijing perceived that Washington wanted Chinese cooperation as never before, it began pushing back hard on concerns of its own. "China senses little drops of blood in the water better than any country," an administration official said. "They sniff out relative changes in power and pursue them."

Obama's China policy implicitly assumes that Beijing is willing and able to begin sharing responsibility with Washington on a range of international issues. However, Chinese foot-dragging on global economic rebalancing, climate change, and curbing the North Korean and Iranian nuclear programs raises doubts about its leaders' readiness, or willingness, to lead.

Finally, Beijing periodically acts in ways that suggest it does not feel bound by the norms of international behavior. Perhaps that should not be surprising. For all its recent expertise at capitalism, China is, after all, a one-party Communist state. It has repressed its ethnic minorities, engaged in seemingly reckless cyber-espionage, and recently and inexplicably revived a border dispute with India. Such behavior constantly threatens to disrupt the administration's China policy.

Thanks to the financial crisis, the global economy was the first substantive item on the Obama White House's U.S.-China agenda. With consumer demand imploding everywhere, the global community especially needed China to prime its economic pump, and Beijing responded. In 2009, China's crisis-related discretionary-spending measures equaled 3.1 percent of its economy, according to the International Monetary Fund.

Yet, Beijing rejected the Obama administration's long-term economic goal of a permanent rebalancing in which the Chinese trade surplus and the U.S. trade deficit would be reduced to more sustainable levels to forestall global financial crises. And absent an agreement on rebalancing trade, economic tensions are only likely to grow. Chinese exports increased nearly 18 percent in December, suggesting that China's trade surplus will rise by the second half of 2010.

An appreciation of the yuan could slow that export surge by making Chinese products more expensive and fueling imports. John Williamson, senior fellow at the Peterson Institute for International Economics in Washington, argues that China's currency is undervalued by about 25 percent. But so far, the Obama administration has failed to persuade Beijing to allow the yuan to appreciate.

Regardless of what happens on the currency front this year, observers expect more trade frictions. In 2009, Washington acted against imports of Chinese tires and steel. More dumping and countervailing duty cases could be on the way.

China is engaging in protectionism of its own, however. In late 2009, Beijing announced plans to give preference in government procurement and eligibility for subsidies to products that contain intellectual property that is developed and owned in China. This practice could make it nearly impossible for U.S. makers of software, telecommunications equipment, and green technologies to qualify for the preferences unless they establish Chinese brands and transfer their research and development to China. The Obama administration's reaction to this provocation is likely to be a major test of its China policy.

China also shares an 880-mile border with North Korea, is home to as many as 30,000 refugees who have fled the regime of Kim Jong Il, and accounts for nearly three-quarters of Pyongyang's foreign trade. This proximity gives Beijing its own priorities in dealing with North Korea. Above all else, the Chinese want stability on their border.

"Beijing deliberately separates its bilateral relationship with North Korea from the nuclear issue, placing the responsibility for nuclear questions on the United States," Asia expert Stephanie Kleine-Ahlbrandt said. As a result, Jonathan Pollack said, "I don't see us on the same sheet of music on this."

In 2009, Beijing reluctantly backed a U.N. Security Council resolution authorizing member states to inspect shipments from North Korea and to destroy goods connected to the North Korean nuclear program. These measures were stronger than previous international efforts to punish Pyongyang. But

China made sure that they fell short of economic sanctions that might destabilize the regime. Also, the resolution was ambiguous on whether states were required to take action. And Beijing has shown no great urgency in pressuring North Korea to get back to the six-party talks.

The new year began on an even sourer note for U.S.-China relations. In January, Google announced that it might pull out of China after discovering massive Chinese hacking of its network infrastructure, which resulted in the theft of intellectual property from at least 20 U.S. companies. Such corporate espionage by the Chinese is not new. So Google's reaction, the unprecedented support it received in the U.S. business community, and Secretary Clinton's subsequent full-throated defense of freedom of expression in China suggest that concern about Chinese cyber-intrusions has reached a new level.

In late January, the Obama administration announced a long-delayed sale of missiles and helicopters to Taiwan. Beijing threatened sanctions against U.S. companies involved in the sale and suspended scheduled exchanges between the Chinese and U.S. militaries.

The Chinese reaction, said Council on Foreign Relations fellow Evan Feigenbaum, "is not about Taiwan. It's about us. It's about their having leverage and exploring its limits to discipline American behavior." Specifically, Beijing wants to head off Washington's selling Taiwan advanced fighter jets that have been on Taipei's shopping list for years.

In the final analysis, a year is hardly enough time to judge any administration's early initiatives. Beijing's U.N. vote on Iran, Hu Jintao's expected state visit to Washington in the late spring or early summer, and the second round of the U.S.-China strategic and economic dialogue to be held in Beijing this summer will all help flesh out a sophomore-year grade for Obama's China policy.

What's Your Opinion?

Do you think—based on this article and your understanding of the relationship between the United States and China—that the two countries really have common interests? Or are the divergences in their interests greater?

Appendixes

The Declaration of Independence

In Congress, July 4, 1776

The Unanimous Declaration of the Thirteen United States of America

When, in the course of human events, it becomes necessary for one people to dissolve the political bands which have connected them with another, and to assume, among the powers of the earth, the separate and equal station to which the laws of nature and of nature's God entitle them, a decent respect to the opinions of mankind requires that they should declare the causes which impel them to the separation.

We hold these truths to be self-evident, that all men are created equal; that they are endowed by their Creator with certain unalienable rights; that among these, are life, liberty, and the pursuit of happiness. That, to secure these rights, governments are instituted among men, deriving their just powers from the consent of the governed; that, whenever any form of government becomes destructive of these ends, it is the right of the people to alter or to abolish it, and to institute a new government, laying its foundation on such principles, and organizing its powers in such form, as to them shall seem most likely to effect their safety and happiness. Prudence, indeed, will dictate that governments long established, should not be changed for light and transient causes; and, accordingly, all experience hath shown, that mankind are more disposed to suffer, while evils are sufferable, than to right themselves by abolishing the forms to which they are accustomed. But, when a long train of abuses and usurpations, pursuing invariably the same object, evinces a design to reduce them under absolute despotism, it is their right, it is their duty, to throw off such government and to provide new guards for their future security. Such has been the patient sufferance of these colonies, and such is now the necessity which constrains them to alter their former systems of government. The history of the present King of Great Britain is a history of repeated injuries and usurpations, all having, in direct object, the establishment of an absolute tyranny over these States. To prove this, let facts be submitted to a candid world:

He has refused his assent to laws the most wholesome and necessary for the public good.

He has forbidden his governors to pass laws of immediate and pressing importance, unless suspended in their operation till his assent should be obtained; and, when so suspended, he has utterly neglected to attend to them.

He has refused to pass other laws for the accommodation of large districts of people, unless those people would relinquish the right of representation in the legislature; a right inestimable to them, and formidable to tyrants only.

He has called together legislative bodies at places unusual, uncomfortable, and distant from the depository of their public records, for the sole purpose of fatiguing them into compliance with his measures.

He has dissolved representative houses repeatedly for opposing, with manly firmness, his invasions on the rights of the people.

He has refused, for a long time after such dissolutions, to cause others to be elected; whereby the legislative powers, incapable of annihilation, have returned to the people at large for their exercise; the state remaining, in the meantime, exposed to all the danger of invasion from without, and convulsions within.

He has endeavored to prevent the population of these States; for that purpose, obstructing the laws for naturalization of foreigners, refusing to pass others to encourage their migration hither, and raising the conditions of new appropriations of lands.

He has obstructed the administration of justice, by refusing his assent to laws for establishing judiciary powers.

He has made judges dependent on his will alone, for the tenure of their offices, and the amount and payment of their salaries.

He has erected a multitude of new offices, and sent hither swarms of officers to harass our people, and eat out their substance.

He has kept among us, in time of peace, standing armies, without the consent of our legislatures.

He has affected to render the military independent of, and superior to, the civil power.

He has combined, with others, to subject us to a jurisdiction foreign to our Constitution, and unacknowledged by our laws; giving his assent to their acts of pretended legislation:

For quartering large bodies of armed troops among us:

For protecting them by a mock trial, from punishment, for any murders which they should commit on the inhabitants of these States:

For cutting off our trade with all parts of the world:

For imposing taxes on us without our consent:

For depriving us, in many cases, of the benefit of trial by jury:

For transporting us beyond seas to be tried for pretended offences:

For abolishing the free system of English laws in a neighboring province, establishing therein an arbitrary government, and enlarging its boundaries, so as to render it at once an example and fit instrument for introducing the same absolute rule into these colonies:

For taking away our charters, abolishing our most valuable laws, and altering, fundamentally, the powers of our governments:

For suspending our own legislatures, and declaring themselves invested with power to legislate for us in all cases whatsoever.

He has abdicated government here, by declaring us out of his protection, and waging war against us.

He has plundered our seas, ravaged our coasts, burnt our towns, and destroyed the lives of our people.

He is, at this time, transporting large armies of foreign mercenaries to complete the works of death, desolation, and tyranny, already begun, with circumstances of cruelty and perfidy scarcely paralleled in the most barbarous ages, and totally unworthy of the head of a civilized nation.

He has constrained our fellow citizens, taken captive on the high seas, to bear arms against their country, to become the executioners of their friends, and brethren, or to fall themselves by their hands.

He has excited domestic insurrections amongst us, and has endeavored to bring on the inhabitants of our frontiers, the merciless Indian savages, whose known rule of warfare is an undistinguished destruction of all ages, sexes, and conditions.

In every stage of these oppressions, we have petitioned for redress, in the most humble terms; our repeated petitions have been answered only by repeated injury. A prince, whose character is thus marked by every act which may define a tyrant, is unfit to be the ruler of a free people.

Nor have we been wanting in attention to our British brethren. We have warned them, from time to time, of attempts made by their legislature to extend an unwarrantable jurisdiction over us. We have reminded them of the circumstances of our emigration and settlement here. We have appealed to their native justice and magnanimity, and we have conjured them, by the ties of our common kindred, to disavow these usurpations, which would inevitably interrupt our connections and correspondence. They, too, have been deaf to the voice of justice and of consanguinity. We must, therefore, acquiesce in the necessity which denounces our separation, and hold them as we hold the rest of mankind, enemies in war, in peace, friends.

We, therefore, the representatives of the United States of America, in general Congress assembled, appealing to the Supreme Judge of the world for the rectitude of our intentions, do, in the name, and by the authority of the good people of these colonies, solemnly publish and declare, that these united colonies are, and of right ought to be, free and independent states: that they are absolved from all allegiance to the British Crown, and that all political connection between them and the state of Great Britain is, and ought to be, totally dissolved; and that, as free and independent states, they have full power to levy war, conclude peace, contract alliances, establish commerce, and to do all other acts and things which independent states may of right do. And, for the support of this declaration, with a firm reliance on the protection of Divine Providence, we mutually pledge to each other our lives, our fortunes, and our sacred honor.

The foregoing Declaration was, by order of Congress, engrossed, and signed by the following members:

JOHN HANCOCK

New Hampshire
Josiah Bartlett
William Whipple
Matthew Thornton

Massachusetts Bay
Samuel Adams
John Adams
Robert Treat Paine
Elbridge Gerry

Rhode Island
Stephen Hopkins
William Ellery

Connecticut
Roger Sherman
Samuel Huntington
William Williams
Oliver Wolcott

New York
William Floyd
Philip Livingston
Francis Lewis
Lewis Morris

New Jersey
Richard Stockton
John Witherspoon
Francis Hopkinson

John Hart
Abraham Clark

Pennsylvania
Robert Morris
Benjamin Rush
Benjamin Franklin
John Morton
George Clymer
James Smith
George Taylor
James Wilson
George Ross

Delaware
Caesar Rodney
George Reed
Thomas M'Kean

Maryland
Samuel Chase
William Paca
Thomas Stone
Charles Carroll, of Carrollton

Virginia
George Wythe
Richard Henry Lee
Thomas Jefferson
Benjamin Harrison
Thomas Nelson, Jr.
Francis Lightfoot Lee
Carter Braxton

North Carolina
William Hooper
Joseph Hewes
John Penn

South Carolina
Edward Rutledge
Thomas Heyward, Jr.
Thomas Lynch, Jr.
Arthur Middleton

Georgia
Button Gwinnett
Lyman Hall
George Walton

Resolved, That copies of the Declaration be sent to the several assemblies, conventions, and committees, or councils of safety, and to the several commanding officers of the continental troops; that it be proclaimed in each of the United States, at the head of the army.

The Constitution of the United States of America[1]

We the People of the United States, in Order to form a more perfect Union, establish Justice, insure domestic Tranquility, provide for the common defence, promote the general Welfare, and secure the Blessings of Liberty to ourselves and our Posterity, do ordain and establish this CONSTITUTION for the United States of America.

Article I

Section 1

All legislative Powers herein granted shall be vested in a Congress of the United States, which shall consist of a Senate and House of Representatives.

Section 2

The House of Representatives shall be composed of Members chosen every second Year by the People of the several States, and the Electors in each State shall have the Qualifications requisite for Electors of the most numerous Branch of the State Legislature.

No Person shall be a Representative who shall not have attained to the Age of twenty-five Years, and been seven Years a Citizen of the United States, and who shall not, when elected, be an Inhabitant of that State in which he shall be chosen.

[Representatives and direct Taxes[2] shall be apportioned among the several States which may be included within this Union, according to their respective Numbers, which shall be determined by adding to the whole Number of free Persons, including those bound to Service for a Term of Years, and excluding Indians not taxed, three fifths of all other Persons.][3] The actual Enumeration shall be made within three Years after the first Meeting of the Congress of the United States, and within every subsequent Term of ten Years, in such Manner as they shall by Law direct. The Number of Representatives shall not exceed one for every thirty Thousand, but each State shall have at Least one Representative; and until such enumeration shall be made, the State of New Hampshire shall be entitled to chuse three, Massachusetts eight, Rhode-Island and Providence Plantations one, Connecticut five, New York six, New Jersey four, Pennsylvania eight, Delaware one, Maryland six, Virginia ten, North Carolina five, South Carolina five, and Georgia three.

When vacancies happen in the Representation from any State, the Executive Authority thereof shall issue Writs of Election to fill such Vacancies.

---

[1] This version, which follows the original Constitution in capitalization and spelling, was published by the United States Department of the Interior, Office of Education, in 1935.

[2] Altered by the Sixteenth Amendment.

[3] Negated by the Fourteenth Amendment.

The House of Representatives shall chuse their Speaker and other Officers; and shall have the sole Power of Impeachment.

Section 3

The Senate of the United States shall be composed of two Senators from each State, chosen by the Legislature thereof, for six Years; and each Senator shall have one Vote.

Immediately after they shall be assembled in Consequence of the first Election, they shall be divided as equally as may be into three Classes. The Seats of the Senators of the first Class shall be vacated at the Expiration of the second Year, of the second Class at the Expiration of the fourth Year, and of the third Class at the Expiration of the sixth Year, so that one-third may be chosen every second Year; and if Vacancies happen by Resignation, or otherwise, during the Recess of the Legislature of any State, the Executive thereof may make temporary Appointments until the next Meeting of the Legislature, which shall then fill such Vacancies.

No Person shall be a Senator who shall not have attained to the Age of thirty Years, and been nine Years a Citizen of the United States, and who shall not, when elected, be an Inhabitant of that State for which he shall be chosen.

The Vice President of the United States shall be President of the Senate, but shall have no vote, unless they be equally divided.

The Senate shall chuse their other Officers, and also a President pro tempore, in the absence of the Vice President, or when he shall exercise the Office of President of the United States.

The Senate shall have the sole Power to try all Impeachments. When sitting for that purpose they shall be on Oath or Affirmation. When the President of the United States is tried, the Chief Justice shall preside: And no person shall be convicted without the Concurrence of two thirds of the Members present.

Judgment in Cases of Impeachment shall not extend further than to removal from Office, and disqualification to hold and enjoy any Office of honor, Trust, or Profit under the United States: but the Party convicted shall nevertheless be liable and subject to Indictment, Trial, Judgment and Punishment, according to Law.

Section 4

The Times, Place and Manner of holding Elections for Senators and Representatives, shall be prescribed in each State by the Legislature thereof; but the Congress may at any time by Law make or alter such Regulations, except as to the Places of Chusing Senators.

The Congress shall assemble at least once in every Year, and such Meeting shall be on the first Monday in December, unless they shall by Law appoint a different Day.

Section 5

Each House shall be the Judge of the Elections, Returns and Qualifications of its own Members, and a Majority of each shall constitute a Quorum to do Business; but a smaller number may adjourn from day to day, and may be authorized to compel the Attendance of absent Members, in such Manner, and under such Penalties, as each House may provide.

Each House may determine the Rules of its Proceedings, punish its Members for disorderly Behaviour, and, with the Concurrence of two thirds, expel a Member.

Each House shall keep a Journal of its Proceedings, and from time to time publish the same, excepting such Parts as may in their Judgment require Secrecy; and the Yeas and Nays of the Members of either House on any question shall, at the Desire of one fifth of those Present, be entered on the Journal.

Neither House, during the Session of Congress, shall, without the Consent of the other, adjourn for more than three days, nor to any other Place than that in which the two Houses shall be sitting.

Section 6

The Senators and Representatives shall receive a Compensation for their Services, to be ascertained by Law, and paid out of the Treasury of the United States. They shall in all Cases, except Treason, Felony, and Breach of the Peace, be privileged from Arrest during their Attendance at the Session of their respective Houses, and in going to and returning from the same; and for any Speech or Debate in either House, they shall not be questioned in any other Place.

No Senator or Representative shall, during the Time for which he was elected, be appointed to any civil Office under the Authority of the United States, which shall have been created, or the Emoluments whereof shall have been increased, during such time; and no Person holding any Office under the United States shall be a Member of either House during his continuance in Office.

Section 7

All Bills for raising Revenue shall originate in the House of Representatives; but the Senate may propose or concur with Amendments as on other bills.

Every Bill which shall have passed the House of Representatives and the Senate, shall, before it becomes a Law, be presented to the President of the United States; if he approve he shall sign it, but if not he shall return it, with his Objections, to that House in which it shall have originated, who shall enter the Objections at large on their Journal, and proceed to reconsider it. If after such Reconsideration two thirds of that House shall agree to pass the bill, it shall be sent, together with the objections, to the other House, by which it shall likewise be reconsidered, and if approved by two thirds of that House, it shall become a Law. But in all such Cases the Votes of both Houses shall be determined by Yeas and Nays, and the Names of the Persons voting for and against the Bill shall be entered on the Journal of each House respectively. If any Bill shall not be returned by the President within ten Days (Sundays excepted) after it shall have been presented to him, the Same shall be a Law, in like Manner as if he had signed it, unless the Congress by their Adjournment prevent its Return, in which Case it shall not be a Law.

Every Order, Resolution, or Vote to which the Concurrence of the Senate and House of Representatives may be necessary (except on a question of Adjournment) shall be presented to the President of the United States; and before the Same shall take Effect, shall be approved by him, or being disapproved by him, shall be repassed by two thirds of the Senate and House of Representatives, according to the Rules and Limitations prescribed in the Case of a Bill.

Section 8

The Congress shall have Power To lay and collect Taxes, Duties, Imposts and Excises, to pay the Debts and provide for the common Defence and general Welfare of the United States; but all Duties, Imposts and Excises shall be uniform throughout the United States;

To borrow money on the credit of the United States;

To regulate Commerce with foreign Nations, and among the several States, and with the Indian Tribes;

To establish a uniform rule of Naturalization, and uniform Laws on the subject of Bankruptcies throughout the United States;

To coin Money, regulate the Value thereof, and of foreign Coin, and fix the Standard of Weights and Measures;

To provide for the Punishment of counterfeiting the Securities and current Coin of the United States;

To establish Post Offices and post Roads;

To promote the Progress of Science and useful Arts, by securing for limited Times to Authors and Inventors the exclusive Right to their respective Writings and Discoveries;

To constitute Tribunals inferior to the Supreme Court;

To define and punish Piracies and Felonies committed on the high Seas, and Offenses against the Law of Nations;

To declare War, grant Letters of Marque and Reprisal, and make Rules concerning Captures on Land and Water;

To raise and support Armies, but no Appropriation of Money to that Use shall be for a longer Term than two Years;

To provide and maintain a Navy;

To make Rules for the Government and Regulation of the land and naval forces;

To provide for calling forth the Militia to execute the Laws of the Union, suppress Insurrections and repel Invasions;

To provide for organizing, arming, and disciplining the Militia, and for governing such Part of them as may be employed in the Service of the United States, reserving to the States respectively, the Appointment of the Officers, and the Authority of training the Militia according to the discipline prescribed by Congress;

To exercise exclusive Legislation in all Cases whatsoever, over such District (not exceeding ten Miles square) as may, by Cession of particular States, and the acceptance of Congress, become the Seat of the Government of the United States, and to exercise like Authority over all Places purchased by the Consent of the Legislature of the State in which the Same shall be, for the Erection of Forts, Magazines, Arsenals, Dock-yards, and other needful Buildings;—And

To make all Laws which shall be necessary and proper for carrying into Execution the foregoing Powers, and all other Powers vested by this Constitution in the Government of the United States, or in any Department or Officer thereof.

Section 9

The Migration or Importation of such Persons as any of the States now existing shall think proper to admit, shall not be prohibited by the Congress prior to the

Year one thousand eight hundred and eight, but a tax or duty may be imposed on such Importation, not exceeding ten dollars for each Person.

The privilege of the Writ of Habeas Corpus shall not be suspended, unless when in Cases of Rebellion or Invasion the public Safety may require it.

No bill of Attainder or ex post facto Law shall be passed.

No capitation, or other direct, Tax shall be laid unless in Proportion to the Census or Enumeration herein before directed to be taken.

No Tax or Duty shall be laid on Articles exported from any State.

No Preference shall be given by any Regulation of Commerce or Revenue to the Ports of one State over those of another: nor shall Vessels bound to, or from, one State, be obliged to enter, clear, or pay Duties in another.

No Money shall be drawn from the Treasury, but in Consequence of Appropriations made by Law; and a regular Statement and Account of the Receipts and Expenditures of all public Money shall be published from time to time.

No Title of Nobility shall be granted by the United States: And no Person holding any Office of Profit or Trust under them, shall, without the Consent of the Congress, accept of any present, Emolument, Office, or Title, of any kind whatever, from any King, Prince, or foreign State.

Section 10

No State shall enter into any Treaty, Alliance, or Confederation; grant Letters of Marque and Reprisal; coin Money; emit Bills of Credit; make any Thing but gold and silver Coin a Tender in Payment of Debts; pass any Bill of Attainder, ex post facto Law, or Law impairing the Obligation of Contracts, or grant any Title of Nobility.

No State shall, without the Consent of the Congress, lay any Imposts or Duties on Imports or Exports, except what may be absolutely necessary for executing its inspection Laws; and the net Produce of all Duties and Imposts, laid by any State on Imports or Exports, shall be for the use of the Treasury of the United States; and all such Laws shall be subject to the Revision and Control of the Congress.

No state shall, without the Consent of Congress, lay any duty of Tonnage, keep Troops, or Ships of War in time of Peace, enter into any Agreement or Compact with another State, or with a foreign Power, or engage in War, unless actually invaded, or in such imminent Danger as will not admit of delay.

Article II

Section 1

The executive Power shall be vested in a President of the United States of America. He shall hold his Office during the Term of four years, and, together with the Vice President, chosen for the same Term, be elected, as follows:

Each State shall appoint, in such Manner as the Legislature thereof may direct, a Number of Electors, equal to the whole Number of Senators and Representatives to which the State may be entitled in the Congress: but no Senator or Representative, or Person holding an Office of Trust or Profit under the United States, shall be appointed an Elector.

[The Electors shall meet in their respective States, and vote by Ballot for two persons, of whom one at least shall not be an Inhabitant of the same State with themselves. And they shall make a List of all the Persons voted for, and of the Number of Votes for each; which List they shall sign and certify, and transmit sealed to the Seat of the Government of the United States, directed to the President of the Senate. The President of the Senate shall, in the Presence of the Senate and House of Representatives, open all the Certificates, and the Votes shall then be counted. The Person having the greatest Number of Votes shall be the President, if such Number be a Majority of the whole Number of Electors appointed; and if there be more than one who have such Majority, and have an equal Number of Votes, then the House of Representatives shall immediately chuse by Ballot one of them for President; and if no Person have a Majority, then from the five highest on the List the said House shall in like Manner chuse the President. But in chusing the President, the Votes shall be taken by States, the Representation from each State having one Vote; a quorum for this Purpose shall consist of a Member or Members from two-thirds of the States, and a Majority of all the States shall be necessary to a Choice. In every Case, after the Choice of the President, the Person having the greatest Number of Votes of the Electors shall be the Vice President. But if there should remain two or more who have equal votes, the Senate shall chuse from them by Ballot the Vice President.][4]

The Congress may determine the Time of chusing the Electors, and the Day on which they shall give their Votes; which Day shall be the same throughout the United States.

No person except a natural-born Citizen, or a Citizen of the United States, at the time of the Adoption of this Constitution, shall be eligible to the Office of President; neither shall any Person be eligible to that Office who shall not have attained to the Age of thirty-five years, and been fourteen Years a Resident within the United States.

In Case of the Removal of the President from Office, or of his Death, Resignation, or Inability to discharge the Powers and Duties of the said Office, the same shall devolve on the Vice President, and the Congress may by Law provide for the Case of Removal, Death, Resignation, or Inability, both of the President and Vice President, declaring what Officer shall then act as President, and such Officer shall act accordingly, until the disability be removed, or a President shall be elected.

The President shall, at stated Times, receive for his Services a Compensation, which shall neither be increased nor diminished during the Period for which he shall have been elected, and he shall not receive within that Period any other Emolument from the United States, or any of them.

Before he enter on the execution of his Office, he shall take the following Oath or Affirmation:—"I do solemnly swear (or affirm) that I will faithfully execute the Office of President of the United States, and will, to the best of my Ability, preserve, protect, and defend the Constitution of the United States."

Section 2

The President shall be Commander in Chief of the Army and Navy of the United States, and of the Militia of the several States, when called into the actual Service

---

[4] Revised by the Twelfth Amendment.

of the United States; he may require the Opinion, in writing, of the principal Officer in each of the executive Departments, upon any subject relating to the Duties of their respective Offices, and he shall have Power to Grant Reprieves and Pardons for Offenses against the United States, except in Cases of Impeachment.

He shall have Power, by and with the Advice and Consent of the Senate, to make Treaties, provided two-thirds of the Senators present concur; and he shall nominate, and by and with the Advice and Consent of the Senate, shall appoint Ambassadors, other public Ministers and Consuls, Judges of the supreme Court, and all other Officers of the United States, whose Appointments are not herein otherwise provided for, and which shall be established by Law: but the Congress may by Law vest the Appointment of such inferior Officers, as they think proper, in the President alone, in the Courts of Law, or in the Heads of Departments.

The President shall have Power to fill up all Vacancies that may happen during the Recess of the Senate, by granting Commissions which shall expire at the End of their next Session.

Section 3

He shall from time to time give to the Congress Information of the State of the Union, and recommend to their Consideration such Measures as he shall judge necessary and expedient; he may, on extraordinary occasions, convene both Houses, or either of them, and in Case of Disagreement between them, with respect to the Time of Adjournment, he may adjourn them to such Time as he shall think proper; he shall receive Ambassadors and other public Ministers; he shall take care that the Laws be faithfully executed, and shall Commission all the Officers of the United States.

Section 4

The President, Vice President and all civil Officers of the United States, shall be removed from Office on Impeachment for, and Conviction of, Treason, Bribery, or other high Crimes and Misdemeanors.

Article III

Section 1

The judicial Power of the United States, shall be vested in one supreme Court, and in such inferior Courts as the Congress may from time to time ordain and establish. The Judges, both of the supreme and inferior Courts, shall hold their Offices during good Behaviour, and shall, at stated Times, receive for their Services, a Compensation, which shall not be diminished during their Continuance in Office.

Section 2

The judicial Power shall extend to all Cases, in Law and Equity, arising under this Constitution, the Laws of the United States, and Treaties made, or which shall be made, under their Authority;—to all Cases affecting ambassadors, other public ministers and consuls;—to all cases of admiralty and maritime Jurisdiction;—to Controversies to which the United States shall be a Party;—to Controversies between two or more states;—between a State and Citizens of another State;[5]—between Citizens of different States—between Citizens of the same State claiming Lands under Grants of different States, and between a State, or the Citizens thereof, and foreign States, Citizens, or Subjects.

In all Cases affecting Ambassadors, other public Ministers and Consuls, and those in which a State shall be Party, the supreme Court shall have original Jurisdiction. In all the other Cases before mentioned, the supreme Court shall have appellate Jurisdiction, both as to Law and Fact, with such Exceptions, and under such Regulations as the Congress shall make.

The trial of all Crimes, except in Cases of Impeachment, shall be by Jury; and such Trial shall be held in the State where the said Crimes shall have been committed; but when not committed within any State, the Trial shall be at such Place or Places as the Congress may by Law have directed.

Section 3

Treason against the United States, shall consist only in levying War against them, or in adhering to their Enemies, giving them Aid and Comfort. No Person shall be convicted of Treason unless on the Testimony of two Witnesses to the same overt Act, or on Confession in open Court.

The Congress shall have power to declare the Punishment of Treason, but no Attainder of Treason shall work Corruption of Blood, or Forfeiture except during the Life of the Person attainted.

Article IV

Section 1

Full Faith and Credit shall be given in each State to the public Acts, Records, and judicial Proceedings of every other State. And the Congress may by general Laws prescribe the Manner in which such Acts, Records and Proceedings shall be proved, and the Effect thereof.

Section 2

The Citizens of each State shall be entitled to all Privileges and Immunities of Citizens in the several States.

A Person charged in any State with Treason, Felony, or other Crime, who shall flee from Justice, and be found in another State, shall on demand of the executive Authority of the State from which he fled, be delivered up, to be removed to the State having Jurisdiction of the crime.

No Person held to Service or Labour in one State, under the Laws thereof, escaping into another, shall, in Consequence of any Law or Regulation therein, be discharged from such Service or Labour, but shall be delivered up on Claim of the Party to whom such Service or Labour may be due.

---

[5] Qualified by the Eleventh Amendment.

Section 3

New States may be admitted by the Congress into this Union; but no new State shall be formed or erected within the Jurisdiction of any other State; nor any State be formed by the Junction of two or more States, or parts of States, without the Consent of the Legislatures of the States concerned as well as of the Congress.

The Congress shall have Power to dispose of and make all needful Rules and Regulations respecting the Territory or other Property belonging to the United States; and nothing in this Constitution shall be so construed as to Prejudice any Claims of the United States, or of any particular State.

Section 4

The United States shall guarantee to every State in this Union a Republican Form of Government, and shall protect each of them against Invasion; and on Application of the Legislature, or of the Executive (when the Legislature cannot be convened) against domestic Violence.

Article V

The Congress, whenever two-thirds of both Houses shall deem it necessary, shall propose Amendments to this Constitution, or, on the Application of the Legislatures of two-thirds of the several States, shall call a Convention for proposing Amendments, which, in either Case, shall be valid to all Intents and Purposes, as part of this Constitution, when ratified by the Legislatures of three-fourths of the several States, or by Conventions in three-fourths thereof, as the one or the other Mode of Ratification may be proposed by the Congress; Provided that no Amendment which may be made prior to the Year One thousand eight hundred and eight shall in any Manner affect the first and fourth Clauses in the Ninth Section of the first Article; and that no State, without its Consent, shall be deprived of its equal Suffrage in the Senate.

Article VI

All Debts contracted and Engagements entered into, before the Adoption of this Constitution, shall be as valid against the United States under this Constitution, as under the Confederation.

This Constitution, and the Laws of the United States which shall be made in Pursuance thereof; and all Treaties made, or which shall be made, under the Authority of the United States, shall be the supreme Law of the Land; and the Judges in every State shall be bound thereby, any Thing in the Constitution or Laws of any State to the Contrary notwithstanding.

The Senators and Representatives before mentioned, and the Members of the several State Legislatures, and all executive and judicial Officers, both of the United States and of the several States, shall be bound by Oath or Affirmation to support this Constitution; but no religious Tests shall ever be required as a qualification to any Office or public Trust under the United States.

Article VII

The Ratification of the Conventions of nine States shall be sufficient for the Establishment of this Constitution between the States so ratifying the same.

Done in Convention by the Unanimous Consent of the States present the Seventeenth Day of September in the Year of our Lord one thousand seven hundred and Eighty seven, and of the Independence of the United States of America the Twelfth. In Witness whereof We have hereunto subscribed our Names.[6]

George Washington
President and deputy from Virginia

New Hampshire
John Langdon
Nicholas Gilman

Massachusetts
Nathaniel Gorham
Rufus King

Connecticut
William Samuel Johnson
Roger Sherman

New York
Alexander Hamilton

New Jersey
William Livingston
David Brearley
William Paterson
Jonathan Dayton

Pennsylvania
Benjamin Franklin
Thomas Mifflin
Robert Morris
George Clymer
Thomas FitzSimmons
Jared Ingersoll
James Wilson
Gouverneur Morris

Delaware
George Read
Gunning Bedford, Jr.
John Dickinson
Richard Bassett
Jacob Broom

Maryland
James McHenry
Daniel of St. Thomas Jenifer
Daniel Carroll

Virginia
John Blair
James Madison, Jr.

North Carolina
William Blount
Richard Dobbs Spaight
Hugh Williamson

South Carolina
John Rutledge
Charles Cotesworth Pinckney
Charles Pinckney
Pierce Butler

Georgia
William Few
Abraham Baldwin

Articles in Addition to, and Amendment of, the Constitution of the United States of America, Proposed by Congress, and Ratified by the Legislatures of the Several States, Pursuant to the Fifth Article of the Original Constitution[7]

Amendment I

Congress shall make no law respecting an establishment of religion, or prohibiting the free exercise thereof; or abridging the freedom of speech, or of the press;

---

[6] These are the full names of the signers, which in some cases are not the signatures on the document.

[7] This heading appears only in the joint resolution submitting the first ten amendments, which are collectively known as the Bill of Rights. They were ratified on December 15, 1791.

or the right of the people peaceably to assemble, and to petition the Government for a redress of grievances.

Amendment II

A well regulated Militia, being necessary to the security of a free State, the right of the people to keep and bear Arms shall not be infringed.

Amendment III

No Soldier shall, in time of peace, be quartered in any house, without the consent of the Owner, nor in time of war, but in a manner to be prescribed by law.

Amendment IV

The right of the people to be secure in their persons, houses, papers, and effects, against unreasonable searches and seizures, shall not be violated, and no Warrants shall issue, but upon probable cause, supported by Oath or affirmation, and particularly describing the place to be searched, and the persons or things to be seized.

Amendment V

No person shall be held to answer for a capital or otherwise infamous crime, unless on a presentment or indictment of a Grand Jury, except in cases arising in the land or naval forces, or in the Militia, when in actual service in time of War or public danger; nor shall any person be subject for the same offence to be twice put in jeopardy of life or limb; nor shall be compelled in any criminal case to be a witness against himself, nor be deprived of life, liberty, or property, without due process of law; nor shall private property be taken for public use, without just compensation.

Amendment VI

In all criminal prosecutions, the accused shall enjoy the right to a speedy and public trial, by an impartial jury of the State and district wherein the crime shall have been committed, which district shall have been previously ascertained by law, and to be informed of the nature and cause of the accusation; to be confronted with the witnesses against him; to have compulsory process for obtaining witnesses in his favour, and to have the Assistance of Counsel for his defence.

Amendment VII

In suits at common law, where the value in controversy shall exceed twenty dollars, the right of trial by jury shall be preserved, and no fact tried by a jury, shall be otherwise reexamined in any Court of the United States, than according to the rules of the common law.

Amendment VIII

Excessive bail shall not be required, nor excessive fines imposed, nor cruel and unusual punishments inflicted.

Amendment IX

The enumeration of the Constitution, of certain rights, shall not be construed to deny or disparage others retained by the people.

Amendment X

The powers not delegated to the United States by the Constitution, nor prohibited by it to the States, are reserved to the States respectively, or to the people.

Amendment XI [1795]

The Judicial power of the United States shall not be construed to extend to any suit in law or equity, commenced or prosecuted against one of the United States by Citizens of another State, or by Citizens or Subjects of any Foreign State.

Amendment XII [1804]

The Electors shall meet in their respective States and vote by ballot for President and Vice-President, one of whom, at least, shall not be an inhabitant of the same State with themselves; they shall name in their ballots the person voted for as President, and in distinct ballots the person voted for as Vice-President, and they shall make distinct lists of all persons voted for as President, and of all persons voted for as Vice-President, and of the number of votes for each, which lists they shall sign and certify, and transmit sealed to the seat of the government of the United States, directed to the President of the Senate;—The President of the Senate shall, in the presence of the Senate and House of Representatives, open all the certificates and the votes shall then be counted;—The person having the greatest number of votes for President, shall be the President, if such number be a majority of the whole number of Electors appointed; and if no person have such majority, then from the persons having the highest numbers not exceeding three on the list of those voted for as President, the House of Representatives shall choose immediately, by ballot, the President. But in choosing the President, the votes shall be taken by states, the representation from each state having one vote; a quorum for this purpose shall consist of a member or members from two-thirds of the states, and a majority of all the states shall be necessary to a choice. And if the House of Representatives shall not choose a President whenever the right of choice shall devolve upon them, before the fourth day of March next following, then the Vice-President shall act as President, as in the case of the death or other constitutional disability of the President.—The person having the greatest number of votes as Vice-President, shall be the Vice-President, if such number be a majority of the whole number of Electors appointed, and if no person have a majority, then from the two highest numbers on the list, the Senate shall choose the Vice-President; a quorum for the purpose shall consist of two-thirds of the whole number of Senators, and majority of the whole number shall be necessary to a choice. But no person constitutionally ineligible to the office of President shall be eligible to that of Vice-President of the United States.

Amendment XIII [1865]

Section 1

Neither slavery nor involuntary servitude, except as a punishment for crime whereof the party shall have been duly convicted, shall exist within the United States, or any place subject to their jurisdiction.

Section 2

Congress shall have power to enforce this article by appropriate legislation.

Amendment XIV [1868]

Section 1

All persons born or naturalized in the United States, and subject to the jurisdiction thereof, are citizens of the United States and of the State wherein they reside. No State shall abridge the privileges or immunities of citizens of the United States; nor shall any State deprive any person of life, liberty, or property, without due process of law; nor deny to any person within its jurisdiction the equal protection of the laws.

Section 2

Representatives shall be apportioned among the several States according to their respective numbers, counting the whole number of persons in each State, excluding Indians not taxed. But when the right to vote at any election for the choice of electors for President and Vice-President of the United States, Representatives in Congress, the Executive and Judicial officers of a State, or the members of the Legislature thereof, is denied to any of the male inhabitants of such State, being twenty-one years of age, and citizens of the United States, or in any way abridged, except for participation in rebellion, or other crime, the basis of representation therein shall be reduced in the proportion which the number of such male citizens shall bear to the whole number of male citizens twenty-one years of age in such State.

Section 3

No person shall be a Senator or Representative in Congress, or elector of President and Vice-President, or hold any office, civil or military, under the United States, or under any State, who, having previously taken an oath, as a member of Congress, or as an officer of the United States, or as a member of any State legislature, or as an executive or judicial officer of any State, to support the Constitution of the

United States, shall have engaged in insurrection or rebellion against the same, or given aid or comfort to the enemies thereof. But Congress may by a vote of two-thirds of each House, remove such disability.

Section 4

The validity of the public debt of the United States, authorized by law, including debts incurred for payment of pensions and bounties for services in suppressing insurrection or rebellion, shall not be questioned. But neither the United States nor any State shall assume or pay any debts or obligation incurred in aid of insurrection or rebellion against the United States, or any claim for the loss or emancipation of any slave; but all such debts, obligations, and claims shall be held illegal and void.

Section 5

The Congress shall have the power to enforce, by appropriate legislation, the provisions of this article.

Amendment XV [1870]

Section 1

The right of citizens of the United States to vote shall not be denied or abridged by the United States or by any State on account of race, color, or previous condition of servitude.

Section 2

The Congress shall have power to enforce this article by appropriate legislation.

Amendment XVI [1913]

The Congress shall have power to lay and collect taxes on incomes, from whatever source derived, without apportionment among the several States, and without regard to any census or enumeration.

Amendment XVII [1913]

The Senate of the United States shall be composed of two Senators from each State, elected by the people thereof, for six years; and each Senator shall have one vote. The electors in each State shall have the qualifications requisite for electors of the most numerous branch of the State legislatures.

When vacancies happen in the representation of any State in the Senate, the executive authority of such State shall issue writs of election to fill such vacancies: Provided, That the legislature of any State may empower the executive thereof to make temporary appointments until the people fill the vacancies by election as the legislature may direct.

This Amendment shall not be so construed as to affect the election or term of any Senator chosen before it becomes valid as part of the Constitution.

Amendment XVIII [1919]

Section 1

After one year from the ratification of this article the manufacture, sale, or transportation of intoxicating liquors within, the importation thereof into, or the exportation thereof from the United States and all territory subject to the jurisdiction thereof for beverage purposes is hereby prohibited.

Section 2

The Congress and the several States shall have concurrent power to enforce this article by appropriate legislation.

Section 3

This article shall be inoperative unless it shall have been ratified as an Amendment to the Constitution by the legislatures of the several States, as provided in the Constitution, within seven years from the date of the submission hereof to the States by the Congress.

Amendment XIX [1920]

The right of citizens of the United States to vote shall not be denied or abridged by the United States or by any State on account of sex.

Congress shall have power to enforce this article by appropriate legislation.

Amendment XX [1933]

Section 1

The terms of the President and Vice-President shall end at noon on the 20th day of January, and the terms of Senators and Representatives at noon on the 3d day of January, of the years in which such terms would have ended if this article had not been ratified; and the terms of their successors shall then begin.

Section 2

The Congress shall assemble at least once in every year, and such meeting shall begin at noon on the 3d day of January, unless they shall by law appoint a different day.

Section 3

If, at the time fixed for the beginning of the term of the President, the President elect shall have died, the Vice-President elect shall become President. If a President shall not have been chosen before the time fixed for the beginning of his term or if the President elect shall have failed to qualify, then the Vice-President elect shall act as President until a President shall have qualified; and the Congress may by law provide for the case wherein neither a President elect nor a Vice-President elect shall have qualified, declaring who shall then act as President, or the manner in which one who is to act shall be selected, and such person shall act accordingly until a President or Vice-President shall have qualified.

Section 4

The Congress may by law provide for the case of the death of any of the persons from whom the House of Representatives may choose a President whenever the right of choice shall have devolved upon them, and for the case of the death of any of the persons from whom the Senate may choose a Vice-President whenever the right of choice shall have devolved upon them.

Section 5

Sections 1 and 2 shall take effect on the 15th day of October following the ratification of this article.

Section 6

This article shall be inoperative unless it shall have been ratified as an amendment to the Constitution by the legislatures of three-fourths of the several States within seven years from the date of its submission.

AMENDMENT XXI [1933]

Section 1

The eighteenth article of amendment to the Constitution of the United States is hereby repealed.

Section 2

The transportation or importation into any State, Territory, or possession of the United States for delivery or use therein of intoxicating liquors, in violation of the laws thereof, is hereby prohibited.

Section 3

This article shall be inoperative unless it shall have been ratified as an amendment to the Constitution by conventions in the several States, as provided in the Constitution, within seven years from the date of the submission hereof to the States by the Congress.

AMENDMENT XXII [1951]

No person shall be elected to the office of the President more than twice, and no person who has held the office of President, or acted as President, for more than two years of a term to which some other person was elected President shall be elected to the office of the President more than once.

But this Article shall not apply to any person holding the office of President when this Article was proposed by the Congress, and shall not prevent any person who may be holding the office of President, or acting as President, during the term within which this Article becomes operative from holding the office of President or acting as President during the remainder of such term.

This article shall be inoperative unless it shall have been ratified as an amendment to the Constitution by the legislatures of three-fourths of the several states within seven years from the date of its submission to the states by the Congress.

Amendment XXIII [1961]

Section 1

The District constituting the seat of Government of the United States shall appoint in such manner as the Congress may direct:

A number of electors of President and Vice-President equal to the whole number of Senators and Representatives in Congress to which the District would be entitled if it were a State, but in no event more than the least populous State; they shall be in addition to those appointed by the States, but they shall be considered, for the purposes of the election of President and Vice-President, to be electors appointed by a State; and they shall meet in the District and perform such duties as provided by the twelfth article of Amendment.

Section 2

The Congress shall have power to enforce this article by appropriate legislation.

Amendment XXIV [1964]

Section 1

The right of citizens of the United States to vote in any primary or other election for President or Vice President, for electors for President or Vice President, or for Senator or Representative in Congress, shall not be denied or abridged by the United States or any state by reason of failure to pay any poll tax or other tax.

Section 2

The Congress shall have the power to enforce this article by appropriate legislation.

Amendment XXV [1967]

Section 1

In case of the removal of the President from office or of his death or resignation, the Vice President shall become President.

Section 2

Whenever there is a vacancy in the office of the Vice President, the President shall nominate a Vice President who shall take office upon confirmation by a majority vote of both Houses of Congress.

Section 3

Whenever the President transmits to the President Pro Tempore of the Senate and the Speaker of the House of Representatives his written declaration that he is unable to discharge the powers and duties of his office, and until he transmits to them a written declaration to the contrary, such powers and duties shall be discharged by the Vice President as Acting President.

Section 4

Whenever the Vice President and a majority of either the principal officers of the executive departments or of such other body as Congress may by law provide, transmit to the President Pro Tempore of the Senate and the Speaker of the House of Representatives their written declaration that the President is unable to discharge the powers and duties of his office, the Vice President shall immediately assume the powers and duties of the office as Acting President.

Thereafter, when the President transmits to the President Pro Tempore of the Senate and the Speaker of the House of Representatives his written declaration that no inability exists, he shall resume the powers and duties of his office unless the Vice President and a majority of either the principal officers of the executive departments or of such other body as Congress may by law provide, transmit within four days to the President Pro Tempore of the Senate and the Speaker of the House of Representatives their written declaration that the President is unable to discharge the powers and duties of his office. Thereupon Congress shall decide the issue, assembling within forty-eight hours for that purpose if not in session. If the Congress, within twenty-one days after receipt of the latter written declaration, or, if Congress is not in session, within twenty-one days after Congress is required to assemble, determines by two-thirds vote of both Houses that the President is unable to discharge the powers and duties of his office, the Vice President shall continue to discharge the same as Acting President; otherwise, the President shall resume the powers and duties of his office.

Amendment XXVI [1971]

Section 1

The right of citizens of the United States, who are eighteen years of age or older, to vote shall not be denied or abridged by the United States or by any State on account of age.

Section 2

The Congress shall have the power to enforce this article by appropriate legislation.

Amendment XXVII [1992]

No law varying the compensation for the service of Senators and Representatives shall take effect until an election of Representatives shall have intervened.

Federalist No. 10

(JAMES MADISON)

Among the numerous advantages promised by a well-constructed union, none deserves to be more accurately developed than its tendency to break and control the violence of faction. The friend of popular governments never finds himself so much alarmed for their character and fate as when he contemplates their propensity to this dangerous vice. He will not fail, therefore, to set a due value on any plan which, without violating the principles to which he is attached, provides a proper cure for it. The instability, injustice, and confusion introduced into the public councils have, in truth, been the mortal diseases under which popular governments have everywhere perished, as they continue to be the favorite and fruitful topics from which the adversaries to liberty derive their most specious declamations. The valuable improvements made by the American constitutions on the popular models, both ancient and modern, cannot certainly be too much admired; but it would be an unwarrantable partiality to contend that they have as effectually obviated the danger on this side, as was wished and expected. Complaints are everywhere heard from our most considerate and virtuous citizens, equally the friends of public and private faith and of public and personal liberty, that our governments are too unstable, that the public good is disregarded in the conflicts of rival parties, and that measures are too often decided, not according to the rules of justice and the rights of the minor party, but by the superior force of an interested and overbearing majority. However anxiously we may wish that these complaints had no foundation, the evidence of known facts will not permit us to deny that they are in some degree true. It will be found, indeed, on a candid review of our situation, that some of the distresses under which we labor have been erroneously charged on the operation of our governments; but it will be found, at the same time, that other causes will not alone account for many of our heaviest misfortunes; and, particularly, for that prevailing and increasing distrust of public engagements and alarm for private rights which are echoed from one end of the continent to the other. These must be chiefly, if not wholly, effects of the unsteadiness and injustice with which a factious spirit has tainted our public administration.

By a faction I understand a number of citizens, whether amounting to a majority or minority of the whole, who are united and actuated by some common impulse of passion, or of interest, adverse to the rights of other citizens, or to the permanent and aggregate interests of the community.

There are two methods of curing the mischiefs of faction: the one, by removing its causes; the other, by controlling its effects.

There are again two methods of removing the causes of faction: the one, by destroying the liberty which is essential to its existence; the other, by giving to every citizen the same opinions, the same passions, and the same interests.

It could never be more truly said than of the first remedy that it was worse than the disease. Liberty is to faction what air is to fire, an aliment without which it instantly expires. But it could not be a less folly to abolish liberty, which is essential to political life, because it nourishes faction than it would be to wish the annihilation of air, which is essential to animal life, because it imparts to fire its destructive agency.

The second expedient is as impracticable as the first would be unwise. As long as the reason of man continues fallible, and he is at liberty to exercise it, different opinions will be formed. As long as the connection subsists between his reason and his self-love, his opinions and his passions will have a reciprocal influence on each other; and the former will be objects to which the latter will attach themselves. The diversity in the faculties of men, from which the rights of property originate, is not less an insuperable obstacle to a uniformity of interest. The protection of these faculties is the first object of government. From the protection of different and unequal faculties of acquiring property, the possession of different degrees and kinds of property immediately results; and from the influence of these on the sentiments and views of the respective proprietors ensues a division of the society into different interests and parties.

The latent causes of faction are thus sown in the nature of man; and we see them everywhere brought into different degrees of activity, according to the different circumstances of civil society. A zeal for different opinions concerning religion, concerning government, and many other points, as well of speculation as of practice; an attachment to different leaders ambitiously contending for pre-eminence and power; or to persons of other descriptions whose fortunes have been interesting to the human passions, have, in turn, divided mankind into parties, inflamed them with mutual animosity, and rendered them much more disposed to vex and oppress each other than to co-operate for their common good. So strong is this propensity of mankind to fall into mutual animosities that where no substantial occasion presents itself the most frivolous and fanciful distinctions have been sufficient to kindle their unfriendly passions and excite their most violent conflicts. But the most common and durable source of factions has been the various and unequal distribution of property. Those who hold and those who are without property have ever formed distinct interests in society. Those who are creditors, and those who are debtors, fall under a like discrimination. A landed interest, a manufacturing interest, a mercantile interest, a moneyed interest, with many lesser interests, grow up of necessity in civilized nations, and divide them into different classes, actuated by different sentiments and views. The regulation of these various and interfering interests forms the principal task of modern legislation and involves the spirit of party and faction in the necessary and ordinary operations of government.

No man is allowed to be a judge in his own cause, because his interest would certainly bias his judgment, and, not improbably, corrupt his integrity. With equal, nay with greater reason, a body of men are unfit to be both judges and parties at the same time; yet what are many of the most important acts of legislation but so many judicial determinations, not indeed concerning the rights of single persons, but concerning the rights of large bodies of citizens? And what are the different classes of legislators but advocates and parties to the causes which they determine? Is a law proposed concerning private debts? It is a question to which the creditors are parties on one side and the debtors on the other. Justice ought to hold the balance between them. Yet the parties are, and must be, themselves the judges; and the most numerous party, or in other words, the most powerful faction must be expected to prevail. Shall domestic manufacturers be encouraged, and in what degree, by restrictions on foreign manufacturers? [These] are questions which would be differently decided by the landed and the manufacturing classes, and probably by neither with a sole regard to justice and the public good.

The apportionment of taxes on the various descriptions of property is an act which seems to require the most exact impartiality; yet there is, perhaps, no legislative act in which greater opportunity and temptation are given to a predominant party to trample on the rules of justice. Every shilling with which they overburden the inferior number is a shilling saved to their own pockets.

It is in vain to say that enlightened statesmen will be able to adjust these clashing interests and render them all subservient to the public good. Enlightened statesmen will not always be at the helm. Nor, in many cases, can such an adjustment be made at all without taking into view indirect and remote considerations, which will rarely prevail over the immediate interest which one party may find in disregarding the rights of another or the good of the whole.

The inference to which we are brought is that the *causes* of faction cannot be removed and that relief is only to be sought in the means of controlling its *effects*.

If a faction consists of less than a majority, relief is supplied by the republican principle, which enables the majority to defeat its sinister views by regular vote. It may clog the administration, it may convulse the society; but it will be unable to execute and mask its violence under the forms of the Constitution. When a majority is included in a faction, the form of popular government, on the other hand, enables it to sacrifice to its ruling passion or interest both the public good and the rights of other citizens. To secure the public good and private rights against the danger of such a faction, and at the same time to preserve the spirit and the form of popular government, is then the great object to which our inquiries are directed. Let me add that it is the great desideratum by which alone this form of government can be rescued from the opprobrium under which it has so long labored and be recommended to the esteem and adoption of mankind.

By what means is this object attainable? Evidently by one of two only. Either the existence of the same passion or interest in a majority at the same time must be prevented, or the majority, having such coexistent passion or interest, must be rendered, by their number and local situation, unable to concert and carry into effect schemes of oppression. If the impulse and the opportunity be suffered to coincide, we well know that neither moral nor religious motives can be relied on as an adequate control. They are not found to be such on the injustice and violence of individuals, and lose their efficacy in proportion to the number combined together, that is, in proportion as their efficacy becomes needful.

From this view of the subject it may be concluded that a pure democracy, by which I mean a society consisting of a small number of citizens, who assemble and administer the government in person, can admit of no cure for the mischiefs of faction. A common passion or interest will, in almost every case, be felt by a majority of the whole, a communication and concert result from the form of government itself; and there is nothing to check the inducements to sacrifice the weaker party or an obnoxious individual. Hence it is that such democracies have ever been spectacles of turbulence and contention; have ever been found incompatible with personal security or the rights of property; and have in general been as short in their lives as they have been violent in their deaths. Theoretic politicians, who have patronized this species of government, have erroneously supposed that by reducing mankind to a perfect equality in their political rights, they would at the same time be perfectly equalized and assimilated in their possessions, their opinions, and their passions.

A republic, by which I mean a government in which the scheme of representation takes place, opens a different prospect and promises the cure for which we are seeking. Let us examine the points in which it varies from pure democracy, and we shall comprehend both the nature of the cure and the efficacy which it must derive from the Union.

The two great points of difference between a democracy and a republic are: first, the delegation of the government, in the latter, to a small number of citizens elected by the rest; secondly, the greater number of citizens and greater sphere of country over which the latter may be extended.

The effect of the first difference is, on the one hand, to refine and enlarge the public views by passing them through the medium of a chosen body of citizens, whose wisdom may best discern the true interest of their country and whose patriotism and love of justice will be least likely to sacrifice it to temporary or partial considerations. Under such a regulation it may well happen that the public voice, pronounced by the representatives of the people, will be more consonant to the public good than if pronounced by the people themselves, convened for the purpose. On the other hand, the effect may be inverted. Men of factious tempers, of local prejudices, or of sinister designs, may, by intrigue, by corruption, or by other means, first obtain the suffrages, and then betray the interests of the people. The question resulting is, whether small or extensive republics are most favorable to the election of proper guardians of the public weal; and it is clearly decided in favor of the latter by two obvious considerations.

In the first place it is to be remarked that however small the republic may be the representatives must be raised to a certain number in order to guard against the cabals of a few; and that however large it may be they must be limited to a certain number in order to guard against the confusion of a multitude. Hence, the number of representatives in the two cases not being in proportion to that of the constituents, and being proportionally greatest in the small republic, it follows that if the proportion of fit characters be not less in the large than in the small republic, the former will present a greater option, and consequently a greater probability of a fit choice.

In the next place, as each representative will be chosen by a greater number of citizens in the large than in the small republic, it will be more difficult for unworthy candidates to practice with success the vicious arts by which elections are too often carried; and the suffrages of the people being more free, will be more likely to center on men who possess the most attractive merit and the most diffusive and established characters.

It must be confessed that in this, as in most other cases, there is a mean, on both sides of which inconveniencies will be found to lie. By enlarging too much the number of electors, you render the representative too little acquainted with all their local circumstances and lesser interests; as by reducing it too much, you render him unduly attached to these, and too little fit to comprehend and pursue great and national objects. The federal Constitution forms a happy combination in this respect; the great and aggregate interests being referred to the national, the local and particular to the State legislatures.

The other point of difference is the greater number of citizens and extent of territory which may be brought within the compass of republican than of democratic government; and it is this circumstance principally which renders factious combinations less to be dreaded in the former than in the latter. The smaller the society, the fewer probably will be the distinct parties and interests composing it; the fewer the distinct parties and interests, the more frequently will a majority be found of the same party; and the smaller the number of individuals composing a majority, and the smaller the compass within which they are placed, the more easily will they concert and execute their plans of oppression. Extend the sphere and you take in a greater variety of parties and interests; you make it less probable that a majority of the whole will have a common motive to invade the rights of other citizens; or if such a common motive exists, it will be more difficult for all who feel it to discover their own strength and to act in unison with each other. Besides other impediments, it may be remarked that, where there is a consciousness of unjust or dishonorable purposes, communication is always checked by distrust in proportion to the number whose concurrence is necessary.

Hence, it clearly appears that the same advantage which a republic has over a democracy in controlling the effects of faction is enjoyed by a large over a small republic—is enjoyed by the Union over the States composing it. Does this advantage consist in the substitution of representatives whose enlightened views and virtuous sentiments render them superior to local prejudices and to schemes of injustice? It will not be denied that the representation of the Union will be most likely to possess these requisite endowments. Does it consist in the greater security afforded by a greater variety of parties, against the event of any one party being able to outnumber and oppress the rest? In an equal degree does the increased variety of parties comprised within the Union increase this security. Does it, in fine, consist in the greater obstacles opposed to the concert and accomplishment of the secret wishes of an unjust and interested majority? Here again the extent of the Union gives it the most palpable advantage.

The influence of factious leaders may kindle a flame within their particular States but will be unable to spread a general conflagration through the other States. A religious sect may degenerate into a political faction in a part of the Confederacy; but the variety of sects dispersed over the entire face of it must secure the national councils against any danger from that source. A rage for paper money, for an abolition of debts, for an equal division of property, or for any other improper or wicked project, will be less apt to pervade the whole body of the Union than a particular member of it, in the same proportion as such a malady is more likely to taint a particular county or district than an entire State.

In the extent and proper structure of the Union, therefore, we behold a republican remedy for the diseases most incident to republican government. And according to the degree of pleasure and pride we feel in being republicans ought to be our zeal in cherishing the spirit and supporting the character of Federalists.

Federalist No. 51

(JAMES MADISON)

To what expedient, then, shall we finally resort, for maintaining in practice the necessary partition of power among the several departments as laid down in the Constitution? The only answer that can be given is that as all these exterior provisions are found to be inadequate, the defect must be supplied, by so contriving the interior structure of the government as that its several constituent parts may, by their mutual relations, be the means of keeping each other in their proper places. Without presuming to undertake a full development of this important idea I will hazard a few general observations which may perhaps place it in a clearer light, and enable us to form a more correct judgment of the principles and structure of the government planned by the convention.

In order to lay a due foundation for that separate and distinct exercise of the different powers of government, which to a certain extent is admitted on all hands to be essential to the preservation of liberty, it is evident that each department should have a will of its own; and consequently should be so constituted that the members of each should have as little agency as possible in the appointment of the members of the others. Were this principle rigorously adhered to, it would require that all the appointments for the supreme executive, legislative, and judiciary magistracies should be drawn from the same fountain of authority, the people, through channels having no communication whatever with one another. Perhaps such a plan of constructing the several departments would be less difficult in practice than it may be in contemplation appear. Some difficulties, however, and some additional expense would attend the execution of it. Some deviations, therefore, from the principle must be admitted. In the constitution of the judiciary department in particular, it might be inexpedient to insist rigorously on the principle; first, because peculiar qualifications being essential in the members, the primary consideration ought to be to select that mode of choice which best secures these qualifications; second, because the permanent tenure by which the appointments are held in that department must soon destroy all sense of dependence on the authority conferring them.

It is equally evident that the members of each department should be as little dependent as possible on those of the others for the emoluments annexed to their offices. Were the executive magistrate, or the judges, not independent of the legislature in this particular, their independence in every other would be merely nominal.

But the great security against a gradual concentration of the several powers in the same department consists in giving to those who administer each department the necessary constitutional means and personal motives to resist encroachments of the others. The provision for defense must in this, as in all other cases, be made commensurate to the danger of attack. Ambition must be made to counteract ambition. The interest of the man must be connected with the constitutional rights of the place. It may be a reflection on human nature that such devices should be necessary to control the abuses of government. But what is government itself but the greatest of all reflections on human nature? If men were angels no government would be necessary. If angels were to govern men, neither external nor internal controls on government would be necessary. In framing a government which is to be administered by men over men, the great difficulty lies in this: you must first enable the government to control the governed; and in the next place oblige it to control itself. A dependence on the people is, no doubt, the primary control on the government; but experience has taught mankind the necessity of auxiliary precautions.

This policy of supplying, by opposite and rival interests, the defect of better motives, might be traced through the whole system of human affairs, private as well as public. We see it particularly displayed in all the subordinate distributions of power, where the constant aim is to divide and arrange the several offices in such a manner as that each may be a check on the other—that the private interest of every individual may be a sentinel over the public rights. These inventions of prudence cannot be less requisite in the distribution of the supreme powers of the State.

But it is not possible to give to each department an equal power of self-defense. In republican government, the legislative authority necessarily predominates. The remedy for this inconveniency is to divide the legislature into different branches; and to render them, by different modes of election and different principles of action, as little connected with each other as the nature of their common functions and their common dependence on the society will admit. It may even be necessary to guard against dangerous encroachments by still further precautions. As the weight of the legislative authority requires that it should be thus divided, the weakness of the executive may require, on the other hand, that it should be fortified. An absolute negative on the legislature appears, at first view, to be the natural defense with which the executive magistrate should be armed. But perhaps it would be neither altogether safe nor alone sufficient. On ordinary occasions it might not be exerted with the requisite firmness, and on extraordinary occasions it might be perfidiously abused. May not this defect of an absolute negative be supplied by some qualified connection between this weaker department and the weaker branch of the stronger department, by which the latter may be led to support the constitutional rights of the former, without being too much detached from the rights of its own department?

If the principles on which these observations are founded be just, as I persuade myself they are, and they be applied as a criterion to the several State constitutions, and to the federal Constitution, it will be found that if the latter does not perfectly correspond with them, the former are infinitely less able to bear such a test.

There are, moreover, two considerations particularly applicable to the federal system of America, which place that system in a very interesting point of view.

First. In a single republic, all the power surrendered by the people is submitted to the administration of a single government; and the usurpations are guarded against by a division of the government into distinct and separate departments. In the compound republic of America, the power surrendered by the people is first divided between two distinct governments, and then the portion allotted to each subdivided among distinct and separate departments. Hence a double security arises to the rights of the people. The different governments will control each other, at the same time that each will be controlled by itself.

Second. It is of great importance in a republic not only to guard the society against the oppression of its rulers, but to guard one part of the society against the injustice of the other part. Different interests necessarily exist in different classes of citizens. If a majority be united by a common interest, the rights of the minority will be insecure. There are but two methods of providing against this evil: the one by creating a will in the community independent of the majority—that is, of the society itself; the other, by comprehending in the society so many separate descriptions of citizens as will render an unjust combination of a majority of the whole very improbable, if not impracticable. The first method prevails in all governments possessing an hereditary or self-appointed authority. This, at best, is but a precarious security; because a power independent of the society may as well espouse the unjust views of the major as the rightful interests of the minor party, and may possibly be turned against both parties. The second method will be exemplified in the federal republic of the United States. Whilst all authority in it will be derived from and dependent on the society, the society itself will be broken into so many parts, interests and classes of citizens, that the rights of individuals, or of the minority, will be in little danger from interested combinations of the majority. In a free government the security for civil rights must be the same as that for religious rights. It consists in the one case in the multiplicity of interests, and in the other in the multiplicity of sects. The degree of security in both cases will depend on the number of interests and sects; and this may be presumed to depend on the extent of country and number of people comprehended under the same government. This view of the subject must particularly recommend a proper federal system to all the sincere and considerate friends of republican government, since it shows that in exact proportion as the territory of the Union may be formed into more circumscribed Confederacies, or States, oppressive combinations of a majority will be facilitated; the best security, under the republican forms, for the rights of every class of citizen, will be diminished; and consequently the stability and independence of some member of the government, the only other security, must be proportionately increased. Justice is the end of government. It is the end of civil society. It ever has been and ever will be pursued until it be obtained, or until liberty be lost in the pursuit. In a society under the forms of which the stronger faction can readily unite and oppress the weaker, anarchy may as truly be said to reign as in a state of nature, where the weaker individual is not secured against the violence of the stronger; and as, in the latter state, even the stronger individuals are prompted, by the uncertainty of their condition, to submit to a government which may protect the weak as well as themselves; so, in the former state, will the more powerful factions or parties be gradually induced, by a like motive, to wish for a government which will protect all parties, the weaker as well as the more powerful. It can be little doubted that if the State of Rhode Island was separated from the Confederacy and left to itself, the insecurity of rights under the popular form of government within such narrow limits would be displayed by such reiterated oppressions of factious majorities that some power altogether independent of the people would soon be called for by the voice of the very factions whose misrule had proved the necessity of it. In the extended republic of the United States, and among the great variety of interests, parties, and sects which it embraces, a coalition of a majority of the whole society could seldom take place on any other principles than those of justice and the general good; whilst there being thus less danger to a minor from the will of a major party, there must be less pretext, also, to provide for the security of the former, by introducing into the government a will not dependent on the latter, or, in other words, a will independent of the society itself. It is no less certain than it is important, notwithstanding the contrary opinions which have been entertained, that the larger the society, provided it lie within a practicable sphere, the more duly capable it will be of self-government. And happily for the republican cause, the practicable sphere may be carried to a very great extent by a judicious modification and mixture of the federal principle.

Glossary

affirmative action Programs designed to ensure that women, minorities, and other traditionally disadvantaged groups have full and equal opportunities in employment, education, and other areas of life.

agency point of view The tendency of bureaucrats to place the interests of their agency ahead of other interests and ahead of the priorities sought by the president or Congress.

agenda setting The power of the media through news coverage to focus the public's attention and concern on particular events, problems, issues, personalities, and so on.

agents of socialization Those agents, such as the family and the media, that have a significant influence on citizens' political socialization.

air wars The fact that modern campaigns are often a battle of opposing televised advertising campaigns.

alienation A feeling of personal powerlessness that includes the notion that government does not care about the opinions of people like oneself.

Anti-Federalists Opponents of the Constitution during the debate over ratification.

apathy A feeling of personal noninterest or unconcern with politics.

appellate jurisdiction The authority of a given court to review cases that have already been tried in lower courts and are appealed to it by the losing party; such a court is called an appeals court or appellate court. (See also **original jurisdiction.**)

authoritarian government A form of government in which leaders, though they admit to no limits on their powers, are effectively limited by other centers of power in the society.

authority The recognized right of an individual or institution to exercise power. (See also **power.**)

autocracy A form of government in which absolute control rests with a single person.

balanced budget When the government's tax revenues for the year are roughly equal to its expenditures.

bill A proposed law (legislative act) within Congress or another legislature. (See also **law.**)

Bill of Rights The first ten amendments to the Constitution. They include such rights as freedom of speech and trial by jury.

bipolar (power structure) A power structure dominated by two powers only, as in the case of the United States and the Soviet Union during the cold war.

block grants Federal grants-in-aid that permit state and local officials to decide how the money will be spent within a general area, such as education or health. (See also **categorical grants.**)

brief A written statement by a party in a court case that details its argument.

budget deficit When the government's expenditures exceed its tax revenues.

budget surplus When the government's tax and other revenues exceed its expenditures.

bureaucracy A system of organization and control based on the principles of hierarchical authority, job specialization, and formalized rules. (See also **formalized rules; hierarchical authority; job specialization.**)

bureaucratic accountability The degree to which bureaucrats are held accountable for the power they exercise.

bureaucratic rule The tendency of large-scale organizations to develop into the bureaucratic form, with the effect that administrators make key policy decisions.

cabinet A group consisting of the heads of the (cabinet) executive departments, who are appointed by the president, subject to confirmation by the Senate. The cabinet was once the main advisory body to the president but no longer plays this role. (See also **cabinet departments.**)

cabinet (executive) departments The major administrative organizations within the federal executive bureaucracy, each of which is headed by a secretary (cabinet officer) and has responsibility for a major function of the federal government, such as defense, agriculture, or justice. (See also **cabinet; independent agencies.**)

candidate-centered politics Election campaigns and other political processes in which candidates, not political parties, have most of the initiative and influence. (See also **party-centered politics.**)

capital-gains tax Tax that individuals pay on money gained from the sale of a capital asset, such as property or stocks.

capitalism An economic system based on the idea that government should interfere with economic transactions as little as possible. Free enterprise and self-reliance are the collective and individual principles that underpin capitalism.

categorical grants Federal grants-in-aid to states and localities that can be used only for designated projects. (See also **block grants.**)

checks and balances The elaborate system of divided spheres of authority provided by the U.S. Constitution as a means of controlling the power of government. The separation of powers among the branches of the national government, federalism, and the different methods of selecting national officers are all part of this system.

citizens' (noneconomic) groups Organized interests formed by individuals drawn together by opportunities to promote a cause in which they believe but that does not provide them significant individual economic benefits. (See also **economic groups; interest group.**)

civic duty The belief of an individual that civic and political participation is a responsibility of citizenship.

civil law Laws governing relations with or between private parties where no criminal act is alleged and where the parties are making conflicting claims or are seeking to establish a legal relationship.

civil liberties The fundamental individual rights of a free society, such as freedom of speech and the right to a jury trial, which in the United States are protected by the Bill of Rights.

civil rights (equal rights) The right of every person to equal protection under the laws and equal access to society's opportunities and public facilities.

civil service system See **merit system.**

clear-and-present-danger test A test devised by the Supreme Court in 1919 to define the limits of free speech in the context of national security. According to the test, government cannot abridge political expression unless it presents a clear and present danger to the nation's security.

clientele groups Special interest groups that benefit directly from the activities of a particular bureaucratic agency and are therefore strong advocates of the agency.

cloture A parliamentary maneuver that, if a three-fifths majority votes for it, limits Senate debate to thirty hours and has the effect of defeating a filibuster. (See also **filibuster.**)

cold war The lengthy period after World War II when the United States and the USSR were not engaged in actual combat (a "hot war") but were nonetheless locked in a state of deep-seated hostility.

collective (public) goods Benefits that are offered by groups (usually citizens' groups) as an incentive for membership but that are nondivisible (e.g., a clean environment) and therefore are available to nonmembers as well as members of the particular group. (See also **free-rider problem; private goods.**)

commerce clause The clause of the Constitution (Article I, Section 8) that empowers the federal government to regulate commerce among the states and with other nations.

common-carrier function The media's function as an open channel through which political leaders can communicate with the public. (See also **partisan**

function; signaling function; watchdog function.)

communism An economic system in which government owns most or all major industries and also takes responsibility for overall management of the economy.

compliance The issue of whether a court's decisions will be respected and obeyed.

concurring opinion A separate opinion written by a Supreme Court justice who votes with the majority in the decision on a case but who disagrees with their reasoning. (See also **dissenting opinion; majority opinion; plurality opinion.**)

confederacy A governmental system in which sovereignty is vested entirely in subnational (state) governments. (See also **federalism; unitary system.**)

conference committees Temporary committees that are formed to bargain over the differences in the House and Senate versions of a bill. The committee's members are usually appointed from the House and Senate standing committees that originally worked on the bill.

constituency The individuals who live within the geographical area represented by an elected official. More narrowly, the body of citizens eligible to vote for a particular representative.

constitution The fundamental law that defines how a government will legitimately operate.

constitutional democracy A government that is democratic in its provisions for majority influence through elections and constitutional in its provisions for minority rights and rule by law.

constitutionalism The idea that there are definable limits on the rightful power of a government over its citizens.

containment A doctrine, developed after World War II, based on the assumptions that the Soviet Union was an aggressor nation and that only a determined United States could block Soviet territorial ambitions.

cooperative federalism The situation in which the national, state, and local levels work together to solve problems.

criminal law Laws governing acts deemed illegal and punishable by government, such as robbery. Government is always a party to a criminal law case; the other party is the individual accused of breaking the law.

de facto discrimination Discrimination on the basis of race, sex, religion, ethnicity, and the like that results from social, economic, and cultural biases and conditions. (See also **de jure discrimination.**)

de jure discrimination Discrimination on the basis of race, sex, religion, ethnicity, and the like that results from a law. (See also **de facto discrimination.**)

decision A vote of the Supreme Court in a particular case that indicates which party the justices side with and by how large a margin.

deficit spending When the government spends more than it collects in taxes and other revenues.

delegates Elected representatives whose obligation is to act in accordance with the expressed wishes of the people whom they represent. (See also **trustees.**)

demand-side economics A form of fiscal policy that emphasizes "demand" (consumer spending). Government can use increased spending or tax cuts to place more money in consumers' hands and thereby increase demand. (See also **fiscal policy; supply-side economics.**)

democracy A form of government in which the people govern, either directly or through elected representatives.

demographic representativeness The idea that the bureaucracy will be more responsive to the public if its employees at all levels are demographically representative of the population as a whole.

denials of power A constitutional means of limiting governmental action by listing those powers that government is expressly prohibited from using.

deregulation The rescinding of excessive government regulations for the purpose of improving economic efficiency.

détente A French word meaning "a relaxing" and used to refer to an era of improved relations between the United States and the Soviet Union that began in the early 1970s.

deterrence policy The idea that nuclear war can be discouraged if each side in a conflict has the capacity to destroy the other with nuclear weapons.

devolution The passing down of authority from the national government to states and localities.

direct primary See **primary election.**

dissenting opinion The opinion of a justice in a Supreme Court case that explains his or her reasons for disagreeing with the majority's decision. (See also **concurring opinion; majority opinion; plurality opinion.**)

dual federalism A doctrine based on the idea that a precise separation of national power and state power is both possible and desirable.

due process clause (of the Fourteenth Amendment) The clause of the Constitution that has been used by the judiciary to apply the Bill of Rights to the actions of state governments.

economic conservatives Those who believe government tries to do too many things that should be left to firms and economic markets. (See also **economic liberals; libertarians; populists; social conservatives; social liberals.**)

economic depression A very severe and sustained economic downturn. Depressions are rare in the United States: the last one was in the 1930s.

economic globalization The increased interdependence of nations' economies. The change is a result of technological, transportation, and communication advances that have enabled firms to deploy their resources across the globe.

economic groups Interest groups that are organized primarily for economic reasons but that engage in political activity in order to seek favorable policies from government. (See also **citizens' groups; interest group.**)

economic liberals Those who believe government should do more to assist people who have difficulty meeting their economic needs on their own. (See also **economic conservatives; libertarians; populists; social conservatives; social liberals.**)

economic recession A moderate but sustained downturn in the economy. Recessions are part of the economy's normal cycle of ups and downs.

economy A system of production and consumption of goods and services that are allocated through exchange among producers and consumers.

effective tax rate The actual percentage of a person's income that is spent to pay taxes.

efficiency An economic principle that holds that firms should fulfill as many of society's needs as possible while using as few of its resources as possible. The greater the output (production) for a given input (for example, an hour of labor), the more efficient the process.

elastic clause See **"necessary and proper" clause.**

Electoral College An unofficial term that refers to the electors who cast the states' electoral votes.

electoral votes The method of voting that is used to choose the U.S. president. Each state has the same number of electoral votes as it has members in Congress (House and Senate combined). By tradition, electoral voting is tied to a state's popular voting; thus, the presidential candidate with the most popular votes overall usually also has the most electoral votes.

elitism The view that the United States is essentially run by a tiny elite (composed of wealthy or well-connected individuals) who control public policy through both direct and indirect means.

entitlement program Any of a number of individual benefit programs, such as social security, that require government to provide a designated benefit to any person who meets the legally defined criteria for eligibility.

enumerated (expressed) powers The seventeen powers granted to the national government under Article I, Section 8 of the Constitution. These powers include taxation and the regulation of commerce as well as the authority to provide for the national defense.

equal-protection clause A clause of the Fourteenth Amendment that forbids any state to deny equal protection of the laws to any individual within its jurisdiction.

equal rights See **civil rights.**

equality The notion that all individuals are equal in their moral worth and are thereby entitled to equal treatment under the law.

equality of opportunity The idea that all individuals should be given an equal chance to succeed on their own.

equality of result The objective of policies intended to reduce or eliminate the effects of discrimination so that members of traditionally disadvantaged groups will have the same benefits of society as do members of advantaged groups.

equity (in relation to economic policy) The situation in which the outcome of an economic transaction is fair to each party. An outcome can usually be considered fair if each party enters into a transaction freely and is not knowingly at a disadvantage.

establishment clause The First Amendment provision that government may not favor one religion over another or favor religion over no religion, and that prohibits Congress from passing laws respecting the establishment of religion.

exclusionary rule The legal principle that government is prohibited from using in trials evidence that was obtained by unconstitutional means (for example, illegal search and seizure).

executive departments See **cabinet departments.**

executive leadership system An approach to managing the bureaucracy that is based on presidential leadership and presidential management tools, such as the president's annual budget proposal. (See also **merit system; patronage system.**)

expressed powers See **enumerated powers.**

externalities Burdens that society incurs when firms fail to pay the full cost of resources used in production. An example of an externality is the pollution that results when corporations dump industrial wastes into lakes and rivers.

factional (minor) party A minor party created when a faction within one of the major parties breaks away to form its own party.

facts (of a court case) The relevant circumstances of a legal dispute or offense as determined by a trial court. The facts of a case are crucial because they help determine which law or laws are applicable in the case.

federalism A governmental system in which authority is divided between two sovereign levels of government: national and regional. (See also **confederacy; unitary system.**)

Federalists Supporters of the Constitution during the debate over ratification.

filibuster A procedural tactic in the U.S. Senate whereby a minority of legislators prevents a bill from coming to a vote by holding the floor and talking until the majority gives in and the bill is withdrawn from consideration. (See also **cloture.**)

fiscal federalism Expenditure of federal funds on programs run in part through states and localities.

fiscal policy A tool of economic management by which government attempts to maintain a stable economy through its taxing and spending decisions. (See also **demand-side economics; monetary policy; supply-side economics.**)

formalized rules A basic principle of bureaucracy that refers to the standardized procedures and established regulations by which a bureaucracy conducts its operations. (See also **bureaucracy.**)

framing The process of selecting certain aspects of reality and making them the most salient part of the communication, thereby conveying a particular interpretation of a situation.

free-exercise clause A First Amendment provision that prohibits the government from interfering with the practice of religion or prohibiting the free exercise of religion.

free-rider problem The situation in which the benefits offered by a group to its members are also available to nonmembers. The incentive to join the group and to promote its cause is reduced because nonmembers (free riders) receive the benefits (e.g., a cleaner environment) without having to pay any of the group's costs. (See also **collective goods.**)

free-trade position The view that the long-term economic interests of all countries are advanced when tariffs and other trade barriers are kept to a minimum. (See also **protectionism.**)

freedom of expression Americans' freedom to communicate their views, the foundation of which is the First Amendment rights of freedom of conscience, speech, press, assembly, and petition.

gender gap The tendency of women and men to differ in their political attitudes and voting preferences.

gerrymandering The process by which the party in power draws election district boundaries in a way that advantages its candidates.

government corporations Bodies, such as the U.S. Postal Service and Amtrak, that are similar to private corporations in that they charge for their services, but different in that they receive federal funding to help defray expenses. Their directors are appointed by the president with Senate approval.

graduated personal income tax A tax on personal income in which the tax rate increases as income increases; in other words, the tax rate is higher for higher income levels.

grants-in-aid Federal cash payments to states and localities for programs they administer.

grants of power The method of limiting the U.S. government by confining its scope of authority to those powers expressly granted in the Constitution.

grassroots lobbying A form of lobbying designed to persuade officials that a group's policy position has strong constituent support.

grassroots party A political party organized at the level of the voters and dependent on their support for its strength.

Great Compromise The agreement of the constitutional convention to create a two-chamber Congress with the House apportioned by population and the Senate apportioned equally by state.

hard money Campaign funds given directly to candidates to spend as they choose.

hierarchical authority A basic principle of bureaucracy that refers to the chain of command within an organization whereby officials and units have control over those below them. (See also **bureaucracy.**)

hired guns The professional consultants who run campaigns for high office.

honeymoon period The president's first months in office, a time when Congress, the press, and the public are more inclined than usual to support presidential initiatives.

ideology A consistent pattern of opinion on particular issues that stems from a core belief or set of beliefs.

ideological (minor) party A minor party characterized by its ideological commitment to a broad and noncentrist philosophical position.

imminent lawless action test A legal test that says government cannot lawfully suppress advocacy that promotes lawless action unless such advocacy is aimed at producing, and is likely to produce, imminent lawless action.

implied powers The federal government's constitutional authority (through the "necessary and proper" clause) to take action that is not expressly authorized by the Constitution but that supports actions that are so authorized. (See also **"necessary and proper" clause.**)

in-kind benefit A government benefit that is a cash equivalent, such as food stamps or rent vouchers. This form of benefit ensures that recipients will use public assistance in a specified way.

inalienable (natural) rights Those rights that persons theoretically possessed in the state of nature, prior to the formation of governments. These rights, including those of life, liberty, and property, are considered inherent and as such are inalienable. Since government is established by people, government has the responsibility to preserve these rights.

independent agencies Bureaucratic agencies that are similar to cabinet departments but usually have a narrower area of responsibility. Each such agency is headed by a presidential appointee who is not a cabinet member. An example is the National Aeronautics and Space Administration. (See also **cabinet departments.**)

individual goods See **private goods.**

individualism The idea that people should take the initiative, be self-sufficient, and accumulate the material advantages necessary for their well-being.

inflation A general increase in the average level of prices of goods and services.

initiative The process by which citizens can place legislative measures on the ballot through signature petitions; if the measure receives a majority vote, it becomes law.

inside lobbying Direct communication between organized interests and policymakers, which is based on the assumed value of close ("inside") contacts with policymakers.

interest group A set of individuals who are organized to promote a shared political interest. (See also **citizens' groups; economic groups.**)

interest-group liberalism The tendency of public officials to support the policy demands of self-interested groups (as opposed to judging policy demands according to whether they serve a larger conception of "the public interest").

internationalist A person who holds the view that the country should involve itself deeply in world affairs. (See also **isolationist.**)

iron triangle A small and informal but relatively stable group of well-positioned legislators, executives, and lobbyists who seek to promote policies beneficial to a particular interest. (See also **issue network.**)

isolationist A person who holds the view that the country should deliberately avoid a large role in world affairs and, instead, concentrate on domestic concerns. (See also **internationalist.**)

issue network An informal network of public officials and lobbyists who have a common interest and expertise in a given area and who are brought together temporarily by a proposed policy in that area. (See also **iron triangle.**)

job specialization A basic principle of bureaucracy that holds that the responsibilities of each job position should be explicitly defined and that a precise division of labor within the organization should be maintained. (See also **bureaucracy.**)

judicial activism The doctrine that the courts should develop new legal principles when judges see a compelling need, even if this action places them in conflict with precedent or the policy decisions of elected officials. (See also **judicial restraint.**)

judicial conference A closed meeting of the justices of the U.S. Supreme Court to discuss and vote on the cases before them; the justices are not supposed to discuss conference proceedings with outsiders.

judicial restraint The doctrine that the judiciary should broadly defer to precedent and the judgment of legislatures. The doctrine claims that the job of judges is to work within the confines of laws set down by tradition and lawmaking majorities. (See also **judicial activism.**)

judicial review The power of courts to decide whether a governmental institution has acted within its constitutional powers and, if not, to declare its action null and void.

jurisdiction (of a congressional committee) The policy area in which a particular congressional committee is authorized to act.

jurisdiction (of a court) A given court's authority to hear cases of a particular kind. Jurisdiction may be original or appellate.

laissez-faire doctrine A classic economic philosophy that holds that owners of businesses should be allowed to make their own production and distribution decisions without government regulation or control.

large-state plan See **Virginia Plan.**

law (as enacted by Congress) A legislative proposal, or bill, that is passed by both the House and Senate and is either signed or not vetoed by the president. (See also **bill.**)

lawmaking function The authority (of a legislature) to make the laws necessary to carry out the government's powers. (See also **oversight function; representation function.**)

laws (of a court case) The constitutional provisions, legislative statutes, or judicial precedents that apply to a court case.

legitimacy (of judicial power) The issue of the proper limits of judicial authority in a political system based in part on the principle of majority rule.

libel Publication of material that falsely damages a person's reputation.

libertarians Those who believe government tries to do too many things that should be left to firms and individuals and who oppose government as an instrument of traditional values. (See also **economic conservatives; social conservatives; economic liberals; social liberals; populists.**)

liberty The principle that individuals should be free to act and think as they choose, provided they do not infringe unreasonably on the rights and freedoms of others.

limited government A government that is subject to strict limits on its lawful uses of powers and hence on its ability to deprive people of their liberty.

living constitution theory A method of interpreting the Constitution that emphasizes the principles it embodies and their application to changing circumstances and needs.

lobbying The process by which interest-group members or lobbyists attempt to influence public policy through contacts with public officials.

logrolling The trading of votes between legislators so that each gets what he or she most wants.

majoritarianism The idea that the majority prevails not only in elections but also in determining policy.

majority opinion A Supreme Court opinion that results when a majority of the justices is in agreement on the legal basis of the decision. (See also **concurring opinion; dissenting opinion; plurality opinion.**)

means test The requirement that applicants for public assistance must demonstrate they are poor in order to be eligible for the assistance. (See also **public assistance.**)

merit (civil service) system An approach to managing the bureaucracy whereby people are appointed to government positions on the basis of either competitive examinations or special qualifications, such as professional training. (See also **executive leadership system; patronage system.**)

military-industrial complex The three components (the military establishment, the industries that manufacture weapons, and the members of Congress from states and districts that depend heavily on the arms industry) that mutually benefit from a high level of defense spending.

momentum (in campaigns) A strong showing by a candidate in early presidential nominating contests, which leads to a buildup of public support for the candidate.

monetary policy A tool of economic management, available to government, based on manipulation of the amount of money in circulation. (See also **fiscal policy.**)

money chase U.S. campaigns are very expensive and candidates must spend a great amount of time raising funds in order to compete successfully.

multilateralism The situation in which nations act together in response to problems and crises.

multinational corporations Business firms with major operations in more than one country.

multiparty system A system in which three or more political parties have the capacity to gain control of government separately or in coalition.

national debt The total cumulative amount that the U.S. government owes to creditors.

natural rights See **inalienable rights.**

"necessary and proper" clause (elastic clause) The authority granted Congress in Article I, Section 8 of the Constitution "to make all laws which shall be necessary and proper" for the implementation of its enumerated powers. (See also **implied powers.**)

negative government The philosophical belief that government governs best by staying out of people's lives, thus giving individuals as much freedom as possible to determine their own pursuits. (See also **positive government.**)

neutral competence The administrative objective of a merit-based bureaucracy. Such a bureaucracy should be "competent" in the sense that its employees are hired and retained on the basis of their expertise and "neutral" in the sense that it operates by objective standards rather than partisan ones.

New Jersey (small-state) Plan A constitutional proposal for a strengthened Congress but one in which each state would have a single vote, thus granting a small state the same legislative power as a larger state.

news The news media's version of reality, usually with an emphasis on timely, dramatic, and compelling events and developments.

news media See **press.**

nomination The designation of a particular individual to run as a political party's candidate (its "nominee") in the general election.

noneconomic groups See **citizens' groups.**

North-South Compromise The agreement over economic and slavery issues that enabled northern and southern states to settle differences that threatened to defeat the effort to draft a new constitution.

objective journalism A model of news reporting that is based on the communication of "facts" rather than opinions and that is "fair" in that it presents all sides of partisan debate. (See also **partisan press.**)

oligarchy Government in which control rests with a few persons.

open party caucuses Meetings at which a party's candidates for nomination are voted on and that are open to all the party's rank-and-file voters who want to attend.

open-seat election An election in which there is no incumbent in the race.

opinion (of a court) A court's written explanation of its decision, which serves to inform others of the legal basis for the decision. Supreme Court opinions are expected to guide the decisions of other courts. (See also **concurring opinion; dissenting opinion; majority opinion; plurality opinion.**)

original jurisdiction The authority of a given court to be the first court to hear a case. (See also **appellate jurisdiction.**)

originalism theory A method of interpreting the Constitution that emphasizes the meaning of its words at the time they were written.

outside lobbying A form of lobbying in which an interest group seeks to use public pressure as a means of influencing officials.

oversight function A supervisory activity of Congress that centers on its constitutional responsibility to see that the executive carries out the laws faithfully and spends appropriations properly. (See also **lawmaking function; representation function.**)

packaging (of a candidate) In modern campaigning, the process of recasting a candidate's record into an appealing image.

partisan function (of the press) Efforts by media actors to influence public response to a particular party, leader, issue, or viewpoint.

partisan press Newspapers and other communication media that openly support a political party and whose news in significant part follows the party line. (See also **objective journalism.**)

party caucus A group that consists of a party's members in the House or Senate and that serves to elect the party's leadership, set policy goals, and determine party strategy.

party-centered politics Election campaigns and other political processes in which political parties, not individual candidates, hold most of the initiative and influence. (See also **candidate-centered politics.**)

party coalition The groups and interests that support a political party.

party competition A process in which conflict over society's goals is transformed by political parties into electoral competition in which the winner gains the power to govern.

party discipline The willingness of a party's House or Senate members to act together as a cohesive group and thus exert collective control over legislative action.

party identification The personal sense of loyalty that an individual may feel toward a particular political party. (See also **party realignment.**)

party leaders Members of the House and Senate who are chosen by the Democratic or Republican caucus in each chamber to represent the party's interests in that chamber and who give some central direction to the chamber's deliberations.

party organizations The party organizational units at national, state, and local levels; their influence has decreased over time because of many factors. (See also **candidate-centered politics; party-centered politics; primary election.**)

party realignment An election or set of elections in which the electorate responds strongly to an extraordinarily powerful issue that has disrupted the established political order. A realignment has a lasting impact on public policy, popular support for the parties, and the composition of the party coalitions. (See also **party identification.**)

patronage system An approach to managing the bureaucracy whereby people are appointed to important government positions as a reward for political services they have rendered and because of their partisan loyalty. (See also **executive leadership system; merit system; spoils system.**)

pluralism A theory of American politics that holds that society's interests are substantially represented through the activities of groups.

plurality opinion A court opinion that results when a majority of justices agree on a decision in a case but do not agree on the legal basis for the decision. In this instance, the legal position held by most of the justices on the winning side is called a plurality opinion. (See also **concurring opinion; dissenting opinion; majority opinion.**)

policy Generally, any broad course of governmental action; more narrowly, a specific government program or initiative.

policy formation The stage of the policy process where a policy is formulated for dealing with a policy problem.

policy implementation (in reference to bureaucracy) The primary function of the bureaucracy; it refers to the process of carrying out the authoritative decisions of Congress, the president, and the courts.

policy implementation (in reference to policy process) The stage of the policy process where a policy is put into effect and evaluated.

political action committee (PAC) The organization through which an interest group raises and distributes funds for election purposes. By law, the funds must be raised through voluntary contributions.

political culture The characteristic and deep-seated beliefs of a particular people.

political movements See **social movements.**

political participation Involvement in activities intended to influence public policy and leadership, such as voting, joining political parties and interest groups, writing to elected officials, demonstrating for political causes, and giving money to political candidates.

political party An ongoing coalition of interests joined together to try to get their candidates for public office elected under a common label.

political socialization The learning process by which people acquire their political opinions, beliefs, and values.

political system The various components of American government. The parts are separate, but they connect with each other, affecting how each performs.

political thinking The careful gathering and sifting of information in the process of forming a knowledgeable view about a political issue.

politics The process through which society settles its conflicts and decides the policies by which it will be governed.

population In a public opinion poll, the people (for example, the citizens of a nation) whose opinions are being estimated through interviews with a sample of these people.

populists Those who believe government should do more to solve the nation's problems and who look to it to uphold traditional values. (See also **economic conservatives; social conservatives; economic liberals; social liberals; libertarians.**)

pork-barrel projects Legislative acts whose tangible benefits are targeted at a particular legislator's constituency.

positive government The philosophical belief that government intervention is necessary in order to enhance personal liberty when individuals are buffeted by economic and social forces beyond their control. (See also **negative government.**)

poverty line As defined by the federal government, the annual cost of a thrifty food budget for an urban family of four, multiplied by three to allow also for the cost of housing, clothes, and other expenses. Families below the poverty line are considered poor and are eligible for certain forms of public assistance.

power The ability of persons or institutions to control policy. (See also **authority.**)

precedent A judicial decision in a given case that serves as a rule of thumb for settling subsequent cases of a similar nature; courts are generally expected to follow precedent.

preemptive war doctrine The idea, espoused by president George W. Bush, that the United States could attack a potentially threatening nation even if the threat had not yet reached a serious and immediate level.

presidential approval ratings A measure of the degree to which the public approves or disapproves of the president's performance in office.

presidential commissions Organizations within the bureaucracy that are headed by commissioners appointed by the president. An example is the Commission on Civil Rights.

press (news media) Those print and broadcast organizations that are in the news-reporting business.

primary election (direct primary) A form of election in which voters choose a party's nominees for public office. In most states, eligibility to vote in a primary election is limited to voters who designated themselves as party members when they registered to vote. A primary is direct when it results directly in the choice of a nominee; it is indirect (as in the case of presidential primaries) when it results in the selection of delegates who then choose the nominee.

prior restraint Government prohibition of speech or publication before the fact, which is presumed by the courts to be unconstitutional unless the justification for it is overwhelming.

private (individual) goods Benefits that a group (most often an economic group) can grant directly and exclusively to the individual members of the group. (See also **collective goods.**)

probability sample A sample for a poll in which each individual in the population has a known probability of being selected randomly for inclusion in the sample. (See also **public opinion poll.**)

problem recognition The stage of the policy process where conditions in society become recognized as a policy problem.

procedural due process The constitutional requirement that government must follow proper legal procedures before a person can be legitimately punished for an alleged offense.

procedural law Laws governing the legal process that define proper courses of action by government or private parties.

proportional representation A form of representation in which seats in the legislature are allocated proportionally according to each political party's share of the popular vote. This system enables smaller parties to compete successfully for seats. (See also **single-member districts.**)

prospective voting A form of electoral judgment in which voters choose the candidate whose policy promises most closely match their own preferences. (See also **retrospective voting.**)

protectionism The view that the immediate interests of domestic producers should have a higher priority (through, for example, protective tariffs) than should free trade between nations. (See also **free-trade position.**)

public assistance Social welfare programs funded through general tax revenues and available only to the financially needy. Eligibility for such a program is established by a means test. (See also **means test; social insurance.**)

public goods See **collective goods.**

public opinion The politically relevant opinions held by ordinary citizens that they express openly.

public opinion poll A device for measuring public opinion whereby a relatively small number of individuals (the sample) is interviewed for the purpose of estimating the opinions of a whole community (the population). (See also **probability sample.**)

public policy A decision of government to pursue a course of action designed to produce an intended outcome.

public policy process The political interactions that lead to the emergence and resolution of public policy issues.

purposive incentive An incentive to group participation based on the cause (purpose) that the group seeks to promote.

realignment See **party realignment.**

reapportionment The reallocation of House seats among states after each census as a result of population changes.

reasonable-basis test A test applied by courts to laws that treat individuals unequally. Such a law may be deemed constitutional if its purpose is held to be "reasonably" related to a legitimate government interest.

recall The process by which citizens can petition for the removal from office of an elected official before the scheduled completion of his or her term.

redistricting The process of altering election districts in order to make them as nearly equal in population as possible. Redistricting takes place every ten years, after each population census.

referendum The process through which the legislature may submit proposals to the voters for approval or rejection.

reform (minor) party A minor party that bases its appeal on the claim that the major parties are having a corrupting influence on government and policy.

registration The practice of placing citizens' names on an official list of voters before they are eligible to exercise their right to vote.

regulation Government restrictions on the economic practices of private firms.

regulatory agencies Administrative units, such as the Federal Communications Commission and the Environmental Protection Agency, that have responsibility for monitoring and regulating ongoing economic activities.

representation function The responsibility of a legislature to represent various interests in society. (See also **lawmaking function; oversight function.**)

representative democracy A system in which the people participate in the decision-making process of government not directly but indirectly, through the election of officials to represent their interests.

republic Historically, the form of government in which representative officials met to decide on policy issues. These representatives were expected to serve the public interest but were not subject to the people's immediate control. Today, the term *republic* is used interchangeably with *democracy.*

reserved powers The powers granted to the states under the Tenth Amendment to the Constitution.

retrospective voting A form of electoral judgment in which voters support the incumbent candidate or party when their policies are judged to have succeeded and oppose the candidate or party when their policies are judged to have failed. (See also **prospective voting.**)

rider An amendment to a bill that deals with an issue unrelated to the content of the bill. Riders are permitted in the Senate but not in the House.

right of privacy A right implied by the freedoms in the Bill of Rights that grants individuals a degree of personal privacy upon which government cannot lawfully intrude. The right gives individuals a level of free choice in areas such as reproduction and intimate relations.

sample In a public opinion poll, the relatively small number of individuals interviewed for the purpose of estimating the opinions of an entire population. (See also **public opinion poll.**)

sampling error A measure of the accuracy of a public opinion poll. It is mainly a function of sample size and is usually expressed in percentage terms. (See also **probability sample.**)

selective incorporation The process by which certain of the rights (for example, freedom of speech) contained in the Bill of Rights become applicable through the Fourteenth Amendment to actions by the state governments.

self-government The principle that the people are the ultimate source and proper beneficiary of governing authority; in practice, a government based on majority rule.

senatorial courtesy The tradition that a U.S. senator from the state in which a federal judicial vacancy has arisen should have a say in the president's nomination of the new judge if the senator is of the same party as the president.

seniority A member of Congress's consecutive years of service on a particular committee.

separated institutions sharing power The principle that, as a way to limit government, its powers should be divided among separate branches, each of which also shares in the power of the others as a means of checking and balancing them. The result is that no one branch can exercise power decisively without the support or acquiescence of the others.

separation of powers The division of the powers of government among separate institutions or branches.

service relationship The situation in which party organizations assist candidates for office but have no power to require them to accept or campaign on the party's main policy positions.

service strategy Use of personal staff by members of Congress to perform services for constituents in order to gain their support in future elections.

signaling (signaler) function The accepted responsibility of the media to alert the public to important developments as soon as possible after they happen or are discovered. (See also **common-carrier function; partisan function; watchdog function.**)

single-issue (minor) party A minor party formed around a single issue of overriding interest to its followers.

single-issue politics The situation in which separate groups are organized around nearly every conceivable policy issue and press their demands and influence to the utmost.

single-member districts The form of representation in which only the candidate who gets the most votes in a district wins office. (See also **proportional representation.**)

slander Spoken words that falsely damage a person's reputation.

small-state plan See **New Jersey Plan.**

social capital The sum of face-to-face interactions among citizens in a society.

social conservatives Those who believe government power should be used to uphold traditional values. (See also **social liberals; economic conservatives; economic liberals; libertarians; populists.**)

social contract A voluntary agreement by individuals to form a government, which is then obligated to work within the confines of that agreement.

social insurance Social welfare programs based on the "insurance" concept, so that individuals must pay into the program to be eligible to receive funds from it. An example is social security for retired people. (See also **public assistance.**)

social liberals Those who believe it is not government's role to buttress traditional values at the expense of unconventional or new values. (See also **social conservatives; economic conservatives; economic liberals; libertarians; populists.**)

social (political) movements Active and sustained efforts to achieve social and political change by groups of people who feel that government has not been properly responsive to their concerns.

socialism An economic system in which government owns and controls many of the major industries.

soft money Campaign contributions that are not subject to legal limits and are given to parties rather than directly to candidates.

solicitor general The high-ranking Justice Department official who serves as the government's lawyer in Supreme Court cases.

sovereignty The ultimate authority to govern within a certain geographical area.

split ticket The pattern of voting in which the individual voter in a given election casts a ballot for one or more candidates of each major party.

spoils system The practice of granting public office to individuals in return for political favors they have rendered. (See also **patronage system.**)

standing committees Permanent congressional committees with responsibility for a particular area of public policy. An example is the Senate Foreign Relations Committee.

stewardship theory A theory that argues for a strong, assertive presidential role, with presidential authority limited only at points specifically prohibited by law. (See also **Whig theory.**)

strict-scrutiny test A test applied by courts to laws that attempt a racial or ethnic classification. In effect, the strict-scrutiny test eliminates race or ethnicity as legal classification when it places minority group members at a disadvantage. (See also **suspect classifications.**)

suffrage The right to vote.

sunset law A law containing a provision that fixes a date on which a program will end unless the program's life is extended by Congress.

supply-side economics A form of fiscal policy that emphasizes "supply" (production). An example of supply-side economics would be a tax cut for business. (See also **demand-side economics; fiscal policy.**)

supremacy clause Article VI of the Constitution, which makes national law supreme over state law when the national government is acting within its constitutional limits.

suspect classifications Legal classifications, such as race and national origin, that have invidious discrimination as their purpose and are therefore unconstitutional. (See also **strict-scrutiny test.**)

symbolic speech Action (for example, the waving or burning of a flag) for the purpose of expressing a political opinion.

totalitarian government A form of government in which the leaders claim complete dominance of all individuals and institutions.

transfer payment A government benefit that is given directly to an individual, as in the case of social security payments to a retiree.

trustees Elected representatives whose obligation is to act in accordance with their own consciences as to what policies are in the best interests of the public. (See also **delegates.**)

two-party system A system in which only two political parties have a real chance of acquiring control of the government.

tyranny of the majority The potential of a majority to monopolize power for its own gain and to the detriment of minority rights and interests.

unilateralism The situation in which one nation takes action against another state or states.

unipolar (power structure) A power structure dominated by a single powerful actor, as in the case of the United States after the collapse of the Soviet Union.

unitary system A governmental system in which the national government alone has sovereign (ultimate) authority. (See also **confederacy; federalism.**)

unit rule The rule that grants all of a state's electoral votes to the candidate who receives most of the popular votes in the state.

veto The president's rejection of a bill, thereby keeping it from becoming law unless Congress overrides the veto.

Virginia (large-state) Plan A constitutional proposal for a strong Congress with two chambers, both of which would be based on numerical representation, thus granting more power to the larger states.

voter turnout The proportion of persons of voting age who actually vote in a given election.

watchdog function The accepted responsibility of the media to protect the public from deceitful, careless, incompetent, and corrupt officials by standing ready to expose any official who violates accepted legal, ethical, or performance standards. (See also **common-carrier function; partisan function; signaler function.**)

Whig theory A theory that prevailed in the nineteenth century and held that the presidency was a limited or restrained office whose occupant was confined to expressly granted constitutional authority. (See also **stewardship theory.**)

whistle-blowing An internal check on the bureaucracy whereby individual bureaucrats report instances of mismanagement that they observe.

writ of certiorari Permission granted by a higher court to allow a losing party in a legal case to bring the case before it for a ruling; when such a writ is requested of the U.S. Supreme Court, four of the Court's nine justices must agree to accept the case before it is granted certiorari.

Notes

Chapter One

[1]Alexis de Tocqueville, *Democracy in America (1835–1840)*, eds. J. P. Mayer and A. P. Kerr (Garden City, N.Y.: Doubleday/ Anchor, 1969), 640.

[2]See John Harmon McElroy, *American Beliefs: What Keeps a Big Country and a Diverse People United* (Chicago: I. R. Dee, 1999); but see Michael B. Katz and Mark J. Stern, *One Nation Divisible: What America Was and What It's Becoming* (New York: Russell Sage Foundation, 2006).

[3]Clinton Rossiter, *Conservativism in America* (New York: Vintage, 1962), 67; see also Robert A. Ferguson, *Reading the Early Republic* (Cambridge, Mass.: Harvard University Press, 2004).

[4]Tocqueville, *Democracy in America*, 310.

[5]James Bryce, *The American Commonwealth*, vol. 2 (New York: Macmillan, 1960), 247–54. First published in 1900.

[6]See Michael Foley, *American Credo: The Place of Ideas in American Politics* (New York: Oxford University Press, 2007).

[7]Paul Gagnon, "Why Study History?" *Atlantic Monthly*, November 1988, 47.

[8]Robert Middlekauff, *The Glorious Cause: The American Revolution, 1763–1789* (New York: Oxford University Press, 2007).

[9]Louis Hartz, *The Liberal Tradition in America* (New York: Harcourt, Brace, 1953), 12; see also Jeffrey Stout, *Democracy and Tradition* (Princeton, N.J.: Princeton University Press, 2004).

[10]James Bryce, *The American Commonwealth*, vol. 2 (Indianapolis, Ind.: Liberty Fund, 1995), 1419.

[11]See Seymour Martin Lipset, *American Exceptionalism: A Double-Edged Sword* (New York: Norton, 1996); Claude Lévi-Strauss, *Structural Anthropology* (Chicago: University of Chicago Press, 1983); Clifford Geertz, *Myth, Symbol, and Culture* (New York: Norton, 1974).

[12]U.S. Census Bureau data, 2006.

[13]Quoted in Ralph Volney Harlow, *The Growth of the United States*, vol. 2 (New York: Henry Holt, 1943), 497.

[14]For a substantial look at Lincoln's positions on slavery, see George M. Fredrickson, *Big Enough to Be Inconsistent: Abraham Lincoln Confronts Slavery and Race* (Cambridge, Mass: Harvard University Press, 2008).

[15]Theodore H. White, *America in Search of Itself: The Making of the President, 1956–1980* (New York: Harper & Row, 1982).

[16]Harold D. Lasswell, *Politics: Who Gets What, When, How* (New York: McGraw-Hill, 1938).

[17]See Charles H. McIlwain, *Constitutionalism: Ancient and Modern* (Ithaca, N.Y.: Cornell University Press, 1983).

[18]Russell Hardin, *Liberalism, Constitutionalism, and Democracy* (New York: Oxford University Press, 1999).

[19]Harold D. Lasswell and Abraham Kaplan, *Power and Society* (New Haven, Conn.: Yale University Press, 1950), 75–77.

[20]Benjamin I. Page and Robert Shapiro, "Effects of Public Opinion on Policy," *American Political Science Review* 77 (March 1983): 178; see also Lawrence R. Jacobs and Robert Shapiro, *Politicians Don't Pander* (Chicago: University of Chicago Press, 2000).

[21]See Robert Dahl, *On Democracy* (New Haven, Conn.: Yale University Press, 2000).

[22]C. Wright Mills, *The Power Elite* (New York: Oxford University Press, 1965).

[23]G. William Domhoff, *Who Rules America? Power and Politics*, 5th ed. (New York, McGraw-Hill, 2005).

[24]See, for example, Dahl, *On Democracy*.

[25]See H. H. Gerth and C. Wright Mills, eds., *From Max Weber: Essays in Sociology* (New York: Oxford University Press, 1958).

[26]Roberto Michels, *Political Parties* (New York: Collier Books, 1962). First published in 1911.

[27]David Easton, *The Political System* (New York: Knopf, 1965), 97.
[28]E. E. Schattschneider, *Two Hundred Million Americans in Search of a Government* (New York: Holt, Rinehart &Winston, 1969), 42.

Chapter Two

[1]Quoted in Charles S. Hyneman, "Republican Government in America," in George J. Graham Jr. and Scarlett G. Graham, eds., *Founding Principles of American Government*, rev. ed. (Chatham, N.J.: Chatham House, 1984), 19.
[2]See Russell Hardin, *Liberalism, Constitutionalism, and Democracy* (New York: Oxford University Press, 1999); A. John Simmons, *The Lockean Theory of Rights* (Princeton, N.J.: Princeton University Press, 1994).
[3]George Bancroft, *History of the Formation of the Constitution of the United States of America*, 3d ed., vol. 1 (New York: D. Appleton, 1883), 166.
[4]Quoted in "The Constitution and Slavery," Digital History Website, December 1, 2003.
[5]Gaillard Hunt, ed., *The Writings of James Madison* (New York: Putnam, 1904), 274; see also Garret Ward Sheldon, *The Political Philosophy of James Madison* (Baltimore: Johns Hopkins University Press, 2000).
[6]See Vincent Ostrom, *The Political Theory of a Compound Republic: Designing the American Experiment* (Lanham, Md.: Lexington Books, 2007).
[7]See *Federalist* Nos. 47 and 48.
[8]Richard Neustadt, *Presidential Power* (New York: Macmillan, 1986), 33.
[9]Henry J. Abraham, *The Judicial Process*, 6th ed. (New York: Oxford University Press, 1993), 320–22.
[10]*Marbury v. Madison*, 1 Cranch 137 (1803).
[11]Martin Diamond, *The Founding of the Democratic Republic* (Itasca, Ill.: Peacock, 1981), 62–71.
[12]*Federalist* No. 10.
[13]Leslie F. Goldstein, "Judicial Review and Democratic Theory: Guardian Democracy vs. Representative Democracy," *Western Political Quarterly* 40 (1987): 391–412.
[14]Benjamin Ginsberg, *The Consequences of Consent* (New York: Random House, 1982), 22.
[15]Robert Dahl, *Pluralist Democracy in the United States* (Chicago: Rand McNally, 1967), 92.
[16]This interpretation is taken from Walter Lippmann, *Public Opinion* (New York: Free Press, 1965), 178–79.
[17]Michael McGeer, *A Fierce Discontent: The Rise and Fall of the Progressive Movement in America, 1870–1920* (New York: Free Press, 2005).
[18]Charles S. Beard, *An Economic Interpretation of the Constitution* (New York: Macmillan, 1941). First published in 1913.
[19]See Randall G. Holcombe, *From Liberty to Democracy* (Ann Arbor: University of Michigan Press, 2002).

Chapter Three

[1]Woodrow Wilson, *Constitutional Government in the United States* (New York: Columbia University Press, 1908), 173.
[2]"NCSL Task Force on No Child Left Behind Report," National Conference of State Legislatures, Denver, Colorado, February 23, 2005; for a broader perspective, see Patrick J. Mcquinn, *No Child Left Behind and the Transformation of Federal Education Policy, 1965–2005* (Lawrence: University Press of Kansas, 2006).
[3]See Samuel Beer, *To Make a Nation: The Rediscovery of American Federalism* (Cambridge, Mass.: Belknap Press of Harvard University, 1993).
[4]*Federalist* No. 2; for the Anti-Federalist view, see Saul Cornell, *The Other Founders* (Chapel Hill: University of North Carolina Press, 1999).
[5]*McCulloch v. Maryland*, 4 Wheaton 316 (1819).
[6]*Gibbons v. Ogden*, 22 Wheaton 1 (1824).
[7]Oliver Wendell Holmes Jr., *Collected Legal Papers* (New York: Harcourt, Brace, 1920), 295–96.
[8]See John C. Calhoun, *The Works of John C. Calhoun* (New York: Russell & Russell, 1968).
[9]*Dred Scott v. Sanford*, 19 Howard 393 (1857).
[10]*U.S. v. Cruikshank*, 92 U.S. 452 (1876).
[11]*Slaughter-House Cases*, 16 Wallace 36 (1873); *Civil Rights Cases*, 109 U.S. 3 (1883).
[12]*Plessy v. Ferguson*, 163 U.S. 537 (1896).

[13]*Santa Clara County v. Southern Pacific Railroad Co.*, 118 U.S. 394 (1886).
[14]*U.S. v. E. C. Knight Co.*, 156 U.S. 1 (1895).
[15]*Hammer v. Dagenhart*, 247 U.S. 251 (1918).
[16]*Lochner v. New York*, 198 U.S. 25 (1905).
[17]Alfred H. Kelly, Winifred A. Harbison, and Herman Belz, *The American Constitution*, 7th ed. (New York: Norton, 1991), 529; but see also Kimberley Johnson, *Governing the American State: Congress and the New Federalism, 1877–1929* (Princeton, N.J.: Princeton University Press, 2006).
[18]James E. Anderson, *The Emergence of the Modern Regulatory State* (Washington, D.C.: Public Affairs Press, 1962), 2–3.
[19]*Schechter Poultry Co. v. United States*, 295 U.S. 495 (1935).
[20]*NLRB v. Jones and Laughlin Steel*, 301 U.S. 1 (1937).
[21]*American Power and Light v. Securities and Exchange Commission*, 329 U.S. 90 (1946).
[22]Louis Fisher, *American Constitutional Law*, 6th ed. (Durham, N.C.: Carolina Academic Press, 2005), 390.
[23]*North American Company v. Securities and Exchange Commission*, 327 U.S. 686 (1946).
[24]*Brown v. Board of Education*, 347 U.S. 483 (1954).
[25]See Thomas Anton, *American Federalism and Public Policy* (Philadelphia: Temple University Press, 1989).
[26]Morton Grodzins, *The American System: A New View of Government in the United States* (Chicago: Rand McNally, 1966).
[27]Rosella Levaggi, *Fiscal Federalism and Grants-in-Aid* (Brookfield, Vt.: Avebury, 1991).
[28]Timothy J. Conlan, *From New Federalism to Devolution* (Washington, D.C.: Brookings Institution, 1998).
[29]*Garcia v. San Antonio Authority*, 469 U.S. 528 (1985).
[30]See Tinsley E. Yarbrough, *The Rehnquist Court and the Constitution* (New York: Oxford University Press, 2000); David L. Hudson, *The Rehnquist Court: Understanding Its Impact and Legacy* (Westport, CT.: onn Praeger, 2006).
[31]*United States v. Lopez*, 514 U.S. 549 (1995).
[32]*Printz v. United States*, 521 U.S. 98 (1997).
[33]*Kimel v. Florida Board of Regents*, 528 U.S. 62 (2000).
[34]*Board of Trustees of the University of Alabama v. Garrett*, 531 U.S. 356 (2002).
[35]*Gonzales v. Raich*, No. 03-1454 (2005).
[36]Patrick M. Garry, *An Entrenched Legacy: How the New Deal Constitutional Revolution Continues to Shape the Role of the Supreme Court* (State College: Pennsylvania State University Press, 2008).
[37]Andrew W. Dobelstein, *Politics, Economics, and Public Welfare* (Englewood Cliffs, N.J.: Prentice-Hall, 1980), 5.
[38]Lloyd A. Free and Hadley Cantril, *The Political Beliefs of Americans* (New York: Simon & Schuster, 1968), 21.
[39]Survey for the Times Mirror Center for the People and the Press by Princeton Survey Research Associates, July 12–27, 1994.

Chapter Four

[1]Julian P. Boyd, ed., *The Papers of Thomas Jefferson*, vol. 12 (Princeton, N.J.: Princeton University Press, 1955), 440.
[2]*Anderson v. Creighton*, 483 U.S. 635 (1987).
[3]*United States v. Carolene Products Co.*, 304 U.S. 144 (1938).
[4]*Schenck v. United States*, 249 U.S. 47 (1919).
[5]*Dennis v. United States*, 341 U.S. 494 (1951); for a broad look at the relationship between issues of national security and liberty, see Geoffrey Stone, *War and Liberty: An American Dilemma: 1790 to the Present* (New York: W. W. Norton, 2007).
[6]See, for example, *Yates v. United States*, 354 U.S. 298 (1957); *Noto v. United States*, 367 U.S. 290 (1961); *Scales v. United States*, 367 U.S. 203 (1961).
[7]*United States v. O'Brien*, 391 U.S. 367 (1968).
[8]*Texas v. Johnson*, 109 S. Ct. 2544 (1989).
[9]*New York Times Co. v. United States*, 403 U.S. 713 (1971).
[10]*Nebraska Press Assn. v. Stuart*, 427 U.S. 539 (1976).
[11]*Barron v. Baltimore*, 7 Peters 243 (1833).
[12]*Gitlow v. New York*, 268 U.S. 652 (1925).
[13]*Fiske v. Kansas*, 274 U.S. 30 (1927); *Near v. Minnesota*, 283 U.S. 697 (1931); *Hamilton v. Regents, U. of California*, 293 U.S. 245 (1934); *DeJonge v. Oregon*, 299 U.S. 253 (1937).
[14]*Near v. Minnesota*, 283 U.S. 697 (1931).
[15]*Brandenburg v. Ohio*, 395 U.S. 444 (1969).
[16]*R.A.V. v. St. Paul*, No. 90-7675 (1992).
[17]*Wisconsin v. Mitchell*, No. 92-515 (1993).

[18]*National Socialist Party v. Skokie*, 432 U.S. 43 (1977).
[19]*Forsyth County v. Nationalist Movement*, No. 91-538 (1992).
[20]*Milkovich v. Lorain Journal*, 497 U.S. 1 (1990); see also *Masson v. The New Yorker*, No. 89-1799 (1991).
[21]*New York Times Co. v. Sullivan*, 376 U.S. 254 (1964).
[22]*Roth v. United States*, 354 U.S. 476 (1957).
[23]*Miller v. California*, 413 U.S. 15 (1973).
[24]*Barnes v. Glen Theatre*, No. 90-26 (1991).
[25]*Stanley v. Georgia*, 394 U.S. 557 (1969).
[26]*Osborne v. Ohio*, 495 U.S. 103 (1990); see also *Ashcroft v. Free Speech Coalition*, No. 00-795 (2002).
[27]*United States v. Williams*, No. 06-694 (2008).
[28]*Denver Area Consortium v. Federal Communications Commission*, No. 95-124 (1996); *Reno v. American Civil Liberties Union*, No. 96-511 (1997); *Ashcroft v. ACLU*, No. 03-0218 (2004).
[29]*Engel v. Vitale*, 370 U.S. 421 (1962).
[30]*Abington School District v. Schempp*, 374 U.S. 203 (1963).
[31]*Wallace v. Jaffree*, 472 U.S. 38 (1985).
[32]*Santa Fe Independent School District v. Does*, No. 99-62 (2000).
[33]*Van Orden v. Perry*, No. 03-1500 (2005).
[34]*McCreary County v. American Civil Liberties Union*, No. 03-1693 (2005).
[35]*Board of Regents v. Allen*, 392 U.S. 236 (1968).
[36]*Lemon v. Kurtzman*, 403 U.S. 602 (1971).
[37]Ibid.
[38]*Mitchell v. Helms*, No. 98-1648 (2000).
[39]*Zelman v. Simmons-Harris*, No. 00-1751 (2002); see also *Locke v. Davey*, No. 02-1315 (2004).
[40]*Locke v. Davey*, No. 02-1315 (2004).
[41]*Hein v. Freedom from Religion*, No. 06-157 (2007).
[42]*Wisconsin v. Yoder*, 406 U.S. 295 (1972); see also *Church of the Lukumi Babalu Aye v. City of Hialeah*, No. 91-948 (1993).
[43]*Edwards v. Aguillard*, 487 U.S. 578 (1987).
[44]*District of Columbia v. Heller*, No. 07-290 (2008).
[45]*Griswold v. Connecticut*, 381 U.S. 479 (1965); for an assessment of the Ninth Amendment, see Daniel A. Farber, *Retained by the People: The "Silent" Ninth Amendment and the Constitutional Rights Americans Don't Know They Have* (New York: Basic Books, 2007).
[46]*Vacco v. Quill*, 117 S.C. 36 (1996); *Washington v. Glucksberg*, No. 96-110 (1997); *Gonzalez v. Oregon*, No. 04-63 (2006).
[47]*Roe v. Wade*, 401 U.S. 113 (1973).
[48]*Gregg v. United States*, No. 00-939 (2001).
[49]*Webster v. Reproductive Health Services*, 492 U.S. 490 (1989); see also *Rust v. Sullivan*, No. 89-1391 (1991).
[50]*Planned Parenthood v. Casey*, No. 91-744 (1992).
[51]*Ayotte v. Planned Parenthood of Northern New England*, No. 04-1144 (2006).
[52]*Stenberg v. Carhart*, No. 99-830 (2000).
[53]*Gonzalez v. Carhart*, No. 05-380 (2007).
[54]*Bowers v. Hardwick*, 478 U.S. 186 (1986).
[55]*Lawrence v. Texas*, 539 U.S. 558 (2003).
[56]*McNabb v. United States*, 318 U.S. 332 (1943).
[57]*Powell v. Alabama*, 287 U.S. 45 (1932).
[58]*Palko v. Connecticut*, 302 U.S. 319 (1937).
[59]*Mapp v. Ohio*, 367 U.S. 643 (1961).
[60]*Gideon v. Wainwright*, 372 U.S. 335 (1963).
[61]*Malloy v. Hogan*, 378 U.S. 1 (1964).
[62]*Miranda v. Arizona*, 384 U.S. 436 (1966); see also *Escobedo v. Illinois*, 378 U.S. 478 (1964).
[63]*Pointer v. Texas*, 380 U.S. 400 (1965).
[64]*Klopfer v. North Carolina*, 386 U.S. 213 (1967).
[65]*Duncan v. Louisiana*, 391 U.S. 145 (1968).
[66]*Benton v. Maryland*, 395 U.S. 784 (1969).
[67]*Dickerson v. United States*, No. 99-5525 (2000).
[68]*Missouri v. Siebert*, 542 U.S. 600 (2004).
[69]*Michigan v. Sitz*, No. 88-1897 (1990).
[70]*Indianapolis v. Edmund*, No. 99-1030 (2001).
[71]*Kyllo v. United States*, No. 99-8508 (2001).
[72]*Ferguson v. Charleston*, No. 99-936 (2001).
[73]*Board of Education of Independent School District No. 92 of Pottawatomie County v. Earls*, No. 01-332 (2002).
[74]*Weeks v. United States*, 232 U.S. 383 (1914).
[75]*Nix v. Williams*, 467 U.S. 431 (1984); see also *United States v. Leon*, 468 U.S. 897 (1984).
[76]*Whren v. United States*, 517 U.S. 806 (1996).
[77]*Hudson v. Michigan*, No. 04-1360 (2006).
[78]*Townsend v. Sain*, 372 U.S. 293 (1963).

[79]*Keeney v. Tamaya-Reyes*, No. 90-1859 (1992); see also *Coleman v. Thompson*, No. 89-7662 (1991).
[80]*Bowles v. Russell*, No. 06-5306 (2007).
[81]*Felker v. Turpin*, No. 95-8836 (1996); but see *Stewart v. Martinez-Villareal*, No. 97-300 (1998).
[82]*Williams v. Taylor*, No. 99-6615 (2000).
[83]*Miller-El v. Cockrell*, No. 01-7662 (2003); *Wiggins v. Smith*, No. 02-311 (2003).
[84]Kurt Heine, "Philadelphia Cops Beat One of Their Own," *Syracuse Herald-American*, January 15, 1995, A13.
[85]Alejandro Del Carmen, *Racial Profiling in America* (Upper Saddle River, N.J.: Prentice-Hall, 2007).
[86]*Wilson v. Seiter*, No. 89-7376 (1991).
[87]*Harmelin v. Michigan*, No. 89-7272 (1991).
[88]*Lockyer v. Andrade*, No. 01-1127 (2003); see also *Ewing v. California*, No. 01-6978 (2003).
[89]*Atkins v. Virginia*, No. 01-8452 (2002); *Panetti v. Quarterman*, No. 06-6407 (2007).
[90]*Roper v. Simmons*, No. 03-633 (2005); *Kennedy v. Louisiana*, No. 07-343 (2008).
[91]*Baze v. Rees*, No. 07-5439 (2008); see also *Hill v. McDonough*, No. 05-8794 (2006).
[92]*Ring v. Arizona*, No. 01-488 (2002).
[93]*Blakely v. Washington*, No. 02-1632 (2004).
[94]"Justices: Judges Can Slash Crack Sentences," CNN.com, December 10, 2007.
[95]*Kimbrough v. United States*, No. 06-6330 (2007).
[96]*Korematsu v. United States*, 323 U.S. 214 (1944).
[97]Case cited in Charles Lane, "In Terror War, 2nd Track for Suspects," *Washington Post*, December 1, 2001, A1.
[98]*Rasul v. Bush*, No. 03-334 (2004); *al-Odah v. United States*, No. 03-343 (2004).
[99]*Hamdi v. Rumsfeld*, No. 03-6696 (2004); see also, *Rumsfeld v. Padilla*, No. 03-1027 (2004).
[100]*Hamdan v. Rumsfeld*, No. 05-184 (2006).
[101]*Boumediene et al. v. Bush*, No. 06-1195 (2008).
[102]Quoted in "Feds Get Wide Wiretap Authority," CBSNEWS.com, November 18, 2002.
[103]See Alpheus T. Mason, *The Supreme Court: Palladium of Freedom* (Ann Arbor: University of Michigan Press, 1962); see also Jeffrey Rosen, *The Most Democratic Branch: How the Courts Serve America* (New York: Oxford University Press, 2006).

Chapter Five

[1]Speech of Martin Luther King Jr. in Washington, D.C., August 2, 1963.
[2]Washington Post wire story, May 14, 1991.
[3]"African-American Health," amednews.com (online newspaper of the American Medical Association), May 1, 2000.
[4]Robert Nisbet, "Public Opinion Versus Popular Opinion," *Public Interest* 41 (1975): 171.
[5]See, for example, Gloria J. Browne-Marshall, *Race, Law, and American Society: 1607 to Present* (New York: Routledge, 2007).
[6]Douglas A. Blackmon, *Slavery by Another Name: The Re-Enslavement of Black Americans from the Civil War to World War II* (New York: Doubleday, 2008).
[7]*Plessy v. Ferguson*, 163 U.S. 537 (1896).
[8]Ada Lois Sipuel Fisher, Danney Gable, and Robert Henry, *A Matter of Black and White: The Autobiography of Ada Lois Sipuel Fisher* (Norman: University of Oklahoma Press, 1996).
[9]*Brown v. Board of Education of Topeka*, 347 U.S. 483 (1954).
[10]See, for example, Alejandro Del Carmen, *Racial Profiling in America* (Upper Saddle River, N.J.: Prentice-Hall, 2007).
[11]Data from National Office of Drug Control Policy, 1997.
[12]See Keith Reeves, *Voting Hopes or Fears?* (New York: Oxford University Press, 1997); Tali Mendelberg, *The Race Card* (Princeton, N.J.: Princeton University Press, 2001).
[13]See Kathleen S. Sullivan, *Women and Rights Discourse in Nineteenth-Century America* (Baltimore, Md.: Johns Hopkins University Press, 2007).
[14]*Tinker v. Colwell*, 193 U.S. 473 (1904).
[15]See Jane Mansbridge, *Why We Lost the ERA* (Chicago: University of Chicago Press, 1986).
[16]*Pennsylvania State Police v. Suder*, No. 03-95 (2004).
[17]*Burlington Northern and Santa Fe Railroad Company v. White*, No. 05-259 (2006).
[18]Jennifer L. Lawless and Richard L. Fox, *It Takes a Candidate: Why Women Don't Run for Office* (New York: Cambridge University Press, 2005).
[19]Lois Duke Whitaker, ed., *Voting the Gender Gap* (Urbana: University of Illinois Press, 2008).

[20]U.S. Department of Education, 2006.
[21]See Sara M. Evans and Barbara Nelson, *Wage Justice* (Chicago: University of Chicago Press, 1989).
[22]U.S. Census Bureau data, 2008; see also Daniel McCool, Susan M. Olson, and Jennifer L. Robinson, *Native Vote: American Indians, the Voting Rights Act, and the Right to Vote* (New York: Cambridge University Press, 2007).
[23]See David E. Wilkins, *American Indian Politics and the American Political System* (Lanham, Md.: Rowman & Littlefield, 2006).
[24]William Evans and Julie Topoleski, "The Social and Economic Impact of Native American Casinos," National Bureau of Economic Research, Working Paper No. 9198, September 2002, Cambridge, Massachusetts.
[25]Sean Page, "Gambling on the Future: US Native American Casinos," BNET web story, December 22, 1997.
[26]James G. Gimpel, "Latinos and the 2002 Election: Republicans Do Well When Latinos Stay Home," Center for Immigration Studies, University of Maryland, January 2003, web download; see also Jorge Ramos, *The Latino Wave: How Hispanics Are Transforming Politics in America* (New York: Harper Paperbacks, 2005); F. Chris Garcia and Gabriel Sanchez, *Hispanics and the U.S. Political System: Moving into the Mainstream* (Upper Saddle River, N.J.: Prentice-Hall, 2007).
[27]James Truslow Adams, *The March of Democracy*, vol. 4 (New York: Scribner's, 1933), 284–85.
[28]*Lau v. Nichols*, 414 U.S. 563 (1974).
[29]See Gordon Chang, ed., *Asian Americans and Politics* (Stanford, Calif.: Stanford University Press, 2001).
[30]*Kimel v. Florida Board of Regents*, No. 98-791 (2000); but see *CBOCS West, Inc. v. Humphries*, No. 06-1431 (2008).
[31]*Board of Trustees of the University of Alabama v. Garrett*, No. 99-1240 (2002); *Tennessee v. Lane*, No. 02-1667 (2004).
[32]See William N. Eskridge Jr., *Dishonorable Passions: Sodomy Laws in America, 1861–2003* (New York: Viking, 2008); Nancy D. Polikoff, *Beyond (Straight and Gay) Marriage: Valuing All Families Under the Law* (Boston: Beacon Press, 2009); Craig A. Rimmerman and Clyde Wilcox, *The Politics of Same-Sex Marriage* (Chicago: University of Chicago Press, 2007).
[33]*Romer v. Evans*, 517 U.S. 620 (1996).
[34]*Lawrence v. Texas*, 539 U.S. 558 (2003).
[35]*Boy Scouts of America v. Dale*, No. 99-699 (2000).
[36]*Craig v. Boren*, 429 U.S. 190 (1976).
[37]*Rostker v. Goldberg*, 453 U.S. 57 (1980).
[38]*United States v. Virginia*, No. 94-1941 (1996).
[39]U.S. Conference of Mayors Report, 1998; see also Survey by Federal Financial Institutions Examination Council, 1998.
[40]V. O. Key Jr., *Southern Politics* (New York: Knopf, 1949), 495.
[41]*Smith v. Allwright*, 321 U.S. 649 (1944).
[42]*League of United Latin American Voters v. Perry*, No. 05-204 (2006).
[43]*Muller v. Johnson*, No. 94-631 (1995); *Bush v. Verg*, No. 94-805 (1996); *Shaw v. Hunt*, No. 94-923 (1996).
[44]*Easley v. Cromartie*, No. 99-1864 (2001).
[45]Terry H. Anderson, *The Pursuit of Happiness: A History of Affirmative Action* (New York: Oxford University Press, 2005).
[46]*University of California Regents v. Bakke*, 438 U.S. 265 (1978).
[47]*Steelworkers v. Weber*, 443 U.S. 193 (1979); *Fullilove v. Klutnick*, 448 U.S. 448 (1980).
[48]*Local No. 28, Sheet Metal Workers v. Equal Employment Opportunity Commission*, 478 U.S. 421 (1986); see also *Local No. 93, International Association of Firefighters v. Cleveland*, 478 U.S. 501 (1986); *Firefighters v. Stotts*, 459 U.S. 969 (1984); *Wygant v. Jackson*, 476 U.S. 238 (1986).
[49]*Adarand v. Pena*, No. 94-310 (1995).
[50]*Gratz v. Bollinger*, No. 02-516 (2003).
[51]*Grutter v. Bollinger*, No. 02-241 (2003).
[52]See J. Edward Kellough, *Understanding Affirmative Action: Politics, Discrimination, and the Search for Justice* (Washington, D.C.: Georgetown University Press, 2006).
[53]*Swann v. Charlotte-Mecklenburg County Board of Education*, 402 U.S. 1 (1971).
[54]Christopher Jencks and Meredith Phillips, eds., *The Black-White Test Score Gap* (Washington, D.C.: Brookings Institution Press, 1998).
[55]*Milliken v. Bradley*, 418 U.S. 717 (1974).
[56]*Board of Education of Oklahoma City v. Dowell*, 498 U.S. (1991).

[57]*Sheff v. O'Neill*, No. 95-2071 (1996).
[58]*Parents Involved in Community Schools v. Seattle*, No. 05-908 (2007); *Meredith, Custodial Parent and Next Friend of McDonald v. Jefferson County Board of Education*, No. 05-915 (2007).
[59]Gunnar Myrdal, *An American Dilemma: The Negro Problem and Modern Democracy* (New York: Harper, 1944).

Chapter Six

[1]V. O. Key Jr., *Public Opinion and American Democracy* (New York: Knopf, 1961), 8.
[2]See Brandice Canes-Wrone, *Who Leads Whom? Presidents, Policy, and the Public* (Chicago: University of Chicago Press, 2005).
[3]See Jeremy Bentham, *An Introduction to the Principles of Morals and Legislation* (Oxford, England: Clarendon Press, 1996). First published in 1789.
[4]Vincent Hutchings, *Public Opinion and Democratic Accountability: How Citizens Learn About Politics* (Princeton, N.J.: Princeton University Press, 2005).
[5]Elisabeth Noelle-Neumann, *The Spiral of Silence*, 2d ed. (Chicago: University of Chicago Press, 1993), ch. 1.
[6]"Study Finds Widespread Misperceptions on Iraq Highly Related to Support for War," web release of the Program on International Policy Attitudes, School of Public Affairs, University of Maryland, October 2, 2003.
[7]Joshua Buntin III, "Start with Civics 101," *Miami Herald*, January 21, 2008, p. 25A.
[8]Survey of Students of the Eight Ivy League Schools by Luntz & Weber Research and Strategic Services, for the University of Pennsylvania's Ivy League Study, November 13–December 1, 1992.
[9]See R. Michael Alvarez and John Brehm, *Hard Choices, Easy Answers* (Princeton, N.J.: Princeton University Press, 2002); see also Samuel L. Popkin, *The Reasoning Voter* (Chicago: University of Chicago Press, 1991).
[10]See Herbert Asher, *Polling and the Public*, 7th ed. (Washington, D.C.: Congressional Quarterly Press, 2007).
[11]Political Arithmetic, May 31, 2007, web release.
[12]M. Kent Jennings and Richard G. Niemi, *Generations and Politics* (Princeton, N.J.: Princeton University Press, 1981).
[13]See Orit Ichilov, *Political Socialization, Citizenship Education, and Democracy* (New York: Teachers College Press, 1990).
[14]Noelle-Neumann, *The Spiral of Silence*.
[15]Jon Western, *Selling Intervention and War: The Presidency, the Media, and the American Public* (Baltimore, Md.: Johns Hopkins University Press, 2005); see also Wojtek Mackiewicz Wolfe, *Winning the War of Words: Selling the War on Terror from Afghanistan to Iraq* (Westport, Conn.: Praeger, 2008).
[16]See, however, Dietram A. Scheufele, Matthew C. Nisbet, and Dominique Brossard, "Pathways to Political Participation: Religion, Communication Contexts, and Mass Media," *International Journal of Public Opinion Research* 15 (Autumn 2003): 300–24.
[17]The classic study of citizen ideology is Philip Converse, "The Nature of Belief Systems in Mass Publics," in David Apter, ed., *Ideology and Discontent* (New York: Free Press, 1965), 206.
[18]Kenneth D. Wald, *Religion and Politics in the United States* (Lanham, Md.: Rowman & Littlefield, 2003).
[19]CNN/USA Today Poll conducted by the Gallup Organization, 1997.
[20]Lois Duke Whitaker, ed., *Voting the Gender Gap* (Urbana: University of Illinois Press, 2008).
[21]Susan A. MacManus, *Young v. Old: Generational Combat in the Twenty-first Century* (Boulder, Colo.: Westview Press, 1996).
[22]See Angus Campbell, Philip Converse, Warren Miller, and Donald Stokes, *The American Voter* (New York: Wiley, 1960), chs. 3 and 4.
[23]Martin P. Wattenberg, *Where Have All the Voters Gone?* (Cambridge, Mass.: Harvard University Press, 2002).
[24]Donald Green, Bradley Palmquist, and Eric Schickler, *Partisan Hearts and Minds* (New Haven, Conn.: Yale University Press, 2002).
[25]See William Domhoff, *Who Rules America?* 5th ed. (New York: McGraw-Hill, 2005).
[26]Benjamin I. Page and Robert Y. Shapiro, "Effects of Public Opinion on Policy," *American Political Science Review* 77 (March 1983): 178; see also Richard Sobel, *The Impact of Public Opinion on U.S. Foreign Policy* (New York: Oxford University Press, 2001); James Stimson, *Tides of Consent: How Public*

Opinion Shapes American Politics (New York: Cambridge University Press, 2004).
[27]Lawrence R. Jacobs and Robert Y. Shapiro, *Politicians Don't Pander* (Chicago: University of Chicago Press, 2000).
[28]Christopher J. Grill, *The Public Side of Representation: A Study of Citizens' View About Representatives and the Representative Process* (Albany: State University of New York Press, 2007).

Chapter Seven

[1]Walter Lippmann, *Public Opinion* (New York: Free Press, 1965), 36.
[2]Quoted in Ralph Volney Harlow, *The Growth of the United States* (New York: Henry Holt, 1943), 312.
[3]Example from Gus Tyler, "One Cheer for the Democrats," *New Leader*, November 3, 1986, 6.
[4]Thomas E. Patterson, *The Vanishing Voter* (New York: Vintage, 2003), p. 10.
[5]Mark N. Franklin, *Voter Turnout and the Dynamics of Electoral Competition in Established Democracies Since 1945* (New York: Cambridge University Press, 2004).
[6]Patterson, *The Vanishing Voter*, 134.
[7]Russell Dalton, "The Myth of the Disengaged American," web publication of the Comparative Study of Electoral Systems, October 2005, 2.
[8]Patterson, *The Vanishing Voter*, 179–80.
[9]*Crawford et al. v. Marion County Election Board et al.*, No. 07-21 (2008).
[10]Ivor Crewe, "Electoral Participation," in David Butler, Howard R. Penniman, and Austin Ranney, eds., *Democracy at the Polls* (Washington, D.C.: American Enterprise Institute, 1981), 251–53.
[11]Richard Boyd, "Decline of U.S. Voter Turnout," *American Politics Quarterly* 9 (April 1981): 142.
[12]David Hill, *American Voter Turnout: An Institutional Perspective* (Boulder, Colo.: Westview Press, 2006).
[13]David C. Leege, Kenneth D. Wald, Brian S. Krueger, and Paul D. Mueller, *The Politics of Cultural Differences* (Princeton, N.J.: Princeton University Press, 2002).
[14]Larry Bartels, *Unequal Democracy: The Political Economy of the Gilded Age* (Princeton, N.J.: Princeton University Press, 2008).
[15]Patterson, *The Vanishing Voter*, 135.
[16]See Bruce Bimber and Richard Davis, *Campaigning Online* (New York: Oxford University Press, 2003); Bruce Bimber, *Information and American Democracy* (New York: Cambridge University Press, 2003); Joe Trippi, *The Revolution Will Not Be Televised* (New York: HarperCollins, 2004).
[17]Dalton, "The Myth of the Disengaged American," 2.
[18]Robert Putnam, *Bowling Alone* (New York: Simon & Schuster, 2000); but see Cliff Zukin et al., *A New Engagement: Political Participation, Civic Life, and the Changing American Citizen* (New York: Oxford University Press, 2006).
[19]See Benjamin Ginsberg, *The Consequences of Consent* (New York: Random House, 1982), ch. 2.
[20]See, for example, Charles J. Stewart, Craig Allen Smith, and Robert E. Denton Jr., *Persuasion and Social Movements*, 5th ed. (Long Grove, Ill.: Waveland Press, 2007).
[21]ABC News/Washington Post poll, March 23, 2003.
[22]Dalton, *Citizen Politics*, 38.
[23]Gallup poll, January 2003.
[24]William Watts and Lloyd A. Free, eds., *The State of the Nation* (New York: University Books, Potomac Associates, 1967), 97.
[25]Robert E. Lane, "Market Justice, Political Justice," *American Political Science Review* 80 (1986): 383; see also Jennifer Nedelsky, *Private Property and the Limits of American Constitutionalism* (New York: Oxford University Press, 1990).
[26]Sidney Verba and Norman Nie, *Participation in America* (New York: Harper & Row, 1972), 131.
[27]Robert Kaplan, "Was Democracy Just a Moment?" *Atlantic Monthly*, December 1997. Retrieved from Atlantic Monthly website.
[28]Daniel Pope, ed., *American Radicalism* (New York: Blackwell, 2001).
[29]Bartels, *Unequal Democracy*.

Chapter Eight

[1]E. E. Schattschneider, *Party Government* (New York: Rinehart, 1942), 1.
[2]See John Aldrich, *Why Parties? The Origin and Transformation of Political Parties in*

America (Chicago: University of Chicago Press, 1995); L. Sandy Maisel, *American Political Parties and Elections* (New York: Oxford University Press, 2007).
[3]E. E. Schattschneider, *The Semisovereign People: A Realist's View of Democracy in America* (New York: Holt, Rinehart & Winston, 1961), 140.
[4]Thomas E. Patterson, *The Vanishing Voter* (New York: Knopf, 2002), ch. 2.
[5]See Richard P. McCormick, *The Second American Party System: Party Formation in the Jacksonian Era* (Chapel Hill: University of North Carolina Press, 1966).
[6]Alexis de Tocqueville, *Democracy in America (1835–1840)*, eds. J. P. Mayer and A. P. Kerr (Garden City, N.Y.: Doubleday/Anchor, 1969), 60.
[7]Aldrich, *Why Parties?* 151.
[8]See Kristi Andersen, *The Creation of a Democratic Majority, 1928–1936* (Chicago: University of Chicago Press, 1979).
[9]See Kevin Phillips, *The Emerging Republican Majority* (New Rochelle, N.Y.: Arlington House, 1969).
[10]See Arthur C. Paulson, *Electoral Realignment and the Outlook for American Democracy* (Boston: Northeastern University Press, 2006).
[11]Gallup Organization, 2008.
[12]Lewis L. Gould, *Grand Old Party* (New York: Random House, 2003); but see also Jacob S. Hacker and Paul Pierson, *Off-Center: The Republican Revolution and the Erosion of American Democracy* (New Haven, Conn.: Yale University Press, 2006).
[13]See John B. Judis and Ruy Teixeira, *The Emerging Democratic Majority* (New York: Scribner, 2002).
[14]See, for example, Everett Carll Ladd, "The Brittle Mandate: Electoral Dealignment and the 1980 Presidential Election," *Political Science Quarterly* 96, No. 1 (Spring, 1981): 1–25.
[15]Clinton Rossiter, *Parties and Politics in America* (Ithaca, N.Y.: Cornell University Press, 1960), 11; see also James H. Fowler and Oleg Smirnov, *Mandates, Parties, and Voters: How Elections Shape the Future* (Philadelphia: Temple University Press, 2007).
[16]Nancy Gibbs and Michael Duffy, "Fall of the House of Newt," *Time*, November 16, 1998, 47.
[17]Jeffrey M. Stonecash, *Political Parties Matter: Realignment and the Return of Partisan Voting* (Boulder; Colo.: Lynne Reinner, 2005).
[18]John Green, Mark Rozell, and William Clyde Wilcox, eds., *The Christian Right in American Politics* (Washington, D.C.: Georgetown University Press, 2003).
[19]Micah L. Sifrey, *Spoiling for a Fight: Third-Party Politics in America* (New York: Routledge, 2003).
[20]Daniel A. Mazmanian, *Third Parties in Presidential Elections* (Washington, D.C.: Brookings Institution, 1984), 143–44.
[21]See Lawrence Goodwyn, *The Populist Movement* (New York: Oxford University Press, 1978).
[22]Lewis L. Gould, *Four Hats in the Ring: The 1912 Election and the Birth of Modern American Politics* (Lawrence: University Press of Kansas, 2008).
[23]See Anthony King, *Running Scared* (New York: Free Press, 1997); but see James E. Campbell, *The American Campaign: U.S. Presidential Campaigns and the National Vote* (College Station: Texas A&M Press, 2008).
[24]See Paul S. Herrnson and John C. Green, eds., *Responsible Partisanship* (Lawrence: University Press of Kansas, 2003).
[25]See Marjorie Randon Hershey, *Party Politics in America*, 13th ed. (New York: Longman, 2009).
[26]David Adamany, "Political Parties in the 1980s," in Michael J. Malbin, ed., *Money and Politics in the United States* (Chatham, N.J.: Chatham House, 1984), 114.
[27]*Senator Mitch McConnell et al. v. Federal Election Commission et al.*, No. 02-1674 (2003).
[28]Michael J. Malbin, *The Election After Reform: Money, Politics, and the Bipartisan Campaign Reform Act* (Lanham, Md.: Rowman & Littlefield, 2006).
[29]Joseph Napolitan, *The Election Game and How to Win It* (New York: Doubleday, 1972); for a contemporary look at the campaigning process, see D. Sunshine Hillygus and Todd G. Shields, *The Persuadable Voter: Wedge Issues in Presidential Campaigns* (Princeton, N.J.: Princeton University Press, 2008).
[30]Federal Elections Commission data, 2008.
[31]David B. Magelby, J. Quin Monson, and Kelly D. Patterson, eds., *Dancing Without Partners: How Candidates, Parties and Interest Groups Interact in the New Campaign Finance*

Environment (Provo, Utah: Brigham Young University Press, 2005).

[32]David Chagall, *The New King-Makers* (New York: Harcourt Brace Jovanovich, 1981).

[33]Lawrence R. Jacobs and Robert Y. Shapiro, *Politicians Don't Pander: Political Manipulation and the Loss of Democratic Responsiveness* (Chicago: University of Chicago Press, 2000).

[34]Emmett H. Buell Jr. and Lee Sigelman, *Attack Politics: Negativity in Presidential Campaigns Since 1960* (Lawrence: University Press of Kansas, 2008). For opposing views on the effect of negative advertising, see Stephen Ansolabehere and Shanto Iyengar, *Going Negative* (New York: Free Press, 1995), and John Geer, *In Defense of Negativity* (Chicago: University of Chicago Press, 2006).

[35]Darrell M. West, *Air Wars: Television Advertising in Election Campaigns,1952–2004*, 4th ed. (Washington, D.C.: Congressional Quarterly Press, 2005), 140–46.

[36]Ibid, 12.

[37]Peter J. Peterson, *Running on Empty: How the Democratic and Republican Parties Are Bankrupting Our Future and What Americans Can Do About It* (New York: Farrar, Straus, and Giroux, 2005).

Chapter Nine

[1]E. E. Schattschneider, *The Semisovereign People: A Realist's View of Democracy in America* (New York: Holt, Rinehart & Winston, 1960), 35.

[2]See Matthew J. Burbank, Ronald J. Hrebenar, and Robert C. Benedict, *Parties, Interest Groups, and Political Campaigns* (Boulder, Colo.: Paradigm, 2008).

[3]Alexis de Tocqueville, *Democracy in America, 1835–1840*, eds. J. P. Mayer and A. P. Kerr (Garden City, N.Y.: Doubleday/Anchor, 1969), bk. 2, ch. 4.

[4]Mancur Olson, *The Logic of Collective Action*, rev. ed. (Cambridge, Mass.: Harvard University Press, 1971), 147; see also Theda Skocpol, *Diminished Democracy* (Norman: University of Oklahoma Press, 2003).

[5]See Jack L. Walker, *Mobilizing Interest Groups in America* (Ann Arbor: University of Michigan Press, 1991).

[6]Olson, *The Logic of Collective Action*, 64.

[7]Christopher J. Bosso, "The Color of Money: Environmental Groups and the Pathologies of Fund Raising," in Allan J. Cigler and Burdett Loomis, *Interest Group Politics*, 4th ed. (Washington, D.C.: Congressional Quarterly Press, 1995), 101–3.

[8]Kay Lehman Schlozman and John T. Tierney, *Organized Interests and American Democracy* (New York: Harper & Row, 1986), 54; see also Jeffrey M. Berry and Clyde Wilcox, *The Interest Group Society*, 5th ed. (New York: Longman, 2008).

[9]Norman J. Ornstein and Shirley Elder, *Interest Groups, Lobbying, and Policymaking* (Washington, D.C.: Congressional Quarterly Press, 1978), 82–86.

[10]See John Mark Hansen, *Gaining Access* (Chicago: Chicago University Press, 1991); Bruce Wolpe and Bertram Levine, *Lobbying Congress* (Washington, D.C.: Congressional Quarterly Press, 1996).

[11]See Paul S. Herrnson, Ronald G. Shaiko, and Clyde Wilcox, *The Interest Group Connection: Electioneering, Lobbying, and Policymaking in Washington*, 2d ed. (Washington, D.C.: Congressional Quarterly Press, 2004).

[12]Quoted in Ornstein and Elder, *Interest Groups, Lobbying, and Policymaking*, 77.

[13]Steve Reinberg, "Debate Builds over Drug Companies' Fees to FDA," *Washington Post*, April 13, 2007, electronic version.

[14]Paul J. Quirk, *Industry Influence in Federal Regulatory Agencies* (Princeton, N.J.: Princeton University Press, 1981); John E. Chubb, *Interest Groups and the Bureaucracy: The Politics of Energy* (Stanford, Calif.: Stanford University Press, 1983), 200–1.

[15]Lee Epstein and C. K. Rowland, "Interest Groups in the Courts," *American Political Science Review* 85 (1991): 205–17.

[16]Richard Davis, *Electing Justice: Fixing the Supreme Court Nomination Process* (New York: Oxford University Press, 2005).

[17]Hugh Heclo, "Issue Networks and the Executive Establishment," in Anthony King, ed., *The New American Political System* (Washington, D.C.: American Enterprise Institute, 1978), 87–124.

[18]Ornstein and Elder, *Interest Groups, Lobbying, and Policymaking*, 88–93.

[19]Quoted in Mark Green, "Political PAC-Man," *The New Republic*, December 13, 1982, 20; see also Richard Skinner, *More Than Money: Interest Group Action in Congressional Elections* (Lanham, Md.: Rowman &

Littlefield, 2006); Mark J. Rozell, Clyde Wilcox, and David Madland, *Interest Groups in American Campaigns*, 2d ed. (Washington, D.C.: Congressional Quarterly Press, 2005).

[20]Quoted in Larry Sabato, *PAC Power: Inside the World of Political Action Committees* (New York: Norton, 1984), 72.

[21]Federal Elections Commission data, 2008.

[22]See Thomas L. Gatz, *Improper Influence* (Ann Arbor: University of Michigan Press, 1996); Gene M. Grossman and Elhanan Helpman, *Interest Groups and Trade Policy* (Princeton, N.J.: Princeton University Press, 2002); Harry L. Wilson, *Guns, Gun Control, and Elections: The Politics and Policy of Firearms* (Lanham, Md.: Rowman & Littlefield, 2006).

[23]Walker, *Mobilizing Interest Groups in America*, 112.

[24]Theodore J. Lowi, *The End of Liberalism: The Second Republic of the United States* (New York: Norton, 1979).

[25]Larry Bartels, *Unequal Democracy: The Political Economy of the New Gilded Age* (Princeton, N.J.: Princeton University Press, 2008).

Chapter Ten

[1]Theodore H. White, *The Making of the President, 1972* (New York: Bantam Books, 1973), 327.

[2]See Bill Kovach and Tom Rosenstiel, *The Elements of Journalism* (New York: Three Rivers Press, 2001).

[3]See Rodger Streitmatter, *Mightier Than the Sword: How the News Media Have Shaped American History* (Westport, Conn.: Praeger, 2008).

[4]Frank Luther Mott, *American Journalism, a History: 1690–1960* (New York: Macmillan, 1962), 114–15; see also Si Sheppard, *The Partisan Press: A History of Media Bias in the United States* (Jefferson, N.C.: McFarland, 2007).

[5]Mott, *American Journalism*, 122–23, 220–27.

[6]Edwin Emery, *The Press and America: An Interpretive History of the Mass Media* (Englewood Cliffs, N.J.: Prentice-Hall, 1977), 350.

[7]Quoted in Mott, *American Journalism*, 529.

[8]Quoted in David Halberstam, *The Powers That Be* (New York: Knopf, 1979), 208–9.

[9]Donald Shaw and Maxwell McCombs, *The Emergence of American Political Issues: The Agenda-Setting Function of the Press* (St. Paul, Minn.: West, 1977).

[10]Bernard C. Cohen, *The Press and Foreign Policy* (Princeton, N.J.: Princeton University Press, 1963), 13.

[11]Thomas E. Patterson, *The American Democracy*, 5th ed. (New York: McGraw-Hill, 2001), 309–10.

[12]Kathleen Hall Jamieson and Karlyn Kohrs Campbell, *The Interplay of Influence*, rev. ed. (Boston: Wadsworth, 2005), 4.

[13]Michael Schudson, *Discovering the News* (New York: Basic Books, 1981).

[14]Michael Schudson, "What Time Means in a News Story." Gannett Center for Media Studies, New York, 1986. Occasional Paper No. 4, 8.

[15]Comment at the annual meeting of the American Association of Political Consultants, Washington, D.C., 1977.

[16]Project for Excellence in Journalism, "Character and the Primaries of 2008," web release, May 29, 2008.

[17]Michael X. Delli Carpini and Scott Keeter, *What Americans Know About Politics and Why It Matters* (New Haven: Conn.: Yale University Press, 1997).

[18]Times Mirror Center for the People and the Press survey, 1994.

[19]W. Lance Bennett, Regina G. Lawrence, and Steven Livingston, *When the Press Fails: Political Power and the News Media from Iraq to Katrina* (Chicago: University of Chicago Press, 2008).

[20]Quoted in David Shaw, "Beyond Skepticism: Have the Media Crossed the Line into Cynicism?" *Los Angeles Times*, April 17, 1996, A1.

[21]Clark Hoyt, "What That McCain Article Didn't Say," *New York Times*, web release, February 24, 2008.

[22]See Scott McClellan, *What Happened: Inside the Bush White House and Washington's Culture of Deception* (New York: Public Affairs, 2008).

[23]Stephen J. Farnsworth and S. Robert Lichter, *The Mediated Presidency: Television News and Presidential Governance* (Lanham, Md.: Rowman & Littlefield, 2006).

[24]Kiku Adatto, "Sound Bite Democracy," Joan Shorenstein Center on the Press, Politics, and Public Policy, Research Paper R-2, Harvard University, Cambridge, Mass., June 1990.

[25]Center for Media and Public Affairs data, 2008
[26]Thomas Patterson, *Out of Order* (New York: Knopf, 1993), ch. 2.
[27]Robert Entman, "Framing: Towards Clarification of a Fractured Paradigm," in Denis McQuail's, ed., *McQuail's Reader in Mass Communication Theory* (London: Sage, 2002); 391–92.
[28]Michael Levy, "Disdaining the News," *Journal of Communication* (1981): 24–31.
[29]Thomas E. Patterson, *The Vanishing Voter* (New York: Knopf, 2002), 59.
[30]Walter Lippmann, *Public Opinion* (New York: Free Press, 1965), 214. First published in 1922.
[31]Greg Mitchell, "E&P/TIPP Poll: Bird in the Hand for Bush?" *Editor & Publisher*, November 6, 2000.
[32]*Editor & Publisher*, online edition, November 1, 2004.
[33]Bernard Goldberg, *Bias: A CBS Insider Exposes How the Media Distort News* (New York: Harper Paperbacks, 2003).
[34]David H. Weaver, Randal A. Beam, Bonnie J. Brownlee, Paul S. Voakes, G. Cleveland Wilhoit, *The American Journalist in the 21st Century* (Mahwah, N.J.: LEA, 2006).
[35]Center for Media and Public Affairs, *Media Monitor*, various dates.
[36]Michael Robinson, "Public Affairs Television and the Growth of Political Malaise," *American Political Science Review* 70 (1976): 409–32.
[37]Center for Media and Public Affairs, *Media Monitor*, various dates.
[38]Ibid.
[39]Mark Rozell, "Press Coverage of Congress," in Thomas Mann and Norman Ornstein, eds., *Congress, the Press, and the Public* (Washington, D.C.: American Enterprise Institute and Brookings Institution, 1994), 109.
[40]Robinson, "Public Affairs Television and the Growth of Political Malaise."
[41]The press's negativity and sensationalism have had another effect as well; they have damaged the press's credibility. According to a 2007 survey conducted by the Center for Public Leadership at Harvard University's John F. Kennedy School of Government, the press has the lowest public confidence rating of any major U.S. institution.
[42]Joseph N. Cappella and Kathleen Hall Jamieson, *Spiral of Cynicism* (New York: Oxford University Press, 1997), 159.
[43]Quoted in Doreen Carvajal, "For News Media, Some Introspection," *New York Times*, April 5, 1998, 28.
[44]Project for Excellence in Journalism, "The Debate Effect," web release, October 27, 2004.
[45]William Cole, ed, *The Most of A. J. Leibling* (New York: Simon, 1963), 7.
[46]See Bruce A. Bimber and Richard Davis, *Campaigning Online: The Internet in U.S. Elections* (New York: Oxford University Press, 2003).
[47]Robinson, "Public Affairs Television and the Growth of Political Malaise."
[48]Donald F. Roberts, Uila G. Foehr, Victoria J. Rideout, and Mollyann Brodie, "Kids and Media at the New Millennium," A Kaiser Family Foundation Report, November 1999, 19.
[49]See David T. Z. Mindich, *Tuned Out: Why Americans Under 40 Don't Follow the News* (New York: Oxford University Press, 2005).
[50]Thomas E. Patterson, "Young People and News," report of the Joan Shorenstein Center on the Press, Politics, and Public Policy, John F. Kennedy School of Government, Harvard University, June, 2007.
[51]Martin P. Wattenberg, *Is Voting for Young People?* (New York: Pearson Longman, 2008), 32.
[52]Ibid. 75–80.

Chapter Eleven

[1]Roger H. Davidson and Walter J. Oleszek, *Congress and Its Members*, 10th ed. (Washington, D.C.: Congressional Quarterly Press, 2008), 4.
[2]See Paul S. Herrnson, *Congressional Elections: Campaigning at Home and in Washington*, 5th ed. (Washington, D.C.: Congressional Quarterly Press, 2008).
[3]See Gary C. Jacobson, *The Politics of Congressional Elections*, 5th ed. (New York: Longman, 2001).
[4]Bruce Cain, John Ferejohn, and Morris P. Fiorina, *The Personal Vote* (Cambridge, Mass.: Harvard University Press, 1987).

[5]Information provided by Clerk of the House.
[6]U.S. Code Online, 2006.
[7]Edward Sidlow, *Challenging the Incumbent: An Underdog's Undertaking* (Washington, D.C.: Congressional Quarterly Press, 2003); David C. W. Parker, *The Power of Money in Congressional Campaigns, 1880–2006* (Norman: University of Oklahoma Press, 2008).
[8]Quoted in Jennifer Babson and Kelly St. John, "Momentum Helps GOP Collect Record Amounts from PACs," *Congressional Quarterly Weekly Report*, December 3, 1994, 3456.
[9]Quoted in "A Tale of Myths and Measures: Who Is Truly Vulnerable?" *Congressional Quarterly Weekly Report*, December 4, 1993, 7; see also Dennis F. Thompson, *Ethics in Congress* (Washington, D.C.: Brookings Institution Press, 1995).
[10]James E. Campbell, *The Presidential Pulse of Congressional Elections* (Lexington: University Press of Kentucky, 1993).
[11]Robert Erikson, "The Puzzle of Midterm Losses," *Journal of Politics* 50 (November 1988): 1011–29.
[12]Linda L. Fowler and Robert D. McClure, *Political Ambition* (New Haven, Conn.: Yale University Press, 1989).
[13]Keith R. Poole and Howard Rosenthal, "Patterns of Congressional Voting," *American Journal of Political Science* 35 (February 1991): 228.
[14]*Congressional Quarterly Weekly Report*, various dates.
[15]Linda Witt, Karen M. Paget, and Glenna Matthews, *Running as a Woman: Gender and Power in American Politics* (New York: Free Press, 1993); Sue Thomas, *How Women Legislate* (New York: Oxford University Press, 1994); Tali Mendelberg, *The Race Card* (Princeton, N.J.: Princeton University Press, 2001).
[16]Steven Smith, *Party Influence in Congress* (New York: Cambridge University Press, 2007); Barbara Sinclair, *Party Wars: Polarization and the Politics of National Policy Making* (Norman: University of Oklahoma Press 2006).
[17]Randall Strahan, *Leading Representatives: The Agency of Leaders in the Politics of the U.S. House* (Baltimore, Md. Johns Hopkins University Press, 2007); David King, *Turf Wars* (Chicago: University of Chicago Press, 1997).
[18]See Stephen E. Frantzich and Steven E. Schier, *Congress: Games and Strategies* (Dubuque, Iowa: Brown & Benchmark, 1995), 127.
[19]See Gerald S. Strom, *The Logic of Lawmaking* (Baltimore, Md.: Johns Hopkins University Press, 1990).
[20]See Barbara Sinclair, *Unorthodox Lawmaking: New Legislative Processes in the U.S. Congress*, 3d ed. (Washington, D.C.: Congressional Quarterly Press, 2007).
[21]See Jon R. Bond and Richard Fleisher, eds., *Polarized Politics: Congress and the President in a Partisan Era* (Washington, D.C.: Congressional Quarterly Press, 2000).
[22]See Gary Orfield, *Congressional Power: Congress and Social Change* (New York: Harcourt Brace Jovanovich, 1975).
[23]James L. Sundquist, "Congress and the President: Enemies or Partners?" in Lawrence C. Dodd and Bruce I. Oppenheimer, eds., *Congress Reconsidered* (New York: Praeger, 1977), 240.
[24]Barry C. Burden, *Personal Roots of Representation* (Princeton, N.J.: Princeton University Press, 2007).
[25]Keith Krehbiel, "Are Congressional Committees Composed of Preference Outliers?" *American Political Science Review* 84 (1990): 149–64; Richard L. Hall and Bernard Grofman, "The Committee Assignment Process and the Conditional Nature of Committee Bias," *American Political Science Review* 84 (1990): 1149–66.
[26]Jason Mycoff, *Confrontation and Compromise: Presidential and Congressional Leadership, 2001–2006* (Lanham, Md.: Rowman & Littlefield, 2007).
[27]Joel A. Aberbach and Mark A. Peterson, eds., *The Executive Branch* (New York: Oxford University Press, 2005), 534–35.
[28]Davidson and Oleszek, *Congress and Its Members*, 7.

Chapter Twelve

[1]Woodrow Wilson, *Constitutional Government in the United States* (New York: Columbia University Press, 1908), 67.
[2]Sidney Milkis and Michael Nelson, *The American Presidency: Origins and Development, 1790–2007*, 5th ed. (Washington, D.C.: Congressional Quarterly Press, 2007).

[3]James W. Davis, *The American Presidency* (New York: Harper & Row, 1987), 13; see also Bruce Ackerman, *The Failure of the Founding Fathers* (Cambridge, Mass.: Belknap Press of Harvard University Press, 2005).
[4]See Barry M. Blechman and Stephen S. Kaplan, *Force Without War* (Washington, D.C.: Brookings Institution, 1978); Arthur M. Schlesinger Jr., *War and the American Presidency* (New York: W. W. Norton, 2004).
[5]*United States v. Belmont*, 57 U.S. 758 (1937).
[6]Robert DiClerico, *The American President*, 5th ed. (Englewood Cliffs, N.J.: Prentice-Hall, 1999), 47.
[7]Quoted in Wilfred E. Binkley, *President and Congress*, 3d ed. (New York: Vintage, 1962), 142.
[8]Theodore Roosevelt, *An Autobiography* (New York: Scribner's, 1931), 383.
[9]See Richard M. Pious, *The American Presidency* (New York: Basic Books, 1979), 83.
[10]Harry S Truman, *Years of Trial and Hope* (New York: Signet, 1956), 535.
[11]See Thomas S. Langston, *The Cold War Presidency: A Documentary History* (Washington, D.C.: Congressional Quarterly Press, 2006).
[12]James Bryce, *The American Commonwealth* (New York: Commonwealth Edition, 1908), 230.
[13]Erwin C. Hargrove, *The Effective Presidency: Lessons on Leadership from John F. Kennedy to George W. Bush* (Boulder, Colo. Paradigm, 2007).
[14]James W. Ceaser, *Presidential Selection: Theory and Development* (Princeton, N.J.: Princeton University Press, 1979).
[15]John S. Jackson and William J. Crotty, *The Politics of Presidential Selection* (New York: Longman, 2001).
[16]See John G. Geer, *In Defense of Negativity* (Chicago: University of Chicago Press, 2006).
[17]John P. Burke, *The Institutionalized Presidency* (Baltimore: Johns Hopkins University Press, 1992); Charles E. Walcott and Karen M. Hult, *Governing the White House* (Lawrence: University Press of Kansas, 1995).
[18]Quoted in Stephen J. Wayne, *Road to the White House, 1992* (New York: St. Martin's Press, 1992), 143; but see Jody C. Baumgartner, *The American Vice Presidency Reconsidered* (Westport, Conn.: Praeger, 2006).
[19]See Barton Gellman and Jo Becker, "Angler: The Cheney Vice Presidency," *Washington Post*, June 24–27, 2007, a four-part series of articles.
[20]See Jeffrey E. Cohen, *The Politics of the United States Cabinet* (Pittsburgh: University of Pittsburgh Press, 1988); Shirley Anne Warshaw, *Powersharing: White House–Cabinet Relations in the Modern Presidency* (Albany: State University of New York Press, 1995).
[21]James Pfiffner, *The Modern Presidency* (New York: St. Martin's Press, 1994), 123.
[22]Quoted in James MacGregor Burns, "Our Super-Government—Can We Control It?" *New York Times*, April 24, 1949, 32.
[23]See Paul C. Light, *Thickening Government: Federal Hierarchy and the Diffusion of Accountability* (Washington, D.C.: Brookings Institution, 1995).
[24]Erwin Hargrove, *The Power of the Modern Presidency* (New York: Knopf, 1974); see also John H. Kessel, *Presidents, the Presidency, and the Political Environment* (Washington, D.C.: Congressional Quarterly Press, 2001); Stephen Skowronek, *Presidential Leadership in Political Time: Reprise and Reappraisal* (Lawrence: University Press of Kansas, 2008).
[25]James P. Pfiffner, *The Strategic Presidency: Hitting the Ground Running*, 2d ed. (Chicago: Dorsey Press, 1996).
[26]Aaron Wildavsky, "The Two Presidencies," *Trans-Action*, December 1966, 7.
[27]Pfiffner, *The Modern Presidency*, ch. 6.
[28]Thomas P. (Tip) O'Neill, with William Novak, *Man of the House: The Life and Political Memoirs of Speaker Tip O'Neill* (New York: Random House, 1987), 297.
[29]Charles O. Jones, *The Presidency in a Separated System* (Washington, D.C.: Brookings Institution Press, 2005).
[30]Richard E. Neustadt, *Presidential Power and the Modern Presidents* (New York: Free Press, 1990), 71–72.
[31]Ibid., 33.
[32]Charlie Savage, "Senator Considers Suit over Bush Law Challenge," *Boston Globe*, June 28, 2006, electronic version.
[33]John E. Mueller, "Presidential Popularity from Truman to Johnson," *American Political Science Review* 64 (March 1970): 18–34; Kathleen Frankovic, "Public Opinion in the 1992 Campaign," in Gerald M. Pomper, ed., *The*

Election of 1992 (Chatham, N.J.: Chatham House, 1993); Chris J. Dolan, *The Presidency and Economic Policy* (Lanham, Md.: Rowman & Littlefield, 2007).

[34]Samuel Kernell, *Going Public: New Strategies of Presidential Leadership*, 3d ed. (Washington, D.C.: Congressional Quarterly Press, 1997), 1; see also Robert M. Eisinger, *The Evolution of Presidential Polling* (New York: Cambridge University Press, 2003); Stephen J. Farnsworth and S. Robert Lichter, *Mediated Presidency: Television News & Presidential Governance* (Lanham, Md.: Rowman & Littlefield, 2005).

[35]Hugh Heclo, "Introduction: The Presidential Illusion," in Hugh Heclo and Lester M. Salamon, eds., *The Illusion of Presidential Government* (Boulder, Colo.: Westview Press, 1981), 2.

[36]Theodore J. Lowi, *The "Personal" Presidency: Power Invested, Promise Unfulfilled* (Ithaca, N.Y.: Cornell University Press, 1985).

Chapter Thirteen

[1]Norman Thomas, *Rule 9: Politics, Administration, and Civil Rights* (New York: Random House, 1966), 6.

[2]James P. Pfiffner, "The National Performance Review in Perspective," working paper 94-4, Institute of Public Policy, George Mason University, 1994, 2.

[3]Ibid., 12.

[4]Max Weber, *Economy and Society*, trans. Guenther Roth and Claus Wittich (New York: Bedminster Press, 1968), 23; see also Paul Du Gay, *The Values of Bureaucracy* (New York: Oxford University Press, 2005).

[5]See Cornelius M. Kerwin, *Rulemaking*, 3d ed. (Washington, D.C.: Congressional Quarterly Press, 2003); Daniel E. Hall, *Administrative Law: Bureaucracy in a Democracy* (Upper Saddle River, N.J.: Prentice Hall, 2005).

[6]Michael Lipsky, *Street-Level Bureaucracy* (New York: Russell Sage Foundation, 1980); see also George Serra, "Citizen-Initiated Contact and Satisfaction with Bureaucracy," *Journal of Public Administration* 5 (April 1995): 175–88.

[7]Paul Van Riper, *History of the United States Civil Service* (Evanston, Ill.: Peterson, 1958), 36.

[8]David H. Rosenbloom, *Federal Service and the Constitution* (Ithaca, N.Y.: Cornell University Press, 1971), 83.

[9]Gregory A. Huber, *The Craft of Bureaucratic Neutrality: Interests and Influence in Governmental Regulation of Occupational Safety* (New York: Cambridge University Press, 2007); Herbert Kaufman, "Emerging Conflicts in the Doctrine of Public Administration," *American Political Science Review* 50 (December 1956): 1060.

[10]Kaufman, "Emerging Conflicts in the Doctrine of Public Administration," 1062.

[11]Quoted in Hugh Heclo, *A Government of Strangers* (Washington, D.C.: Brookings Institution, 1977), 225.

[12]Norton E. Long, "Power and Administration," *Public Administration Review* 10 (Autumn 1949): 269; Joel D. Aberbach and Bert A. Rockman, *In the Web of Politics* (Washington, D.C.: Brookings Institution Press, 2000).

[13]See Heclo, *A Government of Strangers*, 117–18.

[14]Quoted in Aaron Wildavsky, *The Politics of the Budgetary Process*, 4th ed. (Boston: Little, Brown, 1984), 19; see also Dennis D. Riley, *Bureaucracy and the Policy Process: Keeping the Promises* (Lanham, Md.: Rowman & Littlefield, 2005).

[15]Joel D. Aberbach and Bert A. Rockman, "Clashing Beliefs Within the Executive Branch," *American Political Science Review* 70 (June 1976): 461.

[16]See B. Dan Wood and Richard W. Waterman, *Bureaucratic Dynamics* (Boulder, Colo.: Westview Press, 1994); Edward C. Page and Bill Jenkins, *Policy Bureaucracy: Government with a Cast of Thousands* (New York: Oxford University Press, 2005).

[17]See John Brehm and Scott Gates, *Working, Shirking, and Sabotage* (Ann Arbor: University of Michigan Press, 1996).

[18]Long, "Power and Administration," 269; see also John Mark Hansen, *Gaining Access* (Chicago: University of Chicago Press, 1991).

[19]Charles T. Goodsell, *The Case for Bureaucracy*, 2d ed. (Chatham, N.J.: Chatham House, 1985), 55–60; see also B. Guy Peters, *The Politics of Bureaucracy*, 5th ed. (New York: Routledge, 2001).

[20]William T. Gormley Jr. and Steven J. Balla, *Bureaucracy and Democracy* (Washington, D.C.: Congressional Quarterly Press, 2003);

Kevin B. Smith, *Public Administration: Power and Politics in the Fourth Branch of Government* (New York: Oxford University Press, 2006).

[21]See Paul Light, *Thickening Government* (Washington, D.C.: Brookings Institution, 1995); James G. March and Johan P. Olson, "Organizing Political Life: What Administrative Reorganization Tells Us About Government," *American Political Science Review* 77 (June 1983): 281–96.

[22]Donald F. Ketti, *System Under Stress: Homeland Security and American Politics* (Washington, D.C.: Congressional Quarterly Press, 2007).

[23]Kenneth J. Meier, *Regulation* (New York: St. Martin's Press, 1985), 110–11.

[24]See Heclo, *A Government of Strangers.*

[25]See Donald Kettl, *Deficit Politics* (New York: Macmillan, 1992).

[26]See Joel D. Aberbach, *Keeping a Watchful Eye* (Washington, D.C.: Brookings Institution, 1990).

[27]David Rosenbloom, "The Evolution of the Administrative State, and Transformations of Administrative Law," in David Rosenbloom and Richard Schwartz, eds., *Handbook of Regulation and Administrative Law* (New York: Marcel Dekker, 1994), 3–36.

[28]See *Vermont Yankee Nuclear Power Corp. v. National Resources Defense Council, Inc.*, 435 U.S. 519 (1978); *Chevron v. National Resources Defense Council*, 467 U.S. 837 (1984); *Heckler v. Chaney*, 470 U.S. 821 (1985); but see *FDA v. Brown & Williamson Tobacco Co.* (2000).

[29]*Pigeford v. Veneman*, U.S. District Court for the District of Columbia, Civil Action No. 97-1978 (1999).

[30]See Brian J. Cook, *Bureaucracy and Self-Government* (Baltimore, Md.: Johns Hopkins University Press, 1996).

[31]David Osborne and Ted Gaebler, *Reinventing Government: How the Entrepreneurial Spirit Is Transforming the Public Sector* (New York: Addison-Wesley, 1992); see also Elaine Ciulla Kamarck, *End of Government... as We Know It: Making Public Policy Work* (Boulder, Colo.: Lynne Rienner, 2007).

[32]Pfiffner, "The National Performance Review in Perspective," 7; see also David G. Frederickson and H. George Frederickson, *Measuring the Performance of the Hollow State* (Washington, D.C.: Georgetown University Press, 2006).

[33]Ronald C. Moe, "The 'Reinventing Government' Exercise: Misinterpreting the Problem, Misjudging the Results," *Public Administration Review*, March/April 1994, 125–36.

CHAPTER FOURTEEN

[1]*Marbury v. Madison*, 5 U.S. 137 (1803).

[2]*Swann v. Charlotte-Mecklenburg County Board of Education*, 402 U.S. 1 (1971).

[3]*Brown v. Board of Education of Topeka*, 347 U.S. 483 (1954).

[4]*Parents Involved in Community Schools v. Seattle*, No. 05-908 (2007); *Meredith, Custodial Parent and Next Friend of McDonald v. Jefferson County Board of Education*, No. 05-915 (2007).

[5]Linda Camp Keith, "The United States Supreme Court and Judicial Review of Congress, 1803–2001," *Judicature* 9(2007): 166.

[6]Rebecca Mae Salokar, *The Solicitor General: The Politics of Law* (Philadelphia: Temple University Press, 1992); see also Cornell W. Clayton, *The Politics of Justice: The Attorney General and the Making of Legal Policy* (Armonk, N.Y.: Sharpe, 1992).

[7]Henry Glick, *Courts, Politics, and Justice*, 3d ed. (New York: McGraw-Hill, 1993), 120.

[8]Timothy R. Johnson, Paul Wahlbeck, and James Spriggs, "The Influence of Oral Arguments on the U.S. Supreme Court," *American Political Science Review* 100 (2006): 99–113.

[9]Lawrence Baum, *The Supreme Court*, 8th ed. (Washington, D.C.: Congressional Quarterly Press, 2003), 120.

[10]*Gideon v. Wainwright*, 372 U.S. 335 (1963).

[11]See Forest Maltzman, Paul Wahlbeck, and James Spriggs, *The Collegial Game: Crafting Law on the U.S. Supreme Court* (New York: Cambridge University Press, 2000.)

[12]From a letter to the author by Frank Schwartz of Beaver College; this section reflects substantially Professor Schwartz's recommendations to the author, as does the later section that addresses the federal court myth.

[13]*Hutto v. Davis*, 370 U.S. 256 (1982).

[14]*Lawrence v. Texas*, No. 02-102 (2003).

[15]*Bowers v. Hardwick*, 478 U.S. 186 (1986).

[16]See Richard Davis, *Electing Justices* (New York: Oxford University Press, 2005).

[17]See Lee Epstein and Jeffrey Segal, *Advice and Consent: The Politics of Judicial Appointments* (New York: Oxford University Press, 2005).
[18]Robert Scigliano, *The Supreme Court and the Presidency* (New York: Free Press, 1971), 146; see also Lee Epstein and Jack Knight, *The Choices Justices Make* (Washington, D.C.: Congressional Quarterly Press, 1998).
[19]Quoted in Baum, *The Supreme Court*, 37.
[20]See Virginia A. Hettinger et al., *Judging on a Collegial Court: Influences on Federal Appellate Decision Making* (Charlottesville: University of Virginia Press, 2006).
[21]John Gottschall, "Reagan's Appointments to the U.S. Courts of Appeals," *Judicature* 48 (1986): 54.
[22]See Robert A. Carp and Ronald Stidham, *The Federal Courts*, 4th ed. (Washington, D.C.: Congressional Quarterly Press, 2001).
[23]Joseph B. Harris, *The Advice and Consent of the Senate* (Berkeley: University of California Press, 1953), 313.
[24]Quoted in Louis Fisher, *American Constitutional Law* (New York: McGraw-Hill, 1990), 5.
[25]Quoted in Charles P. Curtis, *Law and Large as Life* (New York: Simon & Schuster, 1959), 156–57.
[26]See Lee Epstein and Jack Knight, *The Choices Justices Make* (New York: Longman, 1995); Thomas G. Hansford and James F. Spriggs II, *The Politics of Precedent on the Supreme Court* (Princeton, N.J.: Princeton University Press, 2006).
[27]*Faragher v. City of Boca Raton*, No. 97-282 (1998).
[28]Stephen L. Wasby, *The Supreme Court in the Federal Judicial System*, 4th ed. (Chicago: Nelson-Hall, 1993), 53.
[29]For a helpful explanation of amicus curiae briefs, see Bradley Best, "Amicus Curiae," in David Schultz and John P. Vile, eds., *The Encyclopedia of Civil Liberties in America, Volume 1* (Armonk, N.Y.: M. E. Sharpe, 2005), 33–35.
[30]John Schmidhauser, *The Supreme Court* (New York: Holt, Rinehart & Winston, 1964), 6.
[31]Linda Greenhouse, "In Steps Big and Small, Supreme Court Moved Right," *New York Times*, July 1, 2007, electronic version.
[32]Jeffrey A. Segal and Harold J. Spaeth, *The Supreme Court and the Attitudinal Model Revisited* (New York: Cambridge University Press, 2002).
[33]Linda Greenhouse, "In a Momentous Term, Justices Remake the Law, and the Court," *New York Times*, July 1, 2003, A1.
[34]*Bush v. Gore*, No. 00-949 (2000).
[35]See, however, James L. Gibson, Gregory A. Caldeira, and Lester Kenyatta Spence, "The Supreme Court and the U.S. Presidential Election of 2000," *British Journal of Political Science* 33 (2003): 535–56.
[36]David M. O'Brien, *Storm Center: The Supreme Court in American Politics*, 7th ed. (New York: Norton, 2005), 14–15.
[37]Ross Sandler and David Schoenbrod, *Democracy by Decree* (New Haven, Conn.: Yale University Press, 2003).
[38]Henry J. Abraham, "The Judicial Function Under the Constitution," *News for Teachers of Political Science* 41 (Spring 1984): 14.
[39]Alexander M. Bickel, *The Supreme Court and the Idea of Progress* (New Haven, Conn.: Yale University Press, 1978), 173–81.
[40]Frederic R. Kellogg, *Oliver Wendell Holmes, Jr.: Legal Theory and Judicial Restraint* (New York: Cambridge University Press, 2006).
[41]*Schenck v. United States*, 249 U.S. 47 (1919).
[42]Frank H. Easterbrook, "Do Liberals and Conservatives Differ in Judicial Activism?" *University of Colorado Law Review* 73 (2002): 1401.
[43]Quoted in Linda Greenhouse, "The Justices Decide Who's in Charge," *New York Times*, June 27, 1999, sect. 4, 1.
[44]See Antonin Scalia, *A Matter of Interpretation: Federal Courts and the Law* (Princeton, N.J.: Princeton University Press, 1997).
[45]Remarks by Antonin Scalia at the University of Delaware, April 30, 2007. Reported on the Web by *University of Delaware Daily*.
[46]Stephen Breyer, "Our Democratic Constitution," James Madison Lecture, New York University Law School, New York, October 22, 2001.

Chapter Fifteen

[1]E. E. Schattschneider, *The Semisovereign People* (New York: Holt, Rinehart and Winston, 1960).
[2]Aaron Wildausky, *The Politics of the Budgetary Process*, 4th ed. (Glenview, Ill.: Scott Foresman, 1984).

[3]Marc Allen Eisner, Jeffrey Worsham, and Evan J. Rinquist, *Contemporary Regulatory Policy* (Boulder, Colo.: Lynne Rienner, 2006).

[4]The section titled "Efficiency Through Government Intervention" relies substantially on Alan Stone, *Regulation and Its Alternatives* (Washington, D.C.: Congressional Quarterly Press, 1982).

[5]See Marc Allen Eisner, *Regulatory Politics in Transition*, 2d ed. (Baltimore, Md. Johns Hopkins University Press, 1999).

[6]See Richard A. Harris and Sidney M. Milkis, *The Politics of Regulatory Change* (New York: Oxford University Press, 1996).

[7]Lawrence E. Mitchell, *Corporate Irresponsibility* (New Haven, Conn.: Yale University Press, 2003).

[8]H. Peyton Young, *Equity: In Theory and Practice* (Princeton, N.J.: Princeton University Press, 1995).

[9]"Hill Foes of New Clean Air Rules Unite Behind Moratorium Bill," *Congressional Quarterly Weekly Report* (Spring 1998): 61.

[10]Board on Population Health and Public Health Practice, *The Future of Drug Safety: Promoting and Protecting the Health of the Public* (Washington, D.C.: National Academies Press, 2007).

[11]See Thomas Streeter, *Selling the Air* (Chicago: University of Chicago Press, 1996); Robert McChesney, *The Problem of the Media* (New York: Monthly Review Press, 2004); Christopher J. Bosso, *Environment, Inc.: From Grassroots to Beltway* (Lawrence: University Press of Kansas, 2005).

[12]Rachel Carson, *The Silent Spring* (Boston: Houghton Mifflin, 1962); see also Lester R. Brown, *Plan B2.0: Rescuing a Planet Under Stress and a Civilization in Trouble* (New York: W. W. Norton, 2006).

[13]Robert B. Keiter, *Keeping Faith with Nature* (New Haven, Conn.: Yale University Press, 2003).

[14]*U.S. News & World Report*, June 30, 1975, 25.

[15]*Whitman v. American Trucking Association*, No. 99-1257 (2001).

[16]*Massachusetts v. EPA*, No. 05-1120 (2007).

[17]See Walter A. Rosenbaum, *Environmental Politics and Policy*, 6th ed. (Washington, D.C.: Congressional Quarterly Press, 2004); Norman J. Vig and Michael E. Kraft, eds., *Environmental Policy: New Directions for the Twenty-first Century* (Washington, D.C.: Congressional Quarterly Press, 2003).

[18]Elliot A. Rosen, *Roosevelt, the Great Depression, and the Economics of Recovery* (Charlottesville: University of Virginia Press, 2007).

[19]See Robert Lekachman, *The Age of Keynes* (New York: Random House, 1966); see also Richard Kopke, Geoffrey M. B. Tootell, and Robert K. Trist, eds., *The Macroeconomics of Fiscal Policy* (Cambridge, Mass.: MIT Press, 2006).

[20]See Bruce Bartlett, *Reaganomics: Supply-Side Economics* (Westport, Conn.: Arlington House, 1981).

[21]For opposing views on the success of the tax-cutting strategy, see Gene W. Heck, *Building Prosperity: Why Ronald Reagan and the Founding Fathers Were Right on the Economy* (Lanham, Md.: Rowman & Littlefield, 2007); Bryan D. Jones and Walter Williams, *The Politics of Bad Ideas: The Great Tax-Cut Delusion and the Decline of Good Government in America* (New York: Longman, 2008).

[22]See Richard Duncan, *The Dollar Crisis: Causes, Consequences, Cures*, rev. ed. (New York: John Wiley & Sons, 2005).

[23]U.S. Senate clerk, 2002.

[24]See Allen Schick, *The Federal Budget*, 3d ed. (Washington, D.C.: Brookings Institution Press, 2007).

[25]Alan O. Ebenstein, *Milton Friedman: A Biography* (New York: Palgrave Macmillan, 2007).

[26]Martin Mayer, *FED: The Inside Story of How the World's Most Powerful Financial Institution Drives the Markets* (New York: Free Press, 2001).

Chapter Sixteen

[1]Quoted in E. J. Dionne Jr., "Reflecting on 'Reform,'" *Washington Post*, web download, February 15, 2004.

[2]Press releases of House Committee on Ways and Means and National Conference of State Legislatures, September 19 and June 26, 2002, respectively.

[3]See Felicia Ann Kornbluh, *The Battle for Welfare Rights: Politics and Poverty in Modern America* (Philadelphia: University of Pennsylvania Press, 2007).

[4]Michael Harrington, *The Other America: Poverty in the United States* (New York:

Macmillan, 1962); see also James T. Patterson, *America's Struggle Against Poverty in the Twentieth Century* (Cambridge, Mass.: Harvard University Press, 2000).

[5]Charles Murray, *Losing Ground: American Social Policy, 1950–1980* (New York: Basic Books, 1984).

[6]Signe-Mary McKernan and Caroline Ratcliffe, "Events That Trigger Poverty Entries and Exits," *Social Science Quarterly* 86 (2005): 1146–69.

[7]See Katherine S. Newman, *No Shame in My Game* (New York: Alfred A. Knopf and Russell Sage Foundation, 1999), 41.

[8]V. O. Key Jr., *The Responsible Electorate* (Cambridge, Mass.: Belknap Press of Harvard University, 1966), 43.

[9]Everett Carll Ladd, *American Political Parties* (New York: Norton, 1970), 205.

[10]Institute on Taxation and Economic Policy poll, 2002.

[11]For a general overview of 1950s and 1960s policy disputes, see James Sundquist, *Politics and Policy* (Washington, D.C.: Brookings Institution, 1968).

[12]See Jason DeParle, *American Dream: Three Women, Ten Kids, and a Nation's Drive to End Welfare* (New York: Penguin, 2005).

[13]Quoted in Malcolm Gladwell, "The Medicaid Muddle," *The Washington Post National Weekly Edition*, January 16–22, 1995, 31.

[14]Jill Quadagno, *One Nation, Uninsured: Why the United States Has No National Health Insurance* (New York: Oxford University Press, 2005).

[15]See Christopher Howard, *The Welfare State Nobody Knows* (Princeton, N.J.: Princeton University Press, 2006).

[16]Alberto Alesina and Edward Glaeser, *Fighting Poverty in the U.S. and Europe* (New York: Oxford University Press, 2006).

[17]Robert D. Ebel, Tuan Minh Le, and Zicheng Li Swift, "National Tax Levels and the Rich vs. the Poor," publication of the Tax Policy Center, Washington, D.C., June 6, 2005.

[18]Paul Krugman, "Hey, Lucky Duckies," *New York Times*, December 3, 2002, A31.

[19]Said of George H. W. Bush at the 1988 Democratic Convention. The quote is variously attributed to Ann Richards or Jim Hightower.

[20]For a history of public education, see Joel H. Spring, *The American School 1642–2004* (New York: McGraw-Hill, 2008).

[21]Based on Organization for Economic Cooperation and Development (OECD) data, 2006; see Douglas S. Reed, *On Equal Terms: The Constitutional Politics of Educational Opportunity* (Princeton, N.J.: Princeton University Press, 2003).

[22]Kaiser Family Foundation/Washington Post/Kennedy School of Government poll, September 1999.

[23]See John E. Chubb and Terry M. Moe, *Politics, Markets, and America's Schools* (Washington, D.C.: Brookings Institution, 1990); Tony Wagner and Thomas Vander Ark, *Making the Grade* (New York: Routledge, 2001).

[24]See Jeffrey R. Henig, *Rethinking School Choice* (Princeton, N.J.: Princeton University Press, 1995).

[25]Phi Delta Kappa/Gallup poll, 2002.

[26]See Lee Anderson, *Congress in the Classroom* (College Station: Pennsylvania State University Press, 2007).

[27]See Neal McCluskey, *Feds in the Classroom* (Lanham, Md.: Rowman & Littlefield, 2007).

[28]See, for example, David Hursh, *High Stakes Testing and the Decline of Teaching and Learning* (Lanham, Md.: Rowman & Littlefield, 2008.)

[29]Press release, Congressman John Boehner, January 4, 2003.

[30]Phi Delta Kappa/Gallup poll, 2005.

[31]Stanley Feldman and John Zaller, "The Political Culture of Ambivalence: Ideological Responses to the Welfare State," *American Journal of Political Science* 36, no. 1 (1992): 268–307.

[32]Robert E. Lane, "Market Justice, Political Justice," *American Political Science Review* 80 (1986): 383.

Chapter Seventeen

[1]See Mr. X. (George Kennan), "The Sources of Soviet Conduct," *Foreign Affairs* 25 (July 1947): 566–82.

[2]See Wilson Miscamble, *From Roosevelt to Truman: Potsdam, Hiroshima, and the Cold War* (New York: Cambridge University Press, 2008).

[3]David M. Barrett, *Uncertain Warriors: Lyndon Johnson and His Vietnam Advisors* (Lawrence:

University Press of Kansas, 1993); see also Stanley Karnow, *Vietnam: A History* (New York: Penguin, 1983).

[4]See Dag Henriksen, *NATO's Gamble* (Annapolis, Md.: Naval Institute Press, 2007).

[5]See Mark Sauter and James Carafano, *Homeland Security* (New York: McGraw-Hill, 2005).

[6]West Point speech, June 1, 2002; for an opposing view, see Gary Hart, *The Shield and the Cloak: The Security of the Commons* (New York: Oxford University Press, 2006).

[7]Nick Ritchie, *The Political Road to War with Iraq: Bush, 9/11 and the Drive to Overthrow Saddam* (New York: Routledge, 2007).

[8]See Ofira Seliktar, *The Politics of Intelligence and American Wars with Iraq* (New York: Palgrave Macmillan, 2008).

[9]See Ole Holsti, *Public Opinion and American Foreign Policy* (Ann Arbor: University of Michigan Press, 1996); Richard Sobel, *The Impact of Public Opinion on U.S. Foreign Policy Since Vietnam* (New York: Oxford University Press, 2001).

[10]George C. Wilson, *This War Really Matters: Inside the Fight for Defense Dollars* (Washington, D.C.: Congressional Quarterly Press, 2000).

[11]U.S. government data, various agencies, 2008.

[12]*The World Competitiveness Yearbook* (Lausanne, Switzerland: International Institute for Management Development, 2008).

[13]American Assembly Report (co-sponsored by the Council on Foreign Relations), *Rethinking America's Security* (New York: Harriman, 1991), 9.

[14]Robert Z. Lawrence, *The United States and the WTO Dispute Settlement System* (New York: Council on Foreign Relations, 2007).

[15]Ted C. Fishman, *China, Inc.: How the Rise of the Next Superpower Challenges America and the World* (New York: Scribner, 2005).

[16]John Duffield, *Over a Barrel: The Costs of U.S. Foreign Oil Dependence* (Stanford, Calif.: Stanford Law and Politics, 2007.)

[17]See Joseph S. Nye, *Soft Power: The Means to Success in World Politics* (New York: Public Affairs, 2003); Michael Lind, *The American Way of Strategy* (New York: Oxford University Press, 2006).

[18]Hobart Rowen, "The Budget: Fact and Fiction," *The Washington Post National Weekly Edition*, January 16–22, 1995, 5.

[19]Tom Masland, "Going Down the Aid 'Rathole'?" *Newsweek*, December 5, 1994, 39.

Credits

Photo Credits

Chapter 1 Opener: © Chromosohm Media/Stock Boston; p. 2: © Nicolas Asfouri/AFP/Getty Images; p. 6: © AP Images/Jason DeCrow; p. 12: © AP Images/Ben Curtis; p. 16: © The Granger Collection; p. 17(both): © AP Images

Chapter 2 Opener: © The Granger Collection; p. 27: © AP Images/Ron Edmonds; p. 31: © Bettmann/Corbis Images; p. 37: © The Granger Collection; p. 50: Library of Congress, Prints and Photographs Division (LC-USZ62-62-1304); p. 55: © AP Images/Rogelio V. Solis

Chapter 3 Opener: © The Granger Collection; p. 69: © The Granger Collection; p. 76: © Archivo Iconografico, S.A./Corbis Images; p. 78: © The Granger Collection; p. 80: Library of Congress, Prints & Photographs Division [LC-B811-560]; p. 83: © Ernest C. Withers, Courtesy, Panopticon Gallery, Boston, MA; p. 87: © AP Images/Charlie Riedel; p. 97: © Doug Pensinger/Getty Images

Chapter 4 Opener: © Alan Klehr/Getty Images; p. 110: Library of Congress, Prints & Photographs Division [LC-USZC4-2474]; p. 117: © AP Images/Kimberly Smith, AJC; p. 122: © AP Images/The Florida Times-Union, M. Jack Luedke; p. 127: © AP Images/Jacquelyn Martin; p. 130: © Jeff Greenberg/age fotostock; p. 140: © AP Images/J. Scott Applewhite

Chapter 5 Opener: © AP Images; p. 152: © Charles Moore/Black Star; p. 158: © Topham/The Image Works; p. 161: © AP Images; p. 168: © AP Images/Danny Moloshok

Chapter 6 Opener: © The McGraw-Hill Companies, Inc./Jill Braaten, photographer; p. 193: © Digital Vision Ltd.; p. 198: © Win McNamee/Getty Images; p. 202: © AP Images/Tina Fineberg; p. 209: © Bettmann/Corbis Images; p. 215: © DoD photo by Senior Airman Kenny Holston, U.S. Air Force

Chapter 7 Opener: © Bob Daemmrich/The Image Works; p. 225: © Culver Pictures; p. 234: © The Granger Collection; p. 241: © AP Images/Nati Harnik

Chapter 8 Opener: © Nikki Kahn/The Washington Post/Getty Images; p. 255: Library of Congress, Prints and Photographs Division [LC-USZ62-13016]; p. 256: © Bettmann/Corbis Images; p. 270: Library of Congress, Prints & Photographs Division ; p. 284: © AP Images/Toby Jorrin

Chapter 9 Opener: © Bob Daemmrich/The Image Works; p. 301: Library of Congress, Prints & Photographs Division [LC-USZC4-4642]; p. 305: © Jeff Greenberg/Alamy; p. 310: © AP Images/James Crisp; p. 320: © Monika Graff/The Image Works

Chapter 10 Opener: © Eric Lesser/The New York Times/Redux Pictures; p. 331: © AP Images/Mary Ann Chastain; p. 335: © AP Images/Photo courtesy of Rush Limbaugh; p. 339: © Lionel Bonaventure/AFP/Getty Images; p. 350: © Mark Asnin/Redux Pictures; p. 353: © AP Images/Joseph Kaczmarek; p. 356: © Courtesy, Politico.com

Chapter 11 Opener: © Vanessa Vick/Photo Researchers; p. 373: © Bettmann/Corbis Images; p. 383: Courtesy, Office of the Speaker, Washington, D.C.; p. 388: © Chip Somodevilla/Getty Images; p. 396: © AP Images/J. Scott Applewhite

Chapter 12 Opener: © Punchstock/Brand X Pictures; p. 413: © Greg Mathieson/MAI/Landov; p. 416: © The Granger Collection; p. 419: © UPI/Bettmann/Corbis Images; p. 424: © AP Images/Jae C. Hong; p. 432: © UPI/Bettmann/Corbis Images; p. 438: © U.S. Marine Corps photo by Lance Cpl. Paul Miller; p. 446: © Karl Schumacher/Time & Life Pictures/Getty Images

Chapter 13 Opener: © Medioimages/Getty Images; p. 454: © Joe Raedle/Getty Images; p. 467: © Tetra Images/Getty Images; p. 472: © Marc Bryan-Brown/WireImage/Getty Images; p. 477: © Paul Chinn/San Francisco Chronicle/Corbis

Chapter 14 Opener: © Collection of the Supreme Court of the United States p. 501: © AP Images/ Alex Brandon; p. 506: © Landon Nordeman/Getty Images; p. 510: © AP Images; p. 515: © Stock Montage/Getty Images

Chapter 15 Opener: © Win McNamee/Getty Images; p. 532: © Ryan McVay/Getty Images; p. 535: © Alfred Eisenstaedt/Time Life Pictures//Getty Images; p. 537: © flickr RF/Getty Images; p. 541(both): © NASA; p. 552: © Jeff Kowalsky/Bloomberg/Getty Images

Chapter 16 Opener: © Jim West/The Image Works; p. 564: © AP Images/Paul Beaty; p. 570: © Rene Burri/Magnum Photos; p. 574: © Stockbyte/Veer; p. 587: © Bob Daemmrich/ The Image Works

Chapter 17 Opener: © Robert Nickelsberg/Getty Images; p. 599: © The Michael Barson Collection; p. 604: © AP Images/Greg Baker; p. 611: © AP Images/Mohammad Sajjad; p. 613: © Ed Clark//Time Life Pictures/Getty Images; p. 619: © John Woodworth/PhotoDisc/Getty Images

Index